FROMMER'S

COMPREHENSIVE TRAVEL GUIDE

PORTUGAL '94-'95

by Darwin Porter
Assisted by Danforth Prince

PRENTICE HALL TRAVEL

NEW YORK • LONDON • TORONTO • SYDNEY • TOKYO • SINGAPORE

FROMMER BOOKS

Published by Prentice Hall General Reference
15 Columbus Circle
New York, NY 10023

ISBN 0-671-86797-0
ISSN 1044-2278

Design by Robert Bull Design
Maps by Geografix Inc.

Frommer's Editorial Staff
Editorial Director: Marilyn Wood
Editorial Manager/Senior Editor: Alice Fellows
Senior Editors: Lisa Renaud, Sara Hinsey Raveret
Editors: Charlotte Allstrom, Thomas F. Hirsch, Peter Katucki, Theodore Stavrou
Assistant Editors: Margaret Bowen, Christopher Hollander, Alice Thompson, Ian Wilker
Editorial Assistants: Gretchen Henderson, Douglas Stallings
Managing Editor: Leanne Coupe

Special Sales
Bulk purchases (10+ copies) of Frommer's Travel Guides are available to corporations at special discounts. The Special Sales Department can produce custom editions to be used as premiums and/or for sales promotions to suit individual needs. Existing editions can be produced with custom cover imprints such as a corporate logo. For more information write to: Special Sales, Prentice Hall Travel, 15 Columbus Circle, New York, NY 10023.

Manufactured in the United States of America

CONTENTS

LIST OF MAPS

FOREWORD

by Arthur Frommer

As unlikely as it may seem in the mid-1990s, there still are parts of the Portuguese coast where black-clad women gather at the water's edge at dusk and anxiously gaze out to sea to learn whether their fishermen husbands will safely return that day from the perilous calling in which they are engaged. And there are other locations on these same ancient shores where people mend coarse-string nets, and carry their catch to town on burros with wooden saddles, as if the year were 1894 and not a century later.

The tourists who simply park their modern automobiles a short distance away and walk over unobtrusively to view these scenes will enter a time warp that has no counterpart in Europe other than, perhaps, in Turkey or Greece. Kept poor by a 20th-century dictatorship that clung to power for decades and stunted the nation's growth, Portugal is today among the least prosperous countries of Europe. Gazing over Lisbon from its most prominent hill, it is hard to locate more than a few structures that have been built later than World War II.

Yet as tragic underdevelopment may be to the country's economy, it is a boon for the tourist, and visitors experience here a form of quaintly old-fashioned European life that is fast vanishing from most other parts of western Europe. In the outlying rural sections of Portugal, one comes upon the sort of village life that has disappeared entirely from our own familiar United States, and is usually found only in the pages of 18th- and 19th-century novels. On a motoring trip in the 70s, in the turbulent days after the death of dictator António de Oliveira Salazar, I drove on country roads through these throwbacks into another, slower age, and very quickly relaxed from the anxieties of political events in Lisbon. If ever there were a time-machine for moving into the past, it is Portugal. But . . . the country is beginning to modernize, so it may lose some of its rural charm one day soon.

Try to travel there in the off-season, from November through March, when the weather remains mild in many parts of the country, and hotel prices fall to levels that simply can't be matched any longer in most other European countries. Thousands of American retirees who now pass the winter months on the Algarve coast of Portugal find they spend far less—even including the airfare that brought them there—then they would for equivalent vacations in Miami Beach, Phoenix, or San Diego. From that southernmost "Riviera" of Portugal, it is still possible to make easy excursions to Lisbon, Estoril, or Cascais, or even to drive east, over the Spanish border, to glorious Seville. The great utility of this guidebook is that it describes and gives lodgings-and-meals information for more than a hundred locations along the major touring routes that visitors to Portugal follow. Though the city of Lisbon is exhaustively covered in more than 75 pages of text, it is still only a small part of this comprehensive guide to Portugal, and the other important Portuguese locations are not treated as afterthoughts (as in some guides) but are equally important subjects for careful discussion.

It's a matter of considerable pride for me that nearly 30 years ago, I discovered the writing talents of the book's author, Darwin Porter, and asked him to join our staff. For almost as long as that, he's been researching and writing this guide to Portugal, and his enthusiasm for that land of the Fado (the sad, romantic ballads of singers in prominent cafes of Lisbon) has never diminished. You'll find it in the loving, historical details he inserts into the most practical discussions, his exclamations of delight over particular values in lodgings, the painstaking care with which he chooses small towns and villages as colorful overnight stops on particular driving itineraries. In a country whose currency has been devalued considerably since the last edition of this guidebook was published two years ago, a good guidebook writer can point the way to an unusually pleasant vacation. Assisted by Darwin's judgments, in this thirteenth edition revised by him, we think that just such a rewarding trip awaits you in Portugal. Boa viagem!

AN INVITATION TO READERS

In researching this book, I have come across many remarkable establishments, the best of which I have included here. I am sure that many of you will also come across appealing hotels, inns, restaurants, guesthouses, shops, and attractions. Please don't keep them to yourself. Share your experiences, especially if you want to comment on places that have been included in this edition that have changed for the worse. You can address your letters to:

Darwin Porter
Frommer's Portugal '94–'95
c/o Prentice Hall Travel
15 Columbus Circle
New York, NY 10023

A DISCLAIMER

Readers are advised that prices fluctuate in the course of time and travel information changes under the impact of the varied and volatile factors that affect the travel industry. Neither the author nor the publisher can he held responsible for the experiences of readers while traveling. Readers are invited to write to the publisher with ideas, comments, and suggestions for future editions.

SAFETY ADVISORY

Whenever you're traveling in an unfamiliar city or country, stay alert. Be aware of your immediate surroundings. Wear a moneybelt and keep a close eye on your possessions. Be particularly careful with cameras, purses, and wallets—all of which are favorite targets of thieves and pickpockets.

INTRODUCING PORTUGAL

The geography, history, and politics of Portugal are treated here in a single section, because all three are bonded to each other. Portugal's location at the western edge of the Iberian peninsula helped lure waves of invaders, including Phoenicians, Romans, and Celts. Geography also played a major role in propelling the country into the Age of Exploration, when it conquered territory overseas. During this time, beginning around 1400, Portugal turned outward to the Atlantic Ocean, and for a time it appeared that the little country wanted to claim the vast ocean as its private domain. Other nations demurred, however, and Portugal became involved in international disputes, notably with neighboring Spain. Portugal's heroes from this period, such as Prince Henry the Navigator and Vasco da Gama, helped raise the country from relative insignificance to influential player on the world scene, and remain today important figures in the country's cultural heritage.

1. GEOGRAPHY, HISTORY & POLITICS

GEOGRAPHY

Portugal, which forms part of the Iberian peninsula with Spain, has a coastline of about 500 miles. It is bounded on the south and west by the Atlantic Ocean and on the north and east by Spain. Continental Portugal totals some 34,000 square miles; its Atlantic islands, including Madeira and the Azores, extend the size of the country by another 1,200 square miles. The Azores lie some 700 miles west of Lisbon (Lisboa), the capital of the country. Portugal's population numbers about 10.3 million.

Portugal has four major rivers—the Minho in the north, which separates the country from Spain; the Douro, also in the north, known for vineyards producing port wine; the Tagus, which flows into the Atlantic at Lisbon; and the Guadiana, in the southeast. Part of the Guadiana forms an eastern frontier with Spain.

Northern Portugal, composed of mountainous Trás-os-Montes and Alto Douro, plus Douro Litoral, is the land of *vinho verde* (green wine).

IMPRESSIONS

Wet or fine the air of Portugal has a natural happiness in it, and the people of the country should be as happy and prosperous as any people in the world.
—H. G. WELLS, *A YEAR OF PROPHESYING* (1925)

❓ DID YOU KNOW . . . ?

- In the 15th century, Prince Henry the Navigator, based at Sagres, made notable contributions to the art of navigation on the high seas.
- Under Dom Manuel I (1495–1521), Lisbon was the richest city in Europe.
- Gold and diamonds, discovered in the Portuguese colony of Brazil, financed the baroque art movement that swept the land.
- Lord Byron, who wrote *Childe Harold's Pilgrimage*, found Portugal a fair land that had been "peopled by beasts."
- The Portuguese, although easy-going by nature, become daredevils on the road, leading to the highest accident rate in Europe.
- One of the main staples of the Portuguese economy, other than tourism, is money sent back by emigrants working abroad.
- The Portuguese, as a result of creating an empire, made their language seventh among those of the world.

The coastal strip of Beira Litoral, south of the Douro, is known for pinewoods and cereal production. Further inland and to the east, Beira Alta and parts of the northern rim of Beira Baixa jointly share the Serra da Estrela, the highest mountain range in the country.

The valley of the Tagus cuts through Ribatejo with its flat and fertile fields. Lying southwest of Ribatejo, Alto Alentejo is known for its cork oaks and olive trees. Much of Portugal's wheat comes from the Beja district in Baixo Alentejo.

The terrain of south Portugal, called the Algarve, is most often compared to that of either Andalusia to the east in Spain or to North Africa to the south.

REGIONS IN BRIEF

Costa do Sol This glittering beach-front strip outside Lisbon is a world unto itself, which centers at the chic resorts of Estoril and Cascais. On the northern banks of the mouth of the Tagus is the Portuguese Riviera, long a home to exiled European royalty. This strip should not be confused with Spain's Costa del Sol.

Estremadura The first seeds of the Portuguese empire were planted in this west-central area. This land of contrasts has always looked to the sea for conquest and food. Its chief towns—at least for the visitor—are Óbidos, Nazaré, and Fátima.

Algarve The southern terrain of Portugal attracts the beach lover, so the region overflows with foreign visitors in July and August. This is a Riviera of far greater magnitude than the Costa do Sol; its centers are such resorts as Praia da Rocha, Silves, Albufeira, Vilamoura, Faro, and Monte Gordo, among many others. Sagres, part of the Algarve, is near the extreme southwestern corner of continental Europe.

Alentejo and **Ribatejo** These adjoining areas form the heartland of Portugal. Ribatejo is known for its bull-breeding pastures. The Tagus flows from Spain through the territory. Alentejo, called a "plain of fire and ice," is filled with cork-producing plains.

Coimbra and **the Beiras** The three Beira provinces of central Portugal include Beira Litoral (coastal), Beira Baixa (low), and Beira Alta (high). Together, they take in the university city of Coimbra. Portugal's highest land mass, the Serra da Estrêla, is included in the area.

Porto and **the Douro** Portugal's second city, Porto, is the home of port wine. The Douro, from Rio do Ouro, or "river of gold," flows through some of the world's richest vineyards. Porto is surrounded by several popular resorts, once former fishing villages. These include Póvoa do Varzim.

IMPRESSIONS

If there is one slice of Christendom, one portion of Europe which was made by the sea more than another, Portugal is that slice, that portion, that belt. Portugal was made by the Atlantic.
—HILAIRE BELLOC, *PLACES* (1942)

Minho Region   The northwestern corner of Portugal is almost a land unto itself. The region begins some 25 miles north of Porto; its major centers are Viana do Castelo, Giumaraes, and Braga.

Trás-os-Montes   This far northeastern—and least visited—area of Portugal is a wild, rugged land whose name means "beyond the mountains." It extends south of the Upper Douro at Lamego and stretches north to Spain. Vila Real is a major town here.

Madeira   Located 530 miles southwest of Portugal, Madeira is the peak of a volcanic mass. The wintering English gentry first discovered the island's tourist charms; today it is one of the world's most famous spots. Only 35 miles in length and about 13 miles in breadth at its widest point, the island is an autonomous region of Portugal, with a population of about 253,000.

The Azores   This archipelago spans more than 500 miles from the southeastern tip of Santa Maria to the northwestern extremity of Corvo. The main island is São Miguel, about 760 miles west of Portugal and 2,110 miles east of New York. The chain of the Azores is one of the most isolated in the entire Atlantic Ocean. It constitutes an autonomous region and has some 237,000 inhabitants.

HISTORY

EARLY CIVILIZATION   From about 8,000 to 7,000 B.C., tribes occupied the valley of the Tagus, stretching into Estremadura and Alentejo. Pottery and various artifacts attest to their presence. Neolithic people built hilltop forts that greeted the arrival of the Celtic people around 700 to 600 B.C. Excavations have revealed important settlements in the north of Portugal from this time.

It is believed that those early traders, the Phoenicians, established a trading outpost at Lisbon around 900 B.C. The Carthaginians, in time, recruited Celtic men to fight the growing might of Rome.

ARRIVAL OF THE ROMANS   From 210 B.C. on, the Romans colonized most of Iberia, although they met great resistance from the Celtiberian people of the interior. The Lusitanian leader Viriatus (died about 139 B.C.) looms large in Portuguese history as a freedom fighter who held up the Roman advance. But by the time of Julius Caesar, Portugal had been integrated into the Roman Empire. Roman colonies then included Olisipo (now Lisbon).

Christianity arrived near the end of the 1st century A.D. By the 3rd century, bishoprics had been established at Lisbon, Braga, and elsewhere. Following the decline of the Roman Empire, invaders crossed the Pyrenees into Spain in 409 and eventually made their way to Portugal. The Visigothic empire dominated the peninsula for some two centuries.

MOORS & THE CHRISTIAN RECONQUEST   In 711, a force of Moors arrived in Iberia, and their advance quickly spread to Portugal. They erected settlements in the south instead of the north. The Christian Reconquest—the *Reconquista*—is said to have begun in 718.

In the 11th century, much of northern Portugal was taken from the Moors by Ferdinand the Great, king of León and Castile. Before his death in 1065, Ferdinand set about to reorganize the western territories into Portucale (now Portugal).

DATELINE

- **210 B.C.** Romans invade the peninsula, meeting fierce resistance from the Celtiberian people.
- **60 B.C.** During the reign of Julius Caesar, Portugal is fully integrated into the Roman Empire.
- **A.D. 409** Invaders from across the Pyrenees arrive, establishing a Visigothic empire for some two centuries.
- **711** Moorish warriors arrive in Iberia and conquer Portugal within 7 years.
- **1065** Ferdinand sets about to reorganize western territories into what is now modern Portugal.
- **1143** Afonso Henríques is proclaimed king of Portugal and to drive Moors out of the Algarve.
- **1249** Afonso III completes the

(continues)

DATELINE

Reconquista of the Algarve, as Christians drive out the Moors.

1279–1325 Reign of Dinis, "the poet king"; Castile recognizes Portugal's borders.

1385 Battle of Aljubarrota; João de Avís defeats the Castilians and founds the House of Avís to rule Portugal.

1415 Henry the Navigator sets up a school of navigation in Sagres; Madeira is discovered in 1419, the Azores in 1427.

1488 Bartolomeu Dias rounds the Cape of Good Hope.

1498 Vasco da Gama rounds India's west coast, opening up trade between the west and the east.

1500 Brazil is discovered, marking the high water mark of the reign of Manuel the Fortunate (1495–1521); Portugal is launched on its Golden Age.

1521 Portugal becomes the first of the great maritime world empires, dominating access to the Indian Ocean.

1521–57 Reign of João III, ushering in Jesuits and the Inquisition.

1578 His son, Dom Sebastião, disappears in the
(continues)

BIRTH OF A NATION Ferdinand handed over Portugal to his illegitimate daughter, Teresa. (The land south of the Tagus was at that time still held by the Moors.) Unknowingly, the king of Spain had launched a course of events that was to lead to the birth of another nation.

Teresa was firmly bound in marriage to Henry, a count of Burgundy. Henry accepted his father-in-law's gift of Portugal as his wife's dowry, but upon the king's death, he coveted Spanish territory as well. His own demise cut short further aggrandizement of territory.

Teresa then ruled in Portugal; she cast a disdainful eye on and an interfering nose into her legitimate sister's kingdom in Spain. Teresa lost no time mourning Henry and took a Galician count, Fernão Peres, as her lover. Teresa's refusal to guard her own affair with Peres and stay out of everyone else's affairs led to open strife with León.

Teresa's son, Afonso Henríques, was incensed by his mother's actions. Their armies met at São Mamede in 1128. Teresa lost and was banished along with her lover.

Ungrateful son or not, Afonso Henríques went on to become the "George Washington" of Portugal. In 1143, he was proclaimed king, and official recognition eventually came from the Vatican in 1178. His enemies in Spain temporarily quieted, Afonso turned his eye toward the Moorish territory in the south of Portugal. Supported by the armed might of Crusaders from the north, the Portuguese conquered Santarém and Lisbon in 1147. Upon his death in 1185, Afonso was succeeded by his son, Sancho I, who continued his father's work of consolidating the newly emerged nation. Sancho's heir, Afonso II, ruled for 12 years, beginning in 1211. Like his father and grandfather, he carried on the war against the Moors.

Sancho II was an adolescent when he ascended the throne. He was extremely devout and restored to the clergy much that had been confiscated during his father's reign. He still couldn't pacify the clergy, however, and was eventually excommunicated. His brother, Afonso III, was named king and ruled from 1248 to 1279. During the latter's reign, the Algarve, the southern district of Portugal, was finally taken from the Moors, and the country's capital moved from Coimbra to Lisbon.

Dinis, the son of a bigamous marriage, ruled Portugal from 1279 to 1325. It was during his reign that Castile recognized Portugal's borders. He is sometimes known as "the poet king" or "the farmer king"; he founded the university, in Lisbon, about 1290; it was later moved to Coimbra. Dinis married an Aragonese princess, Isabella, who was later canonized, although evidence indicates the vigorous young king would have preferred a less saintly wife. Isabella was especially interested in the poor. Legend has it that once she was smuggling bread out of the palace to feed them when her husband spotted her and asked what she was concealing. When she showed him, he saw that the bread had miraculously turned into roses.

Afonso IV, the son of these two famous monarchs, is remembered today for having his son's mistress, the legendary Inês de Castro, murdered. Early in life, Afonso's son Prince Dom Pedro (who would later rule as Pedro I), was betrothed to a Spanish princess, but he fell in love with her

PORTUGAL

Atlantic Ocean

SPAIN

0 | 100 km / 62 mi

Valença do Minho
Caminha
Viana do Castelo
Barcelos
Ofir
Braga
Póvoa de Varzim
Porto
Praia da Granja
Espinho
Vila do Conde
Guimarães
Armarante
Bragança
Chaves
Mirandela
Vila Real

MINHO
TRÁS-OS-MONTES E ALTO DOURO
DOURO LITORAL
BEIRA ALTA
BEIRA LITORAL
BEIRA BAIXA
ESTREMADURA
RIBATEJO
ALTO ALENTEJO
BAIXO ALENTEJO
ALGARVE

Aveiro
Viseu
Cantanede
Coimbra
Guarda
Figueira da Foz
Pombal
Leiria
Castelo Branco
Batalha
Fátima
Alcobaça
Tomar
Nazaré
Peniche
Caldas da Rainha
Abrantes
Castelo de Vide
Óbidos
Santarém
Portalegre
Ericeira
Queluz
Sintra
Cascais
Estoril
LISBON
Palmela
Elvas
Badajoz
Estremoz
Vilas Viçosa
Évora
Sesimbra
Setúbal
Alcácer do Sal
Sines
Moura
Beja
Odemira
Alcoutim
Sevilla
Portimão
Cachopa
Tavira
Sagres
Praia da Rocha
Lagos
Albufeira
Faro
Vila Real de Santo António

Lima R.
Cárado R.
Tâmega R.
Sabor R.
Douro R.
Côa R.
Zêzere R.
Tejo (Tagus) R.
Guadiana R.
Sado R.
Mira R.

DATELINE

battle of Morocco, leaving Portugal without an heir.

1581–1640 Philip II of Spain brings Hapsburg rule to Portugal.

1640 João IV, with a nationalist revolution, restores independence and launches the House of Bragança.

1755 A great earthquake destroys Lisbon and parts of Alentejo and the Algarve.

1822 Independence for Brazil is declared.

1908 Carlos I "the painter king," and his son, the crown prince, are assassinated in Lisbon.

1910 The monarchy is ousted as the Portuguese Republic is established.

1916 Portugal enters World War I on the side of the Allies.

1926 The republic collapses, and a military dictatorship under Gomes da Costa is established.

1932–68 António de Oliveira Salazar keeps a tight fist on the government during his long reign as dictator; Portugal is officially neutral in World War II, but Salazar grants the Allies bases in the Azores.

1955 Portugal

(continues)

beautiful lady-in-waiting. Inês was deeply attracted to him, and their affair blossomed. Eventually Inês was banished from the country, although she returned upon the death of the Spanish princess to live openly with Pedro. Jealous sycophants in court persuaded Afonso IV to sanction her murder. Pedro never recovered from the shock of seeing his dead mistress. Patiently he waited until his father died, then he set out to seek revenge. Tracking two of the assassins to Spain, he had them returned by force to Portugal, where he had their hearts torn out. The king announced he had been secretly married to Inês, and according to the story, he had her body exhumed, crowned queen, and seated on the throne, after which he summoned the members of the court to pay her homage and kiss her hand. Inês and, later, Pedro were buried at Alcobaça, where their tombs are frequently visited today.

During Pedro's reign (1357–67), an influential representative body called the Cortes (an assembly of clergy, nobility, and commoners) began to gain ascendancy. The majority of the clergy, greedy for power, fought the sovereign's reform measures, which worked to ally the people more strongly with the crown. During the reign of Pedro's son, Ferdinand I (1367–73), Portugal was invaded by Castilian forces, Lisbon was besieged, and the dynasty faced demise.

In 1383, rather than submit to Spanish rule, the Portuguese people chose the illegitimate son of Pedro as regent. The house of Avís was thereby established. João de Avís (reigned 1383–1433) secured Portuguese independence by defeating Castilian forces at Aljubarrota in 1385. His union with Philippa, granddaughter of Edward III of England, produced a son who oversaw the emergence of Portugal as an empire—Prince Henry the Navigator.

COMING OF A MARITIME EMPIRE Henry's demand for geographical accuracy and his hunger for the East's legendary gold, ivory, enslaved persons, and spices drove him to exploration. Because of his desire to promote Christianity, he joined the fabled Christian kingdom of Prester John to drive the Muslims out of North Africa. Facing him was a "Sea of Darkness" where ships supposedly melted in the equatorial regions, sea serpents flourished, and strange beasts sought to destroy any interloper.

To develop navigational and cartographical techniques, Henry established a community of scholars at Sagres on the south coast of Portugal. He infused the court with his zeal and brought his nation to the culmination of interests that had existed since early contacts with Phoenician and Greek mariners. Henry was responsible for the discovery of Madeira, the Azores, Cape Verde, Senegal, and Sierra Leone, and he established the blueprint for continued exploration during the rest of the century. In 1482, Portuguese ships explored the mouth of the Congo; in 1488, Bartolomeu Dias rounded the Cape of Good Hope; and in 1497, Vasco da Gama reached Calicut (Kozhikode) on India's west coast, clearing the way for trade in spices, porcelain, silk, ivory, and enslaved persons.

The Treaty of Tordesillas, negotiated by João II in 1494

for as yet undiscovered lands in the Western Hemisphere, ensured Portugal's possession of Brazil, which was not discovered until 1500. Utilizing the wealth of the whole empire, Manuel I (the Fortunate; reigned 1495–1521) imprinted his imagination and name upon great monuments of art and architecture. His reign inspired Portugal's Golden Age. By 1521, the country had begun to tap the natural resources of Brazil and had broken the spice-trade monopoly formerly held by the Venetians. As the first of the great maritime world empires, Portugal dominated all access to the Indian Ocean.

João III (reigned 1521–57) ushered in the Jesuits and the Inquisition. When his son Sebastião disappeared in battle in Morocco in 1578, leaving Portugal without an heir, the way was opened for Spanish control. Philip II of Spain claimed the Portuguese throne and began 60 years of Spanish domination. In the East, Portugal's strength had been undermined by Dutch and English traders.

HOUSE OF BRAGANÇA A 1640 nationalist revolution brought a descendant of João I to the throne as João IV. This began the house of Bragança, which lasted into the 20th century, as well as a long series of revolutions and intrigues. João IV arranged an English alliance by having his daughter marry Charles II. For her dowry he "threw in" Bombay and Tangier. In 1668, the Treaty of Lisbon with Spain gave Portugal recognized independence.

On All Saints' Day in 1755, a great earthquake destroyed virtually all Lisbon. In 6 minutes, 15,000 people were killed, thousands of whom had been attending morning masses. The marquês de Pombal, adviser to King José (reigned 1750–77), later reconstructed Lisbon as a safer and more beautiful city. Yet he was an exponent of absolutism, and his 1759 expulsion of the Jesuits earned him powerful enemies throughout Europe. His virtual dictatorship had its beneficial side, however; he curbed the power of the Inquisition and reorganized and expanded industry, agriculture, education, and the military. On the death of his patron, King José, he was exiled from court.

In 1793, Portugal joined a coalition with England and Spain against Napoleon. An insane queen, Maria I (reigned 1777–1816), plus an exiled royal family, facilitated an overthrow by a military junta. The Cortes was summoned; a constitution was drawn up; and Maria's son, João VI (reigned 1816–26), accepted the position of constitu-

DATELINE

joins the United Nations.
• **1974** April "flower revolution" topples the dictatorship; Portugal drifts into near anarchy.
• **1976–83** Sixteen provisional governments reign over a Portugal in chaos, as the empire collapses.
• **1986** Portugal joins the European Community; Mário Soares is elected president (reelected in 1991).
• **1989** Privatization of state-owned companies begins.
• **1992** Portugal holds presidency of European Community.

IN THEIR FOOTSTEPS

Vasco da Gama (ca. 1460–1524) In 1497, this great Portuguese navigator made the first voyage from western Europe around Africa by way of the Cape of Good Hope to the East. This voyage is the subject of the Portuguese epic *Os Lusíadas* by Camões. On a second journey (1502–3), he established colonies at Sofala and Mozambique and was named viceroy of Portuguese Asia in 1524, the last year of his life.

• **Birthplace:** He was born around 1460 at Sines in the former province of Alentejo. Little is known of his early life.

• **Accomplishments:** His discovery of the sea route to India opened up commerce between the West and the East.

• **Resting Place:** He died at Cochin (part of modern India) on December 24, 1524. His tomb is at the Mosteiro des Jerónimos in Bélem.

tional monarch in 1821. João's son, Pedro, declared independence for Brazil in 1822 and became a champion of liberalism in Portugal.

FROM REPUBLIC TO DICTATORSHIP   Between 1853 and 1908, a rumble of republican movements assaulted the very existence of the monarchists. In 1908, Carlos I (reigned 1889–1908), "the painter king," and the crown prince were assassinated at Praça do Comércio in Lisbon. Carlos's successor was overthrown in an outright revolution on October 5, 1910, ending the Portuguese monarchy and making Portugal a republic.

Instability was the watchword of the newly proclaimed republic, with revolutions and uprisings occurring two or three times a year. An attempt to remain neutral in World War I failed when—influenced by its old ally, England—Portugal commandeered German ships in the Lisbon harbor. This action promptly brought a declaration of war from Germany. Portugal entered World War I on the side of the Allies.

The precarious foundations of the republic collapsed in 1926 when a military revolt established a dictatorship, headed by Gomes da Costa. He was followed by António de Carmona, who remained president until 1951, but only as a figurehead. António de Oliveira Salazar became finance minister in 1928 and rescued the country from a morass of economic difficulties. He went on to become the first minister, acting as (but never officially becoming) head of state. In World War II, he asserted his country's neutrality, although he allowed British and American troops to establish bases in the Azores in 1943.

In 1955, Portugal joined the United Nations. Salazar suffered a stroke in 1968 and died in 1970.

MODERN PORTUGAL   The old dictatorship was overthrown on April 25, 1974, in a military coup dubbed the "flower revolution" because the soldiers wore red carnations instead of carried guns. Change swept across the land, and Portugal drifted into near anarchy. Finally, after several years of turmoil, plus frequent failures of provisional governments (there were 16 from 1976 to 1983), a revised constitution came into force in the 1980s (see Politics, below).

Of its once-extensive territorial possessions, only the Madeira group and the Azores in the Atlantic and Macau on the south China coast are still under the flag of Portugal. Macau, however, is scheduled to be returned to China in 1999. The year 1976 marked great change for the country in the realm of rulership. The Azores and Madeira were granted partial autonomy. Macau received broad autonomy, and all the colonial territories in Africa became independent countries—Angola, Cape Verde, Portuguese Guinea, Mozambique, and São Tome and Príncipe (islands in the Gulf of Guinea). The Portuguese colony of East Timor in the Indonesian archipelago was released by Portugal and immediately seized by Indonesia.

Portugal joined the European Community in 1986, but unemployment has remained a serious problem. The country had to resettle some 700,000 refugees from

---

IN THEIR FOOTSTEPS

Luíz Vaz de Camões (1524–80) This poet is the author of *Os Lusíadas* *(The Portuguese)*, the national epic of Portugal, dealing largely with the explorations of Vasco da Gama, who died the year Camões was born. Written in 1572, this work became his masterpiece.

   • **Birthplace:** He was the son of impoverished aristocrats; his early life is undocumented but the subject of much legend. Some claim he was born in Morocco.

   • **Accomplishments:** In addition to his epic, he wrote odes, elegies, satires, epigrams, comedies, and sonnets, including *Filodemo* and *Amphitriões*. He developed Portuguese lyric to its highest point and had an ever-lasting influence on national drama.

   • **Resting Place:** He is buried at the Mosteiro dos Jerónimos in Bélem.

its former African dependencies. Emergency steps to improve agriculture and industry have been called "wrenching."

After a long slump in the 1970s and 1980s, tourism has been on the upswing in mainland Portugal, with visitors coming in by the millions in the 1990s. At the same time, the government tried to stimulate growth by gradually privatizing aspects of government-owned industry, notably banks and other financial institutions, newspapers, petroleum refiners, and food processors.

POLITICS

Portugal is one of the young democracies of Europe. Although, as mentioned above, early attempts had been made at governing it as a republic, Portugal spent much of the 20th century under the monarchy and civilian or military dictatorships. Defining Portugal as a republic engaged in the formation of a classless society, the 1976 constitution (amended 1982 and 1989) calls for presidents to be elected by popular vote for five-year terms. The prime minister is appointed by the president, who also names other members of the government. A unicameral Legislative Assembly is made up of 230 representatives elected by the people to four-year terms. As proof of Portugal's new stability, the country was given the presidency of the European Community (EC) in 1992.

But politics have been chaotic since Dr. Marcelo Caetano replaced dictator Antonio de Oliveiro Salazar after the latter had suffered a stroke. Six years later, in 1974, following discontent in the African colonies of Mozambique and Angola, revolution broke out.

From that time until 1987, Portuguese governments rose and fell much too alarmingly for that country to have any political stability. Moderates elected Gen. Ramalho Eanes as president, in the wake of the revolution, and he was reelected in 1980. He brought the military under control. There had been fear of a right-wing coup to prevent a socialist takeover. However, Eanes three times appointed socialist Mário Soares prime minister. When Monarchists, the Democratic Alliance of Social Democrats, and Christian Democrats obtained a majority in parliament, Eanes appointed Francisco Sá Carneiro as prime minister in 1979. While still in office, the new prime minister was killed in a plane crash.

In the elections of April 25, 1983, Soares's Socialist Party became the biggest single part in the national assembly. To maintain a coalition government, it had secured the support of the Social Democrats. Continuing economic problems led to the collapse of this coalition.

In the 1985 elections, the left-wing vote was divided three ways, the Socialists losing their vanguard position to the PSD, or party of Social Democrats. Their leader,

---

IN THEIR FOOTSTEPS

António de Oliveira Salazar (1889–1970) Politician and minister of finance (1926 and 1928–40), as well as crony and protégé of dictator António de Carmona, he was declared premier of Portugal in 1932; he rewrote the Portuguese constitution along Fascist lines in 1933. After Carmona's death in 1951, Salazar became dictator, living more or less ascetically, suppressing all opposition.

- **Birthplace:** Salazar was born in the small village of Santa Comba, where he adopted the conservative values of his father.
- **Accomplishments:** He modernized Portuguese railways and industries. Celebrated for his cooperation with his contemporary, the Spanish dictator Francisco Franco, Salazar overhauled the country's antiquated finance system, kept revolutionary tendencies to a much-oppressed minimum, and witnessed the beginnings of the dismantling of the once-mighty Portuguese empire.
- **Resting Place:** He is buried in the Panteão Nacional in Lisbon.

Dr. Aníbal Cavaco Silva, became prime minister. In January 1986, Eanes was forced to resign the presidency. He was replaced by Soares, the former socialist prime minister; he became the first civilian president in 60 years.

Although running an administration that has seen its share of political scandal, President Soares won a landslide victory in the January 1991 presidential elections. As head of government, he faces major problems, among them unemployment, inflation, and high infant mortality and illiteracy rates. In the 1990s, the opening up of Eastern Europe has plunged Portugal into even stiffer competition for investment money and trade. Agriculture continues to plague the government, as that industry employs nearly one out of five of the labor force while turning out only a fraction of Portugal's wealth.

2. PORTUGAL'S FAMOUS PEOPLE

Afonso I (Afonso Henríques; 1109?–1185) First king of Portugal, he recognized its potential as a nation rather than as an outlying province of the Castilian kings. Son of Henry of Burgundy, count of Portugal (died 1112) and grandson of Alfonso VI of León and Castile, he seized control from his mother in 1128 and assumed for himself the title of king of a territory considerably smaller than Portugal as mapmakers know it today. Officially recognized by his Castilian cousin Alfonso VII at the treaty of Zamora, he successfully waged war on the Muslims, who then controlled much of the Iberian peninsula. His greatest victories involved capturing Lisbon and Santarém (1147), Beja (1162), Évora (1165), and Juromenha (1166) from the Moors.

Pedro Álvars Cabral (1467 or 1468–1520) Prompted by the maritime success of Vasco da Gama, Manuel I sent Cabral with 13 ships to establish trade with India in 1500. Cabral headed the ships westward in an attempt to avoid the coast of Africa (and thinking the world was much smaller than it actually is), but the expedition was carried by ocean currents and prevailing winds to the coast of Brazil (April 22, 1500). After claiming Brazil for Portugal, Cabral continued his trip toward India; lost four of his ships off the southern tip of South America; and eventually reached Calcutta and Cochin, where he established trading posts on India's uncharted northeastern edge. He returned to Portugal with only four ships. Cabral is an explorer who history has credited as the European colonizer of Brazil and eastern India.

Bartolomeu Dias (ca. 1450–1500) Dias was the navigator chosen by King John in 1487 to lead an exploration into uncharted waters around the tip of Africa. This he accomplished in 1588, thus making him the first known European to sail into the Indian Ocean. The name he gave the southern tip of Africa, Cabo Tormentoso (Cape of Storms), was later changed by King John to Cabo da Bôa Esperança (Cape of Good Hope). His other discoveries included the mouth of the Congo River. Dias died in 1500 when the ship he was commanding foundered in a tropical storm on its way to Brazil.

Sebastião José de Carvalho e Mello (marquês de Pombal; 1699–1782) An aristocrat and politician, he was considered one of the most effective envoys ever sent by Portugal to the courts of Europe. Appointed as Portuguese ambassador first to London and then to Vienna, Pombal strengthened Portugal's legendary friendship with Britain, thereby encouraging a wine trade that continues to this day.

IMPRESSIONS

This small country with its variety of climates and mixture of racial strains, is an assiduous copyist, mimic, and borrower. Any sizable Portuguese town looks like a superstitious bride's finery—something old, something new, something borrowed, and something blue.
—MARY MCCARTHY, February 1955 letter from Portugal, in ON THE COUNTRY (1962)

Famous for his almost unchallenged influence over the benevolent but indolent Joseph Emanuel (reigned 1750-77), he served as Portuguese minister of foreign affairs and eventually conducted much of the day-to-day administration of the country himself. Despite his liberation of the slaves in Brazil and the reduction of the power of the Jesuits, who had spearheaded many of the torments of the Portuguese Inquisition, Pombal is best remembered for his brilliant organization of the rebuilding of Lisbon after a 1755 earthquake reduced much of the capital to rubble.

João Batista da Silva Leitão de Almeida Garrett (1800-54) Considered the greatest of the Portuguese Romantics, Garrett successfully mingled the spirit and pathos of European romanticism with the lyricism and realism of the Portuguese psyche. His best-known dramas include the heavily politicized *Frei Luis de Sousa* (1844). His best-known poems are *Romanceiro (Songbook,* 1850) and *Fôlhas caídas (Fallen Leaves,* 1853), which are considered the greatest collection of love poems in the Portuguese repertoire. Equally well received were *Camões* and *Dona branca (The White Lady),* both released in 1828, and a historical novel set in the 14th century, *O arco de Sant' Ana.*

Henry the Navigator (Henríque o Navegador; 1394-1460) Third son of John I and his English-born queen, Philippa of Lancaster, he is considered one of the most visionary figures in Portuguese history. Serving much of his life as governor of the Algarve, he was never crowned king (leaving that honor to his older brother, Edward), he organized Portuguese expeditions into uncharted regions of Africa long before those of any other European power and established in Sagres an observatory and school of navigation that eventually became the envy of Europe. Influenced by legends of rivers of gold and the existence of isolated Christian empires within central Africa, Henry improved methods of navigation and shipbuilding; compiled the world's best library on the navigational observations of long-dead sailors; and focused the dreams of many generations of Portuguese colonists, explorers, and conquistadores. Although he never physically participated in any of the voyages, the discoveries and colonizations that ensued during his lifetime (Madeira, the Azores, Cape Verde, Senegal, and Sierra Leone) brought unprecedented wealth to Portugal, leading to the eventual foundation of the colonial empire.

João I (John the Great; 1357-1433) Illegitimate son of Peter I, he, by default upon the death of his childless half-brother, Ferdinand, became regent of Portugal and "Defender of the Faith." (João's illegitimacy encouraged claims on the Portuguese throne by the king of Castile, resulting in war and a prolonged siege of Lisbon.) Allying himself with the English, João defeated the Castilians at Aljubarrota in 1385; made a treaty of alliance and friendship with England in 1386; and married Philippa of Lancaster, the English daughter of John of Gaunt, in 1387. The most famous of this union's six sons included King Edward, João's successor, and Prince Henry the Navigator (see above). João's 1415 conquest of Ceuta, in what is now northern Morocco, touched off endless rivalry and bitterness with the Moors and gave Portugal its first taste of a foreign empire.

João II (John the Perfect; 1455-95) King of Portugal from 1481 to 1495 and patron of Bartolomeu Dias (see above), he is best remembered for his restraint in not provoking war with Spain as well as his successful diplomacy at the Treaty of Tordesillas (1494). At that treaty, Portugal gained a claim to the western region of South America, an area later to be colonized as Brazil, leaving the rest of South and Central America (with the approval of the pope, an Aragonese Spaniard) open to the colonial designs of Spain. He also severely limited the power of the feudal nobility, ordering the execution of his powerful opponent, the duke of Bragança.

João IV (John the Fortunate; 1604-56) Son of the duke of Bragança and grandson of the duke of Medina Sidonia, he became the first of the Bragança dynasty after a conspiracy and a bloodless coup d'état evicted the Spanish after their 60-year domination of Portugal. Crowned in 1640, he defeated the Spanish at the epic battle of Montijo four years later, drove the Dutch out of both Angola and Brazil, and reestablished Portugal to a respected position within Europe. He arranged one of the most important weddings of the era: the marriage of his daughter to Charles II of England, offering both Bombay and Tangier to the English as part of her dowry.

João VI (John the Merciful; 1767-1826) Son of Peter II, he married, in 1790,

Carlota, daughter of the Spanish king, in a union he was to regret the rest of his life. In 1792, he took over the Portuguese government because of the insanity of his mother, Queen Maria I, and was formally declared prince regent in 1799. In 1807, the armies of Napoleon invaded Portugal, an event that prompted the evacuation of the prince with his family and court to Brazil. There he remained as the king of Brazil for 14 years, enforcing an aristocratic heirarchy that remains to some extent there to this day. After the death of his mother in 1816, he was declared king of Portugal *in absentia*. Following the defeat of Napoleon and several Portuguese antimonarchical insurrections, he returned to Lisbon, where he assuaged his subjects with democratic and republican reforms. Most of these reforms were thwarted by the rebellion of his reactionary Spanish-born wife, who plotted for the reimposition of a monarchy centered on her son, Dom Miguel.

Ferdinand Magellan (Fernão de Magalhães/Fernando de Magallanes; ca. 1480–1521) An explorer and a navigator, Magellan served in Portuguese expeditions to Malacca and India (1505–12) and to Azamor (1513–14). When no further expeditions were forthcoming for him from Portugal, he offered his services to Spain. In 1517, he received funding from Charles V for an exploration of the Spice Islands (the Moluccas) via the unexplored western route. Two years later, he left Spain with five ships on one of the most celebrated maritime explorations in history. His stops included the La Plata river estuary of Argentina, after which his crew mutinied rather than continue around the stormy tip of South America. (This Magellan suppressed.) Between October and November 1520, he maneuvered around the endless islets and blind channels at the bottom of South America, eventually discovering the channel that led into the open waters of the Pacific. The following March, he discovered Guam, then the Philippines, where he was killed by a treacherous native chief with whom he had made an alliance. The much-diminished expedition, captained after Magellan's death by Basque-born Juan de Elcano, continued from the Philippines around the tip of Africa and back to Spain; it arrived there in 1522 after completing the first circumnavigation of the globe.

Columbano Bordalho Pinheiro (1856–1929) Considered one of the most important of the early 20th-century Portuguese painters, he spent many of his formative years in Paris. Upon returning to Portugal, he infused many of his portraits with aspects of French Romanticism, such as placing a sitter bathed in light against a background of somber clouds.

José Maria Eça de Queirós (1845–1900) Considered the greatest Portuguese novelist, he was a member of the "Generation of '70" group of intellectuals whose passion was the promulgation of realism within art. Containing prose that has been called muscular, satirical, and vibrant, his surprisingly modern works include *O crime do padro Amaro* (*Father Amaro's Crime*), *O primo Basilio* (*Cousin Basil*), and *Maya*. When not writing, he served as the Portuguese consul in Havana (1872–74), London (1874–88), and Paris (1888–1900). Today, his works are required reading for every educated Portuguese.

Amalia Rodrigues (b. 1920) The last great legend of popular music in Europe, she has been called the most famous Portuguese person since Vasco da Gama. Born into a simple Lisbon family, she performed from the age of 18 the melodies of the *fado*. Dressed entirely in black, sparing of gestures and excess ornamentation, Rodrigues is credited almost singlehandedly with the transformation of fado into an international form of poetic expression. Songs that she doesn't write herself are based on love poems from Portuguese literature (including works by Camões and 20th-century poet Pedro Homem de Melo) and evoke a melancholy known to the Portuguese as *saudade*. Her performances, which some Portuguese compare to religious experiences, often rely on inspired improvisations, when it is said that the collective unconscious of the Portuguese people possesses her. Equally fluent in an idiom of traditional folk tunes, Ms. Rodrigues is considered a specialist in the interpretation of such traditional musical forms as *vira, malhão, corrido,* and *fandango.*

António de Sequeira (1768–1837) Portugal's most celebrated early 19th-century artist studied in Rome before returning to Lisbon as official painter at the Portuguese court in 1802. Like his Spanish contemporary, Goya, de Sequeira was passionately involved in politics; when reactionary forces enforced a more despotic rule in Lisbon, he went into voluntary exile, part of which was spent in Paris. Today, he's considered a master of *chiaroscuro* (the balance of light and shadow in a picture). His works show acute perceptions and a strong social commitment without the pessimism of Goya, plus techniques of lighting that show the influence of Rembrandt. Among his most famous works are *The Mocking of Christ* (1830), *Descent from the Cross,* and a sensitive early portrait (1813) of the count of Farrobo.

Gil Vicente (1470?–1536?) Often known as the Portuguese Shakespeare, Vicente was court dramatist to Manuel I and John III. He produced 44 extant plays, some in Portuguese, some in Castilian, and some in a quirky combination of languages and medieval dialects. His works show a powerful lyricism as well as strong talents for satire and comedy. They range from the courtly tragedy *Don Duardos* to the comedic *Farsa de Inês Pereira* and include solemn religious pageants, low farces, and witty comedies.

3. ART, ARCHITECTURE, LITERATURE & MUSIC

ART Two Portuguese artists who gained recognition outside their own country are Nuno Gonçalves and Domingos António de Sequeira. Gonçalves (1482–1552) was court painter to Afonso V. He is especially known for the retable of St. Vincent, a six-panel altarpiece representing 15th-century society that shows Lisbon's patron saint being paid homage by the court and people of Portugal. Sequeira (1768–1837), also subsidized by the court, went from academic neoclassic painting to a technique similar to Goya's. The charcoal drawings done late in his career are his finest works.

All artistic trends have been explored in Portugal, but through the years of restlessness and oppression in this century, many promising painters left the country and have become more closely linked with foreign art.

Sculpture has not been an outstanding art form in Portugal, although a few noteworthy works in ecclesiastical and tomb ornamentation were done in the Middle Ages. Except for the impressive work of sculptors and stonecarvers during the early 16th-century Manueline period, the major departure from the ordinary was in the 18th century: Machado de Castro produced the equestrian statue of Jose I in Lisbon's Praçá do Comércio, plus statuary in Mafra, where he lived and taught.

Later sculptures of merit are the stone *saudade* done by **Soares dos Reis** and the portrait busts of children by Teixeira Lopes. Francisco Franco (*not* the Spanish dictator) is considered the top 20th-century Portuguese sculptor. Not attributed to any individual stone sculptor are two well-known works: the huge *Christ in Majesty* stela overlooking the Tagus River estuary, and the *Padrao dos descobrimentos* (*Monument to the Discoveries*) beside the Tagus, commemorating the 500th anniversary of the 1460 death of Prince Henry the Navigator.

The Portuguese have always preferred working in wood rather than in stone, as some beautiful examples from the late Middle Ages illustrate. Fine, often exotic, wood from the East, Madeira, and Brazil was carved into altarpieces, wallcoverings, and ceilings of cathedrals and palaces. The 16th-century **Coelho family retables** are outstanding examples of wood-carving skill. Fine wood furniture was also turned out by skilled craftsmen.

A distinctive and important Portuguese craft is the making of ceramics called *azulejos.* Because of the decorative design of these tiles, a 15th-century import from Andalusia, they were adopted by the builders in Portugal. Change in fashion has taken this ceramic art from the Moorish polychromatic design to Dutch Delft blue and white (to compete with Dutch imports) back to muted colors. They were mass-produced to meet 18th-century postearthquake rebuilding needs and can be seen in the design of public structures, churches, and private houses put up under the direction of the marquês de Pombal.

Another craft from early days still followed in Portugal is the weaving of

Arraiolos rugs. In the 16th century, Moorish women in the Alentejo district produced the rugs, and they are still woven in Persian-inspired patterns.

ARCHITECTURE   Little ancient architecture has survived in Portugal, with mere traces of Roman, Byzantine, Visigothic, and Moorish building remaining. Castles dating from the 12th century have endured, however—the Bragança citadel is the most outstanding. Fortifications from the 14th century are in Lisbon and Amieira; their architecture is borrowed, respectively, from the city fortresses of Italy and the crusader castles of Syria.

Cathedrals and churches were built in styles ranging from Romanesque to Cistercian (a blend of Romanesque and Gothic) to true Gothic. An example of the last type is the monastery at Batalha, which bears the stamp of the English stonemasons imported to build it. Most of the ecclesiastical structures today are a mixture of architecture and decoration, since they have been changed through the centuries to memorialize successive monarchs. Ornamentation changes have therefore resulted in interiors and facades of Manueline, Palladian, and baroque design.

The style known as **Manueline** (for Manuel I, 1495–1521) was a design unique to Portugal. It was used as decorative architecture on portals, porches, and interiors, mostly to adorn old rather than new structures (except for the Tower of Belém and the Jerónimos Monastery, also at Belém). This flamboyant and exuberant architectural invention, sometimes called Atlantic Gothic, was an expression of Portugal in the age when its seaborne empire flourished.

Since that time, Portuguese architecture has been mostly imitative, following such foreign styles as Renaissance, Palladian, Italianate, baroque, rococo, and Spanish. The use of new or original design has not been encouraged, although *azulejos* (see "Art," above) have been used to some extent for embellishment even in modern times to give a Portuguese flavor to borrowed architectural design. Examples can be seen at the João de Deus and Infanto Santo housing projects and the Calouste Gulbenkian Foundation complex and Exhibition Hall in Lisbon.

LITERATURE   Manuscripts of 12th-century song lyrics are the oldest written Portuguese literature. Many came from the oral poetry recited by the Iberian people in ancient times. The oral lyrics were adopted and adapted by court troubadors, public entertainers, and even clerics and aristocrats. The *cantigas* (lyric songs) were mainly songs of the court. After the rule of Dinis, the *romanceiro,* or Castilian ballad, replaced the lyric songs. Portuguese was used from the 14th century for telling historic tales in poetic form. The lyric tradition of the court troubadors continued off and on until the mid-16th century.

Meanwhile, Portuguese prose began to appear in the chronicles of court life, many with literary merit, like the work of Fernão Lopes in the 15th century. By the 16th century, chroniclers changed their focus to the global discoveries and Portugal's oceanic empire. The nation's ventures in India led also to the writing of travel books. One of the most popular of these was the work of Fernão Mendes Pinto, known as "the Father of All Lies." His *Peregrinacam (Pilgrimage)* and other writings were based more on his colorful imagination than on fact, but they read well.

High on the list of literary figures is Gil Vicente (ca. 1470–1536), father of Portuguese theater. He is acclaimed for his *autos* (religious dramas) and farces. His satirical, often ribald, wit might have signaled the birth of theatrical greatness in the country, but he fell out of favor with the court; soon after his death, his work was drastically censored and some of it destroyed by the Inquisition, which banned secular theater.

Luíz Vaz de Camões (1524–80), Portugal's most famous poet, is a national hero. He was also an explorer in an age when that was the honored vocation; his inspiration was Vasco da Gama, who discovered the sea route to India from 1479 to 1498. Da Gama's exploits were the subject of *Os Lusíadas (The Lusiads),* an epic poem by Camões.

Many Portuguese writers preferred to use the Castilian language during the Habsburg sovereignty over both their country and Spain from 1580 to 1640. However, the most widely circulated work attributed to a 17th-century Portuguese writer was the one that became the prototype of 18th-century epistolary novels. Published in French, *Lettres portugaises (Portuguese Letters)* contained five letters purportedly written by a nun from Beja, Sister Mariana Alcoforado, to her lover, the French chevalier de Chamilly. The letters describe their passionate love affair with lyric clarity.

The Age of the Discoveries was a time of glory for Portugal, and since that time the people have tended to look back to that glory in their literature and their lives. Although some realism can be seen in more recent literary efforts, lyric poetry is still predominant. Romanticism was the only European intellectual movement whose effect is visible in Portuguese literature, as it fit the people's innate mood and their nationalist beliefs. These beliefs, blended with an uncertainty caused by growing unrest early in this century, resulted in a provincialism on the part of Portugal in general that can be seen in its literature. Lyric poetry and historical novels and novellas are expressions of *saudade,* a nostalgia based on a fatalistic melancholy. One turn-of-the-century writer described *saudade* as "the key to understanding the Portuguese soul" and concluded that "progress was not possible for a people whose past will always be more attractive than their futures."

A poet and dramatist who escaped this pall of *saudade* and broadened the scope of Portuguese literature was Fernando Pessoa (1888–1935), who has been called the country's greatest poet after Camões. Some writers who disagreed with Pessoa's metaphysical focus have turned to neorealism, but they are little known outside their own country.

An interesting Portuguese work that has achieved notoriety in recent years— probably exceeded only by that accorded the 17th-century *Portuguese Letters*—is *Nova cartas portuguesas (New Portuguese Letters)*. It is the work of the "Three Marias": Maria Isabel Bareno, Maria Teresa Horta, and Maria Fatima Velho da Costa.

MUSIC Folk songs from ancient times and sacred and secular music from the church and courts have played their part in Portugal. Musical plays and choral pieces evolved eventually into opera, which is still the country's most popular form of classical music. A student of Franz Liszt, Alfredo Keil, was successful as a composer of Romantic opera. Today he is remembered for his patriotic hymn *A Portuguesa,* Portugal's national anthem. Lisbon's opera houses still draw devotees of serious music, although the fare offered is mainly of foreign origin.

The Lisbon Philharmonic, the National Radio System's Symphony Orchestra, and the Gulbenkian Orchestra and Chorus give frequent performances, especially in the capital.

The *saudade* that has influenced the country's literature is most clearly present in the *fado* songs, which are traditional expressions of the sad, romantic, nostalgic mood of Portugal. These are sung by women who are called *fadistas.*

Unless you have experienced the nostalgic sounds of fado, the songs of sorrow, you do not know Portugal—certainly not its soul. The fado is Portugal's most vivid art form; no visit to the country should be planned without at least one night spent in a local tavern where this traditional folk music is heard.

A rough translation of *fado* is "fate," from the Latin *fatum,* meaning "prophecy." Fado usually tells of unrequited love, jealousy, a longing for days gone by. As one expert put it, it speaks of "life commanded by the Oracle, which nothing can change." Fado is also sung by men, who are also called *fadistas.*

Fado found its earliest fame in the 19th century when Maria Severa, the beautiful daughter of a gypsy, took Lisbon by storm, singing her way into the hearts of the people—and especially the heart of the count of Vimioso, an outstanding bullfighter of his day. Legend has it that she is honored by present-day fadistas who wear a black-fringed shawl in her memory.

In this century the most famous exponent of fado has been Amália Rodrigues, who was introduced to American audiences in the 1950s at the New York club La Vie en Rose. She was discovered while walking barefoot and selling flowers on the Lisbon docks, near the Alfama.

Clutching black shawls around themselves, the female fadistas pour out their emotions, from the tenderest whisper of hope to a wailing lament of life's tragedies. As they sing, accompanied by a guitar and a viola, standing against a black gas street lamp, without benefit of backdrops or makeup, they seem to lose all contact with the surrounding world—they just stand there. They seemingly outdo the Rhine's Lorelei in drawing you into their world of tenderness and fire. Though much enjoyment can be derived from understanding the poetic imagery, a knowledge of Portuguese is not essential. The power of the lyrics, the warmth of the voices, and the personalities of the singers communicate a great deal.

---

4. RELIGION & FOLKLORE

RELIGION From its medieval origins, Portugal has been intricately bound in an allegiance to the Church. (The existence of the country itself in the early days of Afonso Henríques probably stemmed from a religion-based hatred of the Moors.) Although they were devout, the Portuguese monarchs never seemed as rabidly fanatical in their faith as their neighbors in Spain. Likewise, although Portugal endured an Inquisition, its purges never ran as deep or were quite as bloody as those of the Spaniards.

Today, although observant of Roman Catholic doctrine and reasonably devout, the country seems more interested in the melancholy passion of the fado and the fanfare of football (soccer) than in the passions of religion. Since the Industrial Revolution and the social unrest that accompanied it, Portugal has maintained an uncomfortable duality between its allegiance to the Roman Catholic Church and a general dislike for clerical directives coming from beyond their village or town. Nonetheless, supplications to God tend to increase during times of trouble: According to an ancient Portuguese proverb, "When food is on the table, the Saints are left in peace."

Despite the influences of socialist politics and a general disillusionment, the Church continues to inspire great loyalty, especially in rural areas and probably more among women than among men. In some villages, especially in the more devout northern sections, at least half of an entire village might be found in church on Sunday.

In rural areas, religion is closely associated with protection of fields, family, households, and domestic animals and used as a kind of appeasement against the many ills that might potentially cause damage. Significantly, some of the most sought after rustic antiques in Portugal are traditional 19th-century ox yokes, lavishly carved from timbers into ornate depictions of Christian imagery, complete with crosses and symbols of fertility to bless and protect the oxen plowing the fields.

Today, despite tendencies within Portugal to both respect and condemn the Church, more than 90% of the people still professes to be Roman Catholic. In 1940, a concordat was signed with the Holy See in Rome, an act that defined the relationship between the Portuguese state and the Catholic Church. The mainland of Portugal today comprises three metropolitan archdioceses under archbishops in Lisbon, Braga, and Évora. There are 20 dioceses. Throughout the country, there is freedom of worship, both public and private.

Despite the decay of allegiance to the Church and the unending diversions of football and politics, the most popular pastime in Portugal involves going on pilgrimages, usually to one or another of the many holy shrines scattered throughout the country. Foremost among them is the shrine of Fátima, whose tenets are discussed more fully on pages 190–91.

FOLKLORE Portugal's Atlantic melancholy, its majestic vistas, and its history's drama and occasional madness have all contributed to a rich body of legend, lore, and folklore. Some of these tales and myths were promoted as idiology that unified the country against the menace of neighboring Spain. Other tales were borrowed from Christian, Moorish, and—in some cases—Celtic mythology that permeated the land in prehistoric times. Even St. Martin of Dume—the Hungarian-trained 5th-century saint credited with converting the Portuguese to Christianity—railed against the Portuguese tendency to rely on charms, divination, good-luck symbols, and invocations of the dead.

The religious and pagan themes run deep. Churches throughout the country are adorned with unusual votive offerings, often made of wax, which hang on strings near the altar or near the votive candles. Intended to promote divine healing for ailments, they are shaped like heads, hands, breasts, babies, pigs, or oxen. They might include yellowing wedding dresses or hair braids and are sometimes the more bizarre (yet touching) sights in a rural chapel. Votives are offered to any of a number of saints in thanks for blessings prayed for and received. If votives are not offered to the saint, it is sometimes believed the saint will take revenge. Today, the Church is more critical of these gifts, but as late as the 1960s, the gift-giving rituals were tolerated and encouraged in many parts of the country.

The phases of the moon are said to be important to the health of vegetables, crops, and babies. The most vigorous of any of these will be sown or conceived, it is believed, during the waxing of the moon. Certain fountains are said to contain healing powers and to conceal the entrances to underground chambers where Enchanted Mooresses are said to be hiding, guarding great treasures. A mother should not breastfeed her infant and eat simultaneously lest the baby grow up to be greedy. And an hours-old infant should not be taken outdoors immediately for fear of inciting the evil eye; rather, it should be placed on a bed near a pair of his or her father's outstretched trousers, the symbol of which will frighten away witches.

A respect for death and bereavement is pervasive. Black is probably the most popular color for clothes in Portugal today, as it is the traditional color for anyone in mourning. Though followed less strictly today than 30 years ago, widows are expected to remain in black for around 7 years after the death of their husbands, and many choose to continue to wear it the rest of their lives. Mourning the loss of a parent is expected to last around 2 or 3 years. Oddly, the loss of a child is not associated with any formal period of mourning.

The land is rife with many different legends as well, some popularized as unifying tales for the Portuguese. Among them is the Rooster of Barcelos, who—although cooked and about to be served as the main course in a magistrate's dinner—crowed ecstatically to prove the innocence of a pilgrim wrongfully accused of theft. Equally touching is the Legend of the Almond Blossoms, which dates from the 10th century's Moorish occupation of the Algarve. A Viking maiden, captured as a child during battle, fell in love with the son of the local Caliph and married him. Despite their joy, only the sight of a field of almond trees, reminiscent of the snow of her native Norway, could keep her happy and healthy in her adopted Moorish home. In gratitude, the Caliph ordered the planting of thousands of almond trees. Today, residents of the Algarve recall this myth every February when the almond trees bloom.

Another legend involves Dom Fuas Ropinho, one of Portugal's founders and the subject of several poems by Camões. The devil, vengeful at the rare instance of facing a virtuous and uncorruptible man, disguised himself as a stag during a hunt and led Dom Fuas to the edge of a steep rocky cliff. Only the image of the Virgin (which appeared suddenly in a blaze of light) caused the hunter to stop, only moments before he'd have been thrown by his horse over the rocks to his death. In 1182, Dom Fuas built near the cliffs a chapel to Our Lady of Nazaré. Rebuilt in the 1500s, it was visited by Vasco da Gama, who prayed there in thanks after discovering the sea route to India in 1498.

Finally, there is the Miracle of the Roses: The Aragonese Princess Isabella spent the bulk of her personal fortune to help the penniless nuns of Santa Clara. Her kind but thrifty husband, Dinis, was about to punish her severely for donating her final funds to the order but was stopped when the loaves of bread Isabella was carrying were miraculously transformed into roses. Since it was January, when roses were out of season, the king fell on his knees in thanks; to everyone's delight, Dinis massively increased her annual income so she could continue to make charitable gifts as she saw fit. Today, the sainted queen is the patron saint of Coimbra, with biannual torchlight processions held in her honor.

Other legends reflect the madness of some of the country's rulers and are in some cases historically true: In the 1300s, Prince Dom Pedro fell in love with one of his wife's ladies-in-waiting, a Spanish-born girl named Inês de Castro. Soon Inês was banished from the country. When Pedro's wife died, Inês returned to live openly with him. Fearing that Inês was fomenting a plot against the monarchy, a group of nobles (including Afonso IV, Pedro's father) arranged to have her killed. Pedro, upon finding her body, became insane. When he ascended the throne 2 years later, he had the hearts of Inês's murderers torn from their bodies, ordered that she be exhumed and dressed in royal clothes, and arranged for her coronation as queen of Portugal in the monastery of Alcobaça. Part of the ceremony involved the obligatory kissing of the skeletal royal hand by all the nobles present. Today, the tomb of Inês that Pedro commissioned for Alcobaça is considered one of the most beautiful in Portugal.

5. CULTURAL & SOCIAL LIFE

THE PEOPLE   The Portuguese have a mixed ethnic ancestry. The blood of the first Ibero-Celtics (later called *Lusitani* by the Romans), Phoenicians, Carthaginians, Romans, Germans, Visigoths, Moors, Jews, Arabs, and Berbers flows in the veins of the Portuguese of today, making a description of the people as being of general Mediterranean stock perhaps the most accurate. A small African minority has appeared in the country as a result of decolonization of Portugal's African territories. The country's districts present a diverse set of social structures; some are classless but impoverished, others have well-defined hierarchical parameters. Despite the declaration in the constitution that the republic is "engaged in the formation of a classless society," social and economic divisions remain, particularly because of the many variations created by land ownership, urban and rural environments, and regional differences.

The Portuguese have developed a character decidedly different from that of the Spanish, their neighbors on the Iberian peninsula. Those who travel among and mingle with the Portuguese usually return home filled with a special warmth for the people, who are easily approachable and helpful. You may find after you've left that you have made several lifetime friends and correspondents.

In Portugal, the family as an institution remains firmly entrenched, even in the aftermath of revolution and upheaval. Many Portuguese have no close friends outside the family unit. The Roman Catholic Church still exerts strong influence over many segments of society; it is rare to meet a non-Catholic Portuguese.

Although city dwellers have become increasingly sophisticated, their counterparts down the economic and social scale, especially in the countryside, tend to retain traditional social roles. Some Portuguese women still work in the fields with the men, sowing seed, guiding oxen, carrying milk jugs, and harvesting. Children often labor in the fields alongside their parents. The wife of a fisherman may help him repair nets and then sell the catch in the streets, returning in the evening to her cottage to do all the housework, cooking, and mending.

In Lisbon, the people dress well, particularly in the business district. In the country you'll still see traditional garb; some older women still wear black shawls draped around their shoulders and carry baskets of produce balanced on their heads.

The Portuguese are a proud people. Life is a little more formal in the industrial north of Portugal; in the south, in the Algarve, the approach seems more casual, and the people's attitudes more relaxed and friendly.

LANGUAGE   Portuguese is a Romance language that evolved mainly from a dialect spoken when Portugal was a province of the Spanish kingdom of León and Castile. Portuguese has developed separately from other Romance dialects, such as those that evolved into Spanish. After Portugal became independent in the 11th century, its borders expanded southward to the sea, and the country took in areas previously governed by Muslim Moors. The language called *Mozarabic,* spoken by the Christians living as Moorish subjects, was integrated into the Portuguese dialect, which created the language of Portugal. The basic language of today, both oral and written, was solidified and perfected in Lisbon, the capital, and Coimbra, the ancient university city. There are, of course, regional variations and pronunciations.

One writer suggested that Portuguese has "the hiss and rush of surf crashing against the bleak rocks of Sagres." If you don't speak it, you'll find French, Spanish, and English commonly spoken in Lisbon, along the Costa do Sol, and in Porto, as well as in many parts of the Algarve. In small villages and towns, hotel staffs and guides usually speak English. The Portuguese people are helpful and patient. Gestures often suffice.

---

6. FOOD & DRINK

FOOD   Meals and Dining Customs   Portuguese food was summed up well by Mary Jean Kempner in her *Invitation to Portugal:* "The best Portuguese food is provincial, indigenous, eccentric, and proud—a reflection of the chauvinism of this complex people. It takes no sides, assumes no airs, makes no concessions or bows to Brillat-Savarin—and usually tastes wonderful."

The basis of much Portuguese cooking is olive oil. Garlic is used extensively. However, if you select anything prepared to order you can request that it be *sem alho* (without garlic).

It's customary in most establishments to order soup (invariably a big bowl filled to the brim), then a fish and a meat course. Potatoes and/or rice are likely to accompany both the meat and the fish platters.

In many restaurants, the chef features a *prato do dia*—that is, a plate of the day—which is actually several listings. These dishes are prepared fresh that day and often are cheaper than the regular offerings.

Dining hours in Portugal are much earlier than they are in Spain. The best time for lunch is between 1 and 2:30pm; for dinner the hours are from 7:30 to 9pm.

Cuisine   Many Portuguese begin their meals with *percébes,* roughly translated as goose barnacles. These little devils are the subject of much controversy. One Lisbon newspaper suggested to tourists that if they "can bear their repulsive appearance," they'll find "an incomparable morsel of delicious seafood" within. Others claim that all they taste from barnacles is brackish seawater.

There will be no controversy among those who begin their meal with *camaraoes* (shrimp). Most restaurants serve a heaping, delectable platter full.

Of course, another way of beginning your repast is to select from the offerings of trays of *acepipes variados,* Portuguese hors d'oeuvres, which might include everything from a sea creature known as "knife" to the inevitable olives and tuna.

From the soup kitchen, the most popular broth is *caldo verde,* literally green broth. Made from cabbage, sausage, potatoes, and olive oil, it is commonly encountered in the north. Another ubiquitous soup is *sopa alentejana,* simmered with garlic and bread among other ingredients. Portuguese cooks are canny, knowing how to gain every last morsel of nutrition from their fish, meat, and vegetables. The fisherpeople make a *sopa de mariscos* by boiling the shells from fish, then richly flavoring the stock and lacing it with white wine.

The first main dish you're likely to encounter on any menu is *bacalhau* (salted codfish), the *o fiel amigo* (faithful friend) to the Portuguese. As you drive through fishing villages in the north, you'll see racks and racks of the fish drying in the sun. Bacalhau has literally saved the lives of thousands from starvation.

Foreigners may not wax as rhapsodical about bacalhau, although it's prepared in imaginative ways, reportedly one for every day of the year. Common ways of serving it include *bacalhau cozido* (boiled with such vegetables as carrots, cabbage, and spinach, then baked), *bacalhau à Bras* (fried in olive oil with onions and potatoes and flavored with garlic), *bacalhau à Gomes de Sá* (stewed with black olives, potatoes, and onions, then baked and topped with a sliced boiled egg), and *bacalhau no churrasco* (barbecued).

Aside from codfish, the classic national dish is *caldeirada*, which was once described as the Portuguese version of a savory Mediterranean bouillabaisse. Prepared at home, it is a simple kettle of fish, with bits and pieces of the latest catch. From the kitchen of a competent chef, it is a pungent stew with choice bits and pieces of fruits of the sea.

Next on the platter is the Portuguese sardine, which many gastronomes have called elegant. This unassuming fish goes by the pompous Latin name of *Clupea pilchardus* and is found off the Atlantic coasts of Iberia as well as France. Many of the sardines come from Setúbal, a city south of the Tagus that is most often visited on a day trip from Lisbon. As you stroll through the alleys of the Alfama or pass along the main streets of small villages throughout Portugal, you'll sometimes see women kneeling in front of braziers on their front doorsteps, grilling these large sardines left behind for domestic consumption. To have them grilled, order *sardinhas assadas*.

Shellfish is one of the great delicacies of the Portuguese table. Its scarcity and the demand of foreign markets have led to astronomical price tags. Tourists devour them and lament later when the bill is presented. The price of lobsters or crabs changes every day, depending on market quotations. Therefore the tariff doesn't appear on the menu; rather, you'll see the abbreviation, "Preco V.," meaning variable price. When the waiter brings one of these crustaceans to your table, ask the price. That way you'll avoid shock when your sin is tallied up.

If you do decide to splurge, make sure you get fresh shellfish. Many of these creatures from the deep, such as king-size crabs, are cooked and then displayed in restaurant windows. If they don't sell that day, I suspect the chef places them there again the next day.

When fresh, *santola* (crab) is a delicacy. It's often served stuffed (*santola recheada*), although this specialty may be too pungent for unaccustomed Western palates. *Amêijoas*, baby clams, are a reliable item of the Portuguese kitchen. *Lagosta* is translated as lobster; in fact, it's really a crayfish, best when served without adornment. If you see the words *piri-piri* on the menu following lobster, rush for the nearest exit. This is a sauce made of hot pepper from Angola. Jennings Parrott once wrote: "After tasting it you will understand why Angola wanted to get it out of the country." However, in fairness, many foreigners accustomed to hot, peppery food like this dish.

A wide variety of good-tasting and inexpensive fish dishes is also available: *salmonette* (red mullet) from Setubal, *robalo* (bass), *lenguado* (sole), and sweet-tasting *pescada* (hake). Perhaps less appealing to the average diner, but preferred by many discriminating palates, are *eiros* (eels), *polvo* (octopus), and *lampreas* (lampreys); the latter is a seasonal feature in the northern Minho district.

Porto residents are known as "tripe eaters." The specialty is *dobrada*, tripe with beans, a favorite of the workers. The *cozido a portuguesa* is another dish much in demand: This stew often employs both beef and pork, along with fresh vegetables and sausages. The chief offering of the beer tavern is *bife na frigideira*, beef in mustard sauce, usually served with a fried egg on top, all piping hot in a brown ceramic dish. Thinly sliced *iscas* (calves' livers) are usually well-prepared and sautéed with onion.

Meat, especially beef and veal, is less satisfying. The best meat in Portugal is *porco* (pork), usually tender and juicy. In particular, order *porco alentejano*, fried pork in a succulent sauce with baby clams, often cooked with herb-flavored onions and tomatoes. In the same province, *cabrito* (roast kid) is another treat, flavored with herbs and garlic. Chicken tends to be hit-or-miss and is perhaps best when spit-roasted a golden brown (*frango no espeto*). In season, game is good, especially *perdiz* (partridge) and *codorniz estufada* (pan-roasted quail).

Cheese (*queijo*) is usually eaten separately and not with fruit as in France. The most common varieties of Portuguese cheese are made from sheep or goat's milk. A popular variety is *queijo da serra* (literally, cheese from the hills). Another much-in-demand cheese is *queijo do Alentejo*, plus *queijo de Azeitao*. Many prefer *queijo Flamengo* (similar to Dutch Gouda).

Locked away in isolated convents and monasteries, nuns and monks created original sweet-tooth concoctions. Many of these dessert specialties have been handed down over the years and are nowadays sold in little pastry shops throughout Portugal. In Lisbon or Porto and a few other Portuguese cities, you can visit a *salao de chá* (tea salon) at 4pm to sample these delicacies. Regrettably, too few restaurants feature regional desserts; many rely on caramel custard or fresh fruit.

Portugal doesn't offer many egg dishes, except for omelets. However, eggs are used extensively in many of the sweets. Although egg yolks cooked in sugar may not appeal to you, you may want to try some of the more original offerings. Perhaps the best known are *ovos moles* (soft eggs sold in colorful barrels) that originate in Aveiro. From the same district capital comes *ovos de fio* (string eggs).

The most typical dessert is *arroz doce*, cinnamon-flavored rice pudding. As mentioned above, flan, or caramel custard, appears on all menus. If you're in Portugal in summer, ask for a peach from Alcobaca. One of these juicy, succulent yellow fruits will spoil all other peaches for you forever. In a first-class restaurant, the waiter will go through an elaborate ritual of peeling it in front of you. Sintra is known for its strawberries, Setubal for its orange groves, the Algarve for its almonds and figs, Elvas for its plums, the Azores for their pineapples, and Madeira for its passionfruit. Some people believe that if you eat too much of the latter, you'll be driven insane.

In this guide, restaurants are listed in price categories. At a **very expensive** restaurant dinner for one (excluding drink and tip) costs more than 6,000$ (about $36); at an **expensive** restaurant, about 3,500$ to 6,000$ ($21–$36); at a **moderate** restaurant, about 1,800$ to 3,500$ ($11–$21); and at an **inexpensive** restaurant, less than about 1,800$ ($11).

DRINKS Drinking water is safe in Lisbon, along the Costa do Sol (Estoril and Cascais), and in Porto. In less-visited towns and villages, you may want to order bottled water. You can ask for it to be with or without "gas."

One of the joys of dining in Portugal is to discover the regional wines. With the exception of port and Madeira, they remain little known to most of the world.

Among the table wines, my personal favorites are from the mountainous wine district known as **Dao.** Its red wines are ruby-colored, and their taste is often described as velvety; its white wines are light and delicate enough to make a fit accompaniment to Portuguese shellfish. From the sandy dunes of the **Colares** wine district, near Sintra, emerges a full-bodied wine made from Ramisco grapes. A Portuguese writer once noted that Colares wine has "a feminine complexion, but a virile energy."

The *vinhos verdes* (green wines) have many adherents. These light wines, low in alcohol content, come from the northwestern corner of Portugal, the **Minho** district. The wine is gaseous since it's made from grapes that are not fully matured. Near Estoril, the **Carcavelos** district produces an esoteric wine commonly served as an apéritif or with dessert. As it mellows, its bouquet becomes more powerful. The **Bucelas** district, near Lisbon, makes a wine from the Arinto grape, among others. Its best-known wine is white, with a bit of an acid taste.

Port wine is produced on the arid slopes of the Douro. Only vineyards within this area are recognized as yielding genuine port. The wine is shipped from Portugal's second-largest city, Porto, which the English have dubbed Oporto. Drunk in tulip-shaped glasses, it comes in many different colors and flavors. The pale dry port makes an ideal apéritif, and you can request it at a time when you might normally order dry sherry. The ruby or tawny port is sweet or medium dry and usually drunk as an after-dessert liqueur. The most valuable port is either vintage or crusted wine. Crusted port does not mean vintage—rather, it takes its name from the decanting of its crust. Vintage port is the very best. In a period of a decade, only 3 years may be declared vintage.

Port is blended to assure a consistency of taste. Cyril Ray called it "one of the heartiest and handsomest of wines." Matured in wooden casks, the wood ports are either white, tawny, or ruby red. At first the wine is a deep ruby; it turns more like the color of straw as it ages.

Port wine "perpetuated and glorified the fame of Porto," as one citizen put it. The first foreigners to be won over by it were the English in the 17th century. In more recent times, however, the French import more of the wine than the British. The grapes are still crushed by barefoot men; but this shouldn't alarm you because the wine is purified before it's bottled.

Its greatest chic was in times gone by, but **Madeira wine** remains popular. It was highly favored by the early American colonists. Made with grapes grown in volcanic soil, it is fortified with brandy before it's shipped out.

The major types of Madeira are Sercial (a dry wine, drunk as an apéritif, once a favorite with characters in Galsworthy novels), Malmsey (the dessert wine the duke of Clarence allegedly asked to drown in to escape torture at the hands of his brother), and Boal (a heady wine used on many occasions, from a banquet following a hunt to a private tête-à-tête). Perhaps one of the finest statements ever made about Madeira wine is the following: "It gives vivacity to a social gathering, profundity to a solitary meditation, helps a man to think well of his friends and to forgive his enemies."

Beer (*cerveja*) is gaining new followers yearly. One of the best of the home brews is sold under the name of Sagres, honoring the town in the Algarve that enjoyed associations with Henry the Navigator.

7. SPORTS & RECREATION

SPORTS

FOOTBALL Football—called soccer in the United States—is the most popular sport in Portugal, and it is taken so seriously that on Sunday afternoons during important matches (with Spain or Brazil, for example), the country seems to come almost to a standstill. It's a fast game played by 2 teams of 11 players for 90 minutes (halves of 45 minutes each). The players are allowed to use only their feet, torsos, and heads to move the ball and score goals by kicking it between two fixed goalposts. Notices for the venue of upcoming matches are prominently posted with hotel concierges, in newspapers, and on bulletin boards throughout whatever city you happen to be in. One of the most-watched teams, incidentally, is that of Porto, which won the European Cup in 1987. Loyalty of Lisbon fans seems equally divided between its two hometown teams, Benfica and Sporting Club.

GOLF With its sun-flooded expanses of underutilized land and its cultural links for many generations to Britain through trade and shared interests, Portugal has developed a passion for golf. Most of the nation's finest courses are relatively new: Since the late 1970s, more than 20 world-class golf courses have been carved out of Portuguese terrain, most in the south (the Algarve), with another half-dozen in the vicinity of Lisbon, four near Porto, and three on Madeira and the Azores. Usually set within sight of the sea, most have deliberately incorporated dramatic topography as part of their layouts, and most were conceived by such world-class golf-course designers as Robert Trent Jones, Henry Cotton, and Frank Pennick. For more information and an overview on golf in Portugal, contact the **Federação Portuguesa de Golf** (Portuguese Golf Federation), Rua Almeida Brandão 39, 1200 Lisboa (tel. 01/674-658).

TENNIS Since the turn of the century, tennis has been played by Portugal's wealthy and by wealthy expatriates, often on private courts set in verdant gardens or within such pockets of posh as Estoril. In recent years, however, a new generation of tennis players, many champions within their respective leagues, have been bred on Portuguese soil, often near Lisbon or near any of the new group of resort hotels cropping up on the Algarve. The resort hotels are keenly aware of the availability of local tennis courts, so most offer a "pro" available for lessons. For more information and an overview on tennis within Portugal, contact the **Federação Portuguesa de Tenis** (Portuguese Tennis Federation), Estadio Nacional, Caxias, 2480 Oeiras (tel. 41/98-472).

RECREATION

NATURE WATCHING The azure skies, golden fields, and gray-green olive groves of Portugal combine to form memorable vistas that can best be appreciated while hiking. This form of recreation is especially suited for birdwatchers who long ago realized that the westermost tip of continental Europe lies along the main routes of birds migrating between the warm wetlands of Africa and the cooler breeding grounds of northern Europe. The moist and rugged terrain of north Portugal is especially suited for nature-watching, particularly around Peneda-Geres, where wild boar, wild horses, and wolves can still be spotted roaming through hills and forests.

HORSEBACK RIDING The Portuguese have prided themselves on their equestrian skills since the earliest battles against the Roman invaders. One of the last of the world's horses bred solely from European stock are the Alter horses, who live for the most part within the Royal Stables at Alter do Chão, in the Portuguese plains. Most of the resorts along the Algarve, plus a few in Cascais, maintain stables stocked with horses for long trail rides through hills, along beaches, and through ancient sunbaked villages. For more information about horseback-riding options within Portugal, contact the **Federação Equestre Portuguesa** (Portuguese Equestrian Federation), Avenida Duque d'Ávila, 9, 1000 Lisboa (tel. 01/67-46-58).

FISHING Portugal isn't the bone-dry desert depicted in many photographs of its southern regions. The north receives abundant rainfall and contains rugged hills and some of the best-stocked streams in Iberia. (Most noteworthy are the Rio Minho, the Ria Vouga, the Ria Lima, and the creeks and lakes of the Sierra de Estrêla.) If you plan on fishing in Portugal, you'll need a license, which can in most circumstances be obtained at the **Direcção Geral das Florestas,** Avenida João Crisostomo 26–28, 1200 Lisboa (tel. 01/53-61-32). Fishing within these inland waters is limited compared to that within the wide blue ocean that faces the 500 miles of Portuguese coastline. Deepsea fishing, in waters richly stocked with fish swept toward Europe on northeastward-flowing ocean currents, turns up abundant catches. Fishing boats can be rented, with and sometimes without a crew, all along the Algarve as well.

HUNTING Some of the best game dishes in Europe are prepared within Iberia. The richest catches in Portugal of quail, partridges, hare, deer, and wild boar are made within the mountainous Trás os Montes, along the Costa Verde, and within the flat and undulating plains of the south-central district. You'll need a license and a certain number of permits to bring firearms into Portugal. Register before you begin hunting at the local town hall and contact the Direcção Geral das Florestas (see "Fishing," above) for a hunting license.

BULLFIGHTS No discussion of Portuguese recreation would be complete without a reference to bullfighting (*La Tourada*). Unlike the rituals observed in Spain and parts of South America, the bull is not killed at the end of the event but released to an ongoing life of grazing and stud duties. The *cavaleiro* (horsemen) dress in 18th-century costumes, which include silk jackets, tricornered hat, and tan riding breeches. Bullfights are held at regular intervals in Lisbon's Campo Pequeño area, across the Tagus in the working-class city of Santarém, throughout the south-central plains, and in the Azores.

WATER SPORTS One of the most famous seagoing nations in the world, Portugal offers many choices. Outside the Algarve, few will be highly organized, although the country's 500 miles of Atlantic coastline are richly peppered with secluded beaches and fishing hamlets. A recent development, especially in the Algarve, is the construction of a series of water parks, where large swimming pools complete with wave-making machines, water slides, and fun fountains amuse hordes of local residents, especially children. Sailing on well-designed oceangoing craft can be arranged at the Cascais Yacht Club, at any of the marinas in the Tagus, near Lisbon, or along the Algarve—particularly near the sprawling new marina at Vilamoura. The surfing along the sunblasted and windswept coast at Guincho has attracted fans from throughout Europe. For information about sailing and water-borne events throughout

Portugal, contact the **Club Naval de Lisboa,** Pav. Náutico, Doca de Belém (tel. 01/63-00-61); the **Federação Portuguesa de Vela** (Portuguese Sailing Federation), Doca de Belém, 1300 Lisboa (tel. 01/641-2152); or the **Federação Portuguesa de Actividades Subaquaticas** (Portuguese Underwater Sports Federation), Rua Almeida Brandão 39, 1200 Lisboa (tel. 01/396-4322).

8. RECOMMENDED BOOKS, FILMS & RECORDINGS

BOOKS
GENERAL & HISTORY

The Portuguese: The Land and Its People, by Marion Kaplan (Viking, 1991), is one of the best surveys of the country to have appeared since the revolution. Here you get a lot of history along with travel information—all the way from the country's Moorish origins to its maritime empire and into the chaotic 20th century. Both the politics and the economy—along with its literary tradition, art, and architecture—are covered.

Beginning in the 1960s, several writers have tried to capture or survey the complete saga of Portuguese history or have focused on limited aspects of the story. Notable examples include *History of Portugal,* volumes I and II, by A. H. de Oliveira (Columbia University Press, 1976); *The Portuguese Seaborne Empire,* by C. R. Boxer (Greenwood Press, 1969); *The Individuality of Portugal,* by Dan Dtsnislawski (Greenwood Press, 1969); and *A History of Spain and Portugal,* by William C. Atkinson (Pelican Books, 1965).

The Discoverers—An Encyclopedia of Explorers and Exploration, edited by Helen Delpar (McGraw-Hill, 1980), is filled with the legend and lore of the great maritime adventurers, notably Vasco de Gama, Ferdinand Magellan, and Prince Henry the Navigator.

FICTION & BIOGRAPHY

The epic poem of Portugal, *O Lusíadas,* written in 1572 by Luíz Vaz de Camões, celebrates the Portuguese "Era of Discoveries" and was written by its premier poet, who is also a national hero. In 1987, Penguin re-released this timeless classic. The best biography on Camões himself still remains Aubrey Bell's *Luís de Camões* (Oxford Press, 1923). (The full name of Camões is spelled differently by various writers).

One of Portugal's best known and most beloved writers, Eça de Queiroz, wrote in the late 19th century. Several of his best-known narratives have been translated into English, notably *The Maias* (St. Martin's Press, 1965), *The Illustrious House of Ramires* (Ohio University Press, 1968), *The Mandarin and Other Stories* (Ohio University Press, 1965), *The City and the Mountains* (Ohio University Press, 1967), *The Relic* (Max Reinhart, 1955), *The Sin of Father Amaro* (Max Reinhart, 1962), and *Dragon's Teeth* (Greenwood Press, 1972). Quieroz (1845–1900) was the most realistic of the novelists of his time, and his works were much admired by Émile Zola in France. His generation became known as "the Generation of 1870," and of his books cited above, *The Maias* is the best known and perhaps the best. Read it even if you have to bypass the others.

The great poet Fernando Pessoa is second only to Camões in the list of illustrious Portuguese writers. Some of his works have been translated into English, including *Selected Poems* (Penguin Books, 1982), *Selected Poems* (University of Texas Press, 1971), and *Selected Poems* (Swallow Press, 1971). Pessoa (1888–1935) is still beloved to the Portuguese, and he appears on their 100-escudo note.

One of modern Portugal's best novelists is José Saramago; his *Balthasar and Blimunda* (Harcourt Brace, 1987) is a magical account of a flying machine and the construction of Mafra Palace—a delightful read. You may want to continue to explore this interesting writer's work by reading *The Year of the Death of Ricardo Reis* (Harcourt Brace, 1991).

FILMS

Unless you speak Portuguese and live in Brazil or mainland Portugal, chances are you are not aware there is a Portuguese-language film industry. Although American films predominate on the screens of Portugal today, occasionally a Portuguese film will "break out" of its language bottleneck and be translated into English or some other language and shown on American or European screens.

A case in point is *Alex*, a 1992 film written and directed by Teresa Villaverde in Portuguese with English subtitles. Starring Ricardo Colares as Alex, it tells of a morose young man recounting events from his childhood. The film is set in the early 1970s and involves the loss of a father who went to war in the African colonies as a devoted family man but returned a "cold and moody enigma."

Historically, the earliest films, beginning in 1908, were documentaries. In 1909, the first feature film, *The Crimes of Diego Alves*, was produced. After World War I, Italian and French directors were attracted to the landscapes (and economics) of Portugal to make feature productions. By 1927, a major mover and shaker had emerged in the film industry: Leitão de Barrios, who made a name in the field of dramatic documentaries, notably his 1929 *Mario de Mar*. In the years preceding World War II, he produced three of his major successes: *The Pupils of the Parish Priest* (1935), *Bocage* (1936), and *Ala Arriba* (1937). Sometimes he turned to Portuguese legend for inspiration, as in his historical films on Inês de Castro and Camões. Actually, only 15 feature films were made in Portugal during the first decade of sound. Dramatized documentaries by nonprofessionals, sometimes using native fisherman and their families, formed the major Portuguese film idiom in the years following World War II.

RECORDINGS

The best overview of the rich repertoire of traditional Portuguese music is sometimes available in the international departments of very large North American record stores. One of the best ways to understand the Portuguese sense of *saudade* (nostalgic longing for lost love and lost greatness) is through its music. The greatest fadista of all time was Amália Rodrigues, whose *Greatest Hits* was released in 1987 through her Portuguese agent, Valentim de Carvalho; it is now widely available in North America's largest record stores. The most evocative tracks on Rodrigues's albums include *"Povo que lavas no rio"* ("People Who Wash Their Clothes in the River"), *"Rapaz da camisola verde"* ("The Boy with the Green Sweater"), *"Naufragio"* ("The Sinking"), and *"Trovo do vento que passa"* ("Searching for the Wind which has Passed"). The lyrics to these were written early in this century by Pedro Homem de Melo. Equally moving are the tracks *"Leonor"* and *"Erros meus"* ("My Mistake"), whose words were written by the Renaissance poet Camões.

One of Portugal's great male fadistas is João Braga, whose CDs *Na paz do teu amor* (*In the Peace of Your Love*), and *Cantiga de mar e mãgoa* (Songs of Pain), both released by Valentim de Carvalho, are favorites today throughout the country. Also highly emotive is a singer known only as Rodrigo, whose albums include *Ha mais marês que marinheiro* (*There Is More Ocean than Sailors*) and *Meu pais recem-nascido* (*My New-born Country*).

Traditional music by other artists, some from the great days of early fado recordings, can be heard on *Fado de Lisbõa* (*Fados from Lisbon*, 1928–1936), distributed by Heritage/Interstate Music Ltd. (HT-CD-14). Music derived from Portuguese celebrations in villages, usually among families at weddings, can be appreciated on *Portuguese Traditional Music* (Au Vidis Records, D-8008). Portuguese instrumentalist Manuel Marques is featured on *Les guitares du Portugal* (Buda Records/Music of the World, 825032). More fado can be appreciated on *Un parfum de fado*, volumes 1 to 3, and *Portugal: The Spirit of Fado* (both distributed by Playa Sound/Au Vidis).

CHAPTER 2

PLANNING A TRIP TO PORTUGAL

This chapter is devoted to the where, when, and how of your trip to Portugal—all those issues required to put your trip together and take it on the road.

In this chapter I concentrate on what you need to do before you go, plus getting to and around Portugal. In addition to helping you decide when to take your vacation, I answer questions you might have about what to take, where to stay, where to gather information, and what documents you need. I also cover various alternative and specialty travel options, such as educational travel; include tips for special travelers; and provide information specifically for British travelers. The chapter ends with a "Fast Facts" section that provides a quick reference for information.

1. INFORMATION, ENTRY REQUIREMENTS & MONEY

SOURCES OF INFORMATION

Before you go, contact one of the overseas offices of the **Portuguese National Tourist Office.** The main office in the United States is at 590 Fifth Ave., **New York,** NY 10036-4704 (tel. 212/354-4403). In Canada, the office is at 600 Bloor St. W., Suite 1005, **Toronto,** ON M4W 3B8 (tel. 416/921-7376). In Great Britain, contact the Portuguese Tourist Office at 1–5 New Bond St., **London** W1Y 0NP (tel. 071/493-3873).

Other useful information sources are newspapers and magazines. To find the latest articles that have been published on your destination, ask for the *Readers' Guide to Periodical Literature* at a library and look under the city/country for listings.

You may also want to obtain a U.S. State Department background bulletin on Portugal. Write to the Superintendent of Documents, U.S. Government Printing Office, Washington, DC 20402 (tel. 202/783-3238) or stop in at a GPO bookstore.

A good travel agent can also be a valuable source of information. If you use one, make sure he or she is a member of the **American Society of Travel Agents** (ASTA). If you are poorly served by a travel agent, write to ASTA's Consumer Affairs Department, 1101 King St., Alexandria, VA 22314.

And, finally, the best sources of all are friends and other travelers who have just returned from Portugal.

ENTRY REQUIREMENTS

U.S., Canadian, British, Australian, New Zealand, and Irish citizens with a valid passport do not need a visa to enter Portugal if they do not plan to stay more than 90 days and do not expect to work there. If you find that you would like to stay more than 90 days, you can apply for an additional stay of 90 days, which as a rule is granted immediately.

CUSTOMS You may be asked how much tobacco you're bringing in; the limit is 200 cigarettes or 50 cigars. One still camera with five unexposed rolls of film is allowed duty free; also allowed are a small movie camera with two reels, a portable tape recorder, a portable record player, a portable musical instrument, and a bicycle (not motor bikes). Campers and sporting types are allowed to bring in one tent and camping accessories (including a kayak not exceeding 18 feet), a pair of skis, two tennis rackets, a tackle set, and a small firearm (for hunting only) with 50 bullets. A normal-size bottle of wine and half a pint of hard alcohol are permitted, as are a "small quantity" of perfume and half a pint of toilet water.

Note: The limits on importing goods are much higher for items bought tax-paid in other European Community countries.

Upon leaving Portugal, U.S. citizens who have been outside their country for 48 hours or more are allowed to bring in $400 worth of merchandise duty free—that is, if they have claimed no similar exemption within the past 30 days. Beyond this free allowance, the next $1,000 worth of merchandise is assessed at a flat rate of 10% duty. If you make purchases in Portugal, it's important to keep your receipts. On gifts, the duty-free limit is $50. Americans 21 or over are allowed to bring in 1 liter of alcohol, 100 cigars (non-Cuban), and 200 cigarettes.

For Canadian citizens, exemptions on returning depend entirely on the length of stay abroad. Canadians who have been outside their country for at least one week are allowed to claim a $300 exemption, which is the only tax-free exemption granted for the entire year. Those out of the country for fewer than 7 days (but a minimum of 48 hours) are allowed a $100 exemption. Regardless of the length of stay, the alcohol and tobacco exemption remains the same: 50 cigars, 200 cigarettes, 1 kilogram (2.2 pounds) of tobacco, and 1.2 liters (40 ounces) of liquor. Personal gifts can be mailed back home at the rate of one per day, but you should write "Unsolicited Gift—Value Under $40" on the package. Canadian Customs publishes a brochure, "I Declare," giving complete details.

MONEY

There are no limits on foreign currency brought into Portugal, though visitors should declare the amount carried. This proves to the Portuguese Customs Office that the currency came from outside the country and therefore the same amount or less can be taken out.

CURRENCY/CASH The basic unit of Portuguese currency is the *escudo* (plural: *escudos*), which is divided into 100 *centavos*. A *conto* is made up of 1,000 escudos. Because of fluctuations in relative values of world currencies, I suggest you check a newspaper or bank for the latest exchange rate before departing.

Portugal is one of the most reasonably priced travel destinations in Europe, although prices have risen dramatically in the past few years. But first-time American visitors often panic at price quotations. The Portuguese escudo is written as 1$00—the dollar sign between the escudo and the centavo. Bank notes are issued for 100, 500, 1,000, 2,000, 5,000, and 10,000 escudos. In coins of silver and copper, the denominations are 1, 2.50, 5, 10, 20, 25, 50, 100, and 200 escudos.

THE ESCUDO & THE U.S. DOLLAR

At this writing, $1 U.S. equaled approximately 165 Portuguese escudos, and this was the rate of exchange used to calculate the dollar values given below and elsewhere in this guide (rounded to the nearest nickel). This rate fluctuates from day to day and may not be the same when you travel. Therefore, the following table should be used only as a general guideline. Always check last-minute quotations.

Escudos	US $	Escudos	US $
5	0.03	1,000	6.10
10	0.06	5,000	30.50
25	0.15	10,000	61.00
50	0.31	25,000	152.50
75	0.46	50,000	305.00
100	0.61	75,000	457.50
200	1.22	100,000	610.00
300	1.83	200,000	1,220.00
400	2.44	300,000	1,830.00
500	3.05	500,000	3,050.00
750	4.58	1,000,000	6,100.00

THE ESCUDO & THE BRITISH POUND

At this writing, £1 equaled approximately 250 Portuguese escudos, and this was the rate of exchange used to calculate the values in the table below. The exchange rate between the British and Portuguese currencies fluctuates from day to day and may not be the same when you travel. Therefore, check last-minute quotations and use this table only as an approximate indicator of relative values.

Escudos	British £	Escudos	British £
5	0.02	1,000	4.00
10	0.04	5,000	20.00
25	0.10	10,000	40.00
50	0.20	25,000	100.00
75	0.30	50,000	200.00
100	0.40	75,000	300.00
200	0.80	100,000	400.00
300	1.20	200,000	800.00
400	1.60	300,000	1,200.00
500	2.00	500,000	2,000.00
750	3.00	1,000,000	4,000.00

TRAVELER'S CHECKS   Traveler's checks are the safest way to carry money while traveling. Most banks will give you a better rate on traveler's checks than for cash. The following are major issuers of traveler's checks.

American Express (tel. toll free 800/221-7282 in the U.S. and Canada) generally charges a 1% commission. Checks are issued commission-free to members of the American Automobile Association (AAA).

Barclay's Bank/Bank of America (tel. toll free 800/221-2426 in the U.S. and

Canada) has a subsidiary, Interpayment Services, that sells Visa traveler's checks in U.S.-dollar and British-pound denominations.

Citicorp (tel. toll free 800/645-6556 in the U.S. and Canada) issues checks in U.S. dollars, British pounds, and German marks.

MasterCard International/Thomas Cook International (tel. toll free 800/223-9920 in the U.S., or 212/974-5695, collect, from the rest of the world), issues checks in about a dozen currencies.

Each of these agencies will refund your checks if they are lost or stolen, upon sufficient documentation and their serial numbers. When purchasing checks ask about refund hotlines; American Express and Bank of America have the greatest number of offices around the world.

CREDIT CARDS Credit cards are used throughout Portugal. Both American Express and Diners Club are widely recognized. If you see the Eurocard or Access sign displayed at an establishment, it means the establishment accepts MasterCard.

Credit cards can save your life when you're abroad, sparing your valuable cash and giving you financial flexibility for large purchases or last-minute changes.

Of course, you may make a purchase with a credit card thinking the amount in local currency will be converted into dollars at a certain rate, only to find the U.S. dollar or British pound has declined by the time your bill arrives, so you're actually paying more for an item than what you had bargained for. But those are the rules of the game. It also can work in your favor if the dollar or pound should rise after you make an escudo-denominated purchase.

CURRENCY EXCHANGE Many hotels in Portugal do not accept dollar- or pound-denominated checks, and if they do, they'll charge for the conversion. In some cases they'll accept countersigned traveler's checks or a credit card, but if you're prepaying a deposit on hotel reservations, it's cheaper and easier to pay with a check drawn on a Portuguese bank.

This can be arranged by a large commercial bank or by a specialist like **Ruesch International,** 1350 I St., Washington, DC 20005 (tel. 202/408-1200, or toll free

WHAT THINGS COST IN LISBON	U.S. $
Taxi from airport to center	7.50
Average Metro ride	.50
Local telephone call	.10
Double room at The Ritz (very expensive)	329.40
Double room at Hotel Eduardo VII (moderate)	106.80
Double room at Residência Nazareth (budget)	51.90
Lunch for one, without wine, at Bachus (moderate)	20.70
Lunch for one, without wine, at O Funil (moderate)	15.20
Dinner for one, without wine, at Tágide (expensive)	65.00
Dinner for one, without wine, at Chester (moderate)	30.50
Dinner for one, without wine, at Leão d'Ouro (moderate)	18.30
Glass of beer	.75
Coca-Cola in a restaurant	.75
Cup of coffee in a cafe	.75
Roll of ASA 100 color film, 24 exposures	6.50
Admission to Museu Nacional dos Coches	2.60
Movie ticket	3.50
Theater ticket	12.50–25.00

800/424-2923), which performs a wide variety of conversion-related tasks, usually for only $2 U.S. per transaction.

If you need a check payable in escudos, call Ruesch's toll-free number, describe what you need, and note the transaction number given to you. Mail your dollar-denominated personal check (payable to Ruesch International) to their office in Washington, D.C. Upon receipt, the company will mail a check denominated in escudos for the financial equivalent, minus the $2 charge. The company, however, does not sell traveler's checks dominated in escudos but can help you with different kinds of wire transfers and conversion of value-added tax (VAT) refund checks. It'll mail brochures and information packets on request.

2. WHEN TO GO — CLIMATE, HOLIDAYS & EVENTS

CLIMATE   "We didn't know we had an April," one Lisbon resident has said, "until *that* song came out." "April in Portugal" is famous—both the song and the season. Summer may be the most popular season, but for the traveler who can chart his or her own course, spring and autumn are the delectable seasons.

For North Americans, the climate of Portugal most closely parallels that of California. The Portuguese consider their climate one of the most ideal in Europe, and it is. There are only slight fluctuations in temperature between summer and winter; the overall mean ranges from 77° Fahrenheit in summer to about 58° Fahrenheit in winter. The rainy season begins in November and usually lasts through January. The proximity of the Gulf Stream allows Portugal's northernmost area, **Minho,** to enjoy mild (albeit very rainy) winters, even though it's at approximately the same latitude as New York City.

Snow brings many skiing enthusiasts to the **Serra de Estrêla** in north-central Portugal. For the most part, however, winter entails only some rain and lower temperatures in other regions. The **Algarve** and especially **Madeira** are exceptions: They enjoy temperate winters. Madeira, in fact, basks in its high season in winter. The Algarve, too, is somewhat of a winter Riviera that attracts sun worshippers from both North America and Europe. Summers in both tend to be long and hot, crystal clear and dry.

Lisbon and Estoril enjoy 46°F to 65°F temperatures in winter, and temperatures between 60°F and 82°F in summer.

Average Daytime Temperature & Monthly Rainfall in Lisbon

Jan Feb Mar Apr May June July Aug Sept Oct Nov Dec

	Jan	Feb	Mar	Apr	May	June	July	Aug	Sept	Oct	Nov	Dec
Temp. (°F)	57	59	63	67	71	77	81	82	79	72	63	58
Rainfall (inches)	4.3	3.0	4.2	2.1	1.7	0.6	0.1	0.2	1.3	2.4	3.7	4.1

HOLIDAYS   Watch these public holidays and adjust your banking needs accordingly: January 1 (New Year's Day and also Universal Brotherhood Day); Carnival in February (dates vary); Good Friday in March or April (dates vary); April 25 (Liberty Day—anniversary of the revolution); May 1 (Labor Day); Corpus Christi in June (dates vary); June 10 (Portugal Day); August 15 (Assumption); October 5 (Proclamation of the Republic); November 1 (All Saints' Day); December 1 (Restoration of Independence); December 8 (Immaculate Conception); and December 25 (Christmas Day). In addition, June 13 (St. Anthony Day) in Lisbon only and June 24 (St. John the Baptist Day) in Porto only are public holidays.

PORTUGAL CALENDAR OF EVENTS

I suggest you verify dates with a tourist office, as festival dates can vary greatly from year to year.

JANUARY

☐ **Festa de São Gonçalo e São Cristovão** at Vila Nova de Gaia, just across the river from Porto. These resemble fertility rites and are two of the most attended religious festivals in Portugal. An image of São Gonçalo is paraded through the narrow streets, as merry-makers beat drums. Boatmen along the Douro ferry a figure of São Cristovão with a huge head down the river. Much port wine is drunk, and cakes baked into phallic shapes are consumed by all, especially unmarried virgin girls. Early January.

FEBRUARY

☐ **Carnival** (Mardi Gras). Festivities are staged throughout the country. Each town has its unique way of celebrating. Masked marchers, flower-bedecked floats, and vehicles satirically decorated mark the occasion. Much food and wine are consumed.

APRIL

☐ **Easter.** Festivities are all over Portugal, with some of the most noteworthy events taking place at Póvoa de Varzim, Ovar, and Braga. The faithful—often colorfully dressed—march in parades.

MAY

☐ **Festas das Cruzes,** at Barcelos on the River Cávado, in the vicinity of Braga. Since 1504, this festival has been celebrated with a "Miracle of the Cross" procession centered around a carpet made of millions of flower petals. Women in colorful regional dress load themselves with large gold chains. A giant firework display on the river signals the festival's end. Early May.

✪ *First Pilgrimage of the year to Fátima*   *In 1930, the Bishop of Leiria authorized pilgrimages to this site. Today, people from all over the world flock here to commemorate the first apparition of the Virgin to the little shepherd children on May 13, 1917.*

   For the last pilgrimage to Fátima, see "October," below.

   Where: *Fátima.* ***When:*** *May 13.* ***How:*** *Call the tourist office in Fátima at 049/53-11-39 for more information. Hotel reservations should be made months in advance, or plan to stay in a neighboring town.*

JUNE

☐ **Feira Nacional da Agricultura** (also known as Feira do Ribatejo). This is the most important agricultural fair in Portugal, staged at Santarém, north of Lisbon on the River Tagus. The best horses and cattle from all provinces are on display here, and the festival is enlivened with horse shows and bullfights. Pavilions sell food from the various regional cuisines. Early June.

JULY

☐ **Colete Encarnado,** at Vila Franca de Xira, north of Lisbon on the River Tagus. Like the more famous *feria* in Pamplona, Spain, this festival involves bull running through narrow streets, followed by the sensational bullfights in what is considered by aficionados the best bullring in Portugal. Fandango dancing along with rodeo-style competition among the Ribatejo *campinos* (Portuguese cowboys) mark the event. First or second Sunday in July.

AUGUST

✪ *Festas da Senhora da Agonia,* in Viana do Castelo, at the mouth of the River Lima, north of Porto. The most spectacular festival in the north is staged to honor "Our Lady of Suffering." A replica of the Virgin is carried through the streets over carpets of flowers. The bishop directs a procession of fishermen to the sea to bless the boats. Float-filled parades make the event not tragic at all, but a time of revelry and celebration, lasting day and night for three days. A blaze of fireworks ends the event.
Where: Viana do Castelo. *When:* Late August. *How:* Call the tourist office at 058/226-20 for exact dates, which vary from year to year. Reserve hotel rooms well in advance or be prepared to stay in a neighboring town.

SEPTEMBER

☐ **Romaria da Nossa Senhora de Nazaré,** at Nazaré, Portugal's most famed fishing village. The event is characterized by folk dancing, singing, and bullfights. The big attraction is the procession carrying the image of Nossa Senhora de Nazaré down to the sea. Early to mid-September.

OCTOBER

☐ **Last Pilgrimage of the Year to Fátima.** Thousands of pilgrims from all over the world descend on Fátima to mark the occasion of the last apparition of the virgin, which is said to have occurred on October 12, 1917.

LISBON
CALENDAR OF EVENTS

Even some small towns in Portugal have more celebrations and festivals than Lisbon. Many Lisboans confine their festival revelry to June.

JUNE

✪ *Festas Dos Santos Populares* Celebrations begin on June 13 and 14 in the Alfama with feasts honoring Saint Anthony. Parades commemorating the city's patron saint are characterized by marchas (walking groups of singers and musicians) along the Avenida da Liberdade and by singing, dancing, the drinking of wine, and the eating of grilled sardines in the Alfama. Vendors peddle pots of sweet basil. On June 23 and 24, at the feast of St. John the Baptist, bonfires brighten the night and participants jump over them. The night of the final celebration is the Feast of Saint Peter on June 29.

When: June 13–29. *Where:* Throughout Lisbon. *How:* The Lisbon tourist office (tel. 01/346-63-07) will supply details about where some of the various events are staged, although much of the action is spontaneous.

☐ **Festas do São Pedro,** in Mintijo, near Lisbon. This festival honoring Saint Peter has been held since medieval times. On the final day there is a blessing of the boats and a colorful procession, with grilled sardines featured as the main item on the menu. Bull breeders bring their beasts in town to release them through the streets to chase foolish young men who are often permanently injured or killed. There are also bullfights. On the final night a pagan rite is still observed, as a skiff is set afire and offered as a sacrifice to the Tagus to appease the spirits. June 28–29.

JULY

☐ **Estoril Festival.** Right outside Lisbon at the seaside resort of Estoril, this festival of classical music is presented at two concert halls that were built for the 500th anniversary of Columbus's first voyage to the New World. For information, write Associação International de Música da Costa do Estoril, Casa dos Arcos, Estrada Marginal, P-2775 Parede, Portugal. July 10–August 7.

3. HEALTH & INSURANCE

HEALTH   Portugal does not offer free medical treatment to visitors, except for citizens of certain countries, such as Great Britain, which have reciprocal health agreements. Nationals from countries like Canada and the United States have to pay for medical services rendered.

You will encounter few health problems traveling in Portugal. The tap water is generally safe to drink, the milk is pasteurized, and health services are good. Occasionally the change in diet may cause some minor diarrhea, so you may want to take some antidiarrhea medicine along.

Carry all your vital medicine in your carry-on luggage and bring enough prescribed medicines to sustain you during your stay. Bring along copies of your prescriptions written in the generic—not brand-name—form. If you need a doctor, your hotel can recommend one or you can contact your embassy or consulate. You can also obtain a list of English-speaking doctors before you leave from the **International Association for Medical Assistance to Travelers (IAMAT)** in the United States at 417 Center St., Lewiston, NY 14092 (tel. 716/754-4883); in Canada at 40 Regal Rd., Guelph, ON N1K 1B5 (tel. 519/836-0102).

If you suffer from a chronic illness, talk to your doctor before taking the trip. For such conditions as epilepsy, diabetes, or a heart condition, wear a Medic Alert Identification Tag, which will immediately alert any doctor to your condition and provide the number of Medic Alert's 24-hour hotline so a foreign doctor can obtain your medical records. For a lifetime membership, the cost is $35. Contact the **Medic Alert Foundation,** P.O. Box 1009, Turlock, CA 95381-1009 (tel. 209/668-3333, or toll free 800/432-5378).

INSURANCE   Before purchasing any additional insurance, check your homeowner's, automobile, and medical insurance policies as well as the insurance provided by credit-card companies and auto and travel clubs. You may have adequate off-premises theft coverage, or your credit-card company may even provide cancellation coverage if the ticket is paid for with its credit card.

Remember that Medicare covers only U.S. citizens traveling in Mexico and Canada. Also note that to submit any claim you must always have thorough documentation, including all receipts, police reports, medical records, and the like.

If you are prepaying for your vacation or are taking a charter or any other flight that has cancellation penalties, look into cancellation insurance.

The following companies will provide further information:

Travel Guard International, 1145 Clark St., Stevens Point, WI 54481 (tel. toll free 800/826-1300), offers a comprehensive 7-day policy that covers basically everything. It costs $52, including emergency assistance, accidental death, trip cancellation and interruption, medical coverage abroad, and lost luggage. However, there are restrictions you should understand before you accept the coverage.

Travelers Insurance Company, Travel Insurance Division, One Tower Square, 10 NB, Hartford, CT 06183-5040 (toll free 800/243-3174), offers travel, accident, and illness coverage from $10 and up, depending on the amount of coverage, for 6 to 10 days; $500 worth of coverage for lost, damaged, or delayed baggage costs $20 for 6 to 10 days; and trip cancellation costs $5.50 for each $100 worth of coverage. Written approval is necessary for cancellation coverage in excess of $10,000.

Mutual of Omaha (Tele-Trip), Mutual of Omaha Plaza, Omaha, NB 68175, offers insurance packages priced from $113 for a 3-week trip. Included in the package are travel-assistance services and financial protection against trip cancellation, trip interruption, flight and baggage delays, accident-related medical costs, accidental death and dismemberment, and medical evacuation coverage. Major credit-card holders can call toll free 800/228-9792 to apply for insurance over the phone.

Healthcare Abroad (MEDEX) offers coverage for between 10 and 90 days at $3 per day; the policy includes accident and sickness coverage up to $100,000. Medical evacuation is also included, along with a $25,000 accidental death and dismemberment compensation. Provisions for trip cancellation and lost or stolen luggage can also be written into this policy for a nominal cost. Contact Healthcare Abroad at Wallach & Co., 107 W. Federal St., P.O. Box 480, Middleburg, VA 22117-0480 (tel. 703/687-3166, or toll free 800/237-6615).

Access America, 6600 W. Broad St., Richmond, VA 23230 (tel. 804/285-3300, or toll free 800/284-8300), offers a comprehensive travel insurance and assistance package, including medical expenses, on-the-spot hospital payments, medical transportation, baggage insurance, trip cancellation/interruption, and collision-damage for a rental car. Its 24-hour hotline connects you to multilingual coordinators who can offer advice and help on medical, legal, and travel problems. Packages begin at $27.

4. WHAT TO PACK

Always pack lightly. Sometimes it's hard to get a porter or baggage cart in rail and air terminals. Also, airlines are increasingly strict about how much luggage you can bring, both carry-on and checked items. Checked baggage should not be more than 62 inches (width, plus length, plus height) or weigh more than 70 pounds. Carry-on luggage shouldn't be more than 45 inches (width, plus length, plus height) and must fit under your seat or in the bin above.

Note also that conservative middle-aged Portuguese people tend to dress up rather than down—and they dress very well indeed, particularly at theaters and concerts. Nobody will bar you for arriving in sports clothes, but you may feel awkward, so include at least one smart suit or dress in your luggage.

Better-class restaurants usually demand that men wear ties and that women not wear shorts or jogging clothing, but those are the only rules enforced.

Pack clothes that "travel well" because you can't always get pressing done at hotels. Be prepared to wash your underwear, socks, and the like in your bathroom and hang them up to dry overnight.

The general rule of packing is to bring four of everything. For men, that means four pairs of socks, four pairs of slacks, four shirts, and four sets of underwear. At least two of these will always be either dirty or drying. Often you'll have to wrap semiwet clothes in a plastic bag as you head for your next destination. Women can follow the same rule.

Take at least one outfit for chilly weather and one for warm weather. Even in summer you may experience suddenly chilly weather in the mountains or along the seacoasts, especially in the north of Portugal. Always take two pairs of walking shoes in case you get your shoes soaked and need that extra pair.

5. TIPS FOR THE DISABLED, SENIORS, SINGLES, FAMILIES & STUDENTS

FOR THE DISABLED Contact **Travel Information Service,** Moss Rehabilitation Hospital, 1200 W. Tabor Rd., Philadelphia, PA 19141-3099 (tel. 215/456-9603), which provides information to telephone callers only.

You may also want to subscribe to *The Itinerary,* P.O. Box 2012, Bayonne, NJ 07002-2012 (tel. 201/858-3400), for $10 a year. This bimonthly travel magazine is filled with news about travel aids for the handicapped, special tours, information on accessibility, and other matters.

You can also obtain a copy of *Air Transportation of Handicapped Persons,* published by the U.S. Department of Transportation. It's free if you write to Free Advisory Circular No. AC12032, Distribution Unit, U.S. Department of Transportation, Publications Division, M-4332, Washington, DC 20590.

You may also want to consider joining a tour for disabled visitors. Names and addresses of such tour operators can be obtained by writing to the **Society for the Advancement of Travel for the Handicapped,** 347 Fifth Ave., New York, NY 10016 (tel. 212/447-7284). Yearly membership dues are $45, $25 for senior citizens and students. Send a self-addressed stamped envelope.

The Federation of the Handicapped, 211 W. 14th St., New York, NY 10011 (tel. 212/747-4268), also operates summer tours for members, who pay a yearly fee of $4.

For the blind, the best information source is the **American Foundation for the Blind,** 15 W. 16th St., New York, NY 10011 (tel. 212/620-2000, or toll free 800/232-5463).

FOR SENIORS Many senior discounts are available, but note that some may require membership in a particular association.

For a copy of *Travel Tips for Older Americans* (publication no. 8970; cost $1), contact the Superintendent of Documents, U.S. Government Printing Office, Washington, DC 20402 (tel. 202/783-5238). Another booklet—this one free—is *101 Tips for the Mature Traveler,* available from Grand Circle Travel, 347 Congress St., Suite 3A, Boston, MA 02210 (tel. 617/350-7500, or toll free 800/221-2610); this travel agency also offers escorted tours and cruises for seniors.

SAGA International Holidays 222 Berkley St., Boston, MA 02116 (tel. toll free 800/343-0273), runs all-inclusive tours for seniors, preferably for those 60 years or older. SAGA was established in the 1950s as a sensitive and highly appealing outlet for aged (mature) tour participants. Insurance and airfare are included in the net price of any of their tours, all of which encompass dozens of locations in Europe and usually last for an average of 17 nights.

In the United States, the best organization to belong to is the **American Association of Retired Persons (AARP),** 601 E St. NW, Washington, DC 20049 (tel. 202/434-2277). Members are offered discounts on car rentals, hotels, and airfares. The association's group travel is provided by the AARP Travel Experience from American Express. Tours may be purchased through any American Express office or travel agent or by calling toll free 800/927-AARP.

Information is also available from the **National Council of Senior Citizens,** 1331 F St. NW, Washington, DC 20004 (tel. 202/347-8800). A nonprofit organization, the council charges a membership fee of $12, for which you receive a monthly newsletter and membership benefits, including travel services. Reduced discounts on hotels and auto rentals are also provided.

Mature Outlook, 6001 N. Clark St., Chicago, IL 60660 (tel. toll free 800/336-6330), is a travel club for people over 50, and it's operated by Sears Roebuck & Co.

Annual membership is available for $9.95, and the outfit issues a bimonthly newsletter featuring hotel discounts.

FOR SINGLES Unfortunately for the 85 million single Americans, the travel industry is geared to couples. Singles often wind up paying the penalty. It pays to travel with someone, and one company that resolves this problem is **Travel Companion,** which matches single travelers with like-minded companions and is headed by Jens Jurgen, who charges between $36 and $66 for a 6-month listing in his well-publicized records. People seeking travel companions fill out forms stating their preferences and needs and receive a minilisting of potential travel partners. Companions of the same or the opposite sex can be requested.

A bimonthly newsletter averaging 34 large pages also gives numerous money-saving travel tips of special interest to solo travelers. A sample copy is available for $4. For an application and more information, contact Jens Jurgen at Travel Companion, P.O. Box P-833 Amityville, NY 11701 (tel. 516/454-0880).

Singleworld, 401 Theodore Fremd Ave., Rye, NY 10580 (tel. 914/967-3334, or toll free 800/223-6490), is a travel agency that operates tours for solo travelers. Two basic types of tours are available: youth-oriented tours for people under 35 and jaunts for those of any age. Annual dues are $25.

Since single supplements on tours usually carry a hefty price tag, a way to get around this is to find a travel agency that allows you to share a room. One such company offering a "guaranteed-share plan" is **Cosmos-Tourama,** 9525 Queens Blvd., Rego Park, NY 11374 (tel. toll free 800/228-0211).

If you're between 45 and 86 and need a travel companion, **Golden Companions,** P.O. Box 754, Pullman, WA 99163 (tel. 208/858-2183), may be the answer. The service was founded in 1987 by Joanne R. Buteau, a research economist and writer. It enables members to meet potential travel companions through a confidential mail network. Once they have "connected," they make their own travel arrangements. The annual $85 membership fee includes a subscription to a bimonthly newsletter, *The Golden Traveler,* which outlines travel discounts and home exchanges.

FOR FAMILIES Advance planning is the key to a successful overseas family vacation. If you have very small children, you should discuss your vacation plans with your family doctor and take along such standard supplies as children's aspirin, a thermometer, Band-Aids, and the like.

On airlines, a special menu for children must be requested at least 24 hours in advance, but if baby food is required, bring your own and ask a flight attendant to warm it to the right temperature. Take along a "security blanket" for your child—a pacifier; a favorite toy or book; or, for older children, something to make them feel at home in different surroundings (a baseball cap, a favorite T-shirt, or some good-luck charm).

Make advance arrangements for cribs, bottle warmers, and seats if you're driving anywhere. Ask your hotel if it stocks baby food, and, if not, take with you and plan to buy the rest in local supermarkets.

Draw up guidelines on bedtime, eating, keeping tidy in the sun, and even shopping and spending—they'll make the vacation more enjoyable.

Babysitters can be found for you at most hotels. You should always insist, if possible, that the hotel secure a babysitter with at least a rudimentary knowledge of English.

Family Travel Times is published ten times a year by TWYCH (Travel With Your Children) and includes a weekly call-in service for subscribers. Subscriptions cost $55 a year and can be ordered by writing to TWYCH, 45 W. 18th St., 7th floor, New York, NY 10011 (tel. 212/206-0688). TWYCH also publishes two nitty-gritty information guides, *Skiing with Children* and *Cruising with Children;* they sell for $29 and $22, respectively, and are discounted to newsletter subscribers. An information packet describing TWYCH's publications and including a recent sample issue is available by sending $3.50 to the above address.

FOR STUDENTS **Council Travel** (a subsidiary of the Council on International Educational Exchange) is America's largest student, youth, and budget travel group, with more than 60 offices worldwide. All bona fide students can go to any Council Travel Office and pay $15 for International Student Identity Cards that entitle holders to generous travel and other discounts.

Discounted international and domestic air tickets are available for student and youth travelers. Eurotrain rail passes, YHA passes, weekend packages, overland safaris, and hostel/hotel accommodations are all bookable from Council Travel.

Council Travel also sells a number of publications for young people considering traveling abroad: *Work, Study, Travel Abroad: The Whole World Handbook; Volunteer: The Comprehensive Guide to Voluntary Service in the U.S. and Abroad,* and *The Teenager's Guide to Study, Travel and Adventure Abroad.*

Council Travel has offices throughout the United States, including the main offices at 205 E. 42nd St., New York, NY 10017 (tel. 212/661-4141). Call toll free 800/GET AN ID to find the location nearest you.

The **IYHF (International Youth Hostel Federation)** was designed to provide clean but bare-bones overnight accommodations for serious budget-conscious travelers. For information, contact American Youth Hostels (AYH)/Hostelling International, 733 15th St. NW, Suite 840, Washington, DC 20005 (tel. 202/783-6161). Membership costs $25 annually; those under 18 pay $10, and those over 54 pay $15.

6. ALTERNATIVE & ADVENTURE TRAVEL

Mass tourism of the kind that has transported vast numbers of North Americans to the most obscure corners of the map has been a by-product of late 20th-century affluence, technology, and democratization.

With the advent of the 1990s, some of America's most respected travel visionaries have perceived a change in the needs of many experienced (sometimes jaded) travelers. There has emerged a demand for specialized travel experiences whose goals and objectives are clearly defined well in advance of departure. There is also an increased demand for organizations that can provide like-minded companions to share and participate in increasingly esoteric travel plans.

Caveat: Under no circumstances is the inclusion of an organization in this section to be interpreted as a guarantee of either its credit worthiness or its competency. Information about these organizations is presented only as a preliminary preview, to be followed by your own investigation should you be interested.

CULTURAL EXCHANGES **Servas** (translated from Esperanto, it means "to serve"), 11 John St., Room 407, New York, NY 10038 (tel. 212/267-0252), is a nonprofit, nongovernment, international, interfaith network of travelers and hosts whose goal is to help build world peace, goodwill, and understanding. They do this by providing opportunities for deeper, more personal contacts among people of diverse cultural and political backgrounds. Servas travelers are invited to share living space with members of communities worldwide, normally staying without charge for visits lasting a maximum of 2 days. Visitors pay a $55 annual fee, plus a $25 deposit for access to lists of international hosts; fill out an application; and are interviewed for suitability by one of more than 200 Servas interviewers throughout the country. They then receive a Servas directory listing the names and addresses of hosts who will allow (and encourage) visitors within their homes.

The **Friendship Force,** 575 South Tower, 1 CNN Center, Atlanta, GA 30303 (tel. 404/522-9490), is a nonprofit organization existing for the sole purpose of fostering friendships among disparate people around the world. Dozens of branch offices lie throughout North America and arrange for en masse visits, usually once a year. Because of group bookings, the price of air transportation to the host country is usually less than what volunteers would pay if they bought an APEX ticket individually. Each participant is required to spend 2 weeks in the host country (host countries are in Europe and also throughout the world). One stringent requirement is that a participant must spend 1 full week in the home of a family as a guest. Most volunteers spend the second week traveling in the host country.

HOME EXCHANGES   For home exchanges, which can be fun and economical, contact the following.

The Invented City, 41 Sutter St., Suite 1090, San Francisco, CA 94104 (tel. 415/673-0347), is an international home-exchange agency. Listings are published three times a year: February, May, and November. A membership fee of $50 allows you to list your home, and you can also give your preferred time to travel, your occupation, and your hobbies.

Intervac U.S., P.O. Box 590504, San Francisco, CA 94119 (tel. 415/435-3497, or toll free 800/756-HOME), is part of the largest worldwide exchange network. It publishes three catalogs a year, containing more than 8,800 homes in more than 36 countries. Members contact one another directly. The $62 cost, plus postage, includes the purchase of all three of the company's catalogs (which will be mailed to you), plus the inclusion of your own listing in whichever one of the three catalogs you select. If you want to publish a photograph of your home, it costs $11 extra. Hospitality and youth exchanges also are available.

Vacation Exchange Club, P.O. Box 650, Key West, FL 33041 (tel. 305/294-3720, or toll free 800/638-3841), will send you four directories a year—in one of which you're listed—for $60.

EDUCATIONAL PROGRAMS   **Elderhostel,** 75 Federal St., Boston, MA 02110 (tel. 617/426-7788), offers an array of university-based summer educational programs for senior citizens throughout the world, including Portugal. Most courses last around 3 weeks and are remarkable values, considering that airfare, accommodations in student dormitories or modest inns, all meals, and tuition are included. Courses include field trips, involve no homework, are ungraded, and emphasize liberal arts. This is not a luxury vacation, but rather an academic fulfillment of a type never possible for senior citizens until several years ago.

Participants must be over 60, but each may take an under-60 companion. Meals consist of solid, no-frills fare typical of educational institutions worldwide. The program provides a safe and congenial environment for older single women, who make up some 67% of the enrollment.

LEARNING THE LANGUAGE   The **National Registration Center for Study Abroad (NRCSA),** P.O. Box 1393, Milwaukee, WI 53201 (tel. 414/278-0631), invites you to experience Portugal in the deepest way—by living and learning the language. NRCSA has helped people of all ages and backgrounds participate in foreign travel and cultural programs since 1968. Full details about how these courses are conducted and the various costs are available by contacting the address above.

7. GETTING THERE

BY PLANE   Although Lisbon is a major European gateway city, in bygone days travelers went to France or England first and then began their Grand Tour, perhaps (but most likely not) stopping over in Portugal.

Air transportation has changed this habit, and more and more sun-seeking travelers are beginning their European adventure in Lisbon. Portugal is, in fact, one of the European countries closest to North America, and it typically costs less to fly from New York to Lisbon than from New York to Paris, Amsterdam, or Frankfurt.

In the paragraphs that follow I'll describe the basic structure of airfares, exploring various methods of cutting your air transportation costs, and then I'll deal with methods of traveling within Portugal once you arrive.

Since deregulation, the airlines have competed fiercely with one another for traffic. To many destinations, one airline now proposes a fare structure; another airline then files a competing and perhaps different fare structure. The competition may or may not result in a uniform price structure for all airlines flying to that particular country.

It all adds up to chaos—but often *beneficial* chaos for the alert traveler willing to study and consider all the fares available. The key to bargain airfares is to shop around.

In what follows I'll point out the current options available for flying directly to Portugal. If you don't want to fly directly to Portugal, then remember to check all the airlines to find the most inexpensive transatlantic fare that coincides with your itinerary and travel plans.

Flying time from New York to Lisbon is about 6½ hours; from Atlanta to Lisbon (with a stopover), 12 hours; from Los Angeles to Lisbon (with a stopover), 15 hours; and from Montreal or Toronto, 8 hours.

Major Airlines   When it was established in 1946, **TAP,** the national airline of Portugal (tel. toll free 800/221-7370), flew only between Lisbon and the then-Portuguese colonies of Angola and Mozambique. Today, TAP flies to four continents and has one of the youngest fleets in the airline industry, with an average age per aircraft of only 4 years in the early 1990s. Its U.S. gateways include JFK, in New York City; Newark, in New Jersey; and Logan, in Boston. In Canada, it services both Toronto and Montreal. In Portugal, it flies to nine destinations, the most popular of which are Lisbon, Porto, Faro, Funchal (Madeira), and Terceira (the Azores).

Service to Portugal is supplemented by flights between JFK and Lisbon on **Delta** (tel. toll free 800/241-4141) and **TWA** (tel. toll free 800/221-2000). Nonstop service from New York to Lisbon is provided daily on TWA and five nights a week on Delta.

Connections can be made from most major points throughout North America on TWA's or Delta's network, but if you live anywhere outside of New York, you must prepare yourself for an airline transfer at JFK.

Air Canada (tel. toll free 800/776-3000) offers three flights a week from both Toronto and Montreal to Lisbon.

TAP also has frequent flights on popular routes connecting Portugal with other major cities in western Europe. Its flights to Lisbon from London are an especially good deal, sometimes priced so attractively that one might combine a sojourn in England with an inexpensive side excursion to Portugal. TAP gives passengers the option of stopping midway across the Atlantic in the Azores and also makes baggage transfers and seat reservations on connecting flights within Portugal much easier.

Regular Fares   All airlines divide their calendar year into three seasons (basic, shoulder, peak), whose dates might vary slightly from airline to airline. TAP declares its basic season as October 18 to December 16 and from December 25 until March 31. The most expensive season, when passengers tend to book most transatlantic flights solidly, stretches between June 16 and August 31. Everything not included within those dates is shoulder season.

The least expensive regular peak-season tickets on TAP between New York and Lisbon, as of this writing, cost $830 for departures and returns on Monday to Thursday, and $880 for departures and returns on Friday, Saturday, and Sunday. This ticket requires a 21-day advance purchase, and a delay of between seven and 21 days before activating the return portion, and the understanding that the fare is not refundable once booked. Shoulder-season fares for the same kind of ticket range from $850 to $900, and low season fares are consistently priced at $600, regardless of the day of the week.

Discounted Fares   One of TAP's most popular tickets is a **Super APEX** fare. Its cost varies according to season, but its price and restrictions are competitive with fares carrying similar restrictions on other airlines. At presstime, a ticket from either New York or Boston to Lisbon, depending on day of week and season of year, ranged from $600 to $880. Tickets must be purchased 21 days before departure, and are not refundable once issued. If your plans are flexible enough, and if you're aware of your anticipated date of return, this might be the ticket for you.

For a bit more money, a **Regular APEX** is available, requiring only a 14-day advance purchase and a stay abroad of 7 to 90 days. Regular APEX tickets are usually refundable minus a $100 penalty for changes in itinerary. At presstime, TAP sold regular APEX tickets, depending on season and flight dates, for between $672 and

$982, round-trip. Most of these fares, as well as many of the applicable restrictions, will probably be matched by TAP's competitors.

For families, one strong attraction at TAP is the fact that **infants under two years** pay only 10% of the adult fare. (About a half-dozen bassinets are available on transatlantic flights, allowing parents to lift infants off their laps onto specially designed brackets during certain segments of the flight.) **Children under 12** pay only 75% of the adult price of most categories of tickets.

At press time, TAP offered a **winter senior citizen fare** from all three of its U.S. gateways to anywhere in Portugal for a reduction of 10% off its published fares. The definition of a senior citizen is a traveler 60 years of age or older. The senior citizen discount also applies to a companion of any age (spouse, grandchild, friend). The maximum stay abroad with this type of ticket is 3 months. Tickets must be purchased at least 14 days before departure.

Subject to change, TAP offers a one-way **youth fare** of between $300 and $440, depending on the season, between New York or Boston and Lisbon. Tickets of this type can only be purchased at the last minute, since they can be booked only within 72 hours of departure. Youth fares are offered only to travelers age 12 to 24, and only if space is available. They cannot be mailed, and must be purchased in person at a travel agent or any TAP counter.

None of the above options takes into account **promotional fares** airlines might initiate by the time you schedule your trip. These are usually particularly attractive during the basic season. At press time, TAP, in a move matched by some competitors, offered a special non-refundable APEX ticket priced at $518 round-trip from November 1 to March 31, and $668 the rest of the year for round-trip passage between New York or Boston and The Azores or Lisbon. Restrictions required a stay abroad of between 7 and 30 days, and tickets needed to be paid for seven days prior to takeoff, or 72 hours after a phone reservation was made, whichever came first. Despite its appeal, restrictions were stiff. Despite the inconveniences, many passengers considered it a bargain price worth the restrictions.

Clients who prefer not to specify when they will return home, or who can't purchase their tickets within 21 days prior to takeoff, usually opt for the **excursion fare** offered by TAP. Costing more than either APEX option, it requires that passengers stay from 7 to 180 days before jetting back to North America. On this ticket, peak season lasts from June 16 to August 31, and there are no restrictions regarding date of return.

The most exclusive, and the most expensive, class of service available on TAP is named after the seafaring pioneers who spread Portugal's empire throughout the world. **Navigator Class** passengers benefit from better service and upgraded food and drink. Navigator Class is TAP's name for business class and is comparable to first class on other major carriers.

Bucket Shops originated in the 1960s in Great Britain, where mainstream airlines gave that (then pejorative) name to resalers of blocks of unsold tickets consigned to them by major transatlantic carriers. "Bucket shop" has stuck as a label, but it might be more polite to refer to them as "consolidators." They exist in many shapes and forms. In its purest sense, a bucket shop acts as a clearinghouse for blocks of tickets that airlines discount and consign during normally slow periods of air travel.

Charter operators (see below) and bucket shops used to perform separate functions, but their offerings in many cases have been blurred in recent times. Many outfits perform both functions.

Tickets are sometimes, but not always, priced at up to 35% less than the full fare. Perhaps your reduced fare will be no more than 20% off the regular fare. Terms of payment can vary—anywhere from 45 days prior to departure to last-minute sales offered in a final attempt by an airline to fill a craft.

Since dealing with unknown bucket shops might be a little risky, it's wise to call the Better Business Bureau in your area to see if complaints have been filed against a company.

Bucket shops abound from coast to coast, but to get you started, here are some recommendations:

FROMMER'S SMART TRAVELER: AIRFARES

1. Take an off-peak flight. That means not only autumn to spring departures, but Monday to Thursday for midweek discounts.
2. Avoid last-minute change of plans that can result in penalties airlines impose for changes in itineraries.
3. Keep checking the airlines and their fares. Timing is everything. A recent spot check of one airline revealed that in just seven days it had discounted a New York-Lisbon fare by $195.
4. Shop all airlines that fly to your destination.
5. Always ask for the lowest fare, not just a discount fare.
6. Ask about frequent-flyer programs to gain bonus miles when you book a flight.
7. Check bucket shops for last-minute discount fares that are even cheaper than their advertised slashed fares.
8. Ask about air/land packages. Land arrangements are often cheaper when booked simultaneously with an air ticket.
9. If a trip to Lisbon is just part of a larger European itinerary that might include Madrid and other capitals, make sure Lisbon is written into your overhaul European flight before you go and not added on once you're there. It's cheaper that way.
10. Fly at a heavy discount as a courier.

In New York, try **TFI Tours International,** 34 West 32nd Street, 12th Floor, New York, NY 10001 (tel. 212-736-1140 in New York State, or toll free 800/825-3834 elsewhere in the U.S.). In Miami, there's **25 West Tours,** 2490 Coral Way, Miami FL 33145 (tel. 305/856-0810 in Miami; toll free 800/423-6954 in Florida, or 800/225-2582 elsewhere in the U.S.). In California, try **Sunline Express Holidays, Inc.,** 607 Market Street, San Francisco, CA 94105 (tel. 415/541-7800 or toll free 800/786-5463). In New England, one of the best possibilities is **Travel Management International,** 18 Prescott St., Suite 4, Cambridge MA 02138 (tel. toll free 800/245-3672), which offers a wide variety of discount fares, including youth fares.

Strictly for reasons of economy (and never for convenience), some travelers are willing to accept the possible uncertainties of taking a **charter flight** to Portugal.

In a strict sense, a charter flight occurs on an aircraft reserved months in advance for a one-time-only transit to some predetermined point. Before paying for a charter, check the restrictions on your ticket or contract. You may be asked to purchase a tour package and pay far in advance. You'll pay a stiff penalty (or forfeit the ticket entirely) if you cancel. Charters are sometimes canceled when the plane doesn't fill. In some cases, the charter-ticket seller will offer you an insurance policy for your own legitimate cancellation (hospital certificate, death in the family, whatever). There is no way to predict whether a ticket to Lisbon will cost less on a charter or in a bucket shop. You'll have to investigate at the time of your trip. *Remember:* Some charter companies have proved unreliable in the past.

Among charter flights operators is **Council Charters,** 205 E. 42nd St., New York, NY 10017 (tel. 212/661-0311, or toll free 800/800-8222). This firm says it can arrange charter seats on regularly scheduled aircraft.

Rebators also compete in the low-cost airfare market. They pass along to passengers part of their commission, though many assess a fee for their services. Most rebators offer discounts that range from 10% to 25%, plus a $25 handling charge. They are not the same as travel agents, although they sometimes offer similar services, including discounted land arrangements and car rentals. Rebators include **Travel Avenue,** 641 Lake St., Suite 201, Chicago, IL 60606 (tel. 312/876-1116, or toll free 800/333-3335) and **The Smart Traveler,** 3111 SW 27th Ave., Miami, FL 33133 (tel. 305/448-3338, or toll free 800/448-3338).

A favorite of spontaneous travelers, **standby fares** leave your departure to the whims of fortune, and the hopes that a last-minute seat will become available. Most airlines don't offer standbys, although some seats are available to London from where you'll have to go by train, plane, or other means to Portugal. These fares are generally offered from April to November only. **Virgin Atlantic Airways** (tel. toll free 800/862-8621) features both a day-of-departure and a day-prior-to-departure stand-by fare from New York to London.

Traveling as a **courier** may not be for everybody. You travel as a passenger and courier, and for this service you'll secure a greatly discounted airfare or sometimes even a free ticket. You're allowed one piece of carry-on luggage only; your baggage allowance is used by the courier firm to transport its cargo (which, by the way, is perfectly legal). As a courier, you don't actually make the merchandise you're "transporting" to Europe, you just carry a manifest to present to Customs. Upon your arrival, an employee of the courier service will reclaim the company's cargo. You fly alone, so don't plan to travel with anybody. Most courier services operate from Los Angeles or New York, but some operate out of other cities, such as Chicago or Miami. Courier services are often listed in the yellow pages or in advertisements in travel sections of newspapers. For a start, check **Halbart,** 147-05 176th St., Jamaica, NY 11434 (tel. 718/656-8189 from 10am to 3pm daily). Another firm to try is **Now Voyager,** 74 Varick St., Suite 307, New York, NY 10013 (tel. 212/431-1616). It has a 24-hour phone system. Now Voyager offers more flights to more destinations. The **International Association of Air Travel Couriers,** P.O. Box 1349, Lake Worth, FL 33460 (tel. 407/582-8320), charges an annual membership of $35. It will send you six issues of its newsletter, *Shoestring Traveler,* and about half a dozen issues of *Air Courier Bulletin,* a directory of air courier bargains around the world. Another advantage of membership is a photo identification card, and the organization acts as a trouble shooter if a courier runs into difficulties.

BY TRAIN   If you're in England, you can spend 2 or 2½ days reaching Lisbon by train. You must go via Paris, departing from London's Victoria Station, taking the rail/Hovercraft/rail service over the English Channel and arriving in a French port, such as Calais or Dieppe, where you continue the rest of the way by train.

Once you're in Paris, the most luxurious way to reach Portugal is by the overnight Paris/Madrid *TALGO* express train, leaving from Gare d'Austerlitz and arriving in Madrid's Chamartín Station, where you have to transfer to the *Lisboa Express* at the same station.

Daily departures from Chamartín at 10:30pm put passengers in Lisbon the next morning at 8:45am. Another train leaves Madrid daily at 11:55am, arriving in Lisbon without a change of trains at 8:06pm. For more complete information about rail connections, contact **Caminhos de Ferro Portugueses,** Calçada do Duque 20, 1200 Lisboa (tel. 01/34-63-181 in Lisbon).

Another train, the *Sud Express,* departs from Gare d'Austerlitz in Paris and goes through to Lisbon and Porto without a change of trains in Spain. The express leaves Paris at 9:30am, arriving in Lisbon the next day at 10:46am. Sleeping cars are available on the run between Irún and Lisbon. Bookings are made through the Portuguese National Railway from one of its representatives (see "By Train" under "Getting Around" later in this chapter).

Note: Completion of the tunnel under the English Channel, scheduled for 1994, will offer new train-travel options. For instance, there will be a train (*Le Shuttle*) connecting Folkestone, England, and Calais, France, in only about 35 minutes.

If you plan to travel a lot on European railroads, you will do well to secure the latest copy of the *Thomas Cook European Timetable of Railroads.* This comprehensive 500-plus-page timetable documents all of Europe's main-line passenger rail services with detail and accuracy. It is available exclusively in North America from Forsyth Travel Library, P.O. Box 2975, Shawnee Mission, KS 66201 (tel. toll free 800/367-7984), at a cost of $24.95, plus $4 postage priority airmail to the United States and $5 (U.S.) for shipments to Canada.

BY BUS   There is no particularly convenient bus service from other parts of Europe to Portugal. Flying, driving, or traveling by rail are the preferred methods. However, the buses that do make the transit—say, from London or France—do offer somewhat lower prices (and significantly less comfort) than equivalent journeys by rail.

The largest bus lines in Europe, **Eurolines, Ltd.,** 52 Grosvenor Gardens, London SW1W OUA (tel. 011/44/71/730-0202), offers bus routes to Portugal that stop at several places in France (including Paris) and Spain along the way. Buses leave from London's Victoria Coach Station every Saturday at 10pm, travel by ferryboat across the English Channel, and arrive in Lisbon two days later at 2:30pm. The bus makes stops every 4 hours for between 60 and 90 minutes each, adding considerably to the transit time. Tickets from London to Lisbon cost £91 ($136.50) one way and £129 ($193.50) round trip.

The same company also offers service from London's Victoria Coach Station to Faro, in Portugal's Deep South, every Monday and Saturday at 10pm. Arrival is 2½ days later, after multiple stops and delays along the way. The cost is £94 ($141) one way and £134 ($201) round trip. Although the phone listed above is the designated sales agent for Eurolines, more detailed information is available directly from Eurolines in the London suburb of Luton, at 011/44/582/404-511.

BY FERRY **Brittany Ferries** operates a service between November and March from Portsmouth (England) to Santander (Spain). Crossing time ranges between 29 and 33 hours. From April through October, the ferry service operates from Plymouth (England) to Santander (crossing time: 23 to 24 hours). Call the company for exact schedules and more information. Bookings are possible from Brittany Ferries, Millbay Docks, Plymouth, England PL1 3EW (tel. 0752/221321 for ferry reservations). From Santander you can drive west to Spain's Galicia, then head south toward Portugal, entering through the Minho district.

BY PACKAGE TOUR Many people never see anything of the Iberian peninsula, except perhaps Spain. You may have wondered about Portugal—whether it's worth a visit, what there is to see and do, and how to get around. One way to get a look at the country and dip briefly into its culture is take an organized tour. Consult a travel agent for the best ones currently offered.

Remember: The advantages of such tours are many. You need not be afraid of traveling alone or with timid companions. Everything is arranged for you—transportation in the countries visited, hotels, service, sightseeing trips, excursions, luggage handling, tips, taxes, and many meals. You're even given time to go shopping or nose around on your own to find interesting attractions. And you may find that some members of your group have interests that are similar to your own, so you can chat and compare notes. Take a copy of this guide along with you, and you'll recognize many places to which you will probably want to return on your own someday.

One company especially familiar with Portugal's terrain and history is **TAP Air Portugal Discovery Vacations,** 399 Market St., Newark, NJ 07105 (tel. toll free 800/247-8686). Established in 1991 as a division of the Portuguese national airline, it offers theme-based tours that show Portugal and its attractions at their most alluring. Examples include a 13-day Route of Columbus tour retracing the itinerary of some of the stops the explorer made on his way to the New World. The price of between $1,500 and $2,000 per person, double occupancy, includes extensive tours of Lisbon, with interludes in both Madeira and the Azores. Other choices include independent 11-day visits with a chauffeur-driven private car to most of the important shrines of Iberia and southern France, including Fátima and Lourdes. Only a handful of this company's options include motorcoach transit between sites. Most options are more loosely structured, perhaps incorporating a self-drive rental car with a preplanned itinerary through the villages and vineyards of Portugal and/or Spain. Overnight accommodations might include stopovers in *pousadas, paradors,* or hotels of whatever level of luxury you specify in advance.

Of special interest are the land-only Romantic Interlude packages, offering stays in some of the most elegant and historic hotels in Portugal. These are priced much less expensively than if you had booked blocks of time there yourself, and they offer levels of luxury most travelers do not automatically associate with a tour company. Per-person rates for a week-long second (or first) honeymoon range from $301 to $1,300, double occupancy, depending on the season and your hotel.

American Express Travel Related Services, with offices throughout the United States and Canada (tel. toll free 800/241-1700 in the U.S. or Canada), features a 7-city Iberian "Sun-Seeker" package, including visits to Lisbon and Faro (capital of the Algarve). Other tours include a 9-city tour of Iberia, lasting 2 weeks and taking in the Algarve (the southern coast of Portugal), Coimbra, Guarda, and Fátima, among other destinations.

TWA Getaway Tours (tel. toll free 800/GETAWAY) are also popular, including a 2-week "Flamenco Package," visiting many destinations in Spain but taking in such Portuguese cities as Lisbon, Coimbra, and Fátima.

Trafalgar Tours, 11 E. 26th St., Suite 1300, New York, NY 10010 (tel. 212/689-8977, or toll free 800/854-0103), has an exceptional schedule of moderately priced 14- to 32-day tours to Spain and Portugal. (Two go to Morocco as well.) Ask about the CostSaver tours, which book you in tourist-class hotels to keep costs trimmed.

8. GETTING AROUND

BY PLANE   Portugal is a small country, and flying from one place to another is relatively easy—that is, where airports exist. The train is the usual method of public transportation. Nevertheless, **TAP Air Portugal** flies four times a day to Faro, in the Algarve, and Porto, the main city of the north. Services to Faro are likely to be increased in the peak summer months of July and August. There are also four flights a day to Funchal, capital of Madeira, plus limited service to the Azores. Airplanes are usually Boeing 727s.

For ticket sales, flight reservations, and information about the city and the country, you can get in touch with the polite personnel of TAP Air Portugal at Praça Marquês de Pombal 3A, 1200 Lisboa (tel. 01/386-40-80).

BY TRAIN   The Portuguese railway system seems underdeveloped compared to those of the more industrialized nations of Western Europe. Still, the connections between the capital and more than 20 major towns are mainly electric and diesel. Express trains run from Lisbon, Coimbra (the university city), and Porto. Leaving from Lisbon's waterfront, electric trains travel along the Costa do Sol (Estoril and Cascais) and on to Queluz and Sintra.

At Lisbon's **Apolónia Station,** connections can be made for international services and the Northern and Eastern Lines. **Rossio** serves Sintra and the Western Lines; and at the **Cais do Sodré** connections are made for the Costa do Sol resorts of Estoril and Cascais. Finally, trains leave from the **Sul e Sueste** for the Alentejo and the Algarve. In addition, express trains connect Lisbon to all the major capitals of Western Europe, and there is a direct link with Seville.

Daily express trains in summer depart Lisbon for the Algarve (except on Sunday). These leave from the **Barreiro Station** (across the Tagus—take one of the frequently departing ferries). Off-season service is reduced to four times weekly. For information about rail travel in Portugal, phone 01/87-60-25 in Lisbon.

Railroad information and tickets for travel between almost any two stations in Europe, including stations throughout Portugal, may be obtained in North America by contacting the representatives of the Portuguese National Railway, **Rail Europe, Inc.** 230 Westchester Ave., White Plains, NY 10604 (tel. 800/848-7245). One of their telephone representatives can sell one-way or round-trip tickets into or out of Portugal, tickets within Portugal, or any of the rail passes available for travel within Portugal and the rest of Europe. It can also arrange couchettes for all-night train rides, and, at the very least, help you plan your itinerary around western Iberia.

Senior Discounts   People who are 65 years or older benefit from the 50% discount policy of the Portuguese Railway Company. These tickets are good all year.

Rail Passes   Many travelers to Europe have for years been taking advantage of one of its greatest travel bargains, the **Eurailpass,** which permits unlimited first-class rail travel in any country in Western Europe (except the British Isles) and also includes Hungary in Eastern Europe. Passes are purchased for periods as short as 15 days or as long as 3 months.

The pass cannot be purchased in Europe, so you must secure one before leaving. It costs $460 for 15 days, $598 for 21 days, $728 for 1 month, $998 for 2 months, and $1,260 for 3 months. Children under 4 travel free if they don't occupy a seat (otherwise, they pay half-fare); children under 12 pay half-fare.

If you're under 26, you can obtain unlimited second-class travel (wherever Eurailpass is honored) on a **Eurail Youthpass,** which costs $508 for 1 month and $698 for 2 months. In addition, a **Eurail Youth Flexipass** is also good for travelers under 26. Three passes are available: $200 for 5 days of travel within 2 months, $348 for 10 days of travel within 2 months, and $474 for 15 days of travel within 2 months.

Groups of three or more can purchase a **Eurail Saverpass** for 15 days of discounted travel in first class for $390. To be entitled to the discount, the members of a group must travel together. The Saverpass is valid all over Europe from April 1 and again from September 30.

Eurail Flexipass allows passengers to visit Europe in first class with more flexibility, offering the same privileges as the Eurailpass. However, it provides a number of individual travel days that can be used over a much longer period of consecutive days. That makes it possible to stay in one city and yet not lose a single day of discounted travel. There are three passes: $298 for 5 days of travel within 2 months, $496 for 10 days of travel within 2 months, and $676 for 15 days of travel within 2 months. Children 4 to 11 pay 50% of the adult fares.

The advantages are tempting: There are no tickets and no supplements—simply show the pass to the ticket collector, then settle back to enjoy the scenery. Seat reservations are required on some trains. Many of the trains have couchettes (sleeping cars), for which an additional fee is charged. Obviously, the 2- or 3-month traveler gets the greatest economic advantages; the Eurailpass is ideal for such extensive trips. Passholders can visit all of Portugal's major sights, then end their vacation in Norway, for example.

Fourteen-day or 1-month voyagers have to estimate rail distance before determining if such a pass is to their benefit. To obtain full advantage of the ticket for 15 days or 1 month, you'd have to spend a great deal of time on the train.

Travel agents in all towns and railway agents in such major cities as New York, Montreal, and Los Angeles sell all these tickets. A Eurailpass is available at the North American offices of CIT Travel Service, the French National Railroads, the German Federal Railroads, and the Swiss Federal Railways.

BY CAR   Many scenic parts of Portugal are isolated from a train or bus station, so it's necessary to have a private car to do serious touring. That way, you're on your own, unhindered by the somewhat fickle train and bus timetables, which often limit your excursions to places close to the beaten track.

There are few superhighways in Portugal, and they are often interrupted by lengthy stretches of traffic-clogged single-lane thoroughfares. The roads, however, provide access to hard-to-reach gems and undiscovered villages.

Rentals   Most visitors opt for an auto-rental plan that provides weekly rentals with unlimited kilometers included in the overall price. Three of North America's major car-rental companies maintain dozens of branches at each of Portugal's most popular commercial and tourist centers, at rates that are usually competitive.

Budget Rent-a-Car (tel. toll free 800/472-3325 in the U.S.) maintains offices in more than a dozen locations in Portugal. The most central and most used are in Lisbon, Faro (the heart of the Algarve), Porto, Praia da Rocha (also a popular Algarve destination), and Madeira. Their least expensive car is a two-door Citroën Ax, which costs about 22,310$ ($136.10) per day. If you decline this option you are responsible for the first 200,000$ ($1,220) of vehicle damage, if you have an accident. On more expensive car rentals at Budget, the insurance cost rises to 1,700$ ($10.40) per day, and renters without it are responsible for the first 500,000$ ($3,050) worth of damage. Because Portugal has one of the highest accident rates in Europe, it is an excellent idea to buy this extra insurance.

Note carefully that some North American credit-card issuers, especially American Express, sometimes agree to pay any financial obligations incurred after an accident involving a client's rented car, but only if the imprint of their card is on the original rental contract. Because of this agreement, some clients opt to decline the extra insurance coverage offered by the car-rental company. To be sure that you qualify for this free insurance, check in advance with your credit-card issuer. Know that even though the card's issuer may eventually reimburse you, you'll still have to fill out some complicated paperwork and usually advance either cash or a credit-card deposit to cover the repair cost.

Budget's least expensive car with automatic transmission is a midsize, costing around 53,530$ ($326.50) per week, with unlimited mileage, without air conditioning. A car with air conditioning is a Ford Scorpio at around 106,180$ ($647.70) per week. Many renters, when faced with the increased cost for a car with automatic transmission or air conditioning, simply opt to drive around Portugal's roads with a stick shift and the windows open.

Avis (tel. toll free 800/331-2112) maintains offices both in downtown Lisbon and at the airport, as well as at around 17 other locations throughout Portugal. The main office is at Avenida Praia da Vitoria 12-C in Lisbon (tel. 01/356-11-76). Tariffs range from around 32,000$ ($195.20) per week for their cheapest car, an Opel Corsa. At the opposite end of the spectrum, a Mercedes 190, Mercedes 200, or Mercedes 300 goes for a year-round rental rate of around 140,000$ ($854) per week, with unlimited mileage. At Avis, the collision damage waiver, depending on the car's value, goes for between 1,550$ and 3,200$ ($9.50 and $19.50) per day. Government tax (VAT) is imposed at a rate of 16% extra.

Hertz (tel. toll free 800/654-3001) has about two dozen locations within Portugal and requires a 3-day advance booking for its least expensive tariffs. Hertz's main office is at Avenida 5 de Outubro 10 in Lisbon (tel. 01/579-027). A Ford Fiesta (or a similar car) with manual transmission and no air conditioning costs around 26,300$ ($160.40) per week, with unlimited mileage, plus 16% tax. Hertz's most expensive car, a Volvo 940, rents for 240,000$ ($1,464) per week. Depending on the value of the car you rent, you'll pay between 1,700$ ($10.40) and 2,200$ ($13.40) per day. The CDW, in most cases, is optional, but if you decline it, you'll be responsible for anywhere from 500,000$ to 1,200,000$ ($3,050 to $7,320) worth of damage. If you decline it, it's wise to be certain that other types of coverage (payment with a certain type of credit card or private insurance with your regular carrier) will reimburse you for accidental car damage.

Gasoline   Unlike the situation only a few years ago, gasoline (petrol to the British) stations are now plentiful throughout the country. However, should you wander far off the beaten track, it is always wise to have a full tank and to get a refill whenever it's available, even if your tank is still more than half full. The government clamps price controls on gas, and it should therefore cost you the same throughout the land. Currently, but subject to change in the life of this edition, gas costs 140$ (90¢) per liter (about ¼ gallon) for 92 octane (normal) or 146$ (95¢) a liter for 97 octane (super)—much more than you'd usually pay within North America. Credit cards are frequently accepted, at least along the principal express routes.

Driver's Licenses   U.S. and Canadian driver's licenses are valid in Portugal, but if you're at least 18 and touring Europe by car, you should probably invest in an international driver's license. In the United States you should apply for one at any local branch of the **American Automobile Association (AAA)**—for a list of local branches, contact the AAA's national headquarters, 1000 AAA Drive, Heathrow, FL 32746-5063 (tel. toll free 800/AAA-HELP). Include two 2-inch by 2-inch photographs, a $10 fee, and a photocopy of your state driver's license. Canadians can get the address of the nearest branch of the **Canadian Automobile Club** by phoning its national office (tel. toll free 800/336-HELP).

Note that your international driver's license is valid only if it's accompanied by an authorized license from your home state or province.

In Portugal, as elsewhere in Europe, in order to drive a car legally you must have in your possession an international insurance certificate, known as a **Green Card** (Carte Verte or Carte Verde). The car-rental agency will provide one as part of your rental contract.

Driving Rules   Continental driving rules apply in Portugal, and international road symbols and signs are used. It is now compulsory to wear safety belts. Speed limits are 55 mph, but only 37 mph in heavily populated or built-up sections. On the limited number of express highways, the speed limit is increased to 75 mph.

Road Maps   The best road maps are published by Michelin, and these are available at many stores and maps shops throughout Europe as well as in the United States and Canada. If you can't find them, you can order them from Michelin Guides and Maps, P.O. Box 3305, Spartanburg, SC 29304-3305 (tel. 803/599-0850 in South Carolina, or toll free 800/423-0485 elsewhere in the U.S.). Maps are updated every year, and always try to obtain the latest copy, as the roads of Portugal are undergoing tremendous change. One of the best Michelin maps to Portugal is #990 (on a scale of 1:1,000,000, or 1 cm = 10 km). On this map scenic routes are outlined in green, and major sights and national parks along the way are also indicated.

Breakdowns   If you rent your car from one of the large companies, such as Avis or Hertz, you'll find 24-hour breakdown service available in Portugal. If you're a member of a major automobile club, such as AA, CAA, or AAA, you can get aid from the **ACP—Automovel Clube de Portugal,** Rua Rosa Araujo 24, 1200 Lisboa (tel. 01/736-121). In the north, the branch office of the club is at Rua Gonçalo Cristovão 2–6, 4000 Porto (tel. 02/316-732).

BY HITCHHIKING   There's no law against hitchhiking, but it isn't commonly practiced. If you decide to hitchhike, do so with discretion. Usually, Portuguese auto insurance doesn't cover hitchhikers. Considering the potential danger to both the passenger and the driver, hitchhiking cannot be recommended by this guide. Certainly no woman alone should attempt to hitchhike in Portugal, and even two women traveling together take great risks.

9. SUGGESTED ITINERARIES

IF YOU HAVE 1 WEEK

Days 1–3 Everybody heads for Lisbon, the gateway to Portugal. Count on using the first day for rest time. On the second, see the highlights of Lisbon, including St. George's Castle and the major attractions of Belém, such as Jerónimos Monastery. On the third day, while still based in Lisbon, explore the environs, heading first to Quelez Palace, 9½ miles from Lisbon, then going on to Sintra, 18 miles from Lisbon.

Days 4–5 Anchor into one of the resorts along the Costa do Sol, principally Cascais or Estoril. This sun coast, also called Coast of Kings, is easily reached from Lisbon. You can relax in the sun or continue to take a number of excursions. The most interesting sights are at Guincho, near the westernmost point in continental Europe, and Mafra, which is Portugal's El Escorial.

Day 6 On your sixth day, head south from Lisbon across the Tagus (see Chapter 9) to an intriguing destination such as Setúbal, 31 miles from Lisbon. After exploring the area and visiting Palmela Castle, you can continue south toward the Algarve. However, if it is running late, seek accommodations in and around Setúbal. Except for a pousada or two, the accommodations on the somewhat barren route between Lisbon and the Algarve are sparse.

Day 7 On your seventh day, you will have reached Sagres, the extreme southwestern corner of Europe, 183 miles south from Lisbon. For a description of what to see and where to stay in the Algarve, refer to Chapter 11.

IF YOU HAVE 2 WEEKS

Spend the first week as outlined above.

Days 8 – 10 Once you've reached the Algarve, settle into your favorite village, town, or resort and explore the full length of the coast. Allow a minimum of 3 days and nights. For example, if you stay at Faro, you will be roughly in the center of the Algarve and can branch out either east or west. The coastline stretches a distance of 100 miles, but it will be slow moving, regardless of which direction you select.

Day 11 On the eleventh day, if you must leave, I recommend that you return to Lisbon via a different route, heading first for Beja, the capital of Baixo Alentejo, 96 miles north from Faro. After a stopover there, you might continue north to Évora, 90 miles to the east of Lisbon, where you may want to spend the night. After exploring Évora the next morning, you can drive west to Lisbon.

Days 12 – 14 From Lisbon, fly to Madeira for a minimum of 3 days to spend time in the sun. Allow a full day for exploring this island, one of the most beautiful in the world.

IF YOU HAVE 3 WEEKS

Spend your first 2 weeks as outlined above.

Day 15 Heading north from Lisbon, stop over at Obidos, 59 miles away. After a visit, the next recommended stopover is at Alcobaça, 67 miles from Lisbon. This former Cistercian monastery was once the richest and most prestigious in Europe. Since accommodations in both these places are extremely limited, your target for the first night should be the well-known fishing village of Nazaré, 77 miles from Lisbon. (*Warning:* Hotel space is extremely tight in summer.)

Day 16 Head for Batalha, the spectacular "Battle Abbey" of Portugal, built in a Gothic-Manueline style and located 73 miles north of Lisbon. From Batalha, drive east to Fátima, the world-famous pilgrimage site, which is 36 miles east of Nazaré and about 88 miles north of Lisbon.

Day 17 Head to Tomar, 85 miles east of Lisbon.

Day 18 Drive north to Coimbra, whose university is among the oldest in the world. The town, 124 miles north of Lisbon, is rich in attractions and makes a suitable overnight stopover.

Day 19 Drive north to Porto, some 175 miles from Lisbon. This is Portugal's second city, home of port wine.

Day 20 I recommend that you at least "dip a toe" into the folkloric Minho district in the far-northern reaches of Portugal; visit Guimaraes, called the "cradle" of Portugal, 31 miles from Porto; and Viana do Castelo, Portugal's northern city of folklore, lying 43 miles north of Porto. Overnight in Viana do Castelo.

Day 21 After that, it's back to Lisbon if you wish, a trip that will absorb most of your final day.

10. WHERE TO STAY

When you check into a hotel, you'll see the official tariffs posted in the main lobby as well as somewhere in your room, perhaps at the bottom of the closet. These rates, dictated by the Directorate of Tourism, are strictly regulated and really are a form of rent control. They include the 13.1% service charge, a 16% value-added tax (VAT), and a tourist tax.

Most hotels will allow you to keep your room or deposit your luggage there until noon. From that point on, the manager can add the cost of an additional full day's rent to your bill.

When checking into a hotel, clear up the all-important question of how many meals, if any, you plan to take in the dining room. Full pension (board) means a room and three meals a day; half board means a room, breakfast, and at least one other meal. It is proper for the hotel clerk to ask which of those main meals, either lunch or dinner, you'll be taking. Those on the half- or full-board plans must pay for a meal even if they miss it. It saves you money to take full or half board, as you are granted a reduction in the overall rate, as opposed to staying at a hotel and taking your meals there à la carte. But the manager is not obliged to grant you a discount on a pension plan unless you are staying at his establishment 2 full days and nights.

Should an infraction such as overcharging occur, you may demand to be given the Official Complaints Book, in which you can write your allegations. The hotel manager is then obligated to turn your comments over to the Directorate of Tourism, where they are reviewed by a staff to see if any punitive action should be taken against the establishment.

Hotels in Portugal are rated from five stars to one. The difference between a five-star hotel and a four-star hotel will not always be apparent to the casual visitor. Often the distinction is based on square footage of bathrooms and other technical differences.

When you go below this level, you enter the realm of the second-class and third-class hotel, the latter comprising the most raw-boned and least-recommended accommodations in Portugal. However, some can be good.

Coastal hotels, especially those in the Algarve, are required to grant off-season (November to February) visitors a 15% reduction on the regular tariff. To attract more off-season business, a number of establishments extend this, starting the reduced rates in mid-October and granting them until April 1.

Unless otherwise indicated, prices in this guide include service and taxes. Breakfast may or may not be included; individual write-ups reflect various hotel policies about breakfast. All references in Portugal to "including breakfast" refer only to a continental breakfast of juice, coffee or tea, croissants, butter, and jam. If you stay at an establishment and order bacon and eggs or other extras, you will likely be billed for these as à la carte items. Hotels are grouped into the following price categories: **very expensive,** more than 41,000$ (about $248) per night for a double room; **expensive,** 20,000$ to 41,000$ ($121–$248); **moderate,** 14,000$ to 20,000$ ($85–$121); **inexpensive,** 9,000$ to 14,000$ ($55–$85); and **budget,** less than 9,000$ ($55). **Parking** rates are per day.

POUSADAS   When traveling through the countryside, it's best to plot your trips so you'll stop over at the government-owned *pousadas* (tourist inns), which range from restored Atlantic coast castles to mountain chalets.

The pousadas, similar to Spain's *paradores,* were originally created for Portuguese holiday-seekers in remote sections of the country. The Portuguese government has fashioned these inns in historic buildings, such as convents, palaces, and castles. Often they stand in beautiful physical settings. Generally (but not always) the pousadas are in regions that do not have too many suitable hotels: everywhere from Henry the Navigator's Sagres to a feudal castle in the walled city of Obidos. The tariffs are moderate; however, a guest can't stay more than 5 days, as there is usually a waiting list. Special terms are granted to honeymoon couples.

Travel agents can make reservations at pousadas, or you can contact **Enatur— Pousadas of Portugal,** Avenida Sta. Joana Princesa 10, 1700 Lisboa (tel. 01/848-1221).

OTHER SPECIAL TYPES OF ACCOMMODATIONS   Tourist inns, not government run, are known as *estalagems.* Often these offer some of the finest accommodations in Portugal, many decorated in the native, or *típico,* style and representing top-notch bargains.

The *residencias* are a form of boardinghouse, except without board. Only a room and breakfast are offered at these establishments. The *pensão* is a Portuguese boardinghouse that charges the lowest tariffs in the country. The deluxe pensão is a misnomer; the term simply means that the pensão enjoys the highest rating in its category. The accommodation is decidedly not luxurious. A luxury pensão is generally the equivalent of a second-class hotel. The boardinghouses are finds for the budget hunter. Many prepare a good local cuisine with generous helpings. For bottom-of-the-barrel type of living, there are both first-class and second-class boardinghouses.

A more recent addition to the accommodations scene are the **solares,** which are mostly spacious country manor houses of the Portuguese aristocracy that are now being restored and opened as guesthouses. Many date from the days of the Discoveries, when navigators brought riches back from all over the world and established lavish homes that have passed down to their heirs. Most of these are along the Costa Verde, between Ponte de Lima and Viana do Castelo, although they are found all over the country—from the coastal area that was the seat of shipbuilding and sailing power to the Alentejo plains.

Information on the solares program is available from the **Portuguese National Tourist Office,** 590 Fifth Ave., New York, NY 10036 (tel. 212/354-4403).

If you prefer to stay on the Costa Verde, you can receive information and assistance from Central Reservations for the Houses (manor houses) of **Delegaçao de Turismo de Ponte de Lima,** Praça da Republica, 4990 Ponte de Lima (tel. 058/94-23-35). You can arrange to go from one solar to the next through this office.

One of the best associations for arranging stays in private homes is the **Associaçao das Casas em Turismo,** Torre D2-8A, Alto da Pampilheira, 2750 Cascais (tel. 01/284-44-64). It has both manor houses and country homes where accommodations can be arranged in all the major tourist districts of the country.

CAMPING & CARAVANS Portugal provides parks for campers and house trailers (caravans) near beaches and in wooded areas all over the country. Some have pools, athletic fields, markets, and restaurants, among other facilities, while many are simply convenient sites with water and toilets away from the hustle and bustle of cities and towns. For a guide to such parks, listing their classification, equipment, and capacity, ask your travel agent or get in touch with **Federaçao Portuguesa de Campismo e Caravanismo,** Avenida 5 de Outubro 15, 1000 Lisboa, (tel. 01/522-715).

RESERVATIONS Advance reservations for peak-season summer travel in Portugal are essential, especially since many of the country's hotels are filled with vacationing Europeans. Unless you're incurably spontaneous, you'll probably be better off in Portugal with some idea of where you'll spend each night, even in low season.

Most hotels require at least a day's deposit before they will reserve a room for you. Preferably, this can be accomplished with an international money order, or, if agreed to in advance, with a personal check. You can usually cancel a room reservation one week ahead of time and get a full refund. A few hotelkeepers will return your money three days before the reservation date, but some will take your deposit and never return it, even if you cancel far in advance. Many budget-hotel owners operate on such a narrow margin of profit that they find just buying stamps for airmail replies too expensive by their standards. Therefore, it's most important that you should enclose a prepaid International Reply Coupon with your payment, especially if you're writing to a budget hotel. Better yet, call and speak to the hotel of your choice, or send a fax.

If you're booking into a chain hotel, such as Sheraton or Meridien, you can call toll free in North America and easily make reservations over the phone. Toll-free 800 numbers are included in hotel write-ups in this guide.

11. FOR BRITISH TRAVELERS

A NOTE ON CUSTOMS

On January 1, 1993, the borders between European Community countries were relaxed as the European markets united. When you're traveling within the EC, this will have a big impact on what you can buy and take home with you for personal use.

If you buy your goods in a duty-free shop, then the old rules still apply—you're allowed to bring home 200 cigarettes and 2 liters of table wine, plus 1 liter of spirits or

2 liters of fortified wine. But now you can buy your wine, spirits, or cigarettes in an ordinary shop in France or Portugal, for example, and bring home *almost* as much as you like. (U.K. Customs and Excise does set theoretical limits.) If you are returning home from a non-EC country, the allowances are the standard ones from duty-free shops. You must declare any goods in excess of these allowances.

GETTING TO EUROPE

BY PLANE   There are no hard and fast rules about where to get the best deals for European flights, but do bear the following points in mind. (1) Daily papers often carry advertisements for companies offering cheap flights. Highly recommended companies include **Trailfinders** (tel. 071/937-5400), which sells discounted fares to Portugal on TAP, and **Avro Tours** (tel. 081/543-0000), which operates charters. (2) In London, there are many **bucket shops** in the neighborhood of Earls Court and Victoria Station that offer cheap fares. For your own protection, make sure that the company you deal with is a member of the IATA, ABTA, or ATOL. (3) **CEEFAX,** a British television information service which is broadcast into many private homes and hotels, runs details of package holidays and flights to Europe and beyond.

BY TRAIN   Many different rail passes are available in the U.K. for travel in Britain and Europe. Unfortunately, one of the most widely used of these passes, the InterRail card, is not valid for travel in Spain or Portugal. (A more comprehensive pass, the well-known Eurailpass, is valid for travel in Portugal and most of the rest of Europe, however, and costs £330 for 15 days of first-class travel and £431 for 21 days of first-class travel.) For information about timetables and availability, stop in at the **International Rail Centre,** Victoria Station, London SW1V 1JY (tel. 071/834-2345).

If you're only interested in a rail ticket good for travel from London directly to Portugal, without intermediary stops, a round-trip fare from London to Lisbon costs £224 in second class and £314 in first class. Its use requires passage by SeaCat or ferryboat across the English channel and a change of trains in Paris. (Trains arrive at the Gare du Nord and depart from a station across town, the Gare d'Austerlitz, requiring a taxi or underground trip in between.) The cost of a foldaway sleeping berth (a couchette, available between Paris and Lisbon only) is an additional £11.90.

Passengers under age 26 with lots of holiday time sometimes opt for a Euro Youth ticket, which allows unlimited stopovers en route between London and Lisbon. Although its second-class, round-trip price of £214 represents a modest savings, it carries burdensome restrictions on its use within Spain, making it less appealing to Hispanophiles.

An especially convenient outlet for buying railway tickets to virtually anywhere lies opposite platform 2 in Victoria Station, London SW1V 1JY. **Wasteels, Ltd.** (tel. 071/834-7066) will provide railway-related services, discuss the various types of fares and rail passes and their various drawbacks, and its staff will probably spend a bit more time with a client during the planning of an itinerary. Depending on circumstances, Wasteels sometimes charges a £5 fee for its services, but for the information available, the money might be well spent.

BY COACH & FERRY   Since the advent of the automobile age, coach travel has competed aggressively with rail travel throughout Europe. **Eurolines,** 52 Grosvenor Gardens, London SW1W 0AU (tel. 071/730-0202), maintains buses which depart from London on Saturday (for Lisbon) and Monday (for Faro) and which each require a change of bus and a change of bus station in Paris en route. Buses are equipped with toilets and reclining seats, are less expensive than the train (£129 round trip to Lisbon and £134 round trip to Faro) and require 41 hours and 45 hours to reach their respective destinations. (By law, drivers are required to stop at regular intervals for rest and refreshment.)

If you're interested in a prearranged motorcoach tour of Portugal that begins and ends near London's Euston Station, contact **Cosmos Tourama, Ltd.,** 17 Holmsdale Rd., Bromley, Kent BR2 9LX (tel. 081/464-3477). Its eight-day Grand Coach Tour of Portugal includes transport from London, a guided drive through the

IMPRESSIONS

*The Portuguese and the English have always been the best of friends because
we can't get no Port Wine anywhere else.*
—CAPT. FREDERICK MARRYAT, *PETER SIMPLE* (1834)

---

countryside, and hotel accommodations for a cost-conscious £418. An additional
week of sunbathing, with hotel accommodation on the Algarve included, brings the
total price to around £558.

BY CAR & FERRY   Taking your car abroad avoids spending on car rentals and
gives you maximum flexibility in setting your own pace and itinerary. **Brittany
Ferries** is one of the U.K.'s largest drive-on ferryboat operators. Many visitors bound
from the U.K. to Portugal opt for a 24-hour waterborne crossing from either
Plymouth (in summer) or Portsmouth (in winter) to Santander, in northwestern Spain.
The company offers two of these crossings per week, with the availability of private
berths in sleeping cabins to make the crossing more comfortable. For information and
reservations, call 0752/221-321. The company also operates ferryboat crossings from
Portsmouth to St. Malo and Caen, in France (tel. 0705/827-701); from Poole
to Cherbourg (tel. 0202/666-466); and from Northern Ireland to Roscoff and St.
Malo (tel. 0752/269-926). Brittany's largest competitor is **P & O Ferries** (tel. 081/
575-8555 or 0304/203-388) which carries cars, passengers, and freight from
Portsmouth to Bilbao, Spain as part of a 30-hour, twice-per-week crossing to Iberia. The
line also sails from Dover to Calais, France, and from Felixstowe to Zeebrugge,
Belgium.

BY SEACAT   Traveling by SeaCat (a form of high-speed motorized catamaran) cuts
your journey time from the U.K. to the continent. A SeaCat trip can be a fun
adventure, especially for first-timers or children, as the vessel is technically "flying"
above the surface of the water. A SeaCat crossing from Folkestone to Bologne is
longer in miles but more timesaving to passengers than the Calais to Dover route used
by conventional ferryboats. SeaCats also travel from the mainland of Britain to the
Isle of Wight, Belfast, and the Isle of Man. For reservations and information, call
HoverSpeed at 0304/240-241.

VIA THE CHANNEL TUNNEL   Scheduled to open in 1994, the "Chunnel" runs
between Folkestone and Calais, France. It will reduce the travel time between England
and France to a brief 30 minutes. Train passengers can use the tunnel on direct routes
to Paris from London's Waterloo Station. If you opt to take a car with you, you'll drive
it into a railway compartment in preparation for the crossing, and drive it away from
the railway yard once you reach the mainland of France. For up-to-the-minute
information, call 0302/270-111.

ALTERNATIVE & ADVENTURE SPECIALISTS

Cycling Tours are a good way to see a country. Although dozens of companies in
Britain offer guided cycling tours on foreign turf, only a handful offer itineraries
through Portugal. An exception is **Cyclists' Tourist Club,** 69 Meadrow,
Godalming, Surrey GU7 3HS (tel. 0483/417-217). It charges £24 a year for
membership, part of which includes information and suggested cycling routes through
Portugal and dozens of other countries.

The appeal of **hillclimbing** and **hiking,** especially in areas of scenic or historic
interest, is almost universal. **Waymark Holidays** (tel. 0753/516-477) offers 14-day
walking tours through the verdant hills of Madeira about four times a year. **Sherpa
Expeditions,** 131a Heston Rd., Hounslow, Middlesex TW5 0RD (tel. 081/577-
7187) offers treks through off-the-beaten-track regions of the world, which in rare
instances might include the hills and mountains of Iberia.

You may have read a lot about **archeology tours**—but most let you look, not dig. A notable and much-respected exception is **Earthwatch Europe** (tel. 0865/311-600), whose more than 150 programs are designed and supervised by well-qualified academic and ecological authorities. At any time, at least 50 of these welcome lay participants in hands-on experience to preserve or document historical, archeological, or ecological phenomena of interest to the global community. At presstime, Portuguese projects included digs uncovering a string of ancient and medieval hill forts across the country.

One final possibility, if your interests are more varied than those items mentioned in this brief list, a phone call to the London headquarters of **IATA** (International Association of Travel Agencies; tel. 081/744-9280) can provide names and addresses of tour operators which specialize in travel relating to your particular interest.

TIPS FOR SPECIAL TRAVELERS

FAMILIES   The best deals for families are often package tours put together by some of the giants of the British travel industry. Foremost among these is **Thomsons Tour Operators.** Through its subsidiary, **Skytours** (tel. 081/200-8733), it offers dozens of air/land packages to Portugal (mostly the Algarve), where a predesignated number of airline seats are reserved for the free use of children under 18 accompanying their parents. To qualify, parents must book airfare and hotel accommodations lasting two weeks or more, and book as far in advance as possible. Savings for families with children can be substantial.

SINGLES   Single people sometimes feel comfortable traveling with groups composed mostly of other singles. One tour operator whose groups are usually composed of at least 50% unattached persons is **Explore, Ltd.** (tel. 0252/344-161), whose well-justified reputation for offering offbeat tours includes 14-day expeditions to five islands of the Azores, and motorcoach tours through the highlights of "Unknown Spain and Portugal." Groups rarely include more than 16 participants, and children under 14 are not allowed.

STUDENTS   Check **Campus Travel,** 52 Grosvenor Gardens, London SW1W 0AG (tel. 071/730-3402), which provides information to student travelers. The **International Student Identity Card (ISIC)** is an internationally recognized proof of student status that will entitle you to savings on flights, sightseeing, food, and accommodations throughout Europe and the world. It costs only £5 and is well worth the cost. **Youth hostels** are the place to stay if you're a student or traveling on a shoestring. You'll need an **International Youth Hostels Association Card,** which you can purchase from the youth hostel store at 14 Southampton Street, London (tel. 071/836-8541), or at Campus Travel (see above).

SENIORS   **Wasteels,** Victoria Station, opposite platform 2, London SW1V 1JY (tel. 071/836-8541), currently provides an over-60s Rail Europe Senior Card. Its price is £5 to any British person with government-issued proof of his or her age, and £19 to anyone with a certificate of age not issued by the British government. With this card, discounts are sometimes available on certain trains within Britain and the rest of Europe. Coach tours often cater to the elderly, with excellent offerings available from such operators as Cosmos Tourama and Thomsons/Skytours (see above).

THE DISABLED   **British Rail** offers discounts of up to 50% on some fares to anyone using a wheelchair and one companion. **RADAR** (Royal Association for Disability and Rehabilitation) publishes two annual holiday guides for the disabled: "Holidays and Travel Abroad" and "Holidays in the British Isles". It also acts as a clearing house for information about travel for and with disabled persons, and provides a number of holiday fact sheets and pamphlets. There is a nominal charge for all publications, available by calling 071/637-5400 or by writing RADAR, 25 Mortimer St., London W1N 8AB.

Another unusual clearing house for data of interest to elderly or infirm travelers is **Holiday Care Service,** 2 Old Bank Chambers, Station Road, Horley, Surrey RH6 9HW (tel. 0293/774-535).

TRAVEL INSURANCE

You might contact **Columbus Travel Insurance Ltd.** (tel. 071/375-0011) or, for students, **Campus Travel** (tel. 071/730-3402). If you're unsure about who provides what kind of insurance and the best deal, contact the **Association of British Insurers,** 51 Gresham St., London EC2V 7HQ (tel. 071/600-333).

FAST PORTUGAL

Your hotel's concierge is usually a reliable dispenser of information, but the following brief summary of some of Portugal's fast facts may prove helpful. For more specific data about Lisbon, see "Fast Facts: Lisbon" in Chapter 3.

American Express   The main office is in Lisbon, where American Express is represented by Star Travel Service, Praça Restauradores 14 (tel. 01/346-03-36). Other American Express representatives can be found at Porto, again Star Travel Service, Avenida Aliados 210 (tel. 02/200-36-37), and at Faro, yet again Star Agency, Rua Conselheiro Bivar 36 (tel. 089/80-55-25).

Babysitters   Check with your hotel's staff for arrangements. Most first-class hotels can provide competent babysitters from lists that the concierge keeps. At smaller establishments, the babysitter is likely to be the daughter of the proprietor. Rates are low. Remember to request a babysitter no later than the morning if you're going out that evening and also request one with at least a minimum knowledge of English.

Business Hours   Most shops are open Monday through Friday from 9am to 1pm and 3 to 7pm and Saturday from 9am to 1pm. Business offices are generally open Monday through Friday from 9am to 1pm and 3 to 5:30pm (sometimes 6pm). The majority of banks are open Monday to Friday from 8:30am to 3:30pm.

Camera/Film   Film is expensive in Portugal, so I suggest you bring in all Customs will allow. There are no special restrictions on taking photographs, except in certain museums.

Cigarettes   The price of American-brand cigarettes (which varies) is always lethal. Bring in at least 200 cigarettes, as allowed by Customs. If you're saving money, try one of the Portuguese brands as an adventure. Many smokers have found Portuguese tobacco excellent.

Climate   See "When to Go," earlier in this chapter.

Crime   See "Safety," below.

Currency   See "Information, Entry Requirements & Money," earlier in this chapter.

Customs   See "Information, Entry Requirements & Money," earlier in this chapter.

Documents Required   See "Information, Entry Requirements & Money," earlier in this chapter.

Driving Rules   See "Getting Around," earlier in this chapter.

Drugs   Illegal drugs are plentiful, almost as much as they are in the United States, although penalties may be more severe if you're caught possessing illegal narcotics. If foreigners are caught selling illegal narcotics, judges may throw the book at them, imposing maximum penalties. Bail for foreigners is rare, and local prosecutors have a high conviction rate. All the U.S., British, and Canadian consulates might do is provide you with a list of local attorneys.

Drugstores   The Portuguese government requires selected pharmacies (*farmácias*) to stay open at all times of the day and night. This is effected by means of a rotation system. Check with your concierge for locations and hours of the nearest drugstores, called *farmácias de servico*. In general, pharmacies in Portugal are open Monday through Friday from 9am to 1pm and 3 to 7pm and Saturday from 9am to 1pm.

Electricity   Many North Americans find their plugs will not fit into sockets in Portugal or Spain, where the voltage is 200 volts AC, 50 cycles. In the unlikely event that you managed to force the plug of your appliance into the outlet, you would destroy your appliance, upset the hotel management, and possibly cause a fire. Don't try. Many hardware stores in North America sell the appropriate converters, and the concierge desks of most hotels will either lend you a converter and adapter or tell you where you can buy one nearby. If you have any doubt about whether you have the appropriate converter, ask questions at your hotel desk before you try to plug anything in.

Embassies/Consulates   If you lose your passport or have some other pressing problem, you'll need to get in touch with the **U.S. Embassy,** on Avenida das Forcas Armadas (Sete Rios), 1600 Lisboa (tel. 01/726-66-00). Hours are Monday through Friday from 8am to 12:30pm and 1:30 to 5pm. If you've lost a passport, the embassy can take photographs for you and help you to obtain the proof of citizenship needed to get a replacement.

The **Canadian Embassy** is at Avenida da Liberdade 144–156, 1200 Lisboa (tel. 01/347-48-92); hours are Monday through Friday from 8:30am to 12:15pm and 1 to 5pm.

The **British Embassy,** Rua São Domingos a Lapa 37, 1200 Lisboa (tel. 01/396-1122), is open Monday through Friday from 10am to 12:30pm and 3 to 4:30pm.

The **Embassy of the Republic of Ireland,** Rua de Imprensa A. Estrela s/n, 1200 Lisboa (tel. 01/396-15-69), is open Monday through Friday from 9:30am to noon and 2:30 to 4:30pm.

The **Australian Embassy,** Av. da Liberdade 244 (second floor), 1200 Lisboa (tel. 01/52-33-50), is open Monday through Thursday from 9am to 12:30pm and 1:30 to 5pm and Friday from 9am to 12:30pm.

New Zealand does not maintain an embassy in Portugal.

Emergencies   For the **police** (or an ambulance) in Lisbon, telephone 115. In case of **fire,** call 32-22-22 or 60-60-60. The Portuguese Red Cross can be reached at 61-77-77. The national **emergency** number in Portugal is 115.

Etiquette   In general, Portugal is considered a polite country. Women often kiss one another once on both cheeks when they meet. Men extend a hand when introduced; if they are good friends, they will often embrace. All services require a visitor to say thank you—*obrigado* for a man and *obrigada* for a woman. "Please" is *por favor*. It's customary to greet people with a *bom dia* in the morning, a *boa tarde* in the afternoon, and a *boa noite* in the evening. Always bring flowers—not wine—if you're invited to someone's home. Stretching—either at the dining table or on the street—for some reason is considered extremely impolite.

Gasoline   See "Getting Around," earlier in this chapter.

Hitchhiking   See "Getting Around," earlier in this chapter.

Holidays   See "When to Go," earlier in this chapter.

Information   See "Information, Entry Requirements & Money," earlier in this chapter, as well as individual city chapters for local information offices.

Language   English is often spoken in the major resorts and at first-class and deluxe hotels, but often in smaller places you'll need the help of a phrase book or dictionary. One of the most helpful is the *Portuguese Phrase Book* published by Berlitz. Crown Publishing also prints the *Useful Common Dictionary: Portuguese-English/English-Portuguese*.

Laundry   Most hotels in this guide provide laundry services, but if you want your garments returned on the same day, you'll often be charged from 20% to 40% more. Simply present your maid or valet with your laundry or dry cleaning (usually lists are provided). *Note:* Materials needing special treatment (such as certain synthetics) should be called to the attention of the person handling your laundry. Some establishments I've dealt with in the past treated every fabric as if it were cotton.

Legal Aid   If you're a foreigner in Portugal, all your consulate can do is advise you of your rights if you run into trouble with the law. The consulate staff will also provide a list of English-speaking lawyers, but, after that, you're thrown on the mercy of the local courts. Consulates do not act like an arbitrator in your behalf, so be duly warned.

Liquor Laws   You have to be 18 to drink. Liquor is sold in most markets, as opposed to in the package stores found in most of the United States. In Lisbon you can drink until dawn. There's always some bar or fado club open serving alcoholic beverages.

Mail   While in Portugal, you may have your mail directed to your hotel (or hotels), to the American Express representative, or to General Delivery (*Poste Restante*) in Lisbon. Your passport must be presented for mail pickups. The **general post office** in Lisbon is at Praça do Comércio (tel. 01/346-32-31); it's open daily from 8am to 10pm.

Maps   If you'd like a map before your trip to plan your itinerary, you can obtain one from Rand McNally, Michelin, or the AAA. These are sold at bookstores all over America. Rand McNally has retail stores at 150 E. 52nd St., New York, NY 10022 (tel. 212/758-7488); 23 E. Madison St., Chicago, IL 60602 (tel. 312/332-4627); and 595 Market St., San Francisco, CA 94105 (tel. 415/777-3131). The U.S. headquarters of Michelin is at P.O. Box 3305, Spartanburg, SC 29304 (tel. 803/599-0850 in South Carolina, or toll free 800/423-0485 elsewhere in the U.S.).

Newspapers/Magazines   The *International Herald Tribune* and *USA Today* are sold at most Lisbon newsstands and in most big cities and resorts, either in major hotels or along the street. If you read Portuguese, the most popular centrist newspaper is the influential *Diário de Noticias*. To the right of center is *O Dia*, to the left is *O'Dario*. The European editions of *Time* and *Newsweek* are sold at most major newsstands.

Passports   See "Information, Entry Requirements & Money," earlier in this chapter.

Pets   Pets brought into Portugal must have the approval of the local veterinarian and a health certificate from your home country.

Radio/TV   Lisbon has two major TV channels—Channel 1 (VHF) and Channel 11 (UHF). Many foreign films are shown, often in English with Portuguese subtitles. For radio, see "Radio" under "Fast Facts: Lisbon" in Chapter 3.

Religious Services   Portugal is a Roman Catholic country, and there are places of worship in every city, town, and village.

Restrooms   All major terminals (airports and railways) have such facilities, and Lisbon has several public ones. However, you can often use the restroom in a cafe or tavern, as there is one on practically every block. It is considered polite to purchase something, however—perhaps a small glass of wine or whatever.

Safety   Whenever you're traveling in an unfamiliar city or country, stay alert. Be aware of your immediate surroundings. Wear a moneybelt and don't sling your camera or purse over your shoulder. This will minimize the possibility of your becoming a victim of crime. Every society has its criminals. It's your responsibility to be aware and alert even in the most heavily touristed areas.

Taxes   Since Portugal and neighboring Spain simultaneously joined the European Community (EC), or Common Market, on January 1, 1986, Portugal has imposed a value-added tax (VAT) on most purchases made within its borders, ranging from 8% to 30%. Known in Portugal as the IVA, its amount is almost always written into the bottom line of the bill for any purchase a foreign visitor might make. Hotel bills are taxed at 8%. Car rentals will be garnished with an additional 16% tax (less than in some other European countries).

Such deluxe goods as jewelry, furs, and expensive imported liquors include a 30% built-in tax. Because a scotch and soda in a Portuguese bar carries this high tax, many imbibers have changed their choice of alcohol from scotch to Portuguese brandy and soda or, more prosaically, beer.

To get an IVA tax refund on those purchases that qualify (ask the shopkeeper), present your passport to the salesperson and ask for the special stamped form. Present the form with your purchases at the booth marked for IVA tax refunds at the airport. You will get your money refunded right there at the booth.

Telegrams/Telex/Fax   At most hotels, the receptionist will help you send one of these messages. Otherwise, go to the nearest post office for assistance.

Telephones   Calling from pay-phone booths in Portugal, providing you have the right change, will allow you to avoid high hotel surcharges. Most booths take 2$5, 5$, and 25$ coins. Put the coins in a slot at the top of the box while you hold the receiver, then dial your number after hearing the dial tone. Once a connection is made, the necessary coins will automatically drop. If enough coins are not available, your connection will be broken. A warning tone will sound and a light over the dial will go on in case more coins are needed. For long-distance (trunk) calls within the country, dial the right trunk code, followed by the number you want.

Telephone calls can also be made at all post offices, which will also send telegrams. Calls to Europe are made by dialing 00, followed by the country code, the area code (not prefaced by 0), then the phone number. The country code for the United States and Canada is 1.

Time Portugal is 6 hours ahead of the United States (eastern time). For the local time in Lisbon, phone 15.

Tipping Portugal has now caught up with the rest of Western Europe. Most service personnel expect a good tip rather than a small one, as in former times.

The hotels add a service charge (known as *servico*), which is divided among the entire staff. But individual tipping is also the rule of the day: 100$ (60¢) to the bellhop for errands run, 100$ (60¢) to the doorman who hails you a cab, 100$ (60¢) to 200$ ($1.20) to the porter for each piece of luggage carried, 500$ ($3.10) to the wine steward if you've dined often at your hotel, and 300$ ($1.80) to the chambermaid.

In first-class or deluxe hotels, the concierge will present you with a separate bill, outlining your little or big extras, such as charges for bullfight tickets. A gratuity is expected in addition to the charge, the amount depending entirely on the number of requests you've put to him or her.

For a normal haircut, you should leave at least 100$ (60¢) behind as a tip. But if your hair is cut at the Ritz, don't dare leave less than 200$ ($1.20). Beauticians and manicurists get at least 200$ ($1.20).

Figure on tipping about 20% of your taxi fare for short runs. For longer treks—for example, from the airport to Cascais—15% is adequate.

Restaurants and nightclubs include a service charge and government taxes. As in hotels, this service is distributed among the entire staff, including the waiter's mistress and the owner's grandfather—so extra tipping is customary. Add about 5% to the bill in a moderately priced restaurant, up to 10% in a deluxe or first-class establishment. For hatcheck in fado houses, restaurants, and nightclubs, tip at least 100$ (60¢). Washroom attendants also get 100$ (60¢).

Water Tap water is generally potable throughout Portugal, but bottled water is always safer. Even if the water in Portugal isn't bad, you are not used to the microbes and can become ill. In rural areas, the water supply may not be purified. Under no circumstances should you swim in or drink from freshwater rivers or streams.

CHAPTER 3
GETTING TO KNOW LISBON

1. ORIENTATION

2. GETTING AROUND

• FAST FACTS: LISBON

3. NETWORKS & RESOURCES

In its golden age it was called the eighth wonder of the world. Travelers returning from a trip to Lisbon reported that its riches rivaled those of Venice.

As one of the greatest maritime centers in history, the Portuguese capital has enjoyed exotic riches from the far-flung corners of its empire. Aside from the wealth of cultural influences, Lisbon stockpiled goods, beginning with its earliest contacts with the Calicut and Malabar coasts. Treasures from Asia brought in on Chinese junks to Indian seaports eventually found their way back to Lisbon: porcelain; luxurious silks; and rubies, pearls, and other rare gems. The abundance and variety of spices from the East—turmeric, ginger, pepper, coconut, cumin, betel— were to rival even Keats's vision of "silken Samarkand."

From the wilds of the Americas came red dye-wood (brazilwood), coffee, gold (discovered there in 1698), and diamonds (first unearthed there in 1729) and other gemstones. All this extensive contact signaled a new era in world trade, with Lisbon sitting at the center of a great maritime empire, a hub of commerce between Europe, Africa, and Asia.

A BIT OF BACKGROUND Many Lisboans claim unabashedly Ulysses founded their city. Others, more scholarly, maintain the Phoenicians or the Carthaginians were the original settlers. The body of the country's patron saint, Vincent, is said to have arrived in Portugal on an abandoned boat, with only two ravens to guide it. It is further alleged the two birds lived in the cathedral tower as late as the 19th century.

The Romans settled in Lisbon in about 205 B.C., later building a fortification on what is now St. George's Castle. The city was captured by the Visigoths in the 5th century A.D., a conquest later followed by centuries of Moorish domination beginning in 714. The first king of Portugal, Afonso Henríques, captured Lisbon from the Moors in 1147. But it wasn't until 1256 that Afonso III moved the capital there, deserting Coimbra, now the major university city of Portugal.

The Great Earthquake occurred at 9:40am on All Saints' Day, November 1, 1755. "From Scotland to Asia Minor, people ran out of doors and looked at the sky, and fearfully waited. It was, of course, an earthquake," as once chronicled a *Holiday* magazine article. Fifty-foot-high tidal waves swept over Algeciras, Spain. The capitals of Europe shook. Churches were packed to overflowing; smoky tapers and incense burned on altars. Twenty-two aftershocks followed. Roofs caved in; hospitals (with more than 1,000 patients), prisons, public buildings, royal palaces, aristocratic town houses, fishermen's cottages, churches, and houses of prostitution—all were toppled. Overturned candles helped ignite a fire that would consume the once-proud capital in 6 days, leaving it a gutted, charred shambles. Voltaire described the destruction in *Candide:* "The sea boiled up in the harbor and smashed the vessles lying at anchor. Whirlwinds of flame and ashes covered the streets and squares, houses collapsed, roofs were thrown onto foundations and the foundations crumbled." All told, 30,000 inhabitants were crushed beneath the tumbling debris.

When the survivors of the initial shocks ran from their burning homes toward the mighty Tagus, they were met with walls of water 40 feet high. Estimates vary, but the final tally of all who died in drownings and the 6-day holocaust that followed is put at around 60,000.

Voltaire cynically commented on the aftermath of the disaster, particularly the *auto-da-fé* that followed: "It was decided by the University of Coimbra that the sight of several people being slowly burned with great ceremony was an infallible means of preventing the earth from quaking."

After the ashes had settled, the marquês de Pombal, the prime minister, ordered that the dead be buried and the city rebuilt at once. To accomplish that ambitious plan, the king gave him powers that were virtually dictatorial.

What Pombal ordered constructed was a city of wide, symmetrical boulevards leading into handsome squares dominated by fountains and statuary. Bordering these wide avenues would be black-and-white mosaic sidewalks, the most celebrated in Europe.

The mixture of the old (pre-earthquake) and the new (post-earthquake) was done so harmoniously that travelers today consider Lisbon one of the most beautiful cities on earth. Under a stark blue sky, the city's medley of pastel-washed houses dazzles, like a city in North Africa. The Tagus, the river flowing through Lisbon, has been called the city's "eternal lover."

Sea gulls take flight from its harbor, where trawlers from Africa unload their freight. Pigeons sweep down on Praça do Comércio, also known as Black Horse Square. From the Bairro Alto (upper city), cable cars carry Lisbon's denizens down to the waterfront. The sidewalks are characteristic black-and-white mosaics forming arabesques. Streets bear colorful names or designations, such as the Rua do Açúcar (Street of Sugar). Fountains abound: One, the Samaritan, dates from the 16th century. The boulevards split through the city to new high-rise apartment houses, while in other quarters laundry hanging from 18th-century houses laps the wind.

It is a city that gives nicknames to everything from its districts (the Chiado, named after a poet) to its kings. Fernando, who built one of the most characteristic walls around Lisbon, was honored with the appellation "the Beautiful."

Many who have never actually been to Lisbon know it well from watching World War II spy movies on TV. It would be only natural, you'd assume, to see Hedy Lamarr slinking around the corner any moment. During World War II, Lisbon, officially neutral, was a hot-bed of intrigue and espionage. It was also a haven for thousands of refugees. Many of those—such as deposed royalty—remained, settling into villas in Estoril and Sintra.

1. ORIENTATION

ARRIVING

BY PLANE Both foreign and domestic flights land at Lisbon's **Portela Airport,** about 4 miles from the heart of the city. For all airport information, telephone 01/841-50-00. A Green Line bus, known as the *Linha Verde,* carries passengers into the city for 260$ ($1.50) for one zone. The bus goes as far as the Santa Apolónia Rail Station. Service is daily every 15 minutes from 7am to 9:20pm. There is no charge for luggage. You can also go by taxi. Passengers line up, British style, in a usually well-organized line at the sidewalk in front of the airport. The average taxi fare from the airport to central Lisbon is 1,200$ ($7.30), including a surcharge for your suitcases and a tip.

For ticket sales, flight reservations, and information about the city and the country, you can get in touch with the polite Lisboa personnel of TAP Air Portugal at Praça Marquês de Pombal 3A (tel. 01/386-10-20, the airline's reservation number).

BY TRAIN Most international rail passengers from Madrid and Paris arrive at the **Santa Apolónia Rail Station,** the major terminal of Lisbon, lying by the Tagus near the Alfama district. Two daily trains make the 10-hour run from Madrid to Lisbon. Rail lines from northern and eastern Portugal also arrive at this station. Other rail terminals include **Rossio,** where you can get trains to Sintra, and the **Cais do Sodré,** with trains to Cascais and Estoril on the Costa do Sol. At a final station, **Sul e Sueste,** you can board trains to the Algarve. For all rail information, at any of the terminals above, call 01/87-60-25.

BY BUS   Buses from all over Portugal, including the Algarve, arrive at the **Rodoviária da Estremadura,** Avenida Casal Ribeiro 18B (tel. 01/57-77-15), which lies near Praça Saldanha, about a 30-minute walk from the Praça dos Restauradores. Buses no. 1, 21, and 32 will deliver you to the Rossio, and bus no. 1 goes on to the Cais do Sodré, if you're checked into a hotel at Estoril or Cascais. At least 10 buses a day leave from Faro, capital of the Algarve, and two *expressos* (express buses) head north every day to Porto. There are 10 daily buses leaving from here to Coimbra, the university city in the north.

BY CAR   International motorists must arrive through Spain, the only nation connected to Portugal via road. You'll have to cross Spanish border points, usually of no great difficulty. Roads are moderately well maintained. From Madrid, if you head west, the main road (N620) from Tordesillas goes southwest by way of Salamanca and Ciudad Rodrigo to reach the Portuguese frontier at Fuentes de Onoro.

If you have a rented car, make sure that your insurance covers Portugal. Driving is on the right side of the road, and international signs and symbols are used. There are 15 border crossings, most open daily from 7am to midnight.

TOURIST INFORMATION

The **Portuguese National Tourist Board** in Lisbon is at Avenida António Augusto de Aguiar 86 (tel. 01/57-50-15). For information about Portugal before heading there, contact the Portuguese National Tourist Office, 590 Fifth Ave., New York, NY 10036-4704 (tel. 212/354-4403).

CITY LAYOUT

MAIN STREETS & SQUARES   Now in its seventh century as the center of the Portuguese nation, Lisbon is the westernmost capital of continental Europe. Part of its legend is that it spreads across seven hills, like Rome. If that statement were ever true, it has long since become historical, as Lisbon now sprawls across more hills than that. Most of it lies on the right (north) bank of the Tagus.

No one ever claimed that getting around Lisbon was easy. Streets rise and fall across the hills, at times dwindling into mere alleyways. But exploring it is well worth the effort.

Lisbon is best approached through its gateway, the **Praça do Comércio,** bordering the Tagus. Like a formal parlor, it is one of the most perfectly planned squares in Europe, rivaled perhaps only by Italy's Piazza dell'Unità d'Italia in Trieste. Before the 1755 earthquake, Commerce Square was known as Terreiro do Paço, the palace grounds, as the king and his court lived in now-destroyed buildings on that site. To confuse matters further, English-speaking residents often refer to it as Black Horse Square, so named because of its statue (actually a bronze green) of José I.

Today the square is the site of the Stock Exchange and various government ministries. Its center is used as a parking lot, which destroys some of the harmonious effect of its *praça*. In 1908, its most monumental event occurred, the reverberations of which were heard around the world. Carlos I and his elder son, Luís Filipe, were fatally shot by an assassin. It would hold on for another 2 years under the rule of a younger prince, but the House of Bragança came to an end that day on Black Horse Square.

Directly west of the square stands the City Hall, fronting the **Praça do Município.** The building was erected in the late 19th century by the architect Domingos Parente.

Heading north from Black Horse or Commerce Square, you enter the hustle and bustle of Praça Dom Pedro IV, popularly known as the **Rossio.** The "drunken" undulation of the sidewalks, with their arabesques of black and white, have led to the appellation, used mainly by tourists, of "the dizzy praça." Here you can sit sipping strong unblended coffee from the former Portuguese provinces in Africa, while a boy gives you one of the cheapest and slickest shoeshines in Europe. The statue on the square is that of the emperor of Brazil, Pedro IV, himself a Portuguese.

Opening onto the Rossio is the **Teatro Nacional Dona Maria II,** a freestanding building whose facade has been preserved. From 1967 to 1970, workmen gutted the interior to rebuild it completely. If you arrive by train, you'll enter the **Estaçao do Rossio,** whose Manueline architectural exuberance is a worthy sight.

Separating the Rossio from the Avenida da Liberdade is the **Praça dos Restauradores,** named in honor of the restoration—that is, when the Portuguese chose their own king and freed themselves from 60 years of Spanish rule. That event is marked by an obelisk.

Lisbon's main avenue is the **Avenida da Liberdade,** a handsomely laid out street dating from 1880 and once called the antechamber of Lisbon. The Avenue of Liberty is like a mile-long park, with shade trees, gardens, and center walks for the promenading crowds. Flanking it are some of the finest shops, headquarters for many major airlines, travel agents, coffeehouses with sidewalk tables, and such important hotels as the Tivoli. The comparable street in Paris would be the Champs-Élysées; in Rome, the Via Veneto.

At the top of the avenue is the **Praça Marquês de Pombal,** with a statue erected in honor of Pombal, the 18th-century prime minister credited with Lisbon's reconstruction in the aftermath of the earthquake.

Proceeding north, you'll enter the splendid **Parque Eduardo VII,** named to honor the son of Queen Victoria, who paid a state visit to Lisbon. In the park is the Estufa Fria, a greenhouse that is well worth a visit.

FINDING AN ADDRESS Finding an address in the old quarters of Lisbon is difficult, as street numbering at times follows no predictable pattern. Therefore, when trying to locate some obscure address, always ask for the nearest cross street before setting out. That will save you much time and frustration.

Addresses consist of a street name followed by a number. Sometimes the floor of the building is given as well: Avenida Casal Ribeiro 18 3°. That means that the building is at number 18 and the particular address is on the third floor. In Lisbon the ground floor is not called the first floor as in the United States; for Americans the third floor is actually the fourth floor. "ESP" after a floor number indicates that you should go left, and "DIR" means head for the right of any floor.

STREET MAPS Arm yourself with a good map before setting out. The best one is published by **Falk,** and it's available at most newsstands and kiosks in Lisbon. Those given away free by tourist offices and hotels aren't adequate, as they don't list the maze of little streets.

NEIGHBORHOODS IN BRIEF

Baixa The business district of Lisbon, Baixa contains much Pombaline-style architecture (referring to the 18th-century prime minister). Many major Portuguese banks are headquartered here. Running south, the main street of Baixa separates the Praça do Comércio from the Rossio. In fact, a triumphal arch leads from the square to **Rua Augusta,** where there are many clothing stores. The two most important streets of Baixa are Rua da Prata ("street of silver") and Rua Aurea, formerly called Rua do Oro ("street of gold"). Silversmiths and goldsmiths are located on these streets.

Chiado If you head west from Baixa, you'll enter a shopping district known as the Chiado. From its perch on a hill, it is traversed by Rua Garrett, named for the noted romantic writer João Batista de Almeida Garrett (1799–1854). Many of the finest shops in the city, such as the Vista Alegre, a china and porcelain house, are here. One coffeehouse in particular, A Brasileira, has been a traditional gathering spot for the Portuguese literati.

Bairro Alto Continuing your ascent, you'll arrive at the Bairro Alto (the upper city). This sector, reached by trolley car, occupies one of the legendary seven hills of Lisbon. Many of its buildings were left fairly intact by the 1755 earthquake. Containing much of the charm and color of the Alfama, it is of interest mainly because it is the center of some of the finest fado cafes in Lisbon, as well as excellent restaurants and unpretentious taverns.

The Alfama   East of the Praça do Comércio lies the oldest district, the Alfama. Saved only in part from the devastation of the earthquake, the Alfama was the Moorish sector of the capital. Centuries later, before the earthquake struck, it was the residential district of aristocrats. Nowadays it is occupied in some parts by stevedores, plus fishermen and their barefoot *varinas* (fishwives). Overlooking the Alfama is **St. George's Castle,** a Visigothic fortification that was later used by the Romans; on the way to the Alfama, on the Rua dos Bacalheiros, stands another landmark, the **Casa dos Bicos** (House of the Pointed Stones)—an early 16th-century town house graced with a facade studded with diamond-shaped stones.

Belém   In the west, on the coastal road to Estoril, is the suburb of Belém (Bethlehem). It contains some of the finest monuments in Portugal, a few of which were built during the Age of Discovery, near the point where the caravels set out to conquer new worlds (at Belém, the Tagus reaches the sea). At one time, before the earthquake, Belém was an aristocratic sector filled with elegant town houses.

Two of the principal attractions in all of Portugal stand here: the **Jerónimos Monastery,** erected in the 16th century in the Manueline style, and the **National Coach Museum,** the finest of its kind in the world. Actually, Belém is Lisbon's museumland, containing also the **Museum of Popular Art,** the **Ethnological Museum,** and the galley-stuffed **Naval Museum.**

Cacilhas   On the south side of the Tagus, where puce-colored smoke billows from factory stacks, is the left-bank settlement of Cacilhas. It is inhabited mainly by the working class, yet it's often visited by right-bank denizens who come here for its seafood restaurants. You can reach the settlement by way of a bridge or a ferryboat, leaving from Praça do Comércio.

The most dramatic way to cross the Tagus is on the **Ponte 25 de Abril,** one of the longest suspension bridges in Europe. Completed in 1966, the bridge helped open Portugal south of the Tagus. The bridge is 7,473 feet long, and its towers are 625 feet high. Standing guard on the left bank is a monumental statue of Christ with arms outstretched.

2. GETTING AROUND

Public transportation is inexpensive but inadequate at times. Yet considering the city's hilly terrain and that many of the streets were designed for donkey carts, the Portuguese manage very well. Even the most skilled chauffeurs, however, have been known to scrape the fenders of their clients' rented limousines while maneuvering through the narrow alleyways.

A lot of the city can be walked, especially by those adept at hill climbing. However, to get from one point to the other—say, from the Alfama to the suburb of Belém—you'll need public transport or your own car.

As Evamarie Doering of Belmont, California, wrote me, "In the 15 years since my last visit there, Lisbon has become one of the noisiest cities I've ever visited. Traffic is outrageous; driving is difficult because of the speed and the tendency of the natives to ride six inches from your rear bumper. The buses, of which there are a great many, are very noisy, and produce volumes of smoke. Honking of car horns seems to be a national pastime."

BY PUBLIC TRANSPORTATION

Tickets valid for 4 to 7 days of travel on all the city's trams, the Metro, buses, funicular, and the Santa Justa Elevator cost 1,155$ (7) or 1,625$ (9.90), respectively.

These discount passes may be purchased at the Santa Justa Elevator, just south of Rossio Square, daily from 8am to 8pm.

METRO Lisbon's Metro stations are designated by large M signs, and the subway system has 24 stations. A single ticket costs 45$ (20¢) per ride if you purchase it from a vending machine, 55$ (30¢) if you purchase it from a toll booth. You can purchase 10 tickets at one time at a toll booth, each ticket costing 50$ (30¢); 10 tickets purchased at a vending machine will sell for only 45$ (20¢) each. One of the most popular trips—and likely to be jam-packed on *corrida* (bullfight) days—is from the Avenida da Liberdade to the Campo Pequeno, the brick building away from the center of the city. Service is daily from 6:30am to 1am.

BUS & TRAM These are among the cheapest in Europe. The trolley cars—*eléctricos*—make the steep run up to the Bairro Alto and are usually painted a rich Roman gold. The double-decker buses, on the other hand, come from London and look as if they need Big Ben in the background to complete the picture. If you're trying to stand on the platform at the back of a jammed bus, by the way, you'll need both hands free to hold on.

At the foot of the Santa Justa Elevator, lying on the Rua Aurea, a stand will give you a schedule pinpointing the zigzagging route of these trams and buses. Your hotel concierge should be of help to you also.

The antedeluvian eléctricos, much like the little cable cars of San Francisco, have become a major tourist attraction. Instead of phasing them out, Lisbon authorities have sent them to Germany, where they were overhauled and refurbished, then shipped back to Portugal. Beginning in 1903, these eléctricos replaced horse-drawn trams. The most interesting ride, from a sightseeing point of view, is on eléctrico 28, which takes you on a fascinating trip through the most history rich part of Lisbon.

You will pay a flat fare of 130$ (70¢) on a bus if you buy the ticket from the driver. The transportation system within the city limits is divided into zones ranging from one to five. The price of your fare depends on how many zones you traverse. You can purchase a book of 10 tickets (*módulos*) for 580$ ($3.50). On an eléctrico a ticket costs 110$ (60¢). Buses and eléctricos run daily from 6am to 1am.

ELECTRIC TRAIN Lisbon is connected with all the towns and villages along the Portuguese Riviera by a smooth-running electric train system. You can board the train at the waterfront **Cais do Sodré Station** in Lisbon and head up the coast all the way to Cascais.

Only one class of seat is offered, and the rides are cheap. Sintra, that third major destination in the environs, is not reached by the electric train. You must go to the **Estação do Rossio Station,** opening onto the Praça Dom Pedro IV or the Rossio, where frequent connections can be made. The one-way fare is one class only. On the Lisbon-Cascais, Lisbon-Estoril, or Lisbon-Sintra run, the one-way fare is 145$ (80¢) per person.

ELEVATOR CAR & FUNICULAR The **Santa Justa Elevator,** just south of Rossio Square, is one of the most convenient methods of transportation in the city, as it links Rua do Ouro with Praça do Carmo, otherwise a steep climb. A one-way fare is 140$ (90¢). Lisbon also has a trio of funiculars, including the Glória, which goes from Praça dos Restauradores to Rua Sao Pedro de Alcantara; the Bica, from the Calcada do Combro to Rua do Boavista; and the Lavra, going from the eastern side of the Avenida da Liberdade to Campo Martires da Pátria. A one-way ticket costs 30$ (10¢).

FERRYBOAT Long before the Ponte 25 de Abril was built, reliable ferryboats chugged across the Tagus, connecting the left bank with the right. They still do, except today they have been rebuilt and remotorized so they are no longer noisy. Many Portuguese who live on the bank opposite Lisbon take the ferryboat to avoid the heavy bridge traffic during rush hour.

Most of these boats leave from Cais de Alfandega (Praça do Comércio) and Cais do Sodré, heading for Cacilhas. A single fare costs 85$ (50¢). However, if you purchase a ticket from a vending machine, the charge is slightly reduced to 82$ (50¢). If you plan to make several trips back and forth across the river, you can purchase a block of 20 *módulos,* using 2 módulos on each trip, which will reduce the one-way passage to 65$ (40¢).

BY TAXI

Taxis in Lisbon tend to be inexpensive and are a popular means of transport for all but the most economy minded of tourists. The taxis usually are diesel-engined Mercedes, charging a basic fare of 135$ (80¢) for the first 480 yards. After that, you'll be assessed another 7$ (5¢) for each additional 117 yards, with 20% additional for night fare from 10pm to 6am. The driver is allowed by law to tack on another 50% to your bill if your luggage weighs more than 66 pounds. Portuguese tip about 20% of an already modest fare.

Many visitors stay at one of the Costa do Sol resort hotels, such as the Palacio in Estoril and the Cidadela in Cascais. If that is your situation, then you'll probably find taxi connections from Lisbon prohibitively expensive. Far preferable for Costa do Sol visitors is the electric train system (see above).

BY CAR

In congested Lisbon, driving is extremely difficult and potentially dangerous, as the city has an alarmingly high accident rate. It always feels like rush hour in Lisbon (theoretically, hours are Monday through Saturday from 8am to 10am, 1 to 2pm, and 4 to 6pm). Parking is seemingly impossible. Save your car rentals for making excursions from the capital. If you drive into Lisbon from another town or city, call ahead and ask at your hotel for the nearest garage or parking possibility. Leave your vehicle there until you're ready to depart Lisbon.

CAR RENTALS   The major international car-rental companies are represented in Lisbon. Car-rental kiosks are found at the airport, or you can rent from one of the offices in the center. These include **Avis,** Avenida Praia da Vitoria 12C (tel. 01/356-76-11), open daily from 8am to 7pm, and **Hertz,** Avenida 5 de Outubro 10 (tel. 57-90-77), open Monday through Friday from 8am to 7pm and Saturday and Sunday from 9am to 1pm and 2 to 7pm. **Europcar,** Avenida António Augusto de Aguiar 24 (tel. 01/53-51-15), is open Monday through Saturday from 8am to 8pm and Sunday from 8 to 6:30pm.

GASOLINE   Lisbon is well stocked with garages and gasoline pumps; some are open around the clock.

PONTE 25 DE ABRIL   This suspension bridge, one of the longest in Europe, connects Lisbon with the district south of the Tagus. For a small car, the toll charge is 55$ (30¢), increasing to 110$ (60¢) for a larger automobile. Not only can you take the bridge to reach Cacilhas, but also you can use it for such cities as Setubal, in the south, and Évora, the old Roman city in the east.

ON FOOT

Central Lisbon is relatively compact, and because of heavy traffic it is best explored by foot. That is virtually the only way to see such districts as the Alfama. However, when you venture farther afield, such as to Belém, you'll need to depend on some of the public transportation outlined above.

FAST ~~FACTS~~   LISBON

Your hotel's concierge usually is a reliable dispenser of information. The following summary of basic information about Lisbon may also prove helpful. See also "Fast Facts: Portugal" in Chapter 2.

American Express   American Express Star Travel Service is the representative of Amex in Portugal, and it will hold or forward mail for you, providing you are a client. There, too, you can buy tickets for tours, exchange currency, and, of course, cash American Express traveler's checks. Its offices are at Praça dos Restauradores 14 (tel. 01/346-03-36); it's open Monday through Friday from 9am to 12:30pm and 2 to 6pm.

Area Code   The area code for Lisbon, Sintra, Estoril, and Cascais is **01.**

Babysitters   Most first-class hotels can provide competent babysitters from lists the concierge keeps. At small establishments, the sitter is likely to be a relative of the proprietor. Rates are low. Remember to request a babysitter early—no later than the morning if you're planning on going out that evening. Also request a sitter with at least a minimum knowledge of English. If you get one fluent in English, count yourself lucky.

Banks   Check with your home bank before your departure, as many banks in Canada and the United States have affiliates in Lisbon. The majority of the banks are open Monday through Friday from 8:30am to 3pm. Three major banks include **Banco Portugues do Atlantico,** Rua Aurea 112 (tel. 01/34-61-321); **Banco Exprito Santo e Comercial de Lisboa,** Avenida da Liberdade 195 (tel. 01/54-12-18); and, at the airport, a branch of **Banco Totta & Açores** (tel. 01/342-62-22), which is open at all hours of the day and night, including holidays. More banks in Lisbon offer night service. For example, **Banco Borges & Irmao,** Avenida da Liberdade 9A (tel. 01/34-21-068) and **Banco Pinto & Sotto Mayor,** Praça dos Restauradores (tel. 01/34-26-222), are open Monday through Friday from 3 to 7:30pm.

Business Hours   Most **shops** are open Monday through Friday from 9am to 1pm and 3 to 7pm. Increasingly, the noon luncheon break is being done away with in many places, with shops remaining open all day. Saturday hours, in general, are from 9am to 1pm. Most **restaurants** serve from noon to 3pm and 7 to 11pm, with or without a weekly closing day, depending on the management. **Offices** in Lisbon, in general, are open Monday through Friday from 9am to 1pm and 3 to either 5:30 or 6pm.

Car Rentals   See "Getting Around," earlier in this chapter.

Climate   See "When to Go" in Chapter 2.

Currency   See "Information, Entry Requirements & Money" in Chapter 2.

Currency Exchange   See "American Express" and "Banks," above. There are currency exchange booths at Santa Apolonia station and at the airport—both open 24 hours a day. The post office (see "Mail," below) will also exchange money.

Dentist   Contact **Centro de Medicina Dentaria,** Calçada Bento da Rocha Cabral (tel. 01/68-41-91). Some of the dentists there speak English.

Doctor   See "Hospitals," below.

Drugstores   A central and well-stocked one is **Farmácia Azevedo,** Rossio 31 (tel. 01/342-74-78). Pharmacies that are closed post a notice indicating the nearest one that's open.

Embassies/Consulates   See "Fast Facts: Portugal" in Chapter 2.

Emergencies   To call the **police** or an **ambulance** in Lisbon, telephone 115. In case of **fire,** call 01/32-22-22. The **Portuguese Red Cross** is reached at 01/30-17-777.

Eyeglasses   One of the city's best-recommended is **Oculista das Avenidas,** Avenida Marqués Tomar 71 (tel. 01/76-42-97), which seems to be the favorite of many residents within its very central downtown neighborhood.

Hairdressers/Barbers   Men can go to any of the big barbershops in the deluxe hotels, such as the Ritz in Lisbon. For women, three hairdressers in Lisbon are particularly recommended: **Cabeleireiro Martins,** 31-1° Avenida Defensores de Chaves (tel. 01/54-89-33); **Cabeleireiro Isabel Queiroz do Vale,** 35-1° Avenida Fontes Pereira de Melo (tel. 01/54-82-38); and **Lúcia Piloto,** Avenida da Liberdade 12 (tel. 01/34-20-535).

Holidays   See "When to Go" in Chapter 2.

Hospitals   In case of a medical emergency, ask at your hotel or call your embassy and ask the staff there to recommend an English-speaking physician; or try the **British Hospital,** Rua Saraiva Carvalho 49 (tel. 01/395-50-67), where the telephone operator, staff, and doctors all speak English.

Hotlines   Drug abuse (tel. 01/726-77-66); **suicide** (tel. 01/54-45-45).

Information   See "Tourist Information," earlier in this chapter.

Laundry/Dry Cleaning   Keeping your clothes clean can be a problem if you're not staying long in Lisbon. Do-it-yourselfers may want to take their clothes to a self-service laundry, **Lavatax,** Rua Francisco Sanches 65A (tel. 01/82-33-92). It's part of a chain that has three other branches in Lisbon, one at Estoril, and one at Cascais. For a dry cleaner, go to **Lavandarias Amoreira,** Shop #1103, Amoreiras Shopping Center, Avenida Eng. Duarte Pacheco (tel. 01/69-23-84).

Libraries   The **Biblioteca Nacional (Lisboa),** Campo Grande 83 (tel. 01/79-50-130), near University City, contains more than two million volumes (books, periodicals, nonbook material) and is open on Monday through Friday from 9:45am to 5:30pm in mid-July to mid-September and on Monday through Saturday from 9:45am to 7:30pm in winter. In addition, the **American Cultural Center,** Avenida Duque de Loulé 22B (tel. 01/57-01-02), has a library of some 8,000 volumes and 132 periodicals. It is open Monday from 2 to 8pm and Tuesday through Friday from 12:30 to 6pm; closed in July.

Lost Property   Go in person to (don't call) the municipal **Governo Civil,** which is next to the San Carlos Opera House. Hours are Monday through Saturday from 9am to noon and 2 to 6pm. For items lost on public transportation, inquire at **Seeção de Achados da PSP,** Olivais Sul, Praça Cidade Salazar Lote 180 (tel. 01/853-54-03), which is open Monday through Friday from 9am to noon and 2 to 6pm.

Luggage Storage/Lockers   These can be found at the **Santa Apolonia** station, located by the river near the Alfama. Lockers cost from 390$ ($2.30) to 850$ ($5.10) for up to 48 hours.

Newspapers/Magazines   See "Fast Facts: Portugal" in Chapter 2.

Photographic Needs   One of the best places to go for your film needs, including processing, is **Fotosport,** Terminal de Rossio, Loja 120 (tel. 01/342-78-70), which is open Monday through Friday from 8am to 10pm and Saturday and Sunday from 9am to 8pm.

Police   Call **115.**

Mail   While in Portugal you may have your mail directed to your hotel (or hotels), to the American Express representative, or to General Delivery (*Poste Restante*) in Lisbon. Your passport must be presented for mail pickups. The **general post office** in Lisbon is at Praça do Comércio (tel. 01/346-32-31); it's open daily from 8am to 10pm.

Radio   English-speaking listeners in Lisbon can pick up the **BBC World Service** and **Voice of America.** Hourly news is broadcast on 648-KHz medium wave and 15.07-MHz short wave. Between 8:30 and 10am daily, Portuguese radio presents English-language programs for tourists—between 558 and 720 KHz/87.9 and 95.7 FM, depending on where you are in the city.

Religious Services   **Roman Catholicism** is the leading religion in Portugal, and you'll find churches everywhere. If you're **Protestant,** a Baptist evangelical church exists in Lisbon. It's the Igreja Evangelica Baptista de Lisboa, Rua Filipe Folque 36B (tel. 01/53-53-62), with Sunday services in Portuguese at 11am and 7:30pm (also at 7:30pm on Wednesday). **Jewish** services are held at the Shaare Tikua Synagogue, Rua Alexandre Herculano 59 (tel. 01/388-15-92). Throughout the year, services are conducted on Friday evening and Saturday morning (call for exact times).

Restrooms   All major terminals (airports and railways) have such facilities, and Lisbon has several public ones. However, you can often use one at a cafe or tavern, as one of these establishments exists practically within every block. It is considered polite to purchase something, however—perhaps a small glass of mineral water.

Safety   Whenever you're traveling in an unfamiliar city or country, stay alert. Be aware of your immediate surroundings. Wear a moneybelt and don't sling your camera or purse over your shoulder. This will minimize the possibility of your becoming a victim of crime. Every society has its criminals. It's your responsibility to be aware and alert even in the most heavily touristed areas. Don't leave anything, especially your luggage, in an unguarded car. In recent years, there have been a lot of break-ins.

Shoe Repairs   Your needs can be answered at **Silva e Neves Lopes,** Rua

Rodrigo da Fonseca 182B (tel. 01/68-70-55), near the Ritz. Hours are Monday through Friday 7am to 8:30pm and Saturday from 7am to 1pm.

Television Lisbon has two major TV channels—Channel 1 (VHF) and Channel 11 (UHF).

Taxes Lisbon imposes no special city taxes. However, a value-added tax (VAT) is added to purchases and services (see "Taxes" under "Fast Facts: Portugal" in Chapter 2).

Taxis See "Getting Around," earlier in this chapter.

Telegrams/Telex/Fax At most hotels the receptionist will help you send a telegram. If not, there is a cable dispatch service, open 24 hours a day, at **Marconi** (the Portuguese Radio Communications Office), Rua S. Juliao 131. To send telegrams from any telephone to points outside Portugal, dial 182 to reach Marconi. To send telegrams within Portugal (your language skills had better be good to handle this one), dial 113 from any telephone. Most foreign visitors leave the logistics of this to the hotel concierge, assuming the hotel offers this service. Telexes and faxes can be sent from most hotels, or you can go to the general post office (see above).

Telephone To make a local call in Lisbon, you can use one of the many telephone booths, but you'll need some coins. You can talk for 3 minutes for 15$ (10¢). For most long-distance telephoning, particularly transatlantic calls, go to the central post office (see "Mail," above). Give an assistant there the number you wish, and he or she will make the call for you, billing you at the end. Some phones are equipped for using calling cards, including American Express and Visa. You can also purchase phone cards from the post office in denominations of 50$ (30¢) and 120$ (70¢).

Transit Info **TAP Air Portugal,** Praça Marquês de Pombal 3A, can be reached at 01/386-40-80. For **airport information,** call 01/841-50-00, and for **train information,** dial 01/87-60-25.

Weather To find out about the weather, if you don't speak Portuguese, ask someone at your hotel desk to translate one of the weather reports that appear daily in the leading newspapers.

3. NETWORKS & RESOURCES

FOR STUDENTS Contact **Tagus,** Praça de Londres 9B (tel. 01/89-15-31), which provides data on low-cost travel not only in Portugal but also in Europe. Always check its discounts against those of other airlines to see just how much of a reduction you are getting. The office is open Monday through Friday from 9am to 6pm and Saturday from 9am to 1pm. Metro: Alameda.

FOR GAY MEN & LESBIANS Before you go to Portugal, you can order *Spartacus*—the international gay guide ($29.95)—from Giovanni's Room, 1145 Pine St., Philadelphia, PA 19107 (tel. 215/923-2960).

Lesbians traveling abroad may want to order a copy of *Ferrari's Places for Women* ($10). It, too, can be ordered from Giovanni's Room.

Gays and lesbians socialize mainly in public bars, restaurants, and clubs, as there is no major social center for them. The many public parks of Lisbon are extremely dangerous after dark. The scene is liveliest in the Bairro Alto, especially along Rua de São Marçel. See also Chapter 7.

FOR WOMEN Women traveling alone or paired with another woman often report sexual harassment when traveling in Iberia, more so in Spain than in Portugal. If you feel threatened, perhaps in a case where a man might be following you, seek help or enter a place of business, which will usually frighten the person away. Or call 115 for the police. For much more detailed advice, including information about safety and health precautions, consult a book like *Handbook for Women Travellers* (1992), by Gemma Moss (Piatkus Publishers, 19).

FOR SENIORS   Before you go, refer to "Tips for Seniors" in Chapter 2. Discounts, if any, for seniors vary from place to place, but it's always a good idea to inquire in advance, especially at cultural presentations, national monuments, and museums and when making ticket purchases on public transportation. TAP Air Portugal, for example, offers those age 60 or more discounts on flights to Lisbon from New York, Boston, and Los Angeles. Delta and TWA make similar discounts. Contact the individual airlines to see what might be offered.

If you're a member of a senior-citizen group—for example, AARP—you might be entitled to discounts at such Lisbon chain hotels as Sheraton or Holiday Inn. However, all these questions have to be answered in advance, as chain hotels often have "blackout" periods during certain busy times when senior citizen discounts don't apply. When seeking discounts, always carry proper identification. A passport is best, although a driver's license or membership card in a recognized senior-citizen group might also serve as identification.

CHAPTER 4

LISBON ACCOMMODATIONS

1. IN THE CENTER
- **FROMMER'S SMART TRAVELER: HOTELS**

2. IN THE BAIRRO ALTO
- **FROMMER'S COOL FOR KIDS: HOTELS**

3. IN THE GRAÇA DISTRICT

4. IN THE BELÉM DISTRICT

Most Lisbon visitors have to make a major decision usually before they arrive: Do they want to stay in a city-proper hotel or at a resort accommodation in the neighboring towns of Estoril and Cascais (see Chapter 8 for recommendations)? Much will depend on their interests.

If it's summer and visitors would like to combine a sea resort holiday with visits to Lisbon's cultural attractions, then a beach resort might be ideal, although there's a bit of a commute into Lisbon. Electric trains, however, run about every 20 minutes or so, so it's entirely possible to combine the amusements of the Costa do Sol with a Lisbon sightseeing jaunt—all while based at the same hotel.

If your interest is primarily in seeing Lisbon's attractions and you're pressed for time, perhaps having no more than two days, then you'll probably opt for the central location of Lisbon. Also, if you're an off-season (November through March) visitor, you probably wouldn't want to be at a sea resort anyway.

In the past few years, Lisbon has seen a lot of hotel building; unfortunately, some of the newer choices, hastily erected, aren't really recommendable and seem to be courting tour groups from around the world. However, beginning in the mid-1980s and continuing into the 1990s, some of the grandest hotels ever built in Lisbon have gone up. Most tend to be at the top of the price scale.

If you can't afford to stay in these world-class hotels, you'll find reasonably priced guesthouses—pensãos—in Portugal. Most of these are no-frills affairs, and often you'll have to share a bath, although many have hot and cold running water in a sink in your room. Sometimes there is a shower. In many cases, the toilet is across the hall.

If you arrive without a reservation, begin your search for a room as early in the day as possible. If you arrive late at night, you may have to take what you can get, often in a much higher price range than you'd like to pay.

1. IN THE CENTER

VERY EXPENSIVE

LE MERIDIEN, Rua Castilho 149, 1000 Lisboa. Tel. 01/69-09-00. Fax 01/69-32-31. 331 rms, 17 suites. A/C MINIBAR TV TEL **Metro:** Rotunda. **Bus:** 1, 2, 9, or 32.
$ Rates (including breakfast): 38,000$ ($231.80) single; 41,000$ ($250.10) double; from 70,000$ ($427) suite. AE, DC, MC, V. **Parking:** 2,900$ ($17.70).
One of the most dramatic major hotels in Lisbon opened in 1985. Each guest room has a wraparound window that overlooks Edward VII Park and lets in the bright Iberian sunshine. The air-conditioned lobby glitters with white marble, polished chromium, and mirrors. A symmetrical entranceway frames the tile-bottomed fountains, whose splashing rises to the top of the sunlit atrium.

Dining/Entertainment: You'll find lots of attractive and interesting public rooms, including a tearoom with Portuguese tiles; the ground-floor Brasserie des Amis with a view of the park and the adjacent boulevard; and the formal, glamorous Restaurant L'Atlantic upstairs. Le Nautique piano bar is upholstered in maroon velvet.

Services: Laundry/valet, babysitting, 24-hour room service.

Facilities: Health club with sauna and massage, car-rental kiosk, business center.

LISBOA SHERATON HOTEL & TOWERS, Rua Latino Coelho 1, 1097 Lisboa. **Tel. 01/57-57-57,** or toll free 800/325-3535 in the U.S. Fax 01/54-71-64. 384 rms, 7 suites. A/C MINIBAR TV TEL **Bus:** 1, 2, 9, or 32.

$ Rates: 40,000$–50,000$ ($244–$305) single; 45,000$–55,000$ ($274.50–$335.50) double; from 100,000$ ($610) suite. Breakfast 2,750$ ($16.80) extra. AE, DC, MC, V. **Parking:** 2,500$ ($15.30).

Lisbon's tallest hotel is easy to spot from most of the major parks and gardens. Originally built in 1972 but renovated several times since, it has its most desirable rooms in the tower. From there, views open onto either the longest bridge in Europe and the Tagus or the cityscape.

Dining/Entertainment: The night begins with live music played in The Lounge, followed by dinner in the Caravela or the Alfama Grill Gourmet Restaurant, both serving a selection of Portuguese and continental dishes. You can enjoy drinks throughout the day and evening on the 26th floor, which has a panoramic view of Lisbon.

Services: Laundry/valet, babysitting, 24-hour room service.

Facilities: Sauna and solarium, car-rental facilities, boutiques, health club, outdoor pool.

THE RITZ, Rua Rodrigo da Fonseca 88, 1200 Lisboa. Tel. 01/69-20-20, or toll free 800/327-0200 in the U.S. Fax 01/69-17-83. 260 rms, 40 suites. A/C MINIBAR TV TEL **Metro:** Rotunda. **Bus:** 1, 2, 9, or 32.

$ Rates (including breakfast): 50,000$ ($305) single; 54,000$ ($329.40) double; from 100,000$ ($610) suite. AE, DC, MC, V. **Parking:** 2,500$ ($15.30).

The Ritz was built in the late 1950s and is operated by Inter-Continental Hotels. Its suites boast the finest decoration you'll see in any major Portuguese hotel. Slender mahogany canopied beds with fringed swags, marquetry desks, satinwood dressing tables with tip-mirrors, and plush carpeting—no wonder the Ritz has been traditionally the preferred choice of celebrated guests. Some of the soundproof modern rooms have terraces opening onto Edward VII Park; each boasts a marble bath with double basin, local and satellite TV, and a radio.

Dining/Entertainment: The main dining room, Veranda, is dignified and pleasant, and from May to October you can take meals out on the attractive Veranda Terrace. The Grill Room is traditionally decorated (see my restaurant recommendations in Chapter 5). The Ritz Bar is a magnet. Lodged in a corner of the hotel, overlooking the terrace and park, it offers everything from a Pimm's No. 1 Cup to a mint julep.

Services: Babysitting, 24-hour room service, laundry/valet.

Facilities: Coffee shop, tearoom, disco, beauty parlor.

HOTEL TIVOLI, Avenida da Liberdade 185, 1298 Lisboa Codex. Tel. 01/52-11-01. Fax 01/57-94-61. 297 rms, 30 suites. A/C MINIBAR TV TEL **Metro:** Avenida. **Bus:** 1, 2, 9, or 32.

$ Rates (including breakfast): 37,500$ ($228.80) single; 44,000$ ($268.40) double; from 50,000$ ($305) suite. AE, DC, MC, V. **Parking:** 1,250$ ($7.60).

Hotel Tivoli has enticing features. First, it's right on the main boulevard of Lisbon. Second, it's large enough to accommodate more than 600 guests—hence, its public facilities are bountiful. Third, its prices are not extravagant, considering the amenities. The two-story-high reception lobby has an encircling mezzanine lounge that is almost arena-size, with comfortable islands of furniture arranged on Oriental rugs. Adjoining the O Terraço restaurant is a homelike salon with a wood-burning fireplace, Oriental rugs, and restrained decor.

The guest rooms contain a mixture of modern and furniture. The larger and best rooms face the front, although those in the rear are quieter.

Dining/Entertainment: The wood-paneled O Zodiaco restaurant offers a buffet for both lunch and dinner; meals are à la carte. The top-floor O Terraço offers a view of Lisbon as well as à la carte meals, with the emphasis on steaks and chops that you select yourself and have cooked on a tile charcoal grill.

Services: Laundry, 24-hour room service, babysitting.

Facilities: Access to Tivoli Club, surrounded by a lovely garden, with pool that can be heated when necessary, tennis court, solarium, bar, and restaurant serving light snacks; business center; boutiques.

EXPENSIVE

HOTEL ALFA LISBOA, Avenida Columbano Bordalo Pinheiro (without number), 1000 Lisboa. Tel. 01/726-21-21. Fax 01/726-30-31. 355 rms, 38 junior suites. A/C MINIBAR TV TEL **Metro:** Sete Rios. **Bus:** 26.

$ Rates (including breakfast): 23,000$–27,500$ ($140.30–$167.80) single; 28,000$–33,000$ ($170.80–$201.30) double; 38,500$ ($234.90) suite. AE, DC, MC, V. **Parking:** 1,000$ ($6.10).

Hotel Alfa Lisboa, removed from the commercial center, is a five-star hotel that has gained popularity with business travelers since it opened. The staff works hard to make visitors comfortable. There's an imposing reception desk in the marble-floored lobby. The guest rooms and suites are well furnished.

Dining/Entertainment: Guests can enjoy an array of drinking and dining facilities. The most formal is the Pombalino Restaurant, with an 18th-century Portuguese palatial decor and international cuisine. The most popular and least expensive selection is A Aldeia, a coffee shop/restaurant decorated in regional Portuguese style. The Labirinto Bar with a nightly piano player is the most popular drinking spot.

Services: Laundry/valet, babysitting, 24-hour room service.

Facilities: Car-rental kiosks, shopping gallery, health club, outdoor pool, solarium, sauna.

HOTEL ALTIS, Rus Castilho 11, 1200 Lisboa. Tel. 01/52-24-96. Fax 01/54-86-96. 307 rms, 13 suites. A/C MINIBAR TV TEL **Metro:** Rotunda. **Bus:** 2.

$ Rates (including breakfast): 26,000$–34,000$ ($158.60–$207.40) single; 32,000$–38,000$ ($195.20–$231.80) double; from 45,000$ ($274.50) suite. AE, DC, MC, V. **Parking:** 1,000$ ($6.10).

A luxurious nine-story modern hotel, with attractively furnished guest rooms and suites, the Altis sits right in Lisbon's commercial and cultural center. The Portuguese hospitality offered by the staff and management—together with the refurnishing of the lobby, public areas, restaurants, and bars—makes for an enjoyable five-star hotel. For example, you can order a drink or a meal night or day. Many services are provided, including laundry and dry-cleaning service right in the hotel. The guest rooms are well equipped, boasting color TVs with eight channels via satellite, radios, and warm contemporary furnishings.

Dining/Entertainment: Three meals a day are served in the Girassol Restaurant, and for lunch or dinner a guest can also choose the Dom Fernando Grill. Continental dishes are featured along with Portuguese regional food. The Piano Bar has live music for dancing, and if you want to see the Lisbon skyline, take the elevator to the top-floor São Jorge Bar.

Services: Laundry/valet, babysitting, 24-hour room service.

Facilities: Indoor heated pool, health club.

AVENIDA PALACE, Rua 1 de Dezembro 123, 1200 Lisboa. Tel. 01/346-01-54. Fax 01/342-28-84. 81 rms, 10 suites. A/C MINIBAR TV TEL **Metro:** Restauradores. **Bus:** 1, 2, 36, or 44.

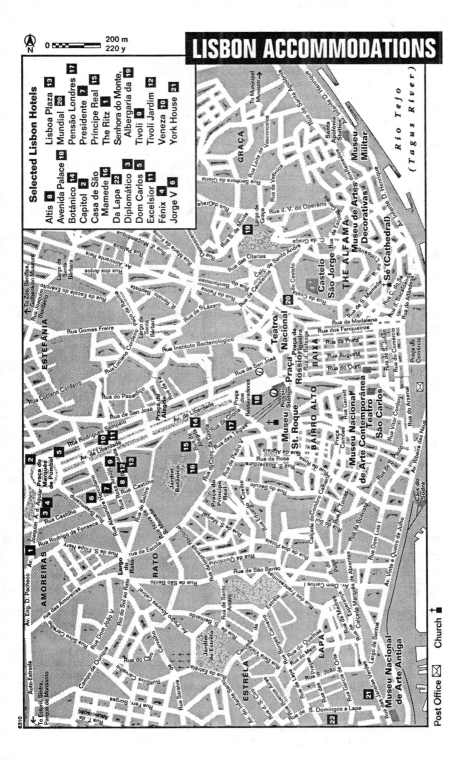

LISBON ACCOMMODATIONS

Selected Lisbon Hotels

Altis **8**	Lisboa Plaza **13**
Avenida Palace **18**	Mundial **20**
Botânico **14**	Pensão Londres **17**
Capitol **2**	Presidente **7**
Casa de São	Príncipe Real **15**
Mamede **16**	The Ritz **1**
Da Lapa **22**	Senhora do Monte,
Diplomático **3**	Albergaria da **19**
Dom Carlos **5**	Tivoli **9**
Excelsior **11**	Tivoli Jardim **12**
Fénix **4**	Veneza **10**
Jorge V **6**	York House **21**

Post Office ⊠ **Church** †∎

$ Rates (including breakfast): 20,000$ ($122) single; 22,000$ ($134.20) double; 35,000$–40,000$ ($213.50–$244) suite. AE, DC, MC, V. **Parking:** Free.

Avenida Palace is a link to the past, a world reflected in crystal and antiques. Built in 1892 in the neo-Manueline style, it lies adjacent to the railway station. The second-floor drawing room attracts those partial to the age of silk-brocade wallcoverings, fringed velvet draperies, crystal chandeliers, marquetry tables, consoles, and hand-woven Portuguese carpets. The location is noisy—right at the Rossio, minutes from fado clubs, restaurants, and some of Lisbon's larger shops.

Major renovations have prevented the Avenida Palace from slipping into disrepair and deterioration. Most guest rooms have been redone. The redecorated rooms are furnished in a traditional manner, with 18th-century antiques or artwork and central heating. The spacious baths are faced in Portuguese marble.

Dining/Entertainment: Breakfast is the only meal served, but the hotel lies literally at the doorstep of dozens of restaurants. The hotel, however, maintains a bar.

Services: Laundry, babysitting, 24-hour room service.

Facilities: Car-rental desk.

DA LAPA, Rua do Pau de Bandeira 4, 1200 Lisboa. Tel. 01/395-00-05.

Fax 01/395-06-65. 83 rms, 16 suites. A/C MINIBAR TV TEL **Bus:** 13 or 27.

$ Rates: 23,000$–27,000$ ($140.30–$164.70) single; 25,000$–29,000$ ($152.50–$176.90) double; 38,000$ ($231.80) suite. Breakfast 1,800$ ($11) extra. AE, DC, MC, V.

Set within a palace built for the count of Valença in 1870, this five-star property is the newest and most talked about in Lisbon. In 1910, the de Valença family sold the villa and its enormous gardens to a wealthy but untitled family who retained it until 1988. After 4½ years of renovation, it reopened in 1992 amid a flurry of publicity and a battalion of prominent Europeans. Today, its lushly manicured gardens (huge by urban standards) lie close to the Tagus, south of the city center, amid most of Portugal's foreign embassies in the Lapa district.

All but about 20 of the accommodations lie in a six-story modern wing built amid the venerable trees of the garden. The guest rooms contain amply proportioned marble surfaces, reproductions of French and English furniture, and a classic design inspired by late 18th-century models. The public areas boast multicolored ceiling frescoes and richly patterned marble floors laid out in sometimes startling geometric patterns.

Dining/Entertainment: The Restaurant Embaixada (recommended separately in Chapter 5) is one of the most sought after in the neighborhood. Sun-flooded lunches and candlelit dinners are served beside the pool in the Pavilhão. The bar is sumptuous and smooth.

Services: Laundry, dry cleaning, concierge, 24-hour room service.

Facilities: Lavishly appointed garden with fountains and water cascades, outdoor pool, business center with translation and secretarial services, fitness center.

HOTEL DIPLOMÁTICO, Rua Castilho 74, 1200 Lisboa. Tel. 01/386-20-41.

Fax 01/52-21-55. 72 rms, 18 suites. A/C MINIBAR TV TEL **Metro:** Rotunda. **Bus:** 2.

$ Rates (including breakfast): 18,000$ ($109.80) single; 21,000$ ($128.10) double; from 23,000$ ($140.30) suite. AE, DC, MC, V. **Parking:** Free.

A first-class hotel, the 11-floor Diplomático lies near the Ritz and Edward VII Park. The two-story lobby and lounge is dominated by a George Bramdeiro mural. The tasteful guest rooms often have small balconies.

Dining/Entertainment: The Park Restaurante serves an array of international dishes along with Portuguese regional specialties. Guitar music accompanies most meals.

Services: Laundry, babysitting, 24-hour room service.

Facilities: Car-rental desk.

HOTEL LISBOA PLAZA, Travessa do Salitre 7, Avenida da Liberdade, 1200 Lisboa. Tel. 01/346-39-22. Fax 01/347-16-30. 94 rms, 12 suites. A/C MINIBAR TV TEL **Metro:** Avenida. **Bus:** 1, 2, 36, or 44.

$ Rates (including breakfast): 22,000$–24,000$ ($134.20–$146.40) single; 24,000$–29,500$ ($146.40–$180) double; 36,000$–45,000$ ($219.60–$274.50) suite. Children under 12 stay free in parents' room. AE, DC, MC, V. **Parking:** 1,500$ ($9.20).

Hotel Lisboa Plaza, in the heart of the city, is a charmer. A family-owned and -operated four-star hotel, the Plaza has many appealing art nouveau touches, including its facade. My favorite rendezvous is the 1900s-style bar with soothing olive colors and tufted leather chairs. The hotel was built in 1953 but completely overhauled in 1988. A well-known Portuguese designer, G. Viterbo, decorated it in a contemporary classic style; modern amenities were added at the time. The guest rooms—with marble baths, hairdryers, and in-house videos—are well styled and comfortable. No-smoking rooms are available. The multilingual staff will introduce you to the hotel.

Dining/Entertainment: Through an art nouveau entrance you approach the Quinta d'Avenida Restaurant, which specializes in a traditional Portuguese cuisine.

Services: Babysitting, 24-hour room service, same-day laundry.

Facilities: Car-rental desks, business services.

HOTEL LUTÉCIA, Avenida Frei Miguel Contreiras 52, 1700 Lisboa. Tel. 01/80-31-21. Fax 01/80-78-18. 151 rms, 8 suites. A/C MINIBAR TV TEL **Metro:** Roma. **Bus:** 27.

$ Rates (including breakfast): 18,000$ ($109.80) single; 21,500$ ($131.20) double; from 35,000$ ($213.50) suite. AE, DC, MC, V.

You'll find the Lutécia in a shopping center, five minutes by subway (go to Roma station) from old Lisbon, toward the airport. Its rooms and suites have distilled beauty and space without excessive adornment; each is furnished with leather-and-wood armchairs, a desk and dressing table, a room-wide headboard, walnut-and-leather paneling complete with pushbuttons, and reading lights. Each tiled bath features a tub/shower combination and large wraparound towels on heated rods. Breakfast is available either on your private balcony or from the buffet in the roof restaurant.

Its 12 stories are set back from a busy thoroughfare, with a formal driveway entrance. The public lounges consume most of the first two floors, although you must take an elevator to the top for the open-view dining room.

Dining/Entertainment: The lobby's Concorde Bar, with decoration based on a picture of Paris's place de la Concorde at the beginning of the 20th century, is ideal for a drink. In the snack bar, a good meal costs around 1,800$ ($11). You can order a three-course menu beginning at 4,900$ ($29.90) in the Panoramic Restaurant.

Services: Laundry/valet, babysitting.

Facilities: Car-rental facilities.

TIVOLI JARDIM, Rua Julio Cesar Machado 7–9, 1200 Lisboa. Tel. 01/53-99-71. Fax 01/355-65-66. 119 rms. A/C MINIBAR TV TEL **Metro:** Avenida. **Bus:** 1, 2, 9, or 32.

$ Rates (including breakfast): 21,900$ ($133.60) single; 28,500$ ($173.90) double. AE, DC, MC, V. **Parking:** Free.

Tivoli Jardim is under the same ownership as its neighbor, the previously recommended Hotel Tivoli. Set behind its namesake, avoiding the traffic noises from Avenida da Liberdade, the structure is adorned with cliff-hanging balconies, two shafts of elevators, and well-styled guest rooms. The walls are white plaster, and the furnishings basic built-in, with reading lights, maid-summoning bells, channel music, comfortable armchairs, and a glass wall (curtained off at night) leading to each balcony. The baths have patterned tile, with a bidet, shower, and tub.

There are adequate public lounges. Portuguese businesspeople have found the Jardim ideal for meeting clients in the cathedral-high lobby, with a wall of glass through which the Iberian sun pours in. Dominating everything is a ceiling-high tapestry in sunburst colors. The tile and marble floors are peacock blue and emerald green, and the staircase leading to the mezzanine is a blood red.

Dining/Entertainment: The dining room is tasteful, with white-brick walls, green tables, and wall niches filled with Portuguese ceramics.

Services: Laundry, babysitting.
Facilities: Use of Tivoli Club in Hotel Tivoli, with pool; car-rental facilities.

MODERATE

HOTEL BOTÁNICO, Rua Mãe d'Agua 16–20, 1200 Lisboa. Tel. 01/342-03-92. Fax 01/342-01-25. 30 rms. A/C MINIBAR TV TEL **Bus:** 1, 2, 9, or 32.
$ Rates: 10,500$–15,000$ ($64.10–$91.50) single; 13,000$–15,000$ ($79.30–$91.50) double. AE, DC, MC, V.

The Botánico perches near a hilltop in a neighborhood dotted with parks and cafes, not far from the Botanical Gardens. A modern cement building with a tasteful wood-accented lobby, it was recently renovated. The guest rooms, though small, are clean and convenient, and each contains a radio. No meals other than breakfast are served.

CAPITOL HOTEL, Rua Eça de Queiroz 24, 1000 Lisboa. Tel. 01/53-68-11. Fax 01/352-61-65. 58 rms. A/C MINIBAR TV TEL **Bus:** 1, 2, 9, or 32.
$ Rates (including breakfast): 14,500$ ($88.50) single; 17,500$ ($106.80) double. AE, DC, MC, V.

This fine little hostelry lies just minutes from the top of Avenida da Liberdade and Praça Marquês de Pombal. It nestles on a quiet street, away from busy boulevards, and opens onto a wedge-shaped park with weeping willows and oaks. The Capitol places the emphasis on roomy, simply furnished chambers with private baths. The more desirable rooms open onto private balconies. On the premises are a bar, snack bar, and restaurant.

DOM CARLOS, Avenida Duque de Loulé 121, 1000 Lisboa. Tel. 01/53-90-71. Fax 01/352-01-28. 56 rms, 17 suites. A/C MINIBAR TV TEL **Metro:** Rotunda. **Bus:** 1, 36, 44, or 45.
$ Rates (including breakfast): 13,500$ ($82.40) single; 16,500$ ($100.70) double; from 21,500$ ($131.20) suite. AE, DC, MC, V.

Just off Praça Marquês de Pombal, Dom Carlos faces its own triangular park, which is dedicated to the partially blind Camilo Castelo Branco, a 19th-century "eternity poet." The curvy facade is all glass, giving guests an indoor/outdoor feeling, reinforced by green trees and beds of orange and red canna. In summer, there is air conditioning; in winter, central heating. The guest rooms are paneled in reddish Portuguese wood. The Nordic-inspired furnishings are softened by an occasional hand-carved cherub. The lobby-lounge is satisfactory, but even more inviting is the mezzanine salon, where sofas and chairs face the park.

Dining/Entertainment: Breakfast is the only meal served. The miniature bar, with leather chairs, is ideal for a tête-à-tête.
Services: Laundry, babysitting.
Facilities: Car-rental desk.

DOM MANUEL, Avenida Duque d'Ávila 189, 1000 Lisboa. Tel. 01/57-61-60. Fax 01/57-69-85. 64 rms. A/C TV TEL **Bus:** 18 or 42. **Metro:** Saldanha or São Sebastião.
$ Rates (including breakfast): 12,000$–14,000$ ($73.20–$85.40) single; 14,000$–16,000$ ($85.40–$97.60) double. AE, DC, MC, V.

This hotel may be small, but it has style, and for such an atmosphere the rates are moderate. The Dom Manuel is a short distance from the heart of Lisbon and the Praça de Espanha on a tree-lined avenue. Its guest lounge, with an open fireplace, is like a salon at a private estate. Flanking sofas are set on an Oriental area rug; on one wall is an Aubusson tapestry, and a picture window looks out onto an interior planter with subtropical greenery. On the mezzanine is an intimate cocktail lounge. You dine on the lower level, which is very Portuguese, with formal leather armchairs and elegant floor torchères. Each guest room is in a restrained modern style, with muted color coordination, a built-in headboard, a desk and armchair, bed lights, and an all-tile bath. Laundry/valet service is available, as is 24-hour room service.

HOTEL EDUARDO VII, Avenida Fontes Pereira de Melo 5, 1000 Lisboa.

Tel. 01/53-01-41. Fax 01/53-38-79. 121 rms, 1 suite. A/C MINIBAR TV TEL **Bus:** 1, 21, or 41.
$ **Rates:** 11,900$–15,300$ ($72.60–$93.30) single; 14,000$–17,500$ ($85.40–$106.80) double; 28,600$ ($174.50) suite. Breakfast 1,000$ ($6.10) extra. AE, DC, MC, V.

This completely renovated hotel commands a desirable location in the commercial and cultural center of Lisbon, one block north of Praça Marquês de Pombal.

It offers many amenities and much comfort. All units are well furnished and maintained. The lovely terrace-style restaurant with a greenhouse wall of windows offers good food and a sweeping view over the city; it specializes in both Portuguese and Brazilian dishes. Nearby, a posh bar offers relaxing end-of-the-day drinks.

HOTEL FÉNIX, Praça Marquês de Pombal 8, 1200 Lisboa. Tel. 01/386-21-21. 123 rms, 4 suites. A/C MINIBAR TV TEL **Metro:** Rotunda.
$ **Rates** (including breakfast): 17,500$ ($106.80) single; 19,500$ ($119) double; 23,500$–40,000$ ($143.40–$244) suite. AE, DC, MC, V.

The Fénix enjoys a front-row position on the circular plaza dedicated to the 18th-century prime minister of Portugal. From most of its guest rooms (all with radios) you can view the trees on the avenue and in Edward VII Park. The hotel is favored by many repeat clients. The brightly furnished and air-conditioned two-floor reception lounge, with a cozy bar/lounge on the mezzanine, is much favored. A plus is the grill room, the Bodegón, worthy of a separate recommendation (see Chapter 5). Laundry service and babysitting are provided.

MUNDIAL HOTEL, Rua Dom Duarte 4, 1100 Lisboa. Tel. 01/886-31-01. Fax 01/87-91-29. 150 rms. A/C MINIBAR TV TEL **Metro:** Rossio.
$ **Rates** (including breakfast): 15,000$–18,200$ ($91.50–$111) single; 18,200$–22,800$ ($111–$139.10) double; 21,450$–28,500$ ($130.80–$173.90) triple. AE, DC, MC, V. **Parking:** Free.

The Mundial is in the heart of everything. The top-floor restaurant offers a view of St. George's Castle and the Alfama and is a short walk from the Rossio, theaters, and shops. The staff is efficient, everything is properly manicured and polished, and the hotel is high on the preference list of European businesspeople. The rooms are comfortable, spacious, and restrained in decor. The tile baths have bidets, shower/tub combinations, and plenty of mirrors and shelf space.

Dining/Entertainment: The Varanda de Lisboa restaurant features a French and a Portuguese cuisine but is known for regional dishes reflecting various districts of Portugal, including Trás-os-Montes, the Algarve, the Minho, and Ribatejo. A pianist entertains at dinner, and the hotel also has a bar.

Services: Laundry, concierge, babysitting, 24-hour room service.
Facilities: Car-rental facilities.

PRÍNCIPE REAL, Rua de Alegria 53, 1200 Lisboa. Tel. 01/346-01-16. Fax 01/342-21-04. 24 rms. A/C MINIBAR TV TEL **Metro:** Rotunda. **Bus:** 2.
$ **Rates** (including breakfast): 18,000$–23,000$ ($109.80–$140.30) double. AE, DC, MC, V.

This modern hotel is reached after a long, steep climb from Avenida da Liberdade. Behind its rather impersonal facade lies a small world of fine living. Guests get acquainted in the bar. Selectivity and care are shown in the individualized guest rooms, which are small but tasteful. The beds are reproductions of fine antiques, with excellent mattresses. Each room is color coordinated, a happy blending of floral fabrics.

Dining/Entertainment: The hotel's restaurant opens onto panoramic views of Lisbon and serves an excellent Portuguese cuisine. There is also a cozy bar downstairs.
Services: Laundry, 24-hour room service.
Facilities: Car-rental facilities.

HOTEL REX, Rua Castilho 169, 1000 Lisboa. Tel. 01/388-21-61. Fax 01/388-75-81. 68 rms, 10 suites. A/C MINIBAR TV TEL **Metro:** Rotunda or Marquês de Pombal. **Bus:** 2, 11, 12, 23, 48, or 53.
$ **Rates** (including breakfast): 12,250$–19,500$ ($74.70–$119) single; 15,000$–

23,400$ ($91.50–$142.70) double; 25,000$–39,000$ ($152.50–$237.90) suite. AE, DC, MC, V. **Parking:** Free.

Sandwiched between its neighbors in a desirable location a few steps from the Ritz and Meridien hotels, this retreat offers a helpful staff and accommodations at prices far below those of its more prestigious competitors. Many guest rooms have spacious balconies, whose panoramic vistas include views of Edward VII Park and the baroque Manueline church on its far edge. The cozy rooms have radios, tile baths, and built-in beds whose wide edges are covered in full-grain lengths of well-rubbed Iberian leather. If you're lucky enough to lodge in one of the suites, you'll enjoy a cozy sitting room with its own breeze-swept terrace, in addition to the comfortable bedroom.

Visible from the large front windows of the elegant lobby, with a high coffered wood-and-plaster ceiling, is an unusual bronze statue of women bearing baskets.

Dining/Entertainment: The top-floor Panoramic Restaurant offers a sweeping view of one of Lisbon's most beautiful parks, as well as the city far below.

Services: Laundry, babysitting, 24-hour room service.

Facilities: Car-rental desk.

HOTEL ROMA, Avenida de Roma 33, 1700 Lisboa. Tel. 01/793-22-44.
Fax 01/793-29-81. 265 rms. A/C TV TEL **Metro:** Roma. **Bus:** 1, 2, 9, or 32.

$ Rates (including breakfast): 11,000$–15,000$ ($67.10–$91.50) single; 15,000$–17,500$ ($91.50–$106.80) double. AE, DC, MC, V. **Parking:** 1,500$ ($9.20).

The Roma, one of the capital's largest reasonably priced hotels, is popular with commercial travelers. On a traffic-clogged boulevard on the northeast side of town, it has a turquoise-and-white-tile facade, with recessed balconies extending from the guest rooms. Each room is comfortably filled with contemporary furnishings, sometimes with a gauzy curtain that separates the sleeping alcove from the living room. The more expensive accommodations are spacious. Any last-minute shopping can be done in the array of shops that fill the marble-floored arcade near the reception desk. There's a pool in the basement, plus a sauna and massage facilities. The hotel has ground-floor and 10th-floor restaurants, serving both French and Portuguese cuisine.

HOTEL VENEZA, Avenida da Liberdade 189, 1200 Lisbon. Tel. 01/352-2618. Fax 01/352-6678. 38 rms. A/C MINIBAR TV TEL **Metro:** Avenida.

$ Prices (including breakfast): 13,000$ ($79.30) single; 16,000$ ($97.60) double. AE, DC, MC, V.

At the turn of the century, the Avenida da Liberdade was lined with private villas whose ornamentation was the pride of Portugal. Today only a handful remain, having been replaced by modern office and apartment buildings. The Veneza, which opened in 1990, occupies one of the few such villas that remain in place. Within, you'll find a grand staircase leading to the three upper floors, a series of modern murals depicting an artist's interpretation of Lisbon, a pleasant staff, and simple guest rooms incongruously furnished in a modern streamlined style. The Veneza contains a bar but serves no meals other than breakfast. Its position adjacent to the better-accessorized Hotel Tivoli ensures its clients access to all the facilities they might need, including several restaurants, an animated bar, a health club, a pool, and a garden.

YORK HOUSE, Rua das Janelas Verdes 32, 1200 Lisboa. Tel. 01/396-24-35. Fax 01/397-27-93. 36 rms. TV TEL **Bus:** 27, 40, 49, 54, or 60.

$ Rates (including breakfast): 14,800$–21,000$ ($90.30–$128.10) single; 16,900$–23,000$ ($103.10–$140.30) double. AE, DC, MC, V. **Parking:** Free on street.

York House mixes the drama of the past with the conveniences of the present. It was once a 16th-century convent and is outside the center of traffic-filled Lisbon, attracting those who want peace and tranquility. Long known to the English and embassy personnel—as well as artists, writers, poets, and professors—it is almost opposite the National Art Gallery, sitting high on a hillside street overlooking the Tagus.

You go past an old iron gate, ascend a flight of stone steps past trailing ivy and rugged walls, and enter through a garden cloister where guests congregate under gnarled trees. Owned and run by José Telles, York House was tastefully furnished by one of the most distinguished designers for theater, opera, and villas in Lisbon. Each guest room has an antique bed, a soft mattress, and 18th- and 19th-century bric-a-brac.

The public rooms boast inlaid chests, coats of armor, carved ecclesiastical figures, paintings, and ornate ceramics. The former monks' dining hall has deep-set windows, large niches for antiques, and—best of all—a combined French/Portuguese cuisine. Guests gather in the two-level lounge for before- or after-dinner drinks.

Mr. Telles has acquired a former **town house** at Janelas Verdes 47 (tel. 01/396-81-44; fax 01/397-27-93), down the street, adjacent to the museum. This aristocratic 18th-century mansion was the home of the late Portuguese novelist Eça de Queiros. Here you can book larger, more luxurious rooms, with abundant closet space and large tile baths. Only breakfast is served here, and main meals are provided at the convent. A total of 17 rooms are rented, costing 14,800$ to 21,000$ ($90.30 to $128.10) for a single and 16,900$ to 23,000$ ($103.10 to $140.30) for a double. The predominantly red Victorian lounge is evocative of turn-of-the-century Lisbon. Breakfast is brought on a tray to your room, to the lounge, or to the rear walled-in terrace with an antique iron spiral staircase whose steps are filled with potted flowering plants.

INEXPENSIVE

CASA DE SÃO MAMEDE, Rua da Escola Politecnica 159, 1200 Lisboa. Tel. 01/39-63-166. 28 rms. TEL **Tram:** 24. **Bus:** 9, 22, or 49.
$ Rates (including breakfast): 7,000$ ($42.70) single; 9,000$ ($54.90) double. No credit cards.

A blue-and-white-tile mural on this establishment's facade depicts St. Mamede (a 12-year-old martyr of the early Christian church) between a lion and a bull. Built in the 1800s as a private villa for the count of Coruche, it was transformed into a hotel in 1945. Today its guest rooms are managed by the Marquês family. Breakfast is served in a sunny second-floor dining room decorated with antique yellow and blue tiles. Although renovated, the rooms retain an aura of their original high-ceilinged and slightly dowdy charm.

HOTEL DO RENO, Avenida Duque d'Ávila 195–197, 1000 Lisboa. Tel. 01/54-81-81. Fax 01/54-67-86. 56 rms. TV TEL **Metro:** São Sebastião. **Bus:** 16.
$ Rates (including breakfast): 8,500$ ($51.90) single; 9,500$ ($58) double; 10,500$ ($64.10) triple. Discounted rates available for children under 8. AE, DC, MC, V. **Parking:** Free.

Hotel do Reno, opened in 1959, lies about a 10-minute taxi ride from the heart of Lisbon. A three-star hotel, it enjoys heavy patronage by Germans and Scandinavians, but it also attracts English and American visitors. There are a large sitting room and a pleasant bar near the main entrance. The guest rooms are contemporary, each with a small sitting area that includes a desk and an armchair, a private bath, a radio, and central heating; most have balconies. Babysitting can be arranged, as can laundry service.

HOTEL EXCELSIOR, Rua Rodrígues Sampaio 172, 1100 Lisboa. Tel. 01/353-71-51. Fax 01/57-87-79. 81 rms. TV TEL **Metro:** Marquês de Pombal. **Bus:** 1, 2, 9, or 32.
$ Rates (including breakfast): 8,500$ ($51.90) single; 10,500$–15,000$ ($64.10–$91.50) double. AE, DC, MC, V. **Parking:** Free on street.

The Excelsior, built in the late 1960s, enjoys a setting one block from Praça Marquês de Pombal, at the entrance to Edward VII Park. Right off the upper regions of Lisbon's major boulevard, it features good-sized guest rooms, most with small sitting areas containing combination desk/dressing tables; all units have radios. In addition to the air-conditioned bar and cocktail lounge with a color TV, the hotel has a spacious breakfast room with large windows. Its restaurant serves both Portuguese and continental dishes.

JORGE V HOTEL, Rua Mouzinho da Silveira 3, 1200 Lisboa. Tel. 01/356-25-25. Fax 01/315-03-19. 47 rms, 6 suites. A/C TV TEL **Metro:** Avenida or Rotunda.

$ Rates (including breakfast): 8,000$ ($48.80) single; 10,000$ ($61) double; 12,000$ ($73.20) triple; 10,000$ ($61) suite. AE, DC, MC, V. **Parking:** Free on street.

The Jorge V is a neat little hotel of modern design, with amenities, inexpensive prices, and a choice location a block off the Avenida da Liberdade. Its facade contains rows of cellular balconies, roomy enough for guests to have breakfast or afternoon "coolers." A tiny elevator takes you to a variety of guest rooms, which aren't generous in size but are comfortable in a compact way; all have small tile baths and radios. Suites that cost the same as doubles are dispensed on a first come, first served basis. Room service is provided until midnight. The reception lounge shares space with a bar. Most favored by guests is the regional-style combination bar/breakfast room of nicely melded aggregate stone and wood paneling.

MIRAPARQUE, Avenida Sidónio Pais 12, 1000 Lisboa. Tel. 01/57-80-70. Fax 01/57-89-20. 100 rms. A/C MINIBAR TV TEL **Bus:** 1, 2, 9, or 32.

$ Rates (including breakfast): 10,250$ ($62.50) single; 11,500$ ($70.20) double; 15,000$ ($91.50) triple. AE, DC, MC, V.

A modern hotel, the Miraparque lies on a secluded quiet street opposite Edward VII Park. The lounges are furnished in simulated brown leather with wood-paneled walls. The tiny bar, with stools and lounge chairs, has a neat and comfortable ambience. The dining room, also wood-paneled, has contemporary chairs and a wall-wide mural. The guest rooms have the same modified contemporary styling, with pastel colors.

PRESIDENTE HOTEL, Rua Alexandre Herculano 13, 1000 Lisboa. Tel. 01/53-95-01. Fax 01/352-02-72. 59 rms. A/C MINIBAR TV TEL **Metro:** Rotunda. **Tram:** 20. **Bus:** 1, 36, 44, or 45.

$ Rates (including breakfast): 10,000$ ($61) single; 12,000$ ($73.20) double. AE, DC, MC, V. **Parking:** 2,000$ ($12.20).

This small-scale establishment lies near Avenida da Liberdade on a busy corner. Built in the late 1960s, it was renovated in 1992. It's recommended for families because it adds an extra bed to any room for 2,000$ ($12.20) and babysitting can be arranged. On the premises are a laundry and a medical service. The general atmosphere, including the furnishings, is of good taste. The guest rooms are small and nicely laid out, with built-in chestnut headboards, radios, and bed lights. Each has double-view windows, a small entry with two closets, a bath tiled in bright colors, and even a valet stand. Room service is provided until midnight. In the wood-paneled mezzanine lounge, only breakfast is served. The modest-size reception lounges are on three levels, connected by wide marble steps.

HOTEL PRÍNCIPE, Avenida Duque d'Ávila 201, 1000 Lisboa. Tel. 01/53-43-14. Fax 01/53-43-14. 68 rms. A/C TV TEL **Metro:** São Sebastião. **Tram:** 20. **Bus:** 41 or 46.

$ Rates (including breakfast): 8,500$–11,000$ ($51.90–$67.10) single; 9,000$–13,000$ ($54.90–$79.30) double. Children under 8 stay at half price in parents' room. AE, DC, MC, V. **Parking:** Free.

Over a quarter of a century old, this place is a favorite with visiting Spanish and Portuguese matadors. The hotel's eight floors are accessible by two elevators. All the large guest rooms have TVs with music (three channels) and private baths, and most open onto their own balconies. The matadors do seem to like the Príncipe's dining room and bar. Don't confuse this hotel with the first-class Príncipe Real, recommended previously. Babysitting and laundry service are available. Room service is offered until midnight.

BUDGET

RESIDÊNCIA ALICANTE, Avenida Duque de Loulé 20, 1000 Lisboa. Tel. 01/353-05-14. Fax 01/352-02-50. 43 rms (36 with bath). TV TEL **Metro:** Picoas or Marquês de Pombal. **Bus:** 1, 2, 9, 32, 36, or 45.

$ Rates (including breakfast): 3,400$ ($20.70) single without bath, 6,600$ ($40.30) single with bath; 4,500$ ($27.50) double without bath, 8,000$ ($48.80) double with bath. AE, DC, MC, V.

Its burnt-orange postwar facade curves around a quiet residential corner in an undistinguished neighborhood. This hotel is nonetheless clean, welcoming, and safe. You register on the street level, with a kindly staff who speak little or no English; then you take a small elevator to one of the four upper floors. Furnishings and room size vary, but most budget-minded visitors find the Alicante an acceptable and reasonable headquarters. The quieter rooms overlook an interior courtyard. Five of the rooms contain air conditioning, which will be turned on for a supplement of 300$ ($1.80) per day.

RESIDÊNCIA AMÉRICA, Rua Tomás Ribeiro 47, 1000 Lisboa. Tel. 01/352-11-77. Fax 01/886-46-48. 56 rms. A/C TEL **Metro:** Picoas. **Bus:** 1, 36, 44, or 45.

$ Rates (including breakfast): 7,500$ ($45.80) single; 8,500$ ($51.90) double. AE, DC, MC, V. **Parking:** 1,500$ ($9.20) nearby.

Built as a bank nearly 40 years ago, Residência América became a comfortable, unpretentious hotel through later renovation. The 1950s-style accommodations all differ in layout and size. The quiet rooms are in back, though they tend to be slightly smaller and darker than those in front. No visitor to the América should leave without checking out the seventh-floor bar, whose leatherette furniture has been there so long

---

FROMMER'S SMART TRAVELER: HOTELS

TIPS FOR VALUE-CONSCIOUS TRAVELERS

1. The price you pay in inexpensive hotels depends on the plumbing. A room with only a shower is much cheaper than one with a private bath. Even cheaper is a room with a sink and a *cabinette de toilet* (toilet and bidet).
2. Consider a package tour (or book land arrangements with your air ticket). You'll often pay 30% less than individual "rack rates" (off-the-street independent bookings).
3. Ask about winter discounts. Some hotels won't grant them, but many will, especially if bookings that week are light.

QUESTIONS TO ASK IF YOU'RE ON A BUDGET

1. Is there a surcharge on either local or long-distance telephone calls? (Often surcharges are lethal, maybe an astonishing 40%. If so, make your calls at the nearest post office.)
2. Is there a garage? What's the charge?
3. Does the hotel include service of 10% or 15% in the rates, or will it be added on at the end of your stay?
4. Are all hotel taxes included in the price, or will they be added on?
5. Is breakfast included in the rates?

it is by now back in style. Having a drink here can be a lot of fun, adding a note of nostalgia to your stay. The América has no restaurant. Laundry service and babysitting are provided.

RESIDÊNCIA IMPERADOR, Avenida 5 de Outubro 55, 1000 Lisboa. Tel. 01/352-48-84. 43 rms. A/C TV TEL **Metro:** Saldanha. **Tram:** 24. **Bus:** 44, 45, or 90.

$ Rates (including breakfast): 7,500$ ($45.80) single; 8,500$ ($51.90) double. AE, DC, MC, V.

The Portuguese-pinewood entranceway of Residência Imperador, not far from the center, is small. However, the guest rooms and upper lounge are adequate in size. Opening onto balconies, the front rooms face a tiny private garden. The units are neatly planned with built-in beds and simple lines; muted colors are used on the walls and in the fabrics. On the top floor are a public room and terrace with a glass front, where breakfast is served.

RESIDÊNCIA NAZARETH, Avenida António Augusto de Aguiar 25, 1000 Lisboa. Tel. 051/54-20-16. Fax 01/356-08-36. 32 rms. A/C MINIBAR TV TEL **Metro:** São Sebastião. **Bus:** 31, 41, or 46.

$ Rates (including breakfast): 6,500$ ($39.70) single; 8,500$ ($51.90) double. AE, DC, MC, V.

You'll recognize this establishment by its dusty-pink facade, on which some of the windows are surrounded with decorative arches raised in low relief. Take an elevator to the fourth-floor landing. There, far from the beauticians, hair stylists, and offices below, has been re-created medieval vaulting you might find in a romanticized version of a Portuguese fortress. The distressed plaster and the wrought-iron lanterns are obvious facsimiles, yet their undeniable charm somehow works wonders on a tired sightseer. Even the spacious bar/TV lounge looks like a vaulted cellar. Light floods in from the windows. Some of the simple guest rooms contain platforms, requiring guests to step up or down to the bath or to the comfortable bed.

RESIDENCIAL O PARADOURO, Avenida Almirante Reis 106, 1100 Lisboa. Tel. 01/81-53-256. Fax 01/815-54-45. 26 rms. TEL **Metro:** Arroios.

$ Rates (including breakfast): 6,500$ ($39.70) single; 7,500$ ($45.80) double. MC, V. **Parking:** 480$ ($2.90).

The Residêncial O Paradouro occupies a somewhat inconvenient location on a busy traffic artery on the east side of town. Once you find it, amid a cluster of commercial and residential buildings, take the elevator to the seventh-floor reception area. The guest rooms are clean and comfortable. Laundry service is provided, as is 24-hour room service. You'll be served breakfast while seated in a wrought-iron garden chair near a big window with a view over a 19th-century villa far below. A bar offers drinks throughout the afternoon.

2. IN THE BAIRRO ALTO

BUDGET

PENSÃO LONDRES, Rua Dom Pedro V 53. 1200 Lisboa. Tel. 01/346-22-03. 39 rms (21 with bath or shower). **Tram:** 20. **Bus:** 15 or 19.

$ Rates (including breakfast): 3,000$ ($18.30) single without shower; 4,200$ ($25.60) double without shower, 5,200$ ($31.70) double with shower. No credit cards.

Originally conceived as a dignified mansion, with high ceilings and ornate moldings, this establishment, set near the belvedere San Pedro de Alcântara, now functions as a slightly battered and unpretentious hotel. The guest rooms contain simple furniture hinting at yesterday's grandeur, with occasional views of the city (especially on the fourth floor).

FROMMER'S COOL FOR KIDS: HOTELS

Hotel Lisboa Plaza *(see page 74)* Right in the heart of Lisbon, this family-owned and -operated hotel offers spacious rooms where children under 12 can stay free if sharing with their parents.

Presidente Hotel *(see page 80)* In the center, near Avenida da Liberdade, this hotel is recommended for families because it adds an extra bed to any room for 2,000$ ($12.20) and can arrange babysitting.

Hotel Príncipe *(see page 80)* Kind to families with children, the staff lets kids under 8 stay at half price in their parents' room and can arrange babysitting. Prices are reasonable, too.

3. IN THE GRAÇA DISTRICT

MODERATE

HOTEL ALBERGARIA DA SENHORA DO MONTE, Calçada do Monte 39, 1100 Lisboa. Tel. 01/886-60-02. Fax 01/87-77-83. 28 rms, 4 suites. A/C TV TEL **Metro:** Socorro. **Tram:** 28. **Bus:** 12, 17, or 35.
$ Rates (including breakfast): 10,500$–12,000$ ($64.10–$73.20) single; 14,000$–17,500$ ($85.40–$106.80) double; from 21,000$ ($128.10) suite. AE, DC, MC, V.

This special little hilltop hotel has a unique character. It's perched near a belvedere, the Miradouro Senhora do Monte, in the Graça district—a spot where knowing Lisboans take their friends for a memorable nighttime view of the city, the Castle of St. George, and the Tagus. Built originally as an apartment house, the hotel has been converted into a clublike establishment, with lots of lavish touches for those seeking an unusual atmosphere. The intimate living room features large tufted sofas and oversize tables and lamps. Multilevel corridors lead to the excellent guest rooms, all of which have verandas. The rooms reveal a decorator's touch, especially the gilt-edged door panels, the grass-cloth walls, and the tile baths with bronze fixtures. Room service and laundry/valet service are available. Breakfast is the only meal served.

4. IN THE BELÉM DISTRICT

MODERATE

HOTEL DA TORRE, Rua dos Jerónimos 8, 1400 Lisboa. Tel. 01/363-01-61. Fax 01/364-59-95. 50 rms. A/C TV TEL **Tram:** 17. **Bus:** 28 or 43.
$ Rates (including breakfast): 11,500$ ($70.20) single; 14,750$ ($90) double. AE, DC, MC, V.
Located in Belém, a suburb of Lisbon, this hotel lies near an estuary of the Tagus. It is suitable primarily for those who want to be in the belt of Lisbon's museumland. The renovated three-story inn is furnished in regional style. The guest rooms have comfortable modern furnishings. The modern lobby contains sunken seating areas, overhead balconies, and large front windows. Regional food is served in the provincial restaurant, São Jerónimo. Laundry/valet service is provided.

LISBON DINING

Lisbon offers a wide range of dining spots. The cuisine in the top establishments is of a high standard, ranking with that of Europe's leading restaurants. Here you'll encounter the best of Portuguese dishes mixed with classics from the continental repertoire. In such establishments, a knowledgeable maître d'hôtel and wine steward will be at your elbow to guide your culinary decisions.

But you needn't pay high prices for top-quality food in Lisbon and its environs. There are many noteworthy regional restaurants that offer Portuguese cooking, even foreign viands, at all price levels—from simple beer-and-steak taverns, to formal town house–style dining rooms, to cliffside restaurants with panoramic views. Aside from the recommendations found in this chapter, you may also want to consider having your evening meal at one of the fado cafes (see Chapter 7).

1. IN THE CENTER

VERY EXPENSIVE

GAMBRINUS, Rua das Portas de Santo Antão 25. Tel. 32-14-66.
  Cuisine: SEAFOOD. **Reservations:** Required. **Metro:** Rossio.
$ Prices: Appetizers 1,000$–3,600$ ($6.10–$22); main courses 3,000$–10,000$ ($18.30–$61). AE, MC, V.
  Open: Daily noon–2am.

Gambrinus, one of the premier restaurants of Lisbon, is the finest choice for fish and shellfish. It's in the congested heart of the city, off the Rossio near the rail station on a little square behind the National Theater. You can arrive early and enjoy an apéritif at the bar in front while munching on "sea creatures." Have your meal while sitting on leather chairs under a cathedral-beamed ceiling, or select a little table beside a fireplace on the raised end of the room. All is dominated by an impressionist tapestry along one wall. There is also an alcove with a stained-glass enclosure.

Gambrinus offers a diversified à la carte menu, accompanied by specialties of the day. The soups are good, especially the bisque of shellfish. The most expensive items are shrimp and lobster dishes. However, you might prefer conch with shellfish thermidor or sea bass *minhota*. If you don't fancy fish and like your dishes *hot*, ask for chicken *piri-piri*. The restaurant also offers elaborate desserts. Coffee with a 30-year-old brandy complements the meal perfectly.

RESTAURANT AVIZ, Rua Serpa Pinto 12B. Tel. 34-28-391.
  Cuisine: PORTUGUESE/INTERNATIONAL. **Reservations:** Required. **Bus:** 15.
$ Prices: Appetizers 2,000$–3,600$ ($12.20–$22); main courses 3,500$–10,000$ ($21.40–$61). AE, DC, MC, V.
  Open: Lunch Mon–Fri noon–3pm; dinner Mon–Sat 7–10:30pm. **Closed:** Aug.

What is now the Aviz was saved from the demolition of the famed hotel of the same name, which in pre-Ritz days was the only deluxe hotel in Lisbon. Mahogany paneling, tufted green-leather chairs, green-marble columns, and crystal create the ambience of a private club. The former hotel staff brought not only parts of the torn-down establishment with them—including all the silver, a meat trolley, and the wall torchères—but also the recipes of the kitchen.

For a beginning, try smoked swordfish; an alternative might be vichyssoise Rothschild, based on creamed prawns. A bevy of main dishes includes *perdreau mode d'Alcântara* (young partridge cooked in Alcântara style), about which Bonaparte's Marshal Junot wrote, "It is the only positive factor that emerged from our ill-fated Iberian invasion campaign." Desserts include Aviz crêpes, flamed in kirsch at the table. A dinner will cost from 8,000$ ($48.80) to 10,000$ ($61) and up, with the emphasis on up. You will be seated in one of three intimate dining rooms, preferably the larger green-and-gold chamber, with its ornate globed chandelier of bronze and frosted glass.

EXPENSIVE

ANTÓNIO CLARA, Avenida da República 38. Tel. 796-63-80.
 Cuisine: PORTUGUESE/INTERNATIONAL. **Reservations:** Required. **Metro:** Entre Campos.
$ Prices: Appetizers 1,800$–3,000$ ($11–$18.30); main courses 2,800$–4,500$ ($17.10–$27.50). AE, DC, MC, V.
 Open: Lunch Mon–Sat noon–3pm; dinner Mon–Sat 7pm–midnight.
Even if it weren't one of the capital's best restaurants, this exquisitely crafted turn-of-the-century art nouveau villa would still be famous as the former home of one of Portugal's most revered architects. It was built in 1890 by Miguel Ventura Terra (1866–1918), whose photograph hangs amid polished antiques and gilded mirrors. The villa's angled tiled wings seem to embrace visitors as they approach the vaguely Moorish facade. The soaring height of the curved staircase and the elegant moldings serve as attractive backdrops for 17th-century wood carvings and belle époque porcelain. You might enjoy a before-dinner drink in the 19th-century saloon, where griffins snarl down from the pink-shaded chandelier. Even the service areas of this house, rarely seen by visitors, contain ceiling frescoes. The dining room is one of the loveliest in Lisbon. Men should wear jackets and ties.

Meals include such specialties as smoked swordfish, paella for two, chateaubriand béarnaise, codfish Clara style, and beef Wellington. A well-coordinated group of wine stewards, headwaiters, and attendants make wine tasting a ceremony. The ground-floor bar, accessible through its own entrance, is perfect for an after-dinner drink. The bar contains an art gallery with frequent special shows.

CLARA, Campo dos Mártires da Pátria 49. Tel. 355-73-41.
 Cuisine: PORTUGUESE/INTERNATIONAL. **Reservations:** Required. **Metro:** Avenida.
$ Prices: Appetizers 1,800$–3,000$ ($11–$18.30); main courses 2,800$–4,200$ ($17.10–$25.60). AE, DC, MC, V.
 Open: Lunch Mon–Sat noon–3:30pm; dinner Mon–Sat 7pm–midnight. **Closed:** Aug 1–15.
In a hillside location amid decaying villas and city squares, this green-tile house contains an elegant hideaway. You might enjoy a drink under the ornate ceiling of the bar, whose locale has functioned over the years as an antiques store, the living room of a private apartment, and the foyer of a palatial house. A piano plays softly at dinner. During lunch, however, you might prefer a seat near the garden terrace's plants and fountain. At night, an indoor seat—perhaps near the large marble fireplace—is more appealing. Specialties include tournedos Clara, stuffed rabbit with red-wine sauce, four kinds of pasta, codfish Clara, filet of sole with orange, pheasant with grapes, and Valencian paella.

ESCORIAL, Rua das Portas de Santo Antão 47. Tel. 346-44-29.
 Cuisine: SPANISH. **Reservations:** Recommended. **Metro:** Rossio.

$ Prices: Appetizers 1,200$–3,000$ ($7.30–$18.30); main courses 3,500$–8,000$ ($21.40–$48.80); fixed-price menu 4,900$ ($29.90). AE, DC, MC, V.
Open: Daily noon–midnight.

Right in the heart of Lisbon's restaurant district, near Praça das Restauradores, this Spanish-owned establishment combines classic Spanish dishes with an inviting ambience. The dining-room walls are paneled in rosewood, with frosted-globe lighting. You can have a before-dinner drink in the Art Room cocktail lounge, which exhibits contemporary Portuguese artists. A menu is printed in English (always look for the course of the day). Your most expensive selection would be from the lobster tank, or you might enjoy a sampling of Portuguese oysters or squid on a skewer. A selection of the chef's specialties is likely to include barbecued baby goat, beef Stroganoff, or partridge casserole.

RESTAURANTE TAVARES, Rua da Misericórdia 37. Tel. 34-21-112.
　Cuisine: PORTUGUESE/CONTINENTAL. **Reservations:** Required. **Bus:** 15.
$ Prices: Appetizers 600$–3,600$ ($3.70–$22); main courses 1,600$–4,200$ ($9.80–$25.60); fixed-price lunch 6,000$ ($36.60); fixed-price dinner 8,000$ ($48.80). AE, DC, MC, V.
　Open: Lunch Mon–Fri 12:30–3pm; dinner Sun–Fri 8–10:30pm.

Restaurante Tavares is a gilt-and-crystal world that offers a palace-style setting and fine cuisine. White-and-gold-paneled walls, three chandeliers, and Louis XV armchairs keep intact the spirit of the 18th century. Actually, Tavares was originally a cafe founded in 1784. When the two Tavares brothers died in the 19th century, half a dozen waiters formed a partnership and took over the restaurant; it is still owned by a group of waiters, who continue its high standards. This is the oldest restaurant in Lisbon, attracting many diplomatic and government heads as well as the literati. However, its reputation as an exclusive bastion of Portuguese society faded with the revolution. Drinks are served in the petite front salon, where you can plan your meal. The wine steward will aid you in your selection (he will try to provide a pleasant wine and will not push the most expensive bottles).

　Your meal might begin with *crêpes de marisco*. A main-course selection might be sole in champagne, a real delicacy, or *tournedos Grand Duc*. Many continental dishes are scattered throughout the menu, including the classic scallops of veal *viennoise*. However, the restaurant nearly always serves such basic Portuguese dishes as sardines and salted codfish, so secure is it in its reputation. To complete your meal, why not try the chef's dessert specialty, a high-rise soufflé, followed by a *café filtro?*

SUA EXCELÊNCIA, Rua do Conde 40–42. Tel. 60-36-14.
　Cuisine: ANGOLAN/PORTUGUESE. **Reservations:** Required. **Bus:** 27 or 49.
$ Prices: Appetizers 700$–2,000$ ($4.30–$12.20); main courses 2,400$–3,900$ ($14.60–$23.80). AE, DC, MC, V.
　Open: Lunch Mon–Tues and Thurs–Fri 1–3pm; dinner Mon–Tues, Thurs–Fri, and Sun 8–10:30pm. **Closed:** Sept.

Sua Excelência is the creation of Francisco Queiroz, who was a travel agent in Angola before he settled in Portugal. He has created his little dream restaurant, with a refined, sedate atmosphere that attracts a discerning clientele. Just ring the bell to announce your arrival and the proprietor will greet you. The atmosphere he has created is somewhat like a fashionable drawing room, with colorful tables placed in an intimate Portuguese provincial decor, made cool by the terra-cotta floor and high painted ceiling.

　Some dishes served are uncommon in Portugal, such as Angolan chicken Moamba. Specialties include prawns *piri-piri* (not unreasonably hot), rollmop sardines, what he proclaims the "best smoked swordfish in Portugal," and clams in at least five recipes. One unusual specialty is "little jacks," a small fish eaten whole: heads, tails, everything; it's served with a well-flavored "paste" made from two-day-old bread. The restaurant is just a block up the hill from the entrance to the National Art Gallery, so it could be visited on a museum/luncheon adventure, even though its ambience is more charming in the evening.

MODERATE

A GÔNDOLA, Avenida de Berna 64. Tel. 797-04-26.
   Cuisine: ITALIAN. **Reservations:** Required. **Metro:** Praça de Espanha. **Bus:** 16 or 26.
$ Prices: Appetizers 800$–1,500$ ($4.90–$9.20); main courses 1,200$–1,800$ ($7.30–$11). AE, DC, MC, V.
   Open: Lunch Mon–Sat 12:30–3pm; dinner Mon–Fri 7:30–10pm.

A Gôndola—Lisbon's "Little Italy"—serves perhaps the finest Italian specialties in town, offering indoor dining as well as al fresco meals in the courtyard.
Although the decor isn't inspired, the food makes the restaurant worth the trip out of the city center. The price of a full dinner is quite a buy when you realize what you get. A first-course selection might be Chaves ham with melon and figs, followed by filet of sole meunière or grilled sardines with pimientos. This is followed by yet another course, ravioli or cannelloni Roman style or veal cutlet milanese. The banquet is topped off by fruit or dessert. This is a convenient choice if you're visiting the Gulbenkian Museum in the area.

ANTÓNIO RESTAURANTE, Rua Tomás Ribiero 63. Tel. 53-87-80.
   Cuisine: PORTUGUESE/INTERNATIONAL. **Reservations:** Not necessary.
   Metro: Picoas. **Bus:** 30, 36, or 38.
$ Prices: Appetizers 600$–1,500$ ($3.70–$9.20); main courses 2,500$–3,600$ ($15.30–$22); fixed-price menu 2,950$ ($18). MC, V.
   Open: Lunch daily noon–4pm; dinner daily 7–10:30pm.

António Restaurante was created especially for Portuguese businesspeople who want a relaxing ambience and good food. A corner establishment, just a bit away from the din of central traffic, it is a refreshing oasis with blue-and-white glazed earthenware tiles, a free-form blue ceiling, white tablecloths topped with blue linen, and even crisp blue jackets on the waiters. The menu is in English. You can start with shellfish soup. Orders of fish, garnished with vegetables, include filets with tomato sauce and baked sole. *Arroz de marisco* (rice with shellfish) is a specialty. From among the fowl and meat dishes, try the breaded chicken with spaghetti or pork with clams Alentejana style. The owner-manager recommends his *açorda de marisco*, a stewlike breaded shellfish-and-egg dish that is a treat. The dessert list is extensive, with even a banana split.

BACHUS, Largo da Trindade 9. Tel. 342-28-28.
   Cuisine: INTERNATIONAL. **Reservations:** Recommended. **Bus:** 15.
$ Prices: Appetizers 950$–1,200$ ($5.80–$7.30); main courses 1,250$–1,900$ ($7.60–$11.60). AE, DC, MC, V.
   Open: Daily noon–2am.
Amusing murals cover the wood-paneled facade of this deluxe restaurant; inside, the decor is elaborate and sophisticated. The ambience is somewhere between that of a private salon in a Russian palace, a turn-of-the-century English club, and a stylized Manhattan bistro. A brass staircase winds around a column of illuminated glass to the dining room. Menu specialties change frequently, depending on the market availability of their ingredients. Full meals might include mixed grill Bachus, chateaubriand with béarnaise, mountain goat, beef Stroganoff, shrimp Bachus, or other daily specials. The wine list is extensive.

BONJARDIM, Travessa de Santo Antão 10. Tel. 342-74-24.
   Cuisine: PORTUGUESE. **Reservations:** Not necessary. **Metro:** Restauradores.
$ Prices: Appetizers 900$–1,900$ ($5.50–$11.60); main courses 1,640$–1,800$ ($10–$11). AE, DC, MC, V.
   Open: Daily noon–11pm.

Bonjardim quite rightly deserves the enthusiastic approval of a Boston traveler: "I was given the names of eight inexpensive restaurants to try in Lisbon during my five-day stay. I ended up trying only two, as I took the rest of my meals at

Bonjardim, sampling a different dish for lunch and dinner every day." Owner/manager Manuel Castanheira caters mostly to families, providing wholesome meals that fit most budgets. So successful has been the operation that he has taken over a building across the street, where the same menu is offered. The location is just east of the Avenida da Liberdade near Praça dos Restauradores.

In the main restaurant, the second-floor air-conditioned dining room is in the rustic Portuguese style, with a beamed ceiling and a tile mural depicting farm creatures. The noonday sun pours in through seven windows. The street-floor dining room, with an adjoining bar for before-meal drinks, has walls of decorative tiles. During your dinner, the aroma of fat chickens roasting to a golden brown on the charcoal spit can only persuade you to try one. An order of this house specialty, *frango no espeto,* is adequate for two, with a side dish of french fries. The cook also bakes hake in the Portuguese style; an alternative dish is pork fried with clams. For dessert, you can order a *cassate.*

Bonjardim also has a nearby self-service cafeteria at Travessa de Santo Antão II (tel. 342-43-89). The Portuguese dishes served here include seafood soup; half a roast chicken with trimmings; garoupa fish *à Bretone,* the chef's specialty; and chocolate mousse, a velvety finish. A meal costs around 1,500$ ($9.20), excluding your drink. The decor is simple, plastic, and efficient. It's open daily from noon to 11:30pm. Reservations aren't needed. Metro: Restauradores. No credit cards accepted.

CASA DA COMIDA, Travessa de Amoireiras 1. Tel. 388-53-76.
   Cuisine: PORTUGUESE/FRENCH. **Reservations:** Required. **Metro:** Rotunda.
$ **Prices:** Appetizers 950$–1,400$ ($5.80–$8.50); main courses 1,800$–2,500$ ($11–$15.30). AE, DC, MC, V.
   Open: Lunch Mon–Fri 1–3:30pm; dinner Mon–Sat 8–11pm. **Closed:** Aug.
   Casa da Comida, off Rua Alexandre Herculano, is recognized by local gourmets as having some of the finest food in Lisbon. If you're in the city on one of the gray rainy days that often occur from December through March, this is an excellent choice for dining, since a roaring fire greets you. At any time of year, however, you will find the food good and the atmosphere pleasant. The dining room is handsomely decorated, the bar is done in period style, and there's a charming walled garden. Specialties include roast kid with herbs, a medley of shellfish Casa da Comida, and pregado with green pepper. An excellent selection of wines is available from the cellar.

CHESTER, Rua Rodrigo da Fonseca 87D. Tel. 65-73-47.
   Cuisine: STEAKS/CONTINENTAL. **Reservations:** Recommended. **Metro:** Rotunda.
$ **Prices:** Appetizers 950$–1,800$ ($5.80–$11); main courses 1,500$–2,800$ ($9.20–$17.10). AE, DC, MC, V.
   Open: Lunch Mon–Fri 12:30–3pm; dinner Mon–Sat 8:30–10:30pm.
Chester, near the Ritz Hotel, is an attractive restaurant and bar, with a good cellar and efficient service. Its specialty is grilled steaks, plus continental dishes. The peppersteak is tempting, the entrecôte with whisky sauce is hearty, and both the rib steak and fondue bourguignonne are prepared for two. You might begin with a crab cocktail and finish with flambéed pineapple. The restaurant is upstairs, and the cozy bar lies below.

CONVENTUAL, Praça das Flores 45. Tel. 60-91-96.
   Cuisine: PORTUGUESE. **Reservations:** Required. **Metro:** Avenida. **Bus:** 100.
$ **Prices:** Appetizers 550$–1,800$ ($3.40–$11); main courses 1,800$–3,000$ ($11–$18.30); fixed-price menu 4,500$ ($27.50). AE, DC, MC, V.
   Open: Lunch Mon–Fri 12:30–3:30pm; dinner Mon–Sat 7:30–11:30pm. **Closed:** Aug.
   In many ways this is one of my favorite Lisbon restaurants, due in large part to the taste and sensitivity of its gracious owner, Mrs. Dina Marquês. It's on one of the loveliest residential squares in town, behind a discreetly plain wooden

door. Once inside, you'll be treated to a display of old panels from baroque churches, religious statues, and bric-a-brac from Mrs. Marqûes's private collection—all in an attractively austere environment whose temperature is kept gratifyingly cool by the building's very old thick stone walls and terra-cotta floor. If you select this place, you'll be in good company, since the prime minister of Portugal comes here. As is appropriate in any establishment even resembling a convent, work stops on Sunday.

Many of the delectably flavored recipes were invented by the owner: creamy coriander soup, stewed partridge in port, duck in rich champagne sauce, a tempting form of grilled monkfish in herb-flavored cream sauce, osso buco, frogs' legs in buttery garlic, and stewed clams in sauce of red peppers, onions, and cream.

EL BODEGÓN, in the Hotel Fénix, Praça Marquês de Pombal 8. Tel. 386-31-55.
    Cuisine: PORTUGUESE/SPANISH/INTERNATIONAL. **Reservations:** Required. **Metro:** Rotunda.
$ Prices: Appetizers 950$–1,200$ ($5.80–$7.30); main courses 1,500$–2,400$ ($9.20–$14.60). AE, DC, MC, V.
    Open: Lunch daily 12:30–3pm; dinner daily 7:30–10:30pm.

Bodegón is a first-class restaurant located in a previously recommended hotel (see Chapter 4). A marble staircase descends to it from street level. After stopping for an apéritif in the bar, you dine in a tavern setting with a beamed ceiling, tile floors, and wood-paneled pillars. Depending on its availability you might enjoy quail, partridge, or fresh salmon from the north of Portugal. You can also order cultivated oysters, which are at their best after October. Among the à la carte selections are fried squid, Valencian paella, and some Italian dishes. For dessert, try, if it's featured, the delectable fresh strawberries from Sintra.

FREI PAPINHAS, Rua Dom Francisco Manuel de Melo 32. Tel. 65-87-57.
    Cuisine: INTERNATIONAL. **Reservations:** Required. **Metro:** São Sebastião.
$ Prices: Appetizers 600$–1,500$ ($3.70–$9.20); main courses 1,200$–2,000$ ($7.30–$12.20). AE, DC, MC, V.
    Open: Lunch daily 12:30–3pm; dinner daily 7–11pm.

Frei Papinhas, near Edward VII Park and just off the Rua Castilho, is an easy walk from the Ritz and Meridien hotels. The restaurant was created by a group of writers and intellectuals who wanted a place where they could meet for really good food and enjoy vigorous conversation at their leisure. They ended up with their own attractive, cozy eating place that offers excellent service. The interior is done in sophisticated country style, relying on such natural elements as a wall of exposed stone, old brick behind the front bar, heavy black beams, and whitewashed walls.

In air-conditioned comfort, you can enjoy an array of international cookery, including fresh fish and game dishes. You might begin with one of the chef's soups, such as vichyssoise or gazpacho, followed by filet of swordfish or pork Alentejo. Racks of the best Portuguese wines are available.

LEÃO D'OURO, Rua 1 de Dezembro 93. Tel. 34-26-195.
    Cuisine: PORTUGUESE. **Reservations:** Not necessary. **Metro:** Rossio.
$ Prices: Appetizers 900$–1,800$ ($5.50–$11); main courses 1,400$–2,200$ ($8.50–$13.40); tourist menu 3,000$ ($18.30). AE, DC, MC, V.
    Open: Lunch Mon–Sat noon–3pm; dinner Mon–Sat 7–10pm.

Leão d'Ouro stands beside the Estaçao do Rossio, the railway station best described as Victorian Gothic. The atmosphere of a large old tavern prevails—high brick arches, a beamed ceiling, and a pictorial tile depicting Portugal's 1640 liberation from Spain. In the late 1980s, this restaurant once more became the fine dining room it was once reputed to be. The waiters are again clad in formal black with black bow ties. You can start your meal with a rich-tasting soup, such as *crème de camarao* (cream of shrimp) or *sopa a alentejana* (made with bread and garlic, among other ingredients). From among the meat dishes, try pork chops prepared in the Alentejana way or filet mignon. A fowl specialty is *frango de churrasco* (barbecued chicken). For dessert, try the *pessegos* (peaches).

O FUNIL [THE FUNNEL], Avenida Elias Garcia 82A. Tel. 796-60-07.

Cuisine: PORTUGUESE. **Reservations:** Recommended. **Metro:** Campo Pequeño. **Bus:** 1, 32, 36, or 38.
$ Prices: Appetizers 250$–1,500$ ($1.50–$9.20); main courses 1,500$–2,200$ ($9.20–$13.40); fixed-price menu 1,800$ ($11). MC, V.
Open: Lunch Tues–Sun noon–3:30pm; dinner Tues–Sat 7–10:30pm.

O Funil specializes in *cozinha Portuguesa* (Portuguese cuisine) and does the cooking so well and so inexpensively that a line forms at the door; it's often hard to get a table. You enter a street-floor tavern with crowded tables, but chances are you'll be directed to the lower level, where you can wait at a tiny bar while a table is made ready. The owners serve their own *vinho da casa* (wine of the house): Try their red Alijo. The kitchen buys good-quality meat and fish fresh daily. The most successful fish dishes are the boiled codfish with a sauce of eggs, flour, olive oil, milk, and cream, and the eels stewed with a sausage of pickled pork, smoked ham, and slices of toast. The most favored meat dishes are mutton stew with boiled potatoes and chicken stuffed with smoked ham. For dessert, try the chocolate pyramid and nut tart.

PABE, Rua Duque de Palmela 27A. Tel. 53-74-84.
Cuisine: PORTUGUESE/INTERNATIONAL. **Reservations:** Required. **Metro:** Rotunda.
$ Prices: Appetizers 800$–2,000$ ($4.90–$12.20); main courses 1,500$–2,800$ ($9.20–$17.10). AE, DC, MC, V.
Open: Daily noon–1am.

Convenient to the Praça Marquês de Pombal, this cozy pub (*Pabé* is Portuguese for *pub*) has done its best to emulate English establishments, with a soft carpet on the floor, mugs hanging over the long bar, a beamed ceiling, coats-of-arms, and engravings of hunting scenes around the walls. Two saloon-type doors lead into a wood-paneled dining room, where you can sup on meat specially imported from the United States. Chateaubriand for two is about the most expensive dish. If you prefer local fare, start off with a shrimp cocktail, then try Portuguese veal liver or *supremo de galinha* (chicken breast with mushrooms). Finish with sherbet. The crowd tends to be a well-groomed Portuguese set as well as resident Yanks and Brits.

RESTAURANT 33, Rua Alexandre Herculano 33A. Tel. 54-60-79.
Cuisine: PORTUGUESE/INTERNATIONAL. **Reservations:** Recommended. **Metro:** Rotunda. **Tram:** 20 or 25. **Bus:** 6 or 9.
$ Prices: Appetizers 700$–2,000$ ($4.30–$12.20); main courses 1,500$–3,000$ ($9.20–$18.30); fixed-price menu 3,250$ ($19.80). MC, V.
Open: Lunch Mon–Fri 12:30–3pm; dinner Mon–Sat 8:30–10pm.

Restaurant 33 is a little discovery. Decorated in a style evocative of an English hunting lodge, it lies near many previously recommended hotels, including the Altis and the Ritz (see Chapter 4). It specializes in an array of dishes, including shellfish rice served in a crab shell, smoked salmon or lobster Tour d'Argent, and peppersteak. You can enjoy a glass of port in the small bar at the entrance while you peruse the menu.

TELHEIRO, Rua Latino Coelho 10A. Tel. 353-40-07.
Cuisine: PORTUGUESE. **Reservations:** Recommended. **Bus:** 30.
$ Prices: Appetizers 750$–950$ ($4.60–$5.80); main courses 1,000$–2,300$ ($6.10–$14); tourist menu 2,000$ ($12.20). AE, DC, MC, V.
Open: Lunch daily noon–3pm; dinner daily 7–10:30pm.

Telheiro, which means "the roof" in Portuguese, is a bistrolike place not far from the Sheraton Hotel. The ceilings are beamed, and you sit on wooden chairs with heart shapes carved out of their backs. The waiters are clad in scarlet waistcoats. Peppers hang from the chandeliers. Pâté, butter, and rolls are placed on your table before you even order. Different specialties are featured every day—perhaps gazpacho, cabbage-and-potato soup, mussels, suckling pig, grilled fresh sea bass or sole, or seafood with rice in a casserole. For dessert, try the fresh Portuguese fruit.

TÍA MATILDE, Rua da Beneficência 77. Tel. 797-27-72.
Cuisine: PORTUGUESE. **Reservations:** Not necessary. **Metro:** Palhavã. **Bus:** 31.

$ Prices: Appetizers 275$–500$ ($1.70–$3.10); main courses 1,500$–3,750$ ($9.20–$22.90); fixed-price menu 4,250$ ($25.90). AE, DC, MC, V.
Open: Lunch Mon–Sat noon–4pm; dinner Mon–Sat 7–10:30pm.

Tía Matilde is a very large and busy place in the Praça de Espanha area. The service here is often hectic, and tourists are rare, but the Portuguese love this one. Here you can sample home cookery and the savory specialties of Ribatejo. Specialties include *cabrito assado* (roast mountain goat), *arroz de frango* (chicken with rice), *bacalhau* (codfish) *à Tía Matilde*, plus a pungent *caldeirada* (fish stew).

INEXPENSIVE

LYCHEE, Rua Barata Salguiero 37. Tel. 52-50-07.
  Cuisine: CHINESE. **Reservations:** Not necessary. **Metro:** Rotunda. **Bus:** 1, 2, 36, 44, or 45.
$ Prices: Appetizers 350$–1,200$ ($2.10–$7.30); main courses 1,000$–1,800$ ($6.10–$11). AE, DC, MC, V.
  Open: Lunch daily noon–3pm; dinner daily 7–10pm.

Lychee is a basement-level restaurant with a decor inspired by the Portuguese dependency of Macau. It is one of the finest Chinese restaurants in the city. An array of specialties is presented for your selection. Typical dishes include shrimp in hot-pepper sauce, fish with black-bean sauce, honey-garlic chicken wings, and deep-fried banana chicken.

TONI DOS BIFES, Avenida Praia da Vitória 50E. Tel. 53-60-80.
  Cuisine: PORTUGUESE. **Reservations:** Not necessary. **Metro:** Picoas.
$ Prices: Appetizers 300$–600$ ($1.80–$3.70); main courses 1,200$–1,800$ ($7.30–$11). No credit cards.
  Open: Daily noon–10:30pm.

Toni dos Bifes is an old Lisbon standby where hungry Portuguese and foreigners have been going for years to get a good, inexpensive, and copious meal. Near the Monumental cinema, the restaurant has a plain but pleasant décor, with a counter on one side of the dining room and small tables on the other. Some tables and chairs are placed outdoors as well, French cafe style, with a glass enclosure. You begin with small portions of pâté, along with butter and toast, bread and a roll, then you can launch into the homemade tomato soup or seafood omelet, followed by a Toni special beefsteak. Other specialties include Toni calamares (squid), grilled or meunière sole, pork Alentejana style, and roast duck. Finish with melon with ham or peach Melba.

VELHA-GOA, Rua Tómas de Anunciaçao 41B. Tel. 60-04-46.
  Cuisine: GOANESE. **Reservations:** Not necessary. **Bus:** 9.
$ Prices: Appetizers 250$–650$ ($1.50–$4); main courses 1,100$–1,800$ ($6.70–$11). AE, DC, MC, V.
  Open: Mon–Fri noon–midnight, Sat 6pm–midnight.

Velha-Goa evokes memories of the Portuguese empire. The Portuguese dependency of Goa was forcibly annexed by India in 1961, but the aura still lingers in this restaurant. The background is Asian, but the cuisine is Goanese. All dishes are prepared according to the taste of the diners—mild, pungent, or *very* pungent. The meal begins with the appetizer, *samuchas*. House specialties include curries—prawns, chicken, Madrasta—but the chef also serves beef and pork chops in case you're dining with someone who doesn't like Indian food. You must arrive before 10:30pm for dinner.

2. IN THE BAIRRO ALTO

MODERATE

PAP' AÇORDA, Rua da Atalaia 57–59. Tel. 346-48-11.
  Cuisine: PORTUGUESE. **Reservations:** Recommended. **Metro:** Rossio.

$ Prices: Appetizers 500$–750$ ($3.10–$4.60); main courses 1,200$–1,800$ ($7.30–$11). MC, V.

Open: Lunch Mon–Fri noon–2:30pm; dinner Mon–Sat 7–10pm.

Pap' Açorda's facade was originally built for a bakery. It welcomes one of Lisbon's most diverse collection of iconoclasts (of all possible life-styles and sexual persuasions) into its pink-and-white interior. Most visitors order a predinner drink at the long and vaguely old-fashioned bar whose marble top dominates the front of the establishment. No one will object if you never get around to actually dining, but if you do, there are two dining rooms in back, one outfitted like a garden. Both are ornamented with Empire-style crystal chandeliers and an occasional decorative lattice set incongruously against a minimalist background. The cuisine could include Spanish-style mussels, shellfish rice, sirloin steak with mushrooms, and a wide array of fish and shellfish dishes. The house specialty, *açorda* (after which the establishment was named), is a traditional dish incorporating coriander, bread, seafood, and eggs.

INEXPENSIVE

BOTA ALTA, Travessa da Queimada 35–37. Tel. 342-79-59.

Cuisine: PORTUGUESE. **Reservations:** Required. **Bus:** 15, 24, or 30.

$ Prices: Appetizers 240$–500$ ($1.50–$3.10); main courses 1,200$–2,200$ ($7.30–$13.40). AE, DC, MC, V.

Open: Lunch Mon–Fri noon–2:30pm; dinner Mon–Sat 7–11:30pm.

Bota Alta, at the very top of a steeply inclined street in the Bairro Alto, boasts a clientele who eagerly crams into its two dining rooms and sometimes stands at the bar waiting for a table to become available. Painted cerulean blue, it contains rustic artifacts as well as lots of original art and photographs. Meals might include beefsteak Bota Alta; several preparations of codfish; and a frequently changing array of daily specials, including Hungarian goulash.

XÊLÊ BANANAS, Praça das Flores 29. Tel. 395-25-15.

Cuisine: PORTUGUESE. **Reservations:** Recommended. **Metro:** Restauradores.

$ Prices: Appetizers 300$–750$ ($1.80–$4.60); main courses 1,200$–1,600$ ($7.30–$9.80). AE, DC, MC, V.

Open: Lunch Mon–Fri 12:30–3pm; dinner Mon–Sat 8–11pm.

Catering to a sophisticated and hip crowd of all possible persuasions, this stylish restaurant lies behind an anonymous-looking facade on a residential 18th-century square. The decor consists of wraparound green-and-brown murals of jungle plants evocative of the Brazilian rain forest, against a cream-colored background of art deco inspiration. Meals might include oysters au gratin, rabbit mousse with walnuts, steak with Roquefort sauce, ox tongue with mushrooms, and several preparations of partridge.

3. IN THE CHIADO DISTRICT

EXPENSIVE

TÁGIDE, Largo da Académia Nacional de Belas Artes 18–20. Tel. 342-07-20.

Cuisine: PORTUGUESE/INTERNATIONAL. **Reservations:** Required. **Metro:** Rossio. **Tram:** 20. **Bus:** 15.

$ Prices: Appetizers 900$–2,800$ ($5.50–$17.10); main courses 2,800$–4,000$ ($17.10–$24.40); fixed-price menu 6,000$ ($36.60). AE, DC, MC, V.

Open: Lunch Mon–Fri 12:30–2:30pm; dinner Mon–Fri 7:30–10:30pm.

Tágide has had a prestigious past: Once the town house of a diplomat, then a major nightclub, it is now one of Lisbon's leading restaurants. Its situation is colorful—up from the docks, atop a steep hill on a ledge overlooking the old part of Lisbon and the Tagus. The dining room has view windows overlooking moored ships and the port. Set into the white-plaster walls are large figures made of blue and white tiles, each of which depicts a famous queen; glittering above are crystal chandeliers.

Both Portuguese dishes and selections from the international repertoire are featured and beautifully served. For an appetizer, I suggest the salmon pâté, cold stuffed crab, or smoked swordfish. Other specialties include suprême of halibut with coriander, pork with clams and coriander, and grilled baby goat with herbs. For dessert, I recommend the stuffed crêpes Tágide.

4. IN THE GRAÇA DISTRICT

MODERATE

RESTAURANTE O FAZ FIGURA, Rua do Paraíso 15B. Tel. 886-89-81.
Cuisine: PORTUGUESE/INTERNATIONAL. **Reservations:** Required. **Metro:** Santa Apolónia.
$ Prices: Appetizers 950$–1,200$ ($5.80–$7.30); main courses 1,300$–1,900$ ($7.90–$11.60). AE, DC, MC, V.
Open: Lunch Mon–Sat 12:30–3pm; dinner Mon–Sat 8pm–midnight.

This is one of the best and most attractively decorated dining rooms in Lisbon, offering faultless service. When reserving a table, ask to be seated on the veranda, where you can order both lunch and dinner overlooking the Tagus. You are given a warm reception and then shown to your table, unless you want to stop for a before-dinner drink in the "international cocktail bar."

5. IN THE BELÉM DISTRICT

MODERATE

SÃO JERÓNIMO, Rua dos Jerónimos 12. Tel. 64-87-97.
Cuisine: PORTUGUESE/INTERNATIONAL. **Reservations:** Recommended.

 FROMMER'S SMART TRAVELER:
RESTAURANTS

VALUE-CONSCIOUS TRAVELERS SHOULD
TAKE ADVANTAGE OF THE FOLLOWING:

1. Fixed-price luncheons or dinners, many of which represent at least a 30% savings off à la carte menus.
2. Daily specials on any à la carte menu; they're invariably fresh and often carry a lower price tag than regular à la carte listings.
3. The house wine; served in a carafe, it's only a fraction of the price of bottled wine. *Note:* Liquor is expensive in Lisbon, and your tab will rise rapidly.
4. Pastas, pizzas, and rice dishes—all exceptional bargains.
5. Eating standing at a cafe or beer tavern, which is less expensive than sitting down.
6. Enjoying a picnic lunch and using the saved money for a really good dinner.

Tram: 16 or 17. **Bus:** 27, 28, or 29.
$ Prices: Appetizers 650$-1,200$ ($4-$7.30); main courses 1,400$-2,500$ ($8.50-$15.30). AE, DC, MC, V.
Open: Lunch Mon-Sat 12:30-3pm; dinner Mon-Sat 7:30-11pm.

A visit to this lighthearted elegant restaurant could be combined with a trip to the famous monastery of the same name. São Jerónimo sits directly to the east of the monastery, behind a big-windowed facade that floods the interior with sunlight. It takes its inspiration from the Roaring '20s, with a French-style decoration; the chairs are by Philippe Starck, and the bar's armchairs are by Carbusier. The waiters wear striped shirts, gray waistcoats, and gray aprons.

INEXPENSIVE

VELA LATINA, Doca Do Bom Sucesso. Tel. 301-71-18.
Cuisine: PORTUGUESE. **Reservations:** Not necessary. **Bus:** 29 or 43.
$ Prices: Appetizers 400$-1,100$ ($2.40-$6.70); main courses 950$-1,950$ ($5.80-$11.90). AE, DC, MC, V.
Open: Lunch Mon-Sat 12:30-3pm; dinner Mon-Sat 8-11pm.

Set within a verdant park, close to the Tagus and the Tower of Belém, this pleasant high-ceilinged restaurant offers well-prepared food, lots of greenery, big windows, and a peaceful sense of calm. Many visitors opt for lunch here after a visit to the Jerónimos Monastery or the Coach Museum. Menu specialties include a wide array of the classic dishes of Portugal, including bean soups, platters of fresh fish, smoked swordfish, roasted lamb, and pork cutlets with herbs and fresh vegetables. Dessert might be flan, fruit tart, or ice cream.

6. IN THE ALFAMA

MODERATE

SANTA CRUZ-MICHEL, Largo de Santa Cruz do Castelo 5. Tel. 886-43-38.
Cuisine: FRENCH. **Reservations:** Required. **Bus:** 37.
$ Prices: Appetizers 850$-1,800$ ($5.20-$11); main courses 1,800$-2,500$ ($11-$15.30). AE, DC, V.
Open: Lunch Mon-Fri 12:30-3pm; dinner Mon-Sat 8-11pm.

Santa Cruz-Michel is a good French bistro with plenty of atmosphere and a hard-to-beat location on the corner of a pocket-size plaza near St. George's Castle. Considered one of the best in Lisbon, the restaurant is made up of three buildings: a barbershop, a blacksmith's shop, and a wine tavern—all renovated and decorated in a tastefully rustic manner. Antique wood chests are used for coffee tables in the tavern portion, and a refectory table holding desserts stands in the walk-in fireplace. On the walls hang everything from zithers to stirrups to ceramics. Chef/owner Michel da Costa, an energetic host with a keen eye for food preparation and service, was trained in southern France. His restaurant provides French gourmet food with *cuisine moderne* overtones. You might begin with saffron-flavored fish soup or goat cheese coated in bread crumbs and tossed into a salad. Main-dish specialties include beef filet Santa Cruz and monkfish medaillons in cognac sauce.

An interesting selection of Portuguese cheeses is always ready to be brought out. However, most diners head immediately for the dessert list (*sobremesas*), loaded with such concoctions as a parfait made with almonds from the Algarve and a hot chocolate sauce. The fresh fruit of the season is also presented, but I personally gravitate to the sorbet with champagne, the most soothing finish to such rich fare. A Portuguese fadista entertains at night.

7. IN THE ALCÂNTARA

EXPENSIVE

CAFÉ ALCÂNTARA, Rua da Cozinha Económica 11. Tel. 363-7176.
   Cuisine: FRENCH/PORTUGUESE. **Reservations:** Recommended. **Bus:** 57.
$ Prices: Appetizers 1,300$–3,900$ ($7.90–$23.80); main courses 2,950$–5,900$ ($18–$36). AE, DC, MC, V.
   Open: Dinner only, daily 8pm–1am.
Established in 1989, this quickly became one of the most exciting dining-and-entertainment complexes in Lisbon. (Its bar and disco facilities are recommended in Chapter 7.) It lies within the solid walls of a 200-year-old warehouse built for the storage of timber, which functioned as a printing factory of movie posters just before its late 1980s reincarnation. Today, the vast premises contains massive columns; trompe-l'oeil murals; oversize mirrors; a color scheme of forest green and bordeaux; exposed marble; ceiling fans; a pair of live trees, dramatic sculpture; simple wooden tables and chairs; and a stylish Portuguese, Brazilian, and international clientele. Menu items are mostly French and include rillettes of salmon, pâté of duckling foie gras, escalopes of fresh salmon with leaf spinach, and lacquered duck. There's also a Portuguese platter of the day, one for each day of the week, which might include fried *bacalau* (codfish) with tomato-based rice or a traditional *feijoada*.

MODERATE

GARE TEJO, Gare Maritima de Alcântara. Tel. 397-6335.
   Cuisine: PORTUGUESE. **Reservations:** Required. **Bus:** 57.
$ Prices: Appetizers 900$–1,650$ ($5.50–$10.10); main courses 1,950$–4,650$ ($11.90–$28.40). AE, DC, MC, V.
   Open: Lunch Mon–Fri noon–3pm; dinner Mon–Sat 7–11pm.
This is one of the newest and most hip and glamorous restaurants in Lisbon, dedicated to the development of Portuguese nouvelle cuisine. Established in 1992, it lies only a few paces from the banks of the Tagus, within what was originally built in the 1930s as one of the city's ferryboat terminals. Big windows overlook the view of river traffic as a polite staff serves such dishes as fresh Atlantic lobster with garlic and herbs "from the kitchen garden"; a seafood platter containing portions of three kinds of fish—fried, grilled, or poached, respectively—each served with a different sauce; roast grouper with new potatoes and baby onions; and a dessert specialty of a modernized form of flan.

8. SPECIALTY DINING

LOCAL FAVORITES

MODERATE

FLORESTA DO GINJAL, Ginjal 7, Cacilhas. Tel. 275-00-87.
   Cuisine: PORTUGUESE/SEAFOOD. **Reservations:** Recommended. **Directions:** Floresta is reached by ferryboat, from Praça do Comércio or from Cais do Sodré; you can buy tickets right on the boat.
$ Prices: Appetizers 250$–750$ ($1.50–$4.60); main courses 800$–3,000$ ($4.90–$18.30). AE, V.
   Open: Lunch daily noon–3pm; dinner daily 7–10:30pm.

Floresta do Ginjal overlooks the waterfront on the left bank of the Tagus. You dine on some of the best-cooked fish dinners in the area while overlooking the river life and hills of Lisbon. The restaurant draws a thriving trade from right-bank Lisbon families, especially on Sunday afternoon. There is a complete Portuguese menu of meat and fowl dishes, but the fish sets the pace. The fishermen's stew, *caldeirada*, is a meal in itself. Another main course might be fried eels or turbot meunière. A dessert favorite is *manjor de principe*, made of eggs and almonds. You can also order strawberries with sugar.

SANCHO, Travessa da Glória 14. Tel. 346-97-80.
   Cuisine: PORTUGUESE. **Reservations:** Recommended. **Metro:** Avenida.
 $ Prices: Appetizers 650$–1,200$ ($4–$7.30); main courses 1,200$–2,500$ ($7.30–$15.30). AE, MC, V.
   Open: Lunch Mon–Sat noon–3pm; dinner Mon–Sat 7–10pm.
Sancho is a cozy rustic-style restaurant just off the Avenida da Liberdade, close to Praça dos Restauradores. The decor is in a classic Iberian style, with a beamed ceiling, a fireplace, leather-and-wood chairs, and stuccoed walls. In summer there is air conditioning.
   Fish gratinée soup is the classic opener. Shellfish is the specialty, and it's always expensive. Main dishes are likely to include the chef's special hake or pan-broiled Portuguese steak. If your palate is made of asbestos, order *churrasco de cabrito* (goat) *au piri-piri*. For dessert, sample crêpes Suzette or perhaps chocolate mousse.

HOTEL DINING

EXPENSIVE

EMBAIXADA, in the Hotel Da Lapa, Rua do Pau de Bandeira 4. Tel. 395-00-05.
   Cuisine: INTERNATIONAL. **Reservations:** Recommended. **Bus:** 13 or 27.
 $ Prices: Appetizers 2,000$–3,000$ ($12.20–$18.30); main courses 3,000$–4,800$ ($18.30–$29.30). Fixed-price luncheon buffet 4,200$ ($25.60) per person. AE, DC, MC, V.
   Open: Lunch daily noon–2:45pm; dinner daily 7:30–11pm.
This is the most upscale and best-recommended restaurant within Lisbon's newest five-star hotel (see Chapter 4). Set within a dignified and elegant dining room with flowered curtains and a view of one of its exclusive neighborhood's most lavishly appointed gardens, it is a favorite of the staff from the many foreign embassies and consulates nearby. Especially popular is the fixed-price luncheon buffet, where an array of international menu items is lavishly displayed in a kind of upscale self-service ritual. The à la carte items are available at lunch and dinner and feature, according to the season, fresh salmon fried with sage, lamb chops with mint sauce, a succulent version of a traditional Portuguese *feijoada*, and beef Wellington.

RITZ GRILL ROOM, in the Ritz Hotel, Rua Rodrigo da Fonseca 88. Tel. 69-20-20.
   Cuisine: FRENCH/PORTUGUESE/INTERNATIONAL. **Reservations:** Recommended. **Metro:** Rotunda.
 $ Prices (including service and taxes): Appetizers 1,800$–3,000$ ($11–$18.30); main courses 2,000$–4,500$ ($12.20–$27.50). AE, DC, MC, V.
   Open: Lunch daily noon–3pm; dinner daily 7:30–10:30pm.
The Ritz Grill Room is in the Ritz Hotel, overlooking the terrace and Edward VII Park, but fortunately set apart from the main lobby. This restaurant features a sophisticated menu; each dish is prepared with the freshest ingredients. You might begin with lobster-and-scampi salad with watercress and orange or vegetable ravioli in morels sauce. Bisque of fresh lobster is regularly featured. Fish courses include fresh salmon cooked in a papillotte with ginger and steamed kingfish stuffed with vegetables. Meat and poultry devotees might be attracted to tournedos with foie gras and Madeira sauce or duck breast with apple-custard vinegar. For dessert, a large variety of pastry is available from the trolley. For a finish, try filtered coffee.

FROMMER'S COOL FOR KIDS: RESTAURANTS

The Big Apple *(see page 98)* Your kids will feel right at home at this tongue-in-cheek version of an American eatery. Not only can they select from one of 18 different burgers (each a meal in itself), but also they can finish with a dessert crêpe.

Hamburger House *(see page 98)* In the heart of Lisbon, this busy eatery dishes up familiar fare, including a wide selection of hamburgers, plus daily specials. It's for the family in a hurry.

Ritz Snack Bar *(see page 99)* Contained within Lisbon's most prestigious hotel, this moderately priced restaurant is a good place to introduce your kids to some regional Portuguese cuisine. If they refuse, they can always find familiar fare on the English menu.

DINING WITH A VIEW
MODERATE

CASA DO LEÃO, Castelo de São Jorge. Tel. 888-01-54.
  Cuisine: INTERNATIONAL. **Reservations:** Recommended. **Bus:** 37.
$ **Prices:** Appetizers 650$–1,200$ ($4–$7.30); main courses 1,200$–3,000$ ($7.30–$18.30). AE, DC, MC, V.
  Open: Daily 12:30–6pm.

My idea of the perfect way to visit the charmingly located Castle of St. George is to stop for a midday meal at this restaurant in a low-slung stone building within the castle walls. You'll pass between a pair of ancient cannons before entering a sun-flooded vestibule where you'll be greeted by the splashing from a dolphin-shaped fountain and the welcoming voice of the uniformed maître d'. Once seated in the spacious blue-tile dining room, beneath soaring brick vaulting, you'll enjoy a panoramic view of the Alfama and the legendary hills of Lisbon. There's even a baronial fireplace, which in cold weather provides an intimate retreat for an apéritif.

Your lunch might include roast duck with orange or grapes, pork chops St. George style, codfish with cream, smoked swordfish from Sesimbra, and an array of the chef's daily specials.

BEER & SHELLFISH TAVERNS
MODERATE

CERVEJARIA BRILHANTE, Rua das Portas de Santo Antão 105. Tel. 346-14-07.
  Cuisine: SEAFOOD. **Reservations:** Not necessary. **Metro:** Rossio. **Bus:** 1, 2, 36, 44, or 45.
$ **Prices:** Appetizers 650$–1,200$ ($4–$7.30); main courses 950$–2,200$ ($5.80–$13.40); tourist menu 1,820$ ($11.10). AE, DC, MC, V.
  Open: Tues–Sun noon–1am.

This is where to go if you enjoy seafood with beer. Lisboans from every walk of life stop off for a stein of beer and *mariscos*. Opposite the Coliseu, the tavern is decorated with stone arches, wood-paneled walls, and pictorial tiles of sea life. You can dine either at the bar or at marble tables. The front window is packed with an appetizing array of king crabs, oysters, lobsters, baby clams, shrimps, even barnacles. And they aren't cheap: The price changes every day, depending on market quotations, and you pay by the kilo.

CERVEJARIA RIBADOURA, Avenida da Liberdade 155. Tel. 54-94-11.

Cuisine: SEAFOOD. **Reservations:** Not necessary. **Metro:** Avenida. **Bus:** 1, 2, 44, or 45.

$ Prices: Appetizers 650$–1,200$ ($4–$7.30); main courses 950$–1,800$ ($5.80–$11). AE, DC, MC, V.

Open: Daily noon–midnight.

Cervejaria Ribadoura is one of the typical shellfish and beer emporiums in central Lisbon, located midway along the city's major boulevard at the corner of the Rua do Salitre. There's a minimum of decor in this tavern-style restaurant. The emphasis is on the varieties of fish: There are more than 50 fish and meat dishes, highlighted by the crustaceans and "sea fruit" recommendations. Try the *bacalhau* (codfish) *à Bras*. You can dine lightly as well, particularly at lunch, on such plates as shrimp omelet. Many diners often follow fish with a meat dish. However, only those who've been trained for at least 25 years on the most mouth-wilting Indian curries should try the sautéed pork cutlets with *piri-piri*, the latter made with red-hot peppers from Angola. A wedge of Portuguese cheese "from the hills" finishes off the meal nicely.

INEXPENSIVE

CERVEJARIA DA TRINDADE, Rua Nova de Trindade 20B. Tel. 342-35-06.

Cuisine: PORTUGUESE. **Reservations:** Not necessary. **Metro:** Rossio. **Tram:** 24. **Bus:** 15, 20, or 100.

$ Prices: Appetizers 78$–1,400$ (50¢–$8.50); main courses 300$–2,400$ ($1.80–$14.60); tourist menu 3,000$ ($18.30). AE, DC, MC, V.

Open: Daily 9am–2am.

Cervejaria da Trindade is a combination German beer hall/Portuguese tavern—the oldest of them all, owned by the brewers of Sagres beer. It's been operating since 1836, having been built on the foundations of the Convento dos Frades Tinos, which had stood here since the 1200s; it was destroyed by the 1755 earthquake. Surrounded by walls tiled with Portuguese scenes, you can order tasty little steaks and heaps of crisp french-fried potatoes. Many of the Portuguese prefer *bife na frigideira*—steak with mustard sauce and a fried egg accompaniment, served in a clay frying pan. The tavern features shellfish, which come from private fish ponds, and the house specialties are *ameijoas* (clams) *à Trindade* and giant prawns. To go with your main course, a small stein of beer does nicely. For dessert, a good selection is a slice of *queijo da serra* (cheese from the mountains) and coffee. Meals are served in the inner courtyard on sunny days.

FAST FOOD

THE BIG APPLE, Avenida Elias Garcia 19B. Tel. 797-55-75.

Cuisine: AMERICAN. **Metro:** Campo Pequeno.

$ Prices: Burgers 800$–1,000$ ($4.90–$6.10); steaks 1,110$–1,400$ ($6.80–$8.50). AE, DC, MC, V.

Open: Lunch daily noon–3pm; dinner daily 7–11pm.

Dozens of tongue-in-cheek accessories adorn the walls and menu of this American-style eatery on a residential neighborhood's tree-lined boulevard. You'll find a Texan's map of the United States (Amarillo appears just south of the Canadian border), and a red, white, and blue checkerboard awning out front. It's simple, pleasant, and clean, and you can order any one of 18 variations of hamburgers, many constituting a meal in themselves. You can also select five kinds of dinner crêpes along with five kinds of temptingly sweet dessert crêpes.

HAMBURGER HOUSE [THE GREAT AMERICAN DISASTER], Praça Marquês de Pombal 1. Tel. 57-61-45.

Cuisine: AMERICAN. **Metro:** Rotunda. **Bus:** 20, 22, or 27.

$ Prices: Burgers 610$–1,020$ ($3.70–$6.20). AE, DC, MC, V.

Open: Lunch daily noon–3pm; dinner daily 7–11pm.

Cramped and sometimes convivial, outfitted in theme-restaurant tones of red, white, and blue, Hamburger House occupies a big-windowed room one floor above street level, at the corner of one of Lisbon's busiest intersections, facing Avenida da Liberdade. To reach it, you'll enter an anonymous-looking commercial arcade within a building devoted to Varig Airlines, then climb a flight of winding steps to the second floor. Hamburger prices depend on their size and their garnishes; full meals can include more substantial fare, such as platters of roast beef and daily specials.

RITZ SNACK BAR, in the Ritz Hotel, Rua Castilho 77C. Tel. 69-20-20.
   Cuisine: PORTUGUESE/INTERNATIONAL. **Metro:** Rotunda.
$ **Prices:** Appetizers 715$–1,700$ ($4.40–$10.40); main courses 1,700$–2,500$ ($10.40–$15.30). AE, DC, MC, V.
   Open: Mon–Sat noon–1:30am.
This is the least expensive of the several restaurants within one of Lisbon's most legendary hotels. Set on several levels, with its own entrance facing Edward VII Park, it offers a polite staff in formal uniforms and a menu that enticingly presents a variety of specialties, including platters of fresh grilled fish and meats. Special emphasis is given to regional Portuguese dishes, which change daily. As a happy ending, the snack bar offers a goodly assortment of tarts, cakes, ice cream "coupes," and cheeses. The menu includes an English version.

VEGETARIAN
INEXPENSIVE

RESTAURANTE A COLMEIA, Rua da Emenda 110. Tel. 347-05-00.
   Cuisine: VEGETARIAN. **Reservations:** Not necessary. **Metro:** Rossio. **Tram:** 28. **Bus:** 15 or 100.
$ **Prices:** Appetizers 100$–250$ ($0.60–$1.50); main courses 400$–700$ ($2.40–$4.30); fixed-price menu 1,200$ ($7.30). No credit cards.
   Open: Mon–Sat noon–8:30pm.

S   On the top floor of a corner building is this center of healthy eating and living offering vegetarian and macrobiotic cuisine. In addition, you'll find a miniature shop where you can purchase such natural ingredients as nuts, raisins, herbs, and even pastries and black breads. You enter on the street floor through an old hall with a stone floor, then ascend scrubbed wooden steps with an old Portuguese tile dado. The top floor has a narrow hallway lined with shelves of books dealing with metaphysics as well as healthful living. At your left is a reception room where you can ask for the dishes of the day and learn the prices. Through the open doors of the two kitchens you'll see the aromatic pastries. The three dining rooms contain large windows.

AFTERNOON TEA

PASTELARIA SALA DE CHA VERSAILLES, Avenida da República 15A. Tel. 54-63-40.
   Cuisine: SANDWICHES/PASTRIES. **Metro:** Campo Pequeno.
$ **Prices:** Sandwiches 210$ ($1.30); pastries 125$–150$ (80¢–90¢). No credit cards.
   Open: Daily 7:30am–10pm.
This is the most famous teahouse in Lisbon, declared part of the "national patrimony." It is claimed that some patrons have been coming here ever since it opened in 1932. In older days, the specialty was Licungo, the famed black tea of Mozambique; you can still order it, but nowadays many drinkers enjoy English brands. However, the Portuguese claim they—not the English—introduced the custom of tea drinking to the English court, after Catherine of Bragança married Charles II in 1662. The decor is rich with chandeliers, gilt mirrors, stained-glass windows, tall stucco ceilings, and black-and-white-marble floors. You can also order milkshakes, mineral water, and fresh orange juice, along with beer and liquor. Snacks come in many varieties, including codfish balls and toasted ham-and-cheese sandwiches.

PASTELARIA BERNARD', Rua Garrett 104. Tel. 347-31-33.

Cuisine: SANDWICHES/SNACKS. **Metro:** Rossio.
$ Prices: Sandwiches 210$ ($1.30); continental breakfast 480$ ($2.90). No credit cards.
Open: Mon–Sat 8am–midnight.

Pastelaria Bernard' is considered the most fashionable teahouse in Lisbon. Dating from the 1800s, it lies in the heart of the Chiado, and in fair weather sidewalk tables are placed outside. During the revolution of 1974, the waiters took it over but couldn't make a go of it until a dressmaker moved in, rescued it, restored it, and reopened it in 1981. Lunch is served in a back room, a full meal of Portuguese specialties such as codfish with almonds. But most visitors come here for tea, served along with sandwiches and snacks. Desserts are famous, including one called *duchesses* (whipped cream cakes). Proper dress is required inside, although tourists in shorts sometimes occupy the outside tables. Since it opens so early, it's a good choice for breakfast as well, perhaps for fresh croissants.

COFFEEHOUSES

How can one go to Lisbon without visiting one of the traditional coffeehouses? It's like a trip to England without taking afternoon tea or to Munich without sampling a stein in a beer hall. To the Portuguese, the coffeehouse is an institution, a democratic parlor where they can drop in for their favorite beverage, abandon their worries, relax, smoke, read the paper, write a letter, or chat with friends about tomorrow's football match or last night's lover.

The coffeehouse in Portugal is no longer revered as it once was. The older and more colorful ones with their turn-of-the-century charm are rapidly being replaced by the 20th-century world of chrome and plastic.

A BRASILEIRA, Rua Garrett 120. Tel. 346-95-41.

Cuisine: SNACKS/SANDWICHES. **Metro:** Rossio.
$ Prices: Snacks 650$–1,500$ ($4–$9.20). No credit cards.
Open: Daily 7:30am–2pm.

One of the oldest coffeehouses in Lisbon is A Brasileira, in the Chiado district. Behind an art nouveau facade, it's a 19th-century emporium, once a favorite gathering place of the literati; today, it still remains dear to some diehard devotees. Guests sit at small tables on chairs made of tooled leather, amid mirrored walls and marble pilasters. Aside from the architectural adornments, there is also a collection of paintings to admire. The cafe has the great Portuguese poet Fernando Pessoa—or rather his statue—sitting on a chair side by side with the customers. A demitasse costs 55$ (30¢), as does a simple glass of beer at the more recently created sidewalk section.

Outside, the street speaks of past associations with men of letters. Garrett, a romantic 19th-century dandy, was one of Portugal's leading poets (the street is named after him). The district itself, the Chiado, was named for another poet. On the square near the cafe a statue honors António Ribeiro, a 16th-century poet. Yet another poet, Bocage of Setúbal, used to frequent this coffeehouse. When once accosted by a bandit, he is said to have replied, "I am going to the Brasileira, but if you shoot me I am going to another world."

PORT WINE TASTING

SOLAR DO VINHO DO PORTO, Rua de São Pedro de Alcântara 45. Tel. 347-57-07.

Cuisine: PORT. **Reservations:** Not necessary. **Bus:** 15 or 100.
$ Prices: Glass of wine 150$–1,600$ (90¢–$9.80). No credit cards.
Open: Mon–Fri 10am–11:30pm, Sat 11am–10:30pm.

A bar devoted exclusively to the drinking and enjoyment of port in all its known types is the Solar, near the Bairro Alto with its fado houses. You enter what appears to be a private living room. In the rear of a large building, it offers a relaxing atmosphere, the feeling enhanced by an open stone fireplace.

Owned and sponsored by the Port Wine Institute, Solar displays many artifacts related to the industry. But the real reason for dropping in here during the day is for its *lista de vinhos*—there are nearly 150 wines to choose from. The location is about 50 feet from the upper terminus of the Gloria funicular.

LATE-NIGHT DINING

Lisboans tend to eat much later than most Americans, Canadians, or Britons. Some restaurants stay open very late indeed, as reflected by such previous recommendations as Gambrinus, Bachus, and Cervejaria da Trindade.

PICNIC FARE & WHERE TO EAT IT

Lisbon has many "green lungs" (public parks) where you can go with your picnic fixings. Of these, the finest is **Parque Eduardo VII,** at the top of Avenida da Liberdade, which has picnic tables.

A good place to stock up on supplies is **Celeiro,** Rua 1 de Dezembro 81 (tel. 342-74-95). To accompany your sandwiches, you'll find a good selection of cheeses and wines, along with fresh fruits and breads. You can also order a roast chicken for 900$ ($5.50) per kilo (2.2 pounds). It's open Monday through Friday from 8:30am to 7pm and Saturday from 8:30am to 1pm. Metro: Rossio.

LISBON ATTRACTIONS

In Lisbon, you'll find that the frame competes with the picture. The Portuguese capital offers many worthwhile attractions, yet few can resist its environs. Many visitors end by using Lisbon only as a base, venturing forth during the day to Lord Byron's "variegated maze of mount and glen" at Sintra; to the sandy beaches along the Portuguese Riviera (Estoril and Cascais); to the monastery and royal palace at Mafra; and even as far north as the fishing village of Nazaré or perhaps Fátima, where three shepherd children claimed to have seen a vision of the Virgin Mary.

One reason Lisbon gets overlooked is that visitors do not budget enough time for it: One or two days simply isn't adequate for Lisbon and the environs. A minimum of five days is needed. A second reason is that Lisbon's attractions remain relatively unknown. Seemingly, every stone in Rome has been documented or recorded by someone. But in talks with literally dozens of visitors, the question most often asked is: "What does one do in Lisbon?"

This chapter hopes to answer that question, specifically with regard to sightseeing. If your time is limited and you can cope only with the most important, then you should explore the **National Coach Museum,** the **Jerónimos Monastery,** and the **Alfama** and the **Castle of St. George.** At least two art museums, although not of the caliber of Madrid's Prado, merit attention: the **Museu Nacional de Art Antiga** and the **Museu Calouste Gulbenkian.**

Those who have sufficient leisure time can visit the **Fundaçao Ricardo Esprito Santo** and watch reproductions of antiques being made or books being gold-leafed. Other choices are seeing the gilded royal galleys at the **Naval Museum,** wandering through the fish market, or exploring the arts and crafts of **Belém's Folk Art Museum.**

The Lisbon voyager will discover, just by walking the streets, a unique city, a capital that extended its power across continents.

SUGGESTED ITINERARIES

IF YOU HAVE 1 DAY This is much too little time, but it's enough to take a walking tour of the Alfama (see later in this chapter), the most interesting district of Lisbon, visiting the 12th-century **Sé** (cathedral), and taking in a view of the city and the River Tagus from the **Santa Luzia Belvedere.** Climax your visit with a call at the **Castelo São Jorge** (St. George's Castle). Taxi to Belém to see the **Mosteiro dos Jerónimos** (Jerónimos Monastery) and the **Torre de Belém.** While at Belém explore one of the major sights of Lisbon, the **Museu Nacional dos Coches** (National Coach Museum).

IF YOU HAVE 2 DAYS Spend Day 1 as outlined above. On Day 2, head for Sintra, the single most visited sight in the environs of Lisbon—Byron called it "glorious Eden." You can spend the day there, as it has many attractions. Try at least to visit the

❓ DID YOU KNOW . . . ?

- Lisbon was the center of the world's last great colonial empire.
- Locals claim their city was founded by the legendary Ulysses.
- The 1755 earthquake killed 30,000 people and left most of the city in ruins.
- In 1955, an Armenian oil magnate from Turkey (Calouste Gulbenkian) bequeathed to Lisbon one of the richest private art collections in the world.
- In 1481, Columbus proposed to João II in Lisbon his plan to sail west but was turned down.
- Henry Fielding, the great English novelist, arrived in 1754 to improve his health but died two months later and is buried in the British cemetery in Lisbon.
- After the Portuguese empire collapsed, refugees from former colonies flooded Lisbon with African food and music.
- Igreja de Santa Engrácia was begun in the 17th century but not completed until 1966.
- Bullfights in Lisbon are called *touradas*. Unlike the Spanish, the Portuguese don't kill their bulls in the ring.
- The Alfama was built Kasbah style, with many streets little more than 8 feet wide.
- Guidebooks consistently credit Alexandre-Gustave Eiffel with the creation of Lisbon's famed Elevador Santa Justa. Actually, a Portuguese designed it.

Palácio Nacional de Sintra and the **Palácio Nacional da Pena.** Return to Lisbon for a night at a fado cafe.

IF YOU HAVE 3 DAYS Spend Days 1 and 2 as outlined above, but on the third day get to see more of Lisbon. A morning passes quickly at the **Museu Calouste Gulbenkian,** one of Europe's treasure troves of art. Have lunch at a *típico* restaurant in the Bairro Alto. In the afternoon see the **Fundaçao Ricardo Esprito Santo** (Museum of Decorative Art) and the **Museu Nacional de Art Antiga** (National Museum of Ancient Art). To climax your day, wander through Parque Eduardo VII.

IF YOU HAVE 5 DAYS Spend Days 1 through 3 as outlined above. On the fourth day, take one of the most interesting excursions from Lisbon (it can be done on an organized tour—see later in this chapter—for comfort, speed, and convenience): Visit the fishing village of **Nazaré** and the walled city of **Óbidos.** Roman Catholic readers might also want to include a visit to the shrine at **Fátima,** although that would make for one very busy day. On the final day, slow your pace a bit, with a morning spent at the beach at **Estoril** on Portugal's Costa do Sol. Then continue along the coast to **Cascais** for lunch. After lunch, wander around this old fishing village now turned into a major resort. Go to **Guincho,** 4 miles along the coast from Cascais, which is near the westernmost point on the European continent and has panoramic views.

1. THE TOP ATTRACTIONS

THE ALFAMA

⭐ The Lisbon of old lives on in the most typical quarter of the city. The wall built by the Visigoths and incorporated into some of the old houses is mute testimony to its ancient past. In East Lisbon, the Alfama was the Saracen sector centuries before its conquest by the Christians.

Some of the buildings were spared from the 1755 earthquake, and the Alfama has retained much of its original charm—characterized by narrow cobblestone streets, cages of canaries chirping in the afternoon sun, fish in baskets balanced on the heads of *varinas*, strings of garlic and pepper inviting you inside típico taverns, old street markets, and charming balconies.

The 19th-century Lisbon historian Norberto de Araújo wrote of "its perpetual resigned human tragedy from the habit of living it." In a colorful description, he pointed up some of its elements: "labyrinth, confused, heaped up, multicolored; twisted and retwisted, lots of embracing narrow streets and kissing eaves; archways, backyards, blind alleys, stairways and terraces; commons and courtyards."

The houses are so close together that in many places it's impossible to stretch your arms to their full length. That proximity was dramatically expressed by the poet Frederico de Brito: "Your house is so close to mine! In the starry night's bliss, to exchange a tender kiss, our lips easily meet, high across the narrow street."

Stevedores, fishmongers, and sailors occupy the Alfama. From the smallest houses, streamers of laundry protrude. The fishwives make early-morning appearances on their iron balconies, where they water their pots of geraniums.

But perhaps the most exciting sight is a little boy racing down a stone stairway in his droopy underwear (or wearing nothing at all) to hug his sailor father. The boy's mother will be preparing a steaming pot of *caldeirada,* the traditional fishermen's stew. When that same boy isn't racing to greet his father or on an errand for his mother, he'll likely join one of Norberto de Araújo's "waves of little truants" who like to attach themselves to visitors. These children appear in ripples, always with an alert eye for a lost tourist. With hands outstretched and eyes soulfully pleading, they beg you to let them lead you to an open street market. Once there, you can wander in a maze of stacks of brightly colored vegetables from the country, bananas from Madeira, pineapple from the Azores, and fish from the sea.

Much of the Alfama's charm lies in its armies of cats roaming the streets at will, asserting their unique rights. It is said that without these cats the sector would be rat infested. Occasionally, a black-shawled old woman, stooping over a brazier grilling sardines in front of her house, will toss one of these felines a fish head.

Once aristocrats lived in the Alfama; their memory is perpetuated by the coats-of-arms of noble families that are slowly decaying on the fronts of some of the 16th-century houses. Some still do live there. One of the surviving members of an old family refuses to move, despite the pleadings of her relatives. "I will always live here," she said. "When I die, then you can remove my body." The best-known aristocratic mansion is the one once occupied by the count of Arcos, the last viceroy of Brazil. Constructed in the 16th century and spared, in part, from the earthquake, it lies on Largo da Salvador.

On your exploration, you'll suddenly come upon a belvedere and be rewarded with an overall perspective of the contrasting styles of the Alfama, from a simple tile-roofed fishmonger's abode to a gaily decorated baroque church. One of the best views is from the belvedere of **Largo das Portas do Sol,** near the Museum of Decorative Art. It's a balcony opening onto the sea, overlooking the typical houses as they sweep down to the Tagus.

One of the oldest churches is **Santo Estevão** (St. Stephen), at the Largo de Santo Estevão. It was originally constructed in the 13th century; the present marble structure dates from the 18th century. Also of medieval origin is the **Church of São Miguel** (St. Michael), at Largo São Miguel, deep in the Alfama on a palm tree–shaded square. The interior is richly decorated, with 18th-century gilt and trompe-l'oeil walls. The church was reconstructed after the earthquake.

Rua da Judiaria (Street of Jews) is yet another reminder of the past. It was settled largely by refugees fleeing Spain to escape the Inquisition.

At night the spirit changes. Street lanterns cast patterns against medieval walls, and the plaintive voice of the fadista is heard until the early-morning hours. Although the Bairro Alto is the traditional fado quarter of Lisbon, the cafes of the Alfama also reverberate with the fadista sound. Amália and Celeste Rodrigues, two celebrated fadistas, got their start in the vicinity of the dockland, selling flowers to tourists arriving on the boats.

The Alfama was well summed up by another Portuguese writer who called it "a sort of old curiosity shop, under a veil of humility here and there, ever inclined to be romantic and childish."

For specific guidance about how to see the Alfama, refer to the walking tour later in this chapter. The Alfama is best explored by day; it can be dangerous to go wandering around the area at night.

SIGHTS OF THE ALFAMA

CASTELO SÃO JORGE (Saint George's Castle), Rua Costa do Castelo.

✪ The local people speak of it as the cradle of their city. Castelo São Jorge in the Alfama district may well have been the spot on which the Portuguese capital began in times too distant to be known. Although it is believed to have predated the Romans, the hilltop was used as a fortress to guard the Tagus and its settlement below.

From the 5th century A.D., it was a Visigothic fortification; it fell in the early 8th century to the Saracens. Many of the walls that still remain were erected during the centuries of Moorish domination. The Moors were in control until 1147, which was a historic year for the Portuguese, for it was then that Afonso Henríques, the first king of the country, chased the Moors out and extended his kingdom south. Even before Lisbon was made the capital of a newly emerging nation, the site was used as a royal palace.

For what many consider the finest view of the Tagus and the Alfama, walk the esplanades and climb the ramparts of the old castle. The castle takes its name in commemoration of an Anglo-Portuguese pact dating from as early as 1371. (Portugal and England have been traditional allies, although their relationship was strained in 1961 when India, a member of the Commonwealth of Nations, seized the Portuguese overseas territories of Goa, Diu, and Damão.)

Huddling close to the protection of the moated castle is a sector that appears almost medieval (many houses still retain their Moorish courtyards, while others have been greatly altered). At the entrance, visitors pause at the Castle Belvedere. The Portuguese refer to this spot as their ancient window overlooking the Alfama, the Serras of Monsanto and Sintra, Ponte 25 de Abril spanning the Tagus, Praça do Comércio, and the tile roofs of the Portuguese capital. In the square stands a heroic statue—sword in one hand, shield in the other—of the first king, Afonso Henríques.

Inside the castle grounds, you can stroll through a setting of olive, pine, and cork trees, all graced by the appearance of a flamingo. When rain is sweeping the city, you'll focus on a cannon and think of the massacres that must have occurred on this blood-soaked hill. On a fair day, you'll perhaps notice that willows weep or oleander bloom. Swans with white bodies and black necks glide in a silence shattered by the bloodcurdling scream of the rare white peacock.

Admission: Free.

Open: Apr–Sept, daily 9am–9pm (Oct–Mar, until 7pm).

CATHEDRAL (SÉ), Largo da Sé. Tel. 86-67-52.

Even tourist brochures admit that this cathedral is not very rich. Characterized by twin towers flanking its entrance, it represents an architectural wedding of Romanesque and Gothic. The facade is severe enough for a medieval fortress, and like many European cathedrals, it has had many architectural fathers. The devastation caused by the 1344 and 1755 earthquakes didn't help either. At one point, the site of the present Sé was allegedly used by the Saracens as a holy mosque. When the city was captured by Christian Crusaders, led by Portugal's first king, Afonso Henríques, the structure was rebuilt. That early date in the 12th century makes the Sé the oldest church in Lisbon.

Inside are many treasures, such as the font where St. Anthony of Padua is said to have been christened in 1195. A notable feature is the 14th-century Gothic chapel of Bartolomeu Joanes. Other things of interest are a crib by Machado de Castro (the 18th-century Portuguese sculptor who did the equestrian statue on Praça do Comércio); the 14th-century sarcophagus of Lopo Fernandes Pacheco; and the original nave and aisles.

To visit the sacristy and cloister requires a guide. The cloister, built in the 14th century by King Dinis, is of ogival construction, with garlands, a Romanesque wrought-iron grille, and tombs with inscription stones. In the sacristy are housed marbles, relics, valuable images, and pieces of ecclesiastical treasure from the 15th and 16th centuries.

Whether you're Roman Catholic or not, you may want to attend a service here. If seen in the morning, the stained-glass reflections on the floor evoke a Monet painting.

Admission: Free.

Open: Daily 9am–noon and 2:30–6pm. **Tram:** 28 (Graça). **Bus:** 37.

SANTO ANTÓNIO DE LISBOA, Largo de Santo António de Sé. Tel. 86-91-45.
St. Anthony of Padua was born in 1195 in a house that stood here. In the crypt, a guide will show you the spot where the saint was allegedly born.

Buried at Padua, Italy, this itinerant Franciscan monk remains the patron saint of Portugal. The devout come to this little church to light candles under his picture. He is known as a protector of young brides and also has a special connection with the children of Lisbon. To raise money to erect the altar at the church, the children of the Alfama built miniature altars with a representation of the patron saint on them. June 12 of every year is designated St. Anthony's Day, a time of merrymaking, heavy eating, and drinking. In the morning are street fires and singing, climaxed by St. Anthony's Feast on the following day.

The original church was destroyed by the 1755 earthquake, and the present building was designed by Mateus Vicente in the 18th century.

Admission: Free.
Open: Tues–Sun 7:30am–12:30pm and 3–7:30pm. **Metro:** Rossio. **Bus:** 37.

BELÉM

At Belém, where the Tagus (*Tejo* in Portuguese) meets the sea, the caravels were launched on their missions: Vasco da Gama to India, Ferdinand Magellan to circumnavigate the globe, and Bartolomeu Dias to round the Cape of Good Hope.

Belém emerged from the Restelo, that point or strand of land from which the ships set sail across the so-called Sea of Darkness. As riches, especially spices, poured back into Portugal, Belém flourished. Great monuments, such as the Belém Tower and Jerónimos Monastery, were built and embellished in the Manueline style.

In time, the royal family established a summer palace here. Much of the character of the district came about when wealthy Lisboans began moving out and erecting town houses. For many years, Belém was a separate municipality. Eventually, however, it became incorporated into Lisbon as a parish. Nowadays it's a major target for sightseers, as it's a virtual monument-studded museumland. For most visitors, the first sight is the Torre de Belém.

SIGHTS IN BELÉM

TORRE DE BELÉM, Praça do Imperio. Tel. 362-00-34.
The quadrangular Tower of Belém is a monument to Portugal's Age of Discovery. Erected between 1515 and 1520 in the Manueline style, the tower is Portugal's classic landmark, often used on documents and brochures as a symbol of the country. A monument to Portugal's great military and naval past, the tower stands on or near the spot where the caravels once set out.

Its architect, Francisco de Arruda, blended Gothic and Moorish elements using such characteristic devices as twisting ropes carved of stone. The coat-of-arms of Manuel I rests above the loggia, and balconies grace three sides of the monument. Along the balustrade of the loggias, stone crosses symbolize the Portuguese Crusaders.

However, the richness of the facade fades once you cross the drawbridge and enter the Renaissance-style doorway. Gothic severity reigns; there are a few antiques, including a 16th-century throne graced with finials, and an inset paneled with pierced Gothic tracery. If you scale the steps leading to the ramparts, you'll be rewarded with a panorama of boats along the Tagus and pastel-washed, tile-roofed old villas in the hills beyond.

Facing the Tower of Belém stands a monument commemorating the first Portuguese to cross the Atlantic by airplane (not nonstop). The date was March 30, 1922, and the flight took pilot Gago Coutinho and navigator Sacadura Cabral from Lisbon to Rio de Janeiro.

At the center of the Praça do Imperio at Belém is the Fonte Luminosa, the Luminous Fountain. The patterns of the water jets, estimated at more than 70 original designs, make an evening show lasting nearly an hour if you want to see all of them.

Admission: 400$ ($2.40) adults; children and those 65 or over free.

Open: Tues–Sun 10am–5pm. **Bus:** 29, 43, or 49.

PADRÃO DOS DESCOBRIMENTOS [Memorial to the Discoveries], Praça da Boa Esperança. Tel. 61-62-60.

Like a prow of one of the Age of Discovery caravels, this memorial stands on the Tagus, looking as if it's ready at any moment to strike out across the Sea of Darkness. Memorable explorers, chiefly Vasco da Gama, are immortalized in stone along the ramps.

At the point where the two ramps meet stands a replica of Henry the Navigator, whose genius opened up new worlds. The memorial was unveiled in 1960, and one of the stone figures is that of a kneeling Philippa of Lancaster, the English mother of Henry the Navigator. Other figures in the frieze symbolize the Crusaders (represented by a man holding a flag with a cross), navigators, monks, cartographers, and cosmographers. At the top of the prow is the coat-of-arms of Portugal at the time of Manuel the Fortunate. The space in front of the memorial is floored with a map of the world in multicolored marble, with the dates of the discoveries set in metal. The continents are in red marble, the oceans are in gray-blue, and the caravels are in still another color.

Admission: Free.
Open: Daily 24 hrs. **Bus:** 29, 43, or 49.

MOSTEIRO DOS JERÓNIMOS [Jerónimos Monastery], Praça do Império. Tel. 362-00-34.

The author Howard La Fay wrote this: "Here, frozen forever in stone, is the blazing noontide of empire. Stylized hawsers writhe in the arches. Shells and coral and fish entwine in every column. Sanctuary lamps glow red above carved African lions."

In an expansive mood of celebration, Manuel I, the Fortunate, ordered this monastery built to commemorate the sailing of Vasco da Gama to India and to give thanks to the Lady Mary for its success. The style of architecture to which the king contributed his name, Manueline, combines flamboyant Gothic and Moorish influences with the dawn of the Renaissance in Portugal.

The monastery was founded in 1502, partially financed by the spice trade that grew following the discovery of the route to India. Originally, a small chapel dedicated to St. Mary had been built on this spot by Henry the Navigator, and although the 1755 earthquake damaged the monastery, it didn't destroy it. Extensive restoration, some of it ill-conceived, was carried out.

The decorated southern doorway is outstanding. Inside, the most interesting architecture is to be seen in the cloister. Every pillar is unique, as each craftsman vied with the others in exuberance of motifs. From the cloister, doors lead to rooms about 7 feet long and 4 feet wide. You walk across the unmarked tombs of unnamed ghosts; other bodies were buried in the walls. The cloister's second tier is approached by a stairway, where monks of old walked in meditation.

The church interior is divided into a trio of naves, noted for their fragile-looking pillars. Some of the ceilings, like those in the monks' refectory, have a ribbed barrel vault. The "palm tree" in the sacristy is also exceptional.

Many of the greatest names in Portuguese history are said to be entombed at the monastery, but none is more famous than Vasco da Gama. The Portuguese also maintain that Luís Vaz de Camões is buried here. Both tombs rest on the backs of lions. Camões was the national poet of Portugal, author of *Os Lusíadas (The Lusiads)*, in which he glorified the triumphs of his compatriots.

Camões epic poetry is said to have inspired a young Portuguese king, Sebastião, to dreams of glory. The foolish king—devoutly, even fanatically, religious—was killed at Alcácer-Kibir, Morocco, in a 1578 crusade against the Muslims. Those refusing to believe that the king was dead formed a cult known as Sebastianism; it rose to minor influence, and four men tried to assert their claim to the Portuguese throne. Each maintained steadfastly, even to death, that he was King Sebastião. Sebastião's remains were allegedly entombed in a 16th-century marble shrine built in the Mannerist style.

Finally, the romantic poet Herculano (1800–54) is buried at Jerónimos, as is Fernando Pessoa.

Admission: To church: Free. To cloisters: June–Sept, 425$ ($2.60); Oct–May, 275$ ($1.70); children and those 65 or over free.
Open: June–Sept, Tues–Sun 10am–5pm. **Bus:** 29, 43, or 49.

MUSEU DE MARINHA [Maritime Museum], Praça do Império. Tel. 362-00-19.

The pageant and the glory that was Portugal on the high seas is evoked for posterity in the Maritime Museum, one of the most important in Europe. Appropriately, it is installed in the west wing of the Mosteiro dos Jerónimos.

These royal galleys re-create an age of opulence that never feared excess. Dragon heads drip with gilt; sea monsters coil with abandon. Of course, assembling a large crew was no problem for kings and queens in those days. Surely Cleopatra floating down the Nile on her barge would have recoiled with jealousy at the sight of the galley Queen Maria I ordered built for the 1785 marriage of her son and successor, Crown Prince João, to the Spanish Princess Carlota Joaquina Bourbon. Eighty dummy oarsmen, elaborately attired in scarlet- and mustard-colored waistcoats, represent the crew.

The museum contains hundreds of models of 15th- to 19th-century sailing ships, the transition from sail to steam, 20th-century warships, merchant marine vessels, fishing boats, river craft, and pleasure boats. In a section devoted to the East is a pearl-inlaid replica of a Dragon Boat used in maritime and fluvial cortèges. Other models include a large reproduction of the frigate *Ulysses*, which dates from December 15, 1792, and an early 20th-century destroyer with two torpedo tubes.

A full range of Portuguese naval uniforms is displayed, from one worn at a Mozambique military outpost in 1896 to a model worn as recently as 1961. In a special room can be seen the queen's stateroom as it was on the royal yacht of Carlos I, the Bragança king who was assassinated at Praça do Comércio in 1908. It was on this craft that his son, Manuel II, and his wife, the queen mother, Amélia, escaped to Gibraltar following the 1910 collapse of the Portuguese monarchy.

Historical exhibits include a letter from Lord Nelson dated October 24, 1799. A large map traces the trail of Brito Capelo and Roberto Ivens through the African continent from 1884 to 1885.

The Maritime Museum also honors some of the early Portuguese aviators. On display is the aquaplane *Santa Cruz*, the first aircraft to cross the South Atlantic. The date was March 30, 1922 ("*Aventura magnífica*" hailed the press), and the captain was Comdr. Sacadura Cabral and the navigator Adm. Gago Coutinho, who invented a new sextant for use by airmen. The flight was from Lisbon to Rio de Janeiro, with stopovers en route. Also displayed is a 1917 airplane, the first one used by Portuguese aviators.

Admission: 250$ ($1.50) adults; children under 10 and those 65 or over free.
Open: Tues–Sun 10am–5pm. **Bus:** 29, 43, or 49.

⭐ MUSEU NACIONAL DOS COCHES [National Coach Museum], Praça Afonso de Albuquerque. Tel. 363-81-64.

Visited by more tourists than any other attraction in Lisbon, the National Coach Museum is considered the finest of its type in the world. Founded by Amélia, wife of Carlos I, it's housed in what was originally an 18th-century riding academy connected to the Belém Royal Palace.

The coaches stand in a former horse ring, and most date from the 17th to the 19th century. Drawing the most interest is a trio of opulently gilded baroque carriages once used by the Portuguese ambassador to the Vatican at the time of Pope Clement XI (1716). Also displayed is a 17th-century coach in which the Spanish Hapsburg king, Phillip II, journeyed from Madrid to Lisbon to see his new possession.

Other coaches include the processional chariot of "Our Lady of Cabo," the coach of João V, the coach of Queen Maria Ana de Austria, as well as Queen Maria's berlinda. Portuguese and foreign harnesses and trappings, all the gala livery, are exhibited on the second floor.

The portrait gallery belonged to the House of Bragança, which ended in 1910. Pictured are such notables as Maria I and a host of minor royalty.

Admission: June–Sept, 425$ ($2.60); Oct–May, 275$ ($1.70).
Open: Tues–Sun 10am–1pm and 2:30–3:30pm. **Closed:** Holidays.
Bus: 29, 43, or 49.

MUSEU DE ARTE POPULAR [Folk Art Museum], Avenida de Brasilia. Tel. 301-12-82.

Nowhere are the folk arts and customs of the Portuguese displayed more dramatically than here. The walls of the building, which previously housed the Regional Center during the 1940 Portuguese World's Exhibition, are painted by contemporary artists, some of the best in Portugal—including Carlos Botelho, Eduardo Anahory, Estrela Faria, Manuel Lapa, Paulo Ferreira, and Tomás de Melo. Their work is supplemented by enlarged photographs of the people of the provinces. The 1948 establishment of the Folk Art Museum was a result of a campaign for ethnic revival directed by António Ferro. The collections—including ceramics, furniture, wickerwork, clothes, farm implements, and painting—are displayed in five rooms that correspond more or less to the provinces, each of which maintains its regional personality.

Entre-Douro and Minho are represented by flowers, musical instruments, goldsmith pieces, Barcelos painted pottery, and Vila Nova de Gaia painted earthenware dolls. Elaborate oxen harnesses are on display, along with farm implements. You can see models of regional boats; fishing tools; embroidered sweaters; Azurara stockings; rugs; a Viana do Castelo weaver's loom; and various items for preparing linen, for spinning, and for knitting. Bilros laces are also on exhibit.

The Trás-os-Montes exhibition gives a survey of the activities of the northeast area. You'll see straw *escrinhos* (baskets), a Vila Real oxcart and a harrow for threshing corn, kitchen items (*transfogueiro* and a piece of furniture, *escano*), black earthenware, and a collection of bedspreads. *Chocalheiros,* the masks worn by men called by the same name who appear on feast days, are interesting displays.

The Algarve, well known to tourists, is represented by palm mats and baskets, a water cart, horse trappings, fishing nets, a manually operated millstone, and line-cut chimneys.

The Beiras room contains a reproduction of the interior of a Monsanto country house, as well as a variety of wicker and straw baskets, fine Molelos black earthenware items, bedspreads, and rugs. Here, too, is a set of tools used in salt making from Aveiro. Of special interest is a *molico* catcher's boat. Molico is seaweed dredged up and used as fertilizer.

The fifth room, containing displays from Estremadura and Alentejo, holds a variety of objects, such as glazed pottery pieces from Leiria and Mafra; Nazaré fishing and clothing items, sculpture, and saints' registries; and a wax dummy modeling the garb of the *campino,* a herdsman who looks after the bulls on the plains. From Alentejo, you'll see a replica of a kitchen, glazed Redondo earthenware, Nisa earthenware, Estremoz polished and striped pottery, and earthenware painted dolls, together with items of shepherds' art and votive paintings.

Admission: 200$ ($1.20) adults; children under 10 free.
Open: Tues–Sun 10am–12:30pm and 2–5pm. **Closed:** Holidays. **Bus:** 14 and 40.

PALÁCIO NACIONAL DE AJUDA, Calçada da Ajuda, near Belém. Tel. 363-70-95.

This early 19th-century palace contains rooms that have not been changed since the days of royal supremacy in Portugal. The palace collection is extensive—of particular note are the Germain silver, the Sormani furniture, and the tapestries.

Admission: 200$ ($1.20) adults; children under 12 and those 65 or over free.
Open: Thurs–Tues 10am–5pm. **Tram:** 18. **Bus:** 14, 42, or 60.

TWO MORE TOP MUSEUMS

Most major Lisbon museums are at Belém, but two major attractions are found in the city: the National Art Gallery and the Gulbenkian Center for Arts and Culture, described below. For a survey of two additional notable museums, the St. Roque Museum of ecclesiastical art and the Archeological Museum in the ruins of the Carmo Church, refer to "More Attractions" in this chapter.

MUSEU NACIONAL DE ARTE ANTIGA (National Museum of Ancient Art), Jardim 9 de Abril. Tel. 396-41-51.

⭐ The country's greatest collection of paintings is housed in the National Museum of Ancient Art, which occupies two connected buildings—a 17th-century palace and an added edifice that was built on the site of the old Carmelite Convent of Santo Alberto. The convent's chapel was preserved and is a good example of the integration of ornamental arts, with gilded carved wood, glazed tiles (*azulejos*), and sculpture of the 17th and 18th centuries.

The museum has many notable paintings, including the famous polyptych from St. Vincent's monastery attributed to Nuno Goncalves between 1460 and 1470. It contains 60 portraits of leading figures of Portuguese history. Other outstanding works are Hieronymus Bosch's triptych, *The Temptation of St. Anthony;* Hans Memling's *Mother and Child;* Albrecht Dürer's *St. Jerome;* and paintings by Velázquez, Zurbarán, Poussin, and Courbet. Paintings from the 15th through the 19th century trace the development of Portuguese art.

The museum also exhibits a remarkable collection of gold- and silversmiths' work, both Portuguese and foreign. Among these is the cross from Alcobaça and the monstrance of Belém, constructed with the first gold brought from India by Vasco da Gama. Another exceptional example is the 18th-century French silver tableware ordered by José I. Diverse objects from Benin, India, Persia, China, and Japan reflect Portuguese expansion overseas. Two excellent pairs of screens depict the Portuguese relationship with Japan in the 17th century. Flemish tapestries, a rich assemblage of church vestments, Italian polychrome ceramics, and sculptures are also on display.

Admission: 200$ ($1.20) adults; children under 14 free; free Sun 10am–1pm.
Open: Tues–Sun 10am–1pm and 2–5pm. **Tram:** Alcântara. **Bus:** 27, 40, 49, or 60.

MUSEU CALOUSTE GULBENKIAN, Avenida de Berna 45A. Tel. 793-51-31.

⭐ Opened in 1969, this museum, part of the Fundaçao Calouste Gulbenkian, houses what one critic called "one of the world's finest private art collections." It was deeded by the Armenian oil tycoon Calouste Gulbenkian, who died in 1955. The modern multimillion-dollar center is in a former private estate that belonged to the count of Vilalva.

The collections cover Egyptian, Greek, and Roman antiquities; a remarkable set of Islamic art, including ceramics and textiles of Turkey and Persia; Syrian glass, books, bindings, and miniatures; and Chinese vases, Japanese prints, and lacquerwork. The European displays include medieval illuminated manuscripts and ivories, 15th- to 19th-century painting and sculpture, Renaissance tapestries and medals, important collections of 18th-century French decorative works, French impressionist painting, René Lalique jewelry, and glassware.

In a move requiring great skill in negotiation, Gulbenkian managed to make purchases of art from the Hermitage in St. Petersburg. Among his most notable acquisitions are two Rembrandts: *Portrait of an Old Man* and *Alexander the Great.* Two other well-known paintings are *Portrait of Hélène Fourment* by Peter Paul Rubens and *Portrait of Madame Claude Monet* by Pierre-Auguste Renoir. In addition, I'd suggest you seek out Mary Cassatt's *The Stocking.* The French sculptor Jean-Antoine Houdon is represented by a statue of *Diana.* Silver made by François-Thomas Germain, once used by Catherine the Great, is here, as well as one piece by Thomas Germain, the father.

As a cultural center, the Gulbenkian Foundation sponsors plays, films, ballet, and musical concerts, as well as a rotating exhibition of works by leading modern Portuguese and foreign artists.

Admission: 200$ ($1.20) adults; children under 10 and those 65 or more free; free Sun.

FROMMER'S FAVORITE LISBON EXPERIENCES

On the Trail of Fado in the Alfama *Fado* means "fate" or "destiny," and its sad lament to lost love and glory is heard nightly in the little houses of the Alfama (also the Bairro Alto). Women swathed in black (called fadistas, as are male fado singers) are accompanied by 12-stringed guitars. Listening to these melancholic, gut-wrenching songs is the quintessential Lisbon experience.

A Day at the Beach Lisbon is not considered a resort, yet it lies near two of the fabled beach resorts of Europe: Estoril and Cascais along the Costa do Sol. An electric train in half an hour or so will deliver you to a day of surf and sun. In the evening you can enjoy the food, fado, and nightlife, even gambling at the Estoril Casino.

Shopping for Handcrafts One of the irresistible reasons to go to Lisbon is to shop till you drop. A nation of artisans displays its finest wares in its capital: ceramics, embroidery (from both the Azores and Madeira), silver, elegant porcelain, gleaming crystal, *azulejos* (tiles), handwoven rugs, and hand-knit sweaters—the list seems endless.

An Afternoon in Sintra Some savvy travelers claim that after visiting Sintra, the rest of Europe becomes a footnote. Follow in the footsteps of Portuguese kings and queens of yore and head for Byron's "glorious Eden." Byron was not alone in proclaiming the village of Sintra as "perhaps the most delightful in Europe." Even the sometimes skeptical Spanish proclaim: "To see the world and yet leave Sintra out/Is, verily, to go blindfold about." Join the Romantics and perhaps you'll come under its spell, too.

Open: June–Oct, Tues, Thurs–Fri, and Sun 10am–5pm; Wed and Sat 2–7:30pm. Nov–May, Tues–Sun 10am–5pm. **Metro:** Sebastião or Palhava. **Tram:** 24. **Bus:** 16, 18, 26, 31, 42, 46, or 56.

2. MORE ATTRACTIONS

THE BAIRRO ALTO

Like the Alfama, the Bairro Alto (upper city) preserves the characteristics of the Lisbon of yore. It once was called the heart of the city, probably for both its location and its houses, streets, and inhabitants. Many of its buildings were left intact during the 1755 earthquake. Today it is the home of some of the finest fado cafes in Lisbon, making it a center of nightlife, but it is also a fascinating place to visit during the day, when its lasting charm of narrow cobblestone streets and alleys, lined with ancient buildings, can be enjoyed.

The Bairro Alto, originally called Vila Nova de Andrade, was started in 1513 when part of the huge Santa Catarina farm was sold to the Andrade family, who sold the land as plots for construction. Early buyers were carpenters, merchants, and ship caulkers, who must have been astute businessmen: At least some of them immediately resold their newly acquired land to aristocrats, and little by little noble families moved to the quarter. The Jesuits followed, moving from their modest College of Mouraria to new headquarters at the Monastery of São Roque, where the *Misericórdia* (social assistance to the poor) of Lisbon is still carried on today. As often happens, the Bairro Alto gradually became a working-class quarter. Today the quarter is also the domain of journalists, since most of the big newspapers have their plants here. Writers and artists have been drawn here to live and work, attracted by the ambience and the good cuisine of local restaurants.

The area is a colorful one. From the windows and balconies, streamers of laundry hang out to dry, and here and there are cages of canaries, parrots, parakeets, and other birds. In the morning the street scene is made up of housewives coming out from their homes to shop for food, probably attracted by the cries of the *varinas* (fishmongers) and other vendors, some pushing creaky, heavily laden carts, and some, usually women, trudging by with baskets of fresh vegetables. Women lounge in doorways or lean on windowsills to watch the world go by.

The Bairro Alto blooms at night, luring visitors and natives with fado, food, discos, and small bars. Lisbon's budget restaurants, the *tascas,* proliferate here, together with more deluxe eateries. Victorian lanterns light the streets, along which people stroll leisurely.

BULLFIGHTING

Bullfighting in Portugal was once the sport of noblemen. In Portuguese bullfights, the bull is not killed, a prohibition instituted in the 18th century by a prime minister, the marquês de Pombal, after the son of the duke of Arcos was killed in the sport. The Portuguese bullfight differs in other respects from the Spanish version. The drama is attended with much ceremony and pageantry, and the major actors are elegantly costumed *cavaleiros,* who charge the bull on horseback, and *macos de forcado,* who grapple with the bull in face-to-face combat—for many, this is the most exciting event.

Warning: The bullfight is not for everyone. Even though the animal is not killed, many readers find the spectacle nauseating and take strong objection to the idea that it is beautiful or an art form. The spears that jab the bull's neck draw blood, of course, making the unfortunate animal visibly weaker. The so-called fight has been labeled "No contest!" One reader wrote, "The animals are frightened, confused, and badgered before they are mercifully allowed to exit. What sport!"

The season is from Easter until around mid-October. Lisbon's 8,500-seat **Praça de Touros,** Campo Pequeno, Avenida da République (tel. 793-20-93; reached on the Metro to its own stop) is the largest ring in the country; it usually presents fights on Thursday and Sunday afternoons in season. These *touradas* and the names of the stars are announced well in advance. Your hotel concierge can be of help to you; many arrange tickets.

Another major bullring is the **Monumental de Cascais,** at Cascais (tel. 73-66-01), the resort lying west of Estoril on the Costa do Sol. The electric train from Lisbon ends its run in Cascais; from the station, an inexpensive taxi will take you to the bullring itself, just outside the town center. The best place to buy tickets is, of course, right at the arena's ticket office. However, for the best seats, it is perhaps advisable to pay the usual 10% commission to an agency. The best one is Agência de Bilhetes para Espectaculos Públicos, whose offices are at Avenida da Liberdade 140 (tel. 32-75-24), Praça dos Restauradores (tel. 36-95-00), and Parque Mayer (tel. 37-25-94). Tickets generally cost 2,000$ ($12.20) to 8,000$ ($48.80).

CHURCHES

"If you want to see all of the churches of Lisbon, you'd better be prepared to stay here for a few months," a guide once told a tourist. What follows is a selection of the most interesting churches.

PANTEÃO NACIONAL [IGREJA DE SANTA ENGRÁCIA; National Pantheon], Campo de Santa Clara. Tel. 888-15-29.

When a builder starts to work on a Portuguese house, the owner will often chide, "Don't take as long as St. Engrácia." Construction on this Portuguese baroque church with its four square towers began in 1682; it resisted the 1755 earthquake but wasn't completed until 1966. Now the Church of Santa Engrácia is so well planned and built that relief and architectural idiosyncracies would have been welcomed. The com-

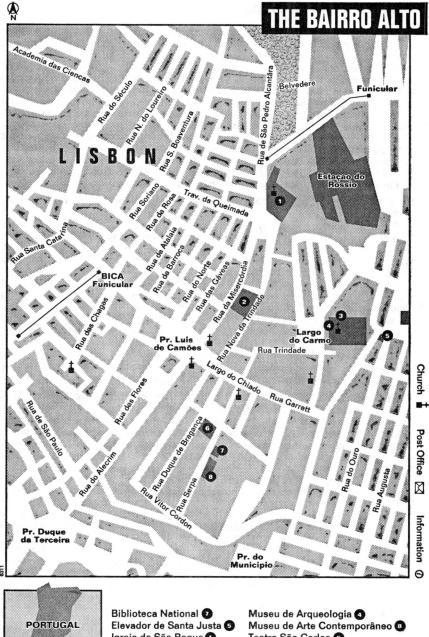

THE BAIRRO ALTO

N

Academia das Ciencas

Rua do Século

Rua N. do Loureiro

Rua S. Boaventura

Rua de São Pedro Alcântara

Belvedere

Funicular

LISBON

Estaçao do
Rossio

Rua Soriano

Rua de Rosa

Trav. da Queimada

Rua da Atalaia

Rua da Barroca

Rua do Norte

Rua das Gáveas

Rua Santa Catarina

BICA
Funicular

Rua da Misercórdia

Rua das Chagas

Rua Nova da Trindade

② Teatro Trindade

Pr. Luis
de Camões

Largo
do Carmo

③
④
⑤

Rua Trindade

Rua das Flores

Largo do Chiado

Rua Garrett

Rua de São Paulo

Rua Alecrim

Rua Duque de Bragança

⑥
⑦
⑧

Rua Serpa

Rua do Ouro

Rua Augusta

Pr. Duque
da Terceira

Rua Vitor Cordon

Pr. do
Municipio

Church ✝

Post Office ⊠

Information ℹ

6311

PORTUGAL

LISBON ★

Biblioteca National ⑦
Elevador de Santa Justa ⑤
Igreja de São Roque ①
Igreja do Carmo ③

Museu de Arqueologia ④
Museu de Arte Contemporâneo ⑧
Teatro São Carlos ⑥
Teatro Trindade ②

pleted building appears pristine and cold, and the state has fittingly turned it into a neoclassic National Pantheon, containing memorial tombs to Portuguese heads of state and other greats and not-so-greats.

Memorials honor Henry the Navigator; Luís Vaz de Camões, the country's greatest poet; Pedro Alvares Cabral, discoverer of Brazil; Afonso de Albuquerque, viceroy of India; Nuño Alvares Pereira, warrior and saint; and Vasco da Gama, of course. Entombed in the National Pantheon are presidents of Portugal and several writers; Almeida Garrett, the outstanding 19th-century literary figure; João de Deus, lyric poet; and Guerra Junquiero, also a poet.

Ask the guards to take you to the terrace for a beautiful view over the river. A visit to the pantheon can be combined with a shopping trip to the Flea Market (walk down the Campo de Santa Clara, heading toward the river).

Admission: 150$ ($0.90) adults; children under 10 free; free Sun.
Open: Tues–Sun 10am–5pm. **Closed:** Holidays. **Bus:** 9 or 46.

MUSEU ARQUEOLÓGICO [Archeological Museum], Largo do Carmo. Tel. 346-04-73.

Standing in its ruins today, you can only imagine the glory of the former 14th-century Carmo Church. On the morning of November 1, 1755, the church was crowded for All Saints' Day. Then the earth shook. The roof cracked and buckled. When the debris was cleared, only a Gothic skeleton remained. For some reason, the Carmo Church was never reconstructed.

Silhouetted against the Lisbon sky are the chancel, apse, and the Great Door, a section of which has been converted into an archeological museum. This museum contains collections of prehistoric weapons and implements, Roman and Visigothic pieces, pottery, statues, *azulejos*, and South American mummies, among other treasures. There are a great number of stone inscriptions in Latin, Hebrew, Arabic, and Portuguese.

Admission: 300$ ($1.80) adults; children under 10 free.
Open: Tues–Sun 10am–6pm. **Directions:** The museum is best reached by taking the Santa Justa elevator from the Rua do Ouro below. **Bus:** 15 or 100.

IGREJA DA SÃO VICENTE DE FORA [St. Vincent Outside the Walls], Largo de São Vicente. Tel. 86-25-44.

In this Renaissance church, the greatest names and some forgotten wives of the House of Bragança were placed to rest. It's really a pantheon. Originally a convent from the 12th century, the church was erected between 1582 and 1627. At that time it was outside the walls of Lisbon. On the morning of the 1755 earthquake, the cupola fell in.

The Braganças assumed power in 1640 and ruled until 1910, when the Portuguese monarchy collapsed and Manuel II and the queen mother, Amélia, fled to England. The body of Manuel II was subsequently returned to Portugal for burial. Amélia, the last queen of Portugal, died in 1951 and was also entombed here, as were her husband, Carlos I, the painter king, and her son, Prince Luís Felipe, both killed by an assassin at Praça do Comércio in 1908.

Aside from the royal tombs, one of the most important reasons for visiting St. Vincent is to see its *azulejos* (glazed earthenware tiles), some of which illustrate the fables of La Fontaine. I suspect no one's officially counted them, but their number is placed at a million. Look for a curious ivory statue of Christ, carved in the former Portuguese province of Goa in the 18th century.

Admission: 150$ (90¢) adults; children under 10 free.
Open: Tues–Sun 10am–1pm and 2:30–5pm. **Bus:** 12 or 28.

MUSEUMS

CENTRO DE ARTE MODERNA [Center for Modern Art], Rua Dr. Nicolau de Bettencourt. Tel. 79-35-131.

Around the corner from the entrance to the Calouste Gulbenkian Museum, the Center for Modern Art is the first major permanent exhibition center of modern Portuguese artists to open in Lisbon. The center shares parklike grounds with the

Gulbenkian Foundation and was, in fact, a gift left in the legacy of the late Armenian oil magnate.

It is housed in a British-designed complex of clean lines and dramatically proportioned geometric forms, with a Henry Moore sculpture in front. The museum owns some 10,000 artworks. It displays the work of many modern Portuguese artists, some of whom enjoy world fame: Souza-Cardoso, Almada, Paula Rego, João Cutileiro, Costa Pinheiro, and Vieira da Silva.

Admission: 200$ ($1.20) adults; children under 10 free; free Sun.

Open: June–Sept, Wed and Sat 2–7:30pm; Tues, Thurs–Fri, and Sun 10am–5pm. Oct–May, Tues–Sun 10am–5pm. **Metro:** Praça de Espanha. **Bus:** 16 or 31.

FUNDAÇÃO RICARDO ESPIRITO SANTO [Museum of Decorative Art], Largo das Portas do Sol 2. Tel. 85-21-83.

The decorative arts school museum is a foundation established in 1953 through the vision and generosity of Dr. Ricardo do Esprito Santo Silva, who endowed it with items belonging to his personal collection and set up workshops of handcrafts in which nearly all activities related to the decorative arts are represented. The handsomely furnished museum is in one of the many aristocratic mansions that used to grace the Alfama. The principal aim of the foundation is the preservation and furtherance of the decorative arts by maintaining the traditional character of the handcrafts while developing the craftspersons' skills and culture. In the workshops you can see how perfect reproductions of furniture and other objects are made in the purest styles. The foundation also restores furniture, books, and Arraiolos rugs. The workshops may be visited on Wednesday.

The museum has been given the appearance of an inhabited palace by placing objects in appropriate surroundings. Visitors can have a fairly accurate picture of what might have been the interior of an upper-class Lisbon home in the 18th and 19th centuries. There are outstanding displays of furniture, Portuguese silver, and Arraiolos rugs, all from the 17th through the 19th century, with 16th-century silver included.

Close to the museum is a bar where visitors may have a rest, snacks, or drinks.

Admission: 200$ ($1.20).

Open: Tues–Sat 10am–1pm and 2:30–5pm. **Tram:** 28. **Bus:** 37.

MUSEU NACIONAL MILITAR [National Military Museum], Caminhos de Ferro. Tel. 888-21-31.

This museum, in front of the Santa Apolónia Station, not far from Terreiro do Paço and Castelo São Jorge (St. George's Castle), is on the site of a shipyard built during the reign of Manuel I (1495–1521). Later, during the reign of João III, a new foundry for artillery was erected that was also used for making gunpowder and storing arms to equip the Portuguese fleet. A fire damaged the buildings in 1726, and the 1755 earthquake destroyed them completely. Rebuilt at the order of José I, the complex was designated as the Royal Army Arsenal. The museum, originally called the Artillery Museum, was created in 1851. Today the facility exhibits not only arms but also painting, sculpture, tiles, and specimens of architecture.

The museum has one of the world's best collections of historical artillery. There are bronze cannons of various periods; one of these is from Diu, weighing 20 tons and bearing Arabic inscriptions. Some iron pieces date from the 14th century. Light weapons, such as guns, pistols, and swords, are displayed in cases.

Admission: 150$ (90¢) adults; 75$ (50¢) children.

Open: Tues–Sat 10am–4pm, Sun 11am–5pm. **Metro:** S. Apolónia. **Bus:** 9, 39, 46, or 90.

MUSEU RAFAEL BORDALO PINHEIRO, Campo Grande 382. Tel. 759-08-16.

Rafael Bordalo Pinheiro was a 19th-century ceramicist and caricaturist, and this museum honors his memory. Actually, it's one of the most esoteric museums in Lisbon and is of little interest to the average North American visitor, unless he or she knows something about Bordalo Pinheiro's day—that is, 19th-century Portuguese life and the scandals of the literati and politicians. In his caricatures he poked fun at some of the most distinguished people of his day.

Bordalo Pinheiro's crustacean and reptilian ceramics are marvelous caricatures. Search out the portrait of Bordalo Pinheiro, by Columbano, the outstanding Portuguese painter who died in 1929.

Admission: 150$ (90¢) adults; children under 18 free; free Sun.

Open: Tues–Sun 10am–1pm and 2–6pm. **Metro:** Campo Grande. **Bus:** 1, 17, 36, or 47.

MUSEU ST. ROQUE, Largo Trindade Coelho. Tel. 346-03-61.

The St. Roque Church was founded in the late 16th century by the Jesuits. With its painted wood ceiling, the church contains a celebrated chapel honoring John the Baptist by Luigi Vanvitelli. The chapel was assembled in Rome in the 18th century with such precious materials as alabaster and lapis lazuli, then dismantled and shipped to Lisbon, where it was reassembled. It was ordered by the Bragança king João V, 9 years before the end of his reign in 1750. The marble mosaics look like a painting. You can also visit the sacristy, rich in paintings illustrating scenes from the lives of the Society of Jesus saints. The Jesuits held great power in Portugal, at one time virtually governing the country for the king.

The St. Roque Museum inside is visited chiefly for its collection of baroque silver. A pair of bronze-and-silver torch holders, weighing about 840 pounds, is considered among the most elaborate in Europe. The 18th-century gold embroidery is a rare treasure, as are the vestments. The paintings are mainly from the 16th century, including one of a double-chinned Catherine of Austria and another of the wedding ceremony of Manuel I. Look for a remarkable 15th-century *Virgin (with Child) of the Plague* and a polished 18th-century conch shell that served as a baptismal font.

Admission: 150$ (90¢); children under 10 free.

Open: Tues–Sun 10am–5pm. **Metro:** Restauradores. **Tram:** 20 or 24. **Bus:** 15 or 100.

OTHER SIGHTS

Those sights in and around Lisbon that could not be categorically listed elsewhere are highlighted below. Some reveal much about the nation's natural resources, geography, climate, inhabitants, and life-style, and it is the knowledge of these that makes you far more than just a tourist passing through.

MARKETS The big market of Ribeira Nova is as close as you can get to the heart of Lisbon. Near the Cais do Sodré, where trains are boarded for the Costa do Sol, an enormous roof shelters a collection of stalls offering the produce you'll be eating later at one of Lisbon's fine restaurants. Foodstuffs are brought in each morning in wicker baskets bulging with oversize carrots, cabbages big enough for shrubbery, and stalks of bananas. Some of the produce arrives by donkey; some by truck; some balanced on the heads of Lisboan women in Mediterranean fashion—all from yesterday's field. The rich soil produces the juiciest of peaches and the most aromatic tomatoes.

"Seeing-eye" fishing boats, many believed to have been based on Phoenician designs, dock at dawn with their catch. The fish are deposited on long marble counters: cod, squid, bass, hake, swordfish. Soon the *varinas* take wicker baskets of the fresh catch, balancing them on their heads, and climb the cobbled streets of the Alfama or the Bairro Alto to sell fish from door to door.

At the market, the mounds of vegetables, fruit, and fish are presided over by hearty, outgoing Portuguese women gaily clad in voluminous skirts and calico aprons. On cue, the vendors begin howling out the value of their wares, stopping only to pose for an occasional snapshot.

Adjoining the market, away from the river, cut-stone streets are flanked with shops selling inexpensive Portuguese clothing. The best buy, if you can locate one, is a distinctively styled cape from the Alentejo district. In three tiers, these capes are often capped with red-fox collars.

ESTUFA FRIA (THE GREENHOUSE) The Portuguese call it their Estufa Fria in handsomely laid out Parque Eduardo VII (tel. 388-22-78), named after Queen

Victoria's son to commemorate his three trips to Lisbon. Against a background of streams and rocks, tropical plants grow in such profusion that some writers have called it a "sylvan glade"; so luxuriant is its growth that it evokes a rain forest.

The park lies at the top of the Avenida da Liberdade, crowned by a statue of the marquês de Pombal, with his "house pet," a lion. There's a 75$ (50¢) admission charge to the greenhouse, which is open daily from 9am to 5:30pm in April through September, daily from 9am to 4:30pm in October through May. Metro: Rotunda. Bus: 2, 11, 12, 27, 32, 38, 44, 45, or 83.

CEMITÉRIO DOS INGLESES [BRITISH CEMETERY]   Up the Rua da Estrêla at one end of the Estrêla Gardens lies the British Cemetery. It's famous as the burial place of Henry Fielding, the novelist (*Tom Jones*) and dramatist. A sick man, Fielding went to Lisbon in 1754 for his health, and the story of that trip is narrated in a posthumous tract, *Journal of a Voyage to Lisbon*. He reached Lisbon in August and died 2 months later. A monument honoring him was erected in 1830. Ring the bell for entry.

AQUEDUTO DAS AGUAS LIVRES [AGUAS LIVRES AQUEDUCT]   An outstanding baroque monument, this aqueduct runs from the Aguas Livres River in Caneças to the Casa da Agua reservoir in Amoreiras. The aqueduct, built under João V in the early 18th century, runs for about 11 miles and is visible from the highway (N7) that leads to Sintra and Estoril. Part of it is underground, but the above-ground section allows some of the 109 stone arches to be seen. The best view is of the 14 arches stretching across the valley of Alcântara from Serafina to the Campolide hills. More information is available by calling the Water Museum, **Museu de Agua,** Rua de Alviela 12 (tel. 83-55-32), which is open Tuesday through Saturday from 10am to 12:30pm and 2 to 5pm.

ELEVADOR DE SANTA JUSTA [SANTA JUSTA ELEVATOR]   For a splendid rooftop view of Lisbon, take the Santa Justa elevator, Rua de Santa Justa, an ornate concoction often attributed to the man who built that tower in Paris, the French engineer Alexandre-Gustave Eiffel. However, the elevator was actually built by a Portuguese engineer, Raoul Mesnier de Ponsard, born to French immigrants in Porto in 1849. He graduated in mathematics and philosophy at Coimbra, then studied in France, Germany, and Switzerland. The elevator goes from Rua Aurea, in the center of the shopping district near Rossio Square, up to the Carmo Church. It operates daily from 7am to 11pm. A ticket costs 140$ (90¢) for everyone; children under 4 are free. Metro: Rossio.

BOTANICAL GARDEN   Connected with the National Costume Museum is the Parque do Monteiro-Mor, Largo Julio de Castilho, Lumiar, one of Lisbon's most beautiful botanical gardens, where you'll find a restaurant (tel. 759-03-18). The park is open June through September daily from 10am to 6pm and October through May daily from 10am to 5:30pm. Admission is 200$ ($1.20); Sunday morning is free; children under 10 are free. Bus: 1 or 36.

3. COOL FOR KIDS

JARDIM ZOOLÓGICO DE LISBOA [Zoological Garden], Parque dos Laranjeiras. Tel. 726-84-47.
Jardim Zoológico, with a collection of some 2,000 animals, enjoys a flower-filled setting in the 65-acre Park of Laranjeiras, about a 10-minute subway ride from the Rossio. There are also a small tram and rowboats.
Admission: 490$ ($3) adults; 300$ ($1.80) ages 3–8.

Open: Daily 10am–6pm. **Metro:** Sete Rios. **Bus:** 15, 16, 16C, 26, 31, 46, 58, 63, or 68.

PLANETÁRIO CALOUSTE GULBENKIAN [CALOUSTE GULBENKIAN PLANTARIUM] Praça do Império. Tel. 362-00-02.

Annexed to the Maritime Museum, the planetarium is open to the public all year, with sessions on Wednesday and Thursday at 11am and 3 and 4pm and on Saturday and Monday at 4 and 5pm. On Monday at 11am is a special session for children when admission is free for everybody. Each session lasts 50 minutes.

Admission: 300$ ($1.80) adults, 200$ ($1.20) children 6–16 (under 6 not allowed). **Bus:** 29, 43, or 49.

AQUÁRIUM VASCO DA GAMA, Rua Direita do Dafundo. Tel. 419-63-37.

Aquárium Vasco da Gama, on the N6, near Alges on the Cascais railway line, has been in operation since 1898. Live exhibits include a pavilion containing eared seals, plus a vast number of tanks for fish and other sea creatures from all over the world. A large portion of the exhibits consists of zoological material brought back by Carlos I on oceanographic expeditions. They include preserved marine invertebrates, water birds, fish, mammals, and some of the king's laboratory equipment.

Admission: Adults June–Sept, 300$ ($1.80), Oct–May, 200$ ($1.20); 100$ (60¢) ages 10–18; children under 10 and adults over 65 free.

Open: June–Oct, daily 10am–6pm; Nov–May, daily 10am–5:30pm. **Metro:** Algés. **Bus:** 23, 29, 50, or 51.

4. WALKING TOURS

WALKING TOUR 1 — THE ALFAMA

Start: Largo do Salvador.
Finish: Miradouro Santa Luzia.
Time: 2 hours; more if you add sightseeing time.
Best Time: Any sunny day.
Worst Time: Twilight or after dark.

The streets of the Alfama are rarely suitable for a car; at times you must walk up steep stone stairs. Once aristocratic, this fabled section of Lisbon has now fallen into seedy decay. Parts of it are like wandering back in a time capsule. Note that the Alfama can be dangerous at night.

A good point to begin your tour is:

1. **Largo do Salvador** (a taxi can take you to this point). Here you'll see a 16th-century mansion that once belonged to the count of Arcos. From there, turn down Rua da Requeira, leading to:
2. **Beco do Carneiro,** the "cul-de-sac of rams." The lane couldn't be narrower. Families live in houses 4 feet (if that much) apart. At the end of the alley, circle back via a flight of steps to your left to:
3. **Largo de Santo Estevão,** named after the church on the site. Round the church and from the back proceed to the:
4. **Pátio das Flores,** via a flight of steps. Here you can see some of the most delightful little houses fronted with characteristic Portuguese tiles (*azulejos*). Walk down the steps to the Rua dos Remedios, cutting right to:
5. **Largo do Chafariz de Dentro,** where you're bound to see Alfama housewives busily gossiping in front of an old fountain. From the square, you connect with:

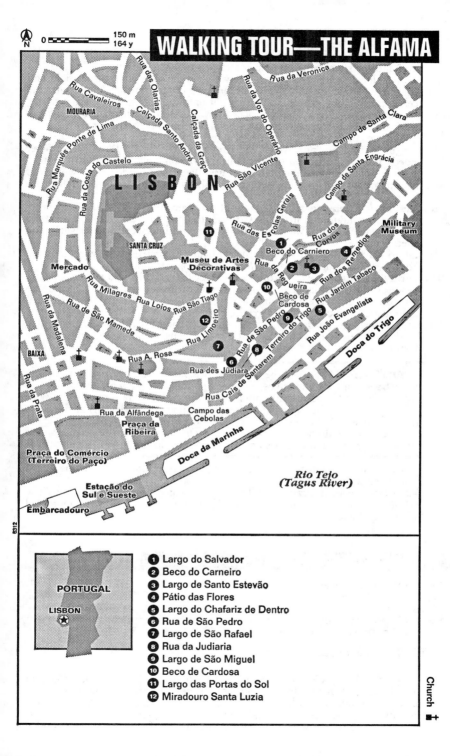

WALKING TOUR—THE ALFAMA

0 ⌐━━━ 150 m
164 y

MOURARIA

Rua Cavaleiros
Rua das Olarias
Calçada Santo André
Calçada da Graça
Rua da Voz do Operário
Rua da Veronica
Rua Marquês Ponte de Lima
Rua da Costa do Castelo
Rua São Vicente
Campo de Santa Clara
Campo de Santa Engrácia
Campo de Santa Engrácia

LISBON

Rua das Escolas Gerais

Rua dos Corvos

Military Museum

SANTA CRUZ

⓫ Largo das Portas do Sol

Mercado

Museu de Artes Decorativas

❶ Largo do Salvador
Beco do Carnieiro
❸ Largo de Santo Estevão
❹ Pátio das Flores
Rua da Regueira
Rua dos Remedios
Rua Jardim Tabaco

Rua Milagres   Rua Loios   Rua São Tiago

Rua de São Mamede

Rua da Madalena

❿ Beco de Cardosa

⓬ Largo de São Miguel ❾
❺ Largo do Chafariz de Dentro
Rua João Evangelista

Doca do Trigo

BAIXA

Rua A. Rosa
Rua Limoeiro
❼
❽ Rua de São Pedro
Terreiro do Trigo
Rua des Judiara

❻

Rua da Prata

Rua Cais de Santarem

Rua da Alfândega

Campo das Cebolas

Praça da Ribeira

Praça do Comércio
(Terreiro do Paço)

Doca da Marinha

Rio Tejo
(Tagus River)

Estação do
Sul e Sueste

Embarcadouro

8312

PORTUGAL

LISBON ★

❶ Largo do Salvador
❷ Beco do Carneiro
❸ Largo de Santo Estevão
❹ Pátio das Flores
❺ Largo do Chafariz de Dentro
❻ Rua de São Pedro
❼ Largo de São Rafael
❽ Rua da Judiaria
❾ Largo de São Miguel
❿ Beco de Cardosa
⓫ Largo das Portas do Sol
⓬ Miradouro Santa Luzia

Church ■✝

6. **Rua de São Pedro,** perhaps the most animated street in the Alfama. Strolling deep into the street, you'll probably attract a trail of children.

Some local taverns will pass before you, and the most adventurous sightseers will venture inside to sample a glass of *vinho verde* (green wine). Later, your head reeling from several glasses, you'll step out onto the narrow street again where, chances are, you'll be virtually knocked down by an old fisherman with saffron- and brown-colored nets draped over his shoulder, as he heads for the sea.

Rua de São Pedro leads into:

7. **Largo de São Rafael,** which will convince you that the 17th century never ended. You pass a *leitaria* (dairy), which now sells milk by the bottle instead of via the old-fashioned method (cows were kept right inside, as the women of the Alfama wanted to make sure their milk was fresh). Right off the square is:

8. **Rua da Judiaria,** so called because of the many Jews who settled there after escaping the Inquisition in Spain. Go back to Largo de São Rafael, crossing to rejoin Rua de Sã Pedro. Walk down the street to the intersection, forking left. You enter:

9. **Largo de Sã Miguel,** with its church richly decorated in the baroque style. From there, walk up Rua da São Miguel, cutting left into:

10. **Beco de Cardosa,** where from some flower-draped balcony a *varina* is bound to scream hell and damnation to her street urchin son if he doesn't come up immediately. At the end of the alley, you connect with Beco Sta. Helena, a continuation, which leads up several flights to:

11. **Largo das Portas do Sol.** On this square is the Museum of Decorative Art, handsomely ensconced in one of the many mansions that used to grace the Alfama.

REFUELING STOP At the Miradouro Santa Luzia are several tiny little **cafe/bars** with outside tables. Visitors from all over the world come here to order coffee and refreshments and soak up the view. There is always plenty of shipping activity in the Tagus. Since these cafes and bars are virtually all the same, select the one with the best view. The best of the lot is **Cerca Moura,** back at Largo das Portas do Sol (see above), as it offers the finest menu of snacks and drinks in the area and also has an "oh, that view" location.

Continue south down Rua Limoeiro until you reach one of the Alfama's most fabled belvederes:

12. **Miradouro Santa Luzia,** a "balcony" from which you can view the sea. The belvedere overlooks the houses of the Alfama as they sweep down in a jumbled pile to the Tagus.

WALKING TOUR 2 —— BAIXA AND THE CENTER

Start: Praça do Comércio.
Finish: Rua Garrett.
Time: 3 hours.
Best Time: Any sunny day except Sunday, when shops are closed.
Worst Time: Monday to Saturday from 7:30 to 9am and 5 to 7pm.

The best place to begin this tour is:

1. **Praça do Comércio** (also known as Terreiro do Paço). This is the waterfront end of Baixa, where the House of Bragança came to an end with the assassination of Carlos I and his elder son, Luís Filipe. Regrettably, employees in the surrounding government buildings use it as a parking lot, thereby destroying its harmony. The square was completed to the design of the marquês de Pombal

1. Praça do Comércio
2. Cais do Sodré
3. Rua Augusta
4. Rossio
5. Avenida de Liberdade
6. Praça dos Restauradores
7. Estação do Rossio
8. Elevador de Santa Justa
9. Largo do Carmo
10. Igreja do Carmo
11. Rua Garrett

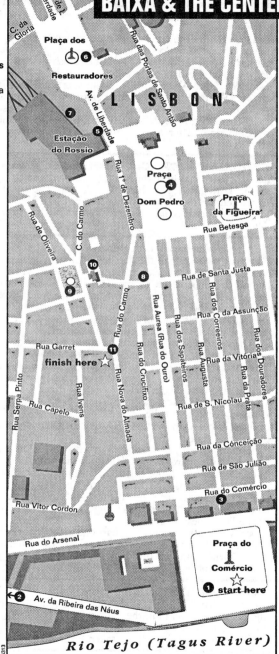

Praça dos Restauradores

LISBON

Plaça dos

Estação do Rossio

Praça Dom Pedro

Praça da Figueira

Rua Betesga

Rua de Santa Justa

Rua de Oliveira

C. do Carmo

Rua da Assunção

Rua Garret

finish here ☆

Rua Nova do Almada

Rua Aurea (Rua do Ouro)

Rua dos Correiros

Rua dos Sapateiros

Rua Augusta

Rua da Vitória

Rua dos Douradores

Rua da Prata

Rua do Crucifixo

Rua de S. Nicolau

Rua Serpa Pinto

Rua Capelo

Rua Ivens

Rua da Cónceição

Rua de São Julião

Rua do Comércio

Rua Vítor Cordon

Rua do Arsenal

Praça do Comércio ☆ start here

Av. da Ribeira das Náus

Rio Tejo (Tagus River)

Church ✝ ■   Post Office ☒   Information ⊙

when he rebuilt Lisbon following the 1755 earthquake. The equestrian statue there is of Dom José, king at the time of the earthquake.

From the square, head west along Avenida da Ribeira das Náus until you reach:
2. Cais do Sodré, the train station. As you walk along you can enjoy views of the Tagus. Once at Cais do Sodré, you will come on an open-air waterfront produce market behind the station. The Ribeiro fish market takes place on this square daily (except Sunday) from dawn in a domed building on the right. *Varinas* (fishwives of the Alfama) still come here to carry away huge baskets of the fresh catch of the day that they deftly balance on their heads.

Return to Praça do Comércio, but this time take a street away from the river, going east along Rua do Arsenal until you reach the northwest corner of Praça do Comércio. After all that walking, especially if it's a hot day, you may need a:

REFUELING STOP   Café Martinho da Arcada, Praça do Comércio 3 (tel. 87-92-59), has been the haunt of the literati since 1782, attracting such greats as the Portuguese poet Fernando Pessoa. The old restaurant here has gone upmarket, but there's still an adjacent cafe and bar. If you're here for lunch, ask for a savory kettle of fish called *cataplana* or clam stew, served in the style of the Algarve.

After dining, head north along:
3. Rua Augusta, one of the best-known shopping streets of Baixa. Leather stores and bookshops, along with embroidery outlets and even home furnishings stores, line the bustling street. Many of the cross streets through this grid have been closed to traffic, making window shopping easier. Glittering jewelry stores, often with some good buys in gold and silver, attract your attention, as do many delis with their vast offerings of Portuguese wine and cheese along with endless arrays of those pastries of which Lisboans are so fond.

The western part of this grid of streets is known as the Chiado. Long known as the most sophisticated shopping district of Lisbon, the area was swept in 1988 by a devastating fire, destroying many shops, particularly those on the periphery of Rua Garrett. As you explore the area directly west of Rua Augusta, you'll see reconstruction still going on.

Rua Augusta leads into the:
4. Rossio, technically called Praça Dom Pedro IV. The Rossio (or principal square of Baixa) dates from the 1200s. During the reign of the dreaded Inquisition, it was the setting of many an *auto-da-fé,* in which Lisboans turned out to witness the torture and death of an "infidel," often a Jew. This was the heart of Pombaline Lisbon as the marquês rebuilt it following the 1755 earthquake. Neoclassical buildings from the 1700s and 1800s line the square, and there is an array of cafes and souvenir shops. The 1840 Teatro Nacional de D. Maria II sits on the north side of the square, occupying the former Palace of the Inquisition. That statue on its facade is of Gil Vicente, "Portugal's Shakespeare," credited with the creation of the Portuguese theater.

Crowds cluster around two baroque fountains at either end of the Rossio. The bronze statue on a column is of Pedro IV, for which the square is named. (He was also crowned king of Brazil as Pedro I.) The tawdry and overly commercial atmosphere of the Rossio is softened by dozens of flower stalls.

REFUELING STOP   Café Nicola, Praça Dom Pedro IV 24–25 (tel. 346-05-79), dates from 1777 but earned its most enduring fame as a gathering place of the Portuguese literati in the 19th century. It is the single most popular cafe in Lisbon. Short on charm, it nevertheless dispenses pastries and endless cups of coffee, plus meals that can be taken both indoors and out.

From the Rossio, proceed to the northwest corner of the square and walk onto the satellite square, Praça da Camara. If you continue north, you'll reach the beginning of the:

5. Avenida de Liberdade, the main street of Lisbon, laid out in 1879. Cutting through the heart of the city, more than 300 feet wide, the avenue runs north for a mile. Once flanked with art deco or belle époque mansions, it has long been hailed as the most splendid boulevard of Lisbon, although much of that long-ago architecture is now gone. Its sidewalks are tesselated in black and white. This is also the heart of Lisbon's cinemaland, along with airline offices, travel agencies, and outlets of various companies located in Lisbon. An open-air *esplanada* is in the center. Almost immediately you come to:

6. Praça dos Restauradores, named for the men who in 1640 revolted against the reign of Spain, an event that led to the reestablishment of the independence of Portugal. An obelisk in the center of the square commemorates that long-ago event. Pálacio Foz, now the Ministry of Information, is also on the square. It was designed by an Italian architect in a deep red.

West of the square is the:

7. Estação do Rossio, the main rail terminus of Lisbon. This is one of the strangest architectural complexes for a rail terminal in Europe. It is built in a mock Manueline style like a lavishly adorned palace. Trains from Sintra and the Estremadura pull right into the virtual heart of the city. Trains leave from a platform an escalador ride above the street-level entrances. A bustling station, it is filled with facilities, including souvenir shops and currency-exchange offices.

At this point if you'd like to walk the long mile of the Avenida da Liberdade, you can do so, all the way to the Praça Marquês de Pombal, with its monument to the prime minister who rebuilt Lisbon. North of the square, you can stroll through Parque Edouard VII. However, if you'd like to see more of the heart of Lisbon, you can continue south from Praça dos Restauradores.

Walk south again along Avenida da Liberdade, following in your previous footsteps, to Praça Dom João da Câmara. Except this time, instead of returning to Rossio, continue directly south along Rua 1 de Dezembro, which will become Rua do Carmo. This street will lead you to the:

8. Elevador de Santa Justa, at the junction of Rua Aurea and Rua de Santa Justa. This elevator, built in 1902 and often falsely attributed to Alexandre-Gustave Eiffel, who designed the fabled tower of Paris, is inside a Gothic-style tower. In no more than a minute you are whisked from Baixa to the Bairro Alto and the:

9. Largo do Carmo, center of the "upper town," which extends to the west of Baixa. Like Baixa, it is laid out in a grid. Instead of following a prescribed walking tour of the Bairro Alto, many visitors at this point prefer to get lost as they wander the narrow cobbled streets of the barrio. The upper town grew up in the 17th century, almost most of the buildings today were constructed in the two centuries following.

On Largo do Carmo stands the former:

10. Igrega do Carmo, a late 14th-century Carmelite church that has been turned into an archeological museum. You can wander through the ruins of the church—once the largest in Lisbon—that was mainly destroyed in the 1755 earthquake.

From Largo do Carmo, head south along Calç. do Sacramento to:

11. Rua Garrett, the principal shopping street of the Chiado. It is lined with department stores and many turn-of-the-century buildings. Shoppers come here, of course, but nostalgia buffs often frequent the street for only one reason, which provides our final:

REFUELING STOP On Saturday and Sunday nights at **A Brasileira,** Rua Garrett 120 (tel. 346-95-41), you can listen to a wandering guitar player serenading the late-night brandy drinkers. This is another of the historic cafes of Lisbon, once catering to the literati, including the Portuguese poet Fernando

Pessoa. This is called the quintessential fin-de-siècle coffeehouse of Lisbon. It's a great place to go for an aromatic cup of strong Brazilian espresso.

5. ORGANIZED TOURS

Lisbon travel agents will book you on organized tours. One of the most popular agencies is **Star Travel,** the representative of American Express at Praça dos Restauradores 14 (tel. 346-03-36).

Touristic Lisbon has two daily departures year round—9:30am and 2:30pm. This 3-hour tour takes in all the highlights, including St. George's Castle and Belém. The cost is 4,500$ ($27.50) per person.

A 10-hour Lisbon, Mafra, Estoril, and Quéluz tour, also operated year round, costs 11,500$ ($70.20), including lunch. Departures are at 9:30am. A half-day tour takes in the highlights of Sintra and Estoril, with departures at 2:30pm, costing 6,500$ ($39.70). An 11-hour tour to Óbidos, Nazaré, and Fátima departs at 8:30am; it costs 12,500$ ($76.30), including lunch.

6. EASY EXCURSIONS

Few people are content to confine their visits to just Lisbon—not with so many major attractions on the city's doorstep. All these attractions are highlighted in Chapter 8. For those who'd like to stay at some of the places in the environs, certainly at Estoril or Cascais, hotels will be previewed, along with plenty of restaurants for those seeking only luncheon stopovers on day trips.

If time is limited, try to visit **Sintra** if nothing else, seeing its two royal palaces. The pink rococo **Quéluz Palace** is a confectionary delight worth visiting. Sintra lies about 18 miles from Lisbon, and Quéluz is 9 miles from Sintra.

A major draw in summer are the neighboring resorts of **Estoril** and **Cascais.** Those with even more time can extend their stay to visit such places as **Mafra Palace** and **Guincho.**

CHAPTER 7

LISBON SAVVY SHOPPING & EVENING ENTERTAINMENT

1. SHOPPING
- **FROMMER'S SMART TRAVELER: SHOPPING**

2. EVENING ENTERTAINMENT

Shopping and nightlife are combined in this chapter, like a horse and carriage, because they are equally essential to appreciating a holiday in Portugal. Instead of looking for one shop, many visitors prefer to tour a district. A good starting point is the Praça do Comércio, the "end" of the Baixa district opening onto the Tagus.

Just north of this district, you can wander the major shopping streets, especially Rua Augusta (see "Shopping Areas," below), hunting what you're looking for or discovering what you thought you didn't need. After that, the Santa Justa elevator in the district will transport you to the Bairro Alto, where you can explore the shops on the hill, notably Rua Garrett.

The Bairro Alto might also be the place to go after dark, especially if you're in search of fado clubs and *típico* restaurants. On the other hand, many visitors prefer to seek out a dining spot or a little fado club in the Alfama. The Bairro Alto is much easier to get around at night. Don't go walking in the Alfama after dark; arrive by taxi at your destination. Reports of night muggings there are commonplace.

Hearing fado music is like listening to the soul of Portugal, and it is the rare visitor who doesn't want to take in this unique art form. These emotionally charged songs are sung by *fadistas* (both men and women; never *fadistos*). Most fado clubs offer typical nightclub food and drink. Go late, as true fadistas don't appear until after 11pm.

Cultural Lisbon is interesting, too. If you don't speak fluent Portuguese most theater is out, however. The opera season extends from mid-September through July, and ballet (sponsored by the Ministry of Culture) is performed by the Companhia Nacional de Bailado during a three-month spring season. Tourist offices in Lisbon can keep you appraised of cultural events.

1. SHOPPING

Portuguese handcrafts often have exotic influences because of the versatility of the Portuguese and their skill in absorbing other styles. The best showing of their work is in Lisbon, for shopkeepers and their buyers hunt out unusual items in the Madeira Islands and the Azores as well as in their own country.

It is still possible to bargain in Lisbon, although it is not looked on kindly in the more prestigious shops. Use both your sixth sense and common sense. A good yardstick is whether a store is managed by its owner, as smaller ones usually are; in owner-managed stores, you might work out a deal.

SHOPPING AREAS Baixa is the major area for browsing, but shops are spread all over the city. Baixa is the district forming downtown Lisbon. **Rua do Ouro** (Street of Gold, where the major jewelry shops can be found), **Rua da Prata** (Street of Silver), and **Rua Augusta** are Lisbon's three principal streets for shopping. The Baixa shopping district lies between the Rossio and the River Tagus.

Rua Garrett is another major shopping artery, found in the Chiado, site of many of the more upmarket shops. Many of these shops were destroyed in a major 1988 fire, and several have not reopened. To reach the area, you can take the Santa Justa elevator near the Rossio.

Antiques lovers gravitate to the **Rua Dom Pedro V** in the Bairro Alto, although other streets with antiques stores include Rua da Misericórdia, Rua São Pedro de Alcântara, Rua da Escola Politécnica, and Rua do Alecrim.

HOURS, SHIPPING & TAXES Most stores open at 9am, close at noon for lunch, reopen at 2pm, and close for the day at 7pm. However, many shopkeepers like to take lunch from 1 to 3pm, so check before making the trip. On Saturday, most stores in Lisbon, and elsewhere in Portugal, are often closed.

Many establishments will crate and ship bulky objects. Any especially large item, such as a piece of furniture, should be sent by ship. Every antiques dealer in Lisbon has lists of reputable maritime shippers. For most small and medium-size shipments, air freight isn't much more expensive than ship. TAP, the Portuguese airline, offers shipping service from Portugal to New York. At any of its gateway cities, TAP can arrange to have your purchase transferred to another airline for shipment.

Remember that all your air cargo shipments will need to clear Customs after they're brought into the United States, Canada, or your home country. This involves some additional paperwork and perhaps a trip to the airport near where you live. It's usually wiser to hire a commercial Customs broker to do the work for you.

Emery Worldwide, a division of CF Freightways, can clear your goods for around $100 for most shipments. For information, you can call toll free in the United States: 800/443-6379.

If you wish to send a package home—usually of a smaller variety—you can do so by packing it in your luggage, unless you're worried about possible breakage. If you are afraid of going beyond your luggage allowance, you can send a package home at most major post offices. Appear with your merchandise, string, and tape at the post office. There are limitations on the duty-free goods you can bring back to the United States. Packages go to the U.S. Customs office upon their arrival in the States.

For Americans, goods valued at less than $50 can be delivered by a postal carrier. If the value of your package is more than $50, you must pay the amount the Customs people assess. Your postal carrier is entitled to collect the additional charges. It is illegal, incidentally, to ship liquor to the United States through the mails.

Items carried with you and purchased abroad are duty free up to $400. Anything beyond that is assessed a duty of 10% up to the nearest $1,000. For example, if you bring back purchases of $1,400, you are allowed a $400 exemption but must pay another $100 for the additional $1,000 of goods.

Value-added tax (called IVA in Portugal) is about 12% to 17% on most items. Foreigners with valid passports can get a refund if their purchases in one store add up to about 11,700$ ($71.30). To be granted this refund, ask the shop at which you purchased the merchandise to fill out a Tax Free Check.

When you leave Portugal, show your purchases (which must be carried by hand and not checked with your luggage) to the Portuguese Custom officials, along with your passport. If everything is in order, your Tax Free Checks will be stamped and you can redeem them at a Tax Refund counter for cash. Tax Refund offices are found at both the airport and the Lisbon harbor.

BEST BUYS Especially good handcrafts buys from the Azores and Madeira can be found in Portugal, including handmade embroideries, such as blouses, napkins, tablecloths, and handkerchiefs; products made of cork, from placemats to cigarette boxes; and *azulejos* (decorative glazed tiles). From Vista Alegre come porcelain and china; there are fishermen's sweaters from Nazaré; local pottery; and, of course, fado records.

Considered a good buy in Portugal, gold is strictly regulated by the government, which requires jewelers to put a minimum of 19¼ karats in jewelry made of this expensive metal. Filigree jewelry in gold and silver is all the rage not only in Lisbon but also elsewhere in Portugal. This art of ornamental openwork made of fine gold or silver wire dates back to ancient times. The most expensive items—often objets d'art—are fashioned from 19¼-karat gold. Depictions of caravels are one of the forms this art expression takes. However, less expensive trinkets are often made of sterling silver, which might be dipped in 24-karat gold.

Portugal is also famous for its Arraiolos carpets. In Alentejo and Ribatejo, you can actually visit the little town of Arraiolos where these fine woolen rugs that have earned an international reputation are sold. Legend says these rugs were first made by Moorish craftsmen expelled from Lisbon in the early 16th century. The designs were said to be in imitation of those from Persia. Some of these carpets eventually find their way into museums.

SHOPPING A TO Z

ANTIQUES

Along both sides of the narrow **Rua de S. José** are treasure troves—shops packed with antiques from all over the world. Antiques dealers from America come here to survey the wares. You'll find ornate spool and carved beds, high-back chairs, tables, wardrobes with ornate carving or of time-seasoned woods, brass plaques, copper pans, silver candelabra, crystal sconces, and chandeliers, plus a wide selection of old wooden figures, silver boxes, porcelain plates, and bowls. But don't count on super bargains.

SOLAR, Rua Dom Pedro V 68–70. Tel. 346-55-22.

Rua Dom Pedro V is another street of antiques shops, of which my personal favorite is Solar. It is stocked with antique tiles salvaged from some of Portugal's historic buildings and manor houses. The condition of the tile varies, of course. Many go back as far as the 15th century. The store also sells antique furniture and pewterware.

ART GALLERIES

GALERIA 111, Campo Grande 113. Tel. 797-74-18.

Galeria 111 is recognized as one of the major art galleries of Lisbon, a distinction it has shared since 1964. Some of the leading contemporary Portuguese artists are on display here in a wide-ranging exhibition of sculpture, painting, and graphics. It also sells drawings, etchings, silk screens, lithographs, art books, and postcards. Annual closing is from August 10 to September 8.

GALERIA SESIMBRA, Rua Castilho 77. Tel. 387-02-91.

Near the Ritz Hotel, this is one of the leading art galleries of Lisbon, operated by one of the most distinguished art dealers of Iberia. Mainly Portuguese artists are displayed here, but foreign artists "who have lived in Portugal long enough to get a feeling for the country" are also exhibited. The finest of Portuguese painting, sculpture, and ceramics are sold here. Its best-known works for sale, however, are Agulha tapestries—composed of a controlled variation of stitching, giving them an advantage over those made on looms. Many artists have turned to this new medium for depth and movement in their work. Their size can range from 10 square feet to the "longest tapestry in the world."

BOOKS

LIBRARIA BERTRAND DO CHIADO, Rua Garrett 73–75. Tel. 346-86-46.

This corner bookstore in the Chiado district has a large selection of titles in English. It also has travel material, such as good maps of Portugal.

CARPETS

CASA QUINTÃO, Rua Ivens 30–34. Tel. 346-58-37.

In Lisbon, the showcase for Arraiolos carpets is Casa Quintao, where rugs are priced by the square foot, according to the density of the stitching. Casa Quintao can reproduce intricate Oriental or medieval designs in rugs or tapestries as well as create any custom pattern. The shop also sells materials and gives instructions on how to make your own carpets and tapestry-covered pillows. The staff seems genuinely willing to help.

CHINA & GLASSWARE

VISTA ALEGRE, Largo do Chiado 18. Tel. 347-54-81.

This company turns out some of the finest porcelain dinner services in the land, along with objets d'art and limited editions for collectors and a range of practical day-to-day tableware. Since its 1824 founding, kings of Portugal used to be frequent customers, and the government still presents Vista Alegre pieces to papal or crowned heads of Europe as mementos of their visits here.

CORK PRODUCTS

CASA DAS CORTIÇAS, Rua da Escola Politécnica 4–6. Tel. 342-58-58.

For something typically Portuguese, try Casa das Cortiças. "Mr. Cork," the original owner, became somewhat of a legend in Lisbon for offering "everything conceivable" that could be made of cork, of which Portugal controls a hefty part of the world market. He is long gone now, but the store carries on. You'll be surprised at the number of items that can be made from cork, including a chess set and a checkerboard. Perhaps a set of six placemats in a two-tone checkerboard style will interest you. For souvenirs, the cork caravels are immensely popular. Other items include a natural cutting board and ice bucket.

EMBROIDERY

CASA REGIONAL DA ILHA VERDE, Rua Paiva de Andrade 4. Tel. 342-59-14.

The specialty here is handmade items, especially embroideries from the Azores—that's why it's called the Regional House of the Green Island. Each piece carries a made-by-hand guarantee. Some of the designs used on the linen placemats with napkins have been in use for centuries. You can get some good buys here.

MADEIRA HOUSE, Rua Augusta 131–135. Tel. 342-68-13.

Madeira House specializes in high-quality cottons, linens, and gift items. Its other location in Lisbon is at Avenida da Liberdade 159.

PRÍNCIPE REAL, Rua da Escola Politécnica 12–14. Tel. 346-59-45.

Príncipe Real specializes in linens elegant enough to grace the tables of monarchs, including that of the late Princess Grace of Monaco. This family-run store produces some of Europe's finest tablecloths and sheets in cotton, linen, and organdy. Although the Rockefellers, Michael Douglas, and the Kennedys have purchased items here from its owner/designer, the merchandise (especially with beneficial escudo exchange rates) is not beyond the means of a middle-class tourist. About two dozen staff members can execute a linen pattern to match a client's favorite porcelain, or the owner can create one of her own designs.

FASHION

ANA SALAZAR, Rua do Carmo 87. Tel. 347-22-89.

In the Chiado district, Ana Salazar, an internationally known name in fashion, is considered the most avant-garde designer for women's clothes in the entire country. Her clothes are worn by the fashion conscious in such cities as New York and Paris. Known for her stretch fabrics, Salazar designs clothes that critics have called "body-conscious yet wearable."

MARKETS

Feira da Ladra, is a place where you can haggle and enjoy the fun of getting a bargain. This open-air street market is like the flea markets of Madrid and Paris. Nearly every possible item that can be purchased is seen here in the street stalls. For the finest pickings, it's best to go in the morning. The vendors peddle their wares on Tuesday and Saturday.

About a 5-minute walk from the waterfront, in the Alfama district, the market sits behind the Maritime Museum, adjoining the Pantheon of São Vicente. Start your browsing at the Campo de Santa Clara. Portable stalls and individual displays are lined up on this hilly street with its tree-lined center.

You can often pick up a bargain here, but you must search diligently through masses of cheap clothing and lots of junk. Everything from brass scales, oil lamps, portable bidets, cow bells, and old coins to Macau china, antique watches, and Angola wood carvings is on display. Take bus no. 12 from Santa Apolónia Station.

SHOPPING MALLS

CENTRO COMERCIAL DAS AMOREIRAS, Avenida Duarte Pacheco. Tel. 69-25-58.

The most spectacular shopping complex in Lisbon, this is the largest in Iberia and the fourth biggest in Europe. You can wander through this Oriental fantasy, exploring the contents of more than 300 shops and boutiques. A huge array of merchandise is offered, including Portuguese fashion, leather goods, crystal, and souvenirs. In addition to several restaurants and snack bars, there is a health center. The location is on a hill at the entrance to Lisbon, lying in back of the old Aguas Livres reservoir. The blue-and-pink towers rise 19 stories and have already changed the skyline of Lisbon. The mall is open daily from 10am to midnight. Take bus no. 11, 15, or 23.

APOLO 70, Avenida Julio Dinis 10. Tel. 797-15-94.

Apolo 70, near the bullring, is a self-contained unit that includes everything from an interior sidewalk cafe to a cinema and a leather shop. Wander for an hour or two among the 38 shops, making purchases at a teenage boutique, getting your photograph blown up to poster size, or having your hair styled by experts; then you can stop in the lower level's cozy bar for a cooling drink. Also on the lower level is a restaurant that vaguely evokes a merry-go-round. Metro: Campo Pequeno.

ESTAÇÃO DO ROSSIO, between Praça dos Restauradores and Praça Dom Pedro IV (Rossio).

There are some 150 boutiques, shops, and snack bars installed in four of the five floors of the Rossio Railway Station, in the heart of downtown Lisbon. The fifth floor is where trains arrive and depart. Banks of escalators whisk you from floor to floor, and shopping in the maze of small shops is easier than walking on the congested streets. Conveniently, the shops are open every day from 9am to midnight. The street floor is deceptively shabby—ignore it and take the escalator to the boutiques. You'll find apparel for men, women, and children, as well as shops specializing in jewelry, fado records, and so forth. There are a pharmacy for "naturalists," beauty parlors, hairdressers, bookstores, leather goods, sweaters, and Portuguese handcrafts.

SILVER, GOLD & FILIGREE

JOALHARIA DO CARMO, Rua do Carmo 87B. Tel. 342-42-00.

Well on its way to being a century old, this is one of the best shops in Lisbon for filigree work. It stocks everything from simple but elegant pendants to models of fully rigged caravelles fashioned entirely from thin strands of gold and/or silver woven together. Some of the gold pieces have been further adorned with either precious or semiprecious stones.

W. A. SARMENTO, Rua Aurea 251. Tel. 342-67-74.

At the foot of the Santa Justa elevator, W. A. Sarmento has been in the hands of the same family for well over a century. The shop has been the favorite place for

---

 FROMMER'S SMART TRAVELER: SHOPPING

1. Read "Hours, Shipping & Taxes," above. There's red tape, but refunds can mean substantial savings.
2. Tune your haggling skills in the open-air markets of Lisbon. You can come up with good buys with strong, steady, and firm bargaining.
3. If you pay cash, some smaller stores will lower the price.
4. Look for sudden sales, when merchandise prices are slashed.
5. Don't assume that because a certain product is "made in Portugal" it's cheaper to buy it in Portugal. It pays to know what something costs at home before you make a substantial purchase.

Lisboans to buy treasured confirmation and graduation gifts, and it has customers among the Costa do Sol aristocracy as well as movie stars and diplomats. They are the most distinguished silver- and goldsmiths in Portugal, specializing in lacy filigree jewelry. For additions to your charm bracelet, Sarmento is the place to go; there are literally dozens of choices. The shop is a member of the tax-free-for-tourists system.

TILE

FÁBRICA CERAMICA VIÚVA LAMEGO, Largo do Intendente 25. Tel. 315-24-01.
Founded in 1849, this shop offers contemporary tile, mostly reproductions of old Portuguese motifs, and also pottery, including an interesting selection of birds and animal motifs. When you reach the address, you'll know you're at the right place: Its facade is decorated with these colorful *azulejos* with figures in their rich plumage and dress.

SANT'ANNA, Rua do Alecrim 95–97. Tel. 342-25-37.
Founded in 1741 in the Chiado district, Sant'Anna is Portugal's leading ceramic center, famous for its *azulejos* (glazed tiles). The showroom is at the Rua do Alecrim location, but you can also visit the factory at Calcada da Boa Hora 96; however, you must telephone ahead to make an appointment at 342-85-81. Some of the designs that decorate the tiles are created by artisans who are among the finest in Europe, and many of them employ designs in use since the Middle Ages. Bargains I bought recently include a group of framed scenic azulejos, a two-holder candelabrum, a tiled hors d'oeuvres tray, and a 3-foot-high ceramic umbrella stand.

2. EVENING ENTERTAINMENT

If you have only one night in Lisbon, spend it at a *fado* club. That same sentiment holds true if you have two or even three nights. The nostalgic sounds of fado, Portuguese "songs of sorrow," are heard at their best in Lisbon, as the Portuguese capital attracts the greatest *fadistas* (fado singers) in the world. However, don't go to hear fado and plan to carry on a private conversation; it's considered bad form. For more information about fado, refer to "Art, Architecture, Literature & Music" in Chapter 1.

Most of the authentic fado clubs are clustered near one another in the Bairro Alto or in the Alfama, between St. George's Castle and the docks. You can "fado hop" between these two typical quarters. Alfama-bound hoppers can ask the taxi driver to deliver them to **Largo do Chafariz,** a small plaza a block from the harbor, and Bairro Alto devotees can get off at **Largo do S. Roque.** Most of my recommendations lie only a short walk from either of these squares.

Fado outshines all other nighttime entertainment in Lisbon. However, for a change of pace, I've included suggestions for other tastes, including discos, bars, and even vaudeville-type places.

For more information about nighttime attractions, go to the tourist office, which has a list of major events being staged in Lisbon. Another helpful source is the **Agência de Bilhetes para Espectáculos Públicos** in the Praça dos Restauradores. It is open daily from 9am to 10pm, and you should show up in person instead of trying to call for information. This agency sells tickets to most theaters and cinemas, except the Teatro Nacional de São Carlos; for those tickets you should go to the theater's own box office (see below).

To obtain information, consult a copy of *What's On in Lisbon,* available at most newsstands. Your hotel concierge is also a good bet for information, since one of his or her duties is reserving seats.

The local newspaper, *Diário de Notícias,* carries all cultural listings, but the information is presented only in Portuguese. No special discount tickets are offered, except students get 50% off on tickets purchased for the national theater (see "Theater" under "The Performing Arts," below).

THE PERFORMING ARTS
OPERA & BALLET

TEATRO NACIONAL DE SÃO CARLOS, Rua Serpa Pinto 9. Tel. 346-84-08.
Teatro Nacional de São Carlos attracts opera and ballet aficionados from all over Europe. Top world companies perform at this 18th-century theater. The season begins in mid-September and extends through July. The box office is open daily from 1 to 7pm. There are no special discounts. Bus: 15 or 100.
Tickets: 500$–10,800$ ($3–$65.80).

CLASSICAL MUSIC

MUSEU DA FUNDAÇÃO CALOUSTE GULBENKIAN, Avenida de Berna 45. Tel. 793-51-31.
From October through June, concerts and recitals—and occasionally ballet—are performed here; sometimes there are also jazz concerts. You'll have to inquire locally about what is happening at the time of your visit. Metro: Sebastião or Palhava. Bus: 16, 18, 26, 31, 42, 46, or 56.
Tickets: Prices vary according to event.

TEATRO MUNICIPAL DE SÃO LUÍS, Rua Antonío Maria Cardoso 40. Tel. 32-71-72.
Chamber-music concerts and symphony presentations are often performed here. Check locally to see if anything is featured. Metro: Estação Cais do Sodré.
Tickets: Prices vary according to event.

THEATER

TEATRO NACIONAL DE D. MARIA II, Praça Dom Pedro IV. Tel. 347-10-78.
This is the most famous theater in Portugal, with a season that usually begins in the autumn and lasts through spring. It presents a repertoire of both Portuguese and foreign plays, and since its a national theater, performances are strictly in Portuguese. Students with valid ID get a 50% discount. Metro: Rossio.
Tickets: 1,000$–4,000$ ($6.10–$24.40).

THE CLUB & MUSIC SCENE
FADO CLUBS

In the clubs listed below, it isn't necessary to have dinner. You can always go later and order just a drink. However, you often have to pay a minimum consumption charge.

The music begins between 9 and 10pm, but it's better to arrive after 11pm. Many of the clubs stay open till 3am, others, till dawn.

A SEVERA, Rua das Gaveas 51. Tel. 346-40-06.

Good food and the careful selection of fadistas make this a perennial favorite. Before he became president, Richard Nixon selected it for a night on the town with his wife, Patricia, leading a congalike line between tables while warbling the refrain, "Severa . . . Severa . . . Severa." Every night top singers, both male and female, appear at this Bairro Alto nightspot, accompanied by guitar and viola music, alternating with folk dancers. In a niche you'll spot a statue honoring the club's namesake, Maria Severa, the legendary 19th-century gypsy fadista. After midnight tourists seem to recede a bit in favor of loyal Lisbon habitués, who request and sometimes join in on their favorite fado number.

The kitchen turns out regional dishes based on recipes from the north of Portugal. For dinner, the favorite main-dish selection is chicken cooked in a clay pot. Before that, you might order *caldo verde*, green-cabbage soup. Another house specialty is stuffed squid. Those less experimental may request the steak of the house, fried in a clay dish. Expect to spend from 9,000$ ($54.90) up for a meal with wine. You can also visit just for drinks, paying the minimum below. The club is open Friday through Wednesday from 8pm to 3:30am. Bus: 20 or 24. Tram: 20 or 24.

Admission (including two drinks): 2,900$ ($17.60).

ADEGA MACHADO, Rua do Norte 91. Tel. 346-00-95.

This spot has passed the test of time and is today one of the favored fado clubs of Portugal. Formerly you could perhaps spot Edward G. Robinson or Vittorio de Sica listening to the incomparable Amália Rodrigues. Alternating with its fadistas are folk dancers whirling, clapping, and singing their native songs in colorful costumes. The dinner hour starts at 8pm, and the doors don't close till 3am, when the last fadista aficionado trails out humming his or her favorite song. The club is open daily; from November to March, it is closed on Monday.

Dinner is à la carte, and the cuisine is mostly Portuguese, with any number of regional dishes. House specialties include chicken in a pot, stuffed squid, steak Machado, roasted baby goat, and pork with clams. For dessert, I'd suggest almond cake made with nuts from the Algarve. Expect to spend 9,000$ ($54.90) for a complete meal. Guests often join the singers and folk dancers, carrying arched garlands of flowers as they parade around the crowded tables, singing "Marcha do Machado." Bus: 15 or 100. Tram: 20 or 24.

Admission (including two drinks): 2,900$ ($17.60).

COTA D'ARMAS, Beco de São Miguel 7. Tel. 295-95-06.

Nightclub cookery isn't always the best in Lisbon, but there is one restaurant that would rank among the top 10 in Lisbon, even if it didn't present a nightly program of "fado and folklore." The elegantly decorated Cota D'Armas is one of the leading attractions for those wishing to venture into the Alfama at night. You can arrive early for dinner, enjoying drinks in the bar decorated in the style of a regional stable. The upstairs dining room is graced with a hand-painted ceiling. The coat-of-arms (the English translation of the restaurant's name) is depicted on the export china of the East India Company. In winter, this setting is made even more inviting by an open fireplace; during dinner, a well-seasoned group of fadistas and guitar players entertain you with Portuguese songs and music. You can also go for lunch, except on Sunday, when it's closed all day. Dinner is served Monday through Saturday. Hours are 12:30 to 3pm and 7:30 to 11:30pm. Meals begin at 900$ ($5.40), mixed drinks are from 600$ ($3.60), and beer is 400$ ($2.40). Tram: 3 or 16. Bus: 9, 12, or 18.

Admission: Free.

LISBOA A NOITE, Rua das Gaveas 69. Tel. 346-85-57.

Electricity fills the air—the tempestuous Fernanda Maria is about to make her first appearance of the evening. Tossing down a shot of whisky offered by a waiter, she stands quietly, tensely clutching her black shawl. Then she comes forward, pauses, scans the audience, and pours forth all the fiery intensity of fado. You, too, may fall under her spell. Success has come to Fernanda—she owns the club.

The 17th-century-style setting is rustic yet luxurious (once this Bairro Alto club was a stable). Creating its present ambience are thick stone-edged arches, heavy hand-hewn beams, blue-and-white-tile walls, a round well with its original bucket, a collection of old engravings, antique guns, and pewter and copper. When it's cold, scented eucalyptus logs crackle in a high fireplace. In the rear is an open kitchen and charcoal grill, with an assemblage of spices, sausages, garlic pigtails, and onions hanging from the beams. It's customary to go here for dinner, enjoying such house specialties as dry codfish Fernanda Maria or steak Lisboa a Noite flambé. The price of an average meal is 9,000$ ($54.90). Hours are Monday through Saturday from 8pm to 3am. Tram: 20 or 24. Bus: 15 or 100.

Admission (including two drinks): 2,750$ ($16.70).

PARREIRINHA DA ALFAMA, Beco do Esprito Santo 1. Tel. 86-82-09.

Seemingly every fadista worth her shawl has sung at this old-time cafe, just a minute's walk from the dockside of the Alfama. It's fado and fado only that enthralls here, not folk dancing. You can order a good regional dinner beginning early, but it's suggested that you go toward the end of the evening and stay late. It's open daily from 8pm to 3am. In the first part of the program, fadistas get all the popular songs out of the way, then settle in to their own more classic favorites.

You can order a filling dinner for 5,000$ ($30.50), and the menu includes specialties from nearly every region of Portugal. The atmosphere is self-consciously taverna, with the walls hung with all sorts of Portuguese provincial oddities and photos of famous people who've been here. The singers selected by the management are first-rate. It's possible to visit just for drinks; mixed drinks cost from 900$ ($5.40). Bus: 37.

Admission (including one drink): 1,700$ ($10.30).

LUSO, Travessa da Queimada 10. Tel. 342-22-81.

Luso has long been one of the most famous and enduring fado and folkloric clubs of the Bairro Alto, although now it's become quite touristy. On a crowded street—often filled with waiting taxis and the sound of honking horns—the entertainment and the regional food are presented most nights to some 160 patrons. Most guests come for the fado and the entertainment, but full dinners are served, costing 4,200$ ($25.60). These are likely to include such specialties as *vieiras de peixe* (fish stuffed in a scallop shell) and *frango na Pucara* (chicken in a casserole). In air-conditioned comfort, guests can visit Monday through Saturday from 8pm to 3am. The show begins at 9:30pm, lasting until 11:05pm. Bus: 100.

Admission (including two national drinks): 2,000$ ($12.20).

DANCE CLUBS

AD LIB, Rua Barata Salgueiro 28. Tel. 356-17-17.

Ad Lib is a posh disco dreamed up by a clique of chaps who wanted an elegant place to drink and dance. On the top floor of a modern building, it doesn't call attention to itself with a sign outside. A uniformed attendant at the formal entrance checks on the intercom system to weed out undesirables. If you're well groomed and not drunk or drugged, you stand a good chance of scaling the citadel; even so, it's wise to telephone in advance.

Upstairs, you'll enter a penthouse with a bar on one level and tables and a dancing area on another. A plant-filled terrace provides a view of Lisbon by night. The decor is Oriental, with fine stone Buddhas from Macau, mirrors, and candles in red bowls. A disc jockey plays the newest continental and American records. Hours are Monday through Saturday from 11pm to 6:30am. Mixed drinks cost 800$ ($4.80) to 1,000$ ($6.10); beer costs 650$ ($3.90). Metro: Avenida.

Admission (including one drink): 8,000$ ($48.80).

THE BAR OF THE CAFÉ ALCÂNTARA/DISCO ALCÂNTARA MAR, Rua da Cozinha Económica 11. Tel. 363-7176.

Although much of the income for this establishment derives from its sophisticated restaurant (see Chapter 5), many habitués of Lisbon's nightlife search it out for its drinking and disco facilities. The bar is a sprawling yet intimate enclave of leather-covered banquettes, convivial chatter, and stiff drinks, priced at around 900$ ($5.50) for a whisky with soda and around 500$ ($3.10) for a beer. After imbibing a few, many night owls head across a narrow bridge to the disco, Alcântara Mar, for an evening of laser lights and electronic music from the far corners of Europe and the United States. The bar is open daily from 8pm to 3am, and the disco is open Wednesday through Sunday from 11pm to 7am. Bus: 57.

Admission to disco: 2,000$ ($12.20) nondiners; 1,200$ ($7.30) patrons of Café Alcântara.

HO LISBOA, Avenida Oscar Monteiro Torres 8B. Tel. 795-1598.

This is the most recent manifestation of a club long noted for an intruiging setting and a high-tech decor. Contained within three floors of flashing lights and electronic gimmicks, it attracts a widely divergent clientele. Mixed drinks cost from 850$ ($5.20) each.

Admission: 2,000$ ($12.20).

KREMLIN, Escadinhas da Praia 5. Tel. 60-87-68.

For at least a part of its history, the cellar-level premises here served as a stables for neighborhood horses and the supplies required to feed them. Today, Kremlin the most energetic and iconoclastic of Lisbon's discos, welcomes a very hip crowd of electronic music lovers who come in costumes probably inspired by counterculture circles throughout Europe. The decor changes about once a month: At presstime, the walls were covered with masks in dozens of variations. Entrance fees vary depending on the "whim" of the doorman when you happen to arrive. Beer costs 550$ ($3.30); a whisky with soda goes for 800$ ($4.80). Kremlin is open nightly from 11:30pm to 4am. Tram: 15, 16, 17, 18, 29, or 30. Bus: 14, 28, 32, 40, or 43.

Admission: 1,000$–5,000$ ($6.10–$30.50).

LOUCURAS, Avenida Pedro Alvares Cabral 35. Tel. 388-11-17.

Loucaras was originally built as a movie theater. Its spacious perimeter welcomes a well-dressed crowd of affluent young people who converse, meet, mingle, and dance to music imported from London, Los Angeles, and New York. The crowd is somewhat more conservative than that within the previously recommended Kremlin, although they have lots of energy available for conversing with newcomers from abroad. The club is open Friday and Saturday from 4 to 8pm, when it caters to a mainly teenage market. It reopens on Friday and Saturday from 11pm to 4am, attracting patrons mostly in their 20s and 30s. A beer costs 500$ ($3.05), a mixed drink from 600$ ($3.60). Bus: 9, 20, or 22. Metro: Rotunda.

Admission: 1,000$ ($6.10).

WHISPERS, Edificio Avíz, Avenida Fontes Pereira de Melo 35. Tel. 315-54-89.

Set near the Sheraton Hotel, this high-energy dance club has long been considered a staple on Lisbon's disco circuit. The latest recorded music is played at high volume (at least on the dance floor) for gyrating crowds. It is open daily from 11pm to 4am. Mixed drinks cost from 900$ ($5.50) each; beer costs from 380$ ($2.30). Metro: Picoas.

Admission (including one drink): 2,500$ ($15.30).

THE BAR SCENE

BACHUS, Largo da Trindade 9. Tel. 342-28-28.

In addition to its role as a restaurant, Bachus offers one of the capital's most convivial watering spots. In an environment filled with Oriental carpets, fine hardwoods, bronze statues, intimate lighting, and very polite uniformed waiters, you can hobnob with some of the most glamorous names in Lisbon. Late-night candlelit suppers are served in the bar. The array of drinks is international, costing from 600$ ($3.60); the spot is a good one in which to unwind in privileged circumstances. Open daily from noon to 2am. Bus: 15.

BORA-BORA, Rua da Madalena 201. Tel. 87-20-43.

A Polynesian bar might seem out of context in Lisbon, but its concept is all the rage in Iberia these days. If you have a yearning for fruited, flaming, and rum-laced drinks, you'll find imaginative variations here. The couches are comfortable and inviting, and you can take in the Polynesian art on the walls. Hamburgers and other fare are available to accompany your Pacific Ocean nectars. Hours are Monday through Saturday from 6pm to 2am. Beer costs 450$ ($2.70); mixed drinks begin at 1,000$ ($6.10). Metro: Rossio.

METRO E MEIO, Avenida 5 de Outubro 174. Tel. 797-59-97.

Metro e Meio can be spotted easily: A giant yellow ruler forms its facade. When renovating, the management discovered several grottolike rooms that had been hidden for decades. Now guests have a choice of rooms, with a central fireplace. The decor is formed by hand-loomed wallhangings, gilt mirrors, statues, hanging lamps, Victorian fringed shades, and contemporary paintings. Recordings are piped in. Whiskies begin at 650$ ($3.90), and you can order sandwiches and hamburgers at 650$ ($3.90) each. The bar stands near the Gulbenkian Museum and can be reached by bus no. 1, 44, or 45. Hours are Monday through Saturday from 6pm to 2am.

THE PANORAMA BAR, in the Lisboa Sheraton Hotel, Rua Latino Coelho 1. Tel. 57-57-57.

The Panorama Bar occupies the top floor of one of Portugal's tallest buildings, the 30-story Lisboa Sheraton. Consequently, the view by day or night features the old and new cities of Lisbon, the mighty Tagus, and many of the towns on the river's far bank. Amid a decor of chiseled stone and stained glass, a polite uniformed staff will serve you. You'll pay from around 1,000$ ($6.10) for a whisky and soda. The bar is open Monday through Friday from 10am to 1:30am and Saturday and Sunday from 4pm to 1:30am. Bus: 1, 2, 9, or 32.

PASSPORT, Rua Nova do Carvalho. Tel. 346-15-07.

The flashing neon sign in front promises bright lights and dancing. Once you're inside, the lights are cooler and the furniture is more Iberian than you might have expected. In many ways the leather, wood, and masonry accents imply a Portuguese village, and there's always the chance to meet new friends. The club is open daily from 10pm to 3:30am. Beer cost 350$ ($2.10); mixed drinks cost 800$ ($4.80). Bus: 1, 44, or 45.

PROCOPIO BAR, Alto de San Francisco 21A. Tel. 65-28-51.

Long a favorite of journalists, politicians, and foreign actors, the once-innovative Procopio has become a tried-and-true staple among Lisbon's watering holes. With a clientele of aging habitués, it might easily become your favorite bar—that is, if you can find it. It lies just off Rua de João Penha, which itself lies off the landmark Praça das Amoreiras. With turn-of-the-century decor, it leans heavily on nostalgia and a sense of Old Iberia. Guests sit on tufted red velvet, enjoying an atmosphere of stained and painted glass and ornate brass hardware. Procopio is open Monday through Saturday from 9pm to 3am, except during the annual August closing. A mixed drink costs from 850$ ($5.20), and beer goes for 350$ ($2.10). Tram: 10, 20, or 24. Bus: 9, 15, or 20.

TEXAS BAR, Rua Nova do Carvalho 24. Tel. 346-36-83.

Remember those movies of port cities showing red-neon lights flashing, drunken sailors staggering down labyrinthine narrow streets, a mixed bag of human flotsam unmatched since Jean Genet wrote of his "whores, thieves, pimps, and beggars"? These rip-roaring scenes live on in Lisbon, in the little streets near the dock area, where sailors hang out at bars named after western American states: Arizona, California, and Texas. The most popular, occasionally drawing some of the Ritz crowd, is the Texas Bar, a gutsy tavern under a bridge. A singer usually warbles a Portuguese version of an old country-and-western hit.

If you're a man alone (if you're a woman alone, stay away), you'll be surrounded on entering by the wildest assemblage of Gravel Gertie look-alikes this side of Barcelona or Marseilles. "Speak English?" is the typical query. One young man trying to escape answered a resounding, "No, Svenska," but a girl was found who spoke lilting Swedish. The Texas Bar accommodates all. When the fleet's in, and some fleet from some port is likely to be in all the time, this waterfront hotspot can be very rowdy. It is open daily from 11am to 4am. Once inside, you can order mixed drinks for 680$ ($4.10) or a beer for 370$ ($2.20). Tram: 17 or 18. Bus: 59.

GAY AND LESBIAN BARS

Though the following establishments cater mainly to gay men, lesbians are also welcome.

MEMORIAL, Rua Gustavo de Matos Sequeira 42. Tel. 396-88-91.

Memorial is near the narrow streets of the Bairro Alto and is considered a "household word" among the gay community of Lisbon. This disco caters mostly to gay men. Both Spanish and Portuguese are spoken by most of the staff, and newcomers will usually be able to strike up a conversation with one of the regulars. It's open Tuesday through Sunday from 10pm to 4am. A beer costs 500$ ($3.05).

Admission: 1,000$ ($6.10).

TRUMPS, Rua da Imprensa Nacionale 104B. Tel. 397-10-59.

Trumps lies near (but not in) the Bairro Alto. Although it tries to cater to both heterosexual and homosexual tastes, most of its clientele is composed of gay men. Contained within a large street-level room, it has a prominent dance floor, a spacious bar, and a staff that speaks French and Spanish. A beer costs 500$ ($3.05). Trumps is open Tuesday through Sunday from 11am to 3:30am. Popular with the expatriate community, this is the most sophisticated gay bar in Lisbon.

Admission: 1,200$ ($7.30) Fri–Sat only.

XEQUE MATE BAR, Rua de São Marçal 170. Tel. 347-28-30.

Xeque Mate mingles the down-home earthiness of an English pub with the futuristic black-and-silver trappings of a gay rendezvous. Set behind a discreet brass plaque on a steeply sloping street lined with 18th-century villas, it imposes no cover charge. Beer costs from 450$ ($2.70), whisky and soda from 600$ ($3.60). Xeque Mate is open nightly from 10pm to between 1:30 and 2am. A taxi is recommended, as public transport is difficult at night.

MORE ENTERTAINMENT

MOVIES   Major motion pictures are shown in Lisbon in their original languages, usually at one of the big cinemas along Avenida da Liberdade. First-run movie houses include **São Jorge,** Avenida da Liberdade 175 (tel. 57-91-44).

VAUDEVILLE   Just off the Avenida da Liberdade, in **Parque Mayer,** is a cluster of vaudeville and music halls, each offering a *revista,* a Portuguese revue similar in some respects to a Spanish *zarzuela.* In the park are a few restaurants and Coney Island–style fun-and-chance stalls, where Lisboans throw darts and win dubious prizes. Here you can feel the entertainment pulse of the people, seeing everything from popular singers to fadistas to acrobats to ballet dancers. Matinees are staged on Sunday at 4pm, and show time is nightly at 9:45pm. Tickets range from a low 650$ ($3.90) for the worst seats (definitely not recommended) to 1,800$ ($10.90) for a grand perch. One reader warns, "Ticket buyers should make sure they're seeking the vaudeville entertainment and not something else. We were at first misdirected to one of the pornographic skinflicks in the same area."

CHAPTER 8

ESTORIL, CASCAIS & SINTRA

The environs of Lisbon are so intriguing that many fail to see the capital itself, lured by Guincho (near the westernmost point in continental Europe), the Mouth of Hell, and Lord Byron's "glorious Eden" at Sintra. A day could be spent drinking in the wonders of the library at the monastery-palace of Mafra (Portugal's El Escorial), dining in the pretty pink rococo palace at Queluz, or enjoying seafood at the Atlantic beach resort of Ericeira.

However, the chief magnet remains the Costa do Sol, the string of beach resorts, such as Estoril and Cascais, that form the Portuguese Riviera on the northern bank of the mouth of the Tagus. In fact, if you arrive in Lisbon when the sun is shining and the air is balmy, you should consider heading for this cabana-studded shoreline. So near to Lisbon is Estoril that it's easy to dart in and out of the capital to see the sights or visit the fado clubs, while you spend your nights in a hotel by the sea. An inexpensive electric train leaving from the Cais do Sodré in Lisbon makes the trip frequently throughout the day and evening, ending its run in Cascais.

The sun coast is sometimes known as A Costa dos Reis, "the coast of kings," because of all the deposed royalty who have settled there—everybody from exiled kings to pretenders, marquesses from Italy, princesses from Russia, and baronesses from Germany. These people may live simply, as did the late Princess Elena of Romania (Magda Lupescu), a virtual recluse in an unpretentious villa; or they may insist on rigid court ambience, as did Umberto, the one-month (1946) king of Italy, who was forced into exile when a plebiscite went against the monarchy. Tending his cows in "baggy trousers and muddy boots" in Sintra was the count of Paris, the pretender to the throne of France; a descendant of Louis Philippe, he was the son of the duke of Guise. In 1969, another pretender, Don Juan, count of Barcelona, lost the Spanish throne when his son, Don Juan Carlos, was named successor by the late Generalísimo Franco. The count was once an officer in the British navy and is now a noted yachtsman. Other nobility include Joanna, the former queen of Bulgaria, and the Infanta Dona Maria Adelaide de Bragança, sister of the Portuguese pretender.

The Riviera is a microcosm of Portugal. Ride out on the train, even if you don't plan to stay there. Along the way you'll pass pastel-washed houses, with red-tile roofs and facades of antique blue and white tiles; miles of modern apartment dwellings; rows of canna, pines, mimosa, and eucalyptus; swimming pools; and in the background, green hills studded with villas, chalets, and new homes.

SEEING ESTORIL, CASCAIS, & SINTRA

Regrettably, the coast, like all major beach coasts in Europe, has become much too overbuilt, which detracts greatly from its charm. It has less traffic on weekdays than it does on Saturday and Sunday, when much of Lisbon drives out. If you have a choice, try to avoid weekends, especially from June through September.

Lisbon, of course, is the aerial gateway for the Costa do Sol and Sintra. Once in

WHAT'S SPECIAL ABOUT ESTORIL, CASCAIS & SINTRA

Towns/Villages
- Sintra, the goal of every tourist who sets foot in Portugal—longtime favorite summer residence of Portugal's kings.
- Estoril, the reigning resort along the Costa do Sol—favorite stamping ground of Europe's deposed royalty.
- Cascais, a humble fishing village whose mild climate and fine sand beach turned it into a bustling resort.

Beaches
- The Estoril Coast—Portugal's "Riviera"—stretching for some 20 miles west of Lisbon, filled with beaches that were once playgrounds of the wealthy but now appeal to all.

Castles & Palaces
- Palácio de Queluz, once a royal palace and inspired by Versailles—known for the fantasy of its decoration.

- Palácio Nacional de Sintra, until 1910 a royal palace, although most of it was constructed during the reign of Manuel the Fortunate.
- Palácio Nacional de Pena, another royal palace built in the mid-19th century in a mélange of styles ranging from Moorish to Baroque.
- Palácio Nacional de Mafra, modeled on Philip II's fabled El Escorial outside Madrid—built with gold and diamonds pouring in from the new colony of Brazil.

Ace Attractions
- Guincho, near the westernmost point on the continent of Europe—called Cabo da Roca. Guincho is known for its seafood restaurants, but the undertow at the beach is treacherous.
- Estoril Casino, glamour hub for international society, opening onto the formal gardens of Parque Estoril.

Lisbon, you can drive or take public transportation. That public transportation to Estoril and Cascais should definitely be the electric commuter train—never a local bus. Trains leave from the waterfront Cais do Sodré station (tel. 01/347-0181) in Lisbon, with departures every 15 to 30 minutes, depending on the time of day.

SUGGESTED 3-DAY ITINERARY

Day 1 While still based in Lisbon, visit the Palace of Queluz in the morning, then spend the rest of the day exploring the royal palaces of Sintra.

Days 2–3 Select either Estoril or Cascais for your hotel base and use it as a center for taking in the relaxed joys of Portugal's Costa do Sol. Spend the morning of the third day exploring Guincho at the westernmost tip of Europe.

1. ESTORIL

8 miles S of Sintra; 15 miles W of Lisbon

GETTING THERE By Train You can take an electric train from the waterfront Cais do Sodré station in Lisbon; the fare is 145$ (90¢) and departures are every 15 to 30 minutes for the half-hour trip. Service is daily from 5:30am to 2:30am.

By Bus As mentioned, you should take the electric train to Estoril; however, once in Estoril you can visit Sintra by bus. Departures from in front of the Estoril rail station are every 45 minutes during the day, costing 260$ ($1.60) for a one-way ticket (trip time: 40 minutes).

By Car From Lisbon, head west on Route 6 and try to avoid driving on weekends. Driving time depends entirely on traffic, which tends to be heavy almost day and night these days. The least traffic is Monday through Friday from 10am to 4pm. Rush hours are brutal, as is the rush to the beach on Saturday and Sunday before 10am and the rush back to Lisbon on Saturday and Sunday between 4 and 6pm. It might be better on your nerves to take the fast electric train and forget about driving along the coast altogether.

ESSENTIALS **Junta Turismo Costa do Estoril** is at Arcadas do Parque (tel. 468-01-13), across from the train station. The **telephone area code** is 01.

This chic resort along the Portuguese Riviera has long basked in its reputation as a playground of monarchs. Fading countesses arrive at the railway station, monarchs in exile drop in at the Palácio Hotel for dinner, the sons of assassinated dictators sunbathe by the pool—and an international joie de vivre pervades the air.

Once Estoril was a figment of the imagination of Fausto Figueiredo, the founding father of the deluxe Palácio and the Casino. Before World War I, Figueiredo envisioned hundreds of people strolling through the marble corridors and down mosaic sidewalks to the ocean as he gazed out over scrub pines and sandy hills. Before World War II, Estoril was firmly entrenched in the resort sweepstakes. As Nazi troops advanced across Europe, many collapsed courts fled to Estoril to wait out the war in a neutral country.

WHAT TO SEE & DO

Parque Estoril, in the center of town, is a magnificent piece of landscaping, a subtropical setting with plants swaying in the breeze. At night, when it's floodlit, fashionable guests go for a stroll. The palm trees studding the grounds have prompted many to call it "a corner of Africa." At the top of the park sits the **casino,** offering not only gambling but also international floor shows, dancing, and movies.

Across the railroad tracks is the beach, where some of the most fashionable women in Europe sun themselves on the peppermint-striped canvas chairs along the Tamariz Esplanade. The atmosphere is cosmopolitan and the beach sandy, unlike the pebbly strand at Nice. If you don't want to swim in the ocean, you can check in at an oceanfront pool for a plunge instead.

To the east is **São João do Estoril,** which also boasts a beach and many handsome private villas. Most visitors go here to dine and dance.

SPORTS & RECREATION In the foothills of Sintra, a 3-minute drive from the casino, lies the ✪ **Clube de Golf do Estoril,** Avenida da República (tel. 01/468-01-76). An attraction for international sports figures, it offers a fairway set against a vista of pine and mimosa. The quality of the course is so acclaimed as one of the finest in Europe that it is selected for international championship matches. Both a 9-hole and an 18-hole course are offered. Golfers play from around 7:30am till sunset daily.

Guests of the Palácio Hotel pay 2,800$ ($7.10) as greens fees (18 holes); others are charged 6,750$ ($41.20) on weekdays and 9,000$ ($54.90) on Saturday and Sunday. Golf clubs can be rented for 3,000$ ($18.30) per 18 holes.

WHERE TO STAY

EXPENSIVE

PALÁCIO HOTEL, Parque Estoril 4, 2765 Estoril. Tel. 01/468-04-00. Fax 01/468-48-67. 134 rms, 28 suites. A/C MINIBAR TV TEL

$ Rates (including breakfast): 18,000$–19,000$ ($109.80–$115.90) single; 20,000$–22,000$ ($122–$134.20) double; from 35,000$ ($213.50) suite. AE, DC, MC, V. **Parking:** Free.

⭐ Palácio Hotel is legendary as a retreat for exiled royalty and as a center of World War II espionage. At its 1930 debut, the Palácio received the honeymooning Japanese crown prince and his new bride. In time, other royalty would follow: Umberto of Italy and Don Juan, the count of Barcelona. During World War II, when people escaped with a case of jewels and the clothes on their back, diamonds, rubies, and gold were accepted instead of money.

The reception rooms are Pompeiian, with sienna-colored marble pillars, bold bands of orange, and handmade carpets. The series of intimate salons is ideal for a tête-à-tête.

The guest rooms are traditional, with fine furnishings plus baths with bidets and heated towel racks. The hotel opens onto the side of Estoril Park, which is capped by the casino. The beach is only a short walk away.

Dining/Entertainment: A major asset of the Palácio is the restaurant-grill Four Seasons (see "Where to Dine," below). You can also enjoy regional and international dishes in the Atlântico Restaurant, preceded by a drink in the Bar Estoril, which features piano entertainment. In the classic central drawing room, with black-and-white checkerboard marble floors, groups of antique furnishings are arranged for guests to have after-dinner coffee.

Services: 24-hour room service, babysitting, laundry/valet.

Facilities: Nearby championship tennis courts, special privileges at hotel's championship golf course, pool.

MODERATE

HOTEL ALVORADA, Rua de Lisboa 3, 2765 Estoril. Tel. 01/468-00-70.
Fax 01/468-72-50. 55 rms. A/C TV TEL
$ Rates (including breakfast): 8,700$ ($53.10) single; 15,000$ ($91.50) double. AE, DC, MC, V. **Parking:** Free.

Hotel Alvorada opened its doors in late 1969 to provide Iberian *pousada*-style living on a small scale, opposite the casino and the formally styled Parque Estoril. Just a 3-minute trek from the sands, it is recommended for its well-styled guest rooms, each of which has a balcony.

The public rooms are personalized and well conceived. Off the reception area, the drinking lounge is decorated with modern Portuguese paintings and provincial-style furnishings. The top-floor solarium offers a panoramic view of the sea. Only breakfast is served.

ESTALAGEM BELVEDERE, Rua Dr. António Martins 8, 2765 Estoril. Tel. 01/466-02-08. Fax 01/467-14-33. 24 rms. TEL
$ Rates (including breakfast): 10,500$ ($64.10) single; 16,600$ ($101.30) double. MC, V. **Parking:** Free. **Closed:** Nov. 14–29.

Estalagem Belvedere was built as a private villa during the Edwardian age and converted into a charming hotel some 25 years ago. It sits in a gracious neighborhood full of faded 19th-century residences, among century-old trees and gardens. Inside, the comfortable public rooms contain Iberian furnishings. Some of the guest rooms have TVs.

Dining/Entertainment: The cozy bar is filled with rustic bric-a-brac, and the dining room serves dinner only, from 7:15 to 10pm daily. The cuisine is both French and Portuguese.

Services: Laundry/valet, babysitting.

Facilities: Outdoor pool, sauna, solarium.

HOTEL ESTORIL-PRAIA, Estrada Marginal, 2765 Estoril. Tel. 01/468-18-11. Fax 01/468-18-15. 91 rms. TEL
$ Rates (including breakfast): 10,000$ ($61) single; 15,000$ ($91.50) double. AE, DC, MC, V. **Parking:** Free on street.

Hotel Estoril-Praia, built in the late 1950s next door to the glamorous Palácio, has

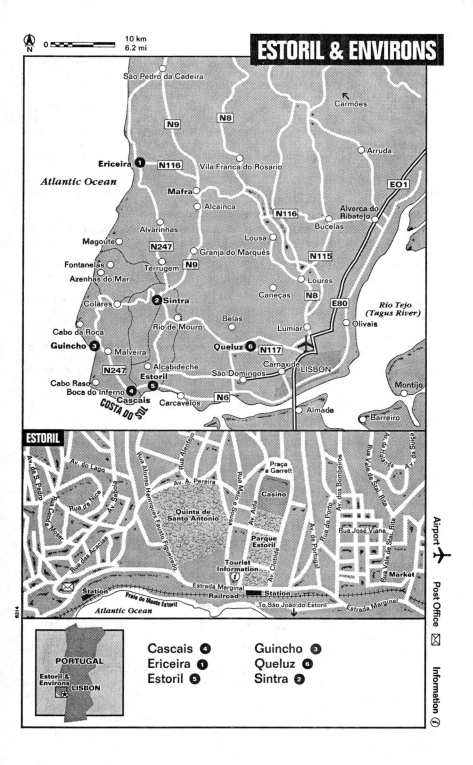

seven floors with walls of glass soaring high. About half the rooms boast good-sized balconies overlooking a view of the water and the casino with its formal gardens. Only a minute or so from the seafront and the electric train station, it is in the center of Estoril's boutique district.

Not only are the guest rooms trim, utilitarian, and uncluttered, but also many have sitting areas, with wood-grained pieces. French doors open onto balconies in most.

Dining/Entertainment: The upper-floor dining room provides unobstructed vistas of the sea and the nearby hills, which are studded with villas. On many evenings a white-capped chef stands in front of his specialty display table. In the marble-floored lounge and bar, good contemporary design prevails, with plenty of museumlike space. Soft tufted-leather chairs are gathered at marble-topped tables. Portuguese cuisine is served. Live music is played in the Bar Estoril every night from 6pm to midnight.

Services: Laundry, babysitting, 24-hour room service.

Facilities: Car-rental facilities, hairdressing salon.

LENNOX COUNTRY CLUB, Rua Eng. Álvaro Pedro Sousa 5, 2765 Estoril. Tel. 01/468-04-24. Fax 01/467-08-59. 34 rms, 3 suites. MINIBAR TEL

$ Rates (including breakfast): 6,350$–15,500$ ($38.70–$94.60) single; 9,400$–23,500$ ($57.30–$143.40) double; 36,000$ ($219.60) suite. AE, DC, MC, V. **Parking:** Free.

Partially because of its emphasis on golf, this hillside hotel seems a lot like a corner of Scotland. As you complete the steep climb to the reception desk, you'll notice a series of Portuguese tiles depicting kilted bagpipers and plaid-covered "bairns" playing golf, in almost a tongue-in-cheek comment on the juxtaposition of the two cultures. There's even a map of the golf course at St. Andrews near the bar, close to the autographed photos of the many championship golfers who have stayed here. The hydrangeas and herbaceous borders in the gardens, coupled with the sunshine, make this place one of the town's prime attractions.

Some of its comfortably attractive accommodations are scattered among a collection of buildings a short walk from the reception area. The most desirable are contained within the main building, which was formerly a private home. Those who like to cook for themselves might be interested in one of the suites, which are equipped with kitchenettes.

Dining/Entertainment: Barbecues are served around the pool every other week, and a band or folkloric group performs at them. The hotel restaurant serves English cuisine, including steak-and-kidney pie, along with regional Portuguese dishes, a complete meal costing 3,300$ ($20.10).

Services: Free transport to nearby golf courses and riding stables, room service, babysitting, laundry.

Facilities: Heated pool.

NEARBY PLACES TO STAY

A satellite of Estoril, **Monte Estoril** lies directly to the west on the road to Cascais, half a mile away. Built across the slope of a hill and containing many moderately priced hotels, it opens onto a vista of Cascais Bay and the Atlantic beyond.

EXPENSIVE

HOTEL ATLÁNTICO, Estrada Marginal 7, Monte Estoril, 2765 Estoril. Tel. 01/468-02-70. Fax 468-36-19. 175 rms. TV TEL

$ Rates (including breakfast): 20,000$ ($122) single; 25,000$–30,000$ ($152.50–$183) double. DC, MC, V. **Parking:** Free.

Hotel Atlántico is a self-contained playground, almost directly on the sandy beach but separated from the shore by the electric train tracks. Its disadvantages are the whizzing coastal-road traffic in front and the train clatter in the rear. However, if you get a room high enough up facing the sea, you can be assured of quiet.

The guest rooms are medium sized and moderately well furnished, with built-in headboards, reading lights, Swedish-style desks and armchairs, and tile baths and showers. Eighty-two are air-conditioned and have minibars.

Dining/Entertainment: The dining room, built cavelike under the width of the hotel, has a view through an all-glass wall overlooking the pool and sea. One TV lounge has video; another lounge offers live music in the evening.

Services: 24-hour room service, laundry, babysitting.

Facilities: Wide sun terrace, with outdoor seawater pool.

ESTORIL EDEN, Avenida Saboia 209, Monte Estoril, 2765 Estoril. Tel. 01/467-05-73. Fax 01/468-01-57. 161 apts. A/C TV TEL

$ Rates: 13,500$ ($82.40) single; 26,500$ ($161.70) double. Breakfast 1,100$ ($6.70) extra. AE, DC, MC, V. **Parking:** 1,000$ ($6.10).

The four-star Estoril Eden is open all year. Built in 1985, this white-walled tower sits on a rocky knoll above the road paralleling the edge of the sea. The soundproof apartments are elegantly decorated, each with a kitchenette, radio, in-house video, and balcony opening onto a sea view. In the studio apartments, the beds are "in the wall," allowing larger living space during the day.

Dining/Entertainment: Dining facilities include the Garden Patio, offering both regional and international cuisine served either à la carte or buffet, plus a poolside cafe/bar, Le Bistrot. You can stock up on food supplies in a minimarket. Live music is presented every Wednesday.

Services: Laundry service.

Facilities: Outdoor and indoor pools, sauna, health club, solarium.

MODERATE

GRANDE HOTEL, Avenida Saboia 488, Monte Estoril, 2765 Estoril. Tel. 01/466-33-01. Fax 01/468-48-34. 77 rms. A/C TV TEL

$ Rates (including breakfast): 10,500$ ($64.10) single; 14,000$ ($85.40) double. Children under 8 stay at 50% discount in parents' room. AE, DC, MC, V.

Grande Hotel is a modern compound just a few minutes up from the beach. It offers seven floors of spacious rooms, about half of which have balconies large enough for breakfast and sunbathing. The large sitting room is popular, with a fireplace and groupings of comfortable furniture. International visitors wander into the open wood-paneled lobby and into the chestnut-fronted drinking lounge.

The guest rooms are furnished in blond modern (bedside tables, chest/desk combinations), the severity lightened by simple color schemes. The better rooms open onto sea views.

Dining/Entertainment: The air-conditioned main dining room is undistinguished yet serves adequate Portuguese meals.

Services: Laundry, babysitting, room service.

Facilities: Pool opening off cocktail terrace, with a view of eucalyptus and palm trees.

INEXPENSIVE

APARTHOTEL TOURING ESTORIL, Rua do Viveiro 538, Monte Estoril, 2765 Estoril. Tel. 01/468-33-85. Fax 01/468-44-70. 99 rms, 6 suites. A/C TEL

$ Rates: 11,000$ ($67.10) single; 12,000$ ($73.20) double; 18,000$ ($109.80) suite. Breakfast 500$ ($3.10) extra. DC, MC, V. **Parking:** Free.

This modern apartment-house complex has accommodations for two or four persons. All are fully equipped with kitchenettes, baths, terraces, radios, and TVs upon request. Laundry service and babysitting are available, and there are a supermarket, hairdresser, and restaurant on the premises. In July and August, guests are entertained by international singing and guitar playing. Facilities include an outdoor pool and a bar.

HOTEL ZENITH, Rua Belmonte 1, Monte Estoril, 2765 Estoril. Tel. 01/468-11-22. Fax 01/468-11-17. 48 rms. TEL

$ Rates (including breakfast): 7,000$ ($42.70) single; 10,000$ ($61) double. MC, V. **Parking:** Free.

You'll find comfortable 1970s accommodations inside this white–and–moss–green tower jutting skyward from a neighborhood of 19th-century villas above the town. The ground-floor bar, encased in burnished tones of hardwood, offers a big-windowed rendezvous to relax in air-conditioned comfort. Each guest room contains a radio as well as access to the rectangular pool whose waterside plants are sheltered from the wind by the bulk of the hotel. There's a TV lounge with a fireplace, along with a basement-level snack bar and restaurant, where meals cost from 1,850$ ($11.30).

WHERE TO DINE
EXPENSIVE

FOUR SEASONS, in the Palácio Hotel, Parque Estoril 4. Tel. 468-04-00.
Cuisine: INTERNATIONAL. **Reservations:** Required.
$ Prices: Appetizers 900$–1,800$ ($5.50–$11); main courses 2,200$–4,500$ ($13.40–$27.50). AE, DC, MC, V.
Open: Dinner only, daily 7:30–11pm.

For fine food, go to the Four Seasons, whose connection with one of Portugal's most famous hotels gives it a vivid cachet. But even if it were independently operated, it would still be one of the finest—and also one of the most expensive—restaurants in the country.

The menus and the service of the Four Seasons depend on just that—the seasons. The dishes, uniforms, linen, china, and glasses are changed four times a year. Other than the handful of intimate tables set imperially on the upper mezzanine, the elaborately decorated tables are grouped around a beautiful but purely decorative Iberian kitchen, whose copper pots and blue tiles lend an appealing rustic touch to an otherwise sophisticated decor. The hushed quiet, the candles, and the rich colors almost invite comparison to an elegant 19th-century Russian home. However, the discreet charm and polite manners of the well-trained staff are distinctively Portuguese.

The international cuisine is superb. For example, for an appetizer you might select the three-cheese crêpes or the lobster bisque or chilled mussel soup. To follow you might have chateaubriand, mussels in cream sauce, grilled beef and monkfish on a skewer, shrimps in garlic butter, or roast duckling with orange sauce. You can enter this place directly from the street or from the hotel lobby after enjoying a drink among the bar's international clientele.

MODERATE

A MARÉ, Estrada Marginal (without number), Monte Estoril. Tel. 468-5570.
Cuisine: PORTUGUESE. **Reservations:** Not necessary.
$ Prices: Appetizers: 200$–900$ ($1.20–$5.50); main courses 1,200$–2,000$ ($7.30–$12.20); shellfish 850$–10,400$ ($5.20–$63.40). AE, DC, MC, V.
Open: Lunch daily noon–3pm; dinner daily 7–11pm.

This is one of the most reliable and best-managed restaurants in Estoril, with a loyal local following. Contained within an old-fashioned villa previously inhabited by a mysteriously deposed countess, it offers a romantic decor and lights that can be lowered, depending on the mood, for greater intimacy. The menu almost always contains at least seven types of fresh fish, which can be prepared in a wide array of styles. (Many visitors prefer filets of these fish prepared simply, fried with parsley and/or herbs and garlic.) Also available is an assortment of fresh shellfish.

ENGLISH BAR, Estrada Marginal. Tel. 468-12-54.
Cuisine: PORTUGUESE. **Reservations:** Recommended.
$ Prices: Appetizers 750$–1,500$ ($4.60–$9.20); main courses 1,900$–3,800$ ($11.60–$23.20). AE, DC, MC, V.
Open: Lunch Mon–Sat noon–4pm; dinner Mon–Sat 7:30–10:30pm. **Closed:** 2nd and 3rd week in Aug.

Many couples come here just to watch the sunsets over the Bay of Cascais. The mock-Elizabethan facade may lead you to think of steak-and-kidney pie and tankards of ale, yet the food is essentially Portuguese, and it's well prepared. Many international dishes are also served.

Try for a window seat in the handsome dining room, with wide-plank floors and comfortable leather-backed wood chairs. There are numerous English-style decorations: heraldic symbols, horsey prints, and bric-a-brac. From the à la carte menu, you can sample such highly recommended dishes as a savory *crème de mariscos* (cream of shellfish soup). The chef's specialty is *cherne na canoa*, turbot served with baby clams and a succulent sauce. In season, you can order *perdiz Serra Morena* (roast partridge). An excellent dessert is a mousse made with nuts.

EVENING ENTERTAINMENT

GAMBLING

ESTORIL CASINO, in Parque Estoril, Praça José Teodoro dos Santos. Tel. 468-45-21.

Occupying a position at the rise of a hill, it opens onto Parque Estoril's formal gardens, which sweep toward the water. The glass walls suggest an international museum of modern art and enclose an inner courtyard, with tile paths, a fountain and pool, and borders of lilac petunias and red carnations. Its complex includes a small movie theater showing films daily, an art gallery selling contemporary paintings, and a few boutiques offering apparel and souvenirs.

The casino accepts your money daily from 3pm to 3am (passport required). An adjoining salon is for one-armed bandits. In the main room you can take your chance at roulette, French banque, chemin de fer, baccarat, blackjack (21), craps, and slot machines.

Admission: 1,000$ ($6.10).

DINNER SHOW

GRAND SALON RESTAURANT, in the Estoril Casino, Parque Estoril, Praça José Teodoro dos Santos. Tel. 468-45-21.

This supper club offers Portuguese and international cuisine daily from 9pm. Dinner will cost you from 9,000$ ($54.90) above the admission price. Specialties include smoked swordfish, pâté, grilled prawns, calves' kidneys flambéed with cognac, and pressed duck. The extravaganza stage show commences at 11pm every night except Monday. On the arena stage, leggy, feathered, and bejeweled dancers strut their wares to good advantage in billowing trains and bespangled bras.

Admission (including two drinks): 4,500$ ($27.50).

DANCE CLUB

FORTE VELHO (Old Fort), Estrada Marginal, São Pedro Cadaveira, São João do Estoril. Tel. 468-13-37.

The very young meet in this very old setting in Forte Velho. The disco was ingeniously conceived, capturing a 17th-century fortress on a cliff above the ocean. It's built of solid rock and offers a central room with fireplace.

Dancing is to records only, and there's an adjoining bar with stools and cozy banquettes, ideal for hand-holding couples. For a change of pace, drinks are carried out on the terrace to the parapet, where imbibers gasp at the steep drop to the surf below. The fun commences at 10pm, though it doesn't really warm up till around midnight. The Old Fort rides the crest until closing at 4am on Tuesday to Sunday. A mixed drink costs from 700$ ($4.30).

Admission: 1,800$ ($11), plus 1,800$ ($11) drink minimum.

COCKTAIL LOUNGE

RAY'S COCKTAIL BAR & LOUNGE, Avenida Saboia 425. Tel. 468-01-06.

This interesting Monte Estoril watering spot is popular with American expatriates, many of whom make it their private club, including the original Ray now that he's retired and has turned it over to Rafael Neves. It's a souped-up decorator extravaganza. Inside you're likely to find a completely universal assemblage of elements—a fátima hand from Tangier, a glass ruby-colored newel post finial, chandeliers dripping with crystal, antique benches, and provincial chairs, plus a heterogeneous mixture of modern art. Everyone seemingly enjoys the drinks (many enjoy quite a few). Most strong drinks cost from 500$ ($3.10). The bar is open daily from 1pm to 2:20am.

2. CASCAIS

4 miles W of Estoril; 19 miles W of Lisbon

GETTING THERE By Train You can reach Cascais by the electric train that begins its run at Lisbon's Cais do Sodré waterfront station and ends at the center of town. Trains to and from Lisbon leave every 15 to 30 minutes. Service is daily from 5:30am to 2:30am. A one-way fare costs 145$ (90¢).

By Bus Take the electric train from Lisbon to Cascais, unless you're coming from Sintra. If you're there, Rodoviária buses depart from Avenida Dr. Miguel Bombarda in Sintra, across from the main train station, heading for Cascais at the rate of 10 per day (trip time: 1 hour), costing 265$ ($1.60) round trip.

By Car From Estoril (see above), continue west along Route 6 for another 4 miles.

ESSENTIALS The **Cascais Tourist Office** is at Avenida Combatentes da Grande Guerra (tel. 486-82-04). The **telephone area code** is 01.

In the 1930s, Cascais was a tiny fishing village that attracted artists and writers to its little cottages. But its history as a resort is old. In fact, it was once known as a royal village because it enjoyed the patronage of Portugal's royal family. When the monarchy died, the military moved in. Gen. António de Fragoso Carmona, president of Portugal until 1951, the man responsible for naming Dr. Salazar as minister of finance, once occupied the 17th-century fort guarding the Portuguese Riviera.

That Cascais is growing is an understatement: It's leapfrogging! At one entrance to the resort, someone wrote the word *City* after Cascais. Even if not officially recognized as such, it is well on its way. Apartment houses, new hotels, and the finest restaurants along the Costa do Sol draw a never-ending stream of visitors every year.

However, the life of the simple fishermen still goes on. Auctions, called *lotas,* at which the latest catch is sold, still take place on the main square, though a modern hotel has sprouted up in the background. In the small harbor, rainbow-colored fishing boats must share space with pleasure craft owned by an international set that flocks to Cascais from early spring until autumn.

The town's tie with the sea is old. If you speak Portuguese, any of the local fishermen, with their weather-beaten faces, will tell you that one of their own, Afonso Sanches, discovered America in 1482 and that Columbus learned of his accidental find, stole the secret, and enjoyed the subsequent acclaim.

Many visitors, both foreign and domestic, drive out to Cascais on a road-clogged summer Sunday to attend the bullfights at the **Monumental de Cascais,** a ring outside the "city" center.

The most popular excursion outside Cascais is to ✪ **Boca de Inferno** (Mouth of Hell). Reached by heading out the highway to Guincho, then turning left toward the sea, the Boca deserves its ferocious reputation. At their peak, thundering waves sweep in with such power and fury they have long ago carved a wide hole, or *boca,* in the cliffs. However, if you should arrive when the sea is calm, you'll wonder why it's called a cauldron. The Mouth of Hell can be a windswept roar if you don't stumble over too many souvenir hawkers.

WHERE TO STAY

Advance reservations are necessary in July and August.

EXPENSIVE

HOTEL ALBATROZ, Rua Frederico Arouca 100, 2750 Cascais. Tel. 01/483-28-21. Fax 01/484-48-27. 37 rms, 3 suites. A/C MINIBAR TV TEL

$ Rates (including breakfast): 20,500$–41,500$ ($125.10–$253.20) single; 23,500$–48,000$ ($143.40–$292.80) double; 33,500$–68,000$ ($204.40–$414.80) suite. AE, DC, MC, V. **Parking:** Free.

The wandering albatross is a bird noted as a master of gliding flight, capable of staying airborne on motionless wings for hours on end. What an appropriate symbol for this treasure along the Costa do Sol. Whether you're seeking rooms or food, the hotel is your "good-luck" choice. Positioned on a rock ledge just above the ocean, it is centered around a neoclassic villa built as a luxurious holiday retreat for the duke of Loulé. It was later acquired in the 19th century by the count and countess de Foz. Sometime in this century it was converted into an inn, and in time the Albatroz received such famous guests as Anthony Eden, Cary Grant, Chief Justice Warren Burger, the duke and duchess of Bedford, Claudette Colbert, William Holden, Amy Vanderbilt, and the former queen of Bulgaria; Prince Rainier and the late Princess Grace visited on more than one occasion.

Today the hotel has benefitted from a tastefully elegant refurbishing that incorporates a lavish use of intricately painted tiles in garlanded patterns of blue and yellow, acres of white latticework, and sweeping expanses of glass. The stone-trimmed 19th-century core has been expanded with a series of terraced balconied additions, each of which contains some of the pristine, elegant guest rooms.

Dining/Entertainment: The à la carte restaurant, serving Portuguese and international cuisine, is one of the finest along the coast (see "Where to Dine," below).

Services: 24-hour room service, babysitting, laundry/valet.

Facilities: Pool, sun terrace.

HOTEL CIDADELA, Avenida 25 de Abril, 2750 Cascais. Tel. 01/483-29-21. Fax 01/486-72-26. 130 rms, 10 suites. A/C MINIBAR TV TEL

$ Rates (including breakfast): 20,000$ ($122) single; 23,000$ ($140.30) double; from 45,000$ ($274.50) suite. AE, DC, MC, V. **Parking:** Free.

Architecturally and decoratively, this hotel is a bastion of good taste. It is elegantly furnished in a restrained manner, spacious in concept in both its private and its public rooms as well as gracious in its reception and its amenities. Many Riviera-bound guests have deserted their old favorites for this holiday rendezvous.

You can reserve a first-class room, built into the central block with balconies, or the Cidadela will place you in womblike comfort in one of its twin-bedded terraced suites or one of its apartmentlike duplexes (the latter usually holds three to six). The rear rooms, sheltered from traffic noise, are preferable.

Each suite is as complete as an apartment: a living room, a dining room, and a fully equipped kitchenette on the lower floor (and there's a supermarket nearby for those who want to whip up their own concoctions), with a staircase leading to the bedrooms, two or three each. Each floor opens onto verandas with garden furniture.

The three major public rooms are pleasantly decorated, the main living room with low modern groups of furniture in warm colors. The hotel divorces itself from the hustle-bustle of summering Cascais and is reached by heading out on a tree-shaded avenue, past restaurants, boutiques, and nightclubs.

Dining/Entertainment: In the good-sized dining room, the sturdy armchairs, upholstered with Portuguese fabric, seat many diners desiring top-quality cooking. You can take lunch or dinner here for 3,200$ ($19.50) extra per person. In the intimate bar, done in blue and gray with "medievalesque" helmets and breast plates, a pianist entertains Wednesday to Monday.

Services: Room service, laundry/valet, concierge.

Facilities: Boutique, hairdresser, garden with large pool.

**ESTALAGEM SENHORA DA GUIA, Estrada do Guincho, 2750 Cascais.
Tel. 01/486-97-85.** Fax 01/486-92-27. 24 rms, 4 suites. A/C MINIBAR TV TEL
$ Rates (including breakfast): 22,000$–26,000$ ($134.20–$158.60) single;
24,000$–28,000$ ($146.40–$170.80) double; 32,000$ ($195.20) suite. AE, DC,
MC, V. **Parking:** Free.

One of the loveliest hotels in the region was opened only a few years ago by the
Ornelas family, who returned to their native Portugal after a sojourn in Brazil.
They settled on the former country villa of one of the most famous fortunes of
Portugal, the Sagres brewery family. The house was built as recently as 1970, but its
thick walls, high ceilings, and elaborately crafted moldings give the impression of a
much older building.

A trio of blond and blue-eyed multilingual siblings embarked on the task of
restoring the house to its former state. Today each of the elegant guest rooms and
suites is tastefully outfitted with reproductions of 18th-century Portuguese antiques,
thick carpets, louvered shutters, spacious modern baths, and many extras. Because of
the villa's position on a bluff above the sea, the views are excellent.

Dining/Entertainment: The sun-washed bar is one of the more alluring rooms
in the house. It's filled with some of the family antiques, many of them English and
acquired during the Ornelas's years in Madeira. Upholstered sofas provide quiet
corners, and there is a fireplace for cold weather. Breakfast is served buffet style under
parasols at the edge of the pool. Lunches and dinners are offered beneath an
African-hardwood ceiling in a formal dining room that remains cool even on the
hottest days.

Services: Room service, concierge.

Facilities: 20% discount at nearby golf and tennis club; horseback riding
arranged on short notice.

**ESTORIL SOL, Parque Palmela, 2750 Cascais. Tel. 01/483-28-31. Fax
01/483-22-80.** 317 rms, 18 suites. A/C MINIBAR TV TEL
$ Rates (including breakfast): 24,000$–30,000$ ($146.40–$183) single; 28,000$–
35,000$ ($170.80–$213.50) double; 50,000$–60,000$ ($305–$366) suite. AE,
DC, MC, V. **Parking:** 1,200$ ($7.30).

Estoril Sol is a luxury high-rise holiday world, perched on a ledge, with the coastal
highway and electric train tracks separating it from the beach. It represents a dream
come true for its late owner, José Teodoro dos Santos, a self-made man who arrived in
Lisbon with less than a dollar in his pocket. A modern land of resort living has been
created, and there are public rooms large enough for a great invasion of sun-seeking
visitors.

The air-conditioned Estoril Sol ended up as one of the largest hotels in Portugal,
with its guest rooms and suites overlooking the sea or the hills beyond. It boasts a
spacious main lounge (a traffic cop would be helpful here), the most expansive veranda
on the peninsula, and a beach reached by an underground passageway.

Dining/Entertainment: The dining facilities include the Ain Restaurant and the
Grill, each serving both Portuguese and French cuisine. A piano player entertains in
the Grill at dinner. The hotel also has a nightclub and a disco.

Services: 24-hour room service; laundry/valet, babysitting.

Facilities: Gymnasium, Olympic-size pool for adults, smaller pool for children,
sauna, solarium, health club with squash courts, facilities for horseback riding and
waterskiing, shopping arcade, service station.

MODERATE

**ESTALAGEM FAROL, Avenida Rey Umberto II de Italia 7, Estrada da
Boca do Inferno 7, 2750 Cascais. Tel. 01/483-01-73.** Fax 01/484-14-47.
14 rms. MINIBAR TV TEL
$ Rates (including breakfast): 10,000$ ($61) single; 12,000$–16,000$ ($73.20–
$97.60) double. AE, DC, MC, V. **Parking:** Free on street.

When the Estalagem Farol was built in the late 19th century, its stone walls housed
the entourage of the count of Cabral. Today its once-aristocratic interior has been
converted into an inn whose allure is only slightly dimmed by the dozens of

Portuguese families who make it the center of their vacation. The owners have converted the back gardens into a stone-ringed concrete slab with a small swimming pool in the center, a few steps from the sea.

One of the favorite places is the richly masculine bar area, where a water view and the handcrafted paneling create an elegant rendezvous. The restaurant is outfitted with Iberian charm. The guest rooms are tastefully furnished and comfortable. Laundry and babysitting can be arranged.

INEXPENSIVE

ALBERGARIA VALBOM, Avenida Valbom 14, 2750 Cascais. Tel. 01/ 486-58-01. Fax 01/486-58-05. 40 rms. A/C TEL
$ Rates (including breakfast): 7,500$ ($45.80) single; 10,500$ ($64.10) double. AE, DC, MC, V. **Parking:** 500$ ($3.10).
Built in 1973, the white-concrete facade with its evenly spaced rows of recessed balconies doesn't offer anything architecturally distinctive. Nonetheless, the interior is warmly and comfortably decorated, and the staff is helpful and polite. You'll find a spacious sienna-colored bar on the premises, along with a sun-washed TV lounge ringed with engravings of fish and conservatively decorated guest rooms. The quieter accommodations look out over the back. The Valbom lies on a commercial-residential street close to the center of Cascais, near the rail station.

CASA PÉRGOLA, Avenida Valbom 13, 2750 Cascais. Tel. 01/484-00-40. Fax 01/483-47-91. 10 rms (5 with bath), 1 suite. A/C
$ Rates (including breakfast): 5,800$ ($35.40) single without bath; 10,000$ ($61) double without bath, 15,000$ ($91.50) double with bath; 17,000$ ($103.70) suite. No credit cards. **Parking:** 1,000$ ($6.10). **Closed:** Nov–Mar.
Built in the 18th century behind a deep and well-planted garden, this elegant villa offers some of the most charming interiors in Cascais. In the center of town, it stands in a neighborhood filled with restaurants and shops. Inside, the wall surrounding its flowers and hanging vines provides a calm from the hectic life outside. This is the domain of Maria de Luz. Her genteel Portuguese staff proudly displays a collection of antique furniture and blue-glazed tiles that surround the elegant second-floor sitting room. Each accommodation is well furnished.

WHERE TO DINE

Outside Lisbon, sprawling Cascais offers the heaviest concentration of high-quality restaurants. Even if you're based in the capital, you should trek out to Cascais to sample the viands—both Portuguese and international dishes. Once you've tasted cognac-simmered lobster, mint-flavored shellfish soup, stuffed cuttlefish, shrimp pâté, and even southern fried chicken, you may become a total refugee from your hotel dining room.

Regrettably, from the customer's—not the owner's—point of view, many Cascais restaurants tend to be overcrowded in summer, as they are so popular and quite reasonably priced. However, since many are excellent, press on to the next recommendation if you can't find a seat at your first choice. What follows is a wide-ranging survey of the best of the lot, in all price ranges.

EXPENSIVE

RESTAURANT ALBATROZ, Rua Frederico Arouca 100. Tel. 483-28-21.
Cuisine: PORTUGUESE/INTERNATIONAL. **Reservations:** Required.
$ Prices: Appetizers 1,200$–1,800$ ($7.30–$11); main courses 3,400$–4,200$ ($20.70–$25.60). AE, DC, MC, V.
Open: Lunch daily 12:30–3pm; dinner daily 7:30–10pm.
One of the finest dining experiences along the Costa do Sol can be found at this elegantly decorated restaurant, part of the most famous hotel along the coast (see "Where to Stay," above). Its summer-style decor is inviting year round. It's best to begin with an apéritif on the covered terrace high above the sea.
Afterward, you'll be ushered into a glistening dining room. There, between walls

pierced by large sheets of glass, under an alternately beamed and lattice-covered ceiling, you can enjoy some of the finest Portuguese and international cuisine in Cascais. Your repast might include poached salmon, partridge stew, chateaubriand, or a savory version of stuffed sole with shellfish. For dessert, your choices will range from crêpes Suzette to an iced soufflé. Accompanying your meal will be a wide selection of Portuguese and international wines.

VISCONDE DA LUZ, in the Jardim Visconde da Luz. Tel. 486-68-48.
   Cuisine: PORTUGUESE. **Reservations:** Required.
$ Prices: Appetizers 950$–1,800$ ($5.80–$11); main courses 1,800$–2,800$ ($11–$17.10). AE, DC, MC, V.
   Open: Lunch Tues–Sun noon–4pm; dinner Tues–Sun 7pm–midnight.
The location of this well-known restaurant is one of its most appealing features: It sits within a low-slung bungalow at the edge of a park in the center of Cascais. The view from the windows encompasses rows of lime trees and towering sycamores where flocks of birds congregate at dusk (be duly warned if you're walking under these trees). Inside, the decor is a modernized form of art nouveau, complete with mirrors, touches of scarlet, and a polite uniformed staff eager to cater to your wishes. Before you enter, you might be interested in looking at the blue-and-white-tile kitchen. The Portuguese food is well prepared with fresh ingredients. A meal might include fried sole, shellfish, pork with clams, seafood curry, and clams in garlic sauce, finished off with almond cake.

MODERATE

BEIRA MAR, Rua das Flores 6. Tel. 483-01-52.
   Cuisine: PORTUGUESE. **Reservations:** Recommended.
$ Prices: Appetizers 750$–1,500$ ($4.60–$9.20); main courses 1,500$–2,300$ ($9.20–$14). AE, MC, V.
   Open: Lunch daily noon–2:30pm; dinner daily 7–10pm.

⑤ Across from the Cascais fish market, this popular little restaurant specializes in the fruits of the sea. As you enter, you're greeted with an old cart showing the rich bounty of produce from Extremadura. Of course, all this hearty fare is meant to be accompanied by the region's fine wines. You'll be seated at immaculate tables, where the service will be both considerate and efficient. Begin with some savory little neck clams or some other kind of shellfish. *Sopa marisco* (shellfish soup) might be another enticing beginning. For a main course, whitefish is crowned with a banana. Grilled sole and many other dishes round out the menu. One reader wrote that dessert was "a crown of freshly picked forest raspberries drizzled with cream." But what "settled the night" was a "tiny crystal of aged port."

EDUARDO, Largo das Grutas 3. Tel. 483-19-01.
   Cuisine: PORTUGUESE/FRENCH. **Reservations:** Recommended.
$ Prices: Appetizers 450$–800$ ($2.70–$4.90); main courses 1,200$–2,500$ ($7.30–$15.30). AE, DC, MC, V.
   Open: Lunch Thurs–Tues noon–3pm; dinner Thurs–Tues 7–11pm.
Rustically decorated with regional artifacts, this pleasant restaurant occupies the street level of a postwar apartment building in the center of Cascais. It's named after its French-born owner, Eduoard de Beukelaer, who turns out a selection of savory Portuguese and French meals. The well-prepared food might include filet steaks, monkfish au gratin, crayfish in butter sauce with capers, and beef Stroganoff.

GIL VICENTE, Rua dos Navegantes 22–30. Tel. 483-20-32.
   Cuisine: PORTUGUESE/FRENCH. **Reservations:** Required.
$ Prices: Appetizers 750$–1,600$ ($4.60–$9.80); main courses 1,600$–3,200$ ($9.80–$19.50). AE, DC, MC, V.
   Open: Lunch Tues–Sun 12:30–3pm; dinner Tues–Sun 7pm–1am. **Closed:** Feb.
This is the kind of bistro you usually find on a back street in a town along the Côte d'Azur. Set on the rise of a hill above the harbor, it was converted from a fisherman's cottage. Both the Portuguese and the French cuisine and the ambience reflect the mood of its owner, who sees to it that excellent meals are served. The name of the

tavern honors the 16th-century father of Portuguese drama—the Iberian Shakespeare, if you will. The decor is simple—a setting of plaster walls, an old stone fireplace, and recessed windows with pots of greenery. An ornate iron washstand has been adapted for condiments, and the walls contain gaily painted heads of old iron bedsteads.

You may be won over by the cooking (pâté, crêpes, shellfish, or grilled chicken and steaks) and the reasonable tariffs. To whet your appetite, try the assortment of hors d'oeuvres, the pâté maison, or the shellfish bisque. At least three main dishes hit the mark every night: sole Colbert, sole delicia, and grilled steak with mushrooms. Among the desserts, you can order fruit salad, chocolate mousse, or banana flambé.

JOHN BULL/BRITANNIA RESTAURANT, Largo Luís de Camões 4A. Tel. 483-01-54.

Cuisine: ENGLISH/PORTUGUESE/AMERICAN. **Reservations:** Required.

$ Prices: Appetizers 650$–1,200$ ($4–$7.30); main courses 1,500$–2,300$ ($9.20–$14). AE, DC, MC, V.

Open: Lunch daily 12:30–3:30pm; dinner daily 7:30–11:30pm.

With its black-and-white-timbered Elizabethan facade, this centrally located pub/restaurant is a wedge of England. In the street-floor John Bull pub, you can order an iced pint of lager. The setting is appropriate—wood paneling, oak beams, a fireplace, crude tavern stools and tables, pewter pots, and ceramic jugs. The meals in the second-floor Britannia Restaurant feature a medley of English and Portuguese, even American, dishes. Southern fried chicken and T-bone steak are familiar Yankee favorites. For English tastes, specialties include cottage pie.

O PIPAS, Rua das Flores 18. Tel. 486-45-01.

Cuisine: PORTUGUESE. **Reservations:** Required.

$ Prices: Appetizers 1,100$–1,950$ ($6.70–$11.90); main courses 2,000$–3,000$ ($12.20–$18.30). AE, DC, MC, V.

Open: Lunch daily noon–3:30pm; dinner daily 7–11:30pm.

If you order shellfish here, a meal can be very expensive; otherwise, this popular restaurant offers well-prepared food at acceptable prices. Many diners consider it the finest independent (outside the hotels) restaurant at the resort. It stands on a teeming street whose pavement is covered with black-and-white mosaics. The decor is Portuguese bistro style, with racks of exposed wine bottles and big picture windows letting in sunlight and views of the busy street outside. The Portuguese menu includes lobster, clams, shellfish of all kinds (including oysters), and several preparations of sole, along with a few meat dishes, especially beef O Pipas.

REIJOS RESTAURANT, Rua Frederico Arouca 35. Tel. 483-00-11.

Cuisine: AMERICAN/PORTUGUESE. **Reservations:** Required for dinner.

$ Prices: Appetizers 350$–1,500$ ($2.10–$9.20); main courses 1,300$–1,950$ ($7.90–$11.90); fixed-price menu 2,800$ ($17.10). AE, DC, MC, V.

Open: Lunch Mon–Sat 12:30–3:30pm; dinner Mon–Sat 7–11pm. **Closed:** Dec 20–Jan 20.

Be warned that this place is likely to be crowded, so you'll have to either wait for a table or abandon all hope in high season. This intimate, informal bistro is that good. The fine foods of two countries, the United States and Portugal, are combined on the menu, and the result is altogether pleasing. An American citizen, Ray Ettinger, long ago teamed with a Portuguese, Tony Brito, to pool their talents in the running of this successful enterprise.

At times to the homesick Mr. Ettinger, nothing is more delectable than roast beef à l'inglese or Salisbury steak with mushroom sauce. Other popular items include lobster thermidor, peppersteak, and shrimp curry. Originating in Macau, two Chinese dishes are prepared at your table: beef with garden peppers and shrimp and cucumbers. Fresh seafood includes sole, sea bass, garoupa, and fresh salmon, as well as the famous *bacalhau a Reijos* (oven-baked dry codfish with cheese sauce). Unlike many European restaurants, Reijos serves fresh vegetables with its main dishes at no extra cost. In addition, it has an outstanding selection of desserts made on the premises by Mr. Ettinger from fresh seasonal ingredients. The service is excellent.

RESTAURANTE ALAUDE, Largo Luís de Camões 8. Tel. 483-02-87.

Cuisine: PORTUGUESE/INTERNATIONAL. **Reservations:** Recommended.
$ Prices: Appetizers 550$–750$ ($3.40–$4.60); main courses 1,200$–1,800$ ($7.30–$11); fixed-price menu 2,250$ ($13.70). AE, DC, MC, V.
Open: Daily 10am–midnight.

The blue-tile facade of this convivial restaurant opens onto a square teeming with vacationing Europeans. Its famous neighbor, the John Bull, frequently serves as the cocktail lounge for clients who eventually stroll over to Alaude for dinner. The square onto which it opens is sometimes so crowded that it's referred to as "the living room of Cascais," offering plenty to see from the vantage point at one of this restaurant's outdoor tables. If you prefer, you can select a seat inside, enjoying one of several well-prepared Portuguese and international specialties. These include sardines in olive oil with tomatoes, several preparations of scampi, clams of the house, and a grilled mélange of shellfish.

RESTAURANTE O BATEL, Travessa das Flores 4. Tel. 483-02-15.
Cuisine: PORTUGUESE. **Reservations:** Required.
$ Prices: Appetizers 200$–950$ ($1.20–$5.80); main courses 1,300$–2,500$ ($7.90–$15.30); fixed-price meal 2,350$ ($14.30). AE, DC, MC, V.
Open: Lunch Thurs–Tues noon–3pm; dinner Thurs–Tues 7–10:30pm.

O Batel fronts the fish market. Styled as a country inn, it doesn't overdo with touristy gimmicks. The atmosphere is semirustic, with rough white walls and beamed ceilings. A display indicates the ingenuity of the chef, his wares enhanced by a basket of figs, plums, peaches, and fresh flowers. The prices are reasonable, and that, balanced with the superb Portuguese cuisine, explains why the tiny tables are usually filled at every meal. Lobster thermidor and lobster stewed in cognac are the house specialties, but the price on these items changes daily. For something less expensive, I recommend Cascais sole with banana, a savory dish of clams with cream, and mixed shellfish with rice. For an appetizer, you can try prawn cocktail. To complete your meal, such desserts as pineapple with Madeira wine are offered. *Wine tip:* Order a Casal Mendes rosé, a cool choice.

EVENING ENTERTAINMENT

FADO CLUB

RODRIGO, Rua de Birre 961, Forte Dom Rodrigo, Estrada de Birre. Tel. 487-13-73.

One of the post popular fadistas in the country today is a singer known only as Rodrigo. His club lies just outside the resort of Cascais, along Rua de Birre. Some of Lisbon's most fashionable people drive out here just to hear Rodrigo sing—he's that good. His voice is haunting and filled with melancholy. The nightclub opens at 8:30pm for dinner, which will cost from 5,000$ ($30.50) to 8,000$ ($48.80), but that is much too early to go, as Rodrigo himself rarely appears before 10pm. Closing time is 2am (it's open Tuesday through Sunday). Be prepared to pay in cash, as credit cards aren't accepted.

Admission (including two drinks): 2,500$ ($15.30).

DANCE CLUBS

PALM BEACH, Praia da Conceição. Tel. 483-08-51.

This hillside disco/restaurant has a rather swank atmosphere and a doorman to weed out undesirables. The disco lies a 10-minute walk from the Cascais rail station. It rides the crest of the wave along the Costa do Sol, drawing a fun-loving young crowd that's well mannered enough to please the management. The club is positioned below the coastal road, its wide windows overlooking the bay at Cascais. You lounge comfortably on banquettes and chairs when not dancing on the mini floor. The atmosphere is informal, and only records are played. Beer goes for 500$ ($3.10), and hard drinks start at 700$ ($4.30). The restaurant, which has a maritime decor and a profusion of plants, overlooks the bay. Here you can order excellent shellfish and

local fish dishes, a meal costing from 3,000$ ($18.30). The Palm Beach also has a pub/cocktail lounge, set up to look like the bridge of a steamboat. Hours are daily from 10:30pm to 4am.
Admission: 1,200$ ($7.30).

VAN GOGO, Travessa Alfarrobeira 9. Tel. 483-33-78.
Van Gogo is a chic playground. Modestly hidden in a corner stone building, it was transformed from a simple fisherman's cottage into a disco, lying a 10-minute walk from the Cascais rail station. A doorman carefully evaluates those who would cross the threshold, using some inner radar I don't understand. You'll encounter a young crowd similar to the one at Juan-les-Pins in France. A seductive atmosphere is created by the black-glass walls, and the customers can rock and roll. Your admission price covers the same amount in drinks. The Van Gogo opens its doors year round at 11pm nightly, closing at 4am.
Admission: 2,500$–3,000$ ($15.30–$18.30).

---

3. GUINCHO

4 miles N of Cascais; 6 miles N of Estoril

GETTING THERE   By Bus   From the train station at Cascais, buses leave for the Praia do Guincho every hour (trip time: 20 minutes).

By Car   From Cascais, continue west along Route 247.

ESSENTIALS   The nearest tourist office is in Cascais (see above). The **telephone area code** is 01.

Guincho means "caterwaul," "screech," "shriek," "yell"—the cry that swallows make while darting among the air currents over the wild sea. These swallows at Guincho are to be seen all year, unlike their fickle fair-weather counterparts at San Juan Capistrano in California. Sometimes at night the sea, driven into a frenzy, howls like a wailing banshee, and that, too, is guincho. The settlement is near the westernmost point on the European continent, known to the Portuguese as **Cabo da Roca.** The beaches are spacious and sandy; the sunshine is incandescent; and the nearby promontories, jutting out amid white-tipped Atlantic waves, are spectacular. The windswept dunes are backed by wooded hills, and to the east the Serra de Sintra is silhouetted on the distant horizon.

Praia do Guincho draws large beach crowds each season. The undertow is treacherous—be forewarned. It's wise to keep in mind the advice of Jennings Parrott, writing in the *International Herald Tribune:* "If you are caught up by the current, don't fight it. Don't panic. The wind forces it to circle, so you will be brought back to shore." A local fisherman, however, advises that you take a box lunch along. "Sometimes it takes several days to make this circle."

One of the primary reasons for coming to Guincho is to sample its seafood restaurants, described below. You can try, for example, the crayfish-size box-jaw lobsters known as *bruxas,* which in Portuguese means "sorcerer," "wizard," "witch doctor," even "nocturnal moth." To be totally Portuguese, you must also sample the barnacles, called *percèbes,* meaning "to perceive," "to understand," "to comprehend." After devouring these creatures, many foreign visitors fail to comprehend or perceive their popularity with the Portuguese. The fresh lobsters and crabs are cultivated in nearby shellfish beds, a fascinating sight.

WHERE TO STAY
EXPENSIVE

HOTEL DO GUINCHO, Praia do Guincho, 2750 Cascais. Tel. 01/487-04-91. Fax 01/487-04-31. 31 rms, 3 suites. A/C MINIBAR TV TEL
$ Rates (including breakfast): 27,500$–31,500$ ($167.80–$192.20) single;

30,000$–34,000$ ($183–$207.40) double; 45,000$ ($274.50) suite. AE, DC, MC, V. **Parking:** Free.

⭐ Hotel do Guincho is a fine choice. In the 17th century, an army of local masons built one of the most forbidding fortresses along the coast, within a few hundred feet of the most westerly point in Europe. The twin towers that flank the vaguely Moorish-looking facade still stand sentinel amid a sun-bleached terrain of sand and rock. Today, however, the inhabitants are more likely to be well-heeled representatives of a more glamorous world. In the past they've included Orson Welles, who was reportedly fascinated by the mist and the surging roar of the waves as they dashed upon the nearby cliffs. The late Princess Grace also found the place intriguing, as have prime ministers of both Italy and Portugal.

You'll enter through an enclosed courtyard, where there's a well that used to provide water for the garrison. The public rooms are filled with all the antique trappings of an aristocratic private home. In cold weather, a fire might be blazing in one of the granite-framed fireplaces, illuminating the thick carpets and the century-old furniture. Each small but comfortable guest room is sheltered behind a thick pine door that's heavily banded with iron. Each room has a vaulted stone ceiling, the keystone of which is carved into one of the 36 different heraldic shields. There are also three small but elegant suites, some with their own fireplaces.

Dining/Entertainment: If you're exploring the coast, the hotel also makes an ideal luncheon or dinner stop. Some celebrities have declared that many of their most perfect meals in Portugal were served here on a sunny afternoon, within sight of the surf a short distance away. The chef prepares such specialties as pâté of pheasant with morels, seafood salad, lobster Newburg, grilled black grouper with tartare sauce, and roast suckling pig Portuguese style. Full à la carte meals begin at 5,000$ ($30.50) and are served daily from 12:30 to 3pm and 7:30 to 11pm.

Services: Laundry, concierge, babysitting, 24-hour room service.
Facilities: Solarium.

INEXPENSIVE

ESTALAGEM DO FORTE MUCHAXO, Praia do Guincho, 2750 Cascais. Tel. 01/487-02-21. Fax 01/487-04-44. 23 rms. TEL
$ Rates (including breakfast): 8,200$–13,200$ ($50–$80.50) single; 9,000$–14,000$ ($54.90–$85.40) double. AE, DC, MC, V. **Parking:** Free.

Some four decades ago, a simple straw hut was set up on rugged wave-dashed rocks, where the proprietor sold brandy and coffee to the fishermen. Gradually, the senior Muchaxo started to cook for them. In time, beach-loving Germans discovered the place, and eventually even royalty arrived wanting to be fed. Nowadays the new has absorbed the old (though the straw shack remains to please traditionalists). The Muchaxo family operates this overblown hacienda, placing emphasis on the rustic blended with a mild dose of the contemporary. The Estalagem is rectangular, with guest-room windows overlooking either the courtyard or the nearby coast and hills. At one side, thrust out onto rock walls, is a pool with terraces and diving boards. After a day of swimming, guests gather in the chalet living room to warm themselves at the huge raised stone fireplace.

Those who want to stay for the night will find a choice of rooms—the best units overlook the sea. Each unit is unique, although most have basic stark-white walls with beamed ceilings.

Dining/Entertainment: There's a choice of two dining rooms: one modern, the other with a bamboo ceiling, staccato black-and-white-covered tables, and hand-painted provincial furniture. People drive from miles around just to sample the Portuguese and French cuisine, highly praised by such discriminating Iberian travelers as author James Michener. The adventurous will begin their meals with barnacles, described previously. The house specialty is lobster Barraca style, but the price is likely to change daily; an order of grilled sea bass is decidedly less expensive. A dish worth recommending is the chateaubriand. However, unless your throat is lined with asbestos, avoid ordering the chicken with *piri-piri* sauce made with hot pepper from Angola. One diner is said to have fainted after tasting this concoction. An excellent finish to a meal would be banana fritters. A typical meal here will cost 5,000$ ($30.50) to 6,000$ ($36.60).

WHERE TO DINE
EXPENSIVE

RESTAURANTE PORTO DE SANTA MARIA, Estrada do Guincho. Tel. **01/487-02-40.**
Cuisine: PORTUGUESE. **Reservations:** Not necessary.
$ Prices: Appetizers 1,200$–2,200$ ($7.30–$13.40); main courses 1,800$– 4,500$ ($11–$27.50). AE, DC, MC, V.
Open: Lunch daily 12:15–3:30pm; dinner daily 7–10:30pm.

If you decide to drive to the isolated stretch of roadside where this restaurant is located, you won't be alone. Hundreds of vacationing Europeans and Portuguese might decide to join you, especially in summer. This restaurant is one of the most appealing of its type along the coast, and it also serves some of the best seafood. A doorman will usher you into the low-lying seafront building whose large windows take in views of the sometimes-treacherous surf.

The beige-and-white decor is highlighted with an enormous aquarium made from white marble and thick sheets of glass, within which crustaceans such as lobsters wave their claws. A central serving table is laden with fruits and flowers. The polite staff serves every conceivable form of shellfish, priced by the gram, as well as such house specialties as grilled sole. Shellfish rice, known as *arroz de mariscos,* is the most popular specialty, and it's usually served to two. You'll probably want to taste the rondelles of pungent sheep's-milk cheese that await the arrival of guests at each table.

4. QUELUZ

9 miles NW of Lisbon

GETTING THERE **By Train** At the Estação Rossio in Lisbon, take the Sintra line to Queluz. Departures during the day are every 15 minutes (trip time: 30 minutes). A one-way fare costs 145$ (90¢). After getting off at Queluz, take a left turn and follow the signs for half a mile to the palace.

By Car From Lisbon, head west along the express highway (A1), which becomes Route 249. Turn off at the exit for Queluz. It usually takes 20 minutes.

ESSENTIALS The nearest tourist office is in Lisbon. The **telephone area code** is 01.

Back in Lisbon, we strike out this time on quite a different excursion. On the highway to Sintra **✪ Palácio de Queluz,** Largo do Palácio, 2745 Lisboa (tel. 01/435-00-39), shimmers in the sunlight, a brilliant example of the rococo in Portugal.

Pedro III ordered its construction in 1747, and the work dragged on until 1787. The architect Mateus Vicente de Oliveira was later joined by French decorator/ designer Jean-Baptiste Robillion; the latter was largely responsible for planning the garden and lakeland setting.

Pedro III had actually adapted an old hunting pavilion that once belonged to the Marquis Castelo Rodrigo. Later the pavilion came into the possession of the Portuguese royal family. Pedro III liked it so much he decided to make it his summer residence. What the visitor of today sees is not exactly what it was in the 18th century. Queluz suffered a lot during the French invasions, and almost all its belongings were transported to Brazil with the royal family. A 1934 fire destroyed a great deal of Queluz, but tasteful and sensitive reconstruction has restored the light-hearted aura of the 18th century.

The topiary effects, with closely trimmed vines and sculptured box hedges, are highlighted by blossoming mauve petunias and red geraniums. Fountain pools on which lilies float are lined with blue *azulejos* and reflect the muted facade, the statuary, and the finely cut balustrades.

Inside, you can wander through the queen's dressing room, lined with painted panels depicting a children's romp; through the Don Quixote Chamber (Dom Pedro was born here and returned from Brazil to die in the same bed); through the Music Room, complete with a French grande pianoforte and an 18th-century English harpsichord; and through the mirrored throne room adorned with crystal chandeliers. The Portuguese still hold state banquets here.

Festooning the palace are all the eclectic props of the rococo era—the inevitable chinoiserie panels (these from the Portuguese overseas province of Macau), Florentine marbles from quarries once worked by Michelangelo, Iberian and Flemish tapestries, Empire antiques, Delft indigo-blue ceramics, 18th-century Hepplewhite armchairs, Austrian porcelains, Rabat carpets, Portuguese Chippendale furnishings, and Brazilian wood pieces (*jacaranda*)—all of exquisite quality. When they visited Portugal, Presidents Eisenhower, Carter, and Reagan were housed in the 30-chambered Pavilion of D. Maria I, as were Elizabeth II (on two occasions) and the Prince and Princess of Wales. These storybook chambers, refurbished by the Portuguese government, are said to have reverberated with the rantings of the grief-stricken monarch Maria I, who, it is alleged, had to be strapped to her bed at times. Before becoming mentally ill, she was a bright, intelligent, and brave woman who did a great job as ruler of her country in a troubled time.

The palace is open Wednesday through Monday (except holidays) from 10am to 1pm and 2 to 5pm. From June through September, admission is 400$ ($2.40); During other months, the charge is 200$ ($1.20). It is free on Sunday morning. Children are admitted free.

WHERE TO DINE

EXPENSIVE

COZINHA VELHA [THE OLD KITCHEN], Palácio Nacional de Queluz, Largo do Palácio. Tel. 435-02-32.
   Cuisine: PORTUGUESE/INTERNATIONAL. **Reservations:** Required.
$ **Prices:** Appetizers 950$–1,800$ ($5.80–$11); main courses 1,900$–4,000$ ($11.60–$24.40). AE, DC, MC, V.
   Open: Lunch daily noon–3pm; dinner daily 7:30–10pm.

If you have only two or three meals in all Portugal, take one at Cozinha Velha. Once it was the kitchen of the palace, built in the grand style; now it has been converted into a colorful dining room favored by gourmets, royalty, and the average visitor seeking a romantic setting for a fine dinner.

The entrance is through a garden patio. The dining room is like a small chapel, with high stone arches, a walk-in freestanding fireplace, marble columns, and the original spits. Along one side is a 20-foot marble table that's a virtual still life of the chef's culinary skill, augmented by baskets of fruit and vases of flowers. You sit on ladderback chairs in a setting of shiny copper, oil paintings, and torchères.

I suggest the hors d'oeuvres for two, followed by a main course such as filet steak, poached sea bass, grilled pork on a spit, or whiting with capers. To finish, you might try the island cheese or vanilla soufflé for two.

5. SINTRA

18 miles NW of Lisbon

GETTING THERE   By Train   Sintra is a 45-minute train ride from the Estação Rossio at the Rossio in Lisbon; a train bound here leaves every 15 minutes. The one-way fare is 145$ (90¢).

By Bus   The bus from Lisbon is not recommended because the service is too slow and too many stops are made en route. However, visitors staying in the Costa do Sol hotels can make bus connections at both Cascais and Estoril.

By Car From Lisbon, head west along A1, which becomes Route 249 on its eastern approach to Sintra.

ESSENTIALS The **Sintra Tourist Office** is at Praça da República 23 (tel. 923-11-57). Sintra is visited on many organized tours departing from both Lisbon and Sintra, but this method allows no time for personal discovery, which is essentially what Sintra is all about. The **telephone area code** is 01.

Warning: Do not leave valuables in unguarded cars and beware of pickpockets and purse snatchers. Not only does Sintra attract virtually every tourist who sets foot on Portuguese soil, but it also attracts those who would prey on tourists—not violence but theft.

SPECIAL EVENTS During June and July, the **Sintra Festival** attracts a large number of music lovers. The program is entirely made up of a piano repertoire from the Romantic period, with the best interpreters of the present international music milieu. The various concerts (about 12) usually take place in the region's churches, palaces (Palácio da Vila, Palácio da Pena, and Palácio de Queluz), and parks and country estates. The tourist office (see above) will furnish complete details.

"It is indeed a fairy-tale setting and gives one the feeling that this is where Sleeping Beauty must have rested all those years." These were the words of a publicist singing the praises of Sintra. Writers have been doing that ever since Portugal's greatest poet, Luís Vaz de Camões, proclaimed its glory in *Os Lusíadas* (*The Lusiads*). Lord Byron called it "glorious Eden" when he and John Cam Hobhouse included Sintra in their 1809 grand tour. English romantics thrilled to its description in the poet's autobiographical *Childe Harold's Pilgrimage*.

Picture a town on a hillside, with decaying birthday-cake villas covered with *azulejos* coming loose in the damp mist hovering like a veil over Sleeping Beauty. What would Sintra be without its luxuriant vegetation? It's all here: camellias for melancholic romantics, ferns behind which lizards dart, pink and purple bougainvillea over garden trelliswork, red geraniums on wrought-iron balconies, eucalyptus branches fluttering in the wind, lemon trees studding the groves, and honey-sweet mimosa scenting the air. Be duly warned: There are those who visit Sintra, fall under its spell, and stay forever.

Sintra is one of the oldest towns in the country. When the Crusaders captured it in 1147, they fought bitterly against the Moors firmly entrenched in their hilltop castle, the ruins of which remain today.

WHAT TO SEE & DO

The specific sights of Sintra are set forth below, but the task of selection is difficult. Byron put it well: "Ah me! What hand can pencil guide, or pen, to follow half on which the eye dilates?"

Horse-drawn carriages are available for rent between the town and the serra. It is well worth trying this means of transport for a most agreeable trip under shady trees to the scenery of which Byron wrote. The carriages start from and return to the large square in front of the National Palace of Sintra.

PALÁCIO NACIONAL DE SINTRA, Largo da Rainha D. Amélia. Tel. 923-00-85.

This was a royal palace until 1910. Its last royal inhabitant was Queen Maria Pía, the Italian grandmother of Manuel II, the last king of Portugal. Much of the palace was constructed in the days of the first Manuel, the Fortunate.

The palace opens onto the central town square. Outside, two conically shaped chimney towers form the most distinctive landmark on the Sintra skyline. Long before the arrival of the Crusaders under Afonso Henríques, this was a summer palace of

Moorish sultans, filled with dancing harem girls who performed in front of bubbling fountains. The original was torn down, and the Moorish style of architecture was incorporated in latter-day versions. The entire effect is rather a conglomeration of styles, with Gothic and the Manueline predominant. The glazed earthenware tiles, *azulejos,* lining many of the chambers are among the best you'll find in Portugal.

The Swan Room was a favorite of João I, one of the founding kings, father of Henry the Navigator and husband of Philippa of Lancaster. It is said that one day the English queen came on her king embracing one of the ladies of the court. Apparently she did not hold a grudge against him for this one indiscretion, but it grew into a court scandal of which the king became painfully aware. Hoping to end speculation and save his wife further embarrassment, he called in his decorators into a room, locked the door, and gave them a secret mission. When the doors were finally opened to the ladies of the court, they marched in to discover that the ceiling was covered with magpies. The symbol of the chattering birds scored a point, and a new subject of gossip was discovered. Guides now call the salon the Chamber of the Magpies.

The Room of the Sirens or Mermaids is one of the most elegant in the palace. In the Heraldic or Stag Room, coats-of-arms of aristocratic Portuguese families and hunting scenes are depicted. From most of these rooms, wide windows look out onto attractive vistas of the Sintra mountain range. Tile-fronted stoves are found in the Old Kitchen, where the feasts of yore were held, especially game banquets during the reign of Carlos I, who was assassinated in 1908.

The palace is rich in paintings and Iberian and Flemish tapestries. But it is at its best when you wander into a tree- and plant-shaded patio and listen to the water of a fountain. Perhaps the young king Sebastião sat here lost in the dreams of glory that would one day take him and his country on an ill-fated mission to North Africa, which would cost him his life.

As you approach the palace, you can buy a ticket at the kiosk on your left.

Admission: June–Sept 400$ ($2.40), Oct–May 200$ ($1.20); 100$ (60¢) children under 10.

Open: Thurs–Tues 10am–12:30pm and 2–4:30pm.

PALÁCIO NACIONAL DA PENA, Estrada de Pena. Tel. 923-02-27.

Towering over Sintra, the Pena Palace appeals to special tastes. On a plateau about 1,500 feet above sea level, it perches like a medieval fortress on one peak, looking at the ruins of the old Moorish castle on the opposite hill. Part of the fun of visiting it is the ride up the verdant winding road, through the Parque das Merendas.

At the top you come on a castle that was called a "soaring agglomeration of towers, cupolas, and battlemented walls" by *National Geographic.* The inspiration behind this castle in the sky was Ferdinand of Saxe-Coburg-Gotha, the husband of Maria II.

Of course, Ferdinand needed a German to help him build this fantasy. While dreams of the Middle Ages danced in his head, Baron Eschwege arrived. You can still see a sculptured likeness of the baron by looking out from the Pena at a huge rock across the way. Romantically, the architect fancied himself a soldier armed with a halberd.

In the early 16th century, Manuel the Fortunate ordered a monastery built on these lofty grounds for the Jerónimos monks. Even today you can visit a cloister and a small ogival chapel that the latter-day builders decided to preserve.

Crossing over a drawbridge, you'll enter the palace proper, whose last royal occupant was Queen Amélia. On a morning in 1910, she clearly saw that the monarchy in Portugal was drawing to an end. Having already lost her husband and her soldier son 2 years before, she was determined not to lose her second offspring, Manuel II. Gathering her most precious possessions and only the small family heirlooms that could be packed quickly, she fled to Mafra where her son waited. She left behind Pena Palace and did not see it again until 1945, when she returned to Portugal under much more favorable conditions. Pena has remained much as Amélia left it, which is part of its fascination; it emerges as a rare record of European royal life in the halcyon days preceding World War I.

Pena Park was designed and planted over 4 years, beginning in 1846. Again,

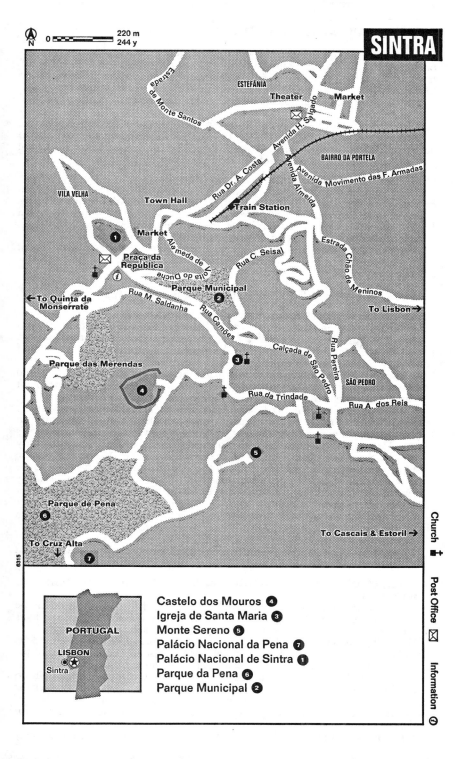

SINTRA

0 ┣━━━━┫ 220 m
        244 y

ESTEFÂNIA
Theater
Market

Estrada de Monte Santos

Avenida H. Salgado

BAIRRO DA PORTELA

Rua Dr. A. Costa

Avenida Almeida

Avenida Movimento das F. Armadas

VILA VELHA
Town Hall
Train Station

Market
1
Praça da República

Alameda de V.

Rua C. Seisal

Estrada Chão de Meninos

Volta op Duche

Parque Municipal
2

Rua M. Saldanha

To Quinta da Monserrate →

Rua Camões

To Lisbon →

Parque das Merendas

Calçada de São Pedro

3

Rua Pereira

SÃO PEDRO

4

Rua da Trindade

Rua A. dos Reis

5

Parque de Pena

6

To Cascais & Estoril →

To Cruz Alta

7

6315

PORTUGAL

LISBON
Sintra

Castelo dos Mouros **4**
Igreja de Santa Maria **3**
Monte Sereno **5**
Palácio Nacional da Pena **7**
Palácio Nacional de Sintra **1**
Parque da Pena **6**
Parque Municipal **2**

Church ✝

Post Office ✉

Information ⊕

Ferdinand was the controlling factor behind the landscaping. What he achieved was one of the most spectacular parks in Portugal, known for the scope of its plant and tree life. For an eye-opening vista of the park and the palace, you can make the ascent to **Cruz Alta.**

Admission: June–Sept 400$ ($2.40); Oct–May 200$ ($1.20); children under 10 free.

Open: Tues–Sun 10am–4:30pm. **Directions:** If you're not driving, you can take a 20-minute taxi or bus ride; the bus departs from Sintra's main square from May to September. If you choose to walk, be warned that it's an arduous trip from the square and will take about 2 hours even if you're in good shape.

CASTELO DOS MOUROS, Calçada dos Clérigos.

The Moorish Castle had been around for a long time when in 1147 Scandinavian crusaders besieged and successfully captured it from its Moorish occupants. It was built sometime between the 8th and 9th century at a position 1,350 feet above sea level. The consort of Maria II, Ferdinand, the German responsible for Pena Palace, attempted restoration in the 19th century, but it was relatively unsuccessful.

There's a parking area for your car, and a guide will send you in the right direction. From the royal tower, the view of Sintra, its palace and castle, and the Atlantic coast is spectacular.

Admission: Free.

Open: June–Sept, daily 9am–6pm; Oct–May, daily 9am–5pm.

PALÁCIO DE MONSERRATE, Estrada de Monserrate.

An Englishman, Sir Francis Cook, set out between 1846 and 1850 to make Lord Byron's dream of a "glorious Eden" a reality. Bringing in landscape artists and flora from everywhere from Africa to Norway, he planned a botanical garden, the rival of which is not to be found in either Spain or Portugal.

The garden scales the slope of a hill—paths cut through to hidden oases—and you'll need to give it the better part of the afternoon. Walking back is rough for all but seasoned hill scalers. However, it's worth the descent.

At the bottom, Cook built his Palácio. It seemed that in his Eden, only a Moorish temple would do. But when Cook died, Monserrate faced a troubled future. An English manufacturer purchased the property and set out virtually to destroy Cook's dreams. He began by selling the palace antiques, and it's said he made so much money on the sale that he was paid back for all the cash he sank into Monserrate. Still he wasn't satisfied. When news leaked out to Lisbon that he was going to subdivide the park and turn it into a housing development of villas, the government belatedly intervened—and well that it did. When you see Monserrate, you'll surely agree that it belongs to all the people, preserved and well maintained.

Lilies float on cool fountains, flowers scent the air, ferns scale the hillside, northern spruce grow tall, and flora from Africa thrives as if it were in its native habitat.

Admission: 100$ (60¢).

Open: June–Sept, daily 10am–6pm; Oct–May, daily 10am–5pm. **Directions:** To reach Monserrate, go out Route EN375 and follow the signs.

CONVENTO DE SANTA CRUZ DOS CAPUCHOS, Estrada de Pena. Tel. 923-01-37.

In 1560, Dom Álvaro de Castro ordered that this unusually structured convent be built along the Estrada de Pena for the Capuchins. Cork was used so extensively in its construction that it is sometimes known as the cork monastery.

You walk up a moss-covered path, like a wayfarer of old approaching for his dole. Ring the bell and a guide (not a monk) will appear to show you in and out of the miniature cells. The convent is in a secluded area, 4½ miles from Sintra.

It appears forlorn and forgotten. Even when it was in use, it probably wasn't too lively. The Capuchins who lived here, perhaps eight in all, had a penchant for the most painstaking of detailed work. For example, they lined the monastery walls with cork-bark tiles and seashells. They also carved a chapel out of rock, using cork for insulation.

A hospital was even installed into the most cramped of quarters. Their monastery is perhaps the coziest in the world. Outside, one of them found time to fresco an altar in honor of St. Francis of Assisi. In 1834, they left suddenly; but fortunately the monastery they left behind wasn't destroyed by vandals.

Admission: 100$ (60¢).

Open: June–Sept, daily 9am–6pm; Oct–May, daily 9am–5pm. **Directions:** It's best reached by taking a taxi from Sintra's main square. There is no bus.

WHERE TO STAY

EXPENSIVE

ESTALAGEM QUINTA DA CAPELA, Monserrate, 2710 Sintra. Tel. 01/ 929-01-70. Fax 01/929-34-25. 8 rms, 3 suites. TEL **Directions:** Follow the signs toward Seteais from Sintra, passing both the hamlet and the gardens of Monserrate, after which you'll see the stone columns and the sign marking the entrance.

$ **Rates** (including breakfast): 14,000$–18,000$ ($85.40–$109.80) single; 21,000$ ($128.10) double; 25,000$ ($152.50) suite. AE, DC, MC, V. **Parking:** Free. **Closed:** Nov–Feb.

Estalagem Quinta da Capela, a complex of two-story stone buildings, was built in the 16th century as a private home for the duke of Cadaval. Much later, the American ambassador to Portugal used it as his weekend retreat before being recalled from his assignment. Today, it is a country inn; ten of its rooms contain TVs. No meals, other than breakfast, are served. The gardens of Monserrate are visible from the breakfast room. A basement-level health club and gym are available, as is a spring-fed pool in the gardens.

HOTEL PALÁCIO DE SETEAIS, Rua Barbosa do Bocage 8, Seteais, 2710 Sintra. Tel. 01/923-32-00. Fax 01/923-42-77. 30 rms. A/C TEL

$ **Rates** (including continental breakfast): 37,000$ ($225.70) single; 40,000$ ($244) double. AE, DC, MC, V. **Parking:** Free.

Lord Byron worked on *Childe Harold's Pilgrimage* in the front garden of this palace converted into a hotel. The establishment is approached via a long private encircling driveway, past shade trees, a wide expanse of lawn, and yew hedges. The stone architecture is formal, dominated by an arched entryway. Seteais looks older than it is, having been built in the late 18th century by a Dutch Gildmeester. It was subsequently taken over and restored by the fifth marquês de Marialva, who sponsored many receptions and galas for the aristocrats of his day.

The *palácio* is on the crest of a hill, with most of its drawing rooms, galleries, and chambers overlooking the formal terraces, flower garden, and vista toward the sea. Upon entering, you'll see a long galleried hall and a staircase with white-and-gilt balustrades and columns leading to the lower-level dining room, drinking lounge, and garden terraces. Along the corridor are tapestries, groupings of formal antique furniture, and hand-woven decorative carpets. On the left is a library with an adjoining music room, furnished with period pieces. The main drawing room is decorated with antiques and a fine mural extending around the cove and onto the ceiling. Large bronze chandeliers with crystal add to the luster. The guest book reads like a *Who's Who.*

Don't just drive up to the entrance and expect to be given shelter. There are only 30 units, so advance reservations are definitely needed. These beautiful rooms are furnished with antiques or reproductions; some contain minibars.

Dining/Entertainment: Lunch or dinner is special in the restaurant Monserrat, and it's possible to come here just for your meal if you make a reservation. In summer, the tables are graced with clusters of pink or blue hydrangea from the garden, and each is set with stemware and silver. The set meal for 8,000$ ($48.80) consists of four courses, with continental and regional dishes. The hors d'oeuvres are among the best, especially the crayfish and fish mousse. The dessert trolley is intriguing—pastries with light rich cream blended with a flaky crust and fruits. After-dinner coffee is taken on the adjoining terrace and loggia or in the dining room. Food is served daily from 12:30 to 2:30pm and 7:30 to 9:30pm. A pianist, harpist, and violinist often entertain.

Services: Laundry, babysitting, room service.
Facilities: Pool, two tennis courts.

MODERATE

QUINTA DE SÃO THIAGO, Estrada de Monserrate, 2710 Sintra. Tel. 01/923-29-23. Fax 01/923-29-23. 10 rms, 2 suites.
$ Rates (including breakfast): 15,000$ ($91.50) single; 16,000$–23,000$ ($97.60–$140.30) double; 28,000$ ($170.80) suite. No credit cards. **Parking:** Free.

$ The Quinta de São Thiago is one of the most desirable places to stay in the Sintra area. Reached along a difficult road, it edges up a side of Sintra mountain. Its origins as a *quinta* go back to some time in the 1500s, and it's always been a private home. Now, in its role as an inn, it's been refurbished and handsomely furnished with antiques. Visited by Lord Byron in 1809, it enjoys a woodland setting. Many of the units open onto views of the Valley of Colares and the water beyond. On a hot day a special delight is the pool, with views of Monserrate and the coastline along the Atlantic.

In the finest British tradition, tea is offered in the parlor, which was transformed from the original kitchen. Dances are held in summer in the music room, and summertime buffets are a feature. Dinner is like eating in the private home of a Portuguese family. The cuisine is both regional and continental. Modern plumbing has been installed, and the quinta guest rooms are comfortably furnished and attractively decorated. It's also recommended that you book ahead for a satisfying dinner in a lovely setting, at a cost of 5,000$ ($30.50), including wine.

HOTEL TIVOLI SINTRA, Praça da República, 2710 Sintra. Tel. 01/923-35-05. Fax 01/923-15-72. 75 rms. A/C MINIBAR TV TEL
$ Rates (including breakfast): 16,500$ ($100.70) single; 19,800$ ($120.80) double. AE, DC, MC, V. **Parking:** Free.

The finest hotel in the center of Sintra is the modern airy Tivoli Sintra, opened in 1981. It lies only a few doors to the right of the Central Hotel (recommended below) and the National Palace and offers an abundance of modern conveniences, including a garage (most important in Sintra). However, the decorator stuck to the typical Portuguese style, and the combination of modern with traditional is successful. The cavernous lobby has floors of marble. Brass lamps are used, and many earth tones are among the colors chosen. The guest rooms are spacious and comfortably furnished, with videos, radios, large beds, and big easy chairs for relaxation. The balconies and the public rooms look out onto a wooded hill, with views of some of Sintra's *quintas* (manor houses). The sight, according to readers Peter and Cynthia Hecker of Berkeley, California, "could have inspired mad Ludwig of Bavaria or at least Walt Disney." The hotel has a restaurant with panoramic views, the Monserrate; a bar; a beauty parlor; and a travel agency. Room service is available to midnight, and laundry and babysitting can be arranged.

INEXPENSIVE

CENTRAL HOTEL, Largo da Rainha D. Amélia 35, 2710 Sintra. Tel. 01/923-09-63. 14 rms (10 with bath). TEL
$ Rates: 11,000$ ($67.10) single without bath; 13,000$ ($79.30) double without bath. 14,500$ ($88.50) double with bath. Breakfast 800$ ($4.90) extra. AE, DC, MC, V.

Central Hotel is for you if you prefer a charming family-owned and -operated village inn offering personalized accommodations and good food. The hotel opens onto the main square of Sintra, facing the National Palace. Because of its location, accommodations facing the square are noisy. The facade is inviting, with decorative blue-and-white tiles and an awning-covered front veranda with dining tables. The interior, especially the guest rooms, reflects an English background. Each room is furnished individually, with a reliance on fine old pieces—like polished wood and inlaid desks. The tiled baths, one to nearly every room, are well designed in cheerful colors.

The Central's restaurant offers a choice of dining on the veranda overlooking the village or in one of the large interior rooms. The cooking is primarily Portuguese, with such main courses as escalopes of veal in Madeira sauce, veal cutlet milanese, beef Portuguese, and chateaubriand for two. A traditional dessert, homemade caramel pudding, makes a smooth finish. You can enjoy a complete dinner for 3,500$ ($21.40) and up. Food is served daily from 12:30 to 3pm and 8 to 9pm.

BUDGET

ESTALAGEM DA RAPOSA, Rua Alfredo Costa 3, 2710 Sintra. Tel. 01/923-04-65. Fax 01/923-57-57. 8 rms. TEL
$ Rates (including breakfast): 7,700$ ($47) single; 8,400$ ($51.20) double. AE, DC, MC, V.

S Estalagem da Raposa was formerly the private home of an old Sintra family. It's been run as an inn for 40 years and is centrally located, within walking distance of the railroad station. The house is set back from the street in a fenced and flowered yard. The inn is owned by a Lisbon family who will make you feel at home immediately. They keep a careful eye on the housekeeping and upkeep of the high-ceilinged rental units. Rooms are furnished with old-fashioned pieces that are homey and comfortable. The maid who keeps the rooms in spotless condition is polite, and she runs right up with a ring of keys to open your door the moment she hears you on the carpeted stairs. You can enjoy regional specialties in the tearoom.

NEARBY PLACE TO STAY

EXPENSIVE

SINTRA ESTORIL HOTEL, no. 9 ao km 6 (Junto ao Autodromo), 2765 Alcabideche. Tel. 01/469-07-21. Fax 01/469-07-40. 187 rms, 5 suites. A/C TV TEL
$ Rates (including breakfast): 17,600$ ($107.40) single; 22,000$ ($134.20) double; 40,000$ ($244.00) suite. AE, DC, MC, V. **Parking:** Free.
Sintra Estoril, in Alcabideche, is a crescent-shaped hotel between Sintra, Cascais, and Estoril. On the outside it looks like a stadium, with encircling balconies. It's not unlike a modern museum inside, with its guest-room balconies opening onto a large playground area, an Olympic-size pool, and tennis and volleyball courts. Its lounges are varied, lofty, and warmly colored. A few public rooms have drama, with shimmering mirrored walls, circular sofas, or a wall of abstract sculpture. Even the guest rooms have their own contemporary character—each with built-in headboards on the two double beds, a radio, piped-in music, and a terrace; some contain minibars.

Dining/Entertainment: Live music is played nightly in the bar, and every Friday evening a folkloric show is presented. The restaurant serves an international cuisine.

Services: 24-hour room service; babysitting, laundry.

Facilities: Sauna, pool, tennis and volleyball courts, playground.

WHERE TO DINE

MODERATE

RESTAURANTE SOLAR S. PEDRO, Praça Dom Fernando II 12, off the Largo da Feira in São Pedro de Sintra. Tel. 923-18-60.
Cuisine: PORTUGUESE/ITALIAN/FRENCH. **Reservations:** Recommended.
$ Prices: Appetizers 450$–1,500$ ($2.70–$9.20); main courses 600$–3,500$ ($3.70–$21.40); fixed-price menu 2,500$ ($15.30).
Open: Lunch Thurs–Tues noon–3pm; dinner Thurs–Tues 7:30–10pm.
Solar S. Pedro is run by the helpful and hospitable Francisco Freitas, who speaks English. His place is a popular rendezvous, as diners are drawn not only to his personality but also to his good selection of Portuguese cuisine, as well as Italian and French specialties. The lobster crêpes are a favorite, and another specialty is a flavorsome filet of sole. Trout with cream and toasted almonds is perfectly balanced. Also excellent is the steak Café Paris. Many of the beef specialties are distinguished as

well, including the peppersteak and the entrecôte with mushrooms. A lovely windowless room, the restaurant is decorated with tiles, wrought-iron, and regional artifacts.

TACHO REAL, Rua da Ferraria 4. Tel. 923-52-77.
   Cuisine: PORTUGUESE/INTERNATIONAL. **Reservations:** Recommended.
   $ Prices: Appetizers 550$–950$ ($3.40–$5.80); main courses 1,200$–2,200$ ($7.30–$13.40). AE, DC, MC, V.
   Open: Lunch Thurs–Tues 12:30–3pm; dinner Thurs–Tues 7:30–10pm. **Closed:** Oct 15–Nov 15.

Sometimes Portuguese diners come all the way from Lisbon to enjoy a well-prepared meal at this restaurant. Fish and meat dishes are deftly handled in the kitchen, and some poultry dishes are also offered. Service is efficient and polite, and English is spoken.

HOTEL TIVOLI SINTRA, Praça da República. Tel. 923-35-05.
   Cuisine: PORTUGUESE/INTERNATIONAL. **Reservations:** Recommended.
   $ Prices: Appetizers 950$–1,500$ ($5.80–$9.20); main courses 1,800$–2,800$ ($11–$17.10). AE, DC, MC, V.
   Open: Lunch daily 12:30–2:30pm; dinner daily 7:30–9:30pm.

Because it's concealed within the concrete-and-glass walls of the town center's most desirable hotel, many visitors might overlook the reliable Tivoli Sintra's impressive possibilities as a dining spot. Actually, it serves some of the finest food in town and prides itself on its associations with two hotels of note in nearby Lisbon. Staffed by a battalion of uniformed waiters, the place is capped with a shimmering metallic ceiling, ringed with dark paneling, and illuminated along one side with floor-to-ceiling panoramic windows. Specialties include tournedos Rossini, a delectable fish soup, filet of turbot elegantly prepared house style with mushrooms and garlic, and seafood.

INEXPENSIVE

RESTAURANT ALCOBAÇA, Rua dos Padarias 7. Tel. 923-16-51.
   Cuisine: PORTUGUESE. **Reservations:** Recommended.
   $ Prices: Appetizers 450$–750$ ($2.70–$4.60); main courses 750$–1,500$ ($4.60–$9.20). MC, V.
   Open: Lunch daily noon–4pm; dinner daily 7–10:30pm. **Closed:** Dec.

Popular with English visitors, this shop-size restaurant occupies two floors of a centrally located building on a steep and narrow pedestrian street. The place is *very* local and consequently provides one of the cheapest meals in town. As you'd expect, Alcobaça serves typical Portuguese cuisine, including roast sardines, *caldo verde*, hake filet with rice, octopus, and Alcobaça chicken.

6. ERICEIRA

13 miles NW of Sintra; 31 miles NW of Lisbon

GETTING THERE By Train You can take the train from Lisbon to Mafra, where connections to Ericeira are available. There is no direct rail service to Ericeira.

By Bus Ericeira is served by Mafrense buses from both Sintra and Lisbon.

By Car From Sintra (see above) continue northwest along Route 247.

ESSENTIALS The **Ericeira Tourist Office** is at Rua Mendes Leal (tel. 631-22). The **telephone area code** is 061.

This fishing port nestles on the Atlantic shore. Its narrow streets are lined with whitewashed houses, accented by pastel-painted corners and window frames. To the east, the mountains of Sintra appear.
   The sea has been giving life to Ericeira for 700 years and continues to do so today.

Not only do the fishermen pluck their food from it, but also it is the sea, especially the beach, that lures streams of visitors every summer, adding a much-needed boost to the local economy. Along the coast lobsters (*lagosta*) are bred in cliffside nurseries, *serração*. Any place in Ericeira, lobster is *la spécialité de la maison*.

In 1584, Mateus Alvares arrived in Ericeira from the Azores, claiming to be King Sebastião (The Desired One), who was killed (some say disappeared) on the battlefields of North Africa. Alvares and about two dozen of his chief supporters were finally executed after their defeat by the soldiers of Philip II of Spain, but he is today remembered as the king of Ericeira. It wasn't until October 1910 that the second monumental event occurred at Ericeira. From the harbor, the fleeing Manuel II and his mother, Amélia, set sail on their yacht to a life of exile in England.

For such a small place, there are quite a few sights of religious and historic interest. The **Church of São Pedro** (St. Peter) and the **Misericórdia** (charitable institution) both contain rare 17th- and 18th-century paintings. The **Hermitage of São Sebastião,** with its Moorish designs, would seem more fitting in North Africa. There is one more hermitage honoring St. Anthony.

The chloride-rich spring waters of **Santa Maria** attract health-spa enthusiasts. However, it is the crescent-shaped sandy **Praja do Sol** that is the favorite of Portuguese and foreign visitors alike.

NEARBY ATTRACTION

PALÁCIO NACIONAL DE MAFRA, 2640 Mafra. Tel. 061/81-18-88.

⭐ This palace, baroque *chef d'oeuvre* of precision craftsmanship, is an ensemble of discipline, grandeur, and majesty. At the peak of its construction, it is said to have employed a working force of 50,000 Portuguese. A small town was built just to house the workers. Its master model was El Escorial, that Daedalian maze constructed by Philip II outside Madrid. Mafra's corridors and complex immurements may not be as impressive, nor as labyrinthine, but the diversity of its contents is amazing. The end product was 880 rooms, housing 300 friars who could look through 4,500 doorways and windows.

That devout king of "peace and prosperity," João V, seemingly couldn't sire an heir, and court gossips openly speculated that he was sterile. One day, he casually mentioned to a Franciscan that if he were rewarded with an heir, he would erect a monastery to the order. Apparently the Franciscans, through what the king considered "divine intervention," came through. João produced his heir and Mafra was born; the work on it began in 1717. Originally it was to house 13 friars, but that figure rapidly mushroomed into 300.

It is said that Mafra, 13 years in the making, was built with the gold and diamonds pouring in from the new colony of Brazil. Seeing it now and considering building methods in those days, one wonders how such a task was ever completed in so short a time.

Its more than 110 chimes, made in Antwerp, can be heard from a distance of 12 to 15 miles when they are played at Sunday recital. Holding the chimes are two towers flanking a basilica, capped by a dome that has been compared to that of St. Paul's in London. The inside of the church is a varied assortment of chapels, 11 in all, expertly crafted with detailed jasper reredos, bas-reliefs, and marble statues from Italy. In the monastery is the pride of Mafra, a 40,000-volume library with tomes 200 and 300 years old, many gold-leafed. Viewed by some more favorably than the world-famed library at Coimbra, the room is a study in gilded light, decorated in what has been called grisaille rococo. In the Museum of Religious Art, the collection of elaborately decorated vestments is outstanding.

Following the omnipresent red Sintra marble, you enter the monks' pharmacy, hospital, and infirmary, the beds without mattresses. Later you can explore the spacious kitchens and the penitents' cells, with the flagellation devices used by the monks.

The summer residence of kings, Mafra was home to such members of Portuguese royalty as the banished Queen Carlota Joaquina. In addition to having a love of painting, Carlos I, the Bragança king assassinated at Praça do Comércio in 1908, was also an avid hunter. In one room, he had chandeliers made out of antlers and upholstery of animal skins. His son, who ruled for 2 years as Manuel II, spent his last night on Portuguese soil at Mafra before fleeing with his mother, Amélia, to England.

You can wander through the trompe-l'oeil–ceilinged audience room, the sewing room of Maria I, and the music room of Carlos. Throughout the apartments hang decaying tapestries, taking their place among antiques, ceramics, and silverware.

Admission: June–Sept 300$ ($1.80); Oct–May 200$ ($1.20); children 11 and under and those 65 or over free.

Open: Wed–Mon 10am–1pm and 2–5pm. **Bus:** An RN bus from Lisbon runs to Mafra, 25 miles northwest of the Portuguese capital.

NEARBY PLACE TO STAY
INEXPENSIVE

HOTEL CASTELÃO, Avenida 25 de Abril, 2640 Mafra. Tel. 061/812-050.
Fax 061/51-698. 34 rms. MINIBAR TV TEL
$ Rates (including breakfast): 8,700$ ($53.10) single; 10,500$ ($64.10) double. AE, DC, MC, V. **Parking:** Free.

For good accommodations, I recommend the Castelão, which has comfortable rooms furnished with radios, easy chairs, reading lamps, and carpeted floors. Guests can relax in a reading room. The hotel has four bars and a typical wine cellar. The restaurant, where well-prepared meals cost from 1,950$ ($11.80), has a panoramic view over the village's main street. The hotel's location is excellent, right in the heart of Mafra.

WHERE TO DINE
MODERATE

O POCO, Calçada da Baleia 10. Tel. 636-69.
$ Prices: Appetizers 550$–1,200$ ($3.40–$7.30); main courses 1,500$–3,300$ ($9.20–$20.10); tourist menu 1,800$ ($11). AE, DC, MC, V.
Open: Lunch daily noon–4pm; dinner daily 7–10pm. **Closed:** Wed in winter.

O Poco serves a wide range of cookery, with Portuguese and international specialties, especially seafood, predominating. Some 50 diners can pack in here, taking a table overlooking the esplanade for a good and filling à la carte meal. Specialties include tournedos in Madeira sauce with fried banana, monkfish with prawns and potatoes, and sole Ericeira style.

PARREIRINHA, Rua Dr. Miguel Bombarda 12. Tel. 621-48.
Cuisine: PORTUGUESE. **Reservations:** Not necessary.
$ Prices: Appetizers 550$–950$ ($3.40–$5.80); main courses 1,000$–1,800$ ($6.10–$11). AE, DC, MC, V.
Open: Lunch Wed–Mon noon–3:30pm; dinner Wed–Mon 7:30–10pm. **Closed:** Nov.

If you're passing through for the day, this is a good restaurant stopover. Lots of seafood dishes, as expected, appear on Parreirinha's menu, but I always gravitate to their tender pork cooked with baby clams. Steak, the most expensive item on the menu, is cooked with a special hot sauce, the recipe for which is known only to the chef. The service is accommodating. You'll want to stick around for supper. Everything tastes better when washed down with a bottle of *vinho verde*.

CHAPTER 9

SOUTH OF THE TAGUS

As continental travelers from Victorian England crossed the Tagus by boat and headed for the scenic wonders on the left bank of Lisbon, chances are they carried a gold-leafed copy of a work by Robert Southey, England's poet laureate. After all, this Lake poet, a much-traveled gentleman, did more than anyone to publicize the glories that awaited his compatriots on the other bank. He virtually made the trek famous when he wrote: "I have never seen such a sublime panorama as the Arrábida Mountains afford, which, constantly changing as we go our way, offer us new beauties at every turn."

Nowadays, the narrow isthmus south of the Tagus is fast booming into a major attraction. Behind the upsurge of interest is the Ponte 25 de Abril, a long suspension bridge that has sped traffic and development to the area so now it is possible to cross the Tagus in minutes. You can then head rapidly across good roads through pine groves to the vertices of the triangle known as "The Land of the Three Castles": Sesimbra, Setúbal, and Palmela. Of course, traditionalists still prefer taking the ferry from Praça do Comércio in Lisbon and docking in Cacilhas.

The isthmus—long cut off from the Portuguese capital—is wild, rugged, lush, and productive. The strip of land plummets toward the sea, stretches along for miles of sandy beaches, and rolls through groves heavy with the odors of ripening oranges and vineyards of grapes used to make muscatel. With craggy cliffs and coves in the background, the crystalline Atlantic is ideal for swimming and skindiving or fishing for tuna, swordfish, and bass.

Sandy beaches double as the sites of fish auctions and leisurely sunbathing. Farther up from the sardine-canning center of Setúbal, the coastline roughens where the Serra of Arrábida meets the sea, resulting in an abundance of caves, grottoes, and precipitous crags.

The land possesses vivid reminders of its past, reflected in Moorish architectural influences, Roman ruins and roads, traces of the Phoenicians, and Spanish fortresses. Mighty castles and humble fishermen's cottages alike shook in November 1755 when an earthquake brought Lisbon to its knees. Signs of that catastrophe are still evidenced in the ruins of the hamlet of Palmela and the lonely walls of Coina Castle.

SEEING THE REGION SOUTH OF THE TAGUS

Its proximity to Lisbon (Setúbal is only 25 miles southeast of the capital) makes this area ideal for a one-day excursion. Yet its unusual inns and moderate tariffs mark it as a place where the budget-minded reader will want to linger.

Because of its proximity to Lisbon and because so many local citizens virtually use

WHAT'S SPECIAL ABOUT THE REGION SOUTH OF THE TAGUS

Great Towns/Villages

- [ ] Sesimbra, a former fishing village that has emerged as a major tourist resort.
- [ ] Setúbal, on the right bank of the Sado River—one of Portugal's largest and most ancient cities.
- [ ] Portinho da Arrábida, a summer stopover because of its good local beaches.
- [ ] Azeitão, a sleepy village lying in the heart of "quinta country"—known for its 16th-century Quinta das Torres mansion.

Beaches

- [ ] Costa da Caparica, on the extensive Setúbal peninsula, south of the Tagus, providing the cleanest ocean swimming close to Lisbon.
- [ ] The peninsula's southernmost beaches, cleaner and less crowded than Caparica—with dozens of sandy coves for swimming and lots of fishing villages.
- [ ] Tróia, a long sandy peninsula, across the Sado River estuary from Setúbal—a pine-studded strip of land that's frequented by sun worshippers in summer

Ace Attractions

- [ ] Serra de Arrábida, a 5,000-foot-high mountain range, now a national park—with wild crags falling steeply into the ocean.
- [ ] "The Land of the Three Castles": Sesimbra, Setúbal, and Palmela—the mandatory stops along the tourist circuit.
- [ ] Cabo Espichel, a salt-encrusted headland and fabled pilgrimage site at the southwestern point of the Setúbal peninsula.

Architectural Highlight

- [ ] Convento de Jesús, Setúbal, ornately decorated—the first example in Portugal of the Manueline style of architecture. Hans Christian Andersen hailed it as "one of the most beautiful small churches that I have ever seen."

this region south of the Tagus as "bedroom communities," the area has an extensive network of ferry connections as well as bus hookups from Lisbon. Train travel is very limited. For those who can afford car rentals, driving is the ideal way to explore the district at your leisure. Otherwise, you can take a bus to the beaches at Caparica in about 45 minutes from Lisbon. Departures are from the Praça de Espanha. These buses go over the Ponte 25 de Abril bridge.

If you take one of the ferries from Lisbon's Praça do Comércio to Cacilhas on the other side of the Tagus, you can catch a bus there for the beaches of Caparica. If you're visiting the peninsula by bus, use Setúbal as your hub; from there you can take local buses to Palmela and Sesimbra.

In summer, a narrow gauge railway runs for 5 miles along the Costa da Caparica, making 20 stops at various beaches along the way. If you go by rail to the peninsula, service is to Setúbal, where you must rely on buses to visit the fishing villages along the southern coast.

SUGGESTED 2-DAY ITINERARY

Day 1 Head south from Lisbon for a day spent exploring the fishing village–cum–resort of Sesimbra. Visit its castle and the Cabo Espichel headland, a famed pilgrimage site.

Day 2 Head east along the foothills of the Serra de Arrábida, stopping for lunch at Portinho da Arrábida. In the afternoon, visit the Convento de Jesus at Setúbal and spend an hour or two at one of the beaches of Tróia, a sandy peninsula across the river. Stay overnight at Setúbal or continue 5 miles east to the government-run inn, Pousada do Castelo de Palmela, but only if you've made reservations.

1. AZEITÃO

9½ miles NW of Setúbal; 15½ miles SE of Lisbon

GETTING THERE   By Car   Because of this village's isolation, you'll need a car. After crossing the Ponte 25 de Abril bridge across the Tagus, continue south along the old road to Setúbal (Route 10) until you see the turnoff for the village of Azeitão.

ESSENTIALS   There is no local tourist office, and the nearest tourist office in Setúbal is not likely to have any information. The **telephone area code** is 065.

This sleepy village lies in the heart of *quinta* country. In Portuguese, a *quinta* means a "farm," "villa," or "country house." At its most meager, it is a simple farmhouse surrounded by lands. At its best, it is a mansion of great architectural style filled with art decorations. Azeitão boasts the best.

Azeitão makes a good base for trekkers, especially those who want to scale the limestone Serra de Arrábida by foot. Others settle for long walks through scented pine woods or silvery olive groves. To cap your day, you can order some Azeitão cheese and a bottle of local muscatel.

WHAT TO SEE & DO

QUINTA DE BACALHOA, Vila Fresca de Azeitão. Tel. 208-00-11.
It is said that Manuel I started the concept of quintas in the early 16th century when he built the Quinta de Bacalhoa, where his mother once lived. In time, it was taken over by the son of Afonso de Albuquerque. At one point in its history the building was owned by the Braganças; it eventually fell into disrepair, and many of its decorations, specifically its antique tiles, were carted off by vandals.

Before World War II, the mansion was purchased by an American woman who worked for years to restore it as much as possible to its original condition. The architecture is characterized by loggias, pavilions, half-moon domes suggesting a Moorish influence, and a trio of pyramided towers. One of the panels of 16th-century *azulejos* (tiles) depicts an innocent Susanna being hotly pursued by lecherous Elders. Some architectural critics have suggested that the palace is the first sign of the Renaissance in Portugal. Bacalhoa is a private villa, but the gardens are open to the public on request.

The quinta's farmland is devoted to vineyards owned by J. M. da Fonseca, International-Vinhos, Lda., makers of Lancers wine. There are two J. M. da Fonseca wineries half a mile apart: the "mother house," as it is called, and a newer plant characterized by white domes. The original winery and warehouses are in the center of Azeitão, as is the classic 19th-century house that was the Fonseca family home. A little museum and public reception room can be visited on the ground floor of the house. The century-old Fonseca wineries have made their product from grapes grown on the slopes of the Arrábida Mountains since the early 19th century, and the fine muscatel for which they have long been known is used in the flavoring and sweetening of white Lancers. Of course, the Fonseca vintners produce other wines you might like to try besides the popular Lancers, much of which is exported. Their top product is a muscatel called Setúbal, rarely sent abroad but considered delectable by wine connoisseurs.

Another 16th-century mansion, **Quinta das Torres,** is open for visits or even a meal or an overnight stay (see "Where to Stay & Dine," below).

Admission: Free; tip expected.
Open (on request): Gardens Mon–Sat 1–5pm.

WHERE TO STAY & DINE
MODERATE

QUINTA DAS TORRES, Estrada Nacional 5, Azeitão, 2900 Setúbal. Tel. 065/208-00-01. 10 rms, 2 suites.

$ Rates (including breakfast): 15,000$ ($91.50) single; 15,000$–18,000$ ($91.50–$109.80) double; 25,000$ ($152.50) suite. MC, V. **Parking:** Free.

A 16th-century baronial mansion of deteriorating elegance, Quinta das Torres has been kept intact for those who desire to step back in time and live quietly. It has been owned by the same family for many generations. The estate is approached through large gates and along a tree-lined driveway; Gradually a pair of square peaked towers framing the entrance terrace comes into view. Each guest room is unique—ranging from smaller chambers to a ballroom-size suite dominated by princess-style brass beds, with a high tester and flouncy ruffles. Some rooms have high shuttered windows, time-mellowed tile floors, antique furnishings, vases of fresh flowers, oil lamps, and niches with saints or madonnas.

The dining room has a covered ceiling, a tall stone fireplace where log fires are lit on chilly evenings, plus elaborate scenic tiles depicting *The Rape of the Sabine Women* and *The Siege of Troy*. The rich-tasting, heavy cuisine is well recommended; a meal will cost around 4,000$ ($24.40). The bill of fare is likely to include smoked filet of pork, steak *au poivre,* and giant prawns. Food is served daily from 1 to 3pm and 7 to 9pm.

---

2. SESIMBRA

16 miles SW of Setúbal; 26½ miles S of Lisbon

GETTING THERE   By Train   It's better to go directly from Lisbon by bus, as rail passengers must first go to Setúbal by train, then double back on a bus from Setúbal to Sesimbra.

By Bus   Carreiras Suburbanas, Lisbon's suburban bus network, operates frequent buses daily from Lisbon to Sesimbra. If you're coming from Setúbal, local buses make frequent runs, the ride taking only 30 minutes.

By Car   From Lisbon, cross the Ponte 25 de Abril bridge, continuing southwest on the A2 expressway to Setúbal. At the junction of Route 378 at Santara, head directly south for the final lap leading into Sesimbra.

By Ferry   You can also get to Sesimbra by taking the ferry from Praça do Comércio wharf in Lisbon, then bus from Cacilhas.

ESSENTIALS   The **Tourist Office** is at Largo de Marinha (tel. 223-57-43). The **telephone area code** is 01.

SPECIAL EVENTS   The year's festivities begin with Carnaval—Mardi Gras (Shrove Tuesday/Pancake Tuesday)—when there is always a cortège that attracts a great number of young people. There is also the typical Cegadas, consisting of a kind of popular burlesque theater, usually made only by men, where the political, economic, or daily-life events of the town, government, or country are satirized.

To promote Sesimbra's gastronomy, in April (no fixed date) there is Festa do Peixe e do Marisco. Apart from special dishes based on fish and shellfish, this event also has music, exhibitions, and contests.

From May 3 to 5, there is a religious festivity: Festas em Honra do Senhor Jesus das Chagas—the celebration of the patron saint of the fishermen. On May 4 is a procession and the blessing of the sea. There is also an exuberant town fair.

From June 23 to 30, the Festivities of the Popular Saints are presented. During this period, the streets are gaily decorated. At night bonfires, marches, and sometimes fado give a joyful atmosphere to the event.

From July 25 to 28, the celebration of the town's patron saint, São Tiago, takes place. The event is marked by several cultural events, including dance.

On the last Sunday of September is another religious feast: Our Lady of the Cape, with a procession and a small fair.

In October (no fixed date) there is the Festival do Mar, an event with cultural, sports, and gastronomic activities.

Among the Portuguese, Sesimbra used to be a closely guarded secret. With justification, it was considered one of the most unspoiled fishing villages in the country. Nowadays, rapid new building and growth have occurred. High-rise buildings overshadow the old life. However, the varinas and fishermen still go about their time-honored task of plucking their livelihood from the Atlantic. Against a backdrop of rocky cliffs, sardines, shellfish, whiting, and the scabbard fish (with its whip-shaped body and daggerlike teeth) lie stretched out in the sun. When the fleet comes in, the day's catch is auctioned at a lota at the harbor (Porto Abrigo). Sesimbra also enjoys popularity as an angling center.

WHAT TO SEE & DO

Far down the beach, beyond the boat-clogged harbor, is the 17th-century **Fortress of St. Teodosio,** built to fortify the region against the pirates who plagued and plundered, carting off the most beautiful women and girls.

A walk along the ruined battlements of the five-towered **Castle of Sesimbra** reduces the village to a nearly immobile miniature. The castle was captured from the Moors in 1165 and rebuilt following the 1755 earthquake, which sent sections of its crenellated walls tumbling to the ground. Enclosed within is a 12th-century church, the oldest monument in Sesimbra.

From Sesimbra, you can head west to the headland of **Cabo Espichel,** with arcaded pilgrim hospices dating from the 1700s. Often violently windswept, with sea gulls circling overhead, this strip of land has been called the "Land's End of Portugal," a reference to the far western extremity of England. A pilgrimage church now in a state of disrepair, Santuario Nossa Senhora do Cabo, occupies space in this melancholy atmosphere. You can inspect its baroque interior with gilded wood and sculpture. Later, you can walk to the edge of the cliffs in back of the church for a spectacular view. *Beware:* There's no guard rail, and it's a sheer drop of 350 feet to the ocean waters. Modern sculpture is placed about in this forlorn setting. At the southern end of the Arrábida chain, this pilgrimage site has been popular since the 13th century. It was here in 1180 that Fuas Roupinho routed the Moors at sea, his forces capturing several enemy ships. From Sesimbra, six buses a day make the 30-minute journey to the southwestern cape.

WHERE TO STAY
MODERATE

HOTEL DO MAR, Rua General Humberto Delgado 10, 2070 Sesimbra. Tel. 01/223-33-26. Fax 01/223-38-88. 168 rms. A/C TEL
$ Rates (including breakfast): 11,300$–32,700$ ($68.90–$199.40) single; 17,300$–34,300$ ($105.50–$209.20) double. Children under 8 stay at 50% discount in parents' room. AE, DC, MC, V. **Parking:** Free.
One of the most unusual self-contained beach-resort hotels south of the Tagus, Hotel do Mar is a beehive construction of units spreading from a high cliff to the water below. The passageways are like continuous art galleries, with contemporary paintings and ceramic plaques and sculpture, and the main lobby houses a glassed-in tropical bird aviary. All the airy guest rooms have private terraces, with views of the

ocean and gardens sweeping down the hillside; some have minibars. Furnishings are streamlined and well selected. Breakfast is served on a flower-filled terrace.

Dining/Entertainment: The hotel restaurant is warmed with wood-grain paneling and overlooks the sea. You might stop off from a day-trip from Lisbon and order a meal for 4,000$ ($24.40) and up. The before-dinner gathering point is a rustically styled bar; after dinner, guests congregate in the living room, which has a fireplace.

Services: Concierge, transfer services, laundry, babysitting, room service.

Facilities: Two tennis courts, beach, outdoor and indoor pools, sauna, solarium.

BUDGET

HOTEL ESPADARTE, Avenida 25 de Abril 11, 2970 Sesimbra. Tel. 01/22-33-189. 80 rms. TEL

$ Rates (including breakfast): 6,000$ ($36.60) single; 8,800$ ($53.60) double. AE, DC, MC, V. **Parking:** Free.

Named after the swordfish that once flourished in local waters, this five-floor hotel, open all year, is right on the esplanade near the water; below the incline ramp are boats and seamen mending their nets. Most of the accommodations have private balconies overlooking the sea. The rooms' sort of 1960s decor is simple but comfortable. The Concha do Mar restaurant specializes in seafood and features a self-service section. In the Bar Miami, guests can dance or watch a movie. There is also a solarium, along with laundry facilities and individual safes.

WHERE TO DINE

MODERATE

RESTAURANTE RIBAMAR, Avenida dos Naufragos. Tel. 223-48-53.

Cuisine: PORTUGUESE. **Reservations:** Recommended.

$ Prices: Appetizers 150$–1,600$ (90¢–$9.70); main courses 1,800$–2,500$ ($10.90–$15.20). MC, V.

Open: Lunch daily noon–3pm; dinner daily 7–10:30pm.

Restaurante Ribamar serves some of the best Portuguese cookery in the area, specializing in fish and shellfish, most of it freshly caught in local waters. Its location is in front of the sea, a short stroll from the beach, with a view of the bay. There is space for about 60 seats outside and 80 inside. The chef's specialty is a platter of mixed fish and shellfish for two. Swordfish, caught in local waters, is also highly valued. Downstairs are two large aquariums where guests can "catch" their own lobster, crayfish, or crab.

3. PORTINHO DA ARRÁBIDA

8 miles SW of Setúbal; 23 miles SE of Lisbon

GETTING THERE By Bus Buses making the run between Sesimbra (see above) and Setúbal (see below) make stops at Portinho da Arrábida.

By Car If you're a motorist, you can explore the foothills of the Serra de Arrábida, stopping for lunch at this fishing village. From Sesimbra, continue along Route 379 in the direction of Setúbal, forking right at the turnoff from Portinho da Arrábida. See below for a warning about parking.

ESSENTIALS The nearest tourist office at Setúbal or Sesimbra will be of little help.

The limestone Arrábida Mountains stretch for about 22 miles, beginning at Palmela and rolling to a dramatic end at Cabo Espichel on the Atlantic. At times, the cliffs and bluffs are so high it seems you have to peer through the clouds to see the purple waters of the Atlantic below.

A Swiss botantist once said the mountain range contained "the most amazing flora to be seen in Europe." The foliage that rims the cliffs and the surrounding areas is lush, subtropical, and wide ranging, including holm oaks, sweet bay, pines, laurel, juniper, cypress, araucaria, magnolia, lavender, myrtle, and pimpernels. A riot of color and fragrance carpets the mountains.

Portinho da Arrábida is at the foot of the serra. This is a favorite oasis with many Lisbon families who rent little multicolored cottages on the beach. If you take a car down here in July and August, you do so at your own risk. There is virtually no parking space, and the road should be one way but isn't. You can be stranded for hours trying to get back up the hill. The other problem is this: To walk down and back could qualify you for the Olympics. Knowing visitors try to park on a wider road above the port, then negotiate the hordes of summer visitors on foot.

The serra is riddled with numerous caves and grottoes, the best known of which is the **Lapa de Santa Margarida.** Of it, Hans Christian Andersen wrote: "It is a veritable church hewn out of the living rock, with a fantastic vault, organ pipes, columns, and altars."

Perched on a hillside like a tiara over Portinho da Arrábida, the **New Convent** dates from the 16th century. You can go to the gate and ring for the caretaker, who may or may not show you around the precincts.

WHERE TO DINE
MODERATE

RESTAURANTE BEIRA-MAR, Portinho da Arrábida. Tel. 208-05-44.
   Cuisine: PORTUGUESE. **Reservations:** Not necessary.
$ **Prices:** Appetizers 450$–1,200$ ($2.70–$7.30); main courses 900$–2,800$ ($5.40–$17); tourist menu 1,950$ ($11.90). No credit cards.
   Open: May–Sept, daily noon–9:30pm; Oct–Nov and Jan–Apr, Thurs–Tues noon–9:30pm. **Closed:** Dec.

A meal here can be your reward for the trek down the hill. The most sought-after warm-weather tables at this airy restaurant are set out on a concrete balcony, a few feet above the port's still waters, near the many fishing vessels. White paper usually serves as the napery for the savory but unpretentiously informal Portuguese meals. Full meals include pork with clams, roast chicken, fish stew, grilled sardines, several preparations of codfish, grilled sole, shellfish rice, and several regional wines.

---

4. SETÚBAL

25 miles SE of Lisbon

GETTING THERE   By Train   There are at least 28 trains per day, linking Lisbon with Setúbal. Trip time is 1½ hours, and a one-way fare costs 235$ ($1.40).

By Bus   Buses from Lisbon arrive at the rate of one every hour or every 2 hours (depending on the time of day). The trip takes an hour, with a one-way ticket costing 470$ ($2.80)—more expensive than the train.

By Car   After crossing the Ponte 25 de Abril bridge from Lisbon, follow the signs to Setúbal along the express highway, A2, until you see the turnoff for Setúbal. The old road (Route 10) to Setúbal is much slower.

ESSENTIALS   The **Setúbal Tourist Office** is at Largo do Corpo Santo (tel. 52-42-84). The **telephone area code** is 065.

On the right bank of the Sado River lies one of Portugal's largest and most ancient cities, said to have been founded by the grandson of Noah. Motorists often include it on their itineraries because of an exceptional inn, the Pousada de São Filipe, installed in a late 16th-century fort overlooking the sea (see "Where to Stay," below). Setúbal is known as the center of Portugal's sardine industry and for the production of the most exquisite muscatel wine in the world. As far back as the days of the Romans and the Visigoths, the aromatic and hearty grapes of this region were praised by connoisseurs.

Orange groves (a jam is made from the fruit), orchards, vineyards, and outstanding beaches (such as the popular Praia da Figueirinha) compose the environs of Setúbal. The white pyramidal mounds you see dotting the landscape are deposits of sea salt drying in the sun, another major commercial asset of this seaside community.

Many artists and writers have come from Setúbal, none more notable than the 18th-century Portuguese poet Manuel Maria Barbosa du Bocage, a forerunner of romanticism. At Praça do Bocage, a monument honors him. In this port, windmills still clack in the countryside, roosters crow, and the "girls of the sardines" seem to speak Portuguese with an Arabic accent.

WHAT TO SEE & DO

CONVENTO DE JESÚS, Praça Miguel Bombarda, off Avenida 22 de Dezembro. Tel. 52-47-72.

The Convento de Jesús is a late 15th-century example of the Manueline style of architecture. Of particular interest are the main chapel and the ornate decorations on the main doorway and the Arrábida marble columns. Each of these columns is actually three columns twisted together like taffy to form a cable or rootlike effect. Somehow they don't seem to hold up the vaulted ceiling but give the illusion of appendages grown down to the floor. Raymond Postgate wrote that the columns "look as if they had been twisted and wrung by a washerwoman," and Hans Christian Andersen recorded that the monument was "one of the most beautiful small churches that I have ever seen." The church has been heavily restored, the latest wholesale renovation from 1969 to 1970.

Admission: Free.

Open: Tues–Sun 10am–12:30pm and 2–6pm. **Bus:** 2, 7, 8, or 20.

MUSEU DA CIDADE (Town Museum), Praça Miguel Bombarda, off Avenida 22 de Dezembro. Tel. 52-47-72.

Adjoining the Convento de Jesús is this unpretentious museum that houses some early 16th-century Portuguese paintings as well as Spanish and Flemish works and a contemporary art section. The museum has a temporary exhibitions gallery where you can see different works.

Admission: Free.

Open: Tues–Sun 10am–12:30pm and 2–6pm. **Bus:** 2, 7, 8, or 20.

PENINSULA DE TRÓIA

Tróia is a long sandy peninsula, across the Sado River estuary from Setúbal. The pine-studded strip of land is the site of one of Portugal's largest tourist enterprises, featuring the **Torralta Tourist Complex** with high-rise apartment-hotels and a par-72, 6,970-yard, 18-hole golf course designed by Robert Trent Jones. The beaches are some of the best south of Lisbon, and the waters are said to be unpolluted. In addition to the golf course, other sporting facilities include seawater swimming pools, watersports facilities, playgrounds for children, and about a dozen tennis courts. It's possible to rent bicycles to tour the island, or you can go horseback riding.

You can rent apartments on the island if you'd like a seaside holiday of a few days. Further information is available by writing **Torralta—CIF, S.A.,** Avenida Duque de Loulé 24, 1098 Lisboa Codex (tel. 01/355-44-79).

At **Cetóbriga,** on the peninsula, ruins of a thriving Roman port have been discovered, with excavations beginning in the mid-19th century. The city, dating from the 3rd and 4th centuries, was destroyed by the ocean, but traces have been unearthed of villas, bathing pools, a fresco-decorated temple, and a place for salt preservation of fish. There is also evidence that long-ago seafarers, the Phoenicians, inhabited the peninsula at one time. Cetóbriga's ruins are about 1½ miles from the site of the present tourist development of Tróia. The scant ruins can be seen opposite the marina.

To reach Tróia from Setúbal, buy a ticket from Transsado, Doca do Comércio (tel. 52-33-84), off Avenida Luisa Todi at the eastern sector of the waterfront. At least 36 ferries ply back and forth throughout the day. Trip time is only 15 minutes, and the cost is 85$ (50¢) for adults and 45$ (30¢) for children. It's also possible to take a car over, costing 400$ ($2.40) each way.

WHERE TO STAY

EXPENSIVE

POUSADA DE SÃO FILIPE, Castelo de São Filipe, 2900 Setúbal. Tel. 065/52-18-44. Fax 065/52-25-38. 14 rms, 1 suite. TV TEL
$ Rates (including breakfast): 22,100$ ($134.80) single; 25,200$ ($153.72) double; 32,000$ ($195.20) suite. AE, DC, MC, V. **Parking:** Free.

This fortress-castle dates back to 1590, when it was built by an Italian architect who came to Portugal during the ill-fated reign of the young king Sebastião. The builder perched it on a hilltop overlooking the town and the harbor. You wind your way up a curving mountain road, passing through a stone arch and past towers to the belvedere. Rooms that once were for the soldiers and the governor have been tastefully and richly furnished with antiques and reproductions. In earlier days there were guns and ammunition, but they have given way to soft beds and ornate Portuguese-crafted headboards. The walls of the chapel and the public rooms contain tile dados depicting scenes from the life of São Filipe and the life of the Virgin Mary. They are dated 1736 and signed by Policarpo de Oliveira Bernardes.

The guest rooms are individually decorated; some are air-conditioned. They are reached via what seems like miles of plant-filled corridors, up wide worn stone steps. The Pousada is reached by taxi from Setúbal, as it is too far for most people to walk.

Dining/Entertainment: You'll find dining pleasant while ensconsed in the restaurant's Windsor-style armchairs. Six alcoved windows open onto a panoramic view. Against a background of tile dado, a primitive tapestry, and photostated engravings, a luncheon or dinner, including many fish specialties, is served. Most guests take this meal when they stop over on a day-trip from Lisbon, paying from 3,300$ ($20.10) to 4,000$ ($24.40). The clients seem to gravitate to the medieval-style lounge, with its coved and arched ceiling, pierced-copper hanging lanterns, tile bar, and husky brass-studded armchairs. The sitting rooms are also intimate, with tile walls, antiques, bowls, engravings, chests, and copper artifacts in the niches.

Services: Laundry service, room service.
Facilities: Car-rental facilities.

INEXPENSIVE

ESPERANÇA HOTEL, Avenida Luisa Todi 220, 2900 Setúbal. Tel. 065/52-51-51. Fax 065/302-83. 64 rms, 12 suites. TEL **Bus:** 2, 7, 8, or 20.
$ Rates (including breakfast): 8,800$ ($53.60) single; 10,000$ ($61) double; from 12,000$ ($73.20) suite. AE, DC, MC, V. **Parking:** Free.

Esperança Hotel stands in the heart of Setúbal, on the main inner street. It's a modern six-story building with basic amenities, a clean-cut lounge, and a reception area with streamlined furnishings—all in a restrained design. Each guest room is done in pastels and has built-in headboards, a dressing table, bedside lighting, and an all-tile bath. All the suites have TVs. The top-floor dining room provides a panoramic view of the area, including the Sado River. The hotel also has a bar and nightclub. Laundry service is provided, and room service is available 24 hours.

WHERE TO DINE

INEXPENSIVE

O BECO, Largo da Misericórdia 24. Tel. 52-46-17.
Cuisine: PORTUGUESE. **Reservations:** Not necessary. **Bus:** 2, 7, 8, or 20.
$ Prices: Appetizers 300$–1,200$ ($1.80–$7.30); main courses 900$–1,750$ ($5.40–$10.60). AE, DC, MC, V.

Open: Lunch Wed–Mon noon–4pm; dinner Wed–Mon 7:15–11pm. **Closed:** Sept 15–Oct 2.

Located in the center of town, O Beco is entered through a narrow passageway that leads to two dining rooms decorated in a typical style with old ovens, regional artifacts, and a fireplace. The service is efficient, the food excellent. The quantities could be smaller and nobody would leave hungry. Shellfish soup is the classic opener. Pork chops are from the acorn-sweetened variety in Alentejo, and a special beefsteak is offered. *Cabrito* (goat) is also good. Two more recommendable regional dishes include a Portuguese stew, *cozido,* and paella. More adventurous seafaring palates will order the grilled squid. A typical dessert is orange tart.

RESTAURANTE BOCAGE, Rua da Marqueza do Faial 8–10. Tel. 52-25-13.
> **Cuisine:** PORTUGUESE. **Reservations:** Not accepted.
> **$ Prices:** Appetizers 350$–1,200$ ($2.10–$7.30); main courses 900$–1,800$ ($5.40–$10.90). AE, DC, MC, V.
> **Open:** Lunch Wed–Mon 12:15–3:30pm; dinner Wed–Sun 7:15–10:30pm.

Old Portugal comes alive for visitors who approach the faded facade of this pink-walled town house, whose doors open onto a corner of the traffic-free main square. Inside you'll find a no-nonsense decor of 1950s-era ceiling fans, a coffered white ceiling, and a green-and-white-terrazzo floor. Most patrons order a fruity muscatel to accompany the array of fresh fish served here. In deference to their almost exclusively local clientele, regional Portuguese cookery is emphasized. A meal is traditionally topped off with a taste of muscatel brandy.

5. PALMELA

5 miles N of Setúbal; 20 miles SE of Lisbon

GETTING THERE By Car From Lisbon, head south along the A2 after crossing Ponte 25 de Abril, exiting at the cutoff marked Palmela. From Setúbal, continue north along A2 to the same exit. (There is no bus or train service.)

ESSENTIALS The nearest tourist office at Setúbal (see above) might have a pamphlet on the *pousada,* not much else for Palmela. The **telephone area code** is 01.

The village of Palmela lies in the heart of a wine-producing region, in the foothills of the Arrábida Mountains. It is famous for its fortress, from which, at a vantage point of 1,200 feet, you'll be rewarded with one of the most extensive and varied views in all Portugal. Over sienna-hued valleys and vineyards heavy with grapes, you can see the capital to the north and the estuary of the Sado to the south.

The position of **Palmela Castle** has long been a strategic point in securing control of the lands south of the Tagus. It was from Palmela that Afonso Henríques, the first king of Portugal, drove out the Moors and established his new nation's domination of the district. The 12th-century fortress was, in its day, a splendid example of medieval military architecture. It is further believed that the Celts founded a castle on this spot in 300 B.C.

Of special interest is the Roman road discovered behind the castle by archeologists. It is the only such road to be unearthed in Portugal and makes for speculation as to its relationship with the Roman beach colonies of Tróia, off Setúbal. You can scale the hill to the castle any time of the day.

WHERE TO STAY & DINE
EXPENSIVE

POUSADA DO CASTELO DE PALMELA, 2950 Palmela. Tel. 01/235-12-26. Fax 01/233-04-40. 28 rms, 2 suites. A/C MINIBAR TV TEL

$ Rates (including breakfast): 22,100$ ($134.81) single; 25,200$ ($153.70) double; 30,600$–35,200$ ($186.60–$214.70) suite. AE, DC, MC, V. **Parking:** Free.

This is one of the last remaining segments of the 12th-century castle. It was built as a monastery within the castle walls in 1482 on orders of João I and dedicated to St. James. The change to use it as a pousada kept it from falling into complete ruin. The conversion was done skillfully and unobtrusively, so the classic look and feel of a cloister have been preserved. It is located on the high crest of a hill, overlooking the valley and sea in the distance. It's traditional in design, a huge square building opening into a large courtyard. The lower-level arches have been glassed in and furnished with lounge chairs.

Each of the guest-room cells has been opened up, enlarged, and given a glamorous up-to-date ambience. They are furnished in the Portuguese manner, with hand-carved pieces and fine fabrics; most open onto views. Near the dining room is a comfortable drawing room with a noteworthy washbasin once used by the monks for their ablutions.

Dining/Entertainment: The dining room, once the refectory of the monastery, is stately yet informal. The pulpit used for the reading of prayers during meals is still standing. The room is large and long, with terra-cotta-tile floors and large windows. The effect is beautiful, light, and elegant. The service is efficient. Portuguese cuisine is offered, with meals costing from 6,000$ ($36.60). Food is served daily from 12:30 to 2:30pm and 7:30 to 9:30pm.

Services: Laundry service, room service.

CHAPTER 10
ESTREMADURA

The first flowers of the Portuguese empire bloomed hundreds of years ago, in these lands north of Lisbon, and the beauty has not been diminished by time. Like the once-white limestone of Battle Abbey (Batalha), this land has been gilded in the sunlight of the passing years.

Estremadura is a land of contrasts. The Atlantic smashes the coast of Guincho, while farther up it can hardly muster a ripple in the snug cover of São Martinho do Porto. These coastal regions are teeming with seafood: nursery-bred lobster, shrimp, crabs, squid, tuna, barnacles, and albacore. The sea is never far from any spot in Estremadura. From many a village's bastion, its shimmer can be seen, a reminder of the source of the land's bounty. In the many examples of Manueline architecture, especially at Batalha, the tie with the sea remains unbroken. The basic nautical designs—ropes, cables, armillary spheres, seascape effects—acknowledge the debt.

SEEING ESTREMADURA

If it is impossible for you to spend several days exploring Estremadura, you can still get a glimpse of it on short day-trips from Lisbon: first to Óbidos, 58 miles north of Lisbon; then to Alcobaça, 67 miles north of Lisbon; on to Nazaré, 81 miles north of Lisbon; back to Batalha, 73 miles north of Lisbon; and finally to Fátima, 87 miles north of the capital. Traveling to these five major places will take you through the heartland of Estremadura.

The fastest way to see the area is by car; the roads are generally good, although traffic can be heavy, especially on summer weekends. Travel by train is not very efficient. Even the major tourist attractions of Estremadura—Nazaré and Fátima—have no direct rail links to Lisbon. Buses, however, service the region for those with plenty of time for exploring and quite a bit of patience.

SUGGESTED 2-DAY ITINERARY

Day 1 Head north from Lisbon to the walled city of Óbidos, where you should spend the night in its famed *pousada* (reserve well in advance). Spend the rest of the day exploring this medieval gem.

Day 2 After a morning visit to Caldas da Rainha, press northwest to Alcobaça to see the monastery there, before journeying to Nazaré for the night. In the morning, retrace your steps through Alcobaça, but head north this time to view the monastery at Batalha before going on to Fátima for the night.

1. ÓBIDOS

58 miles N of Lisbon; 4 miles S of Caldas da Rainha

GETTING THERE By Train From the Estação Rossio Station in Lisbon, commuter trains run to Torres Verdes, where a change of trains is necessary for

WHAT'S SPECIAL ABOUT ESTREMADURA

Great Towns/Villages

☐ Óbidos, a medieval city that the "poet king," Dinis, presented to his wife, Isabella of Aragón, as a present.

☐ Nazaré, Portugal's most famous fishing village—which becomes a popular beach resort every summer.

☐ Fátima, world-famous pilgrimage site—where, it is said, an image of the Virgin Mary appeared.

Beaches

☐ An almost continuous strand of sandy beach goes all the way to the top of Estremadura. The beach at Nazaré is the most frequented, but not necessarily the most hygienic.

Monasteries

☐ Mosteiro de Santa Maria, Alcobaça, a Cisterian monastery from 1152— once the richest and most prestigious in Europe.

☐ Mosteiro de Santa Maria da Vitória, at Batalha, in Gothic-Manueline style—built by the founder of the House of Avíz, João I.

Architectural Highlight

☐ Ramparts of Óbidos, dating from the Moorish occupation but restored over the centuries.

Special Events

☐ The Great Pilgrimages—First Pilgrimage of the Year to Fátima in early to mid-May and Last Pilgrimage of the Year to Fátima (October 12–13), drawing hundreds of faithful pilgrims from around the world to commemorate the apparitions of the Virgin Mary to three shepherd children on May 13, 1917.

Óbidos. Count on about 3 hours of travel. About eight trains per day make the connection, with a one-way fare costing 590$ ($3.60).

By Bus   There are bus connections from Lisbon, but it's harder than getting here by train. Buses leave from Avenida Casal Ribeiro in Lisbon, going to Caldas da Rainha. From there, you have to transfer to another bus to Óbidos. About six buses a day go from Caldas da Rainha to Óbidos (trip time: 20 minutes).

By Car   From Lisbon, the N8 carries motorists north from Lisbon to Óbidos via Torres Vedras.

ESSENTIALS   You'll find the **Óbidos Tourist Office** on Rua Direita (tel. 062/95-92-31). The **telephone area code** is 062.

Years after Afonso Henríques drove the Moors out of Óbidos, the poet king, Dinis, and his saintly wife, Isabella of Aragón, passed by the walls of this medieval borough and were struck by its beauty. The queen likened the village, with its extended walls and gleaming plaster-faced houses, to a jewel-studded crown. Anxious to please, Dinis made her a present of this exquisite village ribboned by a defensive wall. A tradition was established: Instead of giving precious stones, Portuguese royal bridegrooms presented Óbidos to their spouses—and it didn't cost them a penny. And what queen could complain at getting such a gift?

Entered through a tile-coated gatehouse, Óbidos rises on a sugarloaf hill, above a valley of vineyards. Its golden towers, its ramparts (rebuilt in the 12th century and subsequently restored), and its crenellated battlements contrast with bright white houses and the rolling countryside where windmills clack in the breeze. Inside its confines, you will travel back hundreds of years. The narrow streets are either cobbled or made of roughly hewn flagstones. Green shoots lodge in the crannies of the walls, and vines climb the sides of tiled-roofed houses. A loom hums in a candlelit vaulted workshop. It's a living piece of history.

The castle has been converted into a tourist inn *(pousada)*. From its ramparts you can bask in views of Estremadura, the scene so typical you can imagine Afonso Henríques' retinue marching over the hills.

In the Renaissance **Parish Church of Santa Maria,** 10-year-old Afonso V exchanged marriage vows with his cousin, only 8. Inside, the church is lined with blue-and-white *azulejos*. Pause long enough to admire a Renaissance tomb and the paintings of Josefa of Óbidos, a 17th-century artist. The Chapel of St. Lawrence contains relics of saints' hands.

Save some time for browsing through the shops, searching out thick-woven fabrics, regional rugs (both hand- and machine-made), raffia and handmade bags, and the local lace.

WHERE TO STAY
EXPENSIVE

POUSADA DO CASTELO, Paço Real, 2510 Óbidos. Tel. 062/95-91-05.
Fax 062/95-91-48. 6 rms, 3 suites. A/C TEL
$ Rates (including breakfast): 21,100$ ($128.70) single; 25,200$ ($153.70) double; from 30,000$ ($183) suite. AE, DC, MC, V. **Parking:** Free.

For excellent accommodations, I recommend Pousada do Castelo. This Manueline-trimmed stone palace lodged on the ramparts of the walls of Óbidos is firmly rooted in Portugal's history , and today, with the supervision of the government, it is one of the best pousadas in the country. Reached via twisting cobblestone streets through the village, the entrance is through a thick Gothic archway. You ascend farther, into a wide sunny forecourt, and up a grand stone stairway to the main hall. Through the Manueline door, you can go to Foz do Arelho beach, a pleasant resort where the British writer Graham Greene used to spend his vacations.

There are several well-furnished lounges. The fortunate few who stay here enjoy the character of the guest rooms, furnished with antiques or fool-the-eye reproductions. Deeply set windows have tiny monk ledges where you can squat to enjoy the view of the surrounding countryside. Homelike cretonne fabrics cover the beds, and a few rooms contain desks with brass church lamps, armchairs, and ecclesiastical wall plaques.

Dining/Entertainment: Most wayfarers stop just off for the day, partaking of the 3,500$ ($21.30) to 5,250$ ($32) luncheon or dinner. I particularly recommend the roast suckling pig and the chicken cooked in an earthenware pot with red-wine sauce. Try for a table near one of the view windows. The dining room is in the Portuguese quinta style, almost grand yet nicely provincal, with old oak beams, a tile dado, a fireplace, wrought-iron chandeliers, and leather chairs. If you're not staying at the pousada, call ahead for summertime dining reservations. Food is served daily from 12:30 to 3pm and 7:30 to 9:30pm. Fellow guests gather in one of the two drinking lounges for sundown drinks.

Services: Laundry, room service

INEXPENSIVE

ALBERGARIA JOSEFA D'ÓBIDOS, Rue Dom João de Ornelas, 2510 Óbidos. Tel. 062/95-92-28. Fax 062/95-95-33. 38 rms. A/C MINIBAR TV TEL
$ Rates (including breakfast): 7,500$ ($45.70) single; 9,500$ ($57.90) double. AE, DC, MC. **Parking:** Free.

The Albergaria Josefa d'Óbidos, just outside the old town's fortifications, is of recent construction although it looks much older. All guest rooms contain radios; some have wall-to-wall carpeting. Because the inn is set on a hillside, it is entered through two separate main doors.

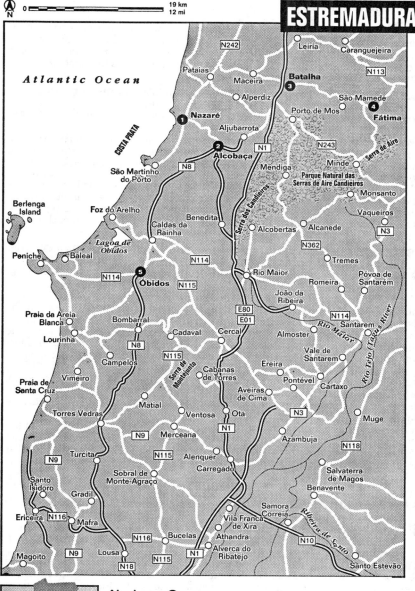

ESTREMADURA

N
0 ⎓ 19 km
12 mi

Atlantic Ocean

N242
Leiria
Caranguejeira
N113
Pataias
Maceira
Batalha ❸
São Mamede
Alperdiz
Porto de Mos
Fátima ❹
Nazaré ❶
Aljubarrota
N1
N243
Minde
Serra de Aire
São Martinho do Pôrto
Alcobaça ❷
N8
Mendiga
Parque Natural das Serras de Aire Candieiros
Monsanto
Berlenga Island
Foz do Arelho
Benedita
Vaqueiros
Caldas da Rainha
Alcobertas
Alcanede
N3
Lagoa de Obidos
Serra dos Candieiros
N362
Peniche
Baleal
N114
Tremes
Óbidos ❺
N115
Rio Maior
Romeira
Póvoa de Santarém
João da Ribeira
N114
Praia da Areia Blanca
Bombarral
E80
E01
Santarem
Cadaval
Cercal
Almoster
Rio Maior
Lourinha
N8
N115
Vale de Santarem
Rio Tejo (Tagus River)
Serra de Montejunta
Cabanas de Torres
Ereira
Campelos
Pontével
Cartaxo
Praia de Santa Cruz
Vimeiro
Aveiras de Cima
Matial
Ventosa
Ota
N3
Muge
Torres Vedras
N1
N9
Merceana
Azambuja
N118
Turcita
N115
Alenquer
Santo Isidoro
Sobral de Monte-Agraço
Carregado
Salvaterra de Magos
N9
Gradil
Benavente
Samora Correia
Ericeira
N116
Mafra
Vila Franca de Xira
N116
Bucelas
Athandra
N10
Ribeira de Sorto
Magoito
N9
Lousa
N115
Alverca do Ribatejo
N18
N1
Santo Estevão

COSTA PRATA

PORTUGAL
Estremadura
⭐ LISBON

Alcobaça ❷
Batalha ❸
Fátima ❹
Nazaré ❶
Óbidos ❺

There's a typical restaurant with a private terrace, which you may want to patronize even if you're not staying there. Meals start at 2,200$ ($13.40). Service is daily from 12:30 to 3pm and 7:30 to 10pm. You can have an apéritif in the bar, which is decorated with reproductions of the works of the artist who is the namesake of this *albergaria*. There is a disco on the ground floor.

ALBERGARIA RAINHA SANTA ISABEL, Rua Direita, 2510 Óbidos. Tel. 062/95-93-23. Fax 062/95-91-15. 20 rms. TV TEL

$ Rates (including breakfast): 8,500$ ($51.80) single; 10,000$ ($61) double. AE, DC, MC, V. **Parking:** Free.

Except for the necessity of negotiating a parking space, many visitors prefer this above many of the other area hostelries. It's on a narrow cobblestone-covered street running through the center of town. It opened as a hotel in 1985, but the building itself, once a private home, is many centuries old. The high-ceilinged lobby is covered with blue, white, and yellow tiles. There's a comfortable sunny bar area filled with leather-covered sofas and Victorian-style chairs. An elevator carries you to your guest room. Most guests drive through the town and deposit their luggage at the reception desk before moving on to park free on the square in front of the village church, about 100 feet away.

ESTALAGEM DO CONVENTO, Rua Dom João de Ornelas, 2510 Óbidos. Tel. 062/95-92-14. Fax 062/95-91-59. 27 rms, 4 suites. MINIBAR TEL

$ Rates (including breakfast): 11,500$ ($70.10) single; 13,500$ ($82.30) double; 16,000$-18,500$ ($97.60-$112.80) suite. AE, MC, V. **Parking:** Free.

This old village nunnery turned inn, owned by chemist Luís de Sousa Garcia, is located outside the town walls. The reception lounge is surely the tiniest on the Iberian peninsula, with a fireplace, a 17th-century chest, torchères, and a pair of gilt angels. The guest rooms have furniture to complement the structure. Although the beds are old, the mattresses are more recent. The rooms open off rambling corridors with chests and benches large enough to hold the trousseaus of a dozen brides.

Dinner guests from the outside are welcomed and can order a 2,500$ ($15.20) table d'hôte or specialties from the à la carte menu, including French onion soup, peppersteak, and crêpes Suzette. The dining room's decor consists of heavy black beams, an open corner stone fireplace, and a brick oven. On sunny days, guests dine on the rear patio, in a garden with a moldy stone wall and tangerine and orange trees. Food is served daily from 12:30 to 2:30pm and 7:30 to 9:30pm. In addition to a bar with hand-hewn beams, there's a living room with leather armchairs, old paintings, an 18th-century desk, and a brass-studded chest dating from 1827. A former wine cellar has been turned into a typical pub.

BUDGET

PENSÃO MARTIM DE FREITAS, Estrada Nacional 8, Arrabalde, 2510 Óbidos. Tel. 062/95-91-85. 6 rms (4 with bath or shower).

$ Rates (including breakfast): 4,000$-5,000$ ($24.40-$30.50) double without bath, 6,000$-7,500$ ($36.60-$45.70) double with bath or shower. MC, V. **Parking:** Free.

The Pensão is outside the walls on the road that leads to Alcobaça and Caldas da Rainha. The accommodating hosts rent simply furnished rooms. Everything is spotless in this establishment, which is generally cited by the Tourist Office to those seeking low-cost accommodations. Breakfast is the only meal served.

WHERE TO DINE
MODERATE

Most visitors to Óbidos like to dine at the Pousada do Castelo (see above). However, you get far better value, less formality, and more local color at one of the typical little restaurants that exist inside or outside the walls.

RESTAURANTE ALCAIDE, Rua Direita. Tel. 95-92-20. Cuisine: RIBATEJAN. **Reservations:** Recommended.

$ Prices: Appetizers 125$–950$ (70¢–$5.80); main courses 1,800$–2,200$ ($10.90–$13.40); fixed-price menu 2,000$ ($12.20). AE, DC, MC, V.
Open: Lunch Tues–Sun 12:30–3:30pm; dinner Tues–Sun 7:30–9:30pm.
Closed: Nov.

My favorite within the walls is Restaurante Alcaide. On a narrow street leading up to the pousada, this little restaurant is known for its regional cookery and good and inexpensively priced wines. Decorated Portuguese tavern style, it opens onto a balcony where the lucky few quickly fill up the tables. As many as 50 guests can be seated at one time. In the afternoon, you can drop in for either tea or a drink.

RESTAURANTE DOM JOÃO V, Largo da Igreja Senhor da Pedra. Tel. 95-91-34.
   Cuisine: EXTREMADURAN. **Reservations:** Not necessary.
$ Prices: Appetizers 450$–650$ ($2.70–$3.30); main courses 1,000$–1,650$ ($6.10–$10). AE, DC, MC, V.
   Open: Lunch Tues–Sun noon–4pm; dinner Tues–Sun 7–11pm. **Closed:** Oct.

Located half a mile west of the center of Óbidos, this restaurant specializes in the regional cuisine of Estremadura, accompanied by good Portuguese wines. The dining room is spacious and clean, and you're invited to look into the kitchen, so you can make your own selection if you find the menu confusing. The helpful staff adds to the enjoyment of dining here, where the food is not fancy but tasty and good value. Parking is possible, an important plus in Óbidos.

---

2. ALCOBAÇA

67 miles N of Lisbon; 10 miles NE of Caldas da Rainha

GETTING THERE   By Train   Trains depart from Lisbon's Estação Rossio Station. The nearest rail connection is at Valado dos Frades, 3 miles away, halfway between Nazaré and Alcobaça. About 14 buses per day make the short run from the train station at Valado dos Frades into Alcobaça, with a one-way ticket costing 115$ (70¢).

By Bus   About 14 buses a day connect Nazaré with Alcobaça; a one-way ticket costs 170$ ($1). There are also three *expressos* a day from Lisbon, the trip taking 2½ hours and costing 880$ ($5.30) one way.

By Car   From Caldas da Rainha, continue northeast along N8 to reach Alcobaça.

ESSENTIALS   The **Alcobaça Tourist Office** is at Praça 25 de Abril (tel. 062/423-77). The **telephone area code** is 062.

The main attraction here is the monastery described below. After your visit, you can explore the nearby market, said to sell the best fruit in all Portugal, especially succulent peaches grown in surrounding orchards originally planted by the Cistercian monks. Many stalls also sell the blue-and-white pottery of Alcobaça.

WHAT TO SEE & DO

MOSTEIRO DE SANTA MARIA (St. Mary Monastery), 2460 Alcobaca. Tel. 4-34-69.

At the apex of its power in the Middle Ages, the Cistercian Mosteiro de Santa Maria was one of the richest and most prestigious in Europe. Begun around 1152, it was founded to honor a vow made by Portugal's first king, Afonso Henríques, should he be victorious over the Moors at Santarém. Alcobaça, at the confluence of the Alcoa and Baça rivers, was built to show his spiritual indebtedness to St. Bernard of Clairvaux, who inspired (others say goaded) many crusaders into battle against the infidel.

Today the monastery, in spite of its baroque facade and latter-day overlay, is a monument to simplicity and majesty. Somehow a sense of other-worldliness pervades as you walk down the 327-foot-long nave. Tall chalk-white clustered columns, like trees, hold up a vaulted ceiling nearly 70 feet high. The transept of Alcobaça shelters the Gothic tombs of two star-crossed lovers, the Romeo and Juliet of Portuguese history: Pedro the Cruel and the ill-fated Spanish beauty, Inês de Castro, his mistress and later (perhaps) his wife. The work of an unknown sculptor, their sarcophagi (although damaged) are considered the greatest pieces of sculpture from 14th-century Portugal.

The oval-faced Inês is guarded and protected by angels hovering over her. Her tomb rests on sculpted animals with human faces, said to represent the assassins who slit her throat. Inês was buried at Alcobaça following a ghoulish ceremony in which the king had her decaying body exhumed and forced his courtiers to kiss her rotted hand and honor her as "the queen of the realm." Around the tomb are panels depicting scenes from the Last Judgment.

Pedro hoped to rise on that day of Resurrection to greet Inês emerging from her sleep of centuries. On a wheel of fortune at his tomb, a sculptor, following his mandate, carved the words *ate o fim do mundo,* meaning "until the end of the world." Guarded by angels, his feet nestled on a dog, Pedro lies in a tomb supported by lions, symbols of his timeless rage and vengeance.

There is much to see at Alcobaça, including the Cloisters of Silence, with their delicate arches, favored by Dinis, the poet king. He sparked a thriving literary colony at the monastery, where the monks were busily engaged in translating ecclesiastical writings. But aside from the tombs and cloisters, the curiosity is the kitchen, through which a branch of the Alcoa River was routed. As in most Cistercian monasteries, the flowing brook was there for sanitation. Chroniclers have suggested that the friars fished for their dinner in the brook and later washed their dishes in it. In the huge chimneyed pit, five or six steers or oxen were roasted at the same time. A 6-ton marble table resting here would probably have accommodated Gargantua and Pantagruel.

Finally, in the 18th-century Salon of Kings are niches with sculptures of some of the rulers of Portugal. An air of melancholy is lent to the scene by the empty niches left waiting for the rulers who were never sculptured. The tiles in the room depict, in part, Afonso Henríques' triumph over the Moors.

Admission: Apr–Sept 300$ ($1.80); Oct–Mar 200$ ($1.20).
Open: Apr–Sept, daily 9am–7pm; Oct–Mar, daily 9am–5pm.

WHERE TO STAY
BUDGET

HOTEL SANTA MARIA, Rua Francisco Zagalo, 2460 Alcobaça. Tel. 062/59-73-95. Fax 062/59-67-15. 31 rms. MINIBAR TV TEL
$ Rates (including breakfast): 5,500$ ($33.50) single; 8,500 ($51.80) double. MC, V. **Parking:** Free.

The most attractive modern hotel in town is on a sloping street just above the flower-dotted plaza in front of the monastery. Its position in a quiet but central part of the historic city is ideal. The combination TV salon/bar/breakfast room is on the ground floor. Each of these rooms is filled with paneling cut into well-polished geometrical shapes and comfortable contemporary chairs, some of which look out over the monastery. If parking is a problem, the hotel will open its garage free. Each guest room contains a radio. Some chambers contain balconies looking out over the square. Only breakfast is served.

WHERE TO DINE
MODERATE

TRINDADE, Praça Dom Afonso Henríques 22. Tel. 062/423-97.
Cuisine: PORTUGUESE. **Reservations:** Not necessary.

$ Prices: Appetizers 550$–990$ ($3.30–$6); main courses 1,500$–1,800$ ($9.10–$10.90). V.
Open: Lunch daily noon–3:30pm; dinner daily 8–10pm. **Closed:** Sept 25–Oct 26; Sat in winter.

Trindade, the most popular restaurant in town, opens onto a side of the monastery, fronting a tree-shaded square. In fair weather, tables are placed on this square, and harried waiters rush back and forth across the street carrying cooling drinks. Trindade has both a full restaurant service and snack-bar facilities. Your meal is likely to include shellfish soup, roast rabbit, or the fresh fish of the day. Roast chicken is also available.

3. NAZARÉ

82 miles N of Lisbon; 8 miles NW of Alcobaça

GETTING THERE   By Train   There is no direct link to Lisbon. About four trains per day head north from Lisbon to Valado dos Frades; the 3-hour trip costs 720$ ($4.30) one way. From Valado dos Frades to Nazaré, it is necessary to take a bus (see below).

By Bus   About a dozen buses a day make the short run between Nazaré and Valado dos Frades (the nearest rail terminal), a one-way ticket costing 115$ (70¢). It is possible to go from Lisbon to Nazaré by bus. Express buses from Lisbon arrive at the rate of five per day, taking only 2 hours, shorter than the train, and costing 950$ ($5.80) one way.

By Car   From our last stopover in Alcobaça (see above), continue northwest along 8-4.

ESSENTIALS   The **Nazaré Tourist Office** is on Avenida da República (tel. 56-11-94). The **telephone area code** is 062.

The inhabitants of Portugal's most famous fishing village live in a unique, tradition-bound, ageless world. Many have never been to Lisbon; indeed, many have never left their village, except perhaps to make the pilgrimage to nearby Fátima.

The people remain insular, even though their village blossoms into a big resort in summer. White tents filled with international visitors dot the crescent-shaped beach. Still the natives go about their time-honored tasks, perhaps pausing to pose for cameras. Nazaré was originally discovered by writers and painters; but in the 1960s seemingly everyone arrived. For that reason, the young who have grown up in a tourist-oriented economy will probably not follow the time-honored folkways of their forebears.

Nazaré is best viewed in winter, because chances are that you won't get to see it in summer. You'll be too busy looking for a parking place (virtually impossible to find) or fighting for a place on the beach in a seething mass of humanity. The problem is that Nazaré is advertised as "the most picturesque" and "the most quaint" fishing village of Portugal. With advertising like that, the hordes arrived and now have almost engulfed the village itself. That, coupled with high-rise construction on every foot of available land, has made people wonder what happened to the fishing village. It's still there—you just have to look harder for it.

Don't expect stunning architectural styles or historic sights. The big attraction is its people and their boats. Claiming descent from Carthaginian and Phoenician ancestors, many of the natives are characterized by aquiline noses and dark brows. They are a gentle, hard-working folk whose classical features are marked and lined by sad, yet noble, countenances.

The villagers' clothes are patch quilts of sun-faded colors. The rugged-looking men appear in rough woolen shirts and trousers, patched in kaleidoscopic rainbow hues, resembling Scottish plaid. Although the origin of this apparel remains unknown, one explanation is that the fishermen picked up the designs from Wellington's troops, who passed this way during the Napoleonic wars. On their heads the men wear long woolen stocking caps, in the dangling ends of which they keep their valuables—a favorite pipe or even a crucifix.

The women are mostly barefoot, wearing embroidered handmade blouses and pleated skirts also made of plaid woolens patched many times. It is customary for married women to don black as a traditional sign of mourning—tasseled black shawls or black capes or cowls; whereas the unmarried girls of the village are traditionally attired in seven petticoats. The government has made it illegal for tourists to count these petticoats, as many were fond of doing in the 1950s.

The boats of the fishermen are Phoenician in design, elongated, slender, and decorated in bold colors. Crudely shaped eyes often appear on the high knifelike prows, eyes supposedly imbued with the magical power to search the deep for fish and to avert storms. Powered by oars, the boats contain lanterns for the dangerous job of fishing after dark. During the gusty days of winter or at high tide, the boats are hauled in and lined up along the waterfront promenade.

While the men are at sea, the women pass their time mending nets, drying sardines on the beach, perhaps nursing children, darning socks, or sewing patches on clothing. At sundown they squat in circles, waiting on the somber shore. When their men come in, the business of sorting out the fish begins. The women trudge up toward the shoreline with heavy baskets balanced precariously on their heads. Some hang nets to dry in the night air; some slice entrails from the silver bodies on the beach; others chase away pestering children . . . and some wait.

Nazaré is divided into two sections: the fishing quarter and the **Sítio,** the latter the almost exclusively residential upper town. Near the beach, you'll find handcraft shops, the markets, restaurants, hotels, and boardinghouses. The main square opens directly onto the sea, and narrow streets lead to the smaller squares, evoking a Medina in a Moorish village. Simple shops hang objects outside their doors, indicating what they sell (for example, a carved wooden cow head would be for a butcher shop). At the farthest point from the cliff and square are the vegetable and fish markets, where auctions are held.

Jutting out over the sea, the promontory of the Sítio is a sheer drop to the ocean and the beach below. It is reached by either a funicular or a goat-steep cobblestone pathway. At the Sítio, the Virgin Mary supposedly appeared in 1182. A young horseback-riding nobleman, Faus Roupinho, was pursuing a wild deer dangerously near the precipice, which was shrouded in mist. The fog lifted suddenly to reveal the Virgin and the chasm below. In honor of this miracle, the nobleman built the **Chapel of Memory.** Today, near the spot, you can go inside the 18th-century structure honoring that alleged event.

WHERE TO STAY

MODERATE

ALBERGARIA MAR BRAVO, Praça Sousa Oliveira 70–71, 2450 Nazaré. Tel. 062/55-11-80. 16 rms. A/C TV TEL

$ Rates (including breakfast): 13,000$–14,700$ ($79.30–$89.60) single; 13,700$–15,400$ ($83.50–$93.90) double. AE, DC, MC, V.

Once this was the simple Pensão Madeira, but it has been completely modernized and turned into the present four-star boarding house. Each guest room is comfortably furnished, and in the reconstruction such modern amenities as private baths and air conditioning were added. The location is ideal, in the center of Nazaré in front of the beach and on the main square. Open year round, it is affiliated with Hotel Praia (see below).

INEXPENSIVE

HOTEL DA NAZARÉ, Largo Afonso Zuquete, 2450 Nazaré. Tel. 062/56-13-11. Fax 062/56-12-58. 52 rms, 1 suite. A/C MINIBAR TV TEL

$ Rates (including breakfast): 12,020$ ($73.30) single; 12,500$ ($76.20) double; 17,400$ ($106.10) suite. AE, DC, MC, V. **Parking:** Free.

Hotel da Nazaré is the runner-up to the Praia (see below). This hotel will not please everybody (and hasn't in the past), yet many patrons count themselves lucky if they can get a room here on a hot summer day. The location is on a busy street set back from the water, about a 3-minute walk from the promenade. The hotel opens onto a tiny plaza, and many of its front guest rooms have private balconies. Open all year, it rents small rooms that are very simply furnished. A rooftop terrace for sun-lounging puts Nazaré and the clifftop Sítio in perspective.

Frankly, the best feature of this hotel is its fourth and fifth floors, which contain restaurant facilities. The dining room opens onto window walls peering out over the village housetops, the rugged cliffs, and the harbor where tomorrow's sardines are being hauled in. Specializing in fish dishes, this dining room is open to the general public. Featured dishes include lobster thermidor, grilled crab, shrimp, and clams in savory sauce. Meals cost from 2,500$ ($15.25).

HOTEL MARÉ, Rua Mouzinho de Albuquerque 8, 2450 Nazaré. Tel. 062/56-12-26. Fax 062/56-17-50. 36 rms, 3 suites.

$ Rates (including breakfast): 10,000$–17,500$ ($61–$106.70) single; 13,000$–20,000$ ($79.30–$122) double; 25,000$ ($152.50) suite. AE, DC, MC, V. **Parking:** Free.

Hotel Maré, a block from the beach, has a modern lobby sheathed in vertical planks of wood, with black-and-white photographs of Nazaré fishermen. The hotel is right in the heart of the fishing port, and its rooms are furnished simply. Usually the person at the desk speaks some English. There's laundry service.

The hotel's sun-flooded restaurant is on the fourth floor, offering a panoramic view. From 12:30 to 3pm and 7 to 10pm daily, guests enjoy meals for 2,250$ ($13.70), including such fare as steak in cream sauce, escalopes of veal in Madeira, and sea bass prepared fisherman's style. On the fifth floor is a bar with comfortable tables. At least half the floor space is devoted to an outdoor sun terrace.

PENSÃO-RESTAURANTE RIBAMAR, Rua Gomes Freire 9, 2450 Nazaré. Tel. 062/55-11-58. 23 rms, 3 suites.

$ Rates (including breakfast): 6,000$–7,000$ ($36.60–$42.70) single; 8,800$–10,000$ ($53.60–$61) double; 11,500$ ($70.10) suite. AE, DC, MC, V. **Parking:** 1,000$ ($6.10).

This genuine old-fashioned village inn has a traditionally styled dining room where candlelit meals are served at night. It's right on the water, with most of its guest rooms opening onto balconies from which you can watch the beaching of the sardine-filled boats. Or you can watch (without being caught staring) the multipetticoated women or the men in their tasseled stocking caps.

A twisting stairway in the rear leads to the old-style rooms, with rattan baskets of pine cones on each landing. Each room is individually decorated, comfortable, and immaculately maintained.

Even if you're passing through just for the day, you may want to try a regional meal in the oak-beamed dining room. A meal is offered for 2,600$ ($15.80) to 3,000$ ($18.30) and includes such specialties as cream of shellfish soup, fish stew (*caldeirada*) Nazaré style, and roast kid. The atmosphere is genial, with ornate tiles, brown chairs, and stark white cloths. Food is served daily from 12:30 to 3pm and 7:30 to 10pm.

HOTEL PRAIA, Avenida Vieira Guimarães 39, 2450 Nazaré. Tel. 062/56-14-23. Fax 062/56-14-36. 41 rms, 4 suites. A/C TV TEL

$ Rates (including breakfast): 12,000$–13,700$ ($73.20–$83.50) single; 12,700$–14,400$ ($77.40–$87.80) double; 18,700$ ($114) suite. AE, DC, MC, V. **Parking:** 1,200$ ($7.30). **Closed:** Dec.

The leading hotel in town (where the competition is not keen) is the Praia. Built in the late 1960s, when Nazaré was being put on the world's tourist maps, the five-floor hotel is decorated in a modern style and located about a 3-minute walk from the sandy beach where the fishing boats and bathing cabins lie. The hotel doesn't have a restaurant on the premises, but guests can patronize the Mar Bravo (see below), owned by the hotel.

WHERE TO DINE

MODERATE

BEIRA-MAR, Avenida da República 40, Tel. 56-14-58.
  Cuisine: PORTUGUESE. **Reservations:** Not necessary.
$ Prices: Appetizers 150$–300$ (90¢–$1.80); main courses 1,500$–2,000$ ($9.10–$12.20); fixed-price menu 1,500$ ($9.10). AE, DC, MC, V.
  Open: Lunch daily noon–3pm; dinner daily 7–10pm. **Closed:** Dec–Feb.
Beira-Mar is one of the best restaurants in the port. In a modern building, it offers typical Portuguese dishes, including the "day's catch." Meat dishes are also available, along with regional soups, but Neptune is king. More than 75 diners can crowd in here on a busy day in summer.

Opening onto the beach, this popular place is also one of the more reasonable inns in town if you're seeking modest accommodations at modest prices—from 7,000$ ($42.70) to 11,000 ($67.10) daily for one of the 15 simply furnished double rooms; singles range from 6,000$ ($36.60) to 9,000$ ($54.90). Guests are received only from March through November.

MAR BRAVO, Praça Sousa Oliveira 75. Tel. 55-11-80.
  Cuisine: PORTUGUESE/FRENCH. **Reservations:** Not necessary.
$ Prices: Appetizers 200$–450$ ($1.20–$2.70); main courses 1,500$–2,500$ ($9.10–$15.20). AE, DC, MC, V.
  Open: Lunch daily noon–4pm; dinner daily 7–10pm.
One of the most frequented of the dozens of restaurants in this bustling village is Mar Bravo, on the corner of the square overlooking the ocean. The decor is tile, with a huge photo of the Nazaré beach covering the back wall. A complete meal consists of soup, followed by a fish or meat dish, and bread. There's a menu in English. À la carte specialties are bass caprice, fish stew *Nazaréna,* and grilled pork. Dessert might be a soufflé, fruit salad, or pudding. Upstairs is a second dining room, with an oceanside view.

4. BATALHA

73 miles N of Lisbon

GETTING THERE By Train   There is no direct rail link to Lisbon. Passengers take a train to the junction at Valado dos Frados, where buses wait to take them the rest of the way to Batalha.

By Bus   From Nazaré (see above), nine buses per day make the 1-hour trip to Batalha, with a one-way ticket costing 410$ ($2.50). If you're going directly to Batalha from Lisbon, you can take one of three *expressos* buses a day, the trip lasting 2 hours and costing 800$ ($4.80) one way.

By Car   From Alcobaça (see above), continue northeast along Route 8.

ESSENTIALS   The **Batalha Tourist Office** is at Largo Paulo VI (tel. 961-80). The **telephone area code** is 044.

Go to Batalha only for one reason: to see the monastery. After that, most visitors are willing to continue on for the night, either to Fátima or Nazaré, where accommodations and dining choices are greater. There are, however, places to sleep and eat in Batalha, the best of which is recommended below. If you're traveling by bus, the Tourist Office (see above) keeps detailed schedules of the best connections possible.

WHAT TO SEE & DO

MOSTEIRO DE SANTA MARIA DA VITÓRIA (Monastery of the Virgin Mary), N8. Tel. 96-497.

The founder of the House of Avíz, João I, vowed on the plains of Aljubarrota in 1385 that if his underequipped and outnumbered army defeated the powerful invading Castilians, he would commemorate his spiritual indebtedness to the Virgin Mary. The result is the magnificent Mosteiro de Santa Maria da Vitória. Designed in the splendid Gothic and Manueline style, it appears as an imposing mass of steeples, buttresses, and parapets when approached from its western facade. Much restored, it is a jewel of finely cut gems in stone.

The western porch, ornamented by a tangled mass of Gothic sculpture of saints and other figures, is capped by a stained-glass window of blue, mauve, and amber. The hue of the limestone has supposedly changed through the ages; today it is a light burnished beige, similar to the color of the facade of the Convent of Christ at Tomar. Napoleon's irreverent army used the stained-glass windows for target practice.

In the Founder's Chapel, completed in 1435, João I and his English queen, Philippa of Lancaster, daughter of John of Gaunt, lie in peaceful repose, their hands entwined. Near that of his parents is the tomb of Prince Henry the Navigator, whose fame eclipsed their own even though he never sat on the throne but spent a great part of his life at his school of navigation at Sagres, on the southern coast of Portugal. Henry's sculpted hands are clasped in prayer. Three of the other princes are also entombed here under a ceiling resembling snow crystals. The Royal Cloister was started by Afonso Domingues and finished by Huguet. These cloisters reveal the beginnings of the nautical-oriented Manueline architecture. (Still a second cloister, the King Afonso Cloister, dates from the 15th century).

The magnum opus of the monastery is the Chapter House, a square chamber whose vaulting is an unparalleled example of the Gothic style, bare of supporting pillars.

The two tombs of Portugal's Unknown Soldiers from World War I are guarded by sentinels and the glow of an eternal flame. In one part of the quadrangle is the Unknown Soldiers Museum, which houses gifts to the fallen warriors from the people of Portugal and from other countries, including a presentation from Maréchal Joffre. Beyond the crypt are the remains of the old wine cellars.

The filigree designs ornamenting the coral-stone entrance to the seven unfinished chapels is stunning. The *capelas,* under an inconstant "sky ceiling," are part of one of the finest examples of the Manueline style, a true extravaganza in stone. It seems a pity that construction was abandoned here so workers and architects for Manuel I could help build his Monastery at Belém. Originally, the chapels were ordered by Dom Duarte, the son of João I, but he died before they could be completed.

Outside in the forecourt, a heroic statue was unveiled in 1968 to Nuno Alvares, who fought with João I on the plains of Aljubarrota.

Admission: May–Sept 400$ ($2.40); Oct–Apr 250$ ($1.50).
Open: May–Sept, daily 9am–6pm; Oct–Apr, daily 9am–5pm.

WHERE TO STAY & DINE
MODERATE

POUSADA DO MESTRE AFONSO DOMINGUES, Largo Mestre Afonso Domingues, 2440 Batalha. Tel. 044/962-61. Fax 044/96-247. 19 rms, 2 suites. A/C MINIBAR TEL
$ Rates (including breakfast): 16,000$ ($97.60) single; 18,000$ ($109.80) double; 23,800$ ($145.18) suite. AE, DC, MC, V. **Parking:** Free.
Filling a big accommodation gap in this part of the country is Pousada do Mestre

Afonso Domingues. It stands right across the square from the Batalha, accommodating guests in well-kept modern comfort. The rooms are of good size. The manager has wisely employed a helpful staff. There's laundry service.

Even if you're not staying overnight in Batalha, you can patronize the first-class dining room, enjoying typically Portuguese fare for 2,200$ ($13.40) to 3,900$ ($23.79) for a complete meal. Food is served daily from 12:30 to 3pm and 7:30 to 10pm.

---

5. FÁTIMA

88 miles N of Lisbon; 36 miles E of Nazaré

GETTING THERE   By Train   A train from Lisbon arrives daily, but it deposits you at a location 12½ miles outside Fátima; however, buses await passengers to take them into Fátima and the pilgrimage sites.

By Bus   When studying bus schedules, note that Fátima is often listed as "Cova da Iria," which leads to a lot of confusion. About three buses a day connect Fátima with Batalha. The trip takes only 40 minutes and costs 210$ ($1.20) one way. Five buses a day also arrive from Lisbon, taking 2½ hours and costing 890$ ($5.40) one way.

By Car   From Batalha (see above), continue east along Route 356 to reach Fátima.

ESSENTIALS   The **Tourist Office** is at Avenida Dom José Alves Correia da Silva (tel. 53-17-37). The **telephone area code** is 049.

This is a world-famous pilgrimage site. Thorny bushes, dwarfed holly, gnarled and twisted olive trees, and a stray oak—the terrain around Fátima is wild, almost primitive, with an aura of barren desolation hanging over the countryside. But if you should go on the 13th of May or October, the drama that unfolds is remarkable. Beginning on the 12th of each of those months, the roads leading to Fátima are choked with pilgrims traveling in donkey-pulled carts, on bicycles, or in automobiles. Usually, however, they go on foot; some even walk on their knees in penance. They camp out till day breaks. In the central square, which is larger than St. Peter's in Rome, a statue of the Madonna passes through the crowd. In the breeze 75,000 handkerchiefs flutter, like thousands of peace doves taking flight.

Then, as many as are able crowd in to visit a small slanted-roof shed known as the **Chapel of the Apparitions.** Inside stands a single white column marking the spot where a small holm oak once grew. It is alleged that an image of the Virgin Mary appeared over this oak on May 13, 1917, when she is said to have spoken to three shepherd children. The oak has long ago disappeared, torn to pieces by souvenir collectors. The oak that now stands near the chapel existed in 1917 but was not connected with the apparition. The original chapel constructed here was dynamited on the night of March 6, 1922, by skeptics who suspected the church of staging the so-called miracle.

While World War I dragged on in Europe, the three devoutly faithful children—Lúcia de Jesús and her cousins, Jacinto Marto and Francisco—claimed they saw the first appearance of "a lady" on the tableland of Cova da Iria. Her coming had been foreshadowed in 1916 by what they would later cite as "an angel of peace," who is said to have appeared before them.

Attempts were made to suppress their story, but news of it spread quickly, eventually generating worldwide enthusiasm, disbelief, and intense controversy. During the July appearance, the lady was reported to have revealed three secrets to them, one of which prefigured the coming of World War II, another connected with Russia's "rejection of God." The final secret, recorded by Lúcia, was opened by church officials in 1960, but they have refused to divulge its contents.

Acting on orders from the Portuguese government, the mayor of a nearby town threw the children into jail and threatened them with torture, even death in burning oil. Still, they would not be intimidated and stuck to their original story. The lady was reported to have made six appearances, the final one on October 13, 1917, when the children were joined by an estimated 70,000 people who witnessed the famous Miracle of the Sun. The day of October 13 had broken to pouring rain and driving winds. Observers from all over the world testified that at noon "the sky opened up" and the sun seemed to spin out of its axis and hurtle toward the earth. Many at the site feared the Last Judgment was upon them. Others later reported they thought the scorching sun was crashing into the earth and would consume it in flames. Many authorities, and certainly the faithful pilgrims, agreed that a major miracle of modern times had occurred. Only the children reported seeing "Our Lady," however.

In the influenza epidemic that swept over Europe after World War I, both Francisco and Jacinto died. Lúcia became a Carmelite nun in a convent at the university city of Coimbra. She returned to Fátima to mark the 50th anniversary of the apparition, when the pope flew in from Rome.

A cold, pristine white basilica in the neoclassic style was erected at one end of the wide square. If you want to go inside, you may be stopped by a guard if you're not suitably dressed. A sign posted outside reads: "The Blessed Virgin Mary, Mother of God, appeared in this place. Therefore, women are asked not to enter the sanctuary in slacks or other masculine attire." Men wearing shorts are also excluded.

Outside Fátima, in the simple and poor village of Aljustrel, you can still see the houses of the three shepherd children.

WHERE TO STAY

When you arrive, everything at first seems to be either a souvenir shop, a boarding house, or a hotel. But on the days of the major pilgrimages, it's virtually impossible to secure a room unless you've reserved months in advance. Those visiting at other times of the year may find the following recommendations suitable.

INEXPENSIVE

HOTEL DE FÁTIMA, Rua João Paulo II, 2495 Fátima. Tel. 049/53-33-51. Fax 049/53-26-91. 133 rms, 9 suites. A/C MINIBAR TV TEL
$ Rates (including breakfast): 10,000$ ($61) single; 12,000$ ($73.20) double; 18,000$ ($109.80) suite. AE, DC, MC, V. **Parking:** 1,000$ ($6.10).
Rated four stars by the government, Hotel de Fátima is a leading accommodation, where many rooms overlook the sanctuary. The ever-increasing invasion of pilgrims to the shrine forced the hotel to enlarge. All rooms have natural wood furnishings in the provincial Portuguese style. The building has three floors, serviced by two elevators.

On the main floor is a cozy reception lounge with a brick fireplace, a large sitting room, plus a dining room where you can order a two-course table d'hôte luncheon or dinner for 3,000$ ($18.30).

HOTEL SÃO JOSE, Avenida Dom José Alves Correia da Silva, 2495 Fátima. Tel. 049/53-22-15. Fax 049/53-21-97. 63 rms, 6 suites. A/C TEL
$ Rates (including breakfast): 7,000$–10,000$ ($42.70–$61) single; 10,000$–12,000$ ($61–$73.20) double; 14,000$ ($85.40) suite. AE, MC, V. **Parking:** Free.
Set beside one of the busiest streets in Fátima, within walking distance of the sanctuary, this modern balconied hotel is large and urban. A uniformed staff will register you in the marble-floored lobby, after which you'll proceed by elevator to a comfortable room. Much that this hotel offers, including its bar and dining room, seems to have a bit more style than some of the other more Spartan hotels in town. Each room has a radio and central heating; six also contain TVs. A set lunch or dinner costs 2,000$ ($12.20).

HOTEL SANTA MARIA, Rua de Santo António, 2495 Fátima. Tel. 049/53-30-15. Fax 049/53-21-97. 60 rms, 6 suites. A/C TV TEL
$ Rates (including breakfast): $7,000–$10,000 ($42.70–$61) single; 10,000$–12,000$ ($61–$73.20) double; 14,000$ ($85.40) suite. AE, MC, V. **Parking:** Free.
This comfortable modern hotel is set on a quiet side street just a few steps east of the park surrounding the sanctuary. Inside you'll find a lobby floored with gray-and-white

marble, lots of exposed wood, and a sunny lounge area with plants that thrive in the light streaming through stained-glass windows. Each modern room, attended by a well-trained staff, contains a balcony and radio. Meals cost from 2,300$ ($14).

BUDGET

HOTEL CINQUENTENÁRIO, Rua Francisco Marto 175, 2495 Fátima. Tel. 049/53-34-65. Fax 049/53-29-92. 132 rms, 14 suites. A/C TV TEL
$ Rates (including breakfast): 5,600$ ($34.10) single; 8,100$ ($49.40) double; 11,500$ ($70.10) suite. AE, DC, MC, V. **Parking:** Free.
This balconied structure, built onto a corner lot a short walk east of the sanctuary, offers comfortable accommodations throughout the year. Inside a heavily patterned series of carpets and wallpapers provide a warmly agreeable, slightly angular decor. Each guest room contains a radio and central heating; only the suites contain minibars. There's a bar on the premises, plus a dining room, serving special Portuguese food. A set menu costs 2,100$ ($12.80).

ESTALAGEM DOM GONÇALO, Rua Jacinto Marto 100, 2495 Fátima. Tel. 049/53-30-62. Fax 049/53-20-88. 42 rms, 3 suites. A/C MINIBAR TV TEL
$ Rates (including breakfast): 6,800$ ($41.40) single; 8,700$ ($53) double; 12,900$ ($78.60) suite. AE, DC, MC, V. **Parking:** 600$ ($3.60).
This modern hotel is set in a large garden at the entrance to town; it serves some of the best food in Fátima, with the biggest portions. Guest rooms are comfortably and attractively furnished.
The restaurant has an à la carte menu, a typical repast going for around 3,000$ ($18.30). You can order the usual selection of fish and meat dishes, along with a mixed salad or a tasty omelet. Food is served daily from noon to 3pm and 7:30 to 9:30pm.

HOTEL REGINA, Rua Dr. Gonego Manuel Formigao, 2495 Fátima. Tel. 049/53-23-03. Fax 049/53-26-63. 100 rms, 2 suites. A/C TV TEL
$ Rates (including breakfast): 6,500$ ($39.65) single; 8,500$ ($51.80) double; 11,050$ ($67.40) triple; 9,000$ ($54.90) suite. AE, DC, MC, V. **Parking:** Free.
The Regina, one of the oldest hotels in Fátima, is a good bet for a conservative, relatively unexciting, yet perfectly adequate hotel. It sits just east of the street bordering the sanctuary. Many of your fellow guests are likely to be elderly Portuguese pilgrims spending a slow-paced holiday. There's a very clean lobby, with an adjacent bar/TV room that is popular just before bedtime. Many guests enjoy their simple meals in the hotel's dining room. The guest rooms are comfortably outfitted. Laundry service is available.

HOTEL TRÊS PASTORINHOS, Rua João Paulo II, 2495 Fátima. Tel. 049/53-34-39. Fax 049/53-24-49. 92 rms, 9 suites. A/C TEL
$ Rates (including breakfast): 6,750$ ($41.10) single; 8,900$ ($54.20) double; 9,950$ ($60.70) suite. AE, DC, MC, V. **Parking:** Free.
This three-star facility, whose name means the Hotel of the Three Shepherd Children, is designed in a holiday style, with its most recently added guest rooms opening onto private balconies that overlook the sanctuary. All rooms have modern facilities. If you're just passing through, you can come in for a multicourse meal costing from 2,300$ ($14). The breakfast rooms open onto sun terraces, edged with pots of flowering plants.

WHERE TO DINE

Fátima has many reliable hotels but few independent restaurants, mainly because those hotels have garnered most of the business.

MODERATE

GRELHA, Rua Jacinto Marto 76. Tel. 53-16-33.
Cuisine: PORTUGUESE. **Reservations:** Not necessary.
$ Prices: Appetizers 650$–950$ ($3.90–$5.80); main courses 1,400$–2,500$ ($8.50–$15.20). AE, DC, MC, V.

Open: Lunch Fri–Wed noon–3pm; dinner Fri–Wed 7–10:30pm. **Closed:** Sept 1–15.

If you'd like an independent eatery, try Grelha, one of the best in town. It offers regional specialties but is known for its grills. In the cooler months, the fireplace is an attraction, and the bar is kept busy year round.

TÍA ALICE, Rua do Adro. Tel. 53-17-37.

Cuisine: PORTUGUESE. **Reservations:** Required.

$ Prices: Appetizers 650$–850$ ($3.90–$5.10); main courses 1,200$–2,600$ ($7.30–$15.80). MC, V.

Open: Lunch Tues–Sun noon–3pm; dinner Tues–Sat 6:30–10pm. **Closed:** July.

Contained within a very old house in the center of town, across from what might be the most famous parish church in Portugal, this restaurant offers a rustic decor and copious portions inspired by the rural traditions of Estremadura. It is unquestionably the finest dining choice in the area. Amid stone walls and beamed ceilings, in a dining room at the top of a flight of wooden stairs, you can enjoy such hearty specialties as broad-bean soups, roast lamb with rosemary and garlic, fried hake with green sauce, chicken, Portuguese sausages, and grilled lamb or pork chops. The restaurant's name translates as "Aunt Alice."

CHAPTER 11
THE ALGARVE

In the ancient Moorish town of Xelb (today called Silves), a handsome and sensitive vizier is said to have once lived. During one of his sojourns into northern lands, he fell in love with and won the hand of a beautiful blonde Nordic princess. After marrying her, he brought her back to the Algarve. Soon the young princess began to pine, finding no solace in the Moor's rose castle. Her young husband finally learned that his new bride's melancholy came from her longing for the snow-covered hills and valleys of her native land. The vizier issued a decree that thousands of almond trees be planted throughout his realm. From that day on, pale-white almond blossoms have blanketed the Algarve in late January and early February. The sight healed the heart of the young princess; on seeing the blossoms, she found she could finally fulfill her marital duties and lived happily ever after in her vizier's sun-drenched kingdom with its sweet-smelling artificial winters . . . or so the story goes.

The maritime province of the Algarve, often called the Garden of Portugal, is the southwesternmost part of Europe, its coastline stretching a distance of 100 miles—all the way from Henry the Navigator's Cape St. Vincent to the border town of Vila Real de Santo Antonio, fronting a once-hostile Spain.

Called Al-Gharb by the Moors, the land south of the *serras* (hills) of Monchique and Caldeirao remains a spectacular anomaly that seems more like a transplanted section of the North African coastline. The winter temperature averages around 60°F, increasing to an average of 74°F in summer. During the day the sky is a pale blue, deepening in the evening to a rich cerulean. The countryside abounds with vegetation: almonds, lemons, oranges, carobs, pomegranates, and figs, the last sending their branches across the ground like the tentacles of an octopus.

Expanses of sun-drenched golden sands contrast harmoniously with sinuous scored rock passageways that open up into high-ceilinged grottoes and sea caves with natural pillars supporting ponderous arches above in-rushing waters. The variety of the coastline provokes wonder: sluggish estuaries, sheltered lagoons, low-lying areas where the cluck of the marsh hen can be heard, long sandy spits, the pounding surf breaking on pine woods, and promontories jutting out into the white-capped aquamarine foam.

Even though most of the towns and villages of the Algarve are more than 150 miles from Lisbon, the great 1755 earthquake was felt here as well. Entire communities were wiped out; however, there remain many Moorish (even Roman) ruins. In the character of its fret-cut chimneys, mosquelike cupolas, and cubist houses, a distinct oriental flavor prevails. However, much of that flavor is gone forever, swallowed by a sea of dreary high-rise apartment blocks surrounding most towns. Years ago Portuguese officials, looking in horror at what happened to Spain's Costa del Sol, promised more limited and controlled development so they wouldn't make "Spain's mistake." That promise, in my opinion, was not kept.

The marketplaces in the shaded arcades of Algarvian villages sell esparto mats,

WHAT'S SPECIAL ABOUT THE ALGARVE

Great Towns/Villages
☐ Sagres, the extreme southwestern "corner" of Europe—opening onto a rugged, barren coast where Henry the Navigator launched Portugal onto "seas of exploration."

☐ Lagos, an ancient port city dating back to the Carthaginians—once the capital of the Algarve.

☐ Albufeira, a former fishing village and cliffside town—now called the "St. Tropez of Algarve."

☐ Faro, today's capital of the Algarve—with an inner city still surrounded by the ruins of its ancient halls.

☐ Silves, which as Xelb was the seat of Muslim culture in the Algarve before it fell to the Christian crusaders from the north.

Beaches
☐ The Algarve coast, with literally hundreds of beaches, the finest in Portugal. The best cove beaches are at Lagos, especially Praia Dona Ana, and other good ones are at Albufeira. Families gravitate to Olhão and Tavira.

☐ Praia da Rocha, a creamy yellow beach that has become the most popular seaside resort in the Algarve.

☐ Praia dos Três Irmãos, 9 miles of burnished golden sand, 3 miles southwest of Portimão—"The Beach of the Three Brothers" in English.

Ace Attractions
☐ Cape St. Vincent, outside Sagres— "the end of the world," according to ancient mariners.

☐ Serra de Monchique, a volcanic block forming a range of green hills where heat and humidity combine to form a lush tropical vegetation.

Ancient Monument
☐ Milreu, first excavated in 1876—extensive Roman ruins from the settlement called *Ossonoba* from the 2nd to the 6th centuries.

Sports
☐ Some of Europe's finest golf courses: Quinta do Logo Golf Club at Quinta do Lago; Vale do Lobo Golf Club at Vale do Lobo, Vilamoura Golf Club at Vilamoura, and Penina Golf Club at Montes de Alvor.

copperwork, pottery, and almond and fig sweets that are sometimes shaped like birds and fish. Through the narrow streets comes the fast sound of little accordions pumping out the rhythmical *corridinho*.

Many former fishing villages—now summer resorts—dot the Algarvian coast, their names tongue twisting: Carvoeiro, Albufeira, Olhão, Portimão. The black clothing of the *varinas* (with embroidery on their apparel, flower-studded hats on their heads), the healthy ruddy faces of the "bullfighters of the sea," and the fishing craft—all create a living bridge with tradition in a land known to Phoenicians, Greeks, Romans, Visigoths, Moors, Christians, and now foreign visitors of every hue, who have changed the old landscape forever.

Sports activities can be pursued year round in the Algarve, and the six championship golf courses between Faro and Lagos lure players from all over the world. Near Almansil is the 27-hole Quinta do Lago course, acknowledged to be one of Europe's top ten. Hotels have tennis courts, and horseback riding can be arranged with any of a number of stables quite near the beaches and in wooded mountain areas. Deep-sea fishing in the ocean waters, beach activities, and surfing attract thousands of vacationers to the Algarvian coast.

SEEING THE ALGARVE

Excellent accommodations are provided in nearly all price levels, the list topped by luxury hotels (some of which have their own championship golf course). The hotels scattered along the coast from Monte Alvor to the Vale do Lobo often have reciprocal meal arrangements.

Budgeteers seek out bargains in the *pensions* (boarding houses) and *estalagems* (inns), some of them in converted mansions and villas. The government owns two *pousadas*—one on the sea at Sagres, the other in the mountains (São Brás de Alportel). In July and August, the Algarve peaks in popularity, and accommodations without reservations made far in advance are difficult to obtain. The population of the Algarve in summer jumps from 300,000 to 800,000 and above, which causes strain almost to the breaking point on water and electrical supplies—and on traffic and tempers.

I find the area much more inviting in the low season, with February and March especially attractive, because of both the scenery and the cheaper, less crowded accommodations.

The flight from Lisbon to the Algarvian airport at Faro takes about 30 minutes. There are daily flights all year leaving Lisbon, with two daily return flights. You can also go by one of the three daily trains. Take the ferryboat at Praça do Comércio in Lisbon, disembarking at Barreiro on the opposite bank of the Tagus, where Algarve-bound trains can be boarded. Three times a week there's a first-class-only special run. A daily motorcoach also leaves from Barreiro to the Algarve, and a drive in your own rented car takes about 5 or 6 hours.

SUGGESTED 8-DAY ITINERARY

Day 1 From Lisbon, head south to the Algarve. Begin your tour in the extreme west, overnighting at Sagres, then work your way east the next morning.

Days 2–3 After exploring Cape St. Vincent in the morning, journey east to Lagos to see that town during the day and have lunch there. Continue east to one of the beach hotels on Praia da Rocha outside Portimão for two days and nights of surf and sand.

Days 4–5 Head east toward Albufeira for a two-night stopover and lunch at Armação de Pêra. Enjoy the many attractions of Albufeira the following day, but if you get bored with the sands visit Vilamoura and Vale do Lobo nearby.

Days 6–7 Base for two nights in Faro, exploring its attractions and branching out on day 7 to see some of the best sights in the environs, including Olhão, Estói, Milreu, and São Brás de Alportel—all of which can be done in one busy day.

Day 8 For a final look at the Algarve, head east toward the Spanish border, lunching at the colorful town of Tavira before spending the night in Monte Gordo, which is better endowed with hotels and attractions than the actual border town Vila Real de Santo António.

1. SAGRES

174 miles S of Lisbon; 21 miles W of Lagos; 71 miles W of Faro

GETTING THERE   By Ferry and Train   From Lisbon's Praça do Comércio you can take a ferry across the Tagus to Barreiro. From there, make connections with the Southern Line Railway on its run to Lagos. At Lagos, buses go to Sagres.

By Bus   Rodoviária buses head west from Lagos (see below) at the rate of 12 per day. Trip time is 1 hour, and a one-way ticket costs 385$ ($2.30).

By Car   Once at Lagos, drive west on Route 125 to Vila do Bispo, where you head south along Route 268 to Sagres.

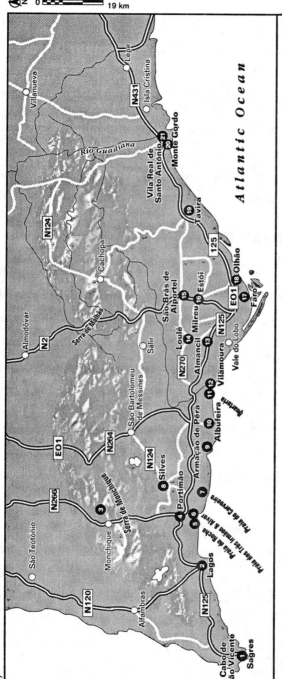

THE ALGARVE

1 Sagres
15 São Brás de Alportel
3 Serra de Monchique
8 Silves
19 Tavira
12 Vilamoura
21 Vila Real de Santo António

20 Monte Gordo
18 Olhão
4 Portimão
5 Praia da Rocha
7 Praia do Carvoeiro
6 Praia dos Três Irmãos & Alvor
11 Quarteira

10 Albufeira
13 Almancil
9 Armação de Pêra
16 Estói & Milreu
17 Faro
2 Lagos
14 Loulé

6317

ESSENTIALS The **Sagres Tourist Office** is at Promóntorio de Sagres (tel. 641-25). The **telephone area code** is 082.

At the extreme southwestern corner of Europe—once called *o fim do mundo* (the end of the world)—Sagres is a rocky escarpment jutting into the Atlantic Ocean, which beats itself into an aquamarine froth on the steep cliffs. It was here that Henry the Navigator, the Infante of Sagres, "dreamed dreams no mortal ever dared to dream before." He also proved that those dreams could come true, launching Portugal and the modern world on the seas of explorations. At Sagres, Henry, son of João I and Philippa of Lancaster, established his school of navigation. Magellan, Diaz, Cabral, and even Vasco da Gama apprenticed at the school founded here.

Henry died in 1460, before the great discoveries of Columbus and Vasco da Gama, but those explorers owed a debt to him. A virtual ascetic, he assembled the best navigators, cartographers, geographers, scholars, sailors, and builders he could muster, infusing them with his rigorous devotion and methodically setting Portuguese caravels on the Sea of Darkness.

WHAT TO SEE & DO

Today, at the reconstructed site of Henry's windswept fortress on Europe's Land's End (nicknamed that after the narrowing westernmost tip of Cornwall, England), you can see a huge stone compass dial that he is alleged to have used in the naval studies pursued at Sagres. At a simple chapel, restored in 1960, sailors are said to have prayed for help before setting out into unchartered waters. The chapel is closed to the public.

Three miles away is the promontory of **Cape St. Vincent,** or Cabo São Vicente. The cape is so named because, according to legend, the body of St. Vincent arrived mysteriously here on a boat guided by ravens. Others claim the body of the patron saint, murdered at Valencia, Spain, washed up on Lisbon's shore. A lighthouse stands here. Sea gulls glide on the air currents; and on the approach, a few goats graze on a hill where even the trees are bent from the gusty wind.

Both the cape and Sagres (especially from the terrace of the pousada), offer a view of the sunset. To the ancient world, the cape was the last explored point, although in time the Phoenicians pushed beyond it. Many mariners thought that when the sun sank beyond the cape, it plunged over the edge of the world. To venture around the promontory was to face the demons of the unknown.

No buses connect the cape with Sagres.

WHERE TO STAY & DINE

The accommodations at Sagres are limited but good.

MODERATE

HOTEL DA BALEEIRA, Sitio da Baleeira, Sagres, 8650 Vila do Bispo. Tel. 082/642-12. Fax 082/644-25. 118 rms. TEL

$ Rates (including breakfast): 11,500$ ($70.10) single; 15,000$ ($91.50) double. AE, DC, MC, V. **Parking:** Free.

In a ship's-bow position, Hotel da Baleeira is a first-class whaleboat (its name in Portuguese) that's spread out above the fishing port with boats tied up in the harbor. The largest hotel on this land projection, it offers guest rooms and seaview balconies. The hotel has nearly doubled the number of its rooms in recent years, although the older ones are quite small, as are the baths. The guest rooms are on the lower level.

Dining/Entertainment: If you're exploring the Algarve and are in Sagres just for the day, you can stop and order a 2,400$ ($14.60) lunch or dinner in a dining room cantilevered toward the sea, where everyone gets a view seat. The chef has his own lobster tanks (no frozen *lagosta* here), and the meals are well prepared and served in an efficient manner. There's also a cocktail lounge.

Services: Laundry, concierge, babysitting, room service.

Facilities: Angular saltwater pool, flagstone terrace, private sandy beach.

POUSADA DO INFANTE, Ponta da Atalaia, 8650 Sagres. Tel. 082/642-22. Fax 082/642-25. 39 rms, 1 suite.

$ Rates (including breakfast): 14,100$–17,300$ ($86–$105.50) single; 16,400$–20,000$ ($100–$122) double; 26,600$ ($162.20) suite. AE, DC, MC, V. **Parking:** Free.

Pousada do Infante seems like a monastery once built by ascetic monks who wanted to commune with nature—you'll be charmed by the rugged beauty of the rocky cliffs, the pounding surf, the sense of the infinity of the ocean. The glistening white-painted government-owned tourist inn with a tile roof is spread along the edge of a cliff protruding rather daringly over the sea. It boasts a long colonnade of arches with an extended stone terrace set with garden furniture, plus a second floor of accommodations with private balconies. Each guest room is furnished with traditional pieces.

The public rooms are generously proportioned, gleaming with marble and decorated with fine tapestries depicting the exploits of Henry the Navigator. Large velvet couches flank the fireplace with tall brass floor lamps.

Dining/Entertainment: The dining room's walls are lined with *azulejos,* and in the corner rests a cone-shaped fireplace with a mounted ship's model. From Portuguese provincial chairs, guests can order the traditional lunch or dinner of the pousadas, which costs 2,750$ ($16.70) to 5,400$ ($32.90), including homemade bread and soup, a fish course, meat with vegetables, and dessert. Have a before-dinner drink on the terrace and watch the oceangoing vessels make their way around the point, heading for faraway ports of call.

Services: Room service.

Facilities: Outdoor saltwater pool, tennis court.

INEXPENSIVE

RESIDENCIA DOM HENRIQUE, Sitio da Mareta, 8650 Sagres. Tel. 082/641-33. 18 rms. TV TEL

$ Rates (including breakfast): 6,000$ ($36.60) single; 10,000$–12,000$ ($61–$73.20) double. No credit cards. **Parking:** Free.

S This sunny two- and three-story hotel with a restaurant is situated dramatically on the *promontório* with the viewpoint above the beach. The view of the cliffs, beach, and sea is so magnificent it's featured on postcards sold in the area. More like a country house, it is a white-stucco building stretched along a small garden. The most expensive doubles open onto the water. Lunch or dinner costs 1,300$ ($7.90). The staff can arrange for boats, waterskiing, and bike rentals. It's also an informal place for afternoon tea, where you can sample some of the regional cakes.

---

2. LAGOS

21 miles E of Sagres; 49 miles W of Faro; 164 miles S of Lisbon

GETTING THERE   By Ferry and Train   From Lisbon, take the ferryboat at Praça do Comércio across the Tagus to Barreiro. There, connections to Lagos can be made on the Southern Line Railway. Five trains per day arrive from Lisbon, taking 6½ hours and costing from 1,500$ ($9.10) to 2,200$ ($13.40) one way, depending on the train.

By Bus   Four buses a day make the run between Lisbon and Lagos, taking 5 hours and costing 1,800$ ($10.90) one way.

By Car   After leaving Sines, go along Route 120 southeast toward Lagos and just follow the signs into the city.

ESSENTIALS   The **Lagos Tourist Office** is at Largo Marquês de Pombal (tel. 082/76-30-31). The **telephone area code** is 082.

What the Lusitanians and Romans called Locobriga and the Moors knew as Zawaia was to become, under Henry the Navigator, a private experimental shipyard of caravels. Edged by the Costa do Ouro (Golden Coast), the Bay of Sagres at one point in its epic history was big enough to allow 407 warships to maneuver with ease.

An ancient port city (one historian traced its origins back to the Carthaginians three centuries before the birth of Christ), Lagos was well known by the sailors of Admiral Nelson's fleet. From Liverpool to Manchester to Plymouth, the sailors spoke wistfully of the beautiful green-eyed, olive-skinned women of the Algarve. Eagerly they sailed into port, looking forward to carousing and drinking the heady Portuguese wine.

Actually, not that much has changed since Nelson's day, and few go to Lagos wanting to know of its history; rather, the mission is to drink deeply of the pleasures of table and beach. In winter, the almond blossoms match the whitecaps on the water, and the climate is often warm enough for sunbathing. In town, the flea market sprawls through narrow streets, the vendors selling such articles as rattan baskets, earthenware pottery, fruits, vegetables, crude furniture, cutlery, knitted shawls, and leather boots.

Less than a mile down the coast, the hustle and bustle of market day is forgotten as the rocky headland of the **Ponta da Piedade** (Point of Piety) appears. This beautiful spot is considered by many the best on the entire coast. Dotted among the colorful cliffs and secret grottoes carved by the waves are the most flamboyant examples of Manueline architecture.

Much of Lagos was razed in the 1755 earthquake, at which time it lost its position as the capital of the Algarve. Today only ruins remain of its former walls of fortification. However, traces of the old are still to be discovered on the back streets.

WHAT TO SEE & DO

IGREJA DE SANTO ANTONIO [Church of St. Anthony], Rua Silva Lopes.

Just off the waterfront sits the 18th-century Church of St. Anthony. Decorating the altar are some of Portugal's most notable rococo gilt carvings. Begun in the 17th century, they were damaged in the earthquake but subsequently restored. What you see today represents the work of many artisans—at times, each of them apparently pursuing a different theme.

Admission: Free.
Open: Daily 9am–5pm.

MUSEU MUNICIPAL DR. JOSÉ FORMOSINHO [Municipal Museum], Rua General Alberto Carlos Silveira. Tel. 76-23-01.

This museum contains replicas of the fret-cut chimneys of the Algarve, three-dimensional cork carvings, 16th-century vestments, ceramics, 17th-century embroidery, ecclesiastical sculpture, a painting gallery, weapons, minerals, and a numismatic collection. An oddity is a sort of believe-it-or-not section displaying among other things an eight-legged calf. In the archeological wing are Neolithic artifacts, along with Roman mosaics found at Boca do Rio near Budens, fragments of statuary and columns, and other remains of antiquity from excavations along the Algarve.

Admission: 200$ ($1.20).
Open: Tues–Sun 9:30am–12:30pm and 2–5pm. **Closed:** Holidays.

ANTIGO MERCADO DE ESCRAVOS [Old Customs House], Praça Infante Dom Henríques.

The Old Customs House stands as a painful reminder of the Age of Exploration. The arcaded slave market, the only one of its kind in Europe, looks peaceful today, but under its four Romanesque arches captives taken from their homelands were sold to the highest bidders. The house opens onto a peaceful square dominated by a statue of Henry the Navigator.

Admission: Free.
Open: Can be viewed at any time.

SPORTS & RECREATION

The Algarve's most westerly golf course is signposted left off EN125 at Odeaxere. Five of this course's 18 holes are on sand dunes bordering the beach. The address is **Clube de Golfe de Palmares,** Companhia de Empreendimentos Turisticos de Lagos, Monte Palmares, Meia Praia (tel. 082/76-29-61).

WHERE TO STAY

EXPENSIVE

HOTEL DE LAGOS, Rua Nova da Aldeia 1, 8600 Lagos. Tel. 082/76-99-20. Fax 082/76-99-20. 36 rms, 11 suites. MINIBAR TV TEL
$ Rates (including breakfast): 24,000$–28,600$ ($146.40–$174.40) double; from 35,550$ ($216.80) suite. AE, DC, MC, V. **Parking:** Free.

A 20th-century castle, Hotel de Lagos has its own ramparts and moats (a swimming pool and a paddling pool). This first-class hotel is spread out over three hilltop acres overlooking Lagos, so no matter which room you're assigned, you'll have a view, even if it's one of a sun-trap courtyard with semitropical greenery. The main room has a hacienda atmosphere, with a background of white-plaster walls, enlivened by sunny colors. Guests gather here in one of the clusters of soft built-in sofas set on carpets. In a corner, logs burn in a fireplace in chilly weather.

Some of the guest rooms have ground-level patios, but most are on the upper six floors. The rooms offer a choice of standard or deluxe, with the average room having a background of stark-white walls contrasted with warm Oriental colors. Most rooms open onto a wedge-shaped balcony where you can eat breakfast.

Dining/Entertainment: Excellent meals are served in an expansive harborview room, decorated in wood paneling. There are also a coffee shop, a piano bar, game rooms, a restaurant, a poolside bar, and two lounge bars.

Services: 24-hour room service.

Facilities: Health club, gymnasium, covered pool. Hotel de Lagos also owns Duna Beach Club on Meia Praia Beach, with a saltwater pool, a restaurant, a snack bar, and three tennis courts; guests are given a free membership during their stay. A private motorcoach makes regularly scheduled trips to the beach club, only 5 minutes from the hotel. Arrangements can be made for golf at nearby Palmares 18-hole course, where guests get a 20% discount on greens fees; for skin diving and sports fishing in the waters along the coast; for horseback riding through nature's garden; for sailing in the bay; and for international floor shows and gambling in the Algarve's casinos.

MODERATE

ALBEGARIA MARINA RIO, Avenida dos Descobrimentos, 8600 Lagos. Tel. 082/76-98-59. Fax 082/76-99-60. 36 rms. A/C TV TEL
$ Rates (including breakfast): 14,600$ ($89) single; 15,000$ ($91.50) double. MC, V.

One of the best in the town center, this four-star hotel stands just opposite the Lagos marina. Its guest rooms are nicely decorated, with many opening onto views of the sea; amenities include hairdryers and radios. On the top floor are a small pool and a sun terrace overlooking the Bay of Lagos. A courtesy bus takes guests in summer to the beaches and provides golfers transportation to the course at Palmares. A buffet breakfast is served in the morning, and a cozy bar is open all day.

HOTEL DA MEIA PRAIA, Estrada Meia Praia, 8600 Lagos. Tel. 082/76-20-01. 66 rms. TEL
$ Rates (including breakfast): 17,000$ ($103.70) double. AE, DC, MC, V. **Parking:** Free. **Closed:** Nov–Mar.

This first-class hotel, located 2½ miles northeast of Lagos, is for those who want sand, sun, and good food rather than an exciting decor. The hotel stands at a point where a hill begins its rise from the sea. Surrounded by private gardens, it fronts railway tracks and a 4-mile-long wide sandy beach. The guests play tennis on two professional hard courts; linger in the informal garden, where white wrought-iron outdoor furniture is scattered under the olive and palm trees; or loll by the large pools (one for adults, one for children). The oceanside guest rooms have balconies with partitions for sunbathing. The furnishings are uncluttered, functional, and modern. The best rooms have sea views. Across the entire all-glass front are the dining room, lounge, and cocktail bar.

INEXPENSIVE

CASA DE SÃO GONÇALO DA LAGOS, Rua Cândido dos Reis 73, 8600 Lagos. Tel. 082/76-21-71. Fax 082/76-39-27. 13 rms. TEL

$ Rates (including breakfast): 9,000$ ($54.90) single; 12,000$–14,000$ ($73.20–$85.40) double. AE, DC, MC, V. **Parking:** Free. **Closed:** Nov–Mar.

This pink town villa, with its fancy iron balconies, dates to the 18th century. At the core of Lagos, close to restaurants and shops, the antique-filled home is almost an undiscovered gem. Most of the public lounges and guest rooms turn, in the Iberian fashion, to the inward peace of a sun-filled patio. Here, surrounded by bougainvillea climbing up balconies, guests order their breakfast, sitting under a fringed parasol and enjoying the splashing of the fountain. All the furnishings are individualized: delicate hand-embroidered linens, period mahogany tables, silver candlesticks, chests with brass handles, inlaid tip-top tables, fine ornate beds from Angola, even crystal chandeliers. During the house's restoration, modern amenities were added.

The luxury pension is in a rambling *casa* (house), with various stairways leading to corridors with fine old prints, engravings, and Portuguese ceramic bowls of flowers set on aged hand-carved chests. Guests enjoy get-togethers in the large living room with its comfortable armchairs drawn up around a fireplace. Here, again, the furnishings are personalized, with a preponderance of antiques.

WHERE TO DINE

EXPENSIVE

ALPENDRE, Rua Antonio Barbosa Viana 71. Tel. 76-27-05.
Cuisine: PORTUGUESE. **Reservations:** Recommended.
$ Prices: Appetizers 750$–1,500$ ($4.50–$9.10); main courses 1,800$–3,200$ ($10.90–$19.50). AE, DC, MC, V.
Open: Lunch daily 12:30–3pm; dinner daily 7–11pm.

One of the most elaborate and sophisticated menus along the Algarve is offered at Alpendre. The food is tasty, but portions aren't large. Service tends to be slow, so don't come here if you're rushed. *Gourmet* magazine called the Alpendre "the most celebrated and luxurious restaurant in Lagos." Your afternoon or evening might begin in the downstairs bar, where you can have a before-dinner drink and sample crunchy Algarvian almonds and olives. Later, you can select from among excellent soups, such as onion au gratin, following with one of the house specialties, such as peppersteak or filet of sole that's sautéed in butter, flambéed with cognac, and served with a sauce of cream, orange and lemon juices, vermouth, and seasonings known only to the chef. Two featured desserts are the mixed fruits flambé and crêpes flambés with coffee, both for two.

MODERATE

A LAGOSTEIRA, Rua 1 de Maio 20. Tel. 76-24-86.
Cuisine: PORTUGUESE. **Reservations:** Recommended.
$ Prices: Appetizers 180$–850$ ($1.10–$5.10); main courses 920$–1,600$ ($5.60–$9.70); fixed-price menu 1,590$ ($9.70). AE, DC, MC, V.
Open: Lunch Mon–Sat 12:30–3pm; dinner Mon–Sat 6:30–10:30pm. **Closed:** Jan 10–31.

A Lagosteira has long been a mecca for knowledgeable diners in Lagos. Its decor is simple, and there's a small bar on one side. From the à la carte menu, the best opener for a big meal is a classic Algarvian fish soup. The most savory opening, however, is clams Lagosteira style. After the fishy beginning, you might happily settle for a sirloin steak grilled over an open fire.

DON SEBASTIÃO, Rua 25 de Abril 20. Tel. 76-27-95.

Cuisine: PORTUGUESE. **Reservations:** Recommended.

$ Prices: Appetizers 280$–1,000$ ($1.70–$6.10); main courses 1,000$–1,500$ ($6.10–$9.15); fixed-price menu 3,300$ ($20.10).

Open: Lunch daily noon–3pm; dinner daily 6:30–10pm. **Closed:** Dec 13–27.

Don Sebastião is a rustically decorated tavern, considered among the finest dining choices in Lagos. Run by Portuguese, it offers a varied menu of local specialties, particularly pork chops with figs or such shellfish dishes as clams and shrimp. Live lobsters are kept on the premises. Often feverish with activity in summer, it features filling and tasty meals, including grills, which are accompanied by one of the best selections of Portuguese vintage wines in the town.

GALEÃO, Rua de Laranjeira 1. Tel. 76-39-09.

Cuisine: REGIONAL/CONTINENTAL. **Reservations:** Recommended.

$ Prices: Appetizers 190$–930$ ($1.10–$5.60); main courses 1,070$–1,635$ ($6.50–$9.90). AE, DC, MC, V.

Open: Lunch Mon–Sat 1–3pm; dinner Mon–Sat 7–10pm. **Closed:** Nov 26–Dec 16.

⑤ The air-conditioned Galeão offers a wide range of dishes, and you can "oversee" the action through an exposed kitchen, which gets very busy in season. Meats are savory, and the fish dishes are well prepared and tasty. Try such dishes as king prawns and garlic, a gratinée of seafood, lobster thermidor, and salmon trout in champagne sauce. You can also order such meat dishes as pork médaillons in curry sauce and sirloin steak Café de Paris.

O TROVADOR, Largo do Convento da Senhora de Gloria 29. Tel. 76-31-52.

Cuisine: INTERNATIONAL. **Reservations:** Recommended.

$ Prices: Appetizers 500$–1,000$ ($3–$6.10); main courses 1,100$–1,950$ ($6.70–$11.90); fixed-price dinner 2,400$ ($14.60). MC, V.

Open: Dinner only, Tues–Sat 7pm–midnight. **Closed:** Dec–Jan.

O Trovador is run by Marion (she's German) and Dave (he's English). It's especially nice off-season, when comfortable chairs are placed around a log-burning fireplace. But at any time of year you get a pleasant atmosphere, good service, and great food. The location is up the hill behind Hotel de Lagos (follow the signs from Rua Vasco da Gama). Among the recommended appetizers are homemade duck-liver pâté, octopus cocktail, fish pâté with a delicate salmon taste, and escargots *bourguignons*. Shellfish dishes are prepared in unique Trovador style. Main courses also include Dave's special—beef casserole cooked in black beer. You might also enjoy Portuguese swordfish. The desserts are all good, but I especially like the homemade cheesecake (not baked) and the coupe Trovador (ice cream).

POUSO DO INFANTE, Rua Alfonso d'Almeida 11. Tel. 76-28-62.

Cuisine: PORTUGUESE. **Reservations:** Required.

$ Prices: Appetizers 450$–900$ ($2.70–$5.40); main courses 1,200$–2,200$ ($7.30–$13.40). AE, DC, MC, V.

Open: Lunch Mon–Sat 12:30–3pm; dinner Mon–Sat 6–11pm. **Closed:** Dec 15–Jan 15; Wed in Oct–June.

This is a pleasant tavern restaurant, with an iron chandelier, walls decorated with local craftwork, and green-painted rustic chairs with straw seats. The fare is not experimental in any way, but it's quite tasty. For example, for an appetizer, you're usually faced with a homemade vegetable soup (generous portions) or classic Portuguese shrimp cocktail. For a main course, you might order that Portuguese oddity, sole with banana, or veal scaloppine with spaghetti. Also worthy as a main-course choice is chicken curry with rice (not always offered) and my personal favorite—lamb in wine sauce. For dessert, the typical Algarvian selection is a smooth almond cake.

3. PORTIMÃO

11 miles E of Lagos; 38 miles W of Faro; 180 miles SE of Lisbon

GETTING THERE   By Train   From Lagos (see above), frequent trains run throughout the day to Portimão (trip time: 40 minutes). Take the Algarve Line.

By Bus   An express bus from Lisbon makes a 4½-hour run, and a bus runs from the beach at Praia da Rocha, 2 miles away.

By Car   The main highway across the southern coast (Route 125) makes a wide arch north on its eastern run to Portimão.

ESSENTIALS   The **Portimão Tourist Office** is at Largo 1° de Dezembro (tel. 236-95). At Praia da Rocha, the Tourist Office is at Avenida Tómas Cabreiro (tel. 082/222-90). The **telephone area code** is 082.

Go here only if you prefer the life of a bustling fishing port and commercial city instead of a hotel perched right on the beach. Ever since the 1930s, Praia da Rocha, 2 miles away, has snared sun-loving traffic. It is today challenged by Praia dos Três Irmãos. But the Algarve is so popular in summer that Portimão long ago developed a base of tourists.

The wafting aroma of the noble Portuguese sardine permeates every street and cafe nook. As a fish-canning center, Portimão leads the Algarve, but it doesn't outpace Setúbal in production. Still, for a change of pace, this town, on an arm of the Arcade River, makes a good stopover center (it also has some fine dining spots). Stroll through its gardens, its shops (especially noted for their pottery), drink the wine of the cafes, and roam down to the quays to see sardines roasting on braziers. The routine activity of the Algarvians is what gives the town its charm. On its left bank, the little whitewashed community of **Ferragudo** is unspoiled, but tame, with a castle.

On Monday through Saturday between 9:30 and 10:30am the fisherman can be seen unloading their boats by tossing up wicker baskets full of freshly caught fish. Fish, fruit, and vegetable markets are held every morning (except Sunday) until 2pm in the market building and open square. On the first Monday of every month, a gigantic day-long regional market is held with gypsies selling local artifacts, pottery, wicker, and even snake oil. Boutiques offering the Algarve's best selection of hand-knit sweaters, hand-painted porcelain, and pottery abound.

Many of the buildings in the town's old quarter date to the mid-18th century, when the town was rebuilt after the devastating 1755 earthquake. While roaming the streets, you can peer into delightful hidden courtyards, some with bread ovens built into the 3-foot-thick walls, blacksmith stables, tinsmiths, sardine-canning factories where sardines are still cleaned and packed by hand, and carpenters' shops.

Portimão is a perfect escape from the summer rush of visitors (mostly European) in the oceanfront towns; the room rates are considerably cheaper here than at nearby Praia da Rocha or Praia dos Três Irmãos.

Even those staying in Portimão head for the beach first thing in the morning. The major attraction is **Praia da Rocha,** a creamy yellow beach that has long been the most popular seaside resort on the Algarve. The beauty of its rock formations led English voyagers to discover it around 1935. At the outbreak of World War II, there were only two small hotels on the Red Coast, interspersed with a few villas, many built by wealthy Portuguese. Nowadays Praia da Rocha is booming, as many have fallen victim to the spell cast by its shoreline and climate.

It is named the Beach of the Rock because of its sculptural rock formations. At the end of the mussel-encrusted cliff, where the Arcade flows into the sea, the ruins of the Fort of St. Catarina lie. The location offers many views of Portimão's satellite, Ferragudo, and of the bay.

You can also visit **Praia dos Três Irmãos** for its beach, even if you prefer not to stay there in a hotel. From Portimão, you can reach it or the tourist development at Alvor by public bus service leaving from the center of Portimão. Service is frequent throughout the day. At Praia dos Três Irmãos, you get 9 miles of burnished golden sand, broken only by an occasional crag riddled with arched passageways. Just 3 miles southwest of Portimão, the "Beach of the Three Brothers" has been discovered by skin divers who explore its undersea grottoes and shoreside cave.

Its neighbor is the whitewashed fishing village of Alvor, where Portuguese and Moorish arts and traditions have mingled since the Arabs gave up their 500 years of occupation. Alvor was a favorite coastal haunt of João II. The gambling casino, the **Casino de Alvor** (tel. 082/231-41), is modest in size compared to the one at Estoril, but it does feature roulette, blackjack, and craps. A restaurant features good food and a floor show nightly at 11pm and 1am.

WHERE TO STAY

Hotels are limited within the center of Portimão and much more plentiful at Praia da Rocha, which has one of the largest concentrations on the Algarve. Praia dos Três Irmãos is the challenger to Praia da Rocha, but it isn't as built up. In summer, don't ever arrive at one of these beachfront establishments without a reservation.

MODERATE

HOTEL GLOBO, Rua 5 de Outubro 26, 8500 Portimão. Tel. 082/41-63-50. Fax 082/831-42. 71 rms. TEL
$ Rates (including breakfast): 13,500$ ($82.35) single; 15,000$ ($91.50) double. AE, DC, MC, V. **Parking:** Free.

In the heart of the old town, the Globo is an island of contemporary living. A first-class hotel, it is recommended for its clean-cut, well-thought-out design. Snug modern balconies overlook the tile rooftops crusted with moss. In 1967, the owner/manager imported an uninhibited architect to turn his inn into a top-notch hotel. Each guest room enjoys good taste in layout and furnishings: matching ebony panels on the wardrobes, built-in headboards, and marble desks.

On the ground floor is an uncluttered, attractive lounge with an adjoining bar. Crowning the top floor is a dining room, the Aquarium, encircled by four glass walls that permit unblocked views of the harbor, ocean, or mountains; its tables are set with crystal stemware and flowers. Guests can also enjoy a rooftop cocktail bar/lounge, Al-Kantor.

INEXPENSIVE

ALBERGARIA MIRADOIRO, Rua Machado Santos 13, 8500 Portimão. Tel. 082/230-11. Fax 082/41-50-30. 32 rms. TEL
$ Rates (including breakfast): 7,000$ ($42.70) single; 9,500$ ($57.95) double. V. **Parking:** Free.

Albergaria Miradoiro benefits from a charmingly central location on a quiet square opposite an ornate Manueline church. Its modern facade is banded with concrete balconies. A few of the simple guest rooms contain terraces. Here you're likely to meet an array of European backpackers eager to converse and share travelers' stories. The hotel is open throughout the year, and motorists can usually find a parking space in the square just opposite.

NEARBY PLACES TO STAY
PRAIA DA ROCHA
Expensive

ALGARVE HOTEL, Avenida Tómas Cabreira, Praia da Rocha, 8500 Portimão. Tel. 082/41-50-01. Fax 082/41-59-99. 220 rms, 4 suites. A/C MINIBAR TV TEL
$ Rates (including breakfast): July–Sept, 28,000$ ($170.80) single; 36,000 ($219.60) double. June, 22,000$ ($134.20) single; 28,000 ($170.80) double. Oct–May, 20,000$ ($122) single; 27,000$ ($164.70) double. From 45,000$ ($274.50) suite. AE, DC, MC, V. **Parking:** Free.

★ The leading hotel in town is strictly for those who love glitter and glamour. With a vast staff at your beck and call, you'll be ensconced in luxury within an elongated block of rooms poised securely on the top ledge of a cliff.

The main lounge is like a sultan's palace: gold-velvet chairs, Oriental carpets, brass-and-teak screens, antique chests, and deep sofas set around a copper-hooded fireplace. The guest rooms have white walls, colored ceilings, intricate tile floors, mirrored entryways, indirect lighting, balconies with garden furniture, and baths with separate showers. Everything is centrally heated. The Yachting, Oriental, Presidential, and Miradouro suites are each a decorator's tour de force in originality.

Dining/Entertainment: Portuguese chefs, with French backgrounds, provide gourmet meals on the à la carte menu served in either the Grill Azul or Das Amendoeiros. Meals in Das Amendoeiros begin at 5,000$ ($30.50), whereas those in the specialty restaurant, Grill Azul, cost from 6,000$ ($36.60). Buffet luncheons in season are served by the pool. A one-of-a-kind nightclub books top-flight entertainers (even Amália Rodrigues on one occasion), in addition to their regular troupe of folk dancers. The club is like an Oriental grotto dug out of a cliff, with three stone walls and a fourth allowing for an oceanic backdrop.

Services: Hairdresser; barbershop; manicurist; laundry/dry cleaning; babysitting; 24-hour room service; social director who plans personalized activities, such as fishing parties on the hotel boat (with seafood stews), games of bridge, barbecues on the beach, mini-golf, volleyball, tennis competitions, waterskiing and deep-sea fishing.

Facilities: Huge kidney-shaped heated pool (plus another one for children), sun deck cantilevered over cliff, sauna, boutiques.

BELA VISTA, Avenida Tómas Cabreira, Praia da Rocha, 8500 Portimão. Tel. 082/240-55. Fax 082/41-53-69. 14 rms. TV TEL
$ Rates (including breakfast): 22,000$ ($134.20) single; 23,000$ ($140.30) double. AE, DC, MC, V. **Parking:** Free.

Bela Vista is an old Moorish-style mansion built during the last century by a wealthy family for use as a summer home. As well as a minaret-type tower at one end of its facade, there's a statue of the Virgin set into the masonry of one of the building's corners. Since 1934, it's been a special kind of hotel, ideal for those who respond to the architecture of the past. Rated first class, it's set on the oceanside, atop its own palisade, with access to a sandy cove where you can swim. The villa is white, with a terra-cotta-tile roof, a coastal landmark spotted by fishermen bringing in their boats at sundown. It's flanked by the owner's home and a simple cliff-edge annex shaded by palm trees.

The attractive structure and its decorations have been preserved, but plastic furniture has been placed into the public lounges. The entry hallway has an art nouveau bronze torchère and a winding staircase, with walls almost covered with 19th-century blue-and-white tiles depicting allegorical scenes from Portuguese history. Guests enjoy get-togethers around a baronial fireplace. In the high-ceilinged dining hall, meals combine Portuguese cuisine with a continental flair. The guest rooms facing the sea, the former master bedrooms, are the most desirable, though all rooms have character. The main house is preferable to the annex. Decorations vary from an inset tile shrine to the Virgin Mary to crystal sconces.

Moderate

JÚPITER, Avenida Tómas Cabreira, Praia da Rocha, 8500 Portimão. Tel. 082/41-50-41. Fax 082/41-53-19. 180 rms. A/C TV TEL
$ Rates (including breakfast): 16,000$ ($97.60) single; 18,500$ ($112.85) double. AE, DC, MC, V. **Parking:** Free.

The Júpiter occupies what might be the most prominent street corner in this bustling summer resort. Its wraparound arcade is filled with boutiques, and in its spacious lobby guests relax, sometimes with drinks, on comfortable couches. The hotel is just across from a wide beach, but it has a pool, covered and heated. The Night Star disco provides late-night diversion beneath a metallic ceiling, while a semiformal restaurant, an informal pub, and a cocktail bar offer food and drink. You can enjoy snacks and light lunches at poolside during summer. The comfortably modern accommodations contain radios and balconies, with views of either the river or the sea.

Budget

PENSÃO TURSOL, Rua Engenheiro Francisco River, Praia da Rocha, 8500 Portimão. Tel. 082/240-46. 23 rms. TEL

$ Rates (including breakfast): $5,500$ ($33.50) single; 7,500$ ($45.70) double. No credit cards. **Parking:** Free. **Closed:** Dec–Jan.

This simple but charming hotel is fronted by a garden rich with flowering vines and shrubs. You'll find it on a street running parallel to the main road beside the beach, in a quiet part of the resort not far from the center. The establishment contains a cool basement bar/TV room filled with leatherette chairs. The staff is helpful. In winter, a fire warms a corner of the dining room; the rest of the year, the windows are thrown open for a view of the surrounding landscape.

RESIDENCIAL SOL, Avenida Tómas Cabreira 10, Praia da Rocha, 8500 Portimão. Tel. 082/240-71. 31 rms. TEL

$ Rates (including breakfast): 4,500$–5,500$ ($27.40–$33.50) single; 6,000$–7,500$ ($36.60–$45.70) double. AE, DC, MC, V. **Parking:** Free.

Partly because of its location near the noisy main street, the painted concrete facade of this establishment appears somewhat bleak. In this case, however, appearances are deceiving, since the guest rooms offer some of the cleanest, most unpretentious, most attractive accommodations in town. Each unit is designed for two and contains radio and exposed wood. The rooms in back are quieter, but the terrace-dotted front units look across the traffic toward a bougainvillea-filled park. The breakfast lounge doubles as a TV room. Laundry and room service are provided.

AT PRAIA DOS TRÊS IRMÃOS

Very Expensive

ALVOR PRAIA, Praia dos Três Irmãos, 8500 Portimão. Tel. 082/45-89-00. Fax 082/45-89-99. 183 rms, 18 suites. A/C MINIBAR TV TEL

$ Rates (including breakfast): 36,200$ ($220.80) single; 42,800$ ($261) double; from 55,000$ ($335.50) suite. AE, DC, MC, V. **Parking:** Free.

⭐ "You'll feel like you're loved the moment you walk in the door," said a well-dressed woman visitor from the Midwest. This citadel of hedonism seems to have more joie de vivre than any hotel on the Algarve. Its position, building, guest rooms, decor, service, and food are ideal. The hotel is so self-contained you may never stray from the premises. Inside, a wide domed airborne staircase leads to a lower level, encircling a Japanese garden and lily pond. On a landscaped crest, the luxury hotel has many of its guest rooms and public rooms exposed to the ocean view, the gardens, and the free-form Olympic-size pool. Gentle walks (or an elevator) lead down the palisade to the sandy beach and the rugged rocks that rise out of the water.

The accommodations are varied, from a cowhide-decorated room evoking Arizona's Valley of the Sun to typical Portuguese rooms with provincial furnishings; all of them contain oversize beds, plenty of clothing space, long desk-and-chest combinations, and well-designed baths with double basins and lots of towels. Many rooms contain private balconies where guests take breakfast facing the view of the Bay of Lagos.

Dining/Entertainment: The bilevel main dining room boasts three glass walls so every guest has an ocean view. The Grill Maisonette is considered separately as a restaurant (see below). Like an exclusive club, the main drinking lounge is equipped with deep leather chairs and decorated with a cubistic modern ceiling.

Services: Babysitting, laundry, 24-hour room service.

Facilities: Reduced greens fees on nearby 18-hole golf course; horseback riding, waterskiing, and tennis; solarium, health club, outdoor pool; boutiques, newsstand, hairdressers, Finnish sauna.

Expensive

DELFIM HOTEL, Praia dos Três Irmãos, 8500 Portimão. Tel. 082/45-89-01. Fax 082/45-89-70. 312 rms, 13 suites. MINIBAR TV TEL

$ Rates (including buffet): 22,700$ ($138.40) single; 27,000$ ($164.70) double; from 45,000$ ($274.50) suite. AE, DC, MC, V. **Parking:** Free.

The developers of this hotel chose their site wisely: near the beach on a scrub-covered hillside whose sands offer a sweeping view of the Algarvian coastline and its dozens of high-rises. With its central tower and identical wings splayed back like a boomerang in flight, the hotel is one of the region's most dramatically modern buildings. In spite of its proximity to the beach, many guests prefer the parasol-ringed pool whose circumference encloses a swim-up bar marooned like an island in its midst. Tennis courts are nearby, as well as an assortment of shops, restaurants, and bars. Each well-furnished guest room contains a private terrace and radio. Only the suites are air-conditioned.

Dining/Entertainment: Portuguese and international cuisine is served, with meals costing from 2,800$ ($17). Piano bar entertainment is offered.

Services: Laundry service, babysitting, 24-hour room service.

AT MONTES DE ALVOR

Expensive

PENINA GOLF HOTEL, Montes de Alvor, 8502 Portimão. Tel. 082/41-54-15. Fax 082/41-50-00. 188 rms, 14 suites. A/C MINIBAR TV TEL

$ Rates (including breakfast): 22,500$ ($137.25) single; 32,000$–34,500$ ($195.20–$210.45) double; from 64,000$ ($390.40) suite. AE, DC, MC, V. **Parking:** Free.

The first deluxe hotel on the Algarve was the Penina Golf, between Portimão and Lagos, founded by a group of hotel entrepreneurs. Nowadays, it has much competition from the other luxury choices. Golfing fans remain loyal to the Penina, however, as it is a major sporting mecca.

Most of the guest rooms contain picture windows and honeycomb balconies providing views of the course and pool or vistas of the Monchique hills. The standard rooms are furnished in a pleasant style, combining traditional pieces with Portuguese provincial spool beds. All rooms are spacious and contain good-sized beds.

Dining/Entertainment: Guests enjoy the Grill Room or the dining room (table d'hôte meals in the latter) for well-prepared repasts capped by dancing.

Services: Laundry, babysitting, 24-hour room service.

Facilities: 36-hole championship golf course; private beach with its own snack bar and changing cabins; changing rooms, lockers, golf school and shops; sauna, billiard room, beauty parlor, barbershop, five hard tennis courts.

WHERE TO DINE

If you're sightseeing in Portimão, you may want to seek out a restaurant there; otherwise, most patrons prefer the even better dining selections along the beaches, especially those as Praia da Rocha and Praia dos Três Irmãos. All the major hotels previously recommended have deluxe or first-class restaurants, sometimes more than one within the same building. There's a wide selection, catering to most pocketbooks.

CENTRAL PORTIMÃO

Moderate

MARINERS, Rua Santa Isabel 28. Tel. 258-48.
Cuisine: INTERNATIONAL. **Reservations:** Not necessary.
$ Prices: Appetizers 295$–895$ ($1.80–$5.40); main courses 995$–1,795$ ($6–$10.90); fixed-price lunch 859$ ($5.20). No credit cards.
Open: Lunch Mon–Sat noon–3pm; dinner Mon–Sat 7–10:30pm. **Closed:** Nov–Apr.

Masses of bougainvillea fill the corners of this restaurant's garden patio. Even without the flowers, you still might be tempted by the vaulted and tile-lined inner room for more formal dining. The owners illuminate much of this place with candlelight, whose glow sparkles on the fine china, good linen, and soothingly repetitive ceiling arches. A relaxing dinner is likely to include peppersteak, filets of plaice in Mornay sauce, mixed grill, lasagne, or hot Indian curry. Less elaborate lunches offer such dishes as beefburgers and fish and chips, served on the patio or in the bar and dining room upstairs.

O BICHO RESTAURANT, Largo Gil Eanes 12. Tel. 229-77.
   Cuisine: ALGARVIAN. **Reservations:** Recommended.
$ **Prices:** Appetizers 250$–1,500$ ($1.50–$9.10); main courses 1,800$–2,800$ ($10.90–$17).
   Open: Lunch daily noon–3pm; dinner daily 7–11pm. **Closed:** Jan 10–20.

O Bicho is one of the best places in the Algarve to order *cataplana*, a typical regional dish consisting of clams, pork, green peppers, tomatoes, and spices, including hot pepper, garlic, and bay leaf. All this is cooked in a special copper pot, also called *cataplana,* which has a lid that seals the mixture in tightly to steam. The owner of this simple eating place has made O Bicho popular with locals and discerning tourists who enjoy the fresh fish dishes.

PRAIA DA ROCHA
Moderate

BAMBOO GARDEN, Edificio Lamego, Avenida Tómas Cabreira. Tel. 830-83.
   Cuisine: CHINESE. **Reservations:** Recommended.
$ **Prices:** Appetizers 960$–1,620$ ($5.80–$9.80); main courses 1,000$–2,300$ ($6.10–$14). AE, DC, MC, V.
   Open: Lunch daily 12:30–3pm; dinner daily 6:30–11:30pm.

Bamboo Garden, which has a classic Asian decor, serves some of the best Chinese food along the coast. In air-conditioned comfort, diners can select from a large menu that includes everything from squid chop suey to prawns with hot sauce. After deciding on a soup or an appetizer (try the spring roll), guests can make their selections from various categories, including chicken, beef, duck, squid, and prawns. You might, for example, prefer fried duck with soybean sauce or chicken with almonds from the Algarve.

SAFARI, Rua António Feu. Tel. 082/41-55-40.
   Cuisine: PORTUGUESE/ANGOLAN. **Reservations:** Recommended.
$ **Prices:** Appetizers 450$–1,200$ ($2.70–$7.30); main courses 1,200$–2,500$ ($7.30–$15.20). AE, DC, MC, V.
   Open: Daily noon–midnight. **Closed:** Nov–Dec.

Safari is a Portuguese-run restaurant with a "taste of Africa" in its cuisine, as its name suggests. Many of its specialties were inspired by the former Portuguese colony of Angola. Built on a cliff overlooking the beach, this good-value restaurant has a glass-enclosed terrace. It is known for its fresh fish and seafood, and many guests in neighboring hotels like to escape the board requirements of their accommodations just to sample one of Safari's good home-cooked meals. The fare includes such delectable dishes as curry Safari, steak Safari, swordfish steak, and shrimp Safari. It's customary to begin your meal with a bowl of savory fish soup.

TITANIC, Edifício Colúmbia, Rua Engenheiro Francisco Bivar. Tel. 223-71.
   Cuisine: INTERNATIONAL. **Reservations:** Recommended, especially in summer.
$ **Prices:** Appetizers 550$–1,200$ ($3.30–$7.30); main courses 1,500$–2,800$ ($9.10–$17). AE, DC, MC, V.
   Open: Lunch daily noon–2pm; dinner daily 7–11pm. **Closed:** Jan.

Complete with gilt and crystal, the 100-seat air-conditioned Titanic is the most elegant restaurant in town. It also serves the best food, an array of international specialties, including live shellfish and flambé dishes. Even though it is named after the ill-fated luxury liner, it is not on the water, but lies in a modern residential complex. You can dine very well here on such appealing dishes as the fish of the day, pork filet with mushrooms, prawns *à la plancha* (grilled) and sole Algarve. Service is among the best at the resort. The kitchen is in open view.

PRAIA DOS TRÊS IRMÃOS

Expensive

GRILL MAISONETTE, in the Alvor Praia Hotel, Praia dos Três Irmãos. Tel. 45-89-00.
  Cuisine: PORTUGUESE/INTERNATIONAL. **Reservations:** Required.
$ Prices: Appetizers 750$–1,500$ ($4.50–$9.10); main courses 1,800$–3,200$ ($10.90–$19.50). AE, DC, MC, V.
  Open: Dinner only, daily 8pm–midnight. **Closed:** Thurs in summer.
The Grill Maisonette takes its rightful place alongside other distinguished restaurants connected with luxury hotels, such as the Ritz Grill in Lisbon. It is among the smartest places for gourmet cuisine along the Algarve coast. The grill, in spite of its spaciousness, has an intimate atmosphere, allowing you plenty of time to peruse the à la carte menu. You might begin with vichyssoise. Main courses are likely to include poached turbot with hollandaise and broiled rib of beef prepared for two. The dessert menu has such delicacies as Rothschild soufflé and crêpes Suzette.

Moderate

RESTAURANTE O BÚZIO, Aldeamento da Prainha, Praia dos Três Irmãos. Tel. 45-85-61.
  Cuisine: INTERNATIONAL. **Reservations:** Required.
$ Prices: Appetizers 300$–1,500$ ($1.80–$9.20); main courses 900$–2,500$ ($5.50–$15.30); fixed-price lunch 1,900$ ($11.60); fixed-price dinner 2,500$ ($15.30). AE, DC, MC, V.
  Open: Lunch daily noon–4pm; dinner daily 7–10:30pm.
Restaurante O Búzio stands at the end of a road encircling a resort development dotted with private condos and exotic shrubbery. In summer, so many cars line the narrow blacktop road that you'd be well advised to park near the resort's entrance, then walk the downhill stretch toward the restaurant.

Lunch and dinner are served in separate locations. Lunch is offered on a shaded hillock overlooking one of the best-landscaped pools on the Algarve. Many visitors enjoy the grassy lawns sloping toward the pool so much they pay an entrance fee and spend the rest of the day beside its waters. If you come only for lunch, there is no entrance fee. You can enjoy a light meal, which might include omelets, salads, hamburgers, or fresh fish. The real allure of the place, however, is after dark. You'll enjoy dinner in a room whose blue curtains reflect the color of the shimmering ocean at the bottom of the cliffs. Your meal might include fish soup, gazpacho, Italian pasta dishes, boiled or grilled fish of the day, peppersteak, and lamb kebabs with saffron-flavored rice. In winter, when it's too cold to eat outside, you can also have lunch in this restaurant.

ESTRADA DE ALVOR

Moderate

O GATO, Urbanização da Quintinha, Lote 10-rc, Estrada de Alvor. Tel. 082/276-74.
  Cuisine: ALGARVIAN/ALETEJAN. **Reservations:** Recommended. **Directions:** Lies on the main road to Praia da Rocha; about 100 yards after the first traffic circle, turn right in the direction of Alvor.
$ Prices: Appetizers 350$–1,500$ ($2.10–$9.10); main courses 1,000$–2,500$ ($6.10–$15.20); fixed-price menu 2,500$ ($15.20). AE, DC, MC, V.
  Open: Lunch daily noon–3pm; dinner daily 7–11pm.

Outside Portimão, one of the best places for dining is O Gato. The skilled chefs turn out a selection of dishes that are first-rate in both their preparation and their ingredients. Menu selections include such classic main dishes as duckling in orange sauce. However, care also goes into regional favorites, including rabbit stew, one of the most savory main courses. A good *cataplana* is also served, or you may prefer any number of fish and shellfish dishes, along with peppersteak and beef Stroganoff. To begin, try a refreshing soup such as gazpacho or razor-thin smoked swordfish served with some of the same accompaniments that usually go with caviar. Meals are served against an attractive backdrop of white walls and mahogany-beam trim. If you're feeling expansive, you can end your repast with one of the flambé desserts.

PORCHES
Moderate

O LEÃO DE PORCHES, Porches. Tel. 082/523-84.
 Cuisine: INTERNATIONAL. **Reservations:** Required.
$ Prices: Appetizers 400$–1,500$ ($2.40–$9.10); main courses 1,500$–2,600$ ($9.10–$15.80); fixed-price dinner 3,400$ ($20.70). MC, V.
 Open: Dinner only, Mon–Sat 7:15–10pm. **Closed:** Jan.

O Leão de Porches lies in a small village, a 3-minute drive from Lagoa on the road (N25) to Faro. Its experienced owner/manager, John Forbes, ran a restaurant in London that enjoyed a worldwide reputation, and he brought his expertise to this place. His cuisine includes such dishes as *cataplana*, roast duck with orange-and-Cointreau sauce, and fresh fish. Another good dish is pork sautéed in butter with red currants and apples and finished with cider and cream. Or you might try oven-braised wild rabbit with red wine, herbs, mushrooms, and onions. You might finish with Irish coffee or one of the homemade ice creams.

4. SILVES

4 miles E of Lagoa

GETTING THERE By Train Trains from Faro pull into the Silves train station, which is a mile from the center of the town.

By Bus The bus station is on Rua da Cruz de Palmeira; eight buses a day arrive from either Silves or Portimão. Trip time is 45 minutes.

By Car Coming east or west along Route 125 (the main road traversing the Algarve), you arrive at the town of Lagoa—not to be confused with Lagos. From here, head north to Silves along Route 124.

ESSENTIALS The **Silves Tourist Office** is on Rua 25 de Abril 26-28 (tel. 422-55). The **telephone area code** is 082.

When you pass through the Moorish-inspired entrance of this hillside town, you'll quickly become aware that Silves is unlike the other towns and villages of the Algarve. It lives in the past, recalling its heyday when it was known as Xelb, the seat of Muslim culture in the south before it fell to the crusaders. Christian warriors and earthquakes have been rough on Silves. However, somehow the Castle of Silves, crowning the hilltop, has held on, although it's seen better days. Once the blood of the Muslims, staging their last stand in Silves, "flowed like red wine," as one Portuguese historian put it. The cries and screams of women and children resounded over the walls. Nowadays the only sound you're likely to hear is the loud rock music coming from the gatekeeper's house.

The red-sandstone castle may date back to the 9th century. From its ramparts you can look down the saffron-mossed tile roofs of the village houses, down the narrow cobbled streets where roosters strut and scrappy dogs sleep peacefully in the doorways. Inside the walls, the government has planted a flower garden, adorning it with golden chrysanthemums and scarlet poinsettias. In the fortress, water rushes through a huge cistern and a deep well made of sandstone. Below are dungeon chambers and labyrinthine tunnels where the last of the Moors hid out before the crusaders found them and sent them to their deaths.

The 13th-century former **Cathedral of Silves** (now a church), down below, was built in the Gothic style. You can wander through its aisles and nave, noting the beauty in their simplicity. Both the chancel and the transept date from a later period, having been built in the flamboyant Gothic style. The Christian architects who originally built it may have torn down an old mosque. Many of the tombs contained here are believed to have been the graves of crusaders who took the town in 1244. The Gothic structure is considered one of the most outstanding religious monuments in the Algarve.

Outside the main part of town, near an orange grove (one of the local Silves boys will surely volunteer as your inexpensive guide), a lonely open-air pavilion shelters a 15th-century stone lacework cross. This ecclesiastical artwork is two-faced, depicting a *pietà* (the face of Christ is destroyed) on one side, the Crucifixion on the other. It has been declared a national monument of incalculable value.

WHERE TO DINE

Silves is most often visited on a day-trip from one of the beach towns to the south. For that reason, many visitors find themselves in Silves at lunchtime. Restaurants here are very simple but also very cheap.

EXPENSIVE

RUI I, Rua Comendador Vilarim 27. Tel. 44-26-82
RUI II, Horta Pocinho Santo. Tel. 44-31-06.
   Cuisine: PORTUGUESE. **Reservations:** Not necessary.
$ Prices: Appetizers 400$–3,000$ ($2.40–$18.30); main courses 1,600$–10,000$ ($9.80–$61); tourist menu 1,400$ ($8.50). MC, V.
   Open: Lunch daily 1–3pm; dinner daily 6–11pm.
Owned by the same entrepreneurs, these twin restaurants pride themselves on seating more customers than any other restaurants in town. Their menus and prices are almost exactly identical, but the availability of certain dishes will vary according to the fresh fish that happen to arrive on the day of your visit. Rui I is the older and more central, while Rui II lies on the southern perimeter of Silves, near the bridge leading to Armação de Pêra. The house specialty is shellfish rice, an herb-laden stew of rice and shellfish priced at 3,500$ ($21.40) per person. Other choices include grilled filet of beef, filet of wild boar, rack of lamb, smoked swordfish, and a choice of traditional desserts.

MODERATE

LADEIRA, Ladeira de São Pedro. Tel. 44-28-70.
   Cuisine: PORTUGUESE. **Reservations:** Not necessary.
$ Prices: Appetizers 250$–500$ ($1.50–$3.10); main courses 850$–1,100$ ($5.20–$6.70); tourist menu 1,400$ ($8.50). MC, V.
   Open: Lunch Mon–Sat noon–3pm; dinner Mon–Sat 6–10pm.
Containing only about 40 seats, this pleasant restaurant is known to virtually everyone in its neighborhood on the western outskirts of Silves. It features grilled fish, home cooking, and regional specialties. If you call in advance, someone will explain its location, often in great detail. Steak Ladeira and mixed-fish *cataplana* are specialties.

5. ARMAÇÃO DE PÊRA

28 miles W of Faro; 195 miles SE of Lisbon

GETTING THERE   By Train   The nearest railway station is at the village of

Alcantarilha, 5 miles away, where five trains arrive daily from Lisbon; Trip time ranges from 5 to 6 hours. Buses at Alcantarilha take passengers the rest of the way.

By Bus   About five buses a day make the 5-hour trip from Lisbon.

By Car   At the town of Alcantarilha on the main coastal route (125), head immediately south to the water and Armação de Pêra.

ESSENTIALS   The **tourist office** is at Avenida Marginal (tel. 082/321-45). The **telephone area code** is 082.

Squat fishermen's cottages make up the core of this ancient village. It rests almost at water's edge on a curvy bay that comes near its Golden Beach, one of the largest along Portugal's southern coast. In the direction of Portimão are rolling low ridges, toward Albufeira's rosy cliffs. Because Armação de Pêra has such a fine beach, it has almost become engulfed in a sea of high-rise buildings, which have virtually eliminated its once rather charming character.

Once Armação de Pêra was utilized by the Phoenicians as a trading post and stopping point for cruises around Cape St. Vincent. Near the center of the resort is a wide beach where fishing boats are drawn up on the sands when a fish auction (*lota*) is held.

While at the resort, you may want to walk out to **Nossa Senhora da Rocha** (Our Lady of the Rock), a Romanesque chapel on a 95-foot-high stone that sticks out into the ocean like the prow of a boat. Underneath are the cathedral-size **sea grottos** (*furnas*). To visit these, you can go down to the beach and flag one of the boats. Unique in the Algarve, the sea caves are entered through a series of arches that frame the sky and ocean from the inside. In their galleries and vaults, where pigeons nest, the splashing and cooing reverberate in the upper stalactite-studded chambers.

WHERE TO STAY
VERY EXPENSIVE

VILALARA, Praia das Gaivotas, 8365 Armação de Pêra. Tel. 082/31-49-10. Fax 082/31-49-56. 86 apts, 50 junior suites. A/C MINIBAR TV TEL

$ Rates (including breakfast): 43,500$ ($265.30) junior suite; 66,000$ ($402.60) one-bedroom apt. AE, DC, MC, V. **Parking:** Free.

The Vilalara is a luxury apartment complex on a cliffside, with a sandy beach—all in all, it's a self-contained miniature resort a mile west of Armação de Pêra. International magazines have acclaimed its good taste, which has attracted diplomats, movie stars, members of royalty, as well as business executives. The complex has an indoor-outdoor informality that is casually chic.

Curving with the contour of the coast, the apartments are built in a serpentine fashion, two floors of one-, two-, and three-bedroom units, each with a private sun-pocket terrace balcony furnished with bamboo and rattan. A long continuous flower box softens the look at the railing. Each apartment is spacious and delightful, with a living room, a fully equipped kitchen, and a veranda with a southern view.

Dining/Entertainment: The major dining focus is the Vilalara Restaurant (see "Where to Dine," below). The hotel contains what it calls a club, with wining and dining facilities and a disco. The snack bar/grill restaurant is near the pool.

Services: Laundry, room service.

Facilities: Health club; solarium; six tennis courts; three pools (one for children); Thalassotherapy Center, specializing in treatments where the sea and its products (such as algae, mud, and sand), are taken into account, plus anticellulite, antismoking, osteopathy, and acupuncture treatments. A team of qualified professionals, including doctors, osteopaths, and therapists, is at hand.

EXPENSIVE

HOTEL DO GARBE, Avenida Marginal, 8365 Armação de Pêra. Tel. 082/31-51-87. Fax 082/31-20-87. 152 rms. A/C TV TEL

$ Rates (including breakfast): 12,500$ ($76.20) single; 21,500$–24,500$ ($131.15–$149.40) double. AE, DC, MC, V. **Parking:** Free.

This self-contained resort enjoys a prime position in the town center, opening onto a soft sand beach. Built block fashion, its white walls, guest-room balconies, and public terraces shine in the summer sun. The public rooms, on several levels, are modern but warmed by their colors and natural elements. In the main sitting room, furnishings are grouped with an eye to the sea view. The immaculately maintained guest rooms combine Nordic and Algarvian features.

Dining/Entertainment: The dining hall turns to the sea. If you're just passing through, you can order lunch or dinner for 2,400$ ($14.60).

Services: Laundry, babysitting, room service, hairdresser.

Facilities: Outdoor pool.

HOTEL DO LEVANTE, 8365 Armação de Pêra. Tel. 082/31-49-00. Fax 082/31-49-99. 41 rms. A/C TV TEL

$ Rates (including breakfast): 18,160$ ($110.70) single; 21,600$ ($131.70) double. AE, DC, MC, V. **Parking:** Free.

Many repeat visitors consider this their favorite hotel on the Algarve. It's contained within a Mediterranean-style villa set on a hill a mile east of the congestion of the resort. From a position near the lobby, visitors have a sweeping view of the sea and the high-rises along the coast. Some of the guest rooms open onto enclosed courtyards, where pines glimmer with festoons of colored lights; others have a view of the sea; all contain radios and private balconies or terraces. Perhaps best of all, a formal garden, laid out in a star-shaped pattern, includes the name of the hotel spelled out amid the greenery.

Dining/Entertainment: A haciendalike dining room, replete with leather-backed chairs and pure white walls, serves well-prepared meals to a largely English or German clientele.

Services: Laundry, babysitting, 24-hour room service.

Facilities: Two pools, shrub-bordered terraces, children's playground.

HOTEL VIKING, Praia da Senhora da Rocha, 8365 Armação de Pêra. Tel. 082/31-48-76. Fax 082/31-48-52. 106 rms, 78 suites. A/C MINIBAR TV TEL

$ Rates (including breakfast): 14,200$ ($86.60) single; 24,000$ ($146.20) double; from 35,000$ ($213.50) suite. AE, DC, MC, V. **Parking:** Free.

The Viking lies about a mile southwest of the town (many signs direct you). It rises in a mass of gray stone and buff-colored concrete between two spits of land jutting into the sea. My favorite place within the grounds is the clifftop pair of pools. There, within a view of the rugged geology that marks this region of Portugal, you can stretch out under bamboo parasols, between the shades of large terra-cotta pots festooned with geraniums and trailing strands of ivy.

Even the geodesic dome of the lobby's skylight illuminates a splashing fountain ringed with glistening slabs of white marble. Each comfortably contemporary guest room contains a private balcony angled toward a view of the sea, plus a marble-covered bath, wall-to-wall carpeting, and a radio.

Dining/Entertainment: There are a replica of a 19th-century cafe set into the windbreak of a cobblestone courtyard, an English pub, a large cocktail bar leading into an enormous dining room, a TV room filled with card tables, a basement-level disco, and an array of indoor and outdoor bars. The hotel puts out lavishly decorated buffets.

Services: Laundry, babysitting, room service.

Facilities: Tennis courts, two pools, "above and below" water sports, beauty salon, sauna, massage facilities, Jacuzzi.

WHERE TO DINE

MODERATE

SANTOLA, Largo da Fortaleza. Tel. 31-23-32.

Cuisine: ALGARVIAN/INTERNATIONAL. **Reservations:** Recommended.
$ Prices: Appetizers 250$–1,400$ ($1.50–$8.50); main courses 950$–2,200$ ($5.80–$13.40). AE, DC, MC, V.
Open: Lunch daily noon–3pm; dinner daily 7pm–midnight.

The long-established Santola has faithful patrons who remember Armação de Pêra when it was just a fishing village. At the edge of the beach, "The Crab" specializes in a wide range of dishes, with the emphasis on seafood. It does excellent charcoal grills and has several continental specialties to tempt diners. From one of its tables you can enjoy a panoramic view. In winter, a fireplace adds the proper glow, and all year round the bar is popular.

VILALARA RESTAURANT, Praia das Gaivotas. Tel. 31-49-10.
    Cuisine: PORTUGUESE/ENGLISH/INTERNATIONAL. **Reservations:** Required.
$ Prices: Appetizers 750$–1,500$ ($4.50–$9.10); main courses 2,000$–3,200$ ($12.20–$19.50). AE, DC, MC, V.
    Open: Dinner only, daily 8–10:30pm.

In this luxury apartment complex, with its splendid flower gardens, Vilalara serves some of the finest food on the Algarve. Service, which is deluxe, is in a restaurant that has a big-windowed panoramic view of the sea and black-painted bamboo chairs and black-and-white decor. The chefs use only top-quality ingredients and prepare dishes with flair. These include the freshest of seafood. An indoor/outdoor grill and its adjacent snack bar are often closed for part of the year, but the restaurant is open all year.

INEXPENSIVE

PANORAMA SOL GRILL, Estrada Praia da Senhora da Rocha. Tel. 082/31-24-24.
    Cuisine: PORTUGUESE. **Reservations:** Required.
$ Prices: Appetizers 450$–750$ ($2.70–$4.50); main courses 800$–1,300$ ($4.80–$7.90). No credit cards.
    Open: Lunch daily 12:30–3pm; dinner daily 6:30–10pm. **Closed:** Nov–Feb; Wed in Mar–Apr.

It's worth the effort it takes to get to the Panorama Sol Grill. You'll find it on a road west of town leading to Hotel do Levante and Hotel Viking. At first you might think that the only available seating is on the simple benches, under sunscreens that have been set up on the outdoor walled-in terrace. No one will object if you want to sit there. However, you'll be rewarded if you continue to climb past the outdoor grill to the top of the stairs, where you'll enter a baronial dining hall. There, within view of a huge stone fireplace, you can eat in more dignified surroundings.

Regardless of where you choose to sit, you'll have to give your menu order at the grill, where the day's catch, as well as an array of meats, is laid out in a refrigerated case for your inspection. Average meals might include silver bass, fresh asparagus, and several preparations of beef, veal, or pork, plus live lobster from the restaurant's aquarium.

---

6. ALBUFEIRA

23 miles W of Faro; 202 miles SE of Lisbon

GETTING THERE By Train Trains connect Albufeira with Faro (see below), which has good connections to and from Lisbon. The train station lies 4 miles from the center, but frequent buses run back and forth from the station to the resort every 30 minutes, for 115$ (70¢) one way.

By Bus Buses run between Albufeira and Faro every hour (trip time: 1½ hours), costing 600$ ($3.70) one way. Seven buses per day link Portimão with Albufeira (trip time: 1 hour), costing 550$ ($3.40) one way.

By Car Albufeira can be reached from east or west along the main Algarvian coastal route, 125. It also lies near the point where the express highway, 264, from the north feeds into the Algarve. The town is well signposted in all directions. Take route 595 to reach Albufeira and the water.

ESSENTIALS The **Tourist Information Office** is on Rua 5 de Outubro (tel. 51-21-44). The **telephone area code** is 089.

This cliffside town—once a fishing village—is the St. Tropez of the Algarve. The lazy life, sunshine, and beaches make it a haven for young people and artists, although the old-time villagers still haven't quite made up their minds as to what they think of the invasion that began in the late 1960s. That migration turned Albufeira into the largest resort in the region. Some of them, however, open the doors of their cottages to those seeking a place to stay. Travelers without the money often sleep in tents on the cliff or under the sky.

The big, bustling resort retains characteristics more readily associated with a North African seaside community. Its streets are steep, the villas staggered up and down the hillside. Albufeira rises above a sickle-shaped beach that shines in the bright sunlight. A rocky grottoed bluff separates the strip used by the sunbathers from the working beach, where brightly painted fishing boats are drawn up on the sand. Access to the beach is through a tunneled rock passageway.

WHERE TO STAY

The town is well supplied with accommodations. However, the tariffs in many of the establishments are more suited to the middle-class pocketbook than that of the young people who favor the place.

EXPENSIVE

CLUBE MEDITERRANEO DE BALAIA, Praia Maria Luisa, 8200 Albufeira.
Tel. 089/58-66-81, or toll free 1/800/CLUB-MED within U.S. Fax 089/58-66-94. 400 rms. A/C TEL
$ Rates (including full board and use of most sports facilities): 22,900$ ($139.70) single per day; 24,700$ ($150.70) double per day; from 150,000$ ($915) to 198,000$ ($1,207.80) per person (double occupancy) per week, depending on season. AE, DC, MC, V. **Parking:** Free.
Set within 40 acres of sun-drenched scrubland, about 4 miles east of Albufeira, this all-inclusive high-rise resort is one of the most stable in the Club Med empire. Favored by vacationers from northern Europe, it encompasses a shoreline of rugged rock formations indented with a series of coves for surf swimming. Each accommodation—containing twin beds, two safes, and piped-in music—offers an understated, uncluttered decor with few frills and roughly textured walls leading to a private balcony or terrace. Many vacationers here appreciate the nearby golf course; others opt to participate in the many semiorganized sports. Meals are usually consumed at communal tables, with many lunchtime buffets and copious amounts of local wine.

Dining/Entertainment: On site are four restaurants, several bars, a late-night disco, and occasional bouts of live entertainment from the staff or from visiting groups of fado or folkloric singers.

Services: Laundry, babysitting.

Facilities: Arranged social and sporting activities through the sports shop—waterskiing, clay-pigeon shooting, practice putting greens; nearby 18-hole golf course; health club; sauna; heated pool.

HOTEL MONTECHORO, Montechoro, 8200 Albufeira. Tel. 089/58-94-23. Fax 089/58-99-47. 302 rms, 40 suites. A/C MINIBAR TV TEL
$ Rates (including breakfast): 20,000$ ($122) single; 22,500$ ($137.30) double; 35,000$ ($213.50) suite. AE, DC, MC, V. **Parking:** Free.
The leading choice in town, the Montechoro, 2 miles northeast of the center of

Albufeira, looks like a hotel you might encounter in North Africa. It's a fully equipped four-star resort complex, with such ample facilities that you might get lost here. Rooms are often done in an extremely modern style.

Dining/Entertainment: Dining facilities include the Restaurant Montechoro and the rooftop Grill Das Amendoeiras. Guests gather in the evening in the Almohade piano bar.

Services: Laundry, dry cleaning, 24-hour room service.

Facilities: Two pools, professional tennis courts, two squash courts, sauna, gymnasium.

MODERATE

HOTEL DE ALDEIA/PATIO DE ALDEIA, Avenida Dr. Francisco Sa Carneiro, Areias de São João, 8200 Albufeira. Tel. 089/58-88-61. Fax 089/58-88-64. Hotel: 128 rms, 5 suites. Patio: 52 apts. A/C TV TEL
$ Rates: Hotel (including breakfast): 12,500$ ($76.30) single; 14,500$ ($88.50) double. Patio (without breakfast): 20,000$ ($122) one-bedroom apt; 23,000$ ($140.30) two-bedroom apt. Lunch or dinner 2,500$ ($15.30) extra per person. AE, DC, MC, V. **Parking:** Free.

Within a 7-minute walk from the ocean, this holiday complex lies in the resort village of Areias de São João, near Golden Beach, about a mile east of Albufeira. Popular with visitors from northern Europe, it's divided into two sections set on opposite sides of the road: The hotel section, containing traditional guest rooms attractively decorated in a simple summer-inspired style, and the patio section, which contains only one- and two-bedroom apartments with kitchenettes. Each unit, regardless of its location, includes maid service, built-in headboards with background music and light switches, strong colors, and ample amounts of rattan and bamboo furniture. Although none of the units has a sea view, you have a choice of pool or mountain views.

Dining/Entertainment: There's a snack bar, plus a piano bar and live entertainment weekly. Across the road is a restaurant if you don't want to cook a meal in your own kitchen.

Services: Laundry, babysitting.

Facilities: Tennis court; mini-golf; sun terraces; two outdoor pools, one reserved for children.

INEXPENSIVE

APARTAMENTOS ALBUFEIRA JARDIM, Cerro da Piedade, 8200 Albufeira. Tel. 089/58-69-78. Fax 089/58-69-77. 460 apts. TEL
$ Rates: 13,500$ ($82.40) studio apt for two; 20,750$ ($126.60) one-bedroom apt for four; 32,750$ ($199.80) two-bedroom apt for six. AE, DC, MC, V. **Parking:** Free.

This establishment is especially popular with northern Europeans, Spaniards, and North Americans who want to linger a while before resuming their tour of the Algarve. Set on a hill high above Albufeira, it was begun in the 1970s as Jardim I and supplemented in the late 1980s with another section a 5-minute walk away, Jardim II. Today, the older (and larger) section offers gardens that are a bit more mature, although visitors enjoy the diversity offered by the restaurants (two), coffee shops (two), tennis courts (three), and pools (five, including two for children) scattered amid the compound's two sections. Laundry service and babysitting are provided.

A minibus makes frequent runs from the apartments to the beach, a 10-minute drive away. The attractively furnished units are contained in buildings with four or five stories. Each unit has a balcony with a view of the faraway ocean and the town. Breakfast is usually prepared by clients in their rooms, unless they opt for a morning eye-opener in one of the coffee shops.

APARTHOTEL AURAMAR, Praia dos Aveiros, 8200 Albufeira. Tel. 089/ 51-33-37. Fax 089/51-33-27. 287 rms. A/C TEL
$ Rates: 10,000$–11,750$ ($61–$71.70) single; 12,000$–13,750$ ($73.20–

$83.90) double. Extra bed 3,000$ ($18.30). Children sharing room with parents 1,500$ ($9.20) per day. Breakfast 900$ ($5.50) extra. AE, DC, MC, V. **Parking:** Free.

One of the resort's largest hotels sits about a mile east of the center, within large gardens on a low cliff overlooking a sandy beach. Built in 1974 like a series of fortresses facing the ocean, the complex is divided into a quartet of three-, four-, and five-story buildings separated by wide stretches of greenery. Because of their self-contained kitchenettes, the guest rooms are suitable for vacationers who prefer to avoid visiting restaurants for each meal. Each room has living-room furnishings and a terrace or balcony and a radio.

Close to the sea cliff is an outstanding recreation area, with the finest pool in the area. Other facilities include two tennis courts, a pool reserved for children, a bookshop, and a minimarket. Car-rental service is available.

Live entertainment is presented four nights a week. There are an informal snack bar and a bar/lounge, and the main building has a restaurant providing Portuguese and international cuisine.

HOTEL BALTUM, Avenida 25 de Abril 26, 8200 Albufeira. Tel. 089/58-91-02. Fax 089/58-61-46. 53 rms, 6 suites. TEL
$ Rates (including breakfast): 5,900$–7,200$ ($36–$43.90) single; 7,050$–11,300$ ($43–$68.90) double; 13,500$–16,500$ ($82.40–$100.70) suite. AE, DC, MC, V. **Parking:** Free.

The Baltum offers modern accommodations that are a one-minute walk from the main beach strip. In the main building, each guest room has central heating; some offer private balconies. Cozy sitting areas—furnished with leather chairs, blond coffee tables, and couches—are available to those willing to spend a few more escudos. The solarium/terrace with its little bar has music. Lunch or dinner costs another 2,200$ ($13.40), and the cuisine is Portuguese. Laundry service is available.

HOTEL BOA-VISTA, Rua Samora Barros 6, 8200 Albufeira. Tel. 089/58-91-75. Fax 089/58-88-36. 85 rms. A/C TV TEL
$ Rates (including breakfast): 10,000$ ($61) single; 12,000$ ($73.20) double. AE, DC, MC, V. **Parking:** Free.

Built in the Algarvian style and set high above the sea outside the center, the "Residence of the Good View" offers two styles of accommodations: one in its amenity-loaded main building, another in its block of furnished efficiencies across the street. The rooms open onto balconies, from which you can look down on the orange-tile-roofed whitewashed cottages to the bay below. The private baths are superb, in gray and white with marble. Traditional wickerwood decor is used, with matching carpets and ceramics. Laundry and 24-hour room service are available. Facilities include a sauna, plus both an indoor and an outdoor pool.

International cuisine is served in the panoramic restaurant/grill bar with a view of the bay. A small band plays three nights a week.

ESTALAGEM DO CERRO, Rua Samora Barros, 8200 Albufeira. Tel. 089/58-61-91. Fax 089/58-61-94. 93 rms. A/C TV TEL
$ Rates (including breakfast): 8,000$ ($48.80) single; 12,000$ ($73.20) double. AE, DC, MC, V. **Parking:** Free.

Estalagem do Cerro, built in 1964, captures Algarvian charm yet doesn't neglect modern amenities. This "Inn of the Craggy Hill" is located at the top of a hill overlooking Albufeira's bay, about a 10-minute walk down to the beach. An older, regional-style building has been recently renovated, but its character has been maintained. It is joined to a modern structure in a similar Moorish style. The tastefully furnished guest rooms have verandas overlooking the sea, pool, or garden.

The inn has an outdoor heated pool in a garden setting. Other facilities include a hairdresser, a sauna, massage facilities, a solarium, a Jacuzzi, and a Turkish bath. There's also a fully equipped gym. Laundry, babysitting, and room service are provided.

A panoramic dining room provides good meals for 1,950$ ($11.90). Here you are served both regional dishes and international specialties in air-conditioned comfort.

Before or after dinner, guests gather in a comfortable modernized bar or its patio. On most nights, guests can dance to disco music, but fado and folkloric shows are also presented.

HOTEL ROCAMAR, Largo Jacinto d'Ayet, 8200 Albufeira. Tel. 089/58-69-90. Fax 089/58-69-98. 91 rms. A/C TEL

$ Rates (including breakfast): 7,000$–7,500$ ($42.70–$45.80) single; 11,500$–13,000$ ($70.20–$79.30) double. AE, DC, MC, V. **Parking:** Free.

You might think this cubistic hotel looks like an updated version of a Moorish castle, a well-ordered assemblage of building blocks, or the partially excavated side of a stone quarry. Built in 1974, it was enlarged in 1991. It rises seven stories above the tawny-colored cliffs that slope down to one of the most inviting beaches along the Algarve. Many of its windows, and all of its balconies, benefit from the view this provides. The hotel is within a 5-minute walk from the town's attractions, yet its more secluded location enables guests to relax within the sun-washed confines of their simple but comfortable rooms. An Iberian-style dining room serves conservative but well-prepared meals, and a contemporary bar offers the possibility of a congenial tête-à-tête. Laundry, babysitting, and room service are available.

HOTEL SOL E MAR, Rua Bernardino de Sousa, 8200 Albufeira. Tel. 089/58-67-21. Fax 089/58-70-36. 74 rms. A/C MINIBAR TV TEL

$ Rates (including breakfast): 10,800$ ($65.90) single; 12,000$ ($73.20) double. AE, DC, MC, V. **Parking:** Free.

Hotel Sol e Mar has a prime location in the heart of Albufeira above the beach. It dates from 1969 and was enlarged in 1975. You'll be deceived by its two-story entrance on the upper palisade. When you walk across the spacious sun-filled lounges to the picture windows and look down, you'll see a six-story drop. Hugging the cliff are guest rooms and a wide stone terrace with garden furniture and parasols. On still a lower level is a sandy beach. There also are two pools, one for children. The guests are a continental crowd with a sprinkling of Americans.

Only six of the rooms are singles, but all contain private balconies. The twins have wooden headboards, locally painted seascapes, slimline armchairs, and plenty of wardrobe space. Laundry, babysitting, and room service are provided.

Diners take their meals in a two-level room, opposite a drinking lounge, a room for card players, and a TV room. After-dinner concerts are played on the electric organ till long past midnight. During the day, guests take the elevator to the lower sun terrace to find swimming; sunbathing; and the Esplanade Café, designed as a Portuguese tavern with Madeira stools, decorative tiles, and hanging anchors. On Tuesday to Sunday nights, guests dance at the Disco Sol e Mar to the latest records.

BUDGET

MAR A VISTA, Cerro da Piedade, 8200 Albufeira. Tel. 089/58-63-54. Fax 089/58-63-54. 46 rms. TEL

$ Rates (including breakfast): 6,000$–7,000$ ($36.60–$42.70) single; 8,000$–9,000$ ($48.80–$54.90) double. AE, DC, MC, V. **Parking:** Free. **Closed:** Oct–Mar

From the crow's nest vantage point of this *estalagem,* you can gaze out over the rooftops of the resort below. The rooftop breakfast room of this first-class inn, decorated in provincial style with blond paneling, takes advantage of the view. The estalagem is composed of two buildings: The principal structure, built in the 1960s, has guest rooms, a bar, and the breakfast room; the second building contains four guest rooms. Most rooms contain private balconies. The walls are hung with interesting prints; the furnishings, although not sumptuous, are typical and comfortable. There are a well-tended walled garden and plenty of parking space. Laundry, babysitting and room service are available.

VILLA RECIFE, Rua Miguel Bombarda 6, 8200 Albufeira. Tel. 089/58-67-47. 92 rms.

$ Rates (including breakfast): 7,000$ ($42.70) single; 8,000$ ($48.80) double. AE, DC, MC, V. **Parking:** None.

Set in the heart of town, Villa Recife is a self-catering hotel entered through the cafe and open-air bar that fills its front garden. Once a week (usually on Friday) a live band entertains on a wooden platform near an encircling wall. All but 14 of its accommodations contain private kitchenettes. The establishment was originally built as a private villa around 1920. Today, the palms and bougainvillea the original owners planted tower over the entranceway, whose walls are covered with blue, white, and yellow *azulejos*. The hotel has been expanded, and now about 20 rooms are contained in the original villa; the majority, however, are found in a modern rear wing, whose design is invisible from the front garden. There, all the studio apartments contain tiny terraces, oak cabinets, and kitchenettes. Facilities include an outdoor pool. Laundry service is available.

NEARBY PLACES TO STAY

PRAIA DA FALÉSIA

Expensive

SHERATON ALGARVE, Praia da Falésia, 8200 Albufeira. Tel. 089/50-19-99, or toll free 800/325-3535 in the U.S. Fax 089/50-19-50. 82 rms, 33 suites. A/C MINIBAR TV TEL

$ Rates: 30,000$–35,000$ ($183–$213.50) single; 35,000$–40,000$ ($213.50–$244) double; 50,000$–75,000$ ($305–$457.50) suite. Breakfast 2,000$ ($12.20) extra. AE, DC, MC, V. **Parking:** Free.

Opened in August 1992, this is one of the newest and most aesthetically pleasing five-star hotels along the Algarve. About 5 miles east of Albufeira, in a residential neighborhood dotted with scrublands and pine forests, the Sheraton was designed to blend tastefully into the rugged landscape of its oceanfront location. Its three-story wings ramble pleasantly through a subtropical garden dotted with copses of the site's original pine trees. Throughout the property, the aesthetic theme incorporates memorabilia (maps, artifacts, navigational aids) of the Age of Discoveries, either painted as frescoes or set into floors as part of multicolored marble mosaics. Conceived as a complete resort incorporating what might be Portugal's newest golf course (nine holes), the hotel caters to a European and international clientele searching for sun and relaxation.

Dining/Entertainment: The resort's most formal restaurant, the Portulano, offers panoramic views, fine continental cuisine, and big-city style (where men are requested to wear jackets). More folkloric is the Alem Mar, specializing in recipes from Portugal and seafood. There's also a beach club, serving sandwiches, salads, and platters of food throughout the daylight hours. Live music from a musical trio is played many evenings in the Jardim Colonial, one of the hotel's handful of hideaway bars.

Services: 24-hour room service, massage, laundry, hairdresser/barber, concierge, postal service.

Facilities: Indoor and outdoor pools, direct access to sandy beach, in-house health club set in replica of 16th-century sailing ship, nine-hole golf course (the Pine Cliffs), three floodlit tennis courts.

PRAIA DA GALÉ

Very Expensive

HOTEL VILLA JOYA, Praia da Galé, 8200 Albufeira. Tel. 089/59-17-95. Fax 089/59-12-01. 13 rms, 3 suites. MINIBAR TEL

$ Rates (including half board): 48,000$ ($292.80) single; 65,000$–89,000$ ($396.50–$542.90) double; 145,000$ ($884.50) suite. AE, DC, MC, V. **Parking:** Free.

This is considered one of the most luxurious and intimate inns in the Algarve, especially favored in Germany, where many magazine articles have praised its sybaritic charms and prominent German-speaking clientele. (Favored by politicians and financiers, it was the site of a sojourn by ex-chancellor Willy Brandt just before his death.) The establishment lies 9 miles west of Albufeira, in a residential neighborhood dotted with other dwellings, but from within the confines of its large gardens, visitors can easily imagine themselves in the open countryside. A footpath leads down to the beach; every accommodation offers a view of the sea as well as a private CD player (TVs are available on request). Personalized and intimate, a 1980s conversion of a Morocco-inspired private villa built during the 1970s, the hotel mingles Saharan and Iberian artifacts with Moorish fabrics and colors. The staff wears caftans and the flowing robes of North Africa, garb that fits appropriately into the dry and sunwashed landscapes of the Algarve.

Dining/Entertainment: The in-house restaurant serves elegant preparations of recipes inspired mostly by France, Germany, and Portugal. Residents tend to stay here on half board, although nonresidents are welcome to dine if they telephone ahead to see if space is available. Meals are served daily from 1 to 3pm and 7:30 to 9pm (last order) for a set price of 9,000$ ($54.90) per person. There's also a bar.

Services: Room service, concierge, laundry.

Facilities: Heated outdoor pool, nearby tennis courts.

WHERE TO DINE
EXPENSIVE

O CABAZ DA PRAIA [Beach Basket], Praça Miguel Bombarda 7. Tel. 51-21-37.
   Cuisine: FRENCH. **Reservations:** Required.
$ **Prices:** Appetizers 700$–1,800$ ($4.30–$11); main courses 1,500$–3,000$ ($9.20–$18.30). AE, MC, V.
   Open: Lunch Fri–Wed noon–2:30pm; dinner Fri–Wed 6:30–11pm.

The Beach Basket, near the Hotel Sol e Mar, sits on a colorful little square near the Church of São Sebastião, which is now a museum. In a former fisherman's cottage, the restaurant has an inviting ambience and good food. With its large sheltered terrace, it offers diners a view over the main Albufeira beach. Main courses, including such favorites as cassoulet of seafood, *salade oceane,* and papillotte of salmon, are served with a selection of fresh vegetables. The restaurant is renowned for its lemon meringue pie.

MODERATE

ALFREDO, Rua 5 de Outubro 9–11. Tel. 51-20-59.
   Cuisine: PORTUGUESE. **Reservations:** Required.
$ **Prices:** Appetizers 650$–900$ ($4–$5.50); main courses 1,000$–1,800$ ($6.10–$11); tourist menu 1,950$ ($11.90). AE, DC, MC, V
   Open: Lunch daily noon–3:00pm; dinner daily 6–11pm.

The pleasant Alfredo serves what are really banquets. Just a minute's stroll from the market square, it is housed in a century-old building that looks as if it's always been an inn. It's full of atmosphere, with crude wooden tables and chairs made for leisurely drinking. The second-floor restaurant is a heavily beamed room with a marble slab floor and simple wooden tables. Ceiling fans create a cooling breeze, and a semivisible kitchen provides all the entertainment many diners require. Your meal might include tuna salad, cataplana clams, and bream or swordfish, as well as tournedos with mushrooms or Portuguese-style steak. The wine of the house, Regengos, is sold by the glass.

A RUÍNA, Cais Herculano. Tel. 51-20-94.
   Cuisine: PORTUGUESE. **Reservations:** Required.
$ **Prices:** Appetizers 650$–950$ ($4–$5.80); main courses 1,100$–2,500$ ($6.70–$15.30). No credit cards.
   Open: Lunch daily 12:30–3pm; dinner daily 7–11pm.

A Ruína sits opposite the fish market. From the arcaded dining room, with its long candlelit wooden tables, you can peer at the fishermen mending their nets. Another cavelike room has more tables and a bar. The decor is unpretentious, and the seafood is fresh. A bowl of good-tasting soup will get you going, then it's on to one of the fish specialties, perhaps grilled fresh tuna. The fish stew, *caldeirada,* is the chef's specialty. Desserts tend to run to custard and mousse.

CAFÉ DORIS, Avenida Dr. Francisco Sá Carneiro, Areias de São João. Tel. 51-24-55.
Cuisine: GERMAN/PORTUGUESE. **Reservations:** Required in summer.
$ Prices: Appetizers 300$–950$ ($1.80–$5.80); main courses 850$–1,800$ ($5.20–$11); tourist menu 1,800$ ($11). MC, V.
Open: Fri–Wed 10am–10pm. **Closed:** Nov–Dec 25.

Café Doris is a rotisserie/crêperie/restaurant, German operated, which turns out some well-prepared crêpes, home-baked cakes, and ice creams. Ice cream comes in many flavors, including one delectable cup with fresh strawberries at 450$ ($3). Rich-tasting goulash-meat soup is always offered as an appetizer. You might follow with the roast pork with onion sauce or a good steak, accompanied by a mixed salad with cream sauce and herbs and lyonnaise potatoes. In addition, Doris has an unusual selection of hot drinks, including coffee Algarve (with Medronho).

FERNANDO, Avenida 25 de Abril, on the main square. Tel. 51-21-16.
Cuisine: PORTUGESE. **Reservations:** Not necessary.
$ Prices: Appetizers 350$–800$ ($2.10–$4.90); main courses 950$–1,500$ ($5.80–$9.20); tourist menu 1,950$ ($11.90). AE, DC, MC, V.
Open: Daily noon–midnight.

Fernando, with a large terrace, temptingly displays good-value tourist menus; there's a pleasant indoor dining room as well. I always go here for the fish of the day, never knowing what I'm going to get. You can always count on a good soup, most often fish based, and, if you're tired of fish, the chef will fix you a simple steak or a Portuguese specialty such as clams with pork. Desserts aren't special, but they're very fattening.

LA CIGALE, Olhos d'Agua. Tel. 50-16-37.
Cuisine: PORTUGUESE. **Reservations:** Required.
$ Prices: Appetizers 650$–950$ ($4–$5.80); main courses 1,100$–2,200$ ($6.70–$13.40). AE, DC, MC, V.
Open: Daily 11am–midnight.

La Cigale stands right on the beach, 4½ miles from Albufeira; its terrace makes it a romantic choice at night. Here is your cliché of the sunny southern coast of Europe. Fortunately, the food matches the atmosphere, enough so that the place draws a lot of diners who have villas on the Algarve—hence, reservations are important. The wine list is fairly distinguished, in keeping with the impressive food. The management seems to operate everything with amiable efficiency. Specialties include clams à la Cigale, sea bass, filet mignon, and a selection of fresh fish depending on the day's catch.

O DIAS, Praça Miguel Bombarda. Tel. 51-52-46.
Cuisine: PORTUGUESE. **Reservations:** Not necessary.
$ Prices: Appetizers 450$–800$ ($2.70–$4.90); main courses 1,000$–2,200$ ($6.10–$13.40). No credit cards.
Open: Lunch Fri–Wed 12:30–2:30pm; dinner daily 7–10:30pm. **Closed:** Jan.

O Dias, near the Beach Basket (recommended above), is a Portuguese-run restaurant with good food and reasonable prices. An outside terrace overlooks the sea—this is, of course, the most desirable setting. Main dishes include various versions of fresh fish and shellfish, including lobster and squid. The charcoal grills are among the most delectable.

O MONTINHO DO CAMPO, Estrada dos Caliços, Montechoro. Tel. 51-39-59.
Cuisine: FRENCH. **Reservations:** Required.
$ Prices: Appetizers 650$–1,200$ ($4–$7.30); main courses 1,400$–2,200$ ($8.50–$13.40); fixed-price menu 3,400$ ($20.70). MC, V.
Open: Dinner Mon–Sat 7–11pm. **Closed:** Nov 15–Dec 15; Jan 8–Feb 8.

O Montinho, located 2 miles northeast of Albufeira, is the finest restaurant in the area. Set behind the already-recommended Hotel Montechoro, this Portuguese *quinta* has a red-tile roof and a covering of ivy and oleander, along with white-stucco walls. Its terrace design looks almost fortified against the parking lot outside. You get an old Iberian feeling here, with raftered ceilings, carved chairs, and Algarvian accents. A host of international visitors comes here nightly to sample the chef's specialties, which include salad with melted goat cheese on toast and walnuts, monkfish lasagne, and duck with orange sauce. Other dishes are changed regularly to offer novelty to the regular clients.

EVENING ENTERTAINMENT

HARRY'S BAR, Praça Central, on the market square. Tel. 51-40-90.
   In the center of the village, Harry's Bar is the place for any bloke who has abandoned his Cotswold tweeds for the lighter threads of the Algarve. Converts swear that Sir Harry's is their Algarvian "local," and after about a quarter of a century, it has earned the reputation of being the Algarve's most popular international rendezvous. The bar merges the ambience of a black-and-white timbered village pub with the coziness of a Portuguese fisherman's cottage.
   Beneath the low natural beams, a comfortable array of Savonarola chairs, crude tables, and wooden settles are found on two levels, divided by wrought-iron railings. The collection of rifles, steins, gleaming copper pots and pans, and earthenware water jugs provides a genuine sense of the past. A bar of herringbone brick and timbers has heel-propping stools, attracting those drawn to the center of the action. Most drinks, such as a rum and Coke, go for 400$ ($2.40), and a beer goes for 250$ ($1.50). Hearty sandwiches and other bar snacks are served as well. It's open daily all year from 6pm to 3am.

---

7. QUARTEIRA

14 miles W of Faro; 191 miles SE of Lisbon

GETTING THERE   By Train   If you're dependent on public transportation, take a plane, bus, or train from Lisbon to Faro (see later in this chapter), then catch one of the frequent connecting bus links between Faro and Quarteira.

By Car   From Albufeira, head east along route 125; from Faro, go west on route 125. Both highways will be signposted at the little secondary road leading south to Quarteira, which is the center for exploring the more extensive tourist developments along Praia de Quarteira and Vilamoura.

ESSENTIALS   The **Tourist Information Office** is along Avenida Infante de Sagres (tel. 31-22-17). The **telephone area code** is 089.

Between Albufeira and Faro, this once-sleepy fishing village used to be known only to a handful of artists who provided amusement for the local fishermen and their *varinas*. Now, with the invasion of outsiders, the traditional way of life has been upset. What was Quarteira has been swallowed up in a sea of high-rise buildings, and the place is now a bustling overgrown resort. The big attraction, of course, is one of the longest beaches along the Algarve, filled in summer not only with vacationing Portuguese but also with hordes of Europeans who descend on Quarteira, also supplying a much-needed boost to the local economy.
   Golfers who don't want to pay the high tariffs at Vale do Lobo or Vilamoura (both of which have 18-hole golf courses) can stay inexpensively in Quarteira at one of the accommodations listed below. The above-mentioned courses are only a 10-minute drive away, and Quarteira lies about 7 miles from the Faro Airport.
   The largest concentration of hotels and restaurants, at least those of quality, are found not in Quarteira or even Praia de Quarteira but in the satellite of Vilamoura, directly west of Quarteira. Frequent buses throughout the day run between Quarteira and Vilamoura. Tourist information, however, should be gathered in Quarteira (see above).

Although the remains of a Roman villa were discovered when builders were working on the local marina, the history of **Vilamoura** is yet to be written. At a central point on the Algarve coast, only 11 miles west of Faro Airport, Vilamoura is an expansive land-development project, the largest private tourist "urbanization" in Europe.

Plans call for a city larger than Faro and an interior lake linked with the bay and ocean by two canals. One can sum up the Vilamoura situation by comparing it to the weather of New England: "If you don't like it now, wait a minute!" There is already a 1,000-boat marina for pleasure boats. At the moment, it is filled with what are called "holiday villages," along with apartment complexes.

Sports get much attention here: two 18-hole golf courses, along with water sports, tennis courts, and a riding center. The yachting set is attracted to the marina, especially in summer, and shops and other tourist facilities, including restaurants and bars, can occupy many a day.

WHERE TO STAY

Vilamoura is a better place to use as a base than the less attractive accommodations along Praia de Quarteira, which is often filled with tour groups.

INEXPENSIVE

ATIS HOTEL, Avenida Paralela a Infante de Sagres, 8125 Quarteira. Tel. 089/38-97-71. Fax 089/38-97-74. 73 rms, 8 suites. A/C TV TEL
$ Rates (including breakfast): 7,500$–10,500$ ($45.80–$64.10) single; 11,500$–14,500$ ($70.20–$88.50) double; 21,500$ ($131.20) suite. AE, DC, MC, V. **Parking:** Free.

The street where you'll find this hotel is so completely lined with high-rise apartment blocks that comparisons are sometimes made to the canyons of Wall Street. Fortunately, many of its balconied rooms look out over the beach, just a short walk away. Horizontal bands of bare concrete curve sinuously around the jutting balconies, many of which are accented with white stripes. A tiny outdoor pool is separated from the sidewalk by a fence. However, many clients prefer to bathe at the beach. There are a cafeteria and a restaurant, along with a darkly paneled bar, plus a TV room on the ground floor. Laundry, babysitting, and room service are offered.

HOTEL DOM JOSÉ, Avenida Infante de Sagres, 8125 Quarteira. Tel. 089/30-27-50. Fax 089/30-27-55. 146 rms. TEL
$ Rates (including breakfast): 12,000$–13,200$ ($73.20–$80.50) double. AE, DC, MC, V. **Parking:** Free.

Hotel Dom José is sometimes completely booked, often by vacationers from Britain, who consider its amenities considerably better than its three-star status would dictate. Its pool is separated from the town's portside promenade by a low wall, behind which a well-developed subculture thrives. At its tallest point, the hotel has eight balconied stories; the outlying wings are shorter, of course. The velvet sofas of the public rooms fill every evening with convivial holiday-makers enjoying drinks, the live music, and the air-conditioned sea view. An aquarium bubbles behind the darkly exotic-looking bar. In another corner of the ground floor, a lattice-covered room contains a wide-screen TV and a garden-style list of salads and sandwiches. There's a seaview restaurant as well. Each of the comfortably furnished double rooms contains a radio, but only 12 are air-conditioned.

NEARBY PLACES TO STAY
VILAMOURA
Expensive

HOTEL ATLANTIS VILAMOURA, Vilamoura, 8125 Quarteira. Tel. 089/38-99-37. Fax 089/38-99-62. 302 rms, 8 suites. A/C MINIBAR TV TEL
$ Rates (including breakfast): 26,000$ ($158.60) single; 35,000$ ($213.50) double; from 45,000$ ($274.50) suite. AE, DC, MC, V. **Parking:** Free.

One of the most stylish hostelries in town is the Atlantis Vilamoura. A Moorish flair is added by the pointed arches accenting the facade. Set away from the congested section of Vilamoura, this Iberian contemporary building boasts gleaming marble, coffered wooden ceilings, and polished mirrors. The guest rooms are well-furnished, each with a seaview veranda.

Dining/Entertainment: The sophisticated bar is dimly lit, with a piano providing evening music. A coffee shop remains open throughout the day.

The food is also excellent, prepared in the large, airy Aries dining room, built on two levels and opening onto the pool and ocean. Lavishly decorated with tiles, it is elegantly appointed, with one of the finest young staffs on the Algarve. A set menu for 4,900$ ($29.90) changes daily, and selections can also be made from an à la carte list. Traditional dishes and Iberian regional specialties are the main fare. Specific dishes are likely to include chicken breast Oscar, roast pork with garlic, or grilled swordfish, preceded by one of the soups or appetizers. Hours are daily from 12:30 to 2:30pm and 7:30 to 10pm.

The premier restaurant of the hotel, Grill Sirius, merits a separate recommendation (see "Where to Dine," below).

Services: Room service, laundry, babysitting.

Facilities: 20% discount at nearby golf course, health club, three tennis courts, outdoor pool, large wind-shaded terrace filled with plants, big indoor pool covered with a dome decorated with bas-reliefs.

DOM PEDRO GOLF HOTEL, Vilamoura, 8125 Quarteira. Tel. 089/38-96-50. Fax 089/31-54-82. 262 rms, 8 suites. A/C MINIBAR TV TEL

$ Rates (including breakfast): 16,000$–22,000$ ($97.60–$134.20) single; 21,000$–26,500$ ($128.10–$161.70) double; from 35,000$ ($213.50) suite. AE, DC, MC, V. **Parking:** Free.

This large hotel of first-class comfort is right in the tourist complex of Vilamoura. The public rooms are sleekly styled, and the guests rooms are pleasantly furnished and carpeted, with private terraces.

Dining/Entertainment: The hotel's band plays for nightly entertainment, and there's a casino. The restaurant serves both Portuguese and international specialties.

Services: Laundry, babysitting, room service.

Facilities: Three pools, including one for children; three tennis courts; sauna; massage; hairdresser; deep-sea fishing or horseback riding arranged; greens fees reduced at various area golf courses.

VILAMOURA MARINOTEL, Vilamoura, 8126 Quarteira Codex. Tel. 089/38-99-88. Fax 089/38-98-69. 385 rms, 8 suites. A/C MINIBAR TV TEL

$ Rates (including breakfast): 28,900$ ($176.30) single; 38,500$ ($234.90) double; 85,000$ ($518.50) suite. AE, DC, MC, V. **Parking:** Free.

A five-star choice, the Marinotel is considered by some the finest deluxe hotel on the Algarve, with some 324 employees for its guest rooms. The Marinotel was a dream long in coming true: It was originally launched in 1974, but construction was delayed because of the revolution and the tight-money situation; however, by spring 1987, the hotel was officially opened and has proved just as popular with the Portuguese as with international visitors. During the slower winter months it becomes a convention hotel, though in summer is overrun with holiday-makers. The hotel employs mainly young Algarvians on its staff.

Rising like a massive pile, the rectangular hotel sits next to the Vilamoura Marina. Each of its attractive and well-furnished guest rooms provides a view, of either the marina or the ocean. The interior, with lounge space for 500, is decorated with both traditional and modern designs. It is characterized by high ceilings and wide-open staircases, with an effective use made of silver, red, and white.

Dining/Entertainment: The hotel's dining facilities are among the best at Vilamoura. Fado, folk dancing, fashion shows, and occasional barbecues round out the program.

Services: Babysitting, laundry, 24-hour room service.

Facilities: Health club, including Jacuzzi and sauna; large pool; direct access to the beach.

Inexpensive

ESTALAGEM DA CEGONHA, Centro Hípico de Vilamoura, 8125 Quarteira. Tel. 089/30-25-77. 9 rms. TEL
$ Rates (including breakfast): 8,800$ ($53.70) single; 11,600$ ($70.80) double. AE, DC, MC, V. **Parking:** Free.

Estalagem da Cegonha, a farmhouse about 400 years ago, stands at Poco de Boliqueime, Vilamoura—about 4½ miles from the golf course, casino, marina, and beach—on the national road between Portimão and Faro. The ancient inn has a peaceful setting, adjoining the riding stables (which charge reasonable rates). A horse-jumping contest is held every year in September. The rooms are large and cozily decorated in a *típico* Portuguese style.

The inn's chef has won an award for regional food; before or after dinner, you can enjoy drinks in one of the comfortable bars. Room service is provided.

VILAMOURA GOLF MOTEL, Vilamoura, 8125 Quarteira. Tel. 089/30-29-77. Fax 089/38-00-23. 21 rms, 31 suites. A/C TV TEL
$ Rates (including breakfast): 10,900$ ($66.50) single; 13,000$ ($79.30) double; from 16,200$ ($98.80) suite. AE, DC, MC, V. **Parking:** Free.

Vilamoura Golf Hotel is for golf enthusiasts, among others. One mile east of Vilamoura's center, it is located on a Frank Pennink championship golf course surrounded by pine trees. Only minutes from the ocean and a marina, it enjoys a tranquil setting that forms part of the biggest tourist complex on the Algarve. Operated by Sointal Casinos do Algarve, it offers well-furnished guest rooms, each with a private terrace. The hotel has many facilities, including a large patio with two pools. The complex is designed in a typical modern Algarvian style, with much use of local materials like dark woods, polished tiles, and Portuguese mosaics. Guests heavily patronize the nearby diversions, including an 18-hole golf course (6,877 yards), tennis courts, and the casino. Laundry and room service are provided.

WHERE TO DINE

MODERATE

RESTAURANTE ATLÂNTICO, Avenida Infante de Sagres 91. Tel. 31-51-42.
Cuisine: PORTUGUESE. **Reservations:** Required.
$ Prices: Appetizers 450-950 ($2.70-$5.80); main courses 1,200$-2,200$ ($7.30-$13.40); tourist menu 1,500$ ($9.20). DC, MC, V.
Open: Lunch Mon-Sat noon-3:30pm; dinner Mon-Sat 6:30-11pm.

You'll find the protective awning of this portside restaurant on the town's main promenade, sitting near a cluster of other restaurants that look very much alike. The place is crowded and popular (often when the others are empty), and it's patronized by an array of international (often scantily clad) diners. The hosts direct a staff of waiters who bring out such specialties as fish soup Algarve style, king prawns Atlântico, peppersteak, clams in their shells, and other regional dishes.

RESTAURANTE O PESCADOR, Largo das Cortés Reais. Tel. 31-47-55.
Cuisine: ALGARVIAN/INTERNATIONAL. **Reservations:** Not necessary.
$ Prices: Appetizers 180-800 ($1.10-$4.90); main courses 750$-1,690$ ($4.60-$10.30). MC, V.
Open: Lunch Fri-Wed 1-3pm; dinner Fri-Wed 7-10pm. **Closed:** Dec 16-Jan 15.

O Pescador ("The Fisherman"), is an unpretentious spot across the parking lot from the fish market, just west of the straw market. Beneath a lattice-accented wooden ceiling, diners enjoy polite service and fresh fish and vegetables. A clean display case contains some of the ingredients that go into the meals. The cuisine is typically Portuguese, including steak, grilled filet of pork, grilled gray mullet, grilled prawns, and fresh hake.

INEXPENSIVE

BONNIE'S WINE BAR, Avenida Infante de Sagres 73. Tel. 31-43-12.
   Cuisine: PORTUGUESE/ENGLISH. **Reservations:** Not necessary.
$ Prices: Bar snacks 600$–900$ ($3.70–$5.50); tourist menu 1,200$ ($7.30);
   beer 300$ ($1.80) per pint; wine 200$ ($1.20) per glass.
   Open: Daily noon–1am.
This outpost of Britain thrives within a cocoon of pine paneling, comfortable
banquettes, foaming mugs of beer, and assorted banners from soccer teams.
Originally established as a purely British pub by died-in-the-wool Anglophiles, it has
since its establishment adopted more and more of the characteristics of south
Portugal, so that now it caters to a crowd of English and Portuguese clients who drink
together, sometimes elbow to elbow. You can order snacks and platters containing
steaks, lasagne, grilled fish, and steak-and-kidney pie. Despite the fact that wine is sold
by the bottle or glass, many customers prefer to drink beer.

NEARBY PLACES TO DINE

VILAMOURA

A shopping-and-dining complex, the **Centro Comercial da Marinha,** across from
the marina, is filled with restaurants, many of dubious quality. Nevertheless, many are
popular more for their colorful location than for their cuisine. The best food is
consistently served at the already-recommended Vilamoura Marinotel.

Expensive

GRILL SIRIUS, in the Hotel Atlantis Vilamoura. Tel. 38-99-37.
   Cuisine: PORTUGUESE/INTERNATIONAL. **Reservations:** Recommended.
$ Prices: Appetizers 950$–2,000$ ($5.80–$12.20); main courses 1,800$–3,500$
   ($11–$21.40). AE, DC, MC, V.
   Open: Lunch daily 12:30–3pm; dinner daily 7:30–10pm.
The most exclusive—and most expensive—dining spot in this hotel is the main-floor
Grill Sirius. It is separated from a chic rendezvous center, the Bar Castor, by a grand
piano on a dais. Live music filters into both areas. This drinking and dining
establishment is the most elegant in Vilamoura. The bar—stylish, modern, and
monochromatic—offers a large variety of drinks and is open daily from 11am to
11pm.
   Overlooking the marina, the Grill Sirius is high-ceilinged, with a sophisticated,
unfussy decor. The chefs prepare a splendid Portuguese and international cuisine, and
the service is formal. You might begin with assorted smoked fish and follow with one
of the seafood specialties, such as lobster cassoulet, turbot in seafood sauce, sea bass
flambé with fennel, or stuffed trout. Meat dishes use only the finest cuts, as reflected
by the T-bone steak and the tournedos stuffed with shrimps and scallops and served
with béarnaise.

EVENING ENTERTAINMENT

CASINO

CASINO DE VILAMOURA (without street name). Tel. 30-29-99.
   Close to the Vilamoura Golf Club and easy to spot, this casino is among the finest
in the Algarve. It features a gambling salon with roulette, blackjack, French banque,
and baccarat. A separate salon is devoted to slot machines. There's also a 600-seat
supper club, with a floor show nightly at 10:30. Here you can order either from a
tourist menu for 6,300$ ($38.40) or à la carte, paying 8,000$ ($48.80) for an average
meal. If you wish to see the show only, the cost is 3,000$ ($18.30), with a first drink
included; subsequent drinks cost from 650$ ($4). The casino is open daily throughout
the year except on December 24 and 25. Tourists must present a valid passport to
enter.
   Admission: 1,000$ ($6.10).

DANCE CLUB

SKIPPER'S DISCO CLUB, Loja 38, Centro Comércial da Marinha. Tel. 31-42-51.

Located in a restaurant-and-shopping complex close to the marina, Skipper's is the most popular stopover on the nighttime rounds. Guests drink at street level in the vaguely nautical bar before descending to dance in the basement to the latest in recorded music. Drinks cost from 700$ ($4.30); beer goes for 400$ ($2.40). You can also order such snacks as beefburgers and sandwiches. Hours are daily from 10pm to 5am.

Admission (including one drink): 500$–1,000$ ($3.10–$6.10).

---

8. ALMANCIL

8 miles W of Faro; 190 miles SE of Lisbon

GETTING THERE   By Train   Faro is the gateway to the eastern Algarve, and since Almancil is the next major town west of that city, Faro makes the best transportation hub for Almancil and its resorts of Vale do Lobo and Quinta da Lago. Go first to Faro by train (see the next section), then take a connecting bus the rest of the way.

By Bus   Almancil is a major stop for buses that leave frequently throughout the day for west Algarve. About 14 buses per day depart from Faro to Albufeira, with stops at Almancil.

By Car   From Faro, head west along route 125; from Albufeira or Portimão, continue east along route 125.

ESSENTIALS   There is no tourist office, but some information is available at Faro (see the next section). The **telephone area code** is 089.

Almancil is a small market town of little tourist interest. Yet it is a center for two of the most exclusive tourist developments along the Algarve: Vale do Lobo, lying 4 miles southeast of Almancil, and Quinta do Lago, lying 6 miles southeast of Almancil.

The name **Vale do Lobo** (Valley of the Wolf) suggests some forlorn spot set amid bleak terrain. Hardly likely! The *Vale*, west of Faro, about a 20-minute drive from the Faro Airport, is the site of a golf course designed by Henry Cotton, the British champion. Some of the holes are played by the sea—which results in many an anxious moment when a shot may hook out over the water a precarious distance from the green. Another nine-hole course and a nine-hole par-three course, a putting green, and a driving range have been installed. The tennis center here is among the best in Europe.

Reached through fig orchards, cork forests, and a valley of tufted pines, the seaside strongly evokes Carmel, California. Pale-golden cliffs jut out over sandy beaches that stretch brilliantly in the distance until they disappear into a faint haze.

Quinta do Lago also has superb facilities and is one of the most elegant "tourist estates" on the Algarve. This pine-covered beachfront property has been the retreat of everybody from movie stars to European presidents. The resort's 27 superb holes of golf are also a potent lure. It is luxury with a definite high price tag (see below).

WHERE TO STAY

VALE DE LOBO

Very Expensive

HOTEL DONA FILIPA, Vale de Lobo, 8136 Almancil. Tel. 089/39-41-41.
Fax 089/39-42-88. 147 rms, 9 junior suites, 6 deluxe suites. A/C MINIBAR TV TEL
$ Rates (including breakfast): 31,850$ ($194.30) single; 42,350$ ($258.30) double;

59,400$ ($362.30) junior suite, 106,000$ ($646.60) deluxe suite. AE, DC, MC, V.
Parking: Free.

⭐ A citadel of ostentatious living, the Dona Filipa is a deluxe golf hotel with such touches as gold-painted palms holding up the ceiling. The grounds are impressive, embracing 450 acres of rugged coastline with steep cliffs, inlets, and sandy bays. The hotel exterior is comparatively uninspired, but a greater dimension was brought to the interior by Duarte Pinto Coelho. Green-silk banquettes, marble fireplaces, Portuguese ceramic lamps, old prints over baroque-style love seats—the flair is lush. Aside from a Chinese room for card playing, the most popular meeting point is the Gothic Bar with its cathedral-like stools, wooden decorations, and matching floor and upholstery fabric in tile patterns. Most guest rooms have balconies.

Dining/Entertainment: Dining is formal and gracious, with a knowledgeable maître d'hôtel and wine steward guiding your selections. International meals cost from 8,000$ ($48.80).

Services: Laundry, 24-hour room service, babysitting.

Facilities: Three tennis courts, pool, free greens fees at São Lorenzo Golf Course, hairdresser.

QUINTA DO LAGO

Very Expensive

QUINTA DO LAGO, Quinta do Lago, 8135 Almancil. Tel. 089/39-66-66, or toll free 800/223-6800 in the U.S. Fax 089/39-63-93. 132 rms, 9 suites. A/C MINIBAR TV TEL

$ Rates (including breakfast): 35,000$–38,500$ ($213.50–$234.90) single; 45,000$–49,500$ ($274.50–$302) double; from 89,500$ ($546) suite. AE, DC, MC, V. **Parking:** Free.

⭐ A pocket of posh living is Quinta do Lago, a sprawling 1,600-acre estate that contains some private plots. The hotel is an investment of Saudi Arabian Prince Faisal, but he has wisely turned over management to the Orient Express staff, which is also a hotel chain. The luxurious Quinta Park Country Club Apartments overlook the seawater lake and are provided with modern comforts.

Dining/Entertainment: The Navegadores is for those who prefer an informal grill room overlooking a pool for both children and adults. There's a modern clubhouse with a restaurant and bar close to the golf driving range and overlooking the Bermuda green of the B1 fairway. The Beach Pavilion offers a menu of snacks, light meals, and drinks. A specialty restaurant serves Italian cuisine. The Patio Club is a sophisticated disco.

Services: Laundry, babysitting, 24-hour room service.

Facilities: Riding center, one of the best in southern Europe; 27-hole golf course, designed by American course architect William F. Mitchell, among the top six in Europe; tennis courts; indoor and outdoor pools; health club; solarium.

WHERE TO DINE

QUINTA DO LAGO

Expensive

MONTINHO'S CASA VELHA, Quinta do Lago. Tel. 39-49-83.
Cuisine: FRENCH/INTERNATIONAL. **Reservations:** Recommended.
$ Prices: Appetizers 650$–1,350$ ($4–$8.20); main courses 1,850$–2,600$ ($11.30–$15.90). AE, MC, V.
Open: Dinner only, Mon–Sat 7–11pm.

⭐ An excellent dining choice that is not part of the massive nearby Quinta do Lago resort is the Casa Velha. Set on a hillside behind its larger neighbor, it overlooks the resort's lake from the premises of a century-old farmhouse that has functioned in one capacity or another as a restaurant since the early 1960s. Cuisine is French, with a scattering of Portuguese and international dishes as well. Specialties include a salad of chicken livers and gizzards with leeks and vinaigrette, smoked swordfish with horseradish, and roasted duck *en service* (the staff presents different parts of the bird throughout the meal, beginning with the thighs *en confit* and ending with the breast *en magret*). Other choices include carefully flavored preparations of sea bass, *délices* of sole, and rack or saddle of lamb *persillé*. The dessert specialty is a "symphony" platter containing a sampling of the various crêpes, tarts, and mousses prepared by the pastry chef.

9. FARO

160 miles SE of Setúbal; 192 miles SE of Lisbon

GETTING THERE   By Plane   Jet plane makes it possible to reach Faro from Lisbon in 30 minutes. For flight information, phone 089/80-02-10. You can take bus no. 16, 17 or 18 from the railway station in Faro to the airport for 125$ (80¢). The bus operates daily from 7:10am to 7:45pm; it leaves every 45 minutes.

By Train   Trains arrive from Lisbon five times a day. The trip takes 7 hours and costs 1,450$ ($8.80) one way. For rail information in Faro, call the train station at Largo Estação (tel. 089/82-26-53).

By Bus   Buses arrive three times a day from Lisbon after a 7-hour journey. The bus station is at Avenida da República (tel. 089/80-33-25); a one-way ticket costs 1,700$ ($10.40).

By Car   Coming from the west, route 25 continues its run to Faro and beyond. From the Spanish border, pick up route 25 west.

ESSENTIALS   The **Tourist Office** is at Rua da Misericórdia 8–12 (tel. 80-36-04). The **telephone area code** is 089.

Flowers brought in from the countryside are plentiful. In the blue lagoon, sailing enthusiasts glide by. A typical old quarter flanks the ruined ramparts that proved all too vulnerable in the past. At the yacht harbor, starlings and sparrows flutter nervously, while children run noisily to the pastry shops to buy stuffed figs and almond cakes. Beyond the waterfront lie the tree-studded avenues and cobbled alleyways of the city.

Once loved by the Romans and later by the Moors, Faro is the main city of the Algarve, where you can sit at a cafe to sample the wine and watch yesterday and today pass by. An old man walks ahead, pulling a donkey on which sits a parasol-shaded girl in a white dress. Brushing past is a German student in shorts, tanned golden by the sun. Faro is a hodgepodge of life and activity: It's been rumbled, sacked, and "quaked" by everybody from Mother Nature to the Earl of Essex, who was Elizabeth I's favorite.

Since Afonso III drove out the Moors for the last time in 1266, Faro has been Portuguese. On its outskirts an international jet airport brings in thousands of visitors every summer. The airport has done more than anything else to speed tourism not only to Faro but also to the Algarve in general.

WHAT TO SEE & DO

The most bizarre attraction is the **Capela d'Ossos** (Chapel of Bones), entered from the rear of the Igreja de Nossa Senhora do Monte do Carmo do Faro, Largo do Carmo, via a courtyard. Erected in the 19th century, this chapel is completely lined with the skulls and bones of human skeletons, an extraordinarily ossicular rococo. In all, it's estimated there are 1,245 human skulls. Hours are daily from 9:30am to 12:30pm and 3 to 5pm. Entrance is free.

The church, built in 1713, contains a gilded baroque altar. Its facade is also baroque, with a bell tower rising from each side. Topping the belfries are gilded mosquelike cupolas connected by a balustraded railing. The upper-level windows are latticed and framed with gold; statues stand in each of the niches on either side of the main portal.

Other religious monuments include the old **Sé** (cathedral), Largo da Sé, built in the Gothic and Renaissance styles (originally a Muslim mosque stood on this site); and the **Igreja da São Francisco,** Largo de São Francisco, with panels of glazed earthenware tiles in milk white and Dutch blue depicting the life of the patron saint.

But most visitors don't come to Faro to look at churches, regardless of how interesting they are. Rather, they take the harbor ferry to the wide white-sand beaches called the **Praia de Faro,** on an islet. The ride is available only in summer. The beach is also connected to the mainland by bridge, a distance of about 3½ miles from the town center. Once there, you can waterski and fish or just rent a deck chair and umbrella and lounge in the sun.

WHERE TO STAY
MODERATE

EVA, Avenida da República, 8000 Faro. Tel. 089/80-33-54. Fax 089/80-23-04. 138 rms, 12 suites. A/C TEL
$ Rates (including breakfast): 11,300$–15,700$ ($68.90–$95.80) single; 13,500$–18,000$ ($82.40–$109.80) double; 19,500$–25,500$ ($119–$155.60) suite. AE, DC, MC, V. **Parking:** Free.
Dominating the harbor like a fortress is Eva, a modern hotel that occupies an entire side of the yacht-clogged harbor. There are direct sea views from most of the guest rooms, which are furnished in a restrained style; some contain minibars. The better rooms open onto the water. Eva's best features are its penthouse restaurant and rooftop pool, supported on 16 posts, with sun terraces and a bar. There is dinner dancing on Saturday. Other facilities include a snack bar, three cocktail bars, and a hairdresser. Laundry, room service, and babysitting can be arranged.

INEXPENSIVE

HOTEL FARO, Praça D. Francisco Gomes, 8002 Faro. Tel. 089/80-32-76. Fax 089/80-35-46. 52 rms, 4 suites. A/C TEL
$ Rates (including breakfast): 8,600$–11,400$ ($52.50–$69.50) single; 9,600$–12,400$ ($58.60–$75.60) double; 15,200$–19,760$ ($92.70–$120.50) suite. AE, DC, MC, V. **Parking:** Free.
The first-class Faro has well-positioned guest rooms opening right onto the bustling harbor. The furnishings in the rooms are comfortable but uninspired, and many contain balconies opening right onto the square, which tends to be noisy until late at night. Each suite has a small sitting room with a sofa bed, suitable for a third person. The light, spacious restaurant serves French and Portuguese dishes complemented by a well-coordinated wine list. The bar provides drinks, which you can order from the mezzanine while surveying the scene below.

BUDGET

HOTEL ALBACOR, Rua Brites de Almeida 25, 8000 Faro. Tel. 089/80-35-93.
$ Rates (including breakfast): 8,000$ ($48.80) single or double. AE, DC, MC, V. **Parking:** Free.
A few of the guest rooms in this well-located hotel contain small balconies; all have a comfortably unpretentious decor that is spotlessly clean. This is a good choice for a budget hotel, so it is likely to be full of a loyal repeat clientele unless you make reservations in advance in high season. There's a bar on the ground floor, plus an elevator. The English-speaking staff is most helpful.

CASA DE LUMENA, Praça Alexandre Herculano 27, 8000 Faro. Tel. 089/80-19-90. Fax 089/80-40-19. 12 rms. TEL

$ Rates (including breakfast): 5,000$–6,000$ ($30.50–$36.60) single; $6,000–9,000$ ($36.60–$54.90) double. AE, DC, MC, V. **Parking:** Free.

Casa de Lumena was once the town house of a reigning sardine family of Faro, but now it's an English-run *pensão* with central heating, sitting on a square shaded by jacaranda trees. At its bar/restaurant, the Grapevine, the international community often meets at lunchtime. The restaurant serves a Portuguese cuisine slightly modified for the international palate. Built at the edge of the sidewalk with wrought-iron gratings at its windows, the Lumena offers renovated and upgraded accommodations, some with TVs. The rooms are of different shapes and furnished in part with pieces inherited with the *casa*. Throughout are antiques, carved chests, satinwood tables, painted dressers, and armoires.

NEARBY PLACE TO STAY

EXPENSIVE

HOTEL LA RÉSERVE, Estrada de Esteval, Santa Bárbara de Nexe, 8000 Faro. Tel. 089/904-74. 20 suites. A/C MINIBAR TV TEL **Directions:** Drive out of Faro on the N125 for 4 miles; follow the sign for "Loulé" straight ahead for another mile to Esteval; turn right at the sign for "Santa Bárbara de Nexe"; 1 mile later you'll see La Réserve on the right.

$ Rates (including breakfast): 30,000$ ($183) single; 40,000$ ($244) double. No credit cards. **Parking:** Free.

The only *Relais & Châteaux* member in Portugal is near a hamlet about 7 miles west of Faro, in its own 6-acre parkland. It offers luxury accommodations in a modern and elegant country-estate atmosphere. The hotel has two pools and a tennis court. Each handsome unit has a southern sea view, private terrace, and radio.

Dining/Entertainment: The hotel has a snack bar, two bars for drinks, and an international restaurant. La Réserve restaurant, in a building adjacent to the hotel, is the finest dining room in the Algarve. The international dinners are carefully presented, and the owners care about the freshness of their meats, fish, and produce. A specialty is smoked swordfish, as fine as any served at Lisbon's more famous Avis. Along with this dish, which is served in razor-thin slices, it is customary to drink a glass of chilled vodka. Try also the Oriental shrimp served on a bed of rice with a fried banana. Local duckling, crisp outside and tender inside, makes a good main course. The best Portuguese wines are on the wine list, including the well-known *vinho verde* (green wine) of the north. Expect to spend from 6,500$ ($39.70) per person for a meal, which you can be sure will be worth it. The restaurant is open Wednesday through Monday from 7 to 11pm. It's important to call for reservations.

Services: Room service, laundry.
Facilities: Tennis courts, pool.

WHERE TO DINE

MODERATE

RESTAURANTE CIDADE VELHA, Rua Domingos Guieiro 19. Tel. 271-45.
Cuisine: PORTUGUESE/INTERNATIONAL. **Reservations:** Required.
$ Prices: Appetizers 450$–950$ ($2.70–$5.80); main courses 1,200$–2,300$ ($7.30–$14). MC, V.
Open: Lunch Mon–Fri 12:30–2pm; dinner Mon–Sat 7:30–11:30pm.

The leading restaurant in town is Cidade Velha, which used to be one of the best-located private homes in Faro; today it serves as a very charming culinary hideaway. You'll find it behind the cathedral, with thick stone walls that were built at least 250 years ago. You'll be invited to enjoy an apéritif in the tiny bar near the entrance.

Your meal will be served in one of a pair of rooms, each with a vaulted brick ceiling. Reservations can either be phoned in or left in person early in the day with one of the vested waiters. Full meals might include such items as crab cakes or smoked swordfish with horseradish sauce, followed by roast rack of lamb with rosemary and mint sauce or roast duck with apricot sauce.

INEXPENSIVE

CAFÉ CHELSEA, Rua de Francisco Gomes 28. Tel. 82-84-95.
  Cuisine: ALGARVIAN/INTERNATIONAL. **Reservations:** Not necessary.
$ Prices: Appetizers 350$–750$ ($2.10–$4.60); main courses 650$–1,000$ ($4–$6.10). AE, DC, MC, V.
  Open: Lunch daily noon–3pm; dinner daily 6:30–11pm.

Café Chelsea, on a stone-paved street thronged with pedestrians, offers a well-preserved cuisine. You can select a table in the open air or between the colorful tile walls of the ground-floor interior. Diners, however, looking for a different kind of atmosphere will press on to the upper-level dining room, where the art nouveau decor includes varied stripes of blue-and-white tiles, touches of scarlet, bentwood chairs and tables, a prominent bar, and big windows looking out over the street. Specialties include Portuguese beefsteak, pork filet, Chelsea hamburgers, Spanish omelets, an array of pasta dishes, and Indian curried prawns, plus an array of salads.

DOIS IRMÃOS, Largo do Terreiro do Bispo 18. Tel. 82-33-37.
  Cuisine: PORTUGUESE. **Reservations:** Required.
$ Prices: Appetizers 350$–650$ ($2.10–$4); main courses 850$–1,500$ ($5.20–$9.20). AE, DC, MC, V.
  Open: Daily noon–11pm.

This popular Portuguese bistro, founded in 1925, has a no-nonsense atmosphere, yet it has its devotees. The menu is as modest as the establishment and its prices, but you get a good choice of fresh fish and shellfish dishes. Ignore the paper napkins and concentrate on the fine kettle of fish placed before you. Clams in savory sauce is a favorite, and sole is regularly featured—but, of course, everything depends on the catch of the day. Service is slow and amiable, and no one seems in a hurry.

EASY EXCURSIONS

ESTÓI & MILREU

A little village some 6 miles northeast of Faro, **Estói** is still mainly unspoiled by throngs of tourists. Buses from Faro service the area. Those who come here are objects of some interest, stared at by old women sheltered behind the curtains of their little houses and followed by begging children. Sometimes you may even see women washing their clothing in a public trough. Garden walls are decaying here, and the cottages are worn by time and the weather.

The principal sight in Estói is the **Palácio do Visconde de Estói,** with a salmon-pink baroque facade. Built in the late 18th century for Francisco José de Moura Coutinho and rescued from near ruin by José Francisco da Silva between 1893 and 1909, it could now use a massive infusion of cash. A palm-lined walk leads to terraced gardens set with orange trees along the balusters.

Statues, busts, vases, and ornamental lakes adorn the terraces; *azulejos* and Roman mosaics adorn the gardens. Stairways, fountains, and belvederes rise beside cypresses, magnolias, patches of lavender, and climbing roses. This has been called a "cross between Versailles and the water gardens of the Villa d'Este near Rome."

The villa is not open to the public, but the grounds can be visited. To enter, ring a bell at the iron gates outside the palm-lined walk. A caretaker will guide you to the gardens. There is no entrance fee, but the caretaker should be tipped.

About half a mile west of Estói is **Milreu,** which was the Roman town of

Ossonoba in the 1st century A.D. Two broken capitals and some fluted columns stand on ground blanketed by buttercups. In classical times the Roman soldiers, seeing the gardens of the Algarve in the spring, decided that a Temple of Venus was in order here, and you see its remains. Around the temple, ruins of baths and houses have been uncovered, with mosaics of interest. Little excavation has been done, however. There is no admission charge, just a lonely field where once a thriving spa existed. The site is open Tuesday through Sunday from 9am to noon and 2 to 5pm.

10. VILA REAL DE SANTO ANTÓNIO

195 miles SE of Lisbon; 53 miles E of Faro; 31 miles W of Huelva (Spain)

GETTING THERE   By Train   Eleven trains per day arrive from Faro, taking 2½ hours and costing 380$ ($2.30) one way. Four trains arrive from Lagos, taking 4½ hours and costing 815$ ($5) one way. To make connections with trains within Spain (an hour ahead of Portuguese time in summer), take a ferryboat from Vila Real de Santo António to Ayamonte (for ferry information, see below). Once you're at Ayamonte, buses from the main square will deliver you to Huelva or Sevilla, where all the Spanish rail system will be at your disposal.

By Bus   It's better to take the bus from Faro to Vila Real. Nine *espressos* per day arrive from Faro, taking 1 hour and costing 620$ ($3.80) one way. Eight buses arrive from Lagos (trip time: 4 hours), costing 860$ ($5.20) one way, and four buses a day pull in from Lisbon (trip time: 7½ hours), costing 1,900$ ($11.60) one way.

BY FERRY   In summer, ferries run between Ayamonte in Spain and Vila Real daily from 7:10am to 1am, costing 130$ (80¢) per passenger or 650$ ($4) per car.

ESSENTIALS   The **Tourist Office** is at Avenida da República (tel. 432-72). The **telephone area code** is 081.

Twenty years after the marquês de Pombal rebuilt Lisbon, which had been destroyed in the great 1755 earthquake, he sent architects and builders to Vila Real de Santo António, where they reestablished the frontier town on the bank opposite Spain. It took only 5 months to build the town. Pombal's motivation was jealousy of Spain. Much has changed, of course, although the Praça de Pombal remains. An obelisk stands in the center of the square, which is paved with inlays of black and white tiles radiating like rays of the sun and is filled with orange trees. Separated from its Iberian neighbor by the Guadiana River, Vila Real de Santo António offers a car-ferry between Portugal and Ayamonte, Spain.

A long esplanade, the Avenida da República, lines the river, and from its northern extremity you can view the Spanish town across the way. Gaily painted horse-drawn carriages take you sightseeing past the shipyards and the lighthouse.

A short drive north on the road to Mertola will take you to the gull-gray castle-fortress of **Castro Marim.** This formidable structure is a legacy of the old border wars between Spain and Portugal. The ramparts and walls watch Spain across the river. Afonso III, who expelled the Moors from this region, founded the original fortress, which was razed by the 1755 earthquake. Inside the walls are the ruins of the Church of São Tiago, dedicated to St. James.

Directly southwest of Vila Real is the emerging resort of **Monte Gordo,** which has the greatest concentration of hotels in the eastern Algarve after Faro.

Monte Gordo is the last in a long line of Algarvian resorts; it lies 2 miles southwest of the frontier town of Vila Real de Santo António at the mouth of the Guadiana River. Its wide beach, one of the finest along the southern coast of Portugal, is backed by pine-studded lowlands.

Sadly, this was once a sleepy little fishing village. Nowadays, the *varinas* urge their sons to work in the hotels instead of the sea, fishing for tips instead of tunny. Monte Gordo has succumbed to the high-rises; it often attracts Spaniards from across the border. One reader described it as a "compact version of Ocean City, Maryland."

Nevertheless, it has many good hotels, and a number of Europeans use it as their place in the Algarvian sun.

WHERE TO STAY

Although Vila Real has hotels, most visitors prefer to stay at the beach at Monte Gordo (see below).

INEXPENSIVE

HOTEL APOLO, Avenida dos Bombeiros Portugueses, 8900 Vila Real de Santo António. Tel. 081/51-24-48. Fax 081/51-24-50. 42 rms. A/C TV TEL
$ Rates (including breakfast): 11,700$ ($71.40) single; 12,000$ ($73.20) double. AE, DC, MC, V. **Parking:** Free.

Hotel Apolo lies on the western edge of town as you enter Vila Real from Monte Gordo or Faro. Near the beach and the river, it attracts vacationers as well as travelers who don't want to cross the Spanish border at night. The hotel is attractive, with a spacious marble-floored lobby leading into a large and tastefully congenial bar scattered with comfortable sofas and flooded with sunlight. Each of the simply furnished guest rooms has a private balcony.

HOTEL GUADIANA, Avenida da República 94, 8900 Vila Real de Santo António. Tel. 081/51-14-82. Fax 081/51-14-78. 37 rms, 5 suites. A/C TV TEL
$ Rates (including breakfast): 7,800$ ($47.60) single; 10,800$ ($65.90) double; from 15,000$ ($91.50) suite. AE, DC, MC, V.

This is the best hotel in town, installed in a mansion classified as a historic national monument. Close to the river and the Spanish border, it is ideally located for exploring the town, less than a mile from Santo António beach and near the beach attractions of Monte Gordo as well. A three-star hotel, the building has been sensitively restored, and an aura of Portuguese tradition remains. Azulejos line some of the walls. The guest rooms are attractively furnished with traditional styling; each, though old-fashioned in decor, has all the modern amenities, such as satellite color TVs and air conditioning. There's a cozy bar, but only breakfast is served.

NEARBY PLACES TO STAY

MONTE GORDO

Expensive

HOTEL DOS NAVEGADORES, Monte Gordo, 8900 Vila Real de Santo António. Tel. 081/51-24-90. Fax 081/51-28-72. 344 rms. A/C TEL
$ Rates (including breakfast): 14,000$ ($85.40) single; 21,000$ ($128.10) double. AE, DC, MC, V. **Parking:** Free.

The sign in front of this large hotel is so discreet you might mistake it for an apartment house. The establishment is popular with vacationing Portuguese and British families, who congregate under the dome covering the atrium's swimming pool, a short distance from the reception desk. In some ways the hotel evokes a Caribbean retreat. You'll find an open bar willing to serve you a fruit-laden drink, along with an array of semitropical plants scattered throughout the wide expanses of the clean and functional public rooms. About three-quarters of the guest rooms have private balconies. The beach is only a 5-minute walk away. There's an array of boutiques in a corridor near the pool, along with a hairdresser. The hotel restaurant serves Portuguese and international dishes. The children's center amuses those between 3 and 12. Babysitting and laundry service are provided.

Moderate

HOTEL ALCÁZAR, Rua de Ceuta, Monte Gordo, 8900 Vila Real de Santo António. Tel. 081/51-21-84. Fax 081/51-22-42. 49 rms, 46 suites.
$ Rates (including breakfast): 13,000$ ($79.30) single; 15,000$ ($91.50) double; 17,000$–23,000$ ($103.70–$140.30) suite. AE, DC, MC, V. **Parking:** Free.

Hotel Alcázar is considered the best in town. Its palm-fringed facade alternates rust-colored brick with curved expanses of white balconies. A free-form pool is built on terraces into the retaining walls that shelter it from the wind and extend the hot-weather season late into autumn. The interior design is a vaguely Arab-style series of repetitive arches and vaults crafted from distressed concrete. The resulting niches offer dozens of intimate cavelike retreats, which at night sparkle from the pinpoint lighting of table lamps handcrafted from sheets of perforated copper. Each unit contains its own sun terrace and a radio. Laundry, babysitting, and room service are provided.

The basement disco is for nighttime roving. One of the sunken living rooms off the main lobby shows recently released video movies. Near the bar, live music ushers in the night from 6pm to midnight. One of the hotel's most alluring spots is under the soaring ceiling of the in-house restaurant, where formal meals are served by a polite staff in a modern setting. Entertainment is presented at various times throughout the week.

Inexpensive

CASABLANCA INN, Rua 7, Monte Gordo, 8900 Vila Real de Santo António. Tel. 081/51-14-44. Fax 081/51-19-99. 42 rms. A/C TEL
$ Rates (including breakfast): 10,100$ ($61.60) single; 13,900$ ($84.80) double. AE, DC, MC, V. **Parking:** Free.

Casablanca Inn is not directly on the beach, but its frontage on a flower-dotted downtown park makes up for it. The owner designed it to look like something you might find in a wealthy part of Morocco. There are a lush flower garden in front, a series of recessed arched balconies, and a format similar to one that a modern Humphrey Bogart might have built in an updated version of *Casablanca*—in fact, the lobby bar is called Rick's and is covered with movie photos of Hollywood's most romantic couple. Each guest room contains a terrace and a radio. At night, the bar is popular with younger people, especially on Wednesday, when live fado music begins at 10:30pm. You can enjoy the bar's cafe terrace for simple lunches daily from 11am to 2pm and for drinks nightly between 5:30pm and 1am. Live organ music is part of the weekly entertainment. The beach is about a 10-minute stroll away.

HOTEL VASCO DA GAMA, Avenida Infante Dom Henríques, Monte Gordo, 8900 Vila Real de Santo António. Tel. 081/51-13-21. Fax 081/51-16-22. 165 rms. TEL
$ Rates (including breakfast): 9,000$–10,200$ ($54.90–$62.20) single; 12,000$–14,400$ ($73.20–$87.80) double. AE, DC, MC, V. **Parking:** Free.

The entrepreneurs here know what their northern guests seek—lots of sunbathing and swimming. Although the hotel enjoys a position on a long, wide sandy beach, it also offers an Olympic pool with high-dive board and nearly an acre of flagstoned sun terrace. Inside is a sky-high oceanfront dining room, with additional tables on the mezzanine, plus several well-furnished lounges with many chair groupings. Other conveniences include two drinking bars and a *boîte* where it's possible to dance to records or combos several nights a week. All the guest rooms are furnished conservatively, and glass doors open onto balconies. Folkloric exhibitions are staged on Monday and Saturday. Laundry service, babysitting, and room service are provided.

Budget

ALBERGARIA MONTE GORDO, Avenida Infante Dom Henríques, Monte Gordo, 8900 Vila Real de Santo António. Tel. 081/421-24. 49 rms, 2 suites.
$ Rates (including breakfast): 5,500$–6,500$ ($33.60–$39.70) single; 6,500$–9,000$ ($39.70–$54.90) double; 11,000$–14,000$ ($67.10–$85.40) suite. No credit cards. **Parking:** Free.

Albergaria Monte Gordo is a streamlined modern building, open to sea and sky, emulating Pueblo architecture. It is across the road from an immense sweep of beach, clean and colorful with the local fishing boats. Thirty guest rooms have private phones. The atmosphere is informal, the staff helpful; many speak English. Decorative touches to the public rooms include fabric and needlework hangings. There are a lively bar and a good restaurant, known for soups and local fish dishes. Nonresidents may enjoy its seaview location and fine service. The peaceful winter atmosphere makes this a place ideal for writers, painters, or people looking for the simple life.

WHERE TO DINE

MODERATE

EDMUNDO, Avenida da República 55. Tel. 446-89.
Cuisine: PORTUGUESE. **Reservations:** Recommended.
$ Prices: Appetizers 350$–700$ ($2.10–$4.30); main courses 1,000$–2,000$ ($6.10–$12.20); tourist menu 1,500$ ($9.20). AE, DC, MC, V.
Open: Lunch Mon–Sat noon–3pm; dinner daily 7–10pm.

Edmundo has long been known in the Algarve, attracting Spaniards who often visit just for the day "for a glimpse of Portugal." One of the most popular restaurants in Vila Real, it overlooks the river and Spain across the water, a view you will enjoy if you get a sidewalk table. The people who run this place are friendly, proud of their repertoire of local cuisine, especially fresh fish. You might begin with shrimp cocktail, then follow with fried sole, crayfish, or sautéed red mullet. You can also order meat dishes, such as lamb cutlets and veal filet.

NEARBY PLACE TO DINE

MONTE GORDO

Moderate

COPACABANA, Avenida Infante Dom Henríques 13. Tel. 415-36.
Cuisine: PORTUGUESE. **Reservations:** Required.
$ Prices: Appetizers 450$–900$ ($2.70–$5.50); main courses 1,200$–2,200$ ($7.30–$13.40). AE, DC, MC, V.
Open: Lunch daily noon–3pm; dinner daily 7–10pm.

Because of its Oriental roof and vivid pink bougainvillea, this indoor/outdoor restaurant looks almost like a piece of Macau-made porcelain. Its entrance is flanked by a pair of feathery pine trees, which give a sparse shade to a few of the tables set out in the courtyard. Under an Oriental arcade, you can watch the chefs working in the heat of an exposed grill. Many patrons prefer to sit outdoors for the sea view just across the street. Others retreat to the wood-walled interior. You can order such Portuguese specialties as fondue of fish for two, grilled chicken, steak Diane, grilled suckling pig, bread-and-egg soup, or swordfish Copacabana, as well as grilled kid and even chiliburgers.

ALENTEJO & RIBATEJO

The adjoining provinces of Alentejo and Ribatejo are the heartland of Portugal: Although Ribatejo is a land of bull-breeding pastures, Alentejo is characterized as a plain of fire and ice.

Ribatejo is the country of the river, where the Tagus, coming from Spain, overflows its banks in winter. It is famed for bluegrass, Arabian horses, and black bulls. The most striking feature, however, is a human one: *campinos,* the region's sturdy horsemen in their stocking caps. Their job is to harness the Arabian pride of their horses and search out the intangible quality of bravery in the bulls. Whether visiting the château of the Templars, rising in the middle of the Tagus at Almourol, or attending an exciting *festa brava,* when the hooves of horses and the rumble of bulls reverberate in the streets of Vila Franca de Xira, you'll marvel at the passion of the people of Ribatejo. Their *fadistas* have long been noted for intensity.

The cork-producing plains of Alentejo (literally, beyond the Tagus) compose the largest province in Portugal—so large, in fact, that the government has divided it into Alto Alentejo in the north (capital: Évora) and Baixo Alentejo in the south (capital: Beja).

In Alentejo, the locals have insulated themselves in tiny-windowed whitewashed houses that keep in heat in the cold winters and coolness during the scorching summers. The least populated of Portuguese provinces, Alentejo possesses seemingly endless fields of wheat and is the world's largest producer of cork (the trees can be stripped only once in 9 years).

In winter, the men are a dramatic sight in their characteristic capes, long brown coats with two short tiered capes, often adorned with red-fox collars. The women are even more colorful, especially when they are working in the rice paddies or wheatfields. Their skirts and patterned undergarments are short so they can wade barefooted into the paddies. Over knitted cowls, with "peek throughs" for their eyes, they wear brimmed felt hats usually studded with flowers.

From the last stopover in the Algarve (see Chapter 11), head north once again, approaching the cities of the plains.

SEEING ALENTEJO & RIBATEJO

A car is best if you can afford it, as there are so many towns to see and even excursions to take from the major cities. There is public transportation, but often you'll have a long, tiresome wait between connections. Both provinces lie on the virtual doorstep of Lisbon, and, in fact, they begin as northern suburbs of the capital.

From Spain, the N521 runs 64 miles west from Caceres to the Portuguese border at Portalegre; or you can take the N4 for 9 miles between the Spanish city of Badajoz and Elvas. In the south of Spain at Seville, the N433 runs to Beja, a distance of 136 miles to the west.

WHAT'S SPECIAL ABOUT ALENTEJO & RIBATEJO

Great Towns/Villages
- ☐ Beja, capital of Baixo Alentejo, founded by Julius Caesar—its fame rests on what may have been a literary hoax.
- ☐ Évora, capital of Alto Alentejo, an architectural phenomenon—one of the most rewarding cities on the tourist circuit.
- ☐ Elvas, "city of the plums"—known for its crenellated fortifications.
- ☐ Marvão, ancient walled hill town—noted for its spectacular views.
- ☐ Tomar, fabled seat of the once notorious quasi-religious order of the Knights Templar.

Ancient Monument
- ☐ Temple of Diana, at Évora, dating from either the 1st or 2nd century A.D.—a survivor of the 1755 earthquake.

Religious Shrine
- ☐ Convento de Cristo, at Tomar—an architectural marvel established in 1320 by the disbanded Knights of Templar.

If you've already explored the Algarve (see Chapter 11), you'll find Alentejo at your doorstep. The best route to take into Alentejo from the south is IP-1, heading north from Albufeira.

Train passengers will find good connections between Lisbon and Évora and Beja. Several trains make the daily run. Once you're there, travel by train through central Portugal is extremely time consuming. Most of the places, even small villages, are served by at least one bus daily. Express buses from Lisbon (Rodoviária Nacional) make connections into such major towns as Évora and Santerém (see specific destinations, below, for more details).

SUGGESTED 4-DAY ITINERARY

Day 1 Assuming you're heading north from the Algarve, go first to the capital at Beja and spend the night.

Days 2–3 Head north from Beja for a two-night stopover in Évora, time enough to explore its monuments.

Day 4 Overnight in Tomar after exploring that interesting city.

1. BEJA

116 miles SE of Lisbon; 47 miles S of Évora

GETTING THERE By Train Five trains per day make the 4-hour journey from Lisbon to Beja for 950$ ($5.80) one way. There are also four daily trains arriving from Évora (see the next section). This journey takes only an hour and costs 535$ ($3.30) one way. If you're in the Algarve (see Chapter 11), you can take one of two trains per day from Faro to Beja, which takes 5½ hours and costs 945$ ($5.80) one way.

By Bus Four *expressos* (express buses) per day make the 3-hour run between Lisbon and Beja; the fare is 1,100$ ($6.70) one way. There are also five buses per day from Évora, taking 2 hours and costing 750$ ($4.60) one way, and five buses per day from Faro, taking 3½ hours and costing 1,080$ ($6.60) one way.

By Car   From Albufeira in the Algarve, take the IP-1 north to the junction with route 263, which heads northeast for the final lap into Beja.

ESSENTIALS   The **Beja Tourist Office** is at Rua Capitão João Francisco de Sousa 25 (tel. 236-93). The **telephone area code** is 084.

The capital of Baixo Alentejo, founded by Julius Caesar and once known as *Pax Julia,* rises like a pyramid above the surrounding fields of swaying wheat. Its fame rests on what many authorities believe to be a literary hoax: In the mid-17th century, in the Convent of Conceição, a young nun named Soror Mariana Alcoforado is said to have fallen in love with a French military officer, identified as the chevalier de Chamilly; he was believed to have seduced her, then to have left Beja forever.

The girl's outpouring of grief and anguish found literary release in the *Five Love Letters of a Portuguese Nun,* published in Paris in 1669. These letters created a sensation and have remained an epistolary classic of self-revelation and remorse ever since. In 1926, F. C. Green wrote "Who Was the Author of the '*Lettres Portugaises*'?" claiming that their true writer was the comte de Guilleragues. However, a modern Portuguese study has submitted evidence that the *Lettres Portugaises* were written by the nun, Sister Alcoforado.

WHAT TO SEE & DO

MUSEU RAINHA D. LEONOR [Queen Leonor Museum], Largo da Conceição. Tel. 084/233-51.

This museum was founded in 1927 and 1928 and presently occupies three buildings in the city of Beja: Convento da Conceição and the churches of Santo Amaro and São Sebastião. The main building was an ancient convent, founded in 1459 by the parents of Portuguese King Manuel I. Favored by royal protection, it became one of the richest and most important convents of that time. Nevertheless, Convento da Conceição is famous throughout the world because of a 17th-century nun, Mariana Alcoforado, who is said to have written here the *Lettres Portugaises,* love letters to the French chevalier de Chamilly.

One of the most important features of the building is precisely what is left of the ancient convent: the church with its baroque decoration and the cloister and chapter house, which present one of the most impressive collections of Spanish and Portuguese tiles from the 15th to the 18th century. Also displayed are statuary and silverwork belonging to the convent patrimony; a good collection of Spanish, Portuguese, and Dutch paintings (15th to 18th century); and the *Escudela de Pero de Faria,* a piece of 1541 Chinese porcelain unique in the world. The first-floor permanent archeological exhibition features various artifacts from the Beja region—it shows the importance of this area from prehistoric to modern times.

Santo Amaro church is one of the oldest churches of Beja, maybe an early Christian foundation. It houses the most important Portuguese Visigothic collection (from Beja and its surroundings).

The church of São Sebastião is a small temple with no great architectural interest. It houses part of the museum's collection of architectural goods from Roman to modern times. It is not open to the public, only to those who make a special request to visit it.

Admission: 100$ (60¢) adults; children free.
Open: Tues–Sun 9:45am–1pm and 2–5:15pm.

CASTELO DE BEJA, Largo Dr. Lima Faleiro.

This castle, which King Dinis built in the early 14th century on the ruins of a Roman fortress, crowns the town. Although some of its turreted walls have been restored, the defensive towers are gone, save for a long marble keep. Traditionally the final stronghold in the castle's fortifications, the old keep appears to be battling the weather and gold fungi. The walls are overgrown with ivy, the last encroachment on

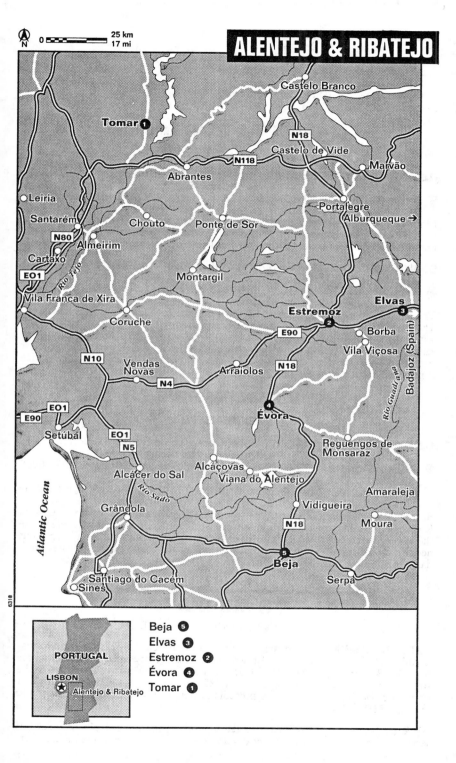

its former glory. From the keep, you can enjoy a view of the provincial capital and the outlying fields.

Admission: 100$ (60¢).

Open: Apr–Sept, daily 10am–1pm and 2–6pm; Oct–Mar, daily 9am–noon and 1–4pm.

WHERE TO STAY

BUDGET

RESIDENCIAL CRISTINA, Rua de Mértola 71, 7800 Beja. Tel. 084/32-30-35. Fax 084/32-98-74. 34 rms. A/C TV TEL

$ Rates (including breakfast): 6,000$ ($36.60) single; 7,600$ ($46.40) double. AE, DC, MC, V. **Parking:** Free.

Many visitors consider Residencial Cristina, the largest hostelry in town, the best place to stay. A helpful management rents simply furnished guest rooms. Everything is immaculately kept. Breakfast is the only meal served.

SANTA BÁRBARA, Rua de Mértola 56, 7800 Beja. Tel. 084/32-20-28. 26 rms. TEL

$ Rates (including breakfast): 4,300$ ($26.20) single; 5,500$–6,000$ ($33.60–$36.60) double. MC, V. **Parking:** Free.

The Santa Bárbara is a little oasis in a town that has few suitable accommodations. The *residencia* is a shiny clean and well-kept bandbox building. It's all small scale, with only a whisper of a reception lobby and elevator. There are two street-level salons, each partially covered with elegant blue-and-yellow tiles. The compact guest rooms are adequate, with carpeting, good beds, and central heating. Laundry service is provided. Breakfast is the only meal served.

WHERE TO DINE

INEXPENSIVE

LUÍS DA ROCHA, Rua Capitão João Francisco de Sousa 63. Tel. 232-67. **Cuisine:** PORTUGUESE. **Reservations:** Not necessary.

$ Prices: Appetizers 350$–750$ ($2.10–$4.60); main courses 950$–1,800$ ($5.80–$11). DC, MC, V.

Open: Lunch daily noon–3:30pm; dinner daily 7–10pm. **Closed:** Sun and May 1–Sept 30.

Beja is rather lacking in first- or even second-class restaurants. However, at Luís da Rocha, on the same street as the tourist office, you can sit downstairs in the cafe where the whole town seems to congregate for coffee and pastries or go upstairs to a spacious neon-lit dining room. You might begin with one of the cream soups, prepared fresh daily, then follow with boiled or fried fish or pork with clams Alentejo style.

---

2. ÉVORA

63 miles SW of Badajoz (Spain); 96 miles E of Lisbon

GETTING THERE   By Train   The train station (tel. 066/221-25 for information) lies a mile from the center of town. Five trains per day arrive from Lisbon; the trip takes 3 hours and costs 695$ ($4.20) one way. One train arrives from Faro in the Algarve; the trip takes 6 hours and costs 1,225$ ($7.50) one way. There are also four trains per day from Beja (see the preceding section), making the 2-hour trip and charging 535$ ($3.30) one way.

By Bus   Rodoviária Nacional, Rua da República (tel. 066/221-21), provides bus service for the area. Seven buses per day arrive from Lisbon; the trip takes 2½ hours and costs 1,000$ ($6.10) one way. And four buses per day make the 5-hour trip from Faro in the Algarve, costing 1,250$ ($7.60) one way. Five buses per day connect Beja with Évora; the trip is 2 hours and costs 750$ ($4.60) one way.

By Car   From Beja (see above), continue north along route 18. The **Évora Tourist Information Office** is at Praça do Giraldo 71 (tel. 226-71). The **telephone area code** is 066.

SPECIAL EVENTS   Évora's major event is the Feira de São João, a folkloric and musical extravaganza when all the handcrafts of the area, including fine ceramics, are displayed as hundreds of people from the Alentejo region come into the city. The event, which occupies the last 10 days of June, is held ostensibly to celebrate the arrival of summer. Food stalls sell regional specialties, and regional dances are presented. The tourist office (see above) will supply more details.

The capital of Alto Alentejo is a historical curio. Considering its size and location, it   is something of an architectural phenomenon. Its builders freely adapted whatever they desired from Mudejar to Manueline, from Roman to rococo. Évora lives up to its reputation as the Museum City. Since it is somewhat close to Lisbon, it is often visited on a day-trip from the capital, but that's a long trek.

Nearly every street in Évora is filled with 16th- and 17th-century houses, many with tile patios. Cobblestones, labyrinthine streets, arcades, squares with bubbling fountains, whitewashed houses, and a profuse display of Moorish-inspired arches characterize the town; all of these used to be enclosed behind medieval walls.

Many conquerors have passed through, and several have left architectural remains. To the Romans at the time of Julius Caesar, Évora was known as Liberalitas Julia. Perhaps its heyday was during the 16th-century reign of João III, when it became the Montmartre of Portugal and avant-garde artists congregated under the aegis of royalty. Included among them were the playwright Gil Vicente.

Évora today is a sleepy provincial capital, perhaps self-consciously aware of its monuments. One local historian actually recommended to an American couple that they see at least 59 monuments. Rest assured that you can capture the essence by seeing only a fraction of that number.

WHAT TO SEE & DO

TEMPLO DE DIANA [Temple of Diana], Praça do Giraldo.

✪ The major monument in Évora is the Temple of Diana, directly in front of the   government-owned *pousada* (see below). Dating from either the 1st or the 2nd   century A.D., it is a light, graceful structure with 14 granite Corinthian columns topped by marble capitals. Of course, no one can prove it actually was dedicated to the goddess, but it is a good guess. Incidentally, the temple withstood the 1755 earthquake, and there is evidence it was once used as a slaughterhouse. Don't fail to walk through the garden for a view of the Roman aqueduct and the surrounding countryside. Since it stands on the open square, it can be viewed at any time.

SÉ [Cathedral], Rua 5 de Outubro. Tel. 066/29-160.

Bulky and heavy, the cathedral of Évora was built in the Roman-Gothic style between 1186 and 1204, although it was notably restored and redesigned over the centuries. The stone facade is flanked by two square towers, both topped by cones, one surrounded by satellite spires. The interior consists of a nave and two aisles. The 18th-century main altar is the finest in town, made of marble in tones of pink, black, and white.

At the sculptured work *The Lady of Mothers,* young women pray for fertility. Once a French couple, whose marriage had up till then produced no children, prayed here, and the wife found herself pregnant by the time she returned to Paris; the next year, the couple returned to Évora, bringing their new child.

The museum houses treasures from the church, the most notable of which is a 13th-century Virgin carved out of ivory (it opens to reveal a collection of scenes from her life). A reliquary is studded with 1,426 precious stones, including sapphires, rubies, diamonds, and emeralds. The most valuable item is a piece of wood said to have come from the True Cross.

In the 14th-century cloister, the medallions of the Apostles include the Star of David, incongruous in a Roman Catholic church. A cross in the ceiling, called the Key of the Cloister, marks the last stone to be set into place.

Admission: 200$ ($1.20) adults; children free.

Open: Tues–Sun 9am–12:30pm and 2–5pm.

IGREJA REAL DE SÃO FRANCISCO [Church of Saint Francis], Rua da República.

This church is visited by those who want to see its ghoulish 16th-century Chapel of Bones (Capela dos Ossos). The chancel walls and central pillars of this stone chapel are lined with human skulls and other parts of skeletons. Alternate legends have it that the bones came from either soldiers who died in a big battle or plague victims. Over the door is the sign: "Our bones who stay here are waiting for yours!" The church was built in the Gothic style with Manueline influences between 1460 and 1510.

Admission: 25$ (20¢).

Open: Mon–Sat 8:30am–1pm and 2:30–6pm, Sun 10–11:30am and 2:30–6pm.

IGREJA NOSSA SENHORA DE GRAÇA [Church of Our Lady of Grace], Largo da Graça.

This church is visited chiefly for its baroque facade, with huge classical nudes over the pillars. Above each group of lazing stone giants is a sphere with a flame atop. These pieces of sculpture are often compared to works by Michelangelo. The church was built in Évora's heyday, during the reign of João III. The central window shaft is flanked by columns and large stone rosettes, the lower level supported by ponderous neoclassic columns.

Admission: 300$ ($1.80).

Open: Tues–Sun 9am–noon and 2–5pm.

UNIVERSIDADE DE ÉVORA, Largo do Colegio.

You may want to visit the ancient university (Universidade de Évora). In 1559, as a result of the cultural flowering of Évora, the university was constructed and placed under the tutelage of the Jesuits. It flourished until the Jesuit-hating marquês de Pombal closed it in the 18th century. The compound wasn't used as a university until 1975.

Through its 17 departments, grouped in five departmental areas and located in various buildings in Évora and Valverde, the University of Évora confers doctorates and administers degree programs at all university levels for its more than 5,000 students.

The double-tiered baroque structure is built around a large quadrangle. The arches are supported by marble pillars, the interior ceilings constructed with brazilwood. The inner courtyard is lined with blue-and-white tiles. Other azulejo representations—depicting women, wild animals, angels, cherubs, and costumed men—contrast with the austere elegance of the classrooms and the elongated refectory.

Admission: Free.

Open (with permission): Mon–Fri 9am–5pm.

IGREJA DE SÃO JOÃO EVANGELISTA [Church of St. John the Evangelist], Praça do Giraldo.

Facing the Temple of Diana and next door to the government-owned pousada, this private Gothic-Mudéjar church is connected to the palace built by the dukes of Cadaval. However, it is open to the public—in fact, it is one of the gems of Évora, although seemingly little visited. It contains a collection of *azulejos* from the 18th century. A guide will show you a macabre sight: an old cistern filled with neatly stacked bones removed from tombs. In the chapel's sacristy are some paintings, including a ghastly rendition of Africans slaughtering a Christian missionary. A curiosity is a painting of a pope that has not only moving eyes but also moving feet. In addition, you can see part of the wall that once completely encircled Évora.

Admission: 125$ (80¢).
Open: Daily 9am–noon and 2–6pm.

MUSEU DE ÉVORA [Museum of Ancient Art], Largo Conde de Vila Flor. Tel. 066/226-04.

⭐ This museum is in the 16th- and 17th-century episcopal palace. Roman, medieval, Manueline, and Luso-Moorish sculptures are displayed on the ground floor. Here you'll see a remnant of a Vestal Virgin in marble, a 14th-century marble Annunciation, and a Holy Trinity in Anca stone, dating from the 1500s. Of major interest on the floor above is a 16th-century Flemish-school polyptych depicting the life of the Virgin, Flemish panels of an altarpiece on the subject of Christ's Passion, and pictures by Portuguese artists of the 16th and 17th centuries.

Admission: 200$ ($1.20); children under 10 free.
Open: Tues–Sun 9am–noon and 2–5pm.

WHERE TO STAY
EXPENSIVE

POUSADA DOS LÓIOS, Largo Conde de Vila Flor, 7000 Évora. Tel. 066/240-51. Fax 066/272-48. 30 rms, 2 suites. TEL

$ **Rates** (including breakfast): 22,100$ ($134.80) single; 25,200$ ($153.70) double; 32,000$–48,600$ ($195.20–$296.50) suite. AE, DC, MC, V. **Parking:** Free.

⭐ One of the finest government-owned tourist inns in Portugal is Pousada dos Lóios. It occupies Lóios Monastery, built in 1485 on the site of the old Évora Castle, which was destroyed during a riot in 1384. A powerful noble, Don Rodrigo Afonso de Melo, founded the monastery and carried on his back two baskets of soil and the first stone for the foundation ceremony. João II, IV, and V used to visit the monastery. The chapter room, with 16th-century doorways in Moorish-Portuguese style, was the place where the official Inquisition reports were kept. After the 1755 earthquake, extensive work was done to repair and preserve the structure. Through the years it was used as a telegraph station, a primary school, an army barracks, and offices. The 1965 opening of the pousada made possible the architectural restoration of the monastery. Its position in the museumlike center of Évora, between the cathedral and the ghostlike Roman Temple of Diana, is prime.

The white-and-gold salon (a one-time private chapel) boasts an ornate Pompeian-style decor and frescoes and is decorated with antique furnishings, hand-woven draperies, crystal chandeliers and sconces, and painted medallion portraits. All guest rooms are furnished in traditional provincial style, with a blending of antique reproductions. Ask for a room in the interior.

Dining/Entertainment: Even if you're not bedding down for the night, like a pilgrim of old, you should at least stop for a regional meal of Alto Alentejo. In winter, meals are served in the main dining hall with its heavy chandeliers. But in fair weather, most guests dine in and around the cloister, at tables set under the Manueline fan-vaulted ceiling and an ornate Moorish doorway leading to the Chapter House. For a complete meal price of 4,000$ ($24.40), you'll get a basket of freshly baked bread and butter; a bowl of hot soup; and a fish dish, such as sole prepared in a herb-flavored tomato sauce and accompanied by mashed potatoes. For your main course, try the acorn-sweetened pork cooked with clams in the Alentejo manner. For dessert, a trolley of assorted pastries is wheeled by. Food is served daily from 12:30 to 2:30pm and 7:30 to 9:30pm.

Services: Laundry, room service.
Facilities: Pool.

INEXPENSIVE

ALBERGARIA VITÓRIA, Rua Diana de Lis 5, 7000 Évora. Tel. 066/271-74. Fax 066/209-74. 48 rms, 3 suites. A/C TV TEL

$ **Rates** (including breakfast): 8,800$ ($53.70) single; 11,300$ ($68.90) double; 15,000$ ($91.50) suite. AE, DC, MC, V. **Parking:** Free.

Set inconveniently near the beltway surrounding the old city, this modern concrete-walled hotel juts above a dusty neighborhood of villas. It sits on the southeastern edge of the city, about a mile from the cathedral, but it could be a handy address in summer when all the central hotels are full. Built in 1985, it contains 45 doubles but only 3 singles, each with a balcony and radio. Only breakfast is served in the dining room, but the Vitória has a bar on the premises.

O RESIDENCIAL SOLAR, Largo da Misericórdia 1, 7000 Évora. Tel. 066/220-31. 27 rms, 1 suite. TV TEL

$ Rates: 6,500$–7,000$ ($39.70–$42.70) single; 9,000$ ($54.90) double; 12,000$ ($73.20) suite. Breakfast 500$ ($3.10) extra. MC, V. **Parking:** Free 8pm–8am.

This is a delightful guesthouse with a touch of grandeur in the form of a stone staircase leading up to a plant-lined entrance decorated with tiles. Your hosts are Mr. and Mrs. Serrabulho, who have recently improved the building by making the guest rooms more comfortable but keeping the original antique atmosphere. The rooms, all in the main building, are clean, traditional, and quite pleasant. You can sit on the terrace nursing a drink and peering through the cloisterlike mullioned veranda. An adjoining rooftop-garden cafe attracts sun worshipers.

HOTEL PLANÍCIE, Rua Miguel Bombarda 40, 7000 Évora. Tel. 066/240-26, or toll free 800/528-1234 in the U.S. Fax 066/298-80. 40 rms, 2 suites. A/C TV TEL

$ Rates (including breakfast): 10,500$–11,300$ ($64.10–$68.90) single; 13,000$–14,000$ ($79.30–$85.40) double; 20,800$ ($126.90) suite. DC, MC, V. **Parking:** Free.

Its symmetry, stone window frames, and severe facade make the Planície resemble an old Tuscan villa. Inside, a tasteful modernization added hundreds of slabs of glistening marble but retained many of the best features of its original construction. Especially appealing is the basement bar's vaulted brick ceiling. Each guest room in this hotel, a member of the Best Western reservation system, has heating. Well-prepared meals, costing from 2,200$ ($13.40), are served in the street-level dining room daily from noon to 3pm and 7 to 10pm.

RESIDENCIAL RIVIERA, Rua 5 de Outubro 49, 7000 Évora. Tel. 066/233-04. Fax 066/20-467. 22 rms. A/C TV TEL

$ Rates (including breakfast): 8,000$ ($48.80) single; 13,000$ ($79.30) double. AE, DC, MC, V. **Parking:** Free.

The Residencial Riviera was built beside the cobblestones of one of the most charming streets in town, about two blocks downhill from the cathedral. Designed as a private villa, it has retained many handcrafted details from the original building, including stone window frames, ornate iron balustrades, and the blue-and-yellow tiles of its foyer. Its guest rooms are quite comfortable.

SANTA CLARA, Travessa da Milheira 19, 7000 Évora. Tel. 066/241-41. Fax 066/265-44. 43 rms. A/C TV TEL

$ Rates (including breakfast): 7,400$ ($45.10) single; 9,600$ ($58.60) double. AE, DC, MC, V. **Parking:** Free.

Santa Clara is another good bet, especially if your requirements are simple. Near the free city car park, it is within walking distance of Évora's major sightseeing attractions. The management rents well-kept guest rooms. The hotel has a good restaurant, serving regional specialties and local wines, with meals priced from 3,100$ ($18.90).

WHERE TO DINE
MODERATE

COZINHA DE ST. HUMBERTO, Rua da Moeda 39. Tel. 242-51.
  Cuisine: ALENTEJAN. **Reservations:** Required.
$ Prices: Appetizers 400$–1,000$ ($2.40–$6.10); main courses 1,200$–2,200$ ($7.30–$13.40); fixed-price lunch 1,900$ ($11.60); fixed-price dinner 2,200$ ($13.40). AE, DC, MC, V.

Open: Lunch daily noon–3:30pm; dinner daily 7–10:30pm. **Closed:** Nov.
This is Évora's most atmospheric restaurant. Hidden away in a narrow side street leading down from Praça do Giraldo, it is rustically decorated with old pots, blunderbusses, standing lamps, a grandfather clock, and kettles hanging from the ceiling. Carnations stand on each table, and you sit in rush chairs or on divans. In warm weather, you can enjoy gazpacho *alentejana*, followed by fried fish with tomato and garlic or pork Évora style (a meal in itself), topped off by regional cheese. A bottle of Borba wine is a good companion with most meals.

FIALHO, Travessa Mascarenhas 14. Tel. 230-79.
   Cuisine: ALENTEJAN. **Reservations:** Recommended.
$ Prices: Appetizers 450$–950$ ($2.70–$5.80); main courses 1,200$–2,100$ ($7.30–$12.80). AE, DC, MC, V.
   Open: Tues–Sun noon–midnight. **Closed:** Sept.

Fialho is considered the most traditional restaurant in Évora. Its entrance is unprepossessing, but the interior will warm you considerably with its decoration in the style of a Portuguese tavern. You get good shellfish dishes along with such fare as pork with baby clams in savory sauce. In season, you might also be able to order partridge. The air-conditioned restaurant seats 80.

GUIÃO, Rua da República 81. Tel. 224-27.
   Cuisine: PORTUGUESE. **Reservations:** Not necessary.
$ Prices: Appetizers 400$–950$ ($2.40–$5.80); main courses 1,100$–2,300$ ($6.70–$14). AE, DC, MC, V.
   Open: Lunch daily noon–3pm; dinner daily 7–11pm. **Closed:** Nov 15–Dec 15.
Guião is a regional tavern that appears on most lists as one of Évora's best three or four restaurants. It lies just off the main square, Praça do Giraldo. Dining is on two levels. The decor exudes Portuguese charm, including a beamed ceiling and antique blue-and-white tiles. Family run, it offers local wines and Portuguese specialties. Meals—hearty and robust fare—are most filling. A typical bill of fare includes grilled squid, grilled fish, swordfish steak, and clams with pork Alentejo style. At certain times of the year, the kitchen prepares partridge.

---

3. ESTREMOZ

28½ miles NE of Évora; 108 miles E of Lisbon

GETTING THERE   By Train   At present there is no train service.

By Bus   The Estremoz bus station is at Rossio Marquês de Pombal (tel. 068/222-82). Six buses arrive here daily from Évora, 1 hour away, and five buses per day also arrive from Portalegre, 1½ hours away.

By Car   From Évora (see the preceding section), head northeast along route 18.

ESSENTIALS   The **Estremoz Tourist Office** is at Rossio Marquês de Pombal (tel. 227-83). The **telephone area code** is 068.

Rising from the Alentejo plain like a pyramid of salt set out to dry in the sun, fortified Estremoz is in the center of the marble-quarry region of Alentejo. Cottages and mansions alike utilize the abundant marble in their windows and apertures or in their balustrades and banisters.

WHAT TO SEE & DO

With enough promenading Portuguese soldiers to man a garrison, the open quadrangle in the center of the Lower Town is called the **Rossio Marquês de Pombal.** The **Town Hall,** with its twin bell towers, opens onto this square, and the walls of its grand stairway are lined with antique azulejos in blue and white, depicting hunting, pastoral, and historical scenes.

The **Estremoz Potteries** turn out the traditional earthenware of the region. It is famous for *moringues,* wide- or narrow-mouthed jars with two spouts and one handle. A type associated with royalty, called kings' jugs, is decorated with marble inlays. Primitive figurines of religious and lay characters are interesting, as are those of animals.

In the 16th-century **Church of St. Mary,** you'll see pictures by Portuguese primitive painters. The church formed part of the ancient fortress. Another church worth a stop is about a mile south of the town on the road to Bencatel, the **Church of Our Lady of the Martyrs** (Nossa Senhora dos Mártires), with beautiful azulejos and an entrance marked by a Manueline arch. Dating from 1844, the church has a nave chevet after the French-Gothic style of architecture.

CASTELO DA RAINHA SANTA ISABEL [Chapel of Queen Saint Isabel], Largo de Dom Dinis. Tel. 226-18.

From the ramparts of its castle, which dates from the 13th-century reign of Dinis, the plains of Alentejo are spread before you. Although one 75-year-old British lady is reported to have walked it, it's best to drive your car to the top of the Upper Town and stop on the Largo de Dom Dinis. The stones of the castle, the cradle of the town's past, were decaying so badly that the city leaders pressed for its restoration in 1970. It was turned into a luxurious *pousada* (see below) that is the best place to stay or dine.

The large imposing keep, attached to a palace, dominates the central plaza. Dinis's saintly wife, Isabella, died in the castle and was unofficially proclaimed a saint by her local followers; even in life, however, one of her detractors wrote, "Poor Dinis!" Also opening onto the marble- and stone-paved largo are two modest chapels and a church. As in medieval days, soldiers still walk the ramparts, guarding the fortress.

MUSEU RURAL DA CASA DO POVO DE SANTA MARIA DE ESTREMOZ [Rural Museum], Rossio Marquês de Pombal. Tel. 068/225-38.

This museum displays the life of people of the Alentejo through models and crafts. It is open for guided tours. The museum is installed in an 18th-century-style building that's part of the property of the Convento das Maltezas de S. João da Penitência, today the Misericórdia (national charity organization).

Admission: 130$ (80¢) adults; children under 12 free.
Open: Tues–Sun 9am–12:30pm and 2–5:45pm.

WHERE TO STAY

EXPENSIVE

POUSADA DA RAINHA SANTA ISABEL, Largo de Dom Dinis, 7100 Estremoz. Tel. 068/226-18. Fax 068/239-82. 33 rms, 3 suites. A/C MINIBAR TEL

$ Rates (including breakfast): 21,100$ ($128.70) single; 25,200$ ($153.70) double; from 35,000$ ($213.50) suite. AE, DC, MC, V. **Parking:** Free.

This is one of the best of the government-owned tourist inns. Within the old castle dominating the town and overlooking the battlements and the Estremoz plain, it is a deluxe establishment, with gold leaf, marble, velvet, and satin mingling with antiques in the guest rooms and corridors. Before his departure for India, Vasco da Gama was received by Dom Manuel in the salon of this castle. In 1698, a terrible explosion followed by fire destroyed the royal residence, but ostentatious alterations were carried out. It became an armory and later was adapted to serve as a barracks, then an industrial school, but its transformation into a castle-pousada has restored it as a historical monument. In perfect style, comfort is provided within the framework of history. Therefore, don't be surprised that prices differ from those of the less regal pousadas.

Dining/Entertainment: The vaulted dining room is cavernous but elegant, offering a menu that is both international and regional. Try, for example, braised duck with olive sauce or vegetable-stuffed partridge. If it's featured, you might want to be daring and order the grilled wild boar with hot-pepper sauce. A meal costs to 4,000$ ($24.40). Food is served daily from 12:30 to 3pm and 7:30 to 10pm.

Services: Laundry, room service.
Facilities: Outdoor pool.

BUDGET

RESIDÊNCIA CARVALHO, Largo da República 27, 7100 Estremoz. Tel. 068/227-12. 18 rms (14 with bath).

$ Rates (including breakfast): 1,750$ ($10.70) single without bath, 3,000$ ($18.30) single with bath; 3,500$ ($21.40) double without bath, 5,800$ ($35.40) double with bath. No credit cards. **Parking:** Free.

Residência Carvalho is clean, simple, and inexpensive—just what you may be looking for in case the pousada is full and you're tired—two likely possibilities. Ten of the rooms have telephones; breakfast is the only meal served.

WHERE TO DINE
MODERATE

ÁGUIAS D'OURO, Rossio Marquês de Pombal 27. Tel. 221-96.
   Cuisine: PORTUGUESE. **Reservations:** Required.
$ Prices: Appetizers 450$–1,000$ ($2.70–$6.10); main courses 1,200$–2,200$ ($7.30–$13.40). AE, DC, MC, V.
   Open: Lunch daily noon–3pm; dinner daily 7–11pm.

Good food and a pleasant ambience are offered at Águias d'Ouro. The Golden Eagle faces the largest square in Estremoz; its mosaic-and-marble balconied facade suggest a doge's palace. On the second floor are several connecting dining rooms with rough white-plaster walls under ceramic brick ceilings, heavy sumptuous black-leather armchairs, and white-draped tables. Your meal begins with a dish of homemade pâté with rye bread. Other offerings include a large bowl of spinach-and-bean soup with crispy croutons and main dishes like stuffed partridge and pork and clams. Chocolate mousse is the featured dessert.

4. ELVAS

7 miles W of Badajoz (Spain); 138 miles E of Lisbon

GETTING THERE   By Train   The Elvas train station is at Fontainhas (tel. 068/62-28-16), 2 miles north of the city. Local buses connect the station to the Praça da República in the center. Four trains a day arrive from Lisbon, taking 5½ hours and charging 900$ ($5.50) one way. From Évora, you can take the twice-daily train, which takes 3 hours and charges 310$ ($1.90) one way. From Badajoz in Spain, there are two trains per day, taking 1 hour and charging 450$ ($2.70) one way.

By Bus   The Elvas bus station is at Praça da República (tel. 068/628-75). Five buses per day make the 4-hour trip from Lisbon for a one-way price of 1,200$ ($7.30). Three buses leave Évora daily to make the 2-hour trip for 780$ ($4.80) one way. From Badajoz there are frequent buses throughout the day. The ride lasts 15 minutes.

By Car   From Estremoz (see the preceding section), continue east toward Spain along route 4.

ESSENTIALS   The **Elvas Tourist Office** is at Praça da República (tel. 62-22-36). The **telephone area code** is 068.

The "city of the plums," known for crenelated fortifications, is characterized by narrow cobblestone streets (pedestrians have to duck into doorways to allow automobiles to inch by) and is surely an anachronism, so tenaciously does it hold on to its monuments and history. The town was held by the Moors until 1226. Later, it was frequently assaulted and besieged by Spanish troops until it was finally defeated in the 1801 War of the Oranges, which was ended by a peace treaty signed at Badajoz. Elvas remained part of Portugal, but its neighbor, Olivença, became Spanish. The Elvas ramparts are an outstanding example of 17th-century fortifications, with fortified gates, curtain walls, moats, bastions, and sloping banks (*glacis*) around them.

Lining the steep hilly streets are tightly packed gold- and oyster-colored cottages topped by tile roofs. Many of the house doors are only 5 feet high. In the tiny windows are numerous canary cages and flowering geraniums. Water is transported to Elvas by the four-tier Aqueduto da Amoreira, built between 1498 and 1622, coming from about 5 miles southwest of the town.

In the Praça Dom Sancho II (honoring the king who reconstructed the town) stands the **Sé (cathedral)**, forbidding and fortresslike. Under a cone-shaped dome, it is decorated with gargoyles, turrets, and a florid Manueline portal. The cathedral opens onto a black-and-white-diamonded square. A short walk up the hill to the right of the cathedral leads to the **Largo Santa Clara,** a small plaza on which was erected an odd Manueline pillory, with four wrought-iron dragon heads.

On the south side of Largo Santa Clara is the **Church of Our Lady of Consolation** (Igreja Nossa Senhora de Consolação), a 16th-century octagonal Renaissance building with a cupola lined in 17th-century *azulejos*.

The **castle,** built by the Moors and strengthened by the Christian rulers in the 14th and 16th centuries, offers a panoramic view of the town and its fortifications, as well as the surrounding country. It's open Friday through Wednesday from 9:30am to 12:30pm and 2:30 to 7pm (it closes at 5:30pm from October 10 to April 30).

WHERE TO STAY

MODERATE

POUSADA DE SANTA LUZIA, Avenida de Badajoz, 7350 Elvas. Tel. 068/62-21-94. Fax 068/62-21-27. 15 rms, 1 suite. A/C MINIBAR TEL

$ Rates (including breakfast): 12,800$ ($78.10) single; 14,400$ ($87.80) double; 19,000$ ($115.90) suite. AE, DC, MC, V. **Parking:** Free.

A major link in the government-inn circuit is Pousada de Santa Luzia, a hacienda-style building just outside the city walls at the edge of a busy highway (Estrada N4). It was built some 50 years ago as a private hotel and is located about a 5-minute walk east of the town center. The bone-white-stucco villa faces the fortifications. The entire ground floor is devoted to a living room, an L-shaped dining salon, and a bar—all opening through thick arches onto a Moorish courtyard with a fountain, a lily pond, and orange trees.

There are some guest rooms on the upper floor, but you can also stay in the nearby annex, a villa with a two-story entrance hall and an ornate staircase. The hotel offers only 15 rooms, so getting in here without a reservation could be difficult.

Meals cost from 3,000$ ($18.30) to 4,000$ ($24.40) and are served daily from noon to 4pm and 8 to 10pm. The menu is extensive. Noteworthy are the fish dishes, including grilled red mullet and fresh oysters. The pousada's restaurant is reputed to be the finest in the area. Laundry service and room service are provided.

INEXPENSIVE

DOM LUÍS, Avenida de Badajoz (along the N4), 7350 Elvas. Tel. 068/62-27-56. Fax 068/62-07-33. 90 rms. A/C TV TEL

$ Rates (including breakfast): 9,200$ ($56.10) single; 11,300$ ($68.90) double. AE, DC, MC, V. **Parking:** Free.

In terms of general amenities, the best selection—certainly the largest in town—is Dom Luís, a well-run hotel with rooms furnished in a modern style. Laundry service and room service are offered.

The hotel also has a good air-conditioned restaurant, seating 130 and serving regional wines and local dishes, with prices beginning at 2,500$ ($15.30). Meals are served daily from 12:30 to 2:30pm and 7:30 to 10pm.

ESTALAGEM DOM SANCHO II, Praça da República 20, 7350 Elvas. Tel. 068/62-26-86. Fax 068/62-47-17. 26 rms. TEL

$ Rates (including breakfast): 6,500$ ($39.70) single; 9,000$ ($54.90) double. AE, DC, MC, V. **Parking:** Free.

Since the pousada is likely to be full, you might try Estalagem Dom Sancho II, which sits proudly on the main square. The location is perfect for walking around the village. Some of the guest rooms open onto the old square, and from your window you can look down on the former town hall and, to the north, the old cathedral. However, one of the rear rooms would be much quieter. The hotel is furnished in period pieces, offering small but adequate units. The excellent dining room serves Portuguese specialties every day; a complete meal costs from 2,000$ ($12.20). A solarium is offered, and room service is provided.

WHERE TO DINE

MODERATE

ESTALAGEM DON QUIXOTE, Route N4, Pedras Negras. Tel. 62-20-14.
   Cuisine: PORTUGUESE. **Reservations:** Recommended.
$ Prices: Appetizers 450$–1,100$ ($2.70–$6.70); main courses 1,300$–2,400$ ($7.90–$14.60). AE, DC, V.
   Open: Lunch daily noon–3pm; dinner daily 7–10:30pm.

Many guests will want to take their meals at the previously recommended pousada. However, a more adventurous choice lies about 2 miles west of Elvas: Estalagem Don Quixote, an isolated compound that is the end point for many a gastronomic pilgrimage in the area. The place is especially busy on weekends, when it adopts a holiday feeling, with lots of convivial chatter and frenzied table service. You can order a drink in the leather-upholstered English-style bar near the entrance. The sprawling sunny dining room greets newcomers with the sight of rows of fresh fish arranged on ice behind glass. Amid an Iberian traditional decor you can order full meals; specialties include shellfish rice, grilled sole, grilled swordfish, roast pork, beefsteak *alentejano,* and at least five kinds of shellfish.

RESTAURANT AQUEDUTO, Avenida de Badajoz. Tel. 62-36-76.
   Cuisine: PORTUGUESE. **Reservations:** Recommended.
$ Prices: Appetizers 350$–900$ ($2.10–$5.50); main courses 1,000$–2,200$ ($6.10–$13.40). AE, DC, MC, V.
   Open: Lunch daily 1–3pm; dinner daily 7–10pm.

Named after the 400-year-old aqueduct that passes nearby, this clean restaurant lies on the eastern outskirts of Elvas, within a stone-sided and much-enlarged farmhouse built about 300 years ago. The ethnic, regional, and hearty cuisine might include fish dishes, lamb, or tasty goatmeat stew. The fruits served here are excellent conclusions to your meal, as is the regional cheese. The staff provides good service.

---

5. TOMAR

40 miles N of Santarém; 85 miles NE of Lisbon

GETTING THERE   By Train   The train station is at Avenida Combatentes da Grande Guerra (tel. 049/31-28-15). Eleven trains arrive daily from Lisbon; the trip takes 2 hours and costs 725$ ($4.40) one way. From Porto, five trains daily make the 4½-hour trip, costing 1,165$ ($7.10) one way.

By Bus   The bus station is on Avenida Combatentes da Grande Guerra, next to the train station. Here six buses a day arrive from Lisbon after a 2-hour trip that costs 1,000$ ($6.10) one way.

By Car   From Santarém, continue northeast along route 3, then cut east at the junction of route 3. When you reach route 110, head north.

ESSENTIALS   The **Tomar Tourist Office** is at Avenida Dr. Cândido Madureira (tel. 31-32-37). The **telephone area code** is 049.

Divided by the Nabão River, historic Tomar was integrally bound to the fate of the notorious quasi-religious order of the Knights Templar. In the 12th century, these powerful and wealthy monks established the beginnings of the Convento de Cristo (see "What to See & Do," below) on a tree-studded hill overlooking the town. Originally a monastery, it evolved into a kind of grand headquarters for the Templars. These knights, who swore a vow of chastity, had fought ferociously at Santarém against the Moors. As a result of their growing military might, they built a massive walled castle at Tomar in 1160. The ruins, especially the walls; can be seen today.

By 1314, the pope was urged to suppress their power, as they had made many enemies and their great riches were coveted by others. King Dinis allowed them to regroup their forces under the new aegis of the Order of Christ. Henry the Navigator became the most famous of the grand masters, using much of their money to subsidize his explorations.

WHAT TO SEE & DO

CONVENTO DE CRISTO [Convent of Christ], atop a hill overlooking the Old Town. Tel. 31-34-81.
From its inception, this monastery underwent five centuries of inspired builders, including Manuel I (the Fortunate). It also saw its destroyers, notably in 1810 when the overzealous troops of Napoleon turned it into a barracks. What remains on the top of the hill, however, is one of Portugal's most brilliant architectural accomplishments.

The portal of the Templars Church, in the Manueline style, depicts everything from leaves to chubby cherubs. Inside is an octagonal church with eight columns, said to have been modeled after the Temple of the Holy Sepulchre at Jerusalem. The mosquelike effect links the Christian and Muslim cultures, as in Córdoba's Mezquita. Howard La Fay called it "a muted echo of Byzantium in scarlet and dull gold." The damage done by the French troops is much in evidence. On the other side, the church is in the Manueline style with rosettes. Throughout you'll see the Templars insignia.

The monastery embraces eight cloisters in a variety of styles. The most notable one, a two-tiered structure built in 1557 by Diogo de Torralva, exhibits perfect symmetry, the almost severe academic use of the classical form that distinguishes the Palladian school. A guide will also take you on a brief tour of a dormitory where the monks lived in cells.

The monastery possesses some of the greatest Manueline stonework. An example is the grotesque west window of the Chapter House. At first, you may be confused by the forms emanating from the window; a closer inspection will reveal a meticulous symbolic and literal depiction of Portugal's sea lore and power. Knots and ropes, mariners and the tools of their craft, silken sails wafting in stone, re-created coral seascapes—all are delicately interwoven in this chef d'oeuvre of the whole movement.

Admission: 300$ ($1.80); children 14 and under free.
Open: Mar–Sept, daily 9:30am–12:30pm and 2–6pm; Oct–Feb, daily 9:30am–12:30pm and 2–5pm.

SENHORA DA CONCEIÇÃO, midway between the Old Town and Convento de Cristo.
On the way up the hill to see the monastery, you can stop off at this chapel, crowned by small cupolas and jutting out over the town. Reached via an avenue of trees, it was built in the Renaissance style in the mid-16th century, and its interior is a forest of white Corinthian pillars.
Admission: Free.
Open: Ask at the tourist office about how to obtain a key for entry.

SÃO JOÃO BAPTISTA, Praça da República.
In the heart of town is this 15th-century church built by Manuel I, with

black-and-white-diamond mosaics and a white-and-gold baroque altar (a chapel to the right is faced with antique tiles). In and around the church are the narrow cobblestone streets of Tomar, where shops sell dried codfish and wrought-iron balconies are hung with bird cages and flowerpots.
Admission: Free.
Open: Daily 9am–5pm.

WHERE TO STAY
MODERATE

HOTEL DOS TEMPLÁRIOS, Largo Cândido dos Reis 1, 2300 Tomar. Tel. 049/32-17-30. Fax 049/32-21-91. 84 rms. A/C TV TEL
$ Rates (including breakfast): 10,400$ ($63.40) single; 16,000$ ($97.60) standard double, 20,000$ ($122) superior double. Children under 8 stay at 50% discount in parents' room. AE, DC, MC, V. **Parking:** Free.

The modern four-star Hotel dos Templários, on the banks of the river, seems incongruously placed in such a small town. Pooling their know-how, five local businessmen created this structure in 1967. The interior is spacious, including the lounges and the terrace-view dining room. The guest rooms are quite suitable. Room service, laundry, and babysitting are provided. Facilities include wide sun terraces, a riverside pool fed by a fountain, a tennis court, and even a greenhouse.

Most guests have breakfast either in their rooms or in a sunny salon overlooking the river. In the evening they gather around the huge living-room fireplace for drinks. If you're passing through, you can stop in for a table d'hôte luncheon or dinner for 3,200$ ($19.50) and up. Hours are daily from 1 to 2:30pm and 8 to 9:30pm.

INEXPENSIVE

HOTEL RESIDENCIAL TRAVADOR, Rua Dr. Joaquim Ribeiro, 2300 Tomar. Tel. 049/32-25-67. Fax 049/32-21-94. 30 rms. A/C TV TEL
$ Rates (including breakfast): 6,000$ ($36.60) single; 9,500$ ($58) double. AE, DC, MC, V. **Parking:** Free.

An inspection of the guest rooms will reveal the high value of a stopover here: Each is outfitted with conservatively patterned wallpaper and lots of well-scrubbed comfort. Built in 1982 by the polite family who still owns it today, the hotel contains a basement with disco music and offers a breakfast-only policy that most visitors find appealing. The location is near the commercial center of town in a neighborhood of apartment buildings.

NEARBY PLACES TO STAY
MODERATE

ESTALAGEM VALE DA URSA, Estrada N238, 6100 Cernache do Bonjardim. Tel. 074/90-981. Fax 074/90-982. 18 rms, 1 suite. TV TEL
$ Rates (including breakfast): 8,000$–12,000$ ($48.80–$73.20) single; 12,000$–17,000$ ($73.20–$103.70) double; 18,000$ ($109.80) suite. **Parking:** Free.

Estalagem Vale da Ursa lies 20 miles northwest of Tomar, 35 miles from the shrine of Fátima, and 100 miles north of Lisbon. Situated near the bridge, over Castelo de Bode, the hotel is a tranquil choice where you can use such facilities as a pool and tennis courts and also fish from the lake's edge. It offers pleasantly furnished guest rooms, each with a private terrace overlooking the lake; five rooms are air-conditioned. The kitchen offers an international as well as a regional cuisine, with meals costing 2,900$ ($17.70) at lunch and 3,000$ ($18.30) at dinner.

POUSADA DE SÃO PEDRO, Castelo de Bode, 2300 Tomar. Tel. 049/38-11-75. Fax 049/38-11-76. 24 rms, 1 suite. A/C MINIBAR TV TEL
$ Rates (including breakfast): 16,000$ ($97.60) single; 18,000$ ($109.80) double; 23,800$ ($145.20) suite. AE, DC, MC, V. **Parking:** Free.

When it was built in the 1950s, this pousada 9 miles southeast of Tomar was used to house teams of engineers working on the nearby dam at Castelo de Bode. After the dam was completed in 1970, the government coverted it into one of the country's most unusual pousadas. In the early 1990s, an annex was built and the establishment was enlarged with the addition of seven accommodations, bringing the total to 25. From the flagstone-covered terrace in back you get a closeup view of Portugal's version of Hoover Dam. It curves gracefully against a wall of water, upon which local residents sail, swim, and sun themselves.

The pousada has a scattering of Portuguese antiques, some of them ecclesiastical, in its stone-trimmed hallways. These corridors lead to unpretentious bedrooms, each with private bath. The public rooms are more alluring than the bedrooms.

The breeze-filled bar near the terrace is decorated a lot like an elegant private living room, with well-upholstered sofas and a fireplace. The pousada serves some of the best food in the area, both international and regional specialties, with meals costing from 3,000$ ($18.30). Hours of service are daily from 12:30 to 2:30pm and 7:30 to 9:30pm.

WHERE TO DINE

MODERATE

BELLA VISTA, Rua Marquês de Pombal and Rua Fonte do Choupo. Tel. 31-28-70.

    Cuisine: PORTUGUESE. **Reservations:** Not necessary.

$ **Prices:** Appetizers 450$–950$ ($2.70–$5.80); main courses 1,100$–2,200$ ($6.70–$13.40). No credit cards.

    Open: Lunch Wed–Mon noon–3pm; dinner Wed–Sun 7–10pm. **Closed:** Nov.
Bella Vista, as its name indicates, is a restaurant boasting a pretty view of the town and a small canal. You can dine outside under a bower or in rustic dining rooms decorated with plates, flowers, plants, and racks to hang your hat on. Meals are simple but plentiful, and the prices are low. Usually the cook makes a fresh pot of vegetable soup every day. For your main course, try fried trout or sole or pork chops with potatoes. About the only exotic item you'll find is chicken curry with rice. Round off your meal with some of the local cheese. Everybody who dines here orders a carafe of the local wine.

CHAPTER 13

COIMBRA & THE BEIRAS

- **WHAT'S SPECIAL ABOUT COIMBRA & THE BEIRAS**
1. **LEIRIA**
2. **FIGUEIRA DA FOZ**
3. **COIMBRA**
4. **BUÇACO**
5. **LUSO**
6. **CÚRIA**
7. **AVEIRO**
8. **CARAMULO**
9. **VISEU**

To many observers, the three provinces of the Beiras, encompassing the university city of **Coimbra,** are the quintessence of Portugal. *Beira* is a Portuguese word meaning "edge" or "border." The trio of provinces includes **Beira Litoral** (coastal), **Beira Baixa** (low), and **Beira Alta** (high).

Embraced in the region is the **Serra da Estrêla,** Portugal's highest landmass—a haven for skiers in winter and a cool retreat in summer. The navigable Mondego River is the main stream of the region and the only major artery in Portugal that has its source within the boundaries of the country.

The granite soil produced by the great range of *serras* blankets the rocky slopes of the Dao and Mondego river valleys and is responsible for the wine of the region: the ruby-red or lemon-yellow Dao.

The Beiras are a subtle land, a sort of Portugal in miniature.

SEEING COIMBRA & THE BEIRAS

Motorists race from Lisbon to Coimbra on the express highway A1 in less than 2 hours; visitors in western Spain find the eastern sector of the Beiras easily accessible. For example, it's only a 55-mile ride on the N620 from the Spanish city of Salamanca to the border crossing at Vilar Formoso.

The Lisbon/Porto/Paris rail line serves such cities as Coimbra, Aveiro, and Guarda. All the major cities of the Beiras enjoy rail links with not only Lisbon and Porto but also Madrid. If you plan to explore the region by rail, Coimbra should be your transportation hub.

The national bus service, Rodoviária Nacional (RN), runs buses linking Lisbon and Coimbra. Once in the Beiras, you'll find a network of buses linking the smaller villages. Local tourist offices will provide copies of bus schedules.

SUGGESTED 6-DAY ITINERARY

Day 1 Head north from Lisbon for an overnight stay in Leiria.

Day 2 Continue north for a morning visit to Conimbriga, then veer west for Figueira da Foz, arriving in time to enjoy its beaches before spending a night at the casino.

Day 3 Head east for Coimbra, where you'll probably find a day is too short to take in its many attractions.

Day 4 Stop for lunch at the palace (now a hotel) at Buçaco or sample roast suckling pig at Mealhada before continuing north for a night at Aveiro.

WHAT'S SPECIAL ABOUT COIMBRA & THE BEIRAS

Great Towns/Villages
- ☐ Coimbra, the "most romantic city of Portugal"—the inspiration for the song "April in Portugal."
- ☐ Aveiro, a town on the lagoon—crisscrossed by myriad canals and spanned by low-arched bridges like Venice.
- ☐ Viseu, capital of Beira Alta—a city of art treasures, palaces, and churches.
- ☐ Figueira da Foz, premier beach resort of the Beiras—noted for its white sands and casino.

Beaches
- ☐ The Beaches of the Beiras—an almost unbroken stretch of sand from Praia de Leirosa in the south all the way to Praia de Espinho in the north.

Ace Attractions
- ☐ Serra de Estrêla, largest national park in Portugal—now one of the country's most popular recreational areas.

- ☐ Luso and Curia, spa towns in the foothills of the Serra de Estrêla—known for their thermal waters.

Ancient Monument
- ☐ Conimbriga, southwest of Coimbra—one of the great Roman archeological finds of Europe.

Museum
- ☐ Machado de Castro National Museum, in Coimbra—a treasure house of antiquities, one of the finest in the north.

Historic Palace
- ☐ Palace Hotel do Buçaco, now open to all—an architectural fantasy once inhabited by the House of Bragança.

Days 5–6 Head east to see the town of Viseu and have lunch there, arriving in Guarda in time to do some exploring before nightfall. While still based in Guarda, spend Day 6 driving through Serra da Estrêla, Portugal's major national park.

---

1. LEIRIA

20 miles N of Alcobaça; 80 miles N of Lisbon

GETTING THERE By Train Leiria is reached after a train ride of 3 hours and 45 minutes from Lisbon. At least two trains a day make the journey.

By Bus Twelve express buses from Lisbon journey to Leiria in just 2 hours, costing 1,050$ ($6.40) one way. You can also take one of eight daily buses arriving from Coimbra (see later in this chapter), a 1-hour trip that costs 750$ ($4.60) one way.

By Car Head north from Lisbon on the express highway A1.

ESSENTIALS The **Leiria Tourist Office** is at Jardim Luís de Camões (tel. 81-47-48). The **telephone area code** is 044.

L ocated on the road to Coimbra, the town of Leiria rests on the banks of the Liz and spreads over the surrounding hills. Many motorists find Leiria a convenient stopping point for the night.
From any point in town, you can see the great **Castelo de Leiria** (Castle of

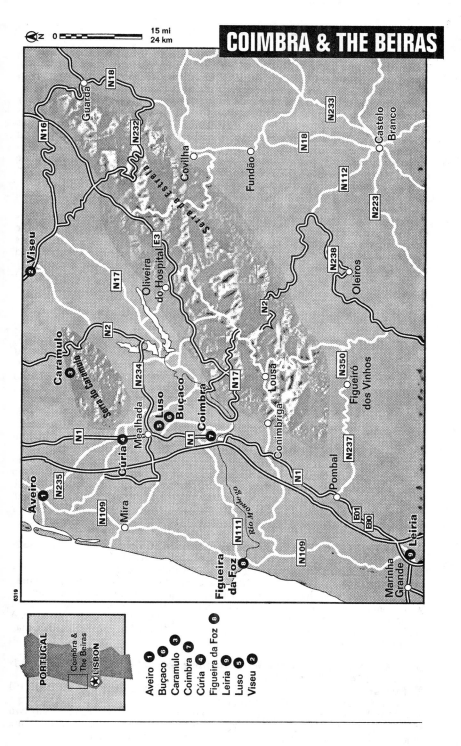

Leiria), once occupied by Dinis, the poet king, and his wife, called Saint Isabella. Tower-topped and imposing still, it has been extensively restored. The castle church, as well as the palace, is Gothic. From an arched balcony, the city and its surroundings can be viewed. The castle lies on the summit of a volcanic outcrop that was practically inaccessible to invaders. The Moors had their defense redoubt on this hill while they were taking possession of the major part of the Iberian peninsula. The fortress was first taken for Portugal in the 12th century by its first king, Afonso Henríques, and was twice recovered by him after the Moors had retaken it, the last recovery being definitive.

To reach the castle, you may take a car right to the front door. On the way to the castle, you might also visit **Igreja de São Pedro,** which dates from the 12th century. Admission to the fortress is 50$ (30¢). It's open April through October from 9am to 6:30pm and daily from 9am to 5pm in other months. For more information, ask at the tourist office.

Around Leiria is one of the oldest state forests in the world. In about 1300, Dinis began the systematic planting of the **Pinhal do Rei,** with trees brought from the Landes area in France. He hoped to curb the spread of sand dunes, which ocean gusts were extending deep into the heartland. The forest, still maintained today, provided timber used to build the caravels to explore the Sea of Darkness.

WHERE TO STAY

INEXPENSIVE

HOTEL EUROSOL, Rua Dom José Alves Correia da Silva, 2400 Leiria. Tel. 044/81-22-01. Fax 044/81-12-05. 135 rms, 7 suites. A/C MINIBAR TV TEL
$ Rates: 6,500$–10,000$ ($39.70–$61) single; 10,000$–12,000$ ($61–$73.20) double; 16,500$ ($100.70) suite. Breakfast 750$ ($4.60) extra. AE, DC, MC, V. **Parking:** Free.
A well-styled 11-story hostelry, the Eurosol competes in position with the stone castle crowning the opposite hill. All the guest rooms offer views, and they rank successfully with those of any first-class hotel in the north: smart yet simple, making use of built-in headboards and wardrobe walls of wood paneling.

The hotel is the social hub of Leiria, attracting businesspeople to its rooftop lounge/bar and dining room. Individual lunches or dinners cost 3,000$ ($18.30) on the four-course table d'hôte. Lighter meals are offered in an adjoining snack bar. The restaurant entrance lounge is decorated with a contemporary wallhanging, depicting the story of the building of the castle. Time your visit to enjoy a dip in the open-air pool, with its tile terrace. There's a lower-level boîte for after-dinner diversions.

SÃO FRANCISCO, Rua São Francisco 26, 2430 Leiria. Tel. 044/82-31-10. Fax 044/81-26-77. 18 rms, 1 suite. A/C MINIBAR TV TEL
$ Rates (including breakfast): 6,000$–8,000$ ($36.60–$48.80) single; 8,000$–10,000$ ($48.80–$61) double; 12,000$ ($73.20) suite. MC, V. **Parking:** Free.
São Francisco lies on the top floor of a 10-story building in the town center, a short walk from the river. Some of the well-maintained guest rooms offer pleasant views of Leiria; each is furnished with a radio, patterned wallpaper, and leatherette furniture. A cubbyhole bar in one of the public rooms serves drinks but no meals other than breakfast.

HOTEL SÃO LUÍS, Rua Henríque Sommer, 2400 Leiria. Tel. 044/81-31-97. Fax 044/81-38-97. 47 rms. A/C TV TEL
$ Rates: 6,000$ ($36.60) single; 7,500$ ($45.80) double. Breakfast 500$ ($3.10) extra. AE, DC, MC, V. **Parking:** Free.
Hotel São Luís is one of the best budget accommodations in Leiria. Ranked only two stars by the government, it is spotlessly maintained, and some of the guest rooms are quite spacious. You don't get a lot of frills here, but you do get comfort and

convenience at a good price. The hotel serves a good breakfast, including ham and fresh fruit along with juice and freshly baked bread (it's the only meal served). Laundry service is provided.

WHERE TO DINE

MODERATE

REIS, Rua Wenceslau de Morais 17. Tel. 248-34.
   Cuisine: PORTUGUESE. **Reservations:** Not necessary.
$ Prices: Appetizers 450$–650$ ($2.70–$4); main courses 1,000$–1,800$ ($6.10–$11). MC, V.
   Open: Lunch Mon–Sat noon–3pm; dinner Mon–Sat 7–10pm.
Considered the best independent restaurant in Leiria, Reis is fairly large, seating 120, with faithful devotees who like both its food and its inexpensive prices. The chef specializes in grills, along with such good regional fare as hearty soups, fresh fish, and meats. In winter, a fireplace makes the Reis more inviting.

2. FIGUEIRA DA FOZ

80 miles S of Porto; 125 miles N of Lisbon; 25 miles W of Coimbra

GETTING THERE   By Train   Trains arrive at Largo Estação (tel. 033/233-13), near the bridge. There are frequent rail connections through Coimbra (see the next section), with 19 trains per day arriving from that university city. Cost for the 40-minute trip is 240$ ($1.50) one way. Eight trains per day arrive from Lisbon (trip time: 3 hours), costing 1,120$ ($6.80) one way.

By Bus   The bus station is the Terminal Rodoviário (tel. 033/230-95), on Largo Luís de Camões. Here three buses per day from Lisbon arrive; the trip takes 3½ hours and costs 1,000$ ($6.10) one way.

By Car   Once you reach Leiria (see previous section), continue north along route 109.

ESSENTIALS   The **Figueira da Foz Tourist Office** is at Avenida 25 de Abril (tel. 226-10). The **telephone area code** is 033.

Old villas on the sea compete with apartment houses. On the north side at the Beach of Brightness, Portuguese families frolic, and the wealthier ones hit the gambling casino at night. Back in the Old Town, fishermen dry cod in the sun; others make their living by reclaiming salt from the marshes and having their wives scoop it up and carry it back to town in wicker baskets on their heads.
   At the mouth of the Mondego River, Figueira da Foz literally means "Fig Tree at the Mouth of the River." How it got that name is long forgotten. North of Cascais and Estoril, Fig Tree is the best-known and oldest resort along the Atlantic coastline of Iberia. Aside from its climate (city leaders claim the sun shines 2,772 hours annually), the most outstanding feature is the town's golden sandy beach, stretching for more than 2 miles.

WHAT TO SEE & DO

Those who don't like the beach can swim in a pool sandwiched between Grande Hotel da Figueira and Estalagem da Piscina on the main esplanade. Should the beach crowds get you down, you can always go for a trek into **Serra da Boa Viagem,** a range of hills whose summit is a favorite vantage point for photographers and sightseers. Bullfights are popular in season; the old-style bullring operates from mid-July to September.

Just 2 miles north of Figueira, bypassed by new construction and sitting placidly on a ridge near the sea, is **Buarcos,** a fishing village far removed from casinos and beaches. From its central square to its stone seawalls, it is unspoiled. Cod dries in wire racks in the sun; streets faintly move with activity; and native women with loaded baskets on their heads, arms akimbo, look out with bright eyes from under dark scarfs.

CASA DO PAÇO, Largo Prof. Victor Guerra 4. Tel. 033/221-59.

Most visitors don't come to Figueira to look at museums, but this is an exceptional one, located at the head office of the Associaçao Comercial e Industrial, a minute's walk from the post office and esplanade. It contains one of the world's greatest collections of Delft tiles, numbering almost 7,000; most depicting warriors with gaudy plumage (some blowing trumpets). The puce-and-blue tiles are detailed and subtly executed. The casa was the palace of Conde Bispo de Coimbra, D. João de Melo, who came here in the last century when Figueira was frequented by royalty, like San Sebastián in Spain.

Admission: Free.
Open: Daily 9:30am–12:30pm and 2–5pm.

WHERE TO STAY
MODERATE

GRANDE HOTEL DA FIGUEIRA, Avenida 25 de Abril, 3080 Figueira da Foz. Tel. 033/221-46. Fax 033/224-20. 91 rms. TV TEL
$ Rates (including breakfast): 12,000$–14,000$ ($73.20–$85.40) single; 14,800$–16,800$ ($90.30–$102.50) double. AE, DC, MC, V. **Parking:** Free.
Grande Hotel da Figueira, on the seafront promenade overlooking the ocean, is the leading choice. Walk across the esplanade for a clean sandy beach at your disposal. Or, as a hotel guest, you have free entrance to the adjoining Olympic-size saltwater pool. The hotel's interior is a world of marble and glass, more like that of a big-city hotel than a resort accommodation. A few of the rooms on the sea have glass-enclosed balconies; most rooms have open balconies, and all have radios. Other facilities include an à la carte restaurant, a piano bar, and a game room. The hotel is open all year.

INEXPENSIVE

APARTHOTEL ATLÂNTICO, Avenida 25 de Abril, 3800 Figueira da Foz. Tel. 033/283-06. Fax 033/224-20. 70 apts. TV TEL
$ Rates: 11,300$ ($68.90) apt for two; 17,000$ ($103.70) apt for four. AE, DC, MC, V. **Parking:** Free.
This towerlike structure rises aside Grande Hotel (see above), with panoramic views over the ocean, the Mondego River, and the beach. Each fully equipped apartment has a living room, bedroom, full bath, kitchenette, and radio. No meals are served. Guests often book in here for a week, shopping for provisions in the nearby supermarket and crossing the busy street to the wide sandy beach. Guests are admitted free to the Olympic-size pool nearby. Laundry service is available, as is babysitting.

ESTALAGEM DE PISCINA, Rua Santa Catarina 7, 3080 Figueira da Foz. Tel. 033/221-46. Fax 033/224-20. 20 rms. TEL
$ Rates (including breakfast): 8,800$ ($53.70) single; 11,600$ ($70.80) double. AE, DC, MC, V. **Parking:** Free. **Closed:** Nov–Apr.
This "Inn of the Swimming Pool" is a bargain for the resort. An intimate and small hotel, it offers comfortable guest rooms, each with a balcony opening onto the pool and sea. The pool area includes a restaurant and snack bar. Laundry, babysitting, and room service are available.

WHERE TO DINE

MODERATE

RESTAURANTE TUBARÃO, Avenida 25 de Abril. Tel. 234-45.
Cuisine: PORTUGUESE. **Reservations:** Not necessary.
$ Prices: Appetizers 450$–950$ ($2.70–$5.80); main courses 1,100$–2,200$ ($6.70–$13.40). No credit cards.
Open: Lunch daily noon–4pm; dinner daily 7–11pm.

People come to Restaurante Tubarão for the food, not the decor. You dine in a large room filled with cloth-covered tables and cooled by revolving ceiling fans. There is a sweeping view of the beach across the esplanade. Some of the tables spill onto the sidewalk, yet because of pedestrian traffic, they are often empty. A cafe in an adjoining room serves drinks throughout the day and night. A battery of hurried waiters will serve you specialties including *gambas a la plancha* (grilled shrimp); grilled codfish; shellfish-flavored rice; seafood soup; and a variety of crab, lobster, and shrimp, priced by weight.

EVENING ENTERTAINMENT

GRANDE CASINO PENINSULAR, Rua Dr. Calado 1. Tel. 033/220-41.

This casino features shows, dancing, a nightclub, and, of course, gambling salons. Expect to pay from 750$ ($4.60) for beverages. You can also dine here: An à la carte meal averages 5,000$ ($30.50); a tourist menu costs 2,200$ ($13.40). The casino show begins at 10:30pm. From May to October, the club is open nightly from 4pm to 4am, and in winter hours are nightly from 3pm to 3am.
Admission (including one drink): 1,500$ ($9.20).

EN ROUTE TO COIMBRA

Between Figueira da Foz and Coimbra, overlooking the fertile Mondego River valley, is the historic village of Montemor-O-Velho (Montemor the Old). Dating from the 8th century, the ruins of the **Castle of Montemor-O-Velho,** 3140 Montemor-O-Velho (tel. 039/683-80), built by the Moors, crown the hilltop. The main road runs scenically past villas, shrines, high walls, and churches. Narrow cobblestone streets will lead you to the restored walls and ramparts, from which there is a fine vista of the valley.

The castle became a royal palace under Sancho I in the 12th century and stood until it was destroyed by the French during Napoleon's first invasion. It witnessed many moments in Portuguese history—perhaps the most infamous being when Afonso IV sanctioned (according to historian Pero Coelho) the plot to kill Inês de Castro, mistress of the king's son. The castle is a moving medieval setting, especially when sparrows play in the air over its time-worn stones. It is open for visitors on Tuesday through Sunday from 10am to 12:30pm and 2 to 5pm. Admission is free. Buses run here from Figueira da Foz.

3. COIMBRA

73 miles S of Porto; 123 miles N of Lisbon

GETTING THERE By Train Coimbra has two rail stations: Estação Coimbra-A, Largo das Ameias (tel. 039/272-63), and Estação Coimbra-B (tel. 039/349-98), 3 miles west of central Coimbra. Coimbra-B station is mainly for trains coming from cities outside the region, whereas regional trains pull into both stations. Frequent shuttles connect the two stations, a bus ride taking only 5 minutes and costing 85$ (50¢). At least 14 trains per day make the 3-hour run north from Lisbon, costing 1,080$ ($6.60) one way. From Figueira da Foz, one train per hour arrives in Coimbra (trip time: 1 hour), costing 240$ ($1.50) one way.

By Bus The bus station is at Avenida Fernão de Magalhães (tel. 039/270-81).

Here 16 buses per day arrive from Lisbon, after a 3-hour trip costing 1,100$ ($6.70) one way. Five buses per day make the 6-hour trip from Porto (see Chapter 14), costing 900$ ($5.50) one way.

By Car From Lisbon, motorists can take the express highway A1 heading north to Coimbra and arrive there in less than 2 hours, if there isn't too much traffic.

ESSENTIALS The **Coimbra Tourist Office** is at Largo da Portagem (tel. 238-86). The **telephone area code** is 039.

Coimbra, called "the most romantic city in Portugal," was the inspiration for the popular song "April in Portugal." On the weather-washed right bank of the muddy Mondego, Coimbra is also the educational center of the country, its university having been founded at Lisbon in 1290.

The students of Coimbra band together in republics that usually rent cramped buildings in the old quarter, some up many flights of winding stairs. The republic isn't very democratic, run as it is on a strict seniority basis. A typical evening's bill of fare in a republic is likely to include grilled sardines, bread, and a glass of wine.

An invitation to one of these student dormitories will give you an insight into Coimbra rarely experienced by the foreign visitor. If you get an invitation, I hope the evening will be capped by the students presenting you with a fado concert. To show your gratitude, if you should happen onto an invitation, offer much-appreciated cigarettes.

WHAT TO SEE & DO

Coimbra's charms and mysteries unfold as you walk up Rua Ferreira Borges, under the Gothic **Arco de Almedina,** with its coat of arms. From that point, you can continue up the steep street, past antiques shops, to the old quarter.

Across the way from the National Museum is the **New Cathedral (Sé Nova),** with a cold 17th-century neoclassic interior. More interesting is the **Old Cathedral (Sé Velha).** At Largo da Sé Velha, the cathedral, founded in 1170, enjoys associations with St. Anthony of Padua. Crenellated and staunch as a fortress, it is entered by passing under a Romanesque portal. Usually a student is there, willing to show you (for a tip, of course) the precincts, including the restored cloister. The pride of this monument is the gilded Flemish retable over the main altar, with a crucifix on top. To the left of the altar is a 16th-century chapel designed by a French artist and containing the tomb of one of the bishops of Coimbra.

VELHA UNIVERSIDADE (University of Coimbra), Largo de Dom Dinis. Tel. 25-403.

The focal point for most visitors, of course, is the University of Coimbra, established in 1537 on orders from João III. Among its alumni are Luís Vas de Camões (the country's greatest poet, author of the national epic, *Os Lusíadas);* St. Anthony of Padua (also the patron saint of Lisbon); and even the late Portuguese dictator, Dr. Salazar, once a professor of economics.

If you'll ignore the cold statuary and architecture on the Largo de Dom Dinis, you can pass under the 17th-century **Porta Pérrea** into the inner core of the academy. The steps on the right will take you along a cloistered arcade, **Via Latina,** to the **Sala dos Capelos,** the site of graduation ceremonies. You enter into a world with a twisted rope ceiling, a portrait gallery of Portuguese kings, red-damask walls, and the inevitable *azulejos.* Afterward, you can visit the **University Chapel,** decorated with an 18th-century organ, 16th-century candelabra, a painted ceiling, 17th-century tiles, and a fine Manueline portal.

BIBLIOTECA GERAL DE UNIVERSIDADE (University Library), Largo de Dom Dinis. Tel. 255-41.

The architectural gem of the entire town is the baroque University Library next door to the University Chapel, with chinoiserie motifs and elaborate decoration. Established between 1716 and 1723 and donated by João V, it shelters more than a million volumes. The interior is composed of a trio of high-ceilinged salons walled by two-story tiers of lacquer-decorated bookshelves. The pale jade and sedate lemon marble inlaid floors complement the jeweled gold and emerald of the profuse gilt. The library tables are ebony and lustrous rosewood, imported from the former colonies in India and Brazil. Three-dimensional ceilings and the zooming telescopic effect of the room structure focus on the large portrait of João V, set against a backdrop of imitation curtains in wood. The side galleries, with their walls of valuable books in law, theology, and humanities of the 16th to the 18th century; the supporting pillars; the intricate impedimenta—all are dazzling, even noble. You may want to save the library for last; after viewing this masterpiece, other sights pale by comparison.

To wind down after leaving the library, walk to the end of the belvedere for a panoramic view of the river—equal to scenes on the Rhine—and the rooftops of the old quarter. On the square stand a statue of João III and the famous curfew-signaling clock of Coimbra, known as *cabra,* meaning goat.

Admission: Free.
Open: Daily 9am–12:30pm and 2–5pm. **Bus:** 1.

MUSEU MACHADO DE CASTRO, Largo Dr. José Rodrigues. Tel. 237-27.

A short walk from the university square leads you here. Named after the greatest Portuguese sculptor of the 18th century, this museum is one of the finest in the north. Built over a Roman building as the Paço Episcopal in 1592, it houses a collection of ecclesiastical sculpture, especially polychrome, much of which dates from the 14th to the 18th century. The other exhibits include vestments, a relic of St. Isabella, paintings, antiques, coaches, silver chalices, old jewelry, embroideries, retables, and 16th-century ceramic representations of the Apostles and Christ.

Admission: 200$ ($1.20) adult; children 16–18 free (must be accompanied by an adult); children 15 and under not admitted.
Open: Tues–Sun 10am–12:30pm and 2–5pm. **Bus:** 1.

IGREJA E MOSTEIRO DE SANTA CRUZ [Church and Monastery of Santa Cruz], Rua Visconde da Luz. Tel. 229-41.

This former monastery was founded in the late 12th century during the reign of Afonso Henríques, Portugal's first king. However, its original Romanesque style gave way to Manueline restorers in 1507. The much popularized "Romeo and Juliet" story of Portugal, involving Pedro the Cruel and Inês de Castro, reached its climax in this church—it was here that Pedro forced his courtiers to pay homage to her royal corpse and kiss her hand.

The lower part of the walls inside are decorated with azulejos. Groined in the profuse Manueline manner, the interior houses the Gothic sarcophagi of Afonso Henríques, his feet resting on a lion, and that of his son, Sancho I. The pulpit nearby is one of the achievements of the Renaissance in Portugal, carved by João de Ruão in the 16th century. The choir stalls preserve, in carved configurations, the symbolism, mythology, and historical import of Portuguese exploration. With its twisted columns and 13th-century tombs, the two-tiered Gothic-Manueline cloister is impressive.

The facade makes Santa Cruz one of the finest monuments in the land. Decorated like an architectural birthday cake, it is topped with finials and crosses, its portal top-heavy with a baroque porch—an unusual blending of styles. It's overadorned but fascinating.

Admission: 150$ (90¢).
Open: Daily 9am–noon and 2–6pm.

NEARBY ATTRACTIONS

On the left bank of the Mondego lie four of the most interesting but least visited attractions of Coimbra.

CONVENTO DE SANTA CLARA-A-VELHA [Convent of St. Clara-a-Velha], Rua de Baixo.

On the silt-laden banks of the Mondego stand the gutted, flooded, and crumbling remains of a 14th-century Gothic convent. This church once housed the body of Coimbra's patron saint, Isabella, although her remains were transferred to the New Convent higher up on the hill. Rising out of the inrushing river, the Roman arches are reflected in the canals, evoking a Venetian scene. You can walk through the upper part only, as the river has already reclaimed the floor. The former convent is reached by crossing the Santa Clara Bridge and turning left down the cobblestone street (Rua de Baixo).

Admission: Free.
Open: Daily 10am–7pm.

CONVENTO DE SANTA CLARA-A-NOVA [Convent of St. Clara-a-Nova], Rua de Baixo.

Commanding a view of right-bank Coimbra, the Convent of St. Clara-a-Nova provides a setting for the tomb of St. Isabella. Built during the reign of João IV, the convent is an incongruous blend of church and military garrison.

The church is noted for a rich baroque interior and Renaissance cloister. In the rear, behind a grille, is the tomb of the saint (usually closed except on special occasions). When her body was removed in 1677, her remains were said to have been well preserved, even though she had died in 1336. Instead of regal robes, she preferred to be buried in the simplest habit of the order of the Poor Clares. At the main altar is the silver tomb (a sacristan will light it for you), which the ecclesiastical hierarchy considered more appropriate after her canonization.

Admission: Free.
Open: Daily 9am–12:30pm and 2–5:30pm.

PORTUGAL DOS PEQUENITOS [Portugal for the Little Ones], Jardim do Portugal dos Pequenitos. Tel. 81-30-21.

At least for youngsters, the main attraction of Coimbra is Portugal dos Pequenitos, reached by crossing Ponte de Santa Clara and heading out Rua António Agusto Gonsalves. It's a mélange of miniature houses from every province of Portugal, including Madeira and the Azores, even the distant foreign lands of Timor and Macau. While there, you'll feel like Gulliver strolling across a Lilliputian world. The re-creations include palaces, an Indian temple, a Brazilian pavilion (with photos of gauchos), a windmill, a castle, and the 16th-century House of Diamonds from Lisbon.

Admission: 300$ ($1.80); children half price.
Open: Apr–Sept, daily 9am–7pm; Oct–Mar, daily 9am–5pm.

QUINTA DAS LAGRIMAS [Garden of Tears], Rua Antonio Augusto Gonçalves. Tel. 44-16-15.

In "sweet Mondego's solitary groves," in the words of Camões, lived Inês de Castro, mistress of Pedro the Cruel, and their three illegitimate children. Although the gardens have been the property of the Osorio Cabral family since the 18th century, they are visited by romantics from many countries. You can't go inside the house, but you can wander through the greenery to the spring fountain, known as the Fonte dos Amores. It was at the quinta on Camões' "black night obscure" that the Spanish beauty was set upon by assassins hired by her lover's father. Pedro returned, finding her in a pool of blood, her throat slit.

(So classic and enduring a Portuguese love story is it that who would want to suggest that it wasn't true or that the murder didn't happen at the Garden of Tears?)

Admission: 100$ (61¢).
Open: Daily 9am–7pm.

WHERE TO STAY
MODERATE

HOTEL ASTORIA, Av. Emídio Navarro 21, 3000 Coimbra. Tel. 039/22055. Fax 039/22057. 64 rms. TV TEL

$ Rates (including breakfast): 13,000$ ($79.30) single; 16,000$ ($97.60) double. AE, DC, MC, V.

When built in 1926, the Astoria was the most upscale and glamorous hotel in

Coimbra, lavish with ornamentation and host to both famous and infamous personalities of Portugal. After years of neglect and decay, it was restored into a clean and somewhat simplified format in 1990. Today, it's considered a comfortable but not overly plush hotel with the faded grandeur of yesteryear—one of the obvious choices for anyone visiting Coimbra. Its cupolas and wrought-iron balcony balustrades rise from a pie-shaped wedge of terrain in the city's congested heart. Five of the guest rooms are air-conditioned, but they're usually reserved in advance for regulars. On the premises is an old-world restaurant, the Amphytryon, a favorite of local businessmen at lunchtime, plus a pleasant bar. Room service is available.

TIVOLI COIMBRA, Rua João Machado 4–5, 3000 Coimbra. Tel. 039/ 269-34. Fax 039/268-27. 90 rms, 10 suites. A/C MINIBAR TV TEL
$ Rates (including breakfast): 15,500$ ($94.60) single; 18,000$ ($109.80) double; 27,000$ ($164.70) suites. AE, DC, MC, V.

Set on a hillside above Coimbra's northern outskirts, a 15-minute walk from the town center, this is the newest and finest hotel in town. Built in 1991, it's a member of one of Portugal's most respected chains, the Tivoli Group, whose hotels in Sintra and Lisbon are among the finest in their four- and five-star category. The guest rooms are conservatively modern, filled with a reassuring number of electronic gadgets and often boasting city views. Room service, babysitting, laundry, and an in-house concierge are available. There are a small garden behind the hotel, an indoor pool in the basement, and a health club with a sauna and Jacuzzi.

The hotel's dignified restaurant, the Porta Férrea, serves well-prepared Portuguese and continental cuisine every day from 1 to 3pm and 7 to 11:30pm. Full meals range from 2,500$ to 4,000$ ($15.30 to $24.40) each. There's also a bar with smooth service from a well-trained staff.

INEXPENSIVE

HOTEL BRAGANÇA, 10 Largo das Ameias, 3000 Coimbra. Tel. 039/ 221-71. Fax 039/361-35. 83 rms. A/C TV TEL
$ Rates (including breakfast): 8,100$ ($49.40) single; 10,350$ ($63.10) double. MC, V.
The Bragança is a bandbox five-floor hotel next door to the railway station. Primarily catering to businesspeople, it does a thriving trade in summer. A few of its guest rooms open onto balconies overlooking the main road; the furnishings are utilitarian. The rooms vary in size. Portuguese meals are served for 1,800$ ($11). Note that nearby parking places are scarce.

DOM LUÍS, Quinta da Verzea, 3000 Coimbra. Tel. 039/44-25-10. Fax 039/81-31-96. 104 rms. A/C MINIBAR TV TEL
$ Rates (including breakfast): 12,400$ ($75.60) single; 14,000$ ($85.40) double. AE, DC, MC, V. **Parking:** Free.
Built in 1989, this is one of the most stylish hotels in the Coimbra area. About half a mile south of the city, it lies on the road heading toward Lisbon. It features a pleasing modern design, brown-marble floors, a restaurant, and comfortable guest rooms. Classified as a three-star hotel, the Dom Luís offers amenities that could justify a four-star rating.

HOTEL OSLO, Avenida Fernão de Magalhães 25, 3000 Coimbra. Tel. 039/290-71. Fax 039/20-614. 33 rms, 2 suites. A/C TV TEL
$ Rates (including breakfast): 10,500$ ($64.10) single; 12,000$ ($73.20) double; 14,000$ ($85.40) suite. AE, DC, MC, V.
Hotel Oslo, on one of the busiest streets in town, was built during the 1960s craze for Scandinavian design and decor. In 1993, it closed for a complete overhaul and was reopened in a revised and upgraded format several months later. The guest rooms today are conservatively modern—unpretentious, simple, and safe. Because of traffic noise, ask for a room at the rear if you're a light sleeper. Laundry service is provided,

and at presstime, plans were being discussed for the installation of a fourth-floor restaurant and bar. Until then, management directs clients to the nearby Dom Pedro, recommended in "Where to Dine," below.

BUDGET

DOMUS, Rua Adelina Veiga 62, 3000 Coimbra. Tel. 039/285-84. 20 rms, 1 suite. TV
$ Rates (including breakfast): 4,500$ ($27.50) single; 6,460$ ($39.40) double; 11,360$ ($69.30) suite. No credit cards.
The Domus lies above an appliance store on a narrow commercial street. Its facade is covered with machine-made golden-brown tiles, and its rectangular windows are trimmed with slabs of marble. The reception desk is at the top of a flight of stairs, one floor above ground level. The staff will check you into one of the usually large and clean rooms, many filled with contrasting patterns of carpeting and wallpaper, creating a functional but cozy family atmosphere. A stereo system plays in the TV lounge, which also doubles as the breakfast room.

HOTEL INTERNATIONAL, Avenida Emídio Navarro 4, 3000 Coimbra. Tel. 039/255-03. 28 rms (11 with shower).
$ Rates: 3,200$ ($19.50) single without shower; 4,500$ ($27.50) double with or without shower. No credit cards. **Parking:** Free.
Hotel International is clean and very simple, unabashedly Portuguese in its mentality and decor. It occupies a once-grand 19th-century building whose interior has been updated over the years. The insignificant lobby is staffed by members of the family who own the property. English is definitely not their second tongue. After registering, you climb a steep series of staircases to rooms that are often tiny, with furniture that is vintage 1920s. Yet it's a welcome relief to find any room in hotel-scarce Coimbra. Seven rooms have phones. Naturally, the doubles with private showers go quickly, as they cost the same as the doubles without showers. No meals are served.

PENSÃO RESIDENCIAL ALENTEJANA, Rua Dr. António Henríques Seco 1, 3000 Coimbra. Tel. 039/259-03. Fax 039/40-51-24. 15 rms. TEL
$ Rates (including breakfast): 5,000$ ($30.50) single; 6,000$ ($36.60) double. AE, DC, MC, V. **Parking:** Free.
Ⓢ This is one of the best boarding houses in this university city. Some accommodations are furnished with antiques. This *pensão* is located in a reconstructed old villa, near Praça da República in the center of Coimbra. The rooms are on the second and third floors. On the first (or ground) floor is a store. Laundry service is available.

WHERE TO DINE
MODERATE

DOM PEDRO, Avenida Emídio Navarro 58. Tel. 291-08.
Cuisine: PORTUGUESE/CONTINENTAL. **Reservations:** Recommended.
$ Prices: Appetizers 550$–950$ ($3.40–$5.80); main courses 1,200$–2,200$ ($7.30–$13.40). DC, MC, V.
Open: Lunch Tues–Sun noon–3:30pm; dinner daily 7–10:30pm.
Dom Pedro stands across the street from the bank of the river, near a congested part of town. After negotiating a vaulted hallway, you'll find yourself in an attractive room whose tables are grouped around a splashing fountain. Above the fountain, the high ceiling is supported by four thick columns connected to one another by a series of arches. This, plus the random tile patterns of birds, animals, and flowers, contributes to an Iberian ambience. In winter, a corner fireplace throws off welcome heat; in summer, the thick walls and terra-cotta floor provide a kind of air conditioning. Full Portuguese and continental meals might include codfish Dom Pedro, trout meunière, peppersteak, and pork cutlet milanese.

O ALFREDO, Avenida João das Regras 32. Tel. 44-15-22.
Cuisine: PORTUGUESE. **Reservations:** Not necessary.

$ Prices: Appetizers 450$–950$ ($2.70–$5.80); main courses 1,100$–2,000$ ($6.70–$12.20). No credit cards.
Open: Lunch daily noon–3pm; dinner daily 7–10pm.

O Alfredo lies on the less populated side of the river on the street that funnels into the Santa Clara bridge. This unobtrusive pink-fronted restaurant looks more like a snack bar than a formal dining establishment. The ambience is pleasant, albeit simple. Full Portuguese meals might feature pork Alentejo style, rice with shrimp, an array of shellfish, Portuguese-style stew, several types of clam dishes, grilled steak, and regional varieties of fish and meat.

PISCINAS, Rua Dom Manuel 2°. Tel. 71-70-13.
Cuisine: PORTUGUESE/CONTINENTAL. **Reservations:** Recommended.
$ Prices: Appetizers 650$–1,000$ ($4–$6.10); main courses 1,300$–2,200$ ($7.90–$13.40). AE, DC, MC, V.
Open: Lunch Tues–Sun noon–3pm; dinner daily 7–10pm.

Considered the best restaurant in Coimbra, Piscinas is hard to reach, lying on the eastern side of town in a sports complex. It's best to go there by taxi, though parking is easily available. On the second floor, the air-conditioned restaurant, seating 230, opens onto a panoramic view. You might begin with shellfish soup or escargots, then follow with one of the main-dish specialties, including beef Piscinas, grilled sole, peppersteak, pork *piri-piri*, or fondue *bourguignonne*. To finish your repast, why not try an Irish coffee? Piano music is played at night.

INEXPENSIVE

CAFÉ NICOLA, Rua Ferreira Borges 35. Tel. 220-61.
Cuisine: PORTUGUESE. **Reservations:** Not necessary.
$ Prices: Appetizers 250$–500$ ($1.50–$3.10); main courses 750$–1,500$ ($4.60–$9.20). No credit cards.
Open: Lunch Mon–Sat 12:30–2pm; dinner Mon–Sat 7:30–10pm.

Café Nicola is a plain modern little second-floor restaurant over an old-fashioned delicatessen/pastry shop. It's Spartan inside, and even the flowers are usually wilted, but tradition is to be respected. Students gather here for strong coffee. The window tables provide box seats for looking at the teeming street. The food is good but plain, and the fish and meat platters are usually large enough to be shared by two. A nourishing bowl of the soup of the day begins most meals. After that, you can order filet of fish, roast chicken, chicken cutlets, or veal croquettes.

DEMOCRÁTICA, Travessa do Rua Nova 5–7. Tel. 237-84.
Cuisine: PORTUGUESE. **Reservations:** Not necessary.
$ Prices: Appetizers 100$–300$ (60¢–$1.80); main courses 680$–1,200$ ($4.10–$7.30); tourist menu 1,160$ ($7.10).
Open: Breakfast Mon–Sat 9:30–11:30am; lunch Mon–Sat 11:30am–3pm; dinner Mon–Sat 7–10pm.

Democrática is a stark restaurant popular with students and travelers on a shoestring budget. This place couldn't be simpler, with a little dining room, tiled walls, and a rear kitchen. The servings are large. The soup has the hearty flavor of the fertile fields of central and north Portugal (it's usually a *caldo verde*). Most likely the fish will be hake, and it's often served with greens and potatoes. A typical dessert would be rice pudding. Everybody orders a carafe of the local wine.

PINTO D'OURO [Golden Chicken], Avenida João das Regras 68. Tel. 44-12-3.
Cuisine: PORTUGUESE. **Reservations:** Not necessary.
$ Prices: Appetizers 350$–600$ ($2.10–$3.70); main courses 800$–1,400$ ($4.90–$8.50). AE, DC, MC, V.
Open: Lunch daily noon–4pm; dinner daily 6:30–11pm.

Pinto d'Ouro is one of the most favored local dining rooms in the district. The bar serving snacks is alluring, though the little tables in the nook adjoining the dining room are preferred. A good dish is clams in wine-garlic sauce. Recently, I began a fine regional repast with *caldo verde*, followed by a large portion of roast *cabrito* (goat) with french fries, rice, and salad; I finished with a huge amount of vine-ripened strawberries sprinkled with sugar, as well as coffee. *Vinho verde* accompanied the meal, and, as an added surprise, I enjoyed fresh goat cheese as an appetizer. Service was fast.

COFFEEHOUSE

CAFÉ SANTA CRUZ, Praça 8 de Maio. Tel. 336-17.
   Cuisine: COFFEE/DRINKS. **Reservations:** Not accepted. **Bus:** 3 or 4.
$ Prices: Coffee 55$ (30¢). No credit cards.
   Open: Winter, Mon–Sat 7am–11pm; summer, Mon–Sat 7am–2am. **Closed:** Sept.

The most famous coffeehouse in Coimbra, perhaps in the north of Portugal, is Café Santa Cruz. It's in a former auxiliary chapel of the cathedral and has a high ceiling supported by flamboyant stone ribbing and vaulting of fitted stone. There's a paneled waiters' station with a marble top handsome enough to serve as an altar in its own right. Now a favorite gathering place in Coimbra, day or night, it has a casual mood; cigarette butts are tossed on the floor. Scores of students and professors come here to read the daily newspapers. There's no bar to stand at, so everyone takes a seat at one of the marble-topped hexagonal tables, sitting on intricately tooled leather chairs. If you order cognac, the shot will overflow the rim of the glass. But most patrons ask for a glass of coffee with milk, which costs 55$ (30¢) at a table.

CONIMBRIGA

One of the great Roman archeological finds of Europe, the village of ✪ Conimbriga lies 10 miles southwest of Coimbra. If you don't have a car, you can reach the site by taking a bus from Coimbra to Condeixa, about a mile from Conimbriga. The bus, Avic Mondego, leaves Coimbra at 9am and returns at 1 and 6pm. From Condeixa, you reach Conimbriga by either walking or hiring a taxi in the village.

The site of a Celtic settlement established in the Iron Age, the village was occupied by the Romans in the late 1st century. Since then and up to the 5th century A.D., the town knew a peaceful life. The site lies near a Roman camp, but the town never served as a military outpost, although it was on a Roman road connecting Lisbon (Roman Olisipo) and Braga (Roman Bracara Augusta). Visitors walk from a small museum (Museu Monográfico) along the Roman road to enter the ruins. The museum contains artifacts from the ruins, including a bust of Augustus Caesar that originally stood in the town's Augustan temple.

Roman mosaics in almost perfect condition have been unearthed in area diggings. The designs are triangular, octagonal, and circular—executed in blood red, mustard, gray, sienna, and yellow. Motifs include beasts from North Africa and delicately wrought hunting scenes. Mosaics displaying mythological themes can be seen in one of the houses. Subjects include Perseus slaying Medusa and the Minotaur of Crete in his labyrinth.

The diggings display to good advantage the complex functional apparatus of Roman ingenuity. Columns form peristyles around reflecting pools, and the remains of fountains stand in courtyards. There are ruins of temples, a forum, patrician houses, water conduits, and drains. Feeding the town's public and private baths were special heating and steam installations with elaborate piping systems. Conimbriga even had its own aqueduct.

The **House of Cantaber** is a large residence, and in its remains you can trace the life of the Romans in Conimbriga. The house was occupied until the family of Cantaber was seized by invaders, who also effectively put an end to the town in the mid-5th century.

Another point of interest is the **House of the Fountains,** constructed before the 4th century, when it was partially destroyed by the building of the town wall. Much of the house has been excavated, and visitors can see remains of early Roman architecture as it was carried out in the provinces. The ruins are open to the public daily from March 15 through September 14 from 9am to 1pm and 2 to 8pm; in off-season, hours are daily from 9am to 1pm and 2 to 6pm. The museum is open only Tuesday through Sunday: Between March 15 and September 14, hours are 10am to 1pm and 2 to 6pm; in off-season, hours are 10am to 1pm and 2 to 5pm. To be admitted to the attraction costs adults 300$ ($1.80) in summer and 200$ ($1.20) in off-season. Children 13 and under are admitted free, and citizens 65 or older get a 50% reduction. For more information, call 039/94-11-77.

---

4. BUÇACO

17½ miles N of Coimbra; 144 miles N of Lisbon

GETTING THERE **By Bus** Buçaco is best explored by car. However, if you're depending on public transportation, you can visit the forest on a day-trip from Coimbra. Buses from Coimbra bound for Viseu make a detour from Luso through the forest and stop at Palace Hotel do Buçaco.

By Car From Coimbra, head northeast along route 110 to the town of Penacova at the foot of the Serra do Buçaco. From there, continue north along a small secondary road to Buçaco (it's signposted).

ESSENTIALS The nearest tourist office is at Luso (see the following section). The **telephone area code** is 031.

The rich, tranquil beauty of Buçaco's forests was initially discovered by a humble order of barefoot Carmelites, following the dictates of seclusion prescribed by their founder. In 1628, they founded a monastery at Buçaco and built it with materials from the surrounding hills. Around the forest they erected a wall to isolate themselves further and to keep women out.

These barefoot friars had a special love for plants and trees, and each year they cultivated the natural foliage and planted specimens sent to them from distant orders. Buçaco had always been a riot of growth: ferns, pines, cork, eucalyptus, and pink and blue clusters of hydrangea. But the friars introduced such exotic additions as the monkey puzzle, a tall Chilean pine with branches so convoluted that monkeys that climb in it become confused. The pride of the forest, however, remains its stately cypresses and cedars.

Such was the beauty of the preserve that a papal bull, issued in 1643, threatened excommunication to anyone who had destroyed a tree. Even though the monastery was abolished in 1834, the forest has been preserved. Filled with natural spring waters, the earth bubbles with many cool fountains, the best known of which is **Fonte Fria** (cold fountain).

The Buçaco forest was the battleground where Wellington defeated the Napoleonic legions under Marshal André Massena. The Iron Duke slept in a simple cloister cell right after the battle. A small **Museu da Guerra Peninsular** (Museum of the Peninsular War) reconstructs much of the drama of this turning point in the Napoleonic invasion of Iberia. It's about half a mile from the hotel (see below). The very slim museum collection consists of engravings, plus a few guns. It is open June 15 through September 15 on Tuesday through Sunday from 9am to 5:30pm; off-season hours are Tuesday through Sunday from 10am to 4pm. Admission is 75$ (50¢).

In the early 20th century, a great deal of the Carmelite monastery was torn down to make way for the royal hunting lodge and palace hotel of Carlos I and his wife, Amélia. He hardly had time to enjoy it, as he was assassinated in 1908. Italian architect Luigi Manini masterminded this neo-Manueline structure of parapets, buttresses, armillary spheres, galleries with flamboyant arches, towers, and turrets. After the fall of the Braganças, wealthy tourists took their afternoon tea by the pools underneath the trellis hung with blossoming wisteria.

One of the best ways to savor Buçaco is to make the 1,800-foot ride to **Cruz Alta** (high cross) by car through the forests and past hermitages. At the summit is a view considered by many to be the best in Portugal.

WHERE TO STAY & DINE

EXPENSIVE

PALACE HOTEL DO BUÇACO, Mata do Buçaco, Buçaco, 3050 Mealhada.
Tel. 031/93-01-01. Fax 031/93-05-09. 60 rms, 6 suites. TV TEL
$ Rates (including breakfast): 20,000$–26,000$ ($122–$158.60) single; 24,000$–30,000$ ($146.40–$183) double; 45,000$–85,000$ ($274.50–$518.50) suite. AE, DC, MC, V. **Parking:** Free.

⭐ This is one of the most nostalgia- and myth-laden buildings in Portugal—a vacation retreat of the Portuguese monarchs that figures prominently in the national psyche. In one of Iberia's most famous farewells, the deposed Amélia said "Good-bye forever" after her final visit to Buçaco in 1945. At that time, the government had permitted the ailing queen a sentimental journey (in a limousine with ladies-in-waiting) to visit all the places where she had spent her reigning years before the simultaneous assassinations of her husband and son in 1908, just before the monarchy's 1910 flight to England.

The palace is an architectural fantasy, ringed with gardens and exotic trees imported from the far corners of the Portuguese empire. The designer borrowed heavily from everywhere: the Jerónimos Monastery in Belém, the Doge's Palace in Venice, and the Graustark Castles of Bavaria. One of the most resplendently grandiose smaller palaces of Europe, it is set in the center of a 250-acre forest, itself the source of many Portuguese legends.

Despite the wear and tear caused by thousands of overnight guests, the structure is still intact and impressive, especially its grand staircase with ornate marble balustrades, its 15-foot-wide bronze torchères, and its walls of blue-and-white *azulelos* depicting important scenes from Portuguese history. There are richly furnished drawing rooms and salons, each a potpourri of architectural whims.

In 1910, the Swiss-born head of the kitchen, the former king's cook, persuaded the government to let him run the palace as a hotel. The most spectacular accommodation is the Queen's suite, which has its own private parlor, dressing room, sumptuous marble bath, and dining room. In some cases, the bath served during the 19th century as adjoining bedrooms for valets or maids. In 1992, many of the guest rooms were upgraded and restored yet still retaining their dignified and comfortably conservative decor. In many cases, air conditioning was added.

Dining/Entertainment: The hotel's high-ceilinged dining room serves lunches from 3,500$ ($21.40) and full dinners from 5,000$ ($30.50).

Services: 24-hour room service, laundry.

---

5. LUSO

19½ miles N of Coimbra; 143 miles N of Lisbon

GETTING THERE   By Train From Coimbra, line 110 extends west to offer daily service to Luso.

By Bus Five buses a day from Coimbra run to Luso on a 1-hour trip. Beginning at 7:45am, departures are about every 2½ hours.

By Car From Coimbra, head north along the Lisbon/Porto motorway, the most important highway in the country, until you come to the signposted turnoff for Luso. Head east for another 3½ miles.

ESSENTIALS The **Luso Tourist Office** is at Rua Emídio Navarro (tel. 931-33). The **telephone area code** is 031.

Luso, a little spa town on the northwestern side of the Buçaco mountain, boasts a mild climate and thermal waters for both drinking and bathing. The radioactive and hypotonic water, low in mineral content, is said to have great efficacy in the treatment of kidney ailments, alimentary complaints, and circulatory problems, as well as respiratory tract or skin allergies.

Besides the health-giving aspects of the spa, it is a resort area, sharing many of its facilities with Buçaco, just 2 miles away. During the spa season, festivities and sports events are held at the casino, nightclub, and tennis courts, as well as on the lake and at the two swimming pools, one of which is heated. Thermal spa enthusiasts flock here generally from June through October.

WHERE TO STAY

INEXPENSIVE

HOTEL EDEN, Emídio Navarro, Lutso, 3050 Mealhada. Tel. 031/93-91-71. Fax 031/93-01-93. 58 rms. A/C TV TEL
$ Rates (including breakfast): 7,200$ ($43.90) single; 10,500$ ($64.10) double. AE, DC, MC, V. **Parking:** Free.

The tone here is set by the modern lobby with a Picasso-style mural covering one of the walls. It was the work of Portuguese artist Jorge do Açor. The Eden stands on a hill above the flowering central garden near what used to be the town's belle époque casino. The guest rooms are pleasantly and comfortably furnished, each with a private balcony. The hotel also has a restaurant, serving good food and wine, with a complete meal costing from 1,700$ ($10.40).

GRANDE HOTEL DAS TERMAS, Rua dos Banhos, Luso, 3050 Mealhada. Tel. 031/93-04-50. Fax 031/93-03-50. 171 rms, 2 suites. TEL
$ Rates (including breakfast): 8,700$–11,300$ ($53.10–$68.90) single; 12,500$–14,200$ ($76.30–$86.60) double; 23,700$ ($144.60) suite. AE, DC, MC, V. **Parking:** Free.

With a backdrop of rolling forests, Grande Hotel das Termas nestles in a valley in the midst of abundant foliage. It is a sprawling establishment adjacent to the spa, offering comfortable, well-proportioned guest rooms with matching furnishings; some rooms open onto private terraces, with views of the tree-covered valley. About 80 rooms are air-conditioned and have TVs.

Guests praise the thermal spa facilities here. The emphasis is on good health. You can swim in a 150-foot Olympic-size pool, lounge and sunbathe on the surrounding grassy terrace, or relax under the weeping willows and bougainvillea arbor. There are hard tennis courts, mini-golf, and a boîte for dancing at night.

The meals available are large (the cuisine is both regional and international), served in a mural-decorated dining room. Try a bottle of full-bodied Messias and wine from nearby Mealhada. Meals cost from 2,800$ ($17.10).

WHERE TO DINE

INEXPENSIVE

RESTAURANT O CESTEIRO, Rua Dr. Lúcio Pais Abranches. Tel. 93-93-60.
Cuisine: PORTUGUESE. **Reservations:** Not necessary.
$ Prices: Appetizers 450$–650$ ($2.70–$4); main courses; 750$–1,500$ ($4.60–$9.20). No credit cards.
Open: Lunch daily noon–2:45pm; dinner daily 7–9:45pm.

This unpretentious restaurant is on the road leading out of town in the direction of Mealhada, about a 5-minute walk from the center. It occupies a spacious room whose facade is covered with a simple sign and plain brown tiles. Inside is a popular bar that does a brisk business with local artisans and farmers. The fare is likely to include duck stew, roast goat, pimiento-flavored pork, and an array of fish dishes, including cod.

6. CÚRIA

7 miles NW of Luso; 16 miles NW of Buçaco; 142 miles N of Lisbon

GETTING THERE   By Bus   Bus connections are made daily from Luso (see the preceding section). Several buses run daily between the train station at Luso and the spa at Cúria.

By Car   From Coimbra, head north along the N1.

ESSENTIALS   The **Cúria Tourist Office** is at Largo da Rotunda (tel. 522-48). The **telephone area code** is 031.

Forming a well-known tourist triangle with Luso and Buçaco is Cúria, in the foothills of the Serra de Estrêla. Its spa has long been a draw to people seeking the curative properties of medicinal waters in a secluded spot. Among its recreation facilities are tennis courts, swimming pools, roller-skating rinks, a lake for boating, cinemas, and teahouses. The season for taking the waters here—calcium sulfated, slightly saline, sodium and magnesium bicarbonated—is from April through October, although June 1 sees the beginning of the largest visitor influx.

In the Bairrada wine-growing district, Cúria offers the fine wines of the region as well as such famous local cuisine as roast suckling pig, roast kid, and sweets.

WHERE TO STAY & DINE
MODERATE

HOTEL DAS TERMAS, Cúria, 3780 Anadia. Tel. 031/51-21-85. Fax 031/51-58-38. 57 rms. A/C TV TEL

$ Rates (including breakfast): 11,500$ ($70.20) single; 17,000$ ($103.70) double. AE, DC, MC, V. **Parking:** Free.

Hotel das Termas is approached via a curving dirt road leading through a parklike setting with lacy shade trees—quiet and secluded. Even the guest rooms have a homelike feeling, with lots of floral chintz, wooden beds, and walls of wardrobe space. One commentator likened Hotel das Termas to the Raffles Hotel in Singapore a few decades ago, with its British colonial atmosphere, along with a decor featuring lots of brass and wicker.

Open all year, the hotel offers facilities for health and relaxation, including a free-form pool encircled with orange trees and umbrella tables. In the park, a rustic wooden bridge leads over a lake to walks and tennis courts.

The lounge is relaxed and casual, furnished with provincial pieces and hand-loomed rugs. The dining hall, with parquet floors and a brick fireplace, is like a tavern, especially when filled with guests who aren't hesitant to chat from table to table.

INEXPENSIVE

PALACE HOTEL DE CÚRIA, 3780 Anadia. Tel. 031/51-21-31. Fax 031/51-55-31. 120 rms. TEL

$ Rates (including breakfast): 6,500$–7,000$ ($39.70–$42.70) single; 8,000$–12,000$ ($48.80–$73.20) double. AE, DC, MC, V. **Parking:** Free. **Closed:** Nov–Mar.

Receiving guests since 1926, Palace Hotel de Cúria is still an elegant accommodation. As you drive past the town's tourist office, you can catch a glimpse of this hotel's facade through a protective grouping of shrubbery. Four female faces, almost outlandishly oversized, gaze enigmatically over the gardens and parasols in front. Their presence, along with the thousands of pounds of stone ornamentation, imply life on a grand scale. Perhaps best of all, the hotel seems to exude a benign air of self-confidence, based on its having served as a temporary retreat for dozens of prestigious cosmopolites over the decades.

The hotel's 60-foot by 107-foot pool is one of the largest in the land. The hotel cooperates richly with the town's spa facilities, which lie a short walk away and are often visited by clients who take the waters as part of a rest cure and holiday. Two tennis courts, billiards, a playground for children, and miniature golf are offered. Horseback riding can also be arranged.

Although it isn't the most famous hotel in Portugal, the Palace is one of the most prestigious, having received in recent years both the president and the prime minister of Portugal, as well as many high-ranking Portuguese politicians.

Between the twin towers of the hotel's Italianate facade are sandwiched the guest rooms, many quite spacious. Room service, laundry, and babysitting are available.

In the bright, airy dining room, an excellent Portuguese and international cuisine is served, with a fixed-price lunch or dinner menu costing 3,300$ ($20.10). Whenever possible, garden-fresh produce, much of it coming from the Beiras, is used.

BUDGET

PENSÃO LOURENÇO, Cúria, 3780 Anadia. Tel. 031/51-22-14. 38 rms. A/C

$ Rates (including breakfast): 4,000$ ($24.40) single; 6,000$ ($36.60) double. No credit cards. **Parking:** Free. **Closed:** Oct–May.

Throughout the spa, a series of signs points motorists to this simple inn, which you'll eventually find in a tree-lined hollow away from the town center. It occupies a pair of buildings set on either side of a narrow road, almost forming its own miniature village. One of the buildings operates a ground-floor cafe whose tables and patrons sometimes spill over into the road. Most of the clients are elderly; many are pensioners who come to Cúria season after season. They form a closely knit community of shared interests and needs.

---

7. AVEIRO

35 miles N of Coimbra; 42 miles S of Porto

GETTING THERE   By Train   The rail station is at Largo Estação (tel. 034/38-11-56). At least 30 trains per day from Porto (see Chapter 14) make the 30-minute run to Aveiro for 430$ ($2.60) one way. There are 22 trains arriving daily from Coimbra; the trip takes an hour and costs 380$ ($2.30) one way. There are also five trains per day from Viseu, a trip that takes 4 hours and costs 680$ ($4.10) one way. Twenty trains per day arrive from Lisbon after a 5-hour trip costing 1,300$ ($7.90) one way.

By Bus   The nearest Rodoviária (national express bus company) station is at Águeda, 12 miles from Aveiro. Buses connect Águeda with the train station at Aveiro.

By Car   Continue north along the A1 toll road from Coimbra to the junction with N235, which leads west to Aveira.

ESSENTIALS   The **Tourist Office** is at Rua João Mendonça 8 (tel. 236-80). The **telephone area code** is 034.

The town on the lagoon, Aveiro is crisscrossed by myriad canals, spanned by low-arched bridges. At the mouth of the Vouga River, it is cut off from the sea by a long sandbar protecting clusters of islets. The architecture is almost Flemish, a good foil for a setting of low willow-reed flatlands, salt marshes, spray-misted dunes, and rice paddies.

On the lagoon, brightly painted swan-necked boats traverse the waters. Called *barcos moliceiros,* these flat-bottomed vessels hold fishermen who harvest seaweed used for fertilizer. They are ever on the lookout for eels, a regional specialty, which they catch in the shoals studded with lotus and water lilies. Outside the town are extensive salt pits, lined with pyramids, fog-white in color.

The surrounding lagoons and many secret pools dotting the landscape make for a boat excursion reminiscent of a trip into Louisiana bayou country. Inquire at the tourist office. The town is quite congested, and many readers have expressed their disappointment on visiting here, citing the incessant whine of the Vespa, as well as the relatively stagnant foul-smelling canal water. Others, however, find it worth the journey.

The **Convent of Jesús**, at the Praça do Milenário, is hailed as the finest example of the baroque style in Portugal. The Infanta Santa Joana, sister of João II and daughter of Afonso V, took the veil here in 1472. Her tomb, an inlaid rectangle of marble quarried in Italy, attracts many pilgrims. Its delicate pale pinks and roses lend it the air of a cherub-topped confection.

The convent, owned by the state and now called the **Museu de Aveiro** (tel. 034/232-97), displays a lock of the saint's hair, her belt and rosary, and a complete pictorial study of her life. A portrait of her, painted in intonaco, is exceptional. But what characterizes the convent is its carved giltwork, lustrous in the chapel, despite the dust.

In this setting is an assortment of 15th-century paintings; royal portraits of Carlos I and Manuel II (the last two Bragança kings); antique ceramics; and 16th-, 17th-, and 18th-century sculpture. There are also some well-preserved 18th- and 19th-century coaches and carriages. After viewing all this, you can walk through the cloisters with their Doric columns. The museum is open Tuesday to Sunday from 10am to 12:30pm and 2 to 5pm, charging 200$ ($1.20) admission; free for children 13 and under.

On the same square is the 15th-century **Church of St. Domingos,** with its blue-and-gold altarpieces and egg-shaped windows flanking the upper part of the nave. The facade, in the Gothic-Manueline style, is decorated with four flame finials. To the right (facing) is a bell tower. There are other churches as well, especially the octagonal **Chapel of Senhor Jesús das Barrocas,** built in 1722.

After a meal of stewed eels and a bottle of hearty Bairrada wine, you might wish to explore some of the settlements along the lagoon, specifically **Ilhavo,** 3 miles south of Aveiro, where you can stop at **Museu do Mar,** Rua Vasco da Gama (tel. 034/32-17-97), an unpretentious gallery offering an insight into the lives of people who live with the sea. Inside you can see seascape paintings, boating paraphernalia, fishing equipment, ship models, and other exhibits. Hours are Wednesday through Saturday from 9am to 12:30pm and 2 to 5:30pm and Sunday and Tuesday from 2 to 5:30pm. Admission is 100$ (60¢).

From Ilhavo, drive 1 mile south to **Vista Alegre,** the famed village of the porcelain works. Such royalty as Britain's Elizabeth II and Spain's Juan Carlos have commissioned pieces of Vista Alegre porcelain for their tables. Lying on a branch of the Aveiro estuary, the village is the site of an open market held here on the 13th of every month, a tradition that dates from the late 1600s.

Fábrica de Porcelana da Vista Alegre, on Largo da Feira (or market square) (tel. 034/32-50-40), is not open to the public, but the factory store receives visitors on Monday through Friday from 9am to 6pm and on Saturday from 9am to 1pm.

Next to the porcelain factory is the **Vista Alegre Museum,** open Tuesday through Friday from 9am to noon and 2 to 4:30pm and Saturday and Sunday from 9am to 12:30pm and 2 to 5:30pm. Admission is free. The museum records the history of porcelain, starting in 1824 when the factory was founded here.

WHERE TO STAY
INEXPENSIVE

HOTEL AFONSO V, Rua Dr. Manuel das Neves 65, 3800 Aveiro. Tel. 034/251-91. Fax 034/38-11-11. 76 rms, 4 suites. MINIBAR TV TEL

$ Rates (including breakfast): 9,170$–12,500$ ($55.90–$76.30) single; 12,500$ ($76.30) double; 14,750$ ($90) suite. AE, MC, V. **Parking:** 400$ ($2.40).

The best place in town is the Afonso V. A recent enlargement and renovation turned its original core into a glossy contemporary structure. If you're driving, you'll find small but well-placed signs directing you to the establishment, which stands in a residential tree-lined neighborhood. The facade is lined with small sea-green tiles. The guest rooms are well furnished.

The hotel has a disco and an English-style pub, as well as an adjacent pair of restaurants (see "Where to Dine," below).

HOTEL IMPERIAL, Rua Dr. Nascimento Leitão, 3800 Aveiro. Tel. 034/221-41. Fax 034/241-48. 107 rms. TV TEL
$ **Rates** (including breakfast): 10,000$ ($61) single; 12,500$ ($76.30) double. AE, DC, MC, V. **Parking:** Free.

Hotel Imperial attracts the local young people, who gravitate to the lower-lounge social center for enjoying drinks and TV or to the open and airy dining room with its two glass walls. They look forward to their Sunday dates here—the 2,150$ ($13.10) dinners or the drinks on the open terrace. Many of the guest rooms and each of the lounges overlooks the Ria de Aveiro and the garden of the Aveiro Museum, the old convent. All the rooms have individually controlled central heating. The furnishings are contemporary, with many built-in features, and the color schemes are soothing.

PALOMA BLANCA, Rua Luís Gomes de Carvalho 23, 3800 Aveiro. Tel. 034/38-19-92. Fax 034/38-18-44. 50 rms. A/C TV TEL
$ **Rates** (including breakfast): 9,300$ ($56.70) single; 12,500$ ($76.30) double. AE, DC, MC, V. **Parking:** Free.

The design of Paloma Blanca, once an aristocratic private villa, is Moorish. An iron fence encloses the three-sided front courtyard, where a splashing fountain is surrounded by mature trees, trailing vines, and hand-painted gold-and-white tiles. The best rooms look out over the third-floor loggia onto a goldfish-filled basin in the garden. You'll find this well-preserved house—known in Portuguese as an *antiga moradia senhorial*—on a busy downtown street leading into the city from Porto. Breakfast is the only meal served. The well-furnished guest rooms are often old-fashioned.

BUDGET

ARCADA HOTEL, Rua Viana do Castelo 4, 3800 Aveiro. Tel. 034/230-01. Fax 034/218-86. 45 rms, 5 suites. TV TEL
$ **Rates** (including breakfast): 5,500$–7,100$ ($33.60–$43.30) single; 7,200$–9,000$ ($43.90–$54.90) double; 11,800$ ($72) suite. AE, DC, MC, V.

The Arcada enjoys an enviable position in the center of Aveiro, with a view of the river traffic in the canal out front. In summer, from your room window you can see the white pyramids of drying salt on the flats. The hotel has been modernized, but the classic beige-and-white facade has remained, and the rooftop is decorated with ornate finials. The hotel occupies the second, third, and fourth floors of the old building. Many of the guest rooms open onto balconies, and each has central heating. Breakfast is the only meal served.

WHERE TO DINE
MODERATE

A COZINHA DO REI, in Hotel Afonso V, Rua Dr. Manuel das Neves 65. Tel. 268-02.
  Cuisine: PORTUGUESE. **Reservations:** Not necessary.
$ **Prices:** Appetizers 550$–950$ ($3.40–$5.80); main courses 1,100$–2,200$ ($6.70–$13.40); snack bar meals from 2,000$ ($12.20). MC, V.
  Open: Daily noon–midnight.

The location of A Cozinha do Rei in this previously recommended hotel adds to its appeal. You'll face a choice as you enter. On the right is an informal snack bar/luncheonette. Meals in the snack bar might include cream of seafood soup, a range of omelets, squid, beefsteak Henri IV, veal cutlets with cream, and several kinds of grilled fish. A refrigerated case near the bar displays the day's catch of fresh fish and shellfish. Across the hallway, on the left as you enter, a more formal restaurant dispenses top-notch meals in a modernized and sun-washed elaboration of a grand restaurant. Service is among the best in town.

RESTAURANTE CENTENÁRIO, Largo do Mercado 9. Tel. 227-98.

Cuisine: PORTUGUESE. **Reservations:** Not necessary.
$ Prices: Appetizers 550$–950$ ($3.40–$5.80); main courses 1,200$–2,000$ ($7.30–$12.20). MC, V.
Open: Daily 9am–midnight.

S Restaurante Centenário stands at the side of the Aveiro's version of Les Halles. From the restaurant's front door, you can see the teeming covered market, whose laborers often stream up to the elongated bar after their early-morning unloadings of fresh produce. Most visitors, however, will gravitate to a napery-covered table for a well-prepared lunch or dinner. The high-ceilinged modern room contains lots of well-polished wood and has a large window opening onto the street. A less-often-used name for the restaurant is "À Casa da Sopa do Mar." As anyone can guess, that shellfish-laden soup is the house specialty. In addition to a steaming bowlful, you can order grilled pork or veal, fried or grilled sole, codfish *brasa,* and an array of other specials.

NEARBY PLACES TO STAY & DINE

MODERATE

POUSADA DA RIA, Bico do Muranzel, 3870 Torreira-Murtosa. Tel. 034/483-32. 19 rms. TV TEL
$ Rates (including breakfast): 16,000$ ($97.60) single; 18,000$ ($109.80) double. AE, DC, MC, V. **Parking:** Free.

The government operates this area *pousada,* located about 18½ miles from Aveiro. The pousada stands on a promontory surrounded on three sides by water. Between the sea and the lagoon, it is a contemporary building where the architect made much use of glass, with rows of balconies on its second floor. You can reach it by going by boat from Aveiro (passengers only) or by taking a long drive via Murtosa and Torreira until you reach this sandy spit. Along the way, you pass Phoenician-style boats in the harbor, sand dunes, and pine trees, not to mention a lot of trucks.

At the pousada, a waterside terrace opens onto views of fishing craft. The inn is popular with Portuguese families on holiday, who often book all its rooms. The guest rooms are compact, furnished with built-in pieces.

If you're stopping for a meal, the cost is 2,750$ ($16.80). The chef's specialty is *caldeirada a ria,* savory fish stew. A sunny Sunday is likely to be bedlam here; otherwise, it's a peaceful haven.

POUSADA DE SANTO ANTÓNIO, Mourisca de Vouga, 3750 Aguedo. Tel. 034/52-32-30. Fax 034/52-31-92. 11 rms, 1 suite. TEL
$ Rates (including breakfast): 16,000$ ($97.60) single; 18,000$ ($109.80) double; 23,800$ ($145.20) suite. AE, DC, MC, V. **Parking:** Free.

S On a rise above the Vouga River stands Pousada de Santo António, a large villa in a fine location near the main Lisbon-Porto highway. One of the first government-run pousadas in Portugal, it was built in 1942 in a design inspired by the farmhouses of the region's wealthy landowners, with a sweeping view over the valley of the River Vouga. The meadowlands and river valley are lush, filling the dining-room and living-room windows with picture-postcard colors. Large natural flagstones make up the front courtyard, ushering you into a renovated villa decorated like a warm provincial inn. All rooms contain striped rugs and floral bedspreads. High headboards on the country-style beds and patterned stone floors give an air of simple comfort. Laundry and room service are available. The outdoor pool and tennis courts are inviting attractions.

The pousada is about 157 miles north of Lisbon, 30 miles north of Coimbra, and 48 miles south of Porto. Caramulo and Talhada's mountains are in the background.

Meals are served daily from 12:30 to 3pm and 7:30 to 10pm. At dinner, whether you begin with *caldeirada* or *caldo verde,* be sure to request, if available, the veal or *bacalhau* (codfish), followed by the fruits of the valley. A meal costs from 3,000$ ($18.30).

BUDGET

HOTEL JOÃO PADEIRO, Rua da República 13, Cacia, 3800 Aveiro. Tel. 034/91-13-26. Fax 034/91-27-51. 22 rms, 4 suites. TV TEL
$ Rates (including breakfast): 4,800$ ($29.30) single; 7,400$ ($45.10) double; 8,700$ ($53.10) suite for two. AE, DC, MC, V. **Parking:** Free.

⑤ Set beside the highway, 4½ miles from Aveiro, the João Padeiro is a sienna-colored building concealing an elegant accommodation. It used to be an unpretentious village cafe until the Simões family transformed it more than a decade ago; now it can serve as an elegantly perfect weekend retreat. You enter a velvet-covered reception area filled with family antiques. A polite staff member will usher you via elevator to the brick-vaulted upstairs hallways and then to your room. Each unit is unique, usually containing some form of antique four-poster bed. Most of the beds are cornered with spindle-turned posts and have elaborately crafted headboards. Each room contains exuberantly flowered wallpaper and a coved ceiling, as well as a hand-crocheted bedspread. Laundry and room service are offered.

The true flavor of the establishment isn't appreciated until dinnertime. You might enjoy an apéritif in the Iberian-style bar, where well-rubbed leather covers the walls and the ceiling is carefully crafted. In cold weather, a sweeping expanse of flagstones, fashioned into a curved fireplace, warms a distant corner of the restaurant. Meals are served in a blue-and-white dining room, with massive Portuguese chests, leather-upholstered chairs, and fresh flowers. The paintings ringing the walls are the work of a well-known Portuguese artist, João de Sousa Araujo.

Meals from a distinguished Portuguese menu are priced from 4,000$ ($24.40). Specialties are likely to include shellfish omelet, house-style filet of sole, goat cooked in wine, fried eels, and lobster curry; try the walnut tart for dessert. The restaurant is open daily for lunch from 12:30 to 3pm and for dinner from 7:30 to 10pm. Closed Christmas.

---

8. CARAMULO

50 miles NE of Coimbra; 174 miles N of Lisbon

GETTING THERE   By Bus   There is no train service to Caramulo. If you're coming by bus from Lisbon, you have to go first to Tondela, from which you can make bus connections into Caramulo. You can also go from Lisbon to Viseu (see the following section), then make a connection by bus to Caramulo, although you'll have to allow at least 5 hours for this trip. One connection is by train from Lisbon to Coimbra (see earlier in this chapter), then a connecting bus to Tondela, and another connecting bus to Caramulo.

By Car   The village is usually approached via Viseu (see the following section). Follow the N2 south for some 15 miles to Tondela, then take a right onto N230 and follow the signposts for Caramulo for about another 12 miles.

ESSENTIALS   The **Tourist Office** is at Estrada Principal do Caramulo (tel. 86-14-37). The **telephone area code** is 032.

Set against a background of mimosa and heather-laden mountains, this tiny resort, midway between Aveiro and Viseu, is a gem and a good vantage point for going to see striking views of the surrounding country. About 2 miles north of town, at the end of a dirt road to the left, is a watchtower from which a panoramic view of the **Serra do Caramulo** unfolds.

WHAT TO SEE & DO

From the tip of this mountain, about 4½ miles from town at Caramulinho, you can see a breathtaking sweep that includes the Lapa, the Estrêla, the Lousa and Buçaco ranges, and the Serras da Gralheira and do Montemura, as well as the coastal plain. To reach the best viewing place on the 3,500-foot-high peak, take Avenida Abel de Lacerda from Caramulo west to the N230-3 road and then go about half a mile on foot.

Another panoramic vista spreads out from the summit of **Cabeço da Neve,** off the same road you'd take to go to Caramulinho.

MUSEU DO CARAMULO, 3475 Caramulo. Tel. 032/86-12-70.

This museum houses at least 60 veteran and vintage cars, including a 1905 four-cylinder De Dion-Bouton, a 1909 Fiat, an 1899 Peugeot, a 1902 Oldsmobile, a 1911 Rolls-Royce, and a 1902 Darracq. These antique cars are restored to perfect condition. A few early bicycles, one dating to 1865, and motorcycles are also exhibited. In addition to the ground-floor car display area, workshop, and library, there is an upper gallery where more vehicles are exhibited. Access to this is gained by a wide staircase at one end of the balustrade formed by crankshafts and camshafts from vintage engines. The museum also contains Portuguese and foreign paintings, sculpture, designs, engravings, the art of the goldsmith, ceramics, antique furniture, and tapestries.

Admission: 500$ ($3.10) adults; 125$ (80¢) children.
Open: Daily 10am–6pm.

WHERE TO STAY & DINE
MODERATE

POUSADA DE SÃO JERÓNIMO, 3475 Caramulo. Tel. 032/86-12-91. Fax 032/86-16-40. 6 rms. A/C TEL
$ Rates (including breakfast): 16,000$ ($97.60) single; 18,000$ ($109.80) double. AE, DC, MC, V. **Parking:** Free.

High as an eagle's nest, Pousada de São Jerónimo is near the crest of a mountain ridge. Its panoramic view is comparable to sights encountered in Switzerland and Austria. The inn is like a spread-out chalet, with an aesthetically pleasing design. You ascend to the reception, living, and dining rooms; one salon flows into another. In winter, guests sit by the copper-hooded fireplace. Beyond the wooden grille is a pleasant dining room, its window wall providing views of the hills.

The guest rooms are small but attractive. Portuguese antiques and reproductions are used—ornate iron headboards and slabs of wood as consoles. Wide windows open onto private balconies where you can take in the vista. Laundry service and babysitting are offered. The pousada also features a private park, a pool, and a playground. If you enjoy fishing, the Agueda and Criz rivers provide trout and *achigas,* a local barbel. From here, you can follow the Besteiros valley, and from its Varandahs, 48 miles along, you can see the impressive Estrêla mountains.

During candlelit dinners, guests sit on hand-carved provincial chairs sampling the country-style cooking. If you're just dropping in, a table d'hôte lunch or dinner goes for 2,700$ ($16.50). Food is served daily from 12:30 to 3pm and 7:30 to 10pm.

NEARBY PLACES TO STAY & DINE
MODERATE

POUSADA DE SANTA BÁRBARA, Póvoa das Quartas, 3400 Oliveira do Hospital. Tel. 038/522-52. Fax 038/505-45. 16 rms. TEL
$ Rates (including breakfast): 16,000$ ($97.60) single; 18,000$ ($109.80) double. AE, DC, MC, V. **Parking:** Free.

On the well-traveled Coimbra-Guarda highway, the best place to stop for food and lodging is Pousada de Santa Bárbara. Although not luxurious, it is suitable for those seeking a mountain spot. Don't be put off by the unimpressive facade. No guest room in the pousada faces the road. It is very well designed, with a fantastic view of the valley from the units, the lounges, and the restaurant. Laundry and room service are offered. Also featured are an outdoor pool and tennis courts.

Oliveira do Hospital, where the Pousada is situated, belonged to the 12th-century

Hospitaler religious Order of St. John of Jerusalem. You can visit Ferreira Chapel, part of the mother church, and there are traces of an ancient Roman village less than 2 miles away. Farther south, you come across Lourosa, whose parish church dates to 912. It is the only one in the country in the Mozarab style. About 12 miles from Povoa das Quartas, in the village of Avo, is the mother church, a pillory, and the ruins of a castle whose handsome facade is almost intact. The River Alva has a plentiful supply of fish and eels.

If you're stopping by the pousada just for lunch or dinner, a set meal in the provincial dining room will cost 3,650$ ($22.30). Food is served daily from 12:30 to 3pm and 7:30 to 10pm. The pousada has one of the best chefs in Portugal. Even the set menu offers a large choice of dishes. My American-style chicken would never have been recognized by an American, but it was superb nonetheless. The trout, however, is the pièce de résistance: Grilled with mushrooms, it's served with the backbone removed and a slice of cured ham. The sweet regional tart evokes a Sintra cheesecake, but with "lashings" of honey and almonds.

INEXPENSIVE

HOTEL URGEIRICA, Urgeirica, 3525 Canas de Senhorim. Tel. 032/67-12-67. Fax 032/67-13-28. 82 rms, 3 suites. A/C MINIBAR TEL

$ Rates (including breakfast): 10,500$ ($64.10) single; 12,000$ ($73.20) double; 18,900$ ($115.30) suite. AE, DC, MC, V. **Parking:** Free.

Hotel Urgeirica is set amid the forested countryside near Canas de Senhorim and connected with all the major Portuguese cities fine highways. The hotel lies about 25 miles from the Estrêla mountains, popular with winter sports enthusiasts, and is 186 miles north of Lisbon, 102 miles southeast of Porto, 50 miles northeast of Coimbra, and 16 miles south of the country town of Viseu. Its baronial granite walls, worthy of a grandee, were erected in 1939 by an English entrepreneur who had just made a fortune mining uranium in the nearby hills. Six years later, realizing the site's potential, he transformed his house into a hotel. It quickly became known as a stylish place to visit, and in time it lured such luminaries as Elizabeth II and Sir Anthony Eden. Nowadays, you'll find a less stylish version, where bartenders still wear uniforms and bow ties, and bowls of flowers are picked hours before in the sprawling gardens. Laundry and babysitting services are provided, and guests can enjoy an outdoor pool and tennis courts.

One of the most amazing aspects of this hotel is the large number of Georgian antiques filling the guest rooms. Their sheer quantities, coupled with high ceilings and English accessories, create the feeling of a sumptuous private house where someone is just about to ring the bell to announce supper.

Even if it's only for a meal, you should consider a stopover here. The bread is baked on the premises, some of the wine comes from nearby vineyards, and formal service is the norm in a vast and impressive dining room lined with five palace-size portraits of British kings. Meals cost from 1,950$ ($11.90) and are served daily from 12:30 to 2:30pm and 7:30 to 9:30pm. A bar whose leather decor and carved oak would be suitable for a private London club allows guests the pleasure of relaxing before fireplaces of chiseled granite, watching pine roots slowly dissolve into ash.

9. VISEU

60 miles E of Aveiro; 57 miles NE of Coimbra; 181 miles NE of Lisbon

GETTING THERE   By Train   The nearest rail station is at Nelas, about 15 miles south of Viseu. Buses connect with the trains pulling into Nelas to take passengers the rest of the way to Viseu.

By Bus   Rodoviária buses arrive from Coimbra at the rate of five per day, taking 2 hours and costing 700$ ($4.30) one way. There are also five buses per day pulling in from Lisbon after a 5-hour run, costing 1,300$ ($7.90) one way.

By Car Viseu lies near the center of the modern expressway, the IP-5, which cuts across Portugal. The IP-5 hooks up with the Lisbon/Porto motorway. Coming from Spain, motorists enter Portugal at the Vilar Formoso customs station, then head west to Viseu.

ESSENTIALS The **Viseu Tourist Board** is at Avenida Gulbenkian (tel. 42-20-14). The **telephone area code** is 032.

The capital of Beira Alta, Viseu is a quiet country town. Yet it is also a city of art treasures, palaces, and churches. Its local hero is an ancient Lusitanian rebel leader, Viriatus. At the entrance of Viseu is the **Cova de Viriato,** where the rebel, a combination Spartacus/Robin Hood, made his camp and plotted the moves that turned back the Roman tide.

Some of the country's most gifted artisans ply their timeless trade in and around Viseu. Where racks creak and looms hum, the busy weaver women create the unique quilts and carpets of Vil de Moinhos. Local artisans of Molelos produce the region's provincial pottery, and women with nimble fingers embroider feather-fine light bone lace.

WHAT TO SEE & DO

There is much to see and explore at random in Viseu: the cubistic network of overlapping tiled rooftops and entwining narrow alleyways and the encroaching macadam streets. However, if your time is limited, head at once to the **Ardo da Sé,** one of the most harmonious squares in Portugal, often referred to as the showplace of Viseu. There you'll find the town's three leading buildings: a cathedral, a museum, and a church.

VISEU SÉ (Cathedral), Largo da Sé.

The severe Renaissance facade of the Viseu Cathedral evokes a fortress. Two lofty bell towers, unadorned stone up to the balustraded summit with crowning cupolas, can be seen from almost any point in or around the town. The second-story windows in the facade, two rectangular and one oval, are latticed and symmetrically surrounded by niches containing religious statuary.

On your right, you will first find the two-story Renaissance cloister adorned with classic pillars and arcades faced with azulejos. The cathedral interior is basically Gothic but infused with Manueline and baroque decorations. Plain, slender Romanesque columns line the nave, supporting the vaulted Manueline ceiling with its nautically roped groining. The basic color scheme inside plays brilliant gilding against muted gold stone. However, the full emphasis is centered on the Roman arched chancel, climaxed by an elegantly carved retable above the main altar. The chancel makes ingenious use of color counterpoint, with copper, green gold, and brownish yellow complementing the giltwork. The ceiling is continued in the sacristy.

Admission: Free.
Open: Daily 9:30am–12:30pm and 2–5:30pm.

MUSEU DE GRÃO VASCO, Largo da Sé. Tel. 032/262-49.

This museum, next door to the cathedral, was named after the 16th-century painter, also known as Vasco Fernandes. The major works of this Portuguese master are displayed here, especially *La Pontecôte,* where the lancelike tongues of fire hurtle toward the saints, some devout, others apathetic.

Admission: 200$ ($1.20) adults; children 14 and under free.
Open: Mon–Sat 9:30am–12:30pm and 2–5pm.

IGREJA DA MISERICÓRDIA (Misericórdia Church), Largo da Sé.

Across the square from the cathedral is this palatial 18th-century church. Its pristine facade contrasts with the cathedral's baroque granite decorations, spirals, large windows and portal frames, balustrades, and matching towers.

Admission: Free.
Open: Mon–Sat 9:30am–12:30pm and 2–5:30pm.

WHERE TO STAY
MODERATE

GRÃO VASCO, Rua Gaspar Barreiros, 3500 Viseu. Tel. 032/42-35-11.
Fax 032/270-47. 107 rms, 3 suites. A/C TV TEL
$ Rates (including breakfast): 13,000$ ($79.30) single; 15,000$ ($91.50) double; 23,000$ ($140.30) suite. AE, DC, MC, V. **Parking:** 500$ ($3.10).
In the heart of town, Grão Vasco, surrounded by gardens and parks, is built motel fashion, with the guest-room balconies overlooking the pool. After days of driving in the hotel-lean environs, you'll find it a pleasure to check into this establishment. Popular with businesspeople, it also attracts tourists, especially in summer. The decor is colorful and contemporary, and the guest rooms are usually large, utilizing Portuguese traditional furnishings.
The dining room with its baronial stone fireplace features good cuisine, with many international dishes. If you're just dropping in, you can sample an à la carte lunch or dinner for 2,500$ ($15.30) to 3,800$ ($23.20).

BUDGET

HOTEL AVENIDA, Avenida Alberto Sampaio 1, 3500 Viseu. Tel. 032/42-34-32. Fax 032/267-43. 40 rms. TEL
$ Rates: 7,000$ ($42.70) single; 8,500$ ($51.90) double. Breakfast 850$ ($5.20) extra. AE, DC, MC, V. **Parking:** Free.
The Avenida is a personalized small hotel right off the Rossio, the main plaza of town. It is the domain of the personable Mario Abrantes da Motto Veiga, who has combined his collection of African and Chinese antiques with pieces of fine old Portuguese furniture. He's created an inviting aura, bound to attract admirers of his eclectic taste. The guest rooms vary in size and character. For example, room 210B boasts a high coved bed and an old refectory table and chair, which includes an adjoining chamber with a wooden spindle bed and a marble-topped chest that is like a nun's retreat. Meals in the plain family-style dining room are well prepared and generous, costing from 2,200$ ($13.40).

WHERE TO DINE
EXPENSIVE

O CORTIÇO, Rua Augusto Hilário 47. Tel. 42-38-53.
Cuisine: PORTUGUESE. **Reservations:** Required.
$ Prices: Appetizers 200$–1,000$ ($1.20–$6.10); main courses 1,500$–5,000$ ($9.20–$30.50); tourist menu 1,500$ ($9.20). AE, DC, MC, V.
Open: Lunch daily noon–2:30pm; dinner daily 7–11pm.
Cortiço will usually be the first name mentioned when you ask a discerning local for a good independent eatery. This is the type of place the Portuguese call *típico*, meaning it is decorated in typical local style and serves good regional cookery. You can dine in one of several rooms for reasonably priced meals. Specialties include *bacalhau* (cod), *cabrito assado* (roast kid), and steak Cortiço.

MODERATE

TRAVE NEGRA, Rua do Loureiros 40. Tel. 261-38.
Cuisine: PORTUGUESE. **Reservations:** Recommended.
$ Prices: Appetizers 450$–950$ ($2.70–$5.80); main courses 1,200$–2,500$ ($7.30–$15.30). AE, DC, MC, V.
Open: Lunch daily noon–3pm; dinner daily 7–10pm.
Trave Negra features well-prepared local cookery of the region. The regional wines are good, too. Before dinner, you can drop into the bar for an apéritif.

CHAPTER 14

PORTO & ENVIRONS

- **WHAT'S SPECIAL ABOUT PORTO & ENVIRONS**
1. **PORTO**
- **DID YOU KNOW . . . ?**
2. **ESPINHO**
3. **VILA DO CONDE**
4. **PÓVOA DO VARZIM**
5. **OFIR & FÃO**

Portugal's second city, Porto is the home of port wine, which is traditionally drunk in tulip-shaped glasses. The grapes that produce the wine come from the vineyards along the arid slopes of the Douro River Valley, many miles inland. At harvest time in autumn, the hills echo with the trilling of flutes and the cadence of drums.

The wine is brought to lodges at **Vila Nora de Gaia,** across the river from Porto, where it is blended, aged, and processed. In the past it was transported on flat-bottomed boats called *barcos rabelos.* With their long trailing rudders and sails flapping in the breeze, these boats with tails skirted down the Douro like swallows. Nowadays they have virtually given way to the train or even the unglamorous truck.

SEEING PORTO & ENVIRONS

An underrated stretch of coastal resorts and fishing villages lies between Porto and the southern reaches of the Minho district. The Atlantic waters, however, are likely to be on the chilly side, even in July and August. The communities along this northern highway of the sun are patronized mainly by the Portuguese. In recent years, these resorts have grown tremendously; they are, however, known more to European vacationers than to Americans (the latter still prefer the Algarve). Even so, a tour of Porto and its coastlines, north and south, is one of the most rewarding tourism targets in the country.

Flying from Lisbon will get you there the fastest, although it takes only 3½ hours to reach Porto by either express train or motorway. Once in Porto, the transportation hub of the area, you can explore the coastal towns by either bus or car.

One of the reasons many visitors arrive is not only to see Porto itself but also to take cruises along the Rio Douro of port wine fame. These trips might be very short, taking in only the famous bridges of Porto and some nearby fishing villages, or they might be more-extended affairs, such as minicruises lasting 1 or 2 days, with food and lodging provided on board. Cruises come in a wide variety of price ranges—beginning at 1,500$ ($9.20) for a simple 1- to 2-hour cruise of Porto itself and ranging all the way to 12,000$ to 24,000$ ($73.20 to $146.40) per person for trips of 1 to 2 days. Of course, summer is the best time to take these cruises, although they operate year round, with a greatly curtailed service in winter. Many prefer to take the cruises in early fall at harvest time.

One of the most reliable cruise companies is **Endouro,** Rua da Reboleira 49, in Porto (tel. 02/32-42-36); however, the tourist office in Porto (see below) provides information about an array of lesser-known companies offering cruises.

WHAT'S SPECIAL ABOUT PORTO & ENVIRONS

Great Towns/Villages

- ☐ Porto, the nation's "second city"—with a wine, a language, and a country named after itself.
- ☐ Espinho, a modern beach resort along the Costa Verde—with a year-round casino.
- ☐ Vila do Conde, at the mouth of the River Ave—a little town long famous for its lace making and embroidery, now a beach resort.
- ☐ Póvoa do Varzim, a holiday city that manages to combine a fishing industry with beach life.
- ☐ Ofir & Fão, north of Porto—two leading summer beach resorts with some of the best sand north of Porto.

Beaches

- ☐ The beaches along the Costa Verde, often cold and windswept but filled with dramatic scenery and white sand—ideal on the right sunny day in summer.
- ☐ Espinho Beach, south of Porto; Póvoa de Varzim; and Ofir—the best meccas for water-sports enthusiasts.

Religious Shrine

- ☐ Sé at Porto—a twin-towered, fortresslike 12th-century cathedral, on a hill overlooking Old Town.

Museum

- ☐ Soares dos Reis National Museum, in Porto—housed in an 18th-century palace, a treasure trove of art of the north.

Ace Attractions

- ☐ Port Wine Cellars at Porto, where wine from the Douro Valley is stored and aged—some 50 or so wine lodges are in the district.
- ☐ Cruises on the Rio Douro, where the grapes for port wine are harvested—an area of great scenic beauty.

Architectural Highlights

- ☐ The bridges of Porto—especially the easternmost Ponte Dona Maria Pía, designed by the famed Alexandre-Gustave Eiffel in 1877; and the western Ponte de Dom Luís I, a two-tiered structure from 1886 that links the upper and lower parts of the city on both sides.

SUGGESTED 4-DAY ITINERARY

Day 1 Most visitors leave only a day for Porto. If that is your case, take our walking tour (see below) and visit the port wine lodges.

Day 2 Spend the day touring the Rio Douro.

Day 3 On this day, explore the beaches and coastline north of Porto. You can easily go as far as Vila do Conde, 17 miles to the north, with its fishing port and long sweep of sand. Póvoa de Varzim, with its long beach, makes a better overnight center, and it has a long beach, too.

Day 4 Head south of Porto for a look at its coast, where a string of family beaches leads all the way to Espinho, a distance of 11 miles. It makes the best center.

---

1. PORTO

195 miles N of Lisbon; 189 miles S of La Corŭna (Spain); 366 miles W of Madrid (Spain)

GETTING THERE   By Plane   Porto (Oporto in English) stretches along the last 3 miles on the right bank of River Douro and is the hub of a communication network in north Portugal. The quickest and easiest method of getting there is by airplane.

TAP, the Portuguese airline, provides quick connection between Lisbon and Porto, and there are daily flights all year. Flights arrive at **Aeroporto das Pedras Rubras** (tel. 02/948-21-41). The main office of **TAP** is at Praça Mouzinho de Albuquerque 105 (tel. 02/608-02-00) in Porto. Buses 44 and 56 run between the airport and the center of Porto; the cost of a one-way bus ticket is 135$ (80¢).

By Train   There are three main railway stations in Porto. They include Estação de São Bento (tel. 02/200-27-22) in the center of the city, only a block from Praça da Liberdade. This station has trains serving the Douro Valley, along with destinations in the north, including Viana de Casteio and Braga. East of the center, but connected to São Bento by rail service, Estação de Campanhã (tel. 02/56-41-41) is one of the most important. It serves the south of Portugal, including Lisbon, as well as international routes. Less important, Estação da Trindade (tel. 02/200-52-24) handles traffic in the immediate environs of Porto, including the beach resort of Póvoa do Varzim and the historic old city of Guimarães (see Chapter 15).

Four trains arrive per day from Lisbon; the trip takes 4½ hours and costs 1,520$ ($9.30) one way. Porto also enjoys 13 trains per day from Viana do Castelo; the trip takes 2 hours and costs 550$ ($3.40) one way. Twelve trains per day arrive from Coimbra, after the 2½-hour trip that costs 725$ ($4.40) one way. International travelers can take one of two daily trains from Madrid to Porto, going via Entroncamento. Trip time is 12 hours, and the cost is 7,000$ ($42.70) one way. One train per day arrives from Paris; the trip takes 27 hours and costs 17,500$ ($106.80) one way.

By Bus   It is also possible to come from Lisbon by bus (there are at least four daily departures). The trip takes 5 hours and costs 1,480$ ($9) one way. Arriving passengers are deposited at the bus depot at Rua Alexandre Herculano 366 (tel. 02/200-68-54). Service is provided by the national bus company, Rodoviário Nacional. There are also 11 buses per day from Coimbra, the trip taking 1½ hours and costing 900$ ($5.50) one way.

By Car   The new Lisbon/Porto superhighway cuts driving time between Portugal's two leading cities to just over 3 hours. For motorists, Porto is the center of the universe, as all major roads in the north fan out from this city. From Spain in the north, the nearest border crossing is at Tuy/Valença do Minho. After that, you can head south for some 78 miles to Porto on the N13.

Porto gave its name not only to port wine but also to the whole country and its language. The name derives from the old settlement of Portus Cale. The Douro, from Rio do Ouro (River of Gold), has always been the source of Porto's life blood. It enjoys many sunny days, yet at times Porto has been called a gray city of mist and rain.

It's set on a rocky gorge that the Douro cut out of a great stone mass. Magazine-writer Ann Bridge says, "The whole thing looks like a singularly dangerous spider's web flung across space." Porto's most interesting quarter is the **Alfândega.** Here the steep narrow streets (hardly big enough for a car to pass through) and the balconied houses evoke Lisbon's Alfama, although the quarter has its own distinctive character. The Alfândega preserves the timeless color of many of the old buildings and cobbled *ruas* lining the riverbank.

Many write off Porto as an industrial city with some spectacular bridges, but that assessment is unfair. The provincial capital and university seat has its own artistic treasures.

ORIENTATION

ARRIVING   A taxi, the most convenient transport from the airport into the center of Porto, costs from 2,500$ to 3,000$ ($15.30 to $18.30). There is also good bus service into the city center from the airport. The nos. 44 and 56 buses run from Praça de Lisboa, with a ticket costing 135$ (80¢).

INFORMATION   One of the most helpful tourist offices in Portugal is the **Porto Tourist Board,** Rua do Clube Fenianos 25 (tel. 02/31-27-40). The office is open in

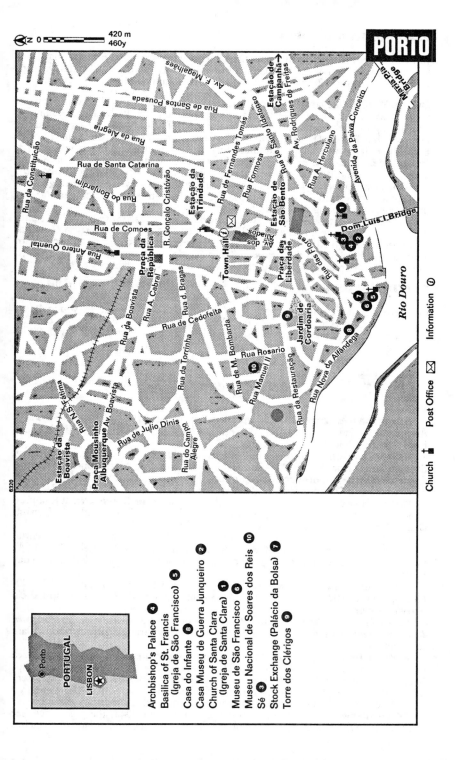

PORTO

Scale: 0 — 420 m / 460 y

PORTUGAL
Porto
LISBON ★

Archbishop's Palace ④
Basilica of St. Francis
(Igreja de São Francisco) ⑤
Casa do Infante ⑧
Casa Museu de Guerra Junqueiro ②
Church of Santa Clara
(Igreja de Santa Clara) ①
Museu de São Francisco ⑥
Museu Nacional de Soares dos Reis ⑩
Sé ③
Stock Exchange (Palácio da Bolsa) ⑦
Torre dos Clérigos ⑨

Church ✝   Post Office ⊠   Information ⓘ

July through September on Monday through Friday from 9am to 7pm, Saturday from 9am to 4pm, and Sunday from 10am to 1pm. Off-season hours are Monday through Friday from 9am to 12:30pm and 2 to 5:30pm and Saturday from 9am to 4pm.

CITY LAYOUT   Regardless of your method of transport, you will need to acquaint yourself with the geography of this rather complicated city. Its bridges are famous. Connecting the right bank to the port wine center of **Vila Nova de Gaia** and the lands south is **Ponte Dona Maria Pía,** an architectural feat of Alexandre-Gustave Eiffel (of Eiffel Tower fame). Another much-needed bridge spanning the Douro is **Ponte de Dom Luís I.** An iron bridge of two roadways, it was completed in 1886 by Teófilo Seyrig, the Belgian engineer inspired by Eiffel. Another bridge, **Ponte da Arrábida,** which opened in 1963, is bright and contemporary. Totally Portuguese in concept and execution, it is one of the largest single-span reinforced-concrete arches in Europe, representing the work of Edgar Cardoso.

The heart of Porto is **Avenida dos Aliados,** a wide *paseo* with a parklike center where families used to go for a stroll. It is bounded on the south by **Praça General Humberto Delgado.** Two major shopping streets of Porto lie on either side of Praça da Liberdade: **Rua Clérigos** and **Rua 31 de Janeiro.** Rua Clérigos leads to the landmark **Torre dos Clérigos,** which to some is the symbol of Porto.

GETTING AROUND   Porto is well serviced by a network of buses, trolleys, and trams; tickets cost from 135$ (80¢). However, if you plan to do extensive touring in the Porto area, it is cheaper to purchase a *Passe Turístico,* which entitles you to 4 days of transportation. The cost is 1,280$ ($7.80). It can be bought at various tobacco shops and kiosks around town. Taxis are available 24 hours a day. Call 02/48-80-61 for radio taxis, or hail one on the street or at a taxi stand.

FAST FACTS   *PORTO*

American Express   The representative in Porto is **Star Travel Service,** Avenida dos Aliados 202 (tel. 02/200-36-37), which is open Monday through Friday from 9am to 12:30pm and 2 to 6pm.

Banks   In general, banks and currency-exchange offices are open Monday through Friday from 8:30 to 11:45am and 1 to 2:45pm. Two central ones are **Banco Espírito Santo & Comércial de Lisboa,** Avenida dos Aliados 45 (tel. 02/32-00-31), and **Banco Pinto & Sotto Mayor,** Praça da Liberdade 26 (tel. 02/32-15-56).

Consulates   In Porto, you will reach the **American Consulate** at Rua Júlio Dinis 826-3 (tel. 02/69-00-08); go to the third floor. There is also a **British Consulate** at Avenida da Boavista 3072 (tel. 02/68-47-89).

Drugstores   Porto is well served by a network of pharmacies. A most central one is the **Farmacia Central do Porto,** 31 de Janeiro 203 (tel. 02/216-84). Otherwise, phone 166 for the location of a 24-hour pharmacy (these change from day to day).

Emergencies   Emergency telephone numbers include **police** (tel. 02/200-68-21), **fire** (tel. 02/48-41-21), **Red Cross** (tel. 02/66-68-72), and **Hospital de Santo António** (tel. 02/200-52-41).

Laundry   On the third floor of the Shopping Center Brasilia is the **Penguin Avenida Boavista** (tel. 02/69-50-32), open Monday through Saturday from 10am to 11pm.

Post Office   If you want to mail a letter, the **main post office** is at Praça General Humberto Delgado (tel. 208-02-51), near the tourist office. It sells stamps Monday through Friday from 9am to 10pm. However, if you had your mail sent general delivery (*poste restante*), it can be picked up daily from 8am to 10pm at Largo 1 de Dezembro. It is also possible to send telegrams and faxes during those hours.

Telephone   It is possible to place long-distance calls at the post office (see above). Otherwise, you can go to the phone office at Praça da Liberdade 62, which is open daily from 8am to 11:30pm. By placing your calls at these public institutions, you avoid hotel surcharges, which can be steep, as much as 40% in some hotels.

WHAT TO SEE & DO

Exploring the sights of Porto requires some probing, but your discoveries will compensate you for the effort. The tourist office suggests that you need at least 3 days to explore Porto, though most foreign visitors don't spend that much time here. Actually, they spend only a day.

For those on a rushed schedule, the most famous sightseeing attractions include a visit to a wine lodge at Vila Nova de Gaia; the panoramic view from the Torre dos Clérigos, with its view of the Douro; a visit to the Sé (cathedral); a stroll through the most important museum, Museu Nacional de Soares dos Reis; a walk through Ribeira, the old quarter, with its little alleyways leading to the harbor (best seen on market days); and if time remains, a visit to the Gothic church of St. Francis, with its stunning baroque interior.

THE TOP ATTRACTIONS
Churches

SÉ [Cathedral], Terreiro de Sé. Tel. 31-90-28.

This cathedral has grown and changed with the city—that is, until about the 18th century. Founded by a medieval queen and designed in a foreboding, basically Romanesque style, it is now a monument to changing architectural tastes. Part of the twin towers, the rose window, the naves, and the vestry are elements of the original 13th-century structure; however, the austere Gothic cloister was added at the end of the 14th century and was later decorated with *azulejos* depicting events from the Song of Solomon. Opening off the cloister is the Chapel of St. Vincent, built in the late 16th century.

The main chapel was erected in the 17th century, and in 1736 the baroque architect Niccolò Nasoni of Italy added the north facade and its attractive loggia. The monumental altar is flanked by twisted columns, the nave by fading frescoes. In the small baroque Chapel of the Holy Sacrament (to the left of the main altar) is an altarpiece fashioned entirely of silver, the work so elaborate that the whole piece gives the illusion of constant movement.

Admission: Free; cloister 100$ (60¢).
Open: Daily 9am–noon and 2–5pm. **Tram:** 1. **Bus:** 15.

IGREJA DE SANTA CLARA [Church of St. Clare], Largo Primeiro de Dezembro. Tel. 31-48-37.

First completed in 1416, the interior was transformed by impassioned 17th-century artists, masters of woodwork and gilding. The number of hours invested is staggering to contemplate. There is hardly a square inch that isn't covered with angels, saints, cherubs, and patterned designs in an architectural scramble of rococo and baroque, one of the most exceptional examples in Portugal. The clerestory windows permit the sunlight to flood in, making a golden crown of the upper regions. In deliberate contrast, the building's facade is squat and plain.

If the keeper of the keys takes a liking to you, he'll take you on a behind-the-scenes tour of the precincts. In the Tribute Room, for example, you'll see a devil carved on the choir stalls. Throughout the tour you will see a hodgepodge of many bad, fading paintings, some not even hung—just propped casually in the corner. But it's intriguing to see what lies beyond all the glitter and glamour out front.

Admission: Free.
Open: Mon–Fri 9:30–11:30am and 3–7:30pm, Sun 9:30am–12:30pm. **Tram:** 1. **Bus:** 15.

? DID YOU KNOW . . . ?

- The favorite dish of a true local is tripe (the stomach of an ox, a sheep, or a goat).
- Afonso Henríques, founding the new kingdom in the 12th century, gave it the name of his homeland: *Portucalia.*
- Port wine, it is said, was the result of a "climatic" accident: Warm weather produced too-sweet grapes, and the resulting wine had to be fortified with brandy.
- A 16th-century convent now holds about 200 million liters of Sandeman port in bottles and oak barrels.
- The 1832 siege of Porto during the "War of Two Brothers," as it was called, forced hungry residents to eat cats and dogs.
- In the mid-1700s, a drunken mob set fire to port wine offices—it was called the *revolta dos borrachos,* or "drunkards' revolt." A total of 25 men were hanged.
- Porto's most famous son was Prince Henry the Navigator, born to a Portuguese king and an English queen.
- Porto became one of the first towns in Iberia to kick out the Moors.
- At the marriage of the daughter of the King of León and Castile to Henry of Burgundy, Porto was included in her "dowry."
- A local earthy maxim shows how residents regard Portugal: "Coimbra sings, Braga prays, Lisbon shows off, and Porto works."

IGREJA DE SÃO FRANCISCO [Church of St. Francis], Praça Infante Dom Henríque. Tel. 200-84-41.

The Gothic Church of St. Francis, reached by steps leading up from the waterfront, was built between 1383 and 1410. But in the 17th and 18th centuries, it underwent extensive rococo dressing. The vault pillars and columns are lined with gilded woodwork: cherubs, rose garlands, fruit cornucopia, and frenzied animals, entwined and dripping with gold. Many of the wide-ribbed Gothic arches are made of marble resembling the Italian forest-green serpentine variety. Soaring overhead, the marble seems to fade and blend mysteriously with the gray-granite columns and floors.

The Romanesque rosette dominates the facade, whose square portal is flanked by double twisted columns. Above the columns, a profusely ornamented niche contains a simple white statue of the patron saint. In the rose window, 12 mullions emanate from the central circle in apostolic symbolism, ending in a swaglike stone fringe. The steps seem to spill out into the square fanlike along the base of the curved walls.

Admission: 100$ (60¢).

Open: Tues–Sat 9am–5pm. **Bus:** 23, 49, or 88.

Museums

CASA MUSEU DE GUERRA JUNQUE-IRO [House and Museum of Guerra Junqueiro], Rua de Dom Hugo 32. Tel. 31-36-44.

The famous Portuguese poet Guerra Junqueiro lived between 1850 and 1923. The house was built by the Italian architect Niccolò Nasoni (1691–1773). Each room is arranged to preserve Junqueiro's private art collection and memorabilia.

The collection includes Georgian and Portuguese silver; Flemish chests; Italian, Oriental, Spanish, and Portuguese ceramics; and ecclesiastical wood and stone carvings. Joining the many examples of religious sculpture are an Italian Renaissance desk, metal plates said to have been made in Nürnberg, a 16th-century Brussels tapestry, and interesting Portuguese furniture.

Admission: 50$ (30¢) adults; children under 10 free; free for everyone Sat–Sun.

Open: Tues–Thurs 10am–12:30pm and 2–5:30pm, Fri–Sat 10am–12:30pm and 2–6pm, Sun 2–5:30pm. **Tram:** 1. **Bus:** 15.

MUSEU DE SÃO FRANCISCO [Museum of St. Francis], Rua da Bolsa 44. Tel. 200-64-93.

The sacristan estimates that 30,000 human skulls have been interred in the cellars here. Even though he may be exaggerating, this dank building was once the burial ground for rich and poor. Nowadays it is a catacomb unique in Portugal.

A section of it looks like an antiques shop. There are paintings, too, one of St. Francis of Assisi worshiping Christ on the Cross. Oddities include some of the first paper money printed in Portugal and an 18th-century ambulance that was really a sedan chair. The Sala de Sessoes adds a note of unexpected elegance: Built in the rich baroque style, it is now a meeting hall with a Louis XIV table and João V chairs. Wherever you go in the room, the painted eyes of framed bishops follow you, watching like Big Brother.

Admission: 350$ ($2.10) adults; children free.
Open: June–Sept, Mon–Sat 9am–5pm; Oct–May, Mon–Sat 9am–noon and 2–7pm. **Tram:** 1. **Bus:** 23, 49, or 88.

MUSEU DE ETNOGRAFIA E HISTÓRIA DO DOURO LITORAL [Ethnological and Historical Museum of Douro Region], Palácio de São João Novo, Largo São João Novo. Tel. 200-20-10.

Reached by steps up from the water is one of the city's leading museums, sheltered on a *típico* square and rarely visited. Culture seekers are usually beset with escudo-hungry children who live in the jumble of dwellings nearby. The museum celebrates the arts, handcrafts, and culture of the Douro River valley. It's a rustic potpourri of spinning wheels, looms, and animal and fish traps nostalgically evoking the simple life-style of the peasant. Roman coins and other artifacts remind you that legions from far afield once marched in and settled on the river banks.

Earthenware jugs from Vita-da-Feira, gold filigree work, a bas-relief of a provincial cottage, and a three-faced Christ are among the exhibits, along with primitive puppets, provincial bedrooms, ceramics, dolls in regional costume, ship models, decorative ox yokes, weathervanes, cannonballs, spears, antique sarcophagi, and even a wine press.

Admission: Free.
Open: Tues–Sat 10am–noon and 2–5pm. **Tram:** 1. **Bus:** 15.

MUSEU NACIONAL DE SOARES DOS REIS [Soares dos Reis National Museum], Rua de Dom Manuel II 56. Tel. 200-71-10.

Created in 1833 by order of Dom Pedro IV, this museum was called the Museu Portuguese when it was opened to the public in 1840. One hundred years later, it was declared a National Museum and was dedicated to Soares dos Reis (1847–89), the noted sculptor from Porto. *Desterrado* and *Flor Agreste* are remarkable sculptures by this artist, but good portraits and allegorical figures can also be seen in the same gallery.

In the foreign painters collection, you'll find Dutch, Flemish, Italian, and French works, including two François Clouets (1522–72) portraits and landscapes by Jean Pillement (1727–1808). The most representative and unified display is that of the Portuguese 19th-century painters, particularly from the Porto School. Henríque Pousão (1859–87) and Silva Porto (1850–93) are represented by fine naturalistic work.

Also displayed in the museum are decorative arts, including ceramics, glassware, gold and silver work, furniture, and other objects.

Admission: 200$ ($1.35) adults; children under 10 free; free for everyone Sun 10am–1pm.
Open: Tues–Sun 10am–12:30pm and 2–5pm. **Bus:** 3, 6, 20, 35, 37, or 41.

MORE ATTRACTIONS

PALÁCIO DA BOLSA [Stock Exchange], Rua da Bolsa. Tel. 200-44-97.

The Stock Exchange is housed in the imposing 19th-century Palácio da Bolsa. It is known for its Moorish Hall, a much-modified pastiche resembling a room in the Alhambra at Granada. The walls, ceiling, and balcony are a gilded mass of patterns and geometrical configurations. The pastel-blue column bases glow in sunlight filtered through intricately latticed octagonal skylights and floral side windows.

Admission: 300$ ($1.80) adults; children under 12 free.
Open: June–Sept, Mon–Fri 9am–6pm, Sat–Sun 10am–noon and 2–5pm; Oct–May, Mon–Fri 9am–5pm, Sat–Sun 10am–noon and 2–4pm. **Tram:** 1. **Bus:** 15.

CASA DO INFANTE [House of the Prince], Rua Nova da Alfândega. Tel. 31-60-25.

Tradition has it that Porto's fabled hometown boy, Prince Henry the Navigator, was born in this house dating from the 1300s. In the 1800s, the building was used as a customs house. Today it contains a Museu Histórico with documents, manuscripts, and various artifacts relating to the history of Porto.

Admission: 150$ (90¢).

Open: Mon–Fri 9am–noon and 2–5:30pm. **Tram: 1. Bus: 15.**

TORRE DOS CLÉRIGOS [Clérigos Tower], Rua dos Clérigos. Tel. 200-17-29.

West of Praça da Liberdade, follow Rua dos Clérigos to the Torre dos Clérigos (Clérigos Tower), which Italian architect Niccolò Nasoni designed in 1754. The tower's six floors rise to a height of some 250 feet, which makes it one of the tallest structures in the north of Portugal. You can climb 225 steps to the top of the belfry, where you'll be rewarded with one of the finest views of Porto and the River Douro. The Italianate baroque Igreja dos Clérigos at the same site was also built by Nasoni and actually predates the tower.

Admission: 50$ (30¢) tower; free, church.

Open: Tower: Mon–Tues and Thurs–Sat 10am–noon and 2–5pm, Sun 10am–5:30pm. Church: Mon–Sat 7:30–9am, 10am–noon, 2–5pm, and 6–7:30pm; Sun 10am–1pm. **Bus: 15.**

Port Wine Lodges

Across the river from Porto, at **Vila Nova de Gaia,** are the port wine lodges. Like the sherry makers at Jerez de la Frontera, Spain, these establishments are hospitable, inviting guests to tour their precincts. Take bus no. 57 or 91 to reach these lodges.

REAL COMPANHIA VINÍCOLA DO NORTE DE PORTUGAL, Rua Azevedo Magalhães. Tel. 30-30-13.

✪ Founded by royal decree in 1756, this is one of the largest of the city's port wine lodges. It is a prime example of the art of wine making, devoted to the blending, aging, and selecting of the region's most famous product. Dating from 1889, the warehouses contain specially treated oaken vats. The wine is bolstered with brandies and vintage wines to maintain its character. The vast cellars, dark, cool, and moist, are the resting place for port that ranges in age from 5 to 70 years. However, the oldest bottle in the company's museum is dated 1765. In one tunnel section alone there are 4 million bottles of Portuguese sparkling wines.

If you wish to learn the intricacies of production and development of port wine, from tasting to decanting, arrive and announce yourself. You'll be guided through the cask- and vat-lined cellars and tunnels. At the company tavern, you can purchase fine wine packed in wicker baskets. Hours are Monday through Friday from 9am to noon and 2 to 5pm.

PORTO SANDEMAN, Largo Miguel Bombarda 3. Tel. 30-40-81.

You can also visit many other port wine centers. Perhaps the most famous is Porto Sandeman, owned by Seagrams of Canada. In a former 16th-century convent, Sandeman was established in 1790 by George Sandeman of Scotland. The House of Sandeman also operates a unique museum, tracing the history of port wine and of Sandeman. Many artifacts displayed date from centuries ago. Visitors can also purchase Sandeman products on the premises, not only wines but also promotional items such as T-shirts, umbrellas, and posters. Hours in April through September are daily from 9:30am to 5pm; hours in October through March are Monday to Friday from 9:30am to 12:30pm and 2 to 5pm.

FERREIRA, Rua da Carvalhosa 19. Tel. 370-00-10.

One of the biggest wine lodges across the river is the legendary Ferreira, which dates from the early 1800s, having been launched by Dona António Adelaide Ferreira. From a modest beginning with only a handful of vineyards, her company rose in power and influence, gobbling up wine estate after wine estate. It is said that at its apex its holdings stretched all the way to the border with Spain, making its owner the richest woman in the nation. This fabled entrepreneur—called *Ferreirinha,* or "Little Ferreira," by the people of Portugal—nearly drowned in the Douro in 1861, but her voluminous petticoat kept her buoyant. (Her companion, an Englishman, baron de Forrester, did drown.) The wine cellar is open from mid-April through mid-October on Monday through Friday from 10am to 12:30pm and 2 to 5:30pm and on Saturday from 10am to noon; off-season hours are Monday through Friday from 10am to noon and 3 to 5pm.

WALKING TOUR —— THE HEART OF PORTO

Start: Terreiro de Sé.
Finish: Estação de São Bento.
Time: 2½ hours.
Best Times: Daily 10am–4pm.
Worst Times: Mon–Fri 8–10am and 4–6pm because of heavy traffic.

The only suitable way to explore the heart of the inner city is on foot. Nearly all major monuments are in the old part of town, and distances between major sights is not far. The often narrow streets are sometimes confusing to the first-time visitor, and even armed with a good map you are likely to get lost from time to time. Long accustomed to entertaining foreigners, the people of Porto are generally friendly and hospitable and will point you in the right direction.

Begin your tour in the heart of the Old Town, at:

1. **Terreiro de Sé,** a square dominated by the Sé (cathedral), which began as a fortress church in the 12th century and was greatly altered in the 1600s and 1700s. Its main facade is flanked with a set of square domed towers. "Cathedral Square," as it is called in English, is also bordered by an 18th-century former episcopal palace that has now been sequestered for municipal offices. Noted for its granite-cased doors and windows, it contains an exceptional stairway inside. Also on the square is a Manueline-style pillory and a statue of Vimara Peres, the warrior of Afonso III of León, who captured ancient Portucale in 868.

   To the rear of the cathedral is one of the most charming and *típico* streets of Porto:
2. **Rua da Dom Hugo.** If you continue along this street, you'll pass the Chapel of Our Lady of Truths. It's invariably closed, but you can peek through the grillework at the gilded rococo altar, with a statue of the Virgin at the center. Along this same street stands the:
3. **Casa Museu de Guerra Junqueiro,** at no. 32, a white mansion—now a museum—that was the home of the poet Guerra Junqueiro (1850–1923). The Italian architect Niccolò Nasoni designed this mansion.

   Rua de Dom Hugo, a narrow street, curves around the eastern side of the Sé. Continue along it until you come to some steep steps. These were carved through some remaining sections of the former town walls that existed in the Middle Ages. This brings you into one of the most colorful, also one of the most poverty stricken, sections of Porto:
4. **The Ribeira district.** Although poverty of any type is not necessarily "picturesque," this decaying neighborhood does have a certain charm for those who wander its back streets. In some cities, the area would be called a slum or ghetto, but in Porto, this district near the waterfront has style. It is filled with arcaded markets, churches, museums, monuments, and once-elegant buildings.

   Regardless of which little alley you take, everything eventually merges onto the:
5. **Cais da Ribeira,** the quayside section of the Ribeira district, opening onto the River Douro. Locals come here to enjoy several low-coast *tascas* (taverns) and seafood restaurants that were constructed into the street-level arcade of the old buildings.

REFUELING STOP Taverna do Bebodos, Cais da Ribeira 24 (tel. 31-35-65). If you're taking this walking tour at midday, make this local favorite (since 1876) your lunch stop. A dining room upstairs opens onto views of the

Douro. Of course, you might happily settle for a glass of the local wine coming from a cask balanced on the bar.

The center of the district is:

6. **Praça da Ribeira,** where locals sit in the sun telling tall tales and where visitors can enjoy the previously previewed port wine lodges across the Douro at Vila Nova de Gaia.

Now head east to the:

7. **Ponte Dom Luís I, or Dom Luís I Bridge,** the middle of the trio of bridges over the River Douro. The iron bridge was designed by Seyrig, a collaborator of Eiffel, in 1886. It has an upper and a lower span, both of which funnel traffic to the port wine lodges in Vila Nova de Gaia, on the other side of the River Douro.

After viewing the bridge and the river, retrace your steps west to Praça da Ribeira. At the north of the square, walk up Rua de São João to:

8. **Feitoria Inglesa (The Factory House of the British Association),** the headquarters of the Port Wine Shippers' Association. One of the most fabled buildings in the Ribeira district, it stands at a point where the Rua Infante Dom Henríque crosses with Rua de São João. The "factory" was designed by British consul John Whitehead in 1786.

Go west along Rua Infante Dom Henríque to the:

9. **Casa do Infante,** standing at the corner of this street where it crosses Rua da Alfândega. Porto-born Henry the Navigator, who launched Portugal on the Age of Discovery, was said to have been born in this house. Follow Rua Infante Dom Henríque to:

10. **Praça do Infante Dom Henríques,** named after Henry the Navigator. At this square you can visit a big covered food market, where tripe is sold in great quantities. Although shunned by much of the Western world, except by Florentines, tripe is said to be the favorite food of the denizens of Porto. The square is graced with a statue of Prince Henry.

The highlight of this square, however, is the:

11. **Igreja de São Francisco,** the Basilica of St. Francis, originally a Gothic church. With its adjacent museum that once was the property of a Franciscan monastery, this church contains the most lavish and most spectacular interior of all the churches of Porto (and the competition is keen).

Behind the church, although facing the square, is Porto's:

12. **Palácio da Bolsa, or Stock Exchange,** taking up a great deal of the site of what used to be a Franciscan monastery. It is known for its oval Arab Room whose stained glass and arabesques are said to imitate the style of the Alhambra in Granada, built by the Moors. The stock exchange stands at the cross streets of Rua da Bolsa and Rua Ferreira Borges.

Follow Rua Ferreira Borges north, veering east to Largo de São Domingos. At the top of this square, continue northeast along:

13. **Rua das Flores,** which some visitors consider the most romantic street of Porto. It's long been known for the quality of its silversmiths, but what makes the street so architecturally striking is its wrought-iron balconies.

The "Street of Flowers" eventually opens onto Praça de Almeida Garrett, named for the famed Portuguese writer. On this square is:

14. **Estação de São Bento,** the most central of the railway stations of Porto. Its grand central hall is decorated with large ceramic tiles—called *azulejos*—which trace the saga of transportation in Portugal. From this terminal you can catch a train to your next destination.

SHOPPING

The capital of the north boasts some of the finest gold- and silversmiths in Portugal. You'll find dozens of shops, especially along **Rua das Flores,** offering displays in their window cases.

PEDRO A. BAPTISTA, Rua das Flores 235. Tel. 200-51-42.

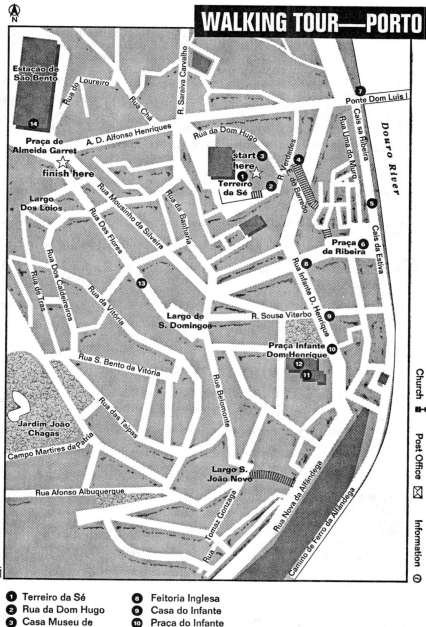

WALKING TOUR—PORTO

① Terreiro da Sé
② Rua da Dom Hugo
③ Casa Museu de Guerra Junqueiro
④ The Ribeira district
⑤ Cais da Ribeira
⑥ Praça da Ribeira
⑦ Ponte Dom Luís I
⑧ Feitoria Inglesa
⑨ Casa do Infante
⑩ Praça do Infante Dom Henríques
⑪ Igreja de São Francisco
⑫ Palácio da Bolsa
⑬ Rua das Flores
⑭ Estação de São Bento

This is the most outstanding shop, offering an unusual collection of antique as well as new jewelry (often based on traditional designs), plus several upper floors of decorator items. In the ground-floor jewelry section, you'll find intricate and delicate lacelike filigree pins, brooches, pillboxes, and bracelets, in both solid gold (19¼ karats) and gold-plated silver. There's also an exquisite silver collection, including elaborately decorated tea services.

The owner buys rare and beautiful antique jewelry that he "offers first to [his] wife." The decorative bric-a-brac collection upstairs features many ornate gilt pieces, such as a 3-foot-high carved-wood church candelabrum and a trestle dining table.

VISTA ALEGRE, Rua Cândido dos Reis 18. Tel. 200-45-54.
One of the finest names in Portuguese porcelain has an outlet in Porto. A wide variety of items is displayed, and shipping can be arranged for this highly fragile merchandise. The prices of this outlet's porcelain vary greatly, depending on the handwork involved, how many colors are used, and often, if a piece is decorated in gold.

SHOPPING CENTER BRASILIA, Praça Mouzinho de Albuquerque 113. Tel. 69-74-25.
The bustle, the multilevel attractions, and the omnipresent marble floors here evoke an upscale shopping complex in South America—but the merchandise and patrons are pure Portuguese. Its main entrance faces the snarling lion and bloodied eagle atop the column of the Praça Mouzinho de Albuquerque, one of the city's busiest commercial centers. This is the most important shopping complex in Porto, laden with all kinds of goods and services—such as shoes, casual wear, sportswear, haute couture, furs, jewelry, electronic gadgets, libraries, toys, ceramics, furniture, supermarket, exchange, and unusual bars and restaurants. In fact, spread before you will be the flashiest array of merchandise in the north of Portugal. It's open until midnight. Bus: 82 or 84.

WHERE TO STAY

Until recently there was a lack of top-rated accommodations in this capital of the north, some of its so-called first-class hotels acceptable only in the direst of emergencies. However, in the 1980s the outlook brightened considerably: With the addition of several new first-class and deluxe hotels and the restoration of some interesting older properties, Porto now provides the most interesting selection of superior accommodations north of Lisbon.

EXPENSIVE

GRANDE HOTEL DE BATALHA, Praça da Batalha 116, 4000 Porto. Tel. 02/200-05-71, or toll free 800/528-12-34 in the U.S. Fax 02/200-24-68. 150 rms. A/C TV TEL **Bus:** 35, 37, or 38.
$ Rates (including breakfast): 18,000$ ($109.80) single; 23,000$ ($140.30) double. AE, DC, MC, V.
Grande Hotel de Batalha, completely restored in 1992, is highly favored by international port wine buyers. A substantial businessperson's hotel in the center of the city, it has comfortable guest rooms with radios and an excellent restaurant featuring Portuguese specialties. The guest rooms have a lighter decorative treatment than the public rooms, yet the lounge, the bar, and the restaurant are quite adequate.

HOTEL INFANTE DE SAGRES, Praça Fillipa de Lancastre 42, 4000 Porto. Tel. 02/201-90-31, or toll free 800/528-12-34 in the U.S. Fax 02/31-49-37. 74 rms. A/C MINIBAR TV TEL **Bus:** 35, 37, or 38.
$ Rates (including breakfast): 30,000$–33,000$ ($183–$201.30) single or double. AE, DC, MC, V. **Parking:** 800$ ($4.90).
⭐ The most traditional choice of visitors to Porto is the plushly furnished Infante de Sagres. The hotel sits immediately to the side of a monumental square flanked by the town hall and Porto's showplace, Avenida dos Aliados. Its rich handcrafted ornamentation convinces most visitors it dates from the 19th century;

actually, it was constructed in 1951 by a wealthy textile manufacturer. Its imposing mass of carved paneling, stained glass, and wrought iron was assembled solely to house the businessman's powerful clients during their trips to Porto.

One of the most beautiful mantelpieces found in any Portuguese hotel sits beneath the circular balcony ventilating the upstairs music room. The fireplace was designed and carved by one of the hotel's former night porters in his spare time over a period of years.

The hotel's rosters are filled with the names of rich and famous clients who once settled themselves into one of the upholstered armchairs in the antique-laden lobbies. They include Princess Anne and Prince Philip, the president of Portugal and many of his cabinet ministers, the governor of São Paulo, and everybody from the president of Zaire to delegations from the People's Republic of China. The hotel maintains one of the highest ratios of employees to guests (1.3 employees per room) in Porto and offers excellent service. The management has created a parasol- and plant-dotted sun terrace within a central courtyard for warm-weather enjoyment. The guest rooms contain large marble-covered baths and elegant, conservative furniture. Laundry and 24-hour room service are available.

The hotel's high-ceilinged dining room, Dona Filipa, serves formal breakfasts, lunches, and dinners in an old-world setting.

HOTEL IPANEMA, Rua Campo Alegre 156, 4100 Porto. Tel. 02/66-80-61. Fax 02/606-33-39. 150 rms. A/C MINIBAR TV TEL

$ Rates (including breakfast): 23,000$ ($140.30) single; from 28,000$ ($170.80) double. AE, DC, MC, V. **Parking:** Free.

The Ipanema, which opened in 1984, is one of the best four-star hotels in Portugal. It is not to be confused with the five-star Ipanema Park Hotel. A sleek modern structure, it has become a feature of the city's skyline, with elongated rows of smoked glass that are visible from the highway stretching toward Lisbon. In fact, one of the establishment's best points is that it's easy to find. Just exit the highway from Lisbon at the signs indicating the direction of Porto, and you'll find it on a cobblestone-covered road leading to the town center, about a mile away. Inside, an attractive and dimly lit bar looks over a plant-filled atrium. The marble-walled lobby contains an unusual collection of Brazilian sculpture, perhaps to honor the hotel's namesake. Each handsomely furnished guest room is accented with cedar and has views over Porto, plus a radio. Meals in the Restaurant Rios are especially popular on Sunday, when a buffet is served.

LE MÉRIDIEN PORTO, Avenida da Boavista 1466, 4100 Porto. Tel. 02/600-19-13. Fax 02/600-20-31. 232 rms, 6 suites. A/C MINIBAR TV TEL **Bus:** Boavista 78.

$ Rates: 26,000$–29,000$ ($158.60–$176.90) single; 29,000$–32,000$ ($176.90–$195.20) double; 55,000$ ($335.50) suite. Breakfast 1,800$ ($11) extra. AE, DC, MC, V. **Parking:** Free.

One of the most dramatically modern hotels in town is fronted with three vertical rows of bay windows stretching to the top of its skyscraping concrete shell. You'll pass beneath a jutting five-sided entrance portico before finding yourself inside this hotel, which is owned by Air France and was designed especially to make both business travelers and vacationers feel at home. Dozens of plants are reflected in the mirrors, which seem to enlarge the marble- and chrome-covered lobby. The musician performing in the modern lobby bar might be accompanied by a synthesizer, making the ambience there smooth and mellow. Opened in 1984, the hotel provides well-furnished guest rooms, each with in-house video movies. Offered to guests are 24-hour room service, laundry and babysitting services, massages, a hairdresser, a health club, and a business center. The hotel stands about 2 miles from the heart of the city.

The basement-level disco is open Monday to Saturday from 10:30pm to 4am. The terrace restaurant is covered separately in my dining recommendations.

TIVOLI PORTO-ATLÂNTICO, Rua Afonso Lopes Vieira 61, 4100 Porto. Tel. 02/69-49-41. Fax 02/606-74-52. 58 rms. A/C MINIBAR TV TEL **Bus:** 3 or 78.

$ Rates (including breakfast): 27,000$ ($164.70) single; 32,000$ ($195.20) double. AE, DC, MC, V. **Parking:** Free.

Tivoli Porto-Atlântico is the residential facility of a complex of commercial buildings on the outskirts of Porto. The hotel's carpeted guest rooms have balconies and all the conveniences of a five-star hostelry. Laundry, babysitting, and 24-hour room service are available. Facilities include a cinema, a gymnasium, an indoor/outdoor pool, and a sauna.

On the premises is a fine restaurant, Foco (see "Where to Dine," below), with efficient and polite service. The warmly paneled bar has comfortable, low-slung leather chairs, and there's an outdoor terrace.

MODERATE

DOM HENRÍQUE, Rua Guedes de Azevedo 179, 4000 Porto. Tel. 02/ 200-57-55. Fax 02/201-94-51. 90 rms, 22 suites. A/C MINIBAR TV TEL **Bus:** 29 or 59.

$ Rates (including breakfast): 12,200$–21,700$ ($74.40–$132.40) single; 13,600$–24,400$ ($83–$148.80) double; from 32,500$ ($198.30) suite. AE, DC, MC, V.

Even though it was conceived for commercial travelers, Dom Henríque is equally accommodating to tourists. In the city center, this recently restored hotel rises 18 floors. Executive suites are available, and although it's considered generally a moderately priced hotel, this establishment has some extra large and amenity-filled guest rooms that are at the "expensive" end of the price scale. Each well-furnished accommodation is equipped with videos, a radio, and a hairdryer. Laundry, babysitting, and room service are available.

Spectacular views can be seen from the hotel's 17th-floor bar, Anrrique, and 18th-floor restaurant/grill, O Navegador. Food is served daily from 12:30 to 2pm and 7:30 to 10pm, with meals costing from 3,400$ ($20.70). On the ground floor, clients can order light meals at the coffee shop, Tábula, which is open daily from 7am to 2am.

PORTO SHERATON, Avenida da Boavista 1269, 4100 Porto. Tel. 02/69-91-41, or toll-free 800/334-84-84 in the U.S. Fax 02/609-14-67. 236 rms, 17 suites. A/C MINIBAR TV TEL **Bus:** Boavista 78. **Tram:** 2.

$ Rates (including breakfast): 15,000$ ($91.50) single; 18,000$ ($109.80) double; from 50,000$ ($305) suite. AE, DC, MC, V. **Parking:** Free.

Opened with a flourish in 1986, this is now considered one of the most stylish and desirable modern hotels in Porto. It rises across the street from its most noteworthy competitor, the Méridien, above the apartments and private villas of the Boavista section, a short distance from the commercial center of the city. Set back from a busy street and ringed with free parking, it was designed with bands of differently hued stone and rows of bronze-colored glass to reflect the sunlight. Inside, leather chairs are arranged in conversational clusters. Each guest room offers a hairdryer, a radio, and video movies. Services include laundry/valet/dry cleaning, babysitting, a beauty parlor and hairdresser, and 24-hour room service. The hotel offers a heated pool, a squash court, and a health club.

The premier restaurant of the hotel, Madruga, provides both international and regional cuisine, with meals costing from 2,900$ ($17.70) to 4,400$ ($26.80). A businessperson's buffet lunch is provided from 12:30 to 3pm on Monday to Friday. In the evening, the chef recommends his gourmet menu, served until 11pm. The lobby's Nautilus Bar is open daily from 9am to 2am. Famous piano tunes are played nightly, as guests sample the finest port from the hotel's port wine cellars.

INEXPENSIVE

ALBERGARIA DE SÃO JOSÉ, Rua da Alegria 172, 4000 Porto. Tel. 02/208-02-61. Fax 02/32-04-46. 43 rms. A/C TV TEL

$ Rates (including breakfast): 8,000$ ($48.80) single; 9,600$ ($58.60) double. AE, DC, MC, V. **Parking:** 800$ ($4.90).

This first-class modern inn has all the facilities you'll need for a pleasant stay in Porto. While the lobby, the lounge, and the bar are decorated in a contemporary style, the guest rooms have antique furnishings that connect you with regional Portugal, plus radios. The carved mahogany beds are old world in their elegance. Breakfast is the only meal served.

ALBERGARIA MIRADOURO, Rua da Alegria 598, 4000 Porto. Tel. 02/57-07-17. Fax 02/57-02-06. 30 rms. A/C TV TEL **Bus:** 29 or 59.
$ Rates (including breakfast): 10,600$ ($64.70) single; 13,000$ ($79.30) double. AE, DC, MC, V. **Parking:** 800$ ($4.90).

The Albergaria Miradouro is like an eagle's nest, a slim 13-floor skyscraper built atop a hill outside the main part of the city. The Miradouro offers vista-scanning rooms (you can watch ships laden with port making their way to the open sea). The small-scale public rooms are tasteful. The lower bar is decorated with wall tiles from Japan and Portugal. Two plush elevators whisk you to an upper bar, with walls opening onto a view. The corner guest rooms are preferred, of course; in each of these, two walls have built-in wardrobes and chests (with a built-in pair of beds), and the walls are glass. In each room you'll find a vestibule, luggage storage, a valet stand, desks, and a sitting room.

HOTEL CASTOR, Rua da Alegria 685, 4000 Porto. Tel. 02/57-00-14. Fax 02/56-60-76. 58 rms. A/C TV MINIBAR TEL **Bus:** 29 or 59.
$ Rates (including breakfast): 11,000$ ($67.10) single; 13,000$ ($79.30) double. AE, DC, MC, V.

Built in the late 1960s, this white-walled hotel lies within a relatively quiet neighborhood in a section of town rarely visited by tourists. Known for its pleasant staff and its scattering of antiques, the Castor boasts a comfortably contemporary interior where two stylish restaurants do a respectable business in their own right, including an Italian-style trattoria offering pizzas along with other specialties. A favorite corner of the hotel is an English-style pub where a large-screen TV shows transmissions from throughout Europe. The format is that of a stylish pub (music is played only on weekends). The conservatively decorated guest rooms contain radios. Laundry, babysitting, and room service are available.

HOTEL SÃO JOÃO, Rua do Bonjardim 120, 4000 Porto. Tel. 02/200-16-62. Fax 02/31-61-14. 14 rms. TV TEL **Transportation:** Near all transportation at the hub of Estação São Bento.
$ Rates (including breakfast): 10,500$–12,000$ ($64.10–$73.20) single; 12,000$–13,000$ ($73.20–$79.30) double. AE, DC, MC, V. **Parking:** Nearby commercial garage.

The São João is in a class by itself: the only hotel-residencia of its type to be rated deluxe by the government. Such a designation shows what a deep imprint human warmth can make on a limited framework, especially when the owners have good taste, a certain flair, and a concern for the welfare of their guests. Accomplishing this is the Baldaque family, who own the top floor of a modern building right in the heart of Porto.

The living room is inviting with its fireplace nook, deep sofa, and antiques, such as a grandfather clock. The main corridor leading to the guest rooms is like an art gallery, with old tapestries, high-back 18th-century chairs, engravings, and large copper bowls of flowers. The guest rooms—all doubles—combine modern with traditional furnishings and have sitting areas.

BUDGET

ALBERGARIA GIRASSOL, Rua Sa da Bandeira 133, 4000 Porto. Tel. 02/200-18-91. Fax 02/208-38-82. 18 rms. TV TEL **Bus:** 35, 37 or 38.
$ Rates (including breakfast): 6,000$ ($36.60) single; 8,000$ ($48.80) double. No credit cards.

The Albergaria Girassol is a modest little inn one flight above street level. The hotel offers nicely designed and furnished guest rooms with built-in headboards. Rooms at the rear are quieter. There's a small TV lounge with soft leather chairs, all tasteful and cozy. You can have your morning meal in a little breakfast room. Laundry and room service are available.

CASTELO DE SANTA CATARINA, Rua de Santa Catarina 1347, 4000 Porto. Tel. 02/49-55-99. Fax 02/410-66-13. 21 rms, 4 suites. TV TEL **Bus:** 49 or 53.

$ Rates (including breakfast): 6,500$ ($39.70) single; 7,500$ ($45.80) double; 9,500$ ($58) suite. No credit cards. **Parking:** Free.

What used to be one of the residential showplaces of Porto is behind a high wall in a commercial neighborhood about a mile from the center. In the 1920s, a Brazilian military officer returned to his native Porto determined to create the most flamboyant villa in town. Drawing on the resources of his influential family, who manufactured ceramic tiles, he created a sprawling compound of greenhouses, terraced gardens, a chapel, and a sumptuous main house. To encircle them, he added a semicircular crescent of servants' quarters. Today the tile-covered exterior walls almost give an encapsulated history of Portugal.

After ringing the bell, you'll be ushered down a labyrinthine series of halls and narrow stairways. To get to your room, you'll pass through opulent but disorganized sitting rooms and ballrooms, illuminated with crystal chandeliers. Each of the small guest rooms contains a set of carved antique furniture, often of rosewood. The plumbing fixtures are designed with a florid, appealing art nouveau flair. Laundry, babysitting, and 24-hour room service are available.

HOTEL PENINSULAR, Rua Sa da Bandeira 21, 4000 Porto. Tel. 02/200-30-12. Fax 02/208-49-84. 52 rms (all with bath or shower). TV TEL **Transportation:** Near all transportation at the hub of Estação de São Bento.

$ Rates (including breakfast): 5,400$ ($32.90) single; 7,200$ ($43.90) double. AE, DC, MC, V.

The only reminder of this building's original purpose as an outbuilding to a nearby church is a lobby mural of a coronation crafted from blue-and-white tiles. Today the building is an unpretentiously pleasant hotel, outfitted with simple and low-cost guest rooms. It stands near the train station of São Bento in the heart of the city. There's a restaurant one floor above the street, which is accessible via a darkly stained stairway near the reception desk. The belle époque facade is marked with an incongruous neon sign. Laundry, babysitting, and 24-hour room service are available, but there is no parking unless you are lucky enough to find a place on the street.

PENSÃO RESIDENCIAL REX, Praça da República 117, 4000 Porto. Tel. 02/200-45-48. 21 rms. TEL **Bus:** 6 or 78.

$ Rates (including breakfast): 6,500$–7,500$ ($39.70–$45.80) single or double. MC, V. **Parking:** Free.

The facade of this establishment fits in gracefully with its location on one of the most beautiful squares of Porto. Its design is a classicized derivation of art nouveau, replete with sea-green tiles, cast-iron embellishments, and Roman-style window treatments. The semimajestic marble staircase leading into the reception area from the street is lined with richly colored paneling. The lobby and the guest rooms are crowned with ornately molded plaster ceilings embellished with painted highlights, and much of the furniture is antique. The bathrooms have been modernized. There's a tiny bar in the TV lounge at the back of the ground floor but no restaurant. The iron gates enclosing an adjacent driveway swing open on request to allow you to park a car.

WHERE TO DINE

When Prince Henry the Navigator was rounding up the cattle in the Douro Valley for his men aboard the legendary caravels, he shipped out the juicy steaks and left the tripe behind. Faced with the tripe, the denizens of Porto responded bravely and began inventing recipes for it. To this day they carry the appellation of tripe eaters, and it has become their favorite local dish. To sample the most characteristic specialty of Porto, you can order *tripas à moda do Porto* (tripe stewed with spicy sausage and string beans). Of course, the city offers other viands, and quite good ones at that.

EXPENSIVE

AQUÁRIO MARISQUEIRO, Rua Rodrigues Sampaio 170. Tel. 200-22-31.
  Cuisine: SEAFOOD. **Reservations:** Required. **Bus:** 7, 77, or 79.
$ **Prices:** Appetizers 600$–1,100$ ($3.70–$6.70); main courses 2,500$–4,000$
  ($15.30–$24.40); fixed-price menu 2,500$ ($15.30). MC, V.
  Open: Mon–Sat 11:30am–11pm.

⭐ Aquário Marisqueiro is one of the finest seafood restaurants in Porto—in fact, it's actually two restaurants connected by a central kitchen. Its location is within sight of the City Hall and close to two leading hotels—the Infante de Sagres and Hotel São João. Marine fare reigns supreme at this "aquarium." Soup made by boiling the shells of *mariscos* is a good beginner. Main fish orders include cod, of course. An excellent fish dish is clams Spanish style, but the house specialty is *açorda* (a type of bread *panada*) of shellfish. The prices of these two dishes vary according to the season. Sole is your safest bet, and trout with ham is even more interesting.

LES TERRASSES, in Le Méridien Porto, Avenida da Boavista 1466. Tel. 600-19-13.
  Cuisine: PORTUGUESE/FRENCH. **Reservations:** Required. **Bus:** Boavista 78.
$ **Prices:** Appetizers 650$–1,200$ ($4–$7.30); main courses 1,400$–3,500$
  ($8.50–$21.40). AE, DC, MC, V.
  Open: Lunch daily 12:30–3pm; dinner daily 7:30–11pm.

Les Terrasses advertises itself as a restaurant/brasserie, but its uniformed maître d'hôtel and its plush gardenlike decor give it the aura of a formal dining room. Located off the lobby of this hotel owned by Air France, it lies nearly 3 miles from the city center. A wooden terrace, covered with lacy cast-iron garden furniture, offers the option of dining under the trees outside. Most guests, however, prefer the air-conditioned interior because of the noise of passing traffic. Tables are separated into semiprivate alcoves. Menu specialties reflect a strong French influence, with the addition of many Portuguese regional dishes. The wine steward will be pleased to suggest a reasonably priced Portuguese vintage to accompany your meal.

PORTUCALE RESTAURANTE, atop the Albergaria Miradouro, Rua da Alegria 598. Tel. 57-07-17.
  Cuisine: PORTUGUESE. **Reservations:** Required. **Bus:** 29 or 59.
$ **Prices:** Appetizers 750$–1,800$ ($4.60–$11); main courses 1,800$–4,200$
  ($11–$25.60). AE, DC, MC, V.
  Open: Lunch daily 12:30–3pm; dinner daily 7:30–10pm.

⭐ The Portucale, perhaps the best restaurant in town, perches on the rooftop of the Albergaria Miradouro. Seemingly the highest point in town, outside the heart of the city, it offers wide views of the river, the boats, and the rooftops. Two elevators zip you to the 13th floor, from which you ascend to the dining room via a spiral staircase, crossing a tiny lily-and-fish pond. Despite the infinity of the panoramic sweep, the restaurant is fairly intimate, its tables set with fine silver, china, and flowers. There's an appetizing pastry cart.

The hand-woven hanging is by Camarinha, the artist who designed the à la carte menu. Specialties of the house include *bacalhau* (dried codfish) *à marinheiro*, *cabrito à serrana* (kid in wine sauce), smoked swordfish, *lomos do pescado*, steak flambé, rice and mushrooms, and homemade cakes.

MODERATE

A BRASILEIRA, Rua do Bonjardim 116. Tel. 200-71-46.
  Cuisine: PORTUGUESE. **Reservations:** Not necessary. **Transportation:**
  Near the transportation hub of Estação de São Bento.
$ **Prices:** Appetizers 150$–1,500$ ($0.90–$9.20); main courses 850$–1,800$
  ($5.20–$11); tourist menu 1,650$ ($10.10). AE, DC, MC, V.
  Open: Mon–Sat noon–11pm.

A Brasileira is an art deco coffeehouse, the virtual social center of Porto, plus a first-class restaurant and a bustling snack bar. In the restaurant part of the complex you can order cream of shellfish soup, then follow with a main dish such as roast chicken, grilled trout, or veal liver; you can finish with chocolate mousse. Specialties include *bolinhos de bacalhau* (codfish).

FOCO, in Hotel Tivoli Porto-Atlântico, Rua Afonso Lopes Vieira 86. Tel. 66-72-48.
   Cuisine: PORTUGUESE. **Reservations:** Recommended. **Bus:** 3 or 78.
$ Prices: Appetizers 650$–1100$ ($4–$6.70); main courses 1,200$–2,500$ ($7.30–$15.30). AE, DC, MC, V.
   Open: Lunch daily 12:30–3pm; dinner daily 7–11pm.
The entrance to this attractive restaurant outside town is adjacent to the already-recommended hotel. It's worth the excursion by taxi or bus from the center, partially because of its unobtrusive and polite but very thorough service. You'll find the establishment within a quadrangle created by a complex of residential apartment buildings, a few minutes' drive past Le Méridien. Before dinner, you can enjoy a drink in one of the low-slung leather chairs in a tiny corner of the restaurant. You'll then be ushered past a screen of plants to a chair in the luxuriously modern dining room. From the windows you'll have a view of the pool. Meals might include trout Transmontana style, grilled squid on a skewer, pork chunks Minho style, roasted kid, smoked salmon, and a daily specialty of the chef.

GARRAFÃO, Rua António Nobre 53, Leça da Palmeira. Tel. 995-17-35.
   Cuisine: PORTUGUESE/SEAFOOD. **Reservations:** Recommended.
$ Prices: Appetizers 650$–1,200$ ($4–$7.30); main courses 1,400$–2,800$ ($8.50–$17.10). AE, DC, MC, V.
   Open: Lunch Mon–Sat noon–5pm; dinner Mon–Sat 7pm–midnight.
Garrafão, a traditional restaurant in the suburbs, overlooks the Praia Boa Nova. Attractively situated, with a pleasant decor, it seats about 100. The prices of the seafood specialties vary according to the season. The Garrafao is known also for its wine cellar, containing a large selection of the best Portuguese wines. À la carte Portuguese specialties feature shrimp omelet, shellfish soup, grilled sole, veal dishes, and caramel custard. The restaurant has a pleasant dining room with windows over the beach.

MESA ANTIGA, Rua de Santo Ildefonso 208. Tel. 200-64-32.
   Cuisine: PORTUGUESE. **Reservations:** Recommended.
$ Prices: Appetizers 450$–1,200$ ($2.70–$7.30); main courses 1,400$–2,200$ ($8.50–$13.40). MC, V.
   Open: Sun–Fri noon–midnight. **Closed:** Sept 15–30.
Mesa Antiga's impeccably crafted blue-and-white tiles combine with its gnarled ceiling beams for a hint of the dignified severity of old Portugal. Above well-ordered rows of dining tables, brass trumpets rise from the curves of brass chandeliers. The food served here, all homemade, is among the best regional cuisine in Porto. Conjured from a tiny kitchen by members of the owner's family, platters emerge steaming hot. Specialties include a delectable version of grilled sole served with fresh and aromatic green sauce, squid on a spit, and an array of daily specials. The most typical dish is tripe prepared in the old-fashioned method of Porto. The restaurant is on a crowded narrow street in the commercial center.

RESTAURANTE CHINÉS, Avenida Vimara Peres 38. Tel. 200-89-15.
   Cuisine: CHINESE. **Reservations:** Not necessary. **Bus:** 15.
$ Prices: Appetizers 450$–900$ ($2.70–$5.50); main courses 1,100$–1,800$ ($6.70–$11). AE, DC, MC, V.
   Open: Lunch daily 12:30–2:30pm; dinner daily 7:30–10:30pm.
Chinés is Porto's leading Chinese restaurant. Housed in a modern building at the entrance to Dom Luís I Bridge, it is a spacious two-level dining room with an incongruous combination of the new and the old. Setting the mood are traditional Chinese lanterns and a dragon mural. For your appetizer you might select egg-flower

soup, fried wonton, or even fried almonds. Main courses include prawns with curry, sweet-and-sour fish, and breast of chicken with pineapple. For dessert, there are many appetizing selections, including bananas with honey.

RESTAURANTE ESCONDIDINHO, Rua Passos Manuel 144. Tel. 200-10-79.
   Cuisine: PORTUGUESE. **Reservations:** Required. **Transportation:** Near the transportation hub of Estação de São Bento.
$ Prices: Appetizers 650$–950$ ($4–$5.80); main courses 1,100$–1,800$ ($6.70–$11). AE, DC, MC, V.
   Open: Lunch Mon–Sat noon–3pm; dinner daily 7–10pm.
Escondidinho (meaning "hidden" or "masked") is a regional tavern, popular with the leading port wine merchants and the English. The entrance alone is a clue, a facade in burnt-orange tile framing an arch leading to the L-shaped dining room. Inside is a world of time-blackened beams and timbers, a corner baronial stone fireplace, and carved wooden shelf brackets holding a collection of antique Portuguese ceramics. The chairs, with their intricate carving and brass studs, are just right for a cardinal or at least a friar. The waiters are old world yet proud of the prevailing informality. They feel free to speak their minds, candidly telling you the day's best dishes.
   The shellfish soup and the charcoaled sardines are always reliable. The chef's special dishes include hake in Madeira sauce and chateaubriand for two. Desserts include kirsch omelet and orange pudding.

RESTAURANTE ORFEU, Rua de Júlio Dinis 928. Tel. 606-43-22.
   Cuisine: PORTUGUESE/CONTINENTAL. **Reservations:** Not necessary.
$ Prices: Appetizers 450$–900$ ($2.70–$5.50); main courses 1,000$–2,100$ ($6.10–$12.80). AE, DC, MC, V.
   Open: Daily 8am–midnight.
Don't confuse this completely competent air-conditioned restaurant with the shabby cafe/snack bar that occupies its street level. Descend stone stairs to reach the basement-level restaurant, which is especially popular with Porto's business community. Once seated at one of the roomy tables, you'll find a battalion of polite waiters ready to take your order. You can select from such dishes as leg of lamb, chateaubriand, partridge, or hare. Calves' kidneys are prepared with Madeira sauce, and for dessert you might like the bananas with cognac.

RESTAURANTE TRIPEIRO, Rua Passos Manuel 195. Tel. 200-58-86.
   Cuisine: PORTUGUESE. **Reservations:** Not necessary. **Bus:** 15.
$ Prices: Appetizers 450$–1,000$ ($2.70–$6.10); main courses 1,100$–2,200$ ($6.70–$13.40). AE, DC, MC, V.
   Open: Lunch Mon–Sat noon–3pm; dinner Mon–Sat 7–10:30pm.
This restaurant's textured stucco walls and elaborately crafted wooden ceiling offer a cool, dark retreat from the glaring sunlight. A group of efficient waiters serves full meals. You can enjoy *vinho verde* (green wine), which is ideal with the specialty of the chef, *tripas* (tripe) *à moda do Porto,* in honor of the namesake of the restaurant. In addition, you might order several preparations of codfish or any of several beef or shellfish dishes (the latter priced by the kilo).

INEXPENSIVE

ABADIA, Rua do Ateneu Comércial do Porto 22. Tel. 200-87-57.
   Cuisine: PORTUGUESE. **Reservations:** Not accepted.
$ Prices: Appetizers 350$–550$ ($2.10–$3.40); main courses 650$–1,200$ ($4–$7.30). No credit cards.
   Open: Oct–May, daily noon–10pm; June–Sept, Mon–Sat noon–10pm.
The large and clean Abadia stands on a short street with a patio entrance. It has an open dining mezzanine. The cook specializes in fresh fish dishes, such as codfish Abadia and codfish Gomes de Sá. He also offers other dishes, such as tripe stew Porto and fried pork. Soups here are hearty and full of flavor. English is definitely not spoken.

TAVERNA DO BEBOBOS, Cais de Ribeira 21–25. Tel. 31-35-65.
  Cuisine: PORTUGUESE. **Reservations:** Required. **Bus:** 15.
$ Prices: Appetizers 250$–650$ ($1.50–$4); main courses 850$–1,800$ ($5.20–$11). No credit cards.
  Open: Lunch Mon–Sat noon–2:30pm; dinner Mon–Sat 7–9:30pm.

⑤ Taverna do Bebobos, located directly on the riverside dock, is perhaps the oldest (founded 1876) and smallest restaurant in Porto. Women sell fish on the quay, and overhead, fluttering from wrought-iron balconies, are lines of laundry. Inside, the ground floor has a service bar with every sort of knickknack on its little tables. A narrow open staircase leads to an intimate dining room upstairs with a corner stone fireplace, a coved ceiling, an iron scale filled with sprouting onions, a 5-foot-high coffee mill, brass and copper pans, ships' lanterns, and a flamboyantly painted pottery crèche. On the tables are hunks of crusty dark bread, and the portions are large enough to be shared. To begin your typically Portuguese meal, you might order a hearty bowl of *caldo verde* or a plate of grilled sardines. For a main course, I'd suggest either trout with ham, regional codfish, or pork prepared Alentejana style (with savory clam sauce). A fruit salad finishes the meal nicely. Because of the small number of tables, it's necessary to have your hotel call and make a reservation for you.

EVENING ENTERTAINMENT

DRINKS [CHEQUERS] PUB, Shopping Center Brasilia, fifth floor, Praça Mouzinho de Albuquerque 113. Tel. 69-73-25.
  This is a watering hole within a massive shopping center. It opens at 1pm but isn't dependent on the whims of shoppers, as it remains open until 2am, long after the last shopper has retreated. The decor is warmly upholstered and modern, and the place is popular with young people, who order beer at 250$ ($1.50) or mixed drinks costing from 600$ ($3.70). A small band plays on Friday and Saturday nights.

MAJESTIC CAFÉ, Rua de Santa Catarina 112. Tel. 200-38-87.
  While in Porto, you shouldn't miss having coffee in one of the old-time "Brazilian" cafes. The local favorite is the Majestic, one of those ornate places where burghers and poets congregated. The wood-and-mirror decor, jasper pillars, and sculpted cherubs over pilasters evoke the craftsmanship of another era. Lining both sides of the oblong room are rows of leather-backed banquettes, in front of which two rows of round-top tables stand. In the rear is a small garden and a counter where coffee is prepared in the old way. A coffee with milk is served in a large glass placed within a bronze holder, so you won't burn your fingers. The cafe was opened in 1922 and is still going strong. You can enjoy the best of port wine and also order light meals, costing from 1,500$ ($9.20). A beer costs from 110$ (70¢). It is open Monday through Saturday from 8am to 11pm.

MAL COZINHADO, Rua do Outeirinho 13. Tel. 208-13-19.
  The real *fado* is in Lisbon, but Porto does offer a club or two where you can hear these typical songs and listen to guitar music. Mal Cozinhado, a *casa de fado* near the river, is the best, with excellent music. The so-called Bad Kitchen also serves food, but in case its name frightens you away you can visit for drinks only. A minimum of 3,200$ ($19.50) is imposed, but it can be spent on drinks. A tourist menu costs 3,500$ ($21.40), although it costs from 7,000$ ($42.70) to dine à la carte. Hours are Monday through Saturday from 8:30pm to 3am.

TWIN'S RESTAURANT/TWIN'S DISCO, Rua do Passeio Alegre 1000. Tel. 618-57-40.
  These establishments are found in one of the most fashionable parts of Porto, the Foz. The restaurant is chic and sophisticated, perhaps more so than any other spot in town. After a satisfying meal, you can enjoy action in the disco club, contained in the same three-story building near the beach at the mouth of the Douro. Reservations are recommended for dinner on the top floor, which is served Monday through Saturday from 8pm to 3:30am, full meals costing from 6,000$ ($36.60) à la carte or 2,500$

($15.30) on the tourist menu. Specialties include crabmeat crêpes, fresh fish, and an array of grilled meats prepared in both classic and modern ways. One floor above the restaurant is a pub where an open fireplace and a piano player compete for attention. Alluring and sedate, the pub is open daily from 8pm to 4am. On the street level, the disco is open nightly from 11pm to 4am. Entrance to its black-and-white precincts costs 1,000$ ($6.10). Once inside, you can spend that amount on drinks, which cost 1,000$ ($6.10) each. The restaurant section closes in August. Tram: 18.

SOLAR DO VINHO DO PORTO [Romantic Museum of Quinta da Maceirinha], Rua de Entre Quintas 220. Tel. 69-11-31.

There's no better way to begin your evening in Porto than by paying a visit here. The establishment is maintained by the Port Wine Institute, a government body that controls the quality of the wine and authorizes its export. Visitors can taste the different types of port on Monday through Friday from 10am to 11:30pm and on Saturday from 11am to 10:30pm. Drinks begin at 100$ (60¢). In this old building, you will also have a view of the Douro. Bus: 78.

EASY EXCURSIONS

The long, busy beach at **Matosinhos,** 5 miles north of Porto, draws large crowds in good weather, although the site is much too industrialized for most international visitors. The bustling little fishing town lies at the mouth of the River Leca. It is reached by following Avenida da Boavista out of the city. Separated by rocky crags are the beaches of Matosinhos, Leca (which also has swimming pools), Cabo do Mundo, Paraso, and Angeiras.

In the town, you can visit the **Church of Bom Jesus of Matosinhos,** whose major treasure is an ancient wooden statue of Christ at the end of the high altar. The statue has made the church a place of annual pilgrimages. The 18th-century church has coats-of-arms, pinnacles, and torches on the exterior.

2. ESPINHO

11 miles S of Porto; 191 miles N of Lisbon

GETTING THERE   By Train   From Porto, southbound trains depart from Estação de São Bento about every hour during the day (trip time: 20 minutes).

By Bus   Southbound buses depart from Porto at the Garage Atlântico, Rua Alexandre Herculano, near Praça de Batalha (tel. 02/72-03-23). Buses heading for Espinho leave about once every hour. Trip time is 30 minutes, costing 225$ ($1.40) one way.

By Car   From Porto, head south along route IC-1.

ESSENTIALS   The **Tourist Office** is at Ángulo das Ruas 6 (tel. 72-09-11). The **telephone area code** is 02.

Espinho is a popular place on the Costa Verde. This modern beach resort offers many activities and is drawing larger crowds of vacationers each year. The town has a range of shops, restaurants, hotels, and campsites in the pinewoods near the sandy beach. Sports enthusiasts will find tennis courts, a bullfighting ring, and an 18-hole golf course.

The big gray **Casino Solverde** at Espinho (tel. 02/72-40-45), open all year, has a restaurant and nightclub in addition to the gaming tables. Here you can play roulette, French banque, baccarat, and slot machines. International cabaret is offered in the nightclub. It is open daily from 3pm to 3am.

Water sports available here include sailing and rowing on the Paramos Lagoon and surfing in the Atlantic. Cabanas line part of the beach, and there are pools in the Solar Atlantico recreation complex overlooking the ocean.

WHERE TO STAY & DINE
MODERATE

HOTEL PRAIAGOLFE, Rua 6, 4500 Espinho. Tel. 02/72-06-30. Fax 02/72-08-88. 133 rms, 6 suites. A/C TV TEL
$ Rates (including breakfast): 15,400$ ($93.90) single; 19,200$ ($117.10) double; 27,750$ ($169.30) suite. AE, DC, MC, V. **Parking:** Free.

The best place to stay in Espinho is the Praiagolfe, a totally renovated accommodation offering many modern comforts. It overlooks the sea, with the railway station about 165 feet away. A fixed-price lunch or dinner here costs from 2,900$ ($17.70). The hotel offers an indoor pool, a squash court, and a health club, as well as a disco. Tennis courts and golf courses are nearby. In summer, the establishment is almost continuously booked, so reservations are imperative.

NEARBY PLACE TO STAY & DINE
MODERATE

HOTEL SOLVERDE/GRANJA, Estrada N109, Praia da Granja, 4400 Vila Nova de Gaia. Tel. 02/72-66-66. Fax 02/72-62-36. 166 rms, 8 suites. A/C MINIBAR TV TEL
$ Rates (including breakfast): 16,200$ ($98.80) single; 18,700$ ($114.10) double; 32,800$ ($200.10) suite. AE, DC, MC, V. **Parking:** Free.

The Solverde/Granja is one of the most luxurious hotels in the north of Portugal. Opened in 1989, it stands on the beach of Granja, about 10 miles south of Porto, less than a mile north of Espinho, and about 20 miles from the Porto airport. The tariffs are among the lowest in Portugal for a five-star hotel with well-furnished guest rooms. Facilities include a grill and a restaurant, a coffee shop, several bars, a disco, a health club, three pools with salt water (one indoors), four tennis courts, and a heliport.

3. VILA DO CONDE

17 miles N of Porto; 212 miles N of Lisbon;
26 miles S of Viana do Castelo; 26 miles S of Póvoa do Varzim

GETTING THERE **By Train** From Porto, northbound trains heading for Vila do Conde depart from the Estação da Trindade several times throughout the day, delivering rail passengers directly to the center of the resort.

By Bus Buses heading for Vila do Conde leave Porto from Autoviação do Minho, Praça Filippa de Lancastre (tel. 200-61-21). Some three to four buses per day depart the station for Vila do Conde. Trip time is 30 minutes, costing 225$ ($1.40) one way.

By Car From Porto, head north along route IC-1.

ESSENTIALS The **Tourist Office** is at Rua 25 de Abril (tel. 64-27-00). The **telephone area code** is 052.

Lying at the mouth of the River Ave, the little town of Vila do Conde—with fortress-guarded sandy beaches, rocky reefs, and charm—has been discovered by summer vacationers. Along the wharfs you may still see piles of rough hand-hewn timbers used in the building of the sardine fleet, for shipbuilding is a traditional industry of the town, and a few wooden-hulled vessels are still made, some for the local fishing fleet and others for use on the cod banks of Newfoundland.

The women of the town have long engaged in the making of lace using a shuttle, a craft handed down from generation to generation. So revered is this activity that a festival, the Feast of St. John, from June 14 to 24, celebrates it with processions by the lacemakers, called *rendilheiras,* together with the *mordomas,* the women who manage the cottage-industry homes; the latter wear magnificent chains and other

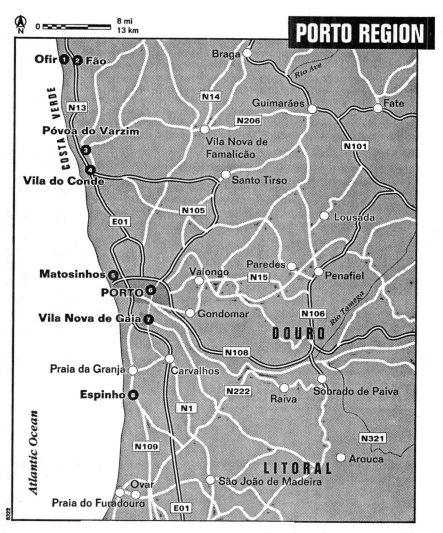

PORTO REGION

0 ⊢⊐⊐⊐⊐⊐ 8 mi
13 km

Ofir ❶ ❷ Fão
Braga
Rio Ave

COSTA VERDE

N13
N14
Guimarães
Fate

Póvoa do Varzim
N206
N101

❸
Vila Nova de Famalicão

❹
Vila do Conde
Santo Tirso

N105
Lousada

E01

N108

Matosinhos ❺
Valongo
Paredes
N15
Penafiel

PORTO ❻

Vila Nova de Gaia ❼
Gondomar
N106
Rio Tâmega

DOURO

N108

Praia da Granja
Carvalhos

Espinho ❽
N222
Raiva
Sobrado de Paiva

N1

Atlantic Ocean

N109
N321
Arouca

LITORAL
São João de Madeira

Ovar
Praia do Furadouro
E01

ornaments of gold. Lacemakers parade through the narrow 16th-century streets of the town. Visitors are welcomed free at **Escola de Rendas,** the lacemaking school on Rua de São Bento (tel. 052/63-35-20). It is open Monday through Friday from 10am to noon and 2 to 7pm and Saturday and Sunday from 3 to 6pm.

The famous hand-knit and hand-embroidered fishermen's sweaters are also made here. The making of sweets (there is a famous confectionery from convent recipes) is another occupation in the town; sweets provide part of the rich local cuisine.

WHAT TO SEE & DO

In addition to the convent listed below, the 16th-century parish church, **Igreja Matriz,** is also worth seeing. It stands in the center of town near the market. Another national monument is the **pillory,** opening onto the Praça Vasco da Gama. Built from 1538 to 1540, it consists of a graceful column, slightly twisted, which recalls many creations from the Manueline art style.

MOSTEIRO DE SANTA CLARA [Convent of St. Clare], north bank of Rio Ave.

This large, squat structure, sitting fortresslike on a hill, was founded in the 14th century. In the upper rooms you can see relics and paintings garnered through the centuries by the Poor Clares. The building is now a charity home. Simplicity and opulence play against each other in a combination of Gothic and Romanesque styles in the structure. The plain altar of its church offers contrast to the gilded stalls behind the communion grilles and the ornately decorated ceilings. A side chapel contains 14th-century sarcophagi. One is the elaborately carved tomb of Dom Afonso Sanche, founder of the convent; the feet of his effigy rest on a lion. Also here are the tomb of his wife, Dona Teresa Martins, topped by a figure dressed in the habit of a Franciscan Tertiary nun, and those of two of their children.

The present monastery was built in the 1700s, accompanied by construction of a 999-arch aqueduct bringing water from nearby Póvoa do Varzim. Part of the water conduit is still visible.

Admission: Free.

Open: Mon–Sat 9am–noon and 2–5pm.

WHERE TO STAY
BUDGET

ESTALAGEM DO BRASÃO, Avenida Dr. João Canavarro, 4480 Vila do Conde. Tel. 052/64-20-16. Fax 052/63-20-28. 26 rms, 4 suites. A/C MINIBAR TV TEL

$ Rates (including breakfast): 4,850$ ($29.60) single; 7,300$ ($44.50) double; 9,000$ ($54.90) suite. AE, DC, MC, V. **Parking:** Free.

Estalagem do Brasão is styled like a gracious *pousada.* Located in the center of the village, it's worth considering if only for its lofty dining room. The compact guest rooms are of contemporary design, with built-in headboards and comfortable armchairs. A set lunch or dinner goes for 2,500$ ($15.30). The chef turns out three specialties on the à la carte menu—codfish Brasão, beef Brasão, and omelet Brasão. There's a combination bar/disco.

WHERE TO DINE
MODERATE

PIONEIRO, Avenida Manuel Barros. Tel. 63-29-12.
  Cuisine: MINHO. **Reservations:** Required.
$ Prices: Appetizers 150$–300$ ($0.90–$1.80); main courses 1,500$–3,000$ ($9.20–$18.30); fixed-price menu 1,500$ ($9.20). AE, DC, MC, V.
  Open: Lunch Tues–Sun noon–3pm; dinner Tues–Sun 7–10pm. **Closed:** Sept 15–30.

There are a number of beachfront restaurants, of which Pioneiro is not only one of the best but also one of the largest. Offering a panoramic view of the water, it can seat up to 265 and specializes in the cookery of the region and fresh shellfish. The chef also prepares roast kid and tripe Porto style.

4. PÓVOA DO VARZIM

39 miles N of Porto; 216 miles N of Lisbon

GETTING THERE By Train From Porto, northbound trains depart every 90 minutes from the Estação da Trindade. The rail station lies outside Póvoa and requires an additional taxi ride into the center. That is why many visitors opt for the bus instead.

By Bus From Porto, buses bound for Póvoa do Varzim leave from the Autoviação do Minho, Praça Filippa de Lancastre (tel. 200-61-21). Trip time is 40 minutes, costing 275$ ($1.70) one way.

By Car From Vila do Conde (see the preceding section), continue north along route 13 for 2 miles.

ESSENTIALS The **Tourist Office** is at Avenida Mouzinho de Albuquerque 160 (tel. 62-46-09). The **telephone area code** is 052.

In this town's big bustling cafe, beneath ornate roofs and gables, skimpily clad tourists idyllically take their afternoon glass of port wine (some have several). Seemingly unaware of them, the town's *pescadores* (fishermen) go on with their work. Franz Villier wrote, "Here the boat-owners are kings, and morality reigns. Drunkards and debauchees may not aspire to the honour of fishing, unless it happens that the owner is one himself."

The southern part of the town is occupied by the fishing industry, which has remained the town's major economic support, despite its emergence as a seaside resort. On weekdays (except holidays), the auction of the fishermen's catch is fascinating to watch, the women selling what their men have brought in. Along the beach in the fishermen's quarter, huge piles of seaweed, drying for use as fertilizer, look like little round thatched huts.

Póvoa do Varzim has developed into a leading resort on the Costa Verde. Its broad, sandy north beaches are dotted with white-canvas tents known as *toldo,* suspended on two poles. Other entertainment amenities include an Olympic-size pool, tennis courts, a roller-skating rink, and a gambling casino.

WHAT TO SEE & DO

The **Casino Monumental,** Avenida de Braga (tel. 052/61-51-51), which has a restaurant offering international cuisine, is open all year daily from 3pm to 3am. The games people play are roulette, French banque, and slot machines. Nightly cabaret with a floor show is presented.

Of interest in the immediate countryside are the "sunken gardens" that farmers have established among the sand dunes. They dug deep into the sand to find moisture for their crops, planting grape vines in the sand heaps above to keep them from sliding down. From these vines, they get a good crop of wine grapes each year, and in the gardens at the bottom they produce many types of vegetables growing right out of the unfriendly sand.

WHERE TO STAY

MODERATE

VERMAR HOTEL, Avenida dos Banhos, 4490 Póvoa do Varzim. Tel. 052/61-55-66. Fax 052/61-51-15. 208 rms. A/C MINIBAR TV TEL
$ Rates (including breakfast): 13,750$ ($83.90) single; 17,000$ ($103.70) double. AE, DC, MC, V. **Parking:** Free.

The most desirable accommodation in town is the Vermar, a high-rise with well-furnished guest rooms. In fact, this is among the leading hotels of Portugal. The service, for example, is among the finest I've encountered in the north. Once you're inside, the heat, the noise, and the traffic of this bustling resort will seem far away. The hotel is about half a mile from the town center, standing back from a road flanking the shoreline.

A stylish and spacious series of ground-floor public rooms contain unusual ceramic murals, several pieces of sculpture ringed with plants, a bar, and a modern dining room. The comfortably low-slung chairs of one of the reading areas look out over the hotel's pair of curved heated pools and the nearby tennis courts. There's even an occasional Portuguese antique scattered amid the greenery and the brown marble of the interior. Each guest room boasts a sun terrace and radio. Laundry, babysitting, and 24-hour room service are available. The Vermar also offers a sauna and a playground.

The hotel contains an excellent restaurant, a grill room, and a bar. The kitchen always seems to satisfy the shellfish lovers who flock here, and much of the harvest from the sea is from local fishermen. Both Portuguese and international dishes are served.

WHERE TO DINE
MODERATE

CASA DOS FRANGOS II, Estrada Nacional 13. Tel. 68-18-80.
  Cuisine: PORTUGUESE/SEAFOOD. **Reservations:** Not necessary.
$ Prices: Appetizers 550$–1,200$ ($3.40–$7.30); main courses 1,200$–2,500$ ($7.30–$15.30). No credit cards.
  Open: Thurs–Tues noon–11pm. **Closed:** Oct.

Everybody's favorite restaurant seems to be Casa dos Frangos II, in spite of its location just north of Póvoa do Varzim on the route to Viana do Castelo. Often a very busy establishment, it is known for its fish stew, a savory kettle of Neptune's delights. Other regional specialties are served as well, and you can enjoy them in air conditioning. Most people gravitate to the *frango no churrasco* (barbecued chicken). You can also order shellfish rice.

5. OFIR & FÃO
29 miles N of Porto; 226 miles N of Lisbon; 22 miles W of Braga

GETTING THERE   By Train   There is no rail service to either Fão or Ofir. Passengers traveling by rail go first to Póvoa do Varzim, then continue the rest of the way north by bus, a distance of 9 miles.

By Bus   From Porto, buses heading for Ofir and Fão depart from Autoviação do Minho, Praça Filippa de Lancastre (tel. 200-61-21). Between three and four buses per day service the area. Trip time is 65 minutes, costing 425$ ($2.60) one way.

By Car   From Póvoa do Varzim, continue north along route 30.

ESSENTIALS   The nearest tourist office is the **Esposende Tourist Bureau,** Avenida Marginal, Esposende (tel. 053/96-13-54). The **telephone area code** is 053.

Once you pass through the pine forests of **Ofir,** you gaze down on a long white-sand spit dotted with windswept dunes and suffused with the sharp cries of sea gulls. The beach is dramatic at any time of the year but exceptional during summer. Ofir is considered by many as the best beach resort between Porto and Viana do Castelo. The White Horse Rocks, according to legend, were formed when fiery steeds from the royal stock of King Solomon were wrecked on the beach.

While Ofir's hotels offer guests every convenience in a secluded setting, the nearest shops and more local color are found 1 to 2 miles inland on an estuary of the Cavado River at **Fão,** which dates back to Roman times. Framed by mountain ridges in the background and a river valley, the village is the sleepy destination of all visitors to Ofir. The *sargaceiros* (literally, "gatherers of sargasso"), with their stout fustian tunics, rake the offshore breakers for the seaweed used in making fertilizer. On the quays, you can lunch on sardines off the smoking braziers. At the end of the day, you can soothe your overdose of sunshine with a mellow glass of port wine.

WHERE TO STAY IN OFIR

The accommodations in Ofir and Fão are among the best along the coast north of Porto.

MODERATE

HOTEL DE OFIR, Avenida Raul de Sousa Martins, Praia de Ofir, 4740 Fão. Tel. 053/98-13-83. Fax 053/98-18-71. 182 rms, 12 suites. A/C TV TEL
$ Rates (including breakfast): 11,800$–16,300$ ($72–$99.40) single; 15,700$–20,200$ ($95.80–$123.20) double; 22,400$–30,800$ ($136.60–$187.90) suite. AE, DC, MC, V. **Parking:** Free.

Hotel de Ofir competes with the resort developments on the Algarve. The hotel is divided into three sections: The older central core contains guest rooms furnished in traditional Portuguese fashion, with reproductions of regional furniture; the adjoining wings are modern. One section is quite luxurious, built motel style right along the dunes, with a row of white tents and a pure-sand beach in full view of the second-floor balconies. There are rather well-styled public rooms for the evening's activities, but the principal focus is on the wide oceanfront terrace, where guests sunbathe. The guest rooms have a well-conceived sense of style, with substantial pieces of furniture placed against pleasantly colored backgrounds; half of them offer minibars. Laundry service, babysitting and room service are available.

The hotel is a resort unto itself, with a vast playground terrace, two pools (one for children), two tennis courts, and a flagstone terrace bordering soft green lawns. The hotel has a bowling alley as well. Guests are given a 50% reduction on greens fees at a nearby golf course.

ESTALAGEM PARQUE DO RIO, Ofir, 4740 Esposende. Tel. 053/98-15-21. Fax 053-98-15-24. 36 rms. A/C TV TEL
$ Rates (including breakfast): 9,100$ ($55.50) single; 14,200$ ($86.60) double. AE, DC, MC, V. **Parking:** Free.

This first-class modern inn on the Cavado River is located in a pine-covered garden, 5 minutes from the main beach. It has two excellent garden pools with surrounding lawns. The resort, planned for those who stay for more than a day, offers a full social life. The amenities include a natural stone fireplace. In the beamed dining room, a snug wood-paneled bar is set against a stone wall, and you'll find several lounges for get-togethers. Each guest room is well conceived, with a private balcony and central heating.

WHERE TO DINE IN OFIR
MODERATE

MARTINS DOS FRANGOS, Rua de São Januário. Tel. 96-18-65.
Cuisine: MINHO. **Reservations:** Not necessary.
$ Prices: Appetizers 450$–950$ ($2.70–$5.80); main courses 1,200$–2,400$ ($7.30–$14.60); tourist menu 1,500$ ($9.20). AE, DC, MC, V.
Open: Daily 9am–midnight.

Martins dos Frangos is among the best of the independents. It's one of the biggest restaurants in the area, seating some 375 diners. Try the barbecued chicken, the grilled meat and fish, the shellfish rice, or one of the house versions of codfish (*bacalhau*). The location is in the town center of Ofir near the river.

CHAPTER 15

THE MINHO REGION

The Minho occupies the verdant northwestern corner of Portugal and is almost a land unto itself. The region begins some 25 miles north of Porto and stretches to the frontier of Galicia in northwestern Spain. In fact, the Minhotons and the Galicians share many characteristics.

Granite plateaus undulate across the countryside, broken by the green valleys of the Minho, Ave, Cávado, and Lima rivers. Bountiful granite quarries stand agape amid the hills. From the great church facades in Braga and Guimarães to the humblest of village cottages, this material has been employed for centuries. Green pasturelands contrast sharply with forests filled with cedars and chestnuts.

The small size of the district and the proximity of one town to another makes hamlet-hopping easy. Even the biggest towns—**Viana do Castelo, Guimarães,** and **Braga**—are provincial. You can sometimes see wooden carts in the streets drawn by pairs of dappled and chocolate-brown oxen. These noble beasts have become subjects for the regional pottery and ceramics for which the Minho (especially Viana do Castelo) are known.

Religious *festas* are excuses for bringing the hardworking people out into the streets for days of merrymaking and celebrations including folk songs, dances, and, of course, displays of traditional costumes. The young girls and women often wear woolen skirts and gaily decorated aprons in floral or geometric designs. Their bodices are pinned with golden filigree and draped with layers of heart- or cross-shaped pendants.

Historically, the Minho was the spawning ground of Portuguese independence. It was from here that Afonso Henríques, the first king, made his plans to capture the south from the Moors. Battlemented castles along the frontier attest to the former hostilities with Spain, and fortresses, ruined sentinels that once protected the river accesses to the heartland, still stand above the coastal villages.

Many visitors consider *pousada*-hopping the most rewarding way of exploring Portugal. Every government-owned inn lies in a characteristic region, as well as a special scenic spot. (The first *pousada,* a place to rest, was founded in the 12th century, offering pilgrims a roof, a bed, and a candle. That hospitality today includes all the amenities of modern comfort.)

SEEING THE MINHO REGION

Porto (see Chapter 14) is the air gateway to the Minho. The city of port wine is also the major center for motorists exploring the north, as all major highways fan out from Porto. A car is the preferred way to see the north if you have only a short time; if you depend on public transportation, you can at least visit some of the major centers by bus and rail, although this is much more time consuming. All the major train routes originate in Porto, taking you north to such centers as Barcelos, Viana do Castelo, and Valença do Minho, with branch lines connecting Guimarães and Braga.

WHAT'S SPECIAL ABOUT
THE MINHO REGION

Great Towns/Villages

☐ Guimarães, called "the cradle of Portugal"—the birthplace of the nation's first king, filled with ancient monuments.

☐ Braga, an old Roman town that's known many rulers, including the Visigoths and the Moors—a noted pilgrimage center today.

☐ Barcelos, a "folkloric" town famed for its regional handcrafts.

☐ Viana do Castelo, capital of the Minho—called a city of folklore because of its pottery and handcrafts.

Beaches

☐ Beaches at Esposende, where Atlantic breezes sweep against a backdrop of pines and sand dunes.

☐ Baroque staircase and shrine of Bom Jesús in Braga—a hilltop pilgrimage site dating from the 18th century.

Ace Attractions

☐ Monte de Santa Luzia, Viana do Castelo—with a famed basilica that is less impressive than the spectacular view of the Minho possible from here.

☐ Costa Verde (Green Coast), north of Porto—small towns and sandy beaches that run all the way to the northern border of Spain.

Ace Attraction

☐ Market Day on Thursday at Barcelos, with a vast regional display of handcrafts—including the highly prized Barcelos cockerels.

SUGGESTED 4-DAY ITINERARY

Day 1 Head northeast from Porto to Guimarães for one of the most rewarding sightseeing days in a historic town.

Day 2 Continue northwest to Braga for a day exploring this pilgrimage center. Spend the night.

Day 3 Head west to Barcelos for a morning of sightseeing and shopping before journeying west again to the beach town of Esposende for a relaxing night.

Day 4 Go north to Viana do Castelo and occupy a busy day exploring the capital of the Minho.

1. GUIMARÃES

30 miles NE of Porto; 43 miles SW of Viana do Castelo;
226 miles N of Lisbon

GETTING THERE By Train Seventeen trains daily make the 1¾-hour run between Porto and Guimarães; the one-way cost is 405$ ($2.50).

By Bus Guimarães is easily reached from Braga (see Section 2 in this chapter), with frequent bus service during the day making the one-hour trip. For information call 053/51-62-29. A one-way bus ticket between Braga and Guimarães costs 300$ ($1.80) (trip time: 45 minutes).

By Car Guimarães lies northwest of Porto via the N105-2 and N105.

ESSENTIALS The **Tourist Office** is at Avenida de Resistência ao Fascismo 83 (tel. 41-24-50). The **telephone area code** is 053.

The cradle of Portugal, Guimarães suffers from a benign malady the French call *embarras de richesses*. At the foot of a range of serras, this first capital of Portugal has successfully preserved a medieval atmosphere in its core.

The city was the birthplace of Afonso Henríques, the first king of Portugal, son of a French nobleman, Henry of Burgundy, and his wife, Teresa, daughter of the king of León and Castile. For her "dowry," Teresa brought the county of Portucale, whose name eventually became Portugal. This consisted of the land lying between the Minho and the Douro, taking in what is now the city of Porto, a handsome gift indeed for the wedding night. Teresa and Henry chose Guimarães as their court, and it was here that Teresa bore Afonso Henríques. The year was 1109 or thereabouts—historians aren't sure.

Henry of Burgundy died 2 years later, and Teresa became regent for the baby king. She soon fell into disfavor with her subjects for having an affair with a count from Galicia and developing strong ties with her native Spain. As a young man, Afonso revolted against the regent's forces outside Guimarães in 1128. A major victory for Afonso came in 1139, when he routed the Moors near Santarém. This led him to break from León and Castile and proclaim himself King of Portucale that same year. Eventually, in 1143, Spain recognized this newly emerged kingdom.

Guimarães also had another famous son, Gil Vicente (1470?–1536?) founder of the Portuguese theater—often referred to as the Shakespeare of Portugal. Although trained as a goldsmith, Vicente was later to entertain the courts of both João II and Manuel I, amusing them with his farces and tragicomedies. He also penned religious dramas.

WHAT TO SEE & DO

If you'd like to step into the Middle Ages for an hour or two, take a stroll down **Rua de Santa Maria,** which has remained essentially unchanged for centuries—except that nowadays you're likely to hear some blaring music, in English no less. Proud town houses, once the residences of the nobility, stand beside humble dwellings. The hand-carved balconies, aged by the years, are most often garnished with iron lanterns (not to mention laundry).

At the end you'll come on a charming square in the heart of the old town, **Largo da Oliveira** (Olive Tree Square). Seek out an odd chapelette in front of a church. Composed of four ogival arches, it is said to mark the spot where in the 6th century Wamba was asked to give up the simple toil of working his fields to become the king of the Goths. Thrusting his olive stick into the tilled soil, he declared he would accept only if his stick sprouted leaves. So it did, and so he did—or that was the tale told.

CASTLE OF GUIMARÃES, Rua Dona Teresa de Noronha.
Dominating the skyline is this 10th-century castle, where Afonso Henríques, Portugal's first king, was born. The castle dates from 996. High-pitched crenels top the strategically placed square towers and the looming keep. The view is magnificent. With the church bells ringing in the distance and roosters crowing early in the morning, the setting seems straight out of the Middle Ages.
Admission: Free.
Open: Tues–Sun 10am–12:30pm and 2–5pm.

IGREJA DE SÃO MIGUEL DE CASTELO [Church of St. Michael of Castelo], Paço dos Duques.
Almost in the shadow of the castle is this squat, rectangular 12th-century Romanesque church where the liberator was baptized. Nearby is a heroic statue of the mustachioed Afonso, his head helmeted, his figure clad in armor, his sword and shield in hand.
Admission: Free.
Open: Irregular hours; take a chance it might be open.

PAÇO DOS DUQUES DE BRAGANÇA [Palace of the Dukes of Bragança], Avenida Conde Dom Henrique. Tel. 41-22-73.
From the keep of the castle you can see the four-winged Paço dos Duques de

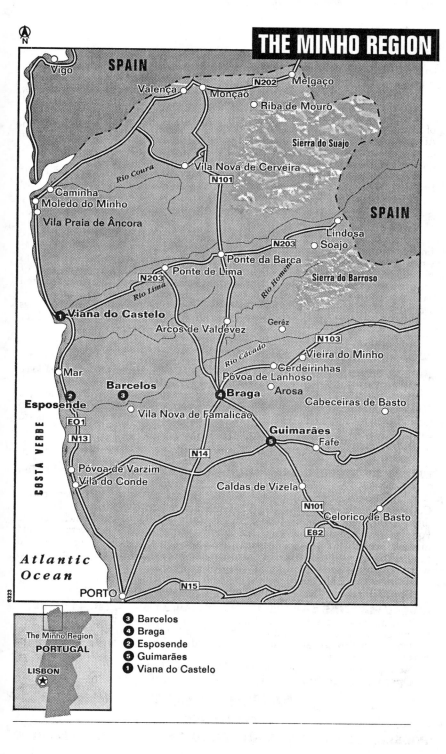

THE MINHO REGION

Bragança. Constructed in the 15th century, it has been heavily restored. Many critics have dismissed the rebuilt structure with contempt. However, if you're not a purist, you may find a guided tour interesting.

Perched on the slope of a hill, the palace possesses a varied assortment of treasures, including a number of portraits—such as that of Catherine of Bragança, who married Charles II of England, the merrie monarch and lover of Nell Gwyn. There are copies of the large Pastrana tapestries depicting scenes from the Portuguese wars in North Africa, scabbards and helmets in the armor room, antiques, Persian hangings, Indian urns, ceramics, and Chinese porcelains. The chapel opens onto the throne chairs of the duke and duchess. Nearby are the double-tiered cloisters.

Admission: June–Sept, 300$ ($1.80); Oct–May, 200$ ($1.20); children under 10 free.

Open: Daily 10am–5:30pm.

SÃO FRANCISCO [Church of St. Francis], Largo de São Francisco. Tel. 41-22-28.

By far the most dramatic interior of any church in town belongs to São Francisco. Entered through a Gothic portal, the spacious interior is faced with Delft-blue and white *azulejos*. Some of the color tones seem to bathe the whole interior in moonlight. In the transept to the right of the main altar is a miniature re-creation of the living room of a church prelate with meticulous detail, from the burgundy-colored cardinal's chapeau resting on a wall sconce to the miniature dog and cat. On the second altar to the right is a polychrome tree of life that represents 12 crowned kings and the Virgin, with her hands clasped and her feet resting on the heads of three cherubs.

Admission: Free.

Open: Daily 9am–noon and 3–6pm.

IGREJA NOSSA SENHORA DA OLIVEIRA [Collegiate Church of the Olive Tree], Largo de Oliveira. Tel. 41-24-65.

This church was originally a 10th-century temple erected by Mumadona, a Galician countess. It has changed with the centuries: Romanesque giving way to Gothic, then to more sterile neoclassicism. Its cloister contains the Museu de Alberto Sampaio.

Admission: Free.

Open: Tues–Sun 10am–12:30pm and 2–5:30pm.

MUSEU DE ALBERTO SAMPAIO, Largo de Oliveira, Rua Alfredo, Tel. 41-24-65.

In the Romanesque cloister and in the buildings of the old monastery of the Collegiate Church of the Olive Tree is this museum. Besides a large silver collection, it displays the tunic worn by João I at the battle of Aljubarrota, which decided Portugal's fate. In addition, there are priestly garments, paintings, ceramics, and medieval sculpture. A fresco illustrates a gloating Salome, rapturous over the severed head of John the Baptist. In one of the rooms, there are pieces from a baroque chapel with enormous wood-carved angels bearing torches.

Admission: 200$ ($1.20) adults; children 14 and under free.

Open: Tues–Sun 10am–12:30pm and 2–5:30pm. **Closed:** Holidays.

MUSEU MARTINS SARMENTO, Rua de Paiva Galvão. Tel. 41-59-69.

This museum, situated partially in the Church of St. Dominic (São Domingos) Gothic cloister, has on display artifacts from the prehistoric (Bronze Age to Iron Age) settlements at Sabroso and Briteiros, excavated by the archeologist for whom the museum was named.

Admission: 250$ ($1.50) adults; children under 12 free.

Open: Tues–Sun 10am–noon and 2–5pm.

WHERE TO STAY
EXPENSIVE

POUSADA DE SANTA MARINHA DA COSTA, Estrada de Penha, 4800

Guimarães. Tel. 053/51-44-53. Fax 053/51-44-59. 49 rms, 2 suites. MINIBAR TV TEL

$ Rates (including breakfast): 22,100$ ($134.80) single; 25,200$ ($153.70) double; 48,600$ ($296.50) suite. AE, DC, MC, V. **Parking:** Free.

Its foundations date from the 12th century, but the restored Pousada de Santa Marinha da Costa is arguably the most impressive pousada in Portugal. It was built in 1154 as an Augustinian convent by Teresa, the mother of Afonso Henríques. The baroque facade was added in the 18th century when the soaring interior hallways and sporting fountains were installed as crowning touches. The ornate Manueline church that occupies part of the building still offers mass on Sunday, but the sprawling ex-convent was never outfitted as stylishly as you'll see it today. The property lies at the end of a winding road about 1¼ miles north of the town center via the N101-2. Signs indicate the direction.

Take the time to explore both the upper hallways and the gardens. One of the favorite rooms is a beautifully furnished large salon. At the end of one of the soaring hallways, a fountain bubbles beneath an intricate wooden ceiling, surrounded by an open arcade that encompasses a view of the faraway mountains.

The guest rooms are a pleasing blend of old stonework, modern plasterwork, plush accessories, and a scattering of Portuguese lithographs. About half the rooms lie within a relatively modern wing attached to the medieval core. These modern rooms, decorated in a traditional Portuguese style of quiet dignity, are air-conditioned; the original (older) rooms are not.

Dining/Entertainment: Meals, costing from 3,000$ ($18.30), are served in the dining room daily from 12:30 to 2:30pm and 7:30 to 9:30pm. A sunken bar, ringed with blue-and-yellow tiles, serves drinks near the anteroom of the vaulted dining room.

Services: Laundry, room service.

MODERATE

POUSADA DE SANTA MARIA DE OLIVEIRA, Rua de Santa Maria, 4800 Guimarães. Tel. 053/51-41-57. Fax 053/51-42-04. 16 rms. A/C TV TEL

$ Rates (including breakfast): 17,300$ ($105.50) single; 20,000$ ($122) double. AE, DC, MC, V. **Parking:** Free.

This is now the second pousada in town, quite different in ambience from Santa Marinha da Costa (see above). It was created when a handful of very old town houses were combined into a single rambling hotel. Many of their original features have been preserved. The street that contains the pousada is so narrow you'll have to park free somewhere within a well-marked lot about 100 feet from the front entrance. It still has a loyal clientele who value its location on one of the most beautiful medieval squares of Portugal, as well as its distinctive country-inn flavor. This establishment exudes a cozy kind of intimate warmth, heightened by the wooden ceilings, tavern bar, and fireplace inside the warmly decorated restaurant, whose windows look out over the square. Laundry, babysitting, and room service are available.

The windows of the comfortably efficient guest rooms usually look out past spindle-turned balustrades over the stone-trimmed city around it. Meals, served daily from 12:30 to 2:30pm and 7:30 to 9:30pm, cost 3,000$ ($18.30). Specialties include a special beef *à la pousada*, fondue for two, and flambé versions of beef and veal.

INEXPENSIVE

FUNDADOR DOM PEDRO HOTEL, Avenida Dom Afonso Henríques, 740, 4800 Guimarães. Tel. 053/51-37-81. Fax 053/51-37-86. 63 rms. A/C MINIBAR TV TEL

$ Rates (including breakfast): 13,000$ ($79.30) single; 14,000$ ($85.40) double. AE, DC, MC, V. **Parking:** Free.

This city-center hotel offers comfortable guest rooms equipped with piped-in music. The Dom Pedro, along with the previous recommendations, makes a night in

Guimarães a lot more palatable than it was in days of yore. The hotel isn't necessarily great on style, but it's modern, functional, and well kept; as a further compensation, it boasts fine service. Two elevators take you to the rooms. The hotel, inaugurated in 1980, has a penthouse bar with snacks.

WHERE TO DINE
MODERATE

MIRAPENHA, Estrada de Fafe. Tel. 51-65-32.
 Cuisine: PORTUGUESE. **Reservations:** Not necessary.
$ Prices: Appetizers 350$–650$ ($2.10–$4); main courses 950$–1,800$ ($5.80–$11); tourist menu 1,700$ ($10.40). No credit cards.
 Open: Lunch Sun–Fri 12:30–2:30pm; dinner Sun–Fri 8–10pm.
Mirapenha is a typical restaurant just outside town, a reasonably priced taxi ride's distance away. Fine local food is served, including specialties like *bacalhau* (codfish) *à Mirapenha*, *bife à Mirapenha* (steak), and other regional dishes.

INEXPENSIVE

EL REI, Praça de São Tiago 20. Tel. 41-90-96.
 Cuisine: MINHO. **Reservations:** Not necessary.
$ Prices: Appetizers 350$–850$ ($2.10–$5.20); main courses 950$–1,500$ ($5.80–$9.20). V.
 Open: Lunch Mon–Sat noon–2:30pm; dinner Mon–Sat 7–10:30pm.
In an enviable position in the heart of the medieval sector, this little restaurant opens onto the rear of the former Town Hall and the previously recommended Pousada de Santa Maria da Oliveira. It is patronized heavily by locals, plus the occasional foreign visitors, who enjoy its good fish and meat dishes. Try the hake filets or the house-style steak. Service is efficient, albeit sometimes rushed. The walls have been decorated with local artists' work, which is for sale.

VIRA BAR, Alameda 25. Tel. 41-41-16.
 Cuisine: PORTUGUESE. **Reservations:** Recommended.
$ Prices: Appetizers 450$–650$ ($2.70–$4); main courses 750$–1,500$ ($4.60–$9.20). AE, DC, MC, V.
 Open: Lunch daily noon–3pm; dinner daily 7–10pm.
Many people think Vira Bar is the best restaurant outside the pousadas. It is certainly one of the most pleasant in town, seating 70 diners in air-conditioned comfort. Alternatively, it warms them with a fireplace in winter. A good local cuisine is served. Regional wines accompany most menus.

---

2. BRAGA
31 miles N of Porto; 228 miles N of Lisbon

GETTING THERE By Train The train station is on Largo Estação (tel. 053/22-166). Thirteen trains per day arrive from Porto after a 1½-hour trip costing 560$ ($3.40) one way. From Coimbra, twelve trains per day make the 4-hour trip costing 905$ ($5.50) one way. If you're in the north, you can take one of 11 trains from Viana do Castelo, which arrive in Braga after 2 hours and a one-way charge of 380$ ($2.30).

By Bus The bus station is at Central de Camionagem (tel. 053/61-60-80), a few blocks north of the heart of town. Buses arrive every 30 minutes throughout the day from Porto; the trip takes 1½ hours and costs 530$ ($3.20) one way. From Guimarães, there are 11 buses per day; the trip takes an hour and costs 300$ ($1.80). From Lisbon, four buses make the 8-hour trip daily, costing 1,720$ ($10.50) one way.

By Car From Guimarães (see the preceding section), head northwest along the N101 to Braga.

ESSENTIALS The **Braga Tourist Office** is at Avenida da Liberdade (tel. 225-50). The **telephone area code** is 053.

Nearly everywhere you look in Braga there's a church, a palace, a garden, or a fountain. Known to the Romans as Bracara Augusta, it also resounded to the footsteps of other conquerors—the Suevi, the Visigoths, and the Moors. For centuries, it has been an archepiscopal see and a pilgrimage site (the Visigoths are said to have renounced their heresies here).

WHAT TO SEE & DO

SÉ (Cathedral of Braga), Sé Primaz. Tel. 233-17.

Inside the town, interest focuses on the Sé, which was built in the 12th century by Count Henry of Burgundy and Dona Teresa. Following his demise, she was chased out of town because of an illicit love affair; but in death Henry and Teresa were reunited in their tombs in the Chapel of Kings.

The Sé didn't escape subsequent decorative and architectural styles. The north triple-arched facade is austere and dominating, with a large stone-laced Roman arch flanked by two smaller Gothic ones. What appear to be the skeletons of cupolas top the facade's dual bell towers, which flank a lofty rooftop niche containing a larger-than-life statue of the Virgin and Child. Under a carved baldachin in the apse is a statue of "Our Lady of the Milk"—that is, the Virgin breast-feeding the infant Jesus. The statue is in the Manueline style—but somehow pious, restrained.

Once inside the structure, you'll believe you've entered one of the darkest citadels of Christendom. However, if you can see them, the decorations are profuse, particularly a pair of huge 18th-century gilded organs. In the 1330 Capela da Gloria is the sarcophagus of Archbishop Dom Gonçalo Pereira, with an unctuous expression on his face, carved by order of the prelate himself.

You can visit the **Treasury of the Cathedral** and the **Museum of Sacred Art,** an upstairs repository of Braga's most precious works of art. Included are elaborately carved choir stalls from the 18th century, embroidered vestments from the 16th through the 18th century, a 14th-century statue of the Virgin and a Gothic chalice from the same period, plus the *custódia* of Dom Gaspar de Bragança. In the cloister is a *pietà*, a reflection of human grief.

Admission: Museum and treasury only: 200$ ($1.20) adults; children under 10 free. Cathedral: free.

Open: June–Sept, daily 8:30am–6:30pm; Oct–May, daily 8:30am–12:30pm and 1:30–5:30pm.

MUSEU DOS BISCAINHOS, Rua dos Biscainhos. Tel. 276-45.

This museum is in Biscainhos Palace, a building from the 17th and 18th centuries that for about 300 years has been the house of a noble family. The original gardens—including the baroque ornamental garden, an orchard, and a kitchen garden—are still there. The museum's interior has painted and ornamented ceilings and walls with panels of figurative and neoclassic tiles. Its exhibition rooms contain collections of Portuguese furniture and pottery; glassware; silverware; textiles; and Portuguese, Oriental, and Dutch Delft porcelain.

Admission: 400$ ($2.40) adults; children 14 and under free.

Open: Tues–Sun 10am–12:15pm and 2–5:30pm. **Closed:** Holidays.

BOM JESÚS DO MONTE, 3 miles southeast of Braga via N103-3.

Bom Jesús do Monte is a hilltop pilgrimage site reached via foot, a 960$ ($5.90) funicular ride, or a car ride along a tree-lined roadway. A baroque granite double staircase dating from the 18th century may look exhausting; but if it's any consolation, pilgrims often climb it on their knees. Less elaborate than the stairway of Remédios at Lamego, the stairs at Bom Jesús (Good Jesus) are nevertheless equally impressive. On the numerous landings are gardens, grottoes, small chapels, sculptures, and allegorical stone figures set in fountains.

Admission: Free.
Open: Daily 8am–8pm.

WHERE TO STAY

INEXPENSIVE

HOTEL TURISMO DE BRAGA, Praceta João XXI, Avenida da Liberdade, 4700 Braga. Tel. 053/61-22-00. Fax 053/61-22-11. 132 rms. A/C TV TEL
$ Rates (including breakfast): 9,000$ ($54.90) single; 11,600$ ($70.80) double. AE, DC, MC, V. **Parking:** Free.

The best hotel in town, the Turismo de Braga is in an 11-story 1950s building fronted with flowering gardens and a parking lot. As you face the sprawling building, you'll find its entrance beneath an arcade that also shelters some cafes. Inside, all is air-conditioned calm and comfort. The two-story lobby is set below a spacious lounge bar/restaurant, where you can enjoy a drink and a meal in a warmly burnished wood-paneled ambience. Each comfortable guest room contains a spacious balcony, whose walls are covered with blue-and-white tiles. There are a rooftop pool and an eighth-floor snack bar for residents. The hotel stands on a busy corner of traffic arteries, just outside the most densely populated section of Braga.

BUDGET

HOTEL JOÃO XXI, Avenida João XXI 849, 4700 Braga. Tel. 053/61-66-30. Fax. 053/61-66-31. 28 rms. A/C MINIBAR TV TEL
$ Rates (including breakfast): 6,000$ ($36.60) single; 7,000$ ($42.70) double. AE, DC, MC, V. **Parking:** Free.

This is a good stopover hotel in its bracket (second class). On a tree-shaded avenue leading to Bom Jésus do Monte, it stands opposite the leading first-class hotel of Braga. The entry to this modern little six-floor hotel is a salute to the 19th century. The tiny street-floor reception room is decorated à la Louis XVI. The social center of the hotel is the living room/lounge with well-selected furnishings featuring an open fireplace for the nippy months. At the sixth-floor restaurant you can order breakfast or an evening meal; the latter costs from 3,500$ ($21.40) per person. The guest rooms are in a warm modern decor, furnished with semitraditional pieces, with the accent on neatness and efficiency; the singles have double beds.

NEARBY PLACES TO STAY: BOM JESÚS DO MONTE

Many visitors to Braga prefer to stay high on the hill overlooking the city at the sanctuary of Bom Jesús do Monte. If you're interested in views and don't mind mingling with a lot of pilgrims, then you might want to do the same. The views at night are among the most exciting in the north of Portugal.

INEXPENSIVE

HOTEL DO ELEVADOR, Bom Jesús do Monte, 4700 Braga. Tel. 053/67-66-11. Fax 053/67-66-79. 24 rms. A/C TV TEL
$ Rates (including breakfast): 10,950$ ($66.80) single; 12,800$ ($78.10) double. AE, DC, MC, V. **Parking:** Free.

Hotel do Elevador is not unlike a private hillside villa—furnished in a plush manner with antiques, paintings, and objets d'art—except for the guest rooms, which have contemporary appointments. At your table, with a view, the price of a complete lunch or dinner costs 2,650$ ($16.20).

HOTEL DO PARQUE, Bom Jesús do Monte, 4700 Braga. Tel. 053/67-65-48. Fax 053/67-66-79. 45 rms, 4 suites. A/C MINIBAR TV TEL
$ Rates (including breakfast): 10,950$ ($66.80) single; 12,800$ ($78.10) double; 18,700$ ($114.10) suite. AE, DC, MC, V. **Parking:** Free.

Hotel do Parque was a turn-of-the-century villa that reopened in 1987 as one of the best hotels in the Braga area. Furnished in a high standard traditional style, it offers well-furnished guest rooms equipped with all the modern amenities. Set on elegantly maintained grounds, the hotel serves dinner, costing 2,850$ ($17.40) to 3,900$ ($23.80). The cuisine is of the Minho but also of France. Guests enjoy drinks in the hotel bar or relax in a spacious sitting room with an open fireplace.

NEARBY PLACES TO STAY: EAST OF BRAGA
MODERATE

POUSADA DE SÃO BENTO, Caniçada do Minho, 4850 Vieria do Minho. Tel. 053/64-71-90. 30 rms. A/C TV TEL
$ Rates (including breakfast): 17,300$ ($105.50) single; 20,000$ ($122) double. AE, DC, MC, V. **Parking:** Free.

Pousada de São Bento overlooks the winding road that runs between Caldeirinhas and Pontes do Rio Caldo. The pousada was originally built as the opulent private villa of an engineer who supervised the construction of a nearby dam; it was later enlarged. Undeniably romantic, it has stone walls and smallish windows that remind some guests of an alpine chalet, except for the masses of vines trailing across its facade. Inside, a cathedral ceiling is supported by decoratively massive wooden trusses, creating a kind of canopy over a pair of granite fireplaces. Laundry and room service are available. The pool is a magnet for guests.

The landscape is so beautiful that you may prefer to make the pousada a base from which to explore. This area abounds in luxuriant vegetation and rippling waterfalls, and there's lots of game in the wooded areas. The park of Peneda-Gerês and the ancient stone cloisters of Santa Maria do Bouro and Our Lady of Abadia are easy sightseeing targets. The pousada, on the Braga-Gerês highway, is 16 miles from Vieria do Minho at Caniçada do Minho and about 18½ miles east of Braga.

Meals, served daily from 12:30 to 2:30pm and 7:30 to 9:30pm, cost 2,750$ ($16.80) to 3,650$ ($22.30).

INEXPENSIVE

CASA DE REQUEIXO, Frades 4800, Póvoa de Lanhoso. Tel. 053/63-11-13. 4 rms. **Transportation/Directions:** From Braga, take an unnumbered bus marked VENDAS NOVAS or CHAVES. Motorists should go on the national highway EN-103 from Braga to Chaves, getting off at the "20 km" signposted stop in the village of Frades.
$ Rates (including breakfast): 8,000$ ($48.80) single; 9,000$ ($54.90) double. No credit cards. **Parking:** Free.

★ At Frades, near Póvoa de Lanhoso, east of Braga, is the most romantic place to stay. The Casa de Requeixo is an elegant massive stone mansion of the 16th and 17th centuries. From a base here, you can explore the area by taking one of several itineraries in either the Minho or the National Park of Peneda-Gêres. Dr. Manuel Artur Norton has beautifully furnished guest rooms, each with a large living room, a dining room, and a kitchen. The quinta combines the best qualities of the past with modern-day comfort and offers both in a bucolic setting.

It's also possible to dine nearby with typically Portuguese meals served at either Restaurante Victor or Restaurante Gaucho, including wine from local vineyards. After dinner, guests return to the casa for coffee and a glass of port wine to cap the evening.

WHERE TO DINE
MODERATE

A MARISQUEIRA, Rua Castelo 3. Tel. 221-52.
Cuisine: SEAFOOD. **Reservations:** Not necessary.
$ Prices: Appetizers 300$–900$ ($1.80–$5.50); main courses 1,000$–2,000$ ($6.10–$12.20); tourist menu 1,800$ ($11). No credit cards.
Open: Lunch daily noon–3pm; dinner daily 7–10pm.
Established during the 1930s in the center of town, this is one of the best-known and best-reputed restaurants in Braga. (It is not to be confused with another restaurant,

Marisqueira Braga, adjacent to Hotel João XXI.) Within an old-fashioned and *típico* setting lined with handpainted *azulejos,* you can order some of the best shellfish dishes in the region, as well as such regional favorites as oven-cooked roast kid and grilled filet of sole. An array of wines from the Douro region might accompany your meal.

O CANTINHO DO CAMPO DAS HORTAS, Largo da Senhora da Boa Luz. Tel. 61-40-03.
Cuisine: PORTUGUESE. **Reservations:** Recommended.
$ Prices: Appetizers 450$–950$ ($2.70–$5.80); main courses 1,000$–2,300$ ($6.10–$14). No credit cards.
Open: Lunch daily noon–2:30pm; dinner daily 7–10:30pm.

⑤ In a former privately owned town house, opening onto the Campo das Hortas, this newest challenger to the restaurants of Braga is already acclaimed as the finest dining choice in the city. It has a long list of habitués drawn from all walks of city life—ranging from the mayor to the highest church official. It seems busiest at lunch, when members of the business community book most of the tables. Regional wines accompany most meals in this small and bustling place. A regular à la carte menu is featured, but in-the-know diners always ask about the daily specials. Portions are generous, and the cooking is rather rich. Roast *cabrito* (or kid) is in season in June, but the eternal year-round favorite is *bacalhau* (dried salt cod), prepared in an infinite number of ways. Braga chefs secretly guard their recipes for this "faithful friend."

O INÁCIO, Campo das Hortas 4. Tel. 61-32-25.
Cuisine: PORTUGUESE. **Reservations:** Recommended.
$ Prices: Appetizers 650$–1,000$ ($4–$6.10); main courses 1,200$–2,000$ ($7.30–$12.20). AE, DC, MC, V.
Open: Lunch Sat–Thurs noon–3pm; dinner Sat–Thurs 7:30–10pm. **Closed:** First week Oct.

⑤ An old stone structure, O Inácio—the most popular restaurant in town—has rugged walls and hand-hewn beams. In the colder months a fire burns in an open hearth. The decor is rustic, with regional pottery and oxen yokes. Your host will often advise about his Portuguese specialties of the day. Usually these are *bacalhau* (codfish) *à Inácio, papas de sarrabulho* (a regional stew), and *bife na cacarola* (pot roast). Roast kid is also featured occasionally. Most fish dishes (and they're fresh) are good alternative choices. The dessert surprise is a rum omelet soufflé. The owner has a well-stocked wine cellar and, in my opinion, serves the best cuisine in Braga.

3. BARCELOS

14 miles W of Braga; 227 miles N of Lisbon

GETTING THERE By Train The train station is on Avenida Alcaides de Faria. Train connections are possible from Braga, at the rate of 13 per day; the trip takes 1¼ hours and costs 250$ ($1.50) one way. Fifteen trains a day arrive from Viana do Castelo after a 1-hour trip that costs 300$ ($1.80) one way.

By Bus The bus station is on Avenida Dr. Sidónio Pais (tel. 053/81-43-10). Ten buses a day arrive here from Braga after the 30-minute trip, costing 315$ ($1.90) one way.

By Car From Braga, follow the N103 due west.

ESSENTIALS The **Tourist Office** is at Largo da Porta Nova (tel. 81-18-82). The **telephone area code** is 053.

Barcelos is a sprawling river town that rests on a plateau ringed by green hills. Wrought-iron street lanterns glimmer late in the evening long after the market in the open square of **Campo da República** has closed down. Barcelos does not feature any single major attraction, only itself, taken as a whole, with its ensemble of sights and curiosities—and that is more than enough.

WHAT TO SEE & DO

✪ **Market day,** on Thursday, held in the fountain-centered **Campo da República,** almost 450 yards square, is a major event. You can purchase such local handcrafts as rugs, dyed pillows stuffed with chicken feathers, Portuguese chandeliers, crochet work, local pottery, and Barcelos cockerels. These hand-painted earthenware cocks are the most characteristic souvenirs of Portugal and often seem a symbol of the country. The worship of the Barcelos rooster derives from a legend concerning a Gallego who was sentenced to hang despite his protestations of innocence. In a last-hour appeal to the judge (who was having dinner at the time), the condemned man made a bold statement: If his manifestation of innocence were true, the roasted rooster resting on the magistrate's plate would get up and crow. Suddenly, a gloriously scarlet-plumed cockerel rose from the plate, crowing loud and long. The man was acquitted, of course.

Opening onto the tree-studded main square are some of the finest buildings in Barcelos. The 18th-century **Igreja do Terço** resembles a palace more than a church, with a central niche facade topped by finials and a cross. The interior tilework around the baroque altar depicts scenes of monks at labor and a moving rendition of the Last Supper. Also fronting the *campo,* with its fountain, is the **Hospital da Misericórdia,** a long formal 17th-century building, behind a spiked fence, which takes up almost half a side of the square.

Of more interest, however, is the small octagonal **Temple of Senhor da Cruz,** with a tile-faced cupola. An upper balustrade, punctuated by large stone finials and a latticed round window about the square portal, provide contrast to the austerity of the walls. The interior is more sumptuous, with crystal, marble, and gilt.

Overlooking the swirling Cávado River are the ruins of the **Palace of the Braganças,** dating from 1786. The original palace site, as well as the town of Barcelos itself, was bestowed on Nuno Alvares by João I as a gift in gratitude for his bravery in the 1385 battle at Aljubarrota.

On the facade is a representation of the palace, re-created in splendor. You can wander through the ruins, which have been turned into an archeological museum, left relatively unguarded and filled with sarcophagi, heralded shields, and an 18th-century tile fountain. A museum of ceramics underneath the palace encapsulates the evolution of that handcraft (look for the blood-red ceramic oxen, with their lyre-shaped horns).

The shadow from the high palace chimney stretches across the old pillory in the courtyard below. The structure even exceeds in height the bell tower of the adjoining **Igreja Matriz.** Fronting the river, this Gothic church contains a baroque altar and an interior whose sides are faced with multicolored tiles. The altar is an array of cherubs, grapes, gold leaf, and birds.

SHOPPING

CENTRO DO ARTESANATO DE BARCELOS, Largo de Porta Nova. Tel. 81-18-82.

✪ This unique shopping center is tucked away in a provincial town, but it displays some of the best regional handcrafts at the most compelling prices of any shop I've encountered in the north. It's an age-old stone tower, opposite the Church of São da Cruz. On its street level and upper floor is found a wide display of goods.

Outstanding (and worth the trip to Barcelos) is the collection of witty and sophisticated ceramics from the heirs of Rosa Ramalho, who was known as the Grandma Moses of Portuguese ceramics. Some of these figures were influenced by Picasso. Ms. Ramalho created figures depicting eerie people, some looking as if they stepped out of a painting by Hieronymus Bosch. She put the heads of wolves on nuns, gave goats six legs, and so forth, all in muted forest green or butterscotch brown.

In addition, there is a good selection of the ceramic red-combed Barcelos cockerels, with many variations on the traditional motif in red and black. Local wares include black-ceramic candlesticks, earthenware bowls traditionally used for *caldo verde*, hand-knitted pillows, handmade rugs in bold stripes, and hand-loomed bedspreads. As a novelty, the rugs and pillows made from flamboyantly dyed chicken feathers may attract you.

Open: Daily 10am–noon and 9–5:30pm.

WHERE TO STAY

INEXPENSIVE

ALBERGARIA CONDES DE BARCELOS, Avenida Alcaides de Faria, 4750 Barcelos. Tel. 053/81-10-61. 30 rms.

$ Rates (including breakfast): 6,300$ ($38.40) single; 9,700$ ($59.20) double. AE, DC, MC, V. **Parking:** Free.

Albergaria Condes de Barcelos has a delightful pousada style with furnishings made by local artisans. Beds are intricately carved. The inn, a part of a three-story complex, stands mostly on thick pillars, in the Corbusier manner, and has an inner courtyard. The hotel is just a little way from the center of town, within walking distance of the artisan sales museum. Natural wood paneling is used generously in the dining room, the main lounge, and the bar/lounge. Laundry and room service are offered.

BUDGET

PENSÃO RESIDENCIAL DOM NUNO, Avenida Dom Nuno Alvares Pereira 76, 4750 Barcelos. Tel. 053/81-50-84. Fax 053/81-63-36. 27 rms. TEL

$ Rates (including breakfast): 7,000$ ($42.70) double. No credit cards. **Parking:** Free.

The Dom Nuno is preferred by many visitors over Albergaria Condes de Barcelos (see above). Located on a quieter street, about halfway between the tourist zone of the village and the Condes de Barcelos, it offers attractively furnished doubles. Everything has a bright, modern look. This is one of the friendliest little inns you are likely to find in this part of Portugal. The hotel has a bar and offers room service.

WHERE TO DINE

MODERATE

ARANTES RESTAURANT, Avenida da Liberdade 33. Tel. 81-16-45.
Cuisine: PORTUGUESE. **Reservations:** Not necessary.

$ Prices: Appetizers 450$–950$ ($2.70–$5.80); main courses 950$–1,800$ ($5.80–$11); tourist menu 2,100$ ($12.80). No credit cards.

Open: Lunch daily noon–3pm; dinner daily 7–10pm.

This is one of the most visible restaurants in town, set in the commercial center—a large, bustling, much-frequented staple for local merchants and entrepreneurs. Although the ambience is not particularly intimate and the service might be either too rushed or too slow (depending on the mood of the staff and local business on the day of your arrival), it usually serves well-flavored and copious portions of both Portuguese and regional dishes. These might include bean soup, roasted lamb, grilled fish, a limited selection of shellfish, and fresh vegetables from nearby farms. An array of wines, mostly from the Douro, might accompany your meal.

DOM ANTÓNIO, Rua Dom António Barroso 87. Tel. 81-22-85.
Cuisine: PORTUGUESE. **Reservations:** Not necessary.

$ Prices: Appetizers 450$–850$ ($2.70–$5.20); main courses 950$–1,900$ ($5.80–$11.60); tourist menu 1,800$ ($11). AE, MC, V.

Open: Daily noon–midnight.

One of the town's local favorites was founded in the mid-1980s on the street level of a very old town house in the historic heart of Barcelos. Within a deliberately rustic interior, aided by a polite staff, you can enjoy soups, *bacalhau Dom António* (a popular house specialty concocted from codfish, onions, and potatoes), shellfish rice, grilled salmon, and grilled steaks.

4. ESPOSENDE

12½ miles S of Viana do Castelo; 30 miles N of Porto;
228 miles N of Lisbon

GETTING THERE   By Train   From Porto, northbound trains depart during the day from the Estação da Trindade. They leave every 90 to 120 minutes throughout the day.

By Bus   The trip by bus from Porto to Esposende takes about an hour. In Porto, about three or four buses per day leave from the Autoviação do Minho, Praça Filippa de Lancastre (tel. 02/200-61-21).

By Car   From Porto, take the IC-1 north.

ESSENTIALS   The **Esposende Tourist Office** is at Avenida Marginal (tel. 96-13-54). The **telephone area code** is 053.

Esposende is a beach-resort town where the pines and sand dunes are swept by the Atlantic breezes and cows graze in nearby pastures. The surrounding countryside is no longer as unspoiled as it used to be, although you'll still see an occasional ox cart in the street. The area has been extensively developed, and there's a wide new road running along the seafront. Men and women in fustian clothes and broad-brimmed hats work the vineyards in the foothills. The beach is large and fine, lining both sides of the Cavado estuary. Small fishing vessels plod up the river carrying anglers to the bass upstream. Recent archeological diggings have revealed the remains of a Roman city and necropolis, but that doesn't seem to have disturbed Esposende in the least.

WHERE TO STAY

INEXPENSIVE

ESTALAGEM ZENDE, Estrada Nacional 13, 4740 Esposende. Tel. 053/ 96-18-85. Fax 053/96-50-18. 25 rms. A/C TV TEL
$ Rates (including breakfast): 9,000$ ($54.90) single; 11,000$ ($67.10) double. AE, DC, MC, V. **Parking:** Free.
Estalagem Zende is rated a luxury inn by the government. It lies on the main road to Viana do Castelo, right outside Esposende. Thirty percent of the well-maintained guest rooms have minibars. The hotel offers a solarium. Laundry and room service are available.
   The inn has a good restaurant, Martins, and cocktail bar, and it serves some of the best food in Esposende. A meal costs from 2,200$ ($13.40) and up. In winter, fire blazes on the hearth. Food is served daily from 12:30 to 3pm and 7:30 to 10pm.

HOTEL SAUVE MAR, Avenida Eng. Arantes e Oliveira, 4740 Esposende. Tel. 053/96-54-45. Fax 053/96-52-49. 66 rms. A/C TEL
$ Rates (including breakfast): 10,000$ ($61) single; 11,000$ ($67.10) double. AE, DC, MC, V. **Parking:** Free.
A semimodern hotel on the river, the Sauve Mar attracts budgeteers who don't want to pay for the superior first-class accommodations at neighboring Ofir and Fão (see Chapter 14). The lodgings are pleasant and comfortable. It's also possible to visit just for a meal, which will cost from 3,000$ ($18.30). The food served here is among the

best at the resort. One reader found the barbecued chicken "the best (he's) tasted in Portugal." The Sauve Mar is open all year, although you may have the place to yourself off-season.

WHERE TO DINE

For the finest dining, consider the restaurants of the hotels previously recommended, especially that of Hotel Sauve Mar.

MODERATE

RESTAURANT MARTINS, Estrada Nacional. Tel. 053/96-18-55.
 Cuisine: SEAFOOD. **Reservations:** Not necessary.
 $ Prices: Meals from 3,000$ ($18.30). AE, DC, MC, V.
 Open: Lunch daily noon–3pm; dinner daily 7–10:30pm.
Set in the heart of Esposende, this large and bustling restaurant specializes in Portuguese seafood, often grilled lightly and seasoned with local garlic and herbs. Specialties include roasted goat, smoked swordfish, grilled filets of sole, shellfish rice, and several preparations of codfish. You can also order platters of shellfish, which will, of course cost more than equivalent portions of chicken, lamb, beef, or veal.

5. VIANA DO CASTELO

44 miles N of Porto; 241 miles N of Lisbon; 15½ miles N of Esposende

GETTING THERE   By Train   The train station is along Avenida Combatentes (tel. 058/82-22-96 for information). Here, 12 trains per day arrive from Porto; the trip takes 2½ hours and costs 505$ ($3.10) one way.

By Bus   The bus station, Central de Camionagem, is at the eastern edge of the city (tel. 058/25-047). Buses arrive every hour from Porto after a 2½-hour trip costing 660$ ($4) one way. There are also two buses daily from Lisbon, making the 6-hour trip at a cost of 2,000$ ($12.20) one way. From Braga, eight buses per day arrive, taking 1½ hours and costing 530$ ($3.20) one way.

By Car   From Porto or Esposende, continue north along the IC-1.

ESSENTIALS   The **Viana do Castelo Tourist Office** is at Rua de Hospital Velho (tel. 82-26-20). The **telephone area code** is 058.

Viana do Castelo sits between an estuary of the Lima River and a base of rolling hills. This is northern Portugal's city of folklore. The setting is enhanced by an occasional ox cart with wooden wheels clacking along the stone streets. Some of the boatmen of the city, their faces weather-beaten, can be seen near the waterfront, offering to sell visitors a slow cruise along the riverbanks.

But for the best view, scale the **Monte de Santa Luzia,** reached by a funicular ride or, if you have a car, along a twisting road. From Hotel de Santa Luzia at the summit, a great view unfolds, including Alexandre-Gustave Eiffel's bridge spanning the Lima.

Viana do Castelo is noted for its pottery and regional handcrafts (many can be purchased in the Friday market). It is even better known for its regional dress, best seen at the annual *festa* (the Friday, Saturday, and Sunday nearest August 20) of Nossa Senhora de Agonia (Our Lady of Agony), when the women wear strident orange, scarlet, and Prussian blue, with layers of golden necklaces with heart- and cross-shaped pendants.

WHAT TO SEE & DO

The town center is **Praça da República,** one of the handsomest squares in Portugal. At its heart is the much-photographed **Chafariz Fountain,** constructed in the 16th century, with water spewing from the mouths of its figures. The most impressive building on the square is the **Misericórdia,** a dour, squat three-story structure, unique in the country. The lower level is an arcade composed of five austere Roman arches, whereas the two upper levels are ponderous Renaissance balconies. All are crowned by a rooftop crucifix. Each level's four supporting pillars are primitive caryatidlike figures between which are interspersed bright red geraniums in flower boxes. Adjoining the Charity Hospital is a church fronting Rua da Bandeira. Inside is a combination of pictorial tiles made in 1714, ornate baroque altars, a painted ceiling, and wood carvings.

The other building dominating the square is the old **Town Hall,** constructed over an arcade made up of three wide and low Gothic arches. The crenel-topped facade displays a royal coat-of-arms and wrought-iron balcony windows above each arch. Originally the Paços do Concelho, it was constructed during the reign of Manuel I and completed under João III. From the small sidewalk tables and chairs, you can observe the square's activities and sample pastries, such as *torta de Viana.*

Igreja Matriz, down Rua de Sacadura Cabral at Largo do Instituto Histórico do Minho, was begun by João I in 1285 and completed in 1433. Dominated by a large Gothic arched portal, the facade is flanked by two battlemented towers. The interior archway is carved with granite figures, acanthus leaves, and simplistic statuary with moon-shaped faces. The inside is cold but with an excellent trompe l'oeil ceiling.

WHERE TO STAY

MODERATE

HOTEL DO PARQUE, Praça da Galiza, 4900 Viana do Castelo. Tel. 058/82-86-05. Fax 058/82-86-12. 123 rms. TV TEL
$ Rates (including breakfast): 10,850$–11,750$ ($66.20–$71.70) single; 12,950$–15,500$ ($79–$94.60) double. AE, DC, MC, V. **Parking:** Free.
This four-star hotel sits at the base of the bridge crossing the Lima River on the edge of town. It has a motel/miniresort flavor, with lounges overlooking two pools. On its rooftop is a panoramic restaurant, serving regional and international dishes, and adjoining it is a solarium with a refreshment area. Intermixed with the main-floor lounge is an interior winter garden. The lounges have soft leather armchairs. For evening entertainment there is a disco*boîte.* The guest rooms are quite contemporary, with plenty of built-in furnishings, heating, piped-in music, and balconies.

HOTEL SANTA LUZIA, Monte de Santa Luzia, 4900 Viana do Castelo. Tel. 058/82-88-89. Fax 058/82-88-92. 55 rms. TEL
$ Rates (including breakfast): 16,000$ ($97.60) single; 18,000$ ($109.80) double. AE, DC, MC, V. **Parking:** Free.
Some 3½ miles from the center, the Santa Luzia sits on a wooded hillside high above the most congested part of the city. It stands just behind the illuminated dome of the neo-Byzantine Basilica de Santa Luzia. Built in 1895, the hotel has neoclassical details and granite balconies, giving it the appearance of a royal palace, especially when it is floodlit at night. To reach it, you have to negotiate winding cobblestone roads, which, because of their curves, take motorists through a forest. Once at the summit, you'll find a view over the city and the river that is the best in the region.

In 1986, the hotel was completely renovated, an art deco sheen added to the high-ceilinged public rooms. It has long expanses of glistening marble, stylish accessories from the Jazz Age, a comfortable bar/restaurant, and spacious and comfortably furnished guest rooms arranged along both sides of enormous and echoing hallways. Fixed-price meals in the dining room begin at 3,000$ ($18.30) and are served daily from 12:30 to 3pm and 7:30 to 10pm. There's an outdoor pool sunk into one of the hotel's gardens.

HOTEL VIANA SOL, Largo Vasco da Gama, 4900 Viana do Castelo. Tel. 058/82-89-95. Fax 058/82-89-97. 65 rms, 1 suite. TV TEL
$ Rates (including breakfast): 9,700$–15,000$ ($59.20–$91.50) single; 11,500$–

20,000$ ($70.20–$122) double; 25,000$ ($152.50) suite. AE, DC, MC, V. **Parking:** Free.

Set behind a dignified granite-and-stucco facade, near a commemorative column and fountain in the town center, this well-designed hotel opened in 1986. In contrast to its elegantly severe exterior, its spacious public rooms are sheathed with layers of white marble, capped with mirrored ceilings, and illuminated with a three-tiered atrium lit with a skylight and filled with plants. The lobby bar lies near a pagoda-shaped fountain. The guest rooms are well furnished. There's a restaurant on the premises, plus a pool, a health club, tennis courts, and squash courts.

INEXPENSIVE

HOTEL AFONSO III, Avenida Dom Afonso III 494, 4900 Viana do Castelo. Tel. 058/82-90-01. Fax 058/266-38. 89 rms, 1 suite. TEL
$ Rates (including breakfast): 7,200$–8,600$ ($43.90–$52.50) single; 9,900$–11,800$ ($60.40–$72) double; 15,000$ ($91.50) suite. AE, DC, MC, V. **Parking:** Free.

This first-class hotel opened in 1971. Over half of the attractively furnished guest rooms are graced with private balconies, and most contain TVs. The contemporary decor consists mainly of black-and-white marble, with a lobby sheathed with nautically inspired designs crafted from richly grained hardwood. The overall tone is both simple and sophisticated. The seventh-floor restaurant provides a panoramic view over the Lima River; meals cost 2,800$ ($17.10). Other facilities include a convention hall, a *boîte,* a bar, and pools. Laundry and 24-hour room service are available.

HOTEL ALIANÇA, Avenida dos Combatentes da Grande Guerra, 4900 Viana do Castelo. Tel. 058/82-94-98. 26 rms. TV TEL
$ Rates (including breakfast): 8,000$ ($48.80) single; 9,000$ ($54.90) double. MC, V. **Parking:** Free.

The Aliança was built in the 18th century, but its facade was restored in 1962, leaving a streamlined stucco sheathing with granite window trim. It sits on the corner of the town's main street at the edge of the river, within sight of the loading derricks and cranes. This is by no means a stylish or upscale hotel, but its slightly dowdy charm and the sincere concern of the Portuguese family who run it more than compensate. Each guest room is likely to have a high ceiling, slightly frayed furniture, and a blandly old-fashioned color scheme, along with 1930s accessories. Laundry and room service are available.

BUDGET

RESIDENCIAL VIANA MAR, Avenida dos Combatentes da Grande Guerra 215, 4900 Viana do Castelo. Tel. 058/82-89-62. Fax 058/82-89-62. 36 rms (16 with bath). TEL
$ Rates (including breakfast): 5,000$ ($30.50) single without bath; 8,000$ ($48.80) double with bath. AE, DC, MC, V. **Parking:** Free.

Residencial Viana Mar is on the main commercial thoroughfare of town behind a granite facade whose severity is relieved by colorful awnings. Inside, near the nondescript reception area, lies a sunken bar. Each guest room has basic furnishings. A few of the hotel's rooms are contained in two nearby annexes. Only breakfast is served.

NEARBY PLACES TO STAY

The most romantic way to stay in and around Viana do Castelo is not at one of the hotels recommended above but at one of the antique *quintas* in the environs. In these restored manor houses you can stay with the Portuguese aristocracy. You can make reservations through **Delegaçao de Turismo de Ponte de Lima, TURIHAB— Associaçao Turismo de Habitaçao,** Praça da República, 4990 Ponte de Lima (tel. 058/94-27-29; fax 058/74-14-44). Payment is made by check sent directly to the owners, with 50% prepayment required when your reservation is made. A minimum stay of 3 nights is required, and bookings must be made at least 3 days before your planned arrival. The environs of Viana do Castelo have some of the most elaborate and stylized quintas and manor houses in all of Portugal. A random sampling of the best ones follow.

EXPENSIVE

PAÇO D'ANHA, Anha, 4900 Viana do Castelo. Tel. 058/32-24-59. Fax 058/32-39-04. 6 apts. TV TEL
$ Rates (including breakfast): 22,000$ ($134.20) apt for four. AE, DC, MC, V. **Parking:** Free.

The Paço d'Anha has centuries of tradition. A fine example of Portuguese aristocratic architecture, it is in a beautiful setting near the Atlantic coast, with pinewoods, lawns, and vineyards where the fine and fruity Paço d'Anha Vinho Verde white wine is produced. In the annexes next to the main building are six apartments, each with two double beds and a bath. Guests can use the facilities available at the farm, including a tennis court. They can take walks in the surrounding gardens and woods and visit the 17th-century manor and cellars. There's always a supply of wood available for the fireplaces.

INEXPENSIVE

CASA DE REQUEIJO, Lugar de Requeijo, 4970 Arcos de Valdevez. Tel. 058/652-72. Fax 058/633-10. 10 rms.
$ Rates (including breakfast): 10,000$ ($61) single; 13,500$ ($82.40) double. DC, MC, V. **Parking:** Free.

⭐ Ideally suited as a base for touring the north of Portugal, about 25 miles from Viana do Castelo, this is a 16th-century manor house surrounded by a crenellated wall that local scholars say is typical of the 18th century. The house was actually conceived as an outbuilding to a much older and partially ruined 1250 "mother house," which stands nearby. The complex is owned by the family of Alberto Alves Pereira and his wife, Catherine, the charming on-site managers who are the 46th generation of their family to control the place.

The building overlooks the River Vez, reputedly the least polluted river in Europe, which is well-stocked with fish and allows swimmers to swim long distances up and down its sylvan length. There's a pool on the premises, plus a miniflotilla of river craft for use (free) by guests. You'll also find a family chapel, a TV lounge, a cocktail lounge, Ping-Pong tables, a tennis court, a piano, and tables for card playing in the living room. Many hikers and bicyclists (including sports-minded groups from the United States) use the Casa de Requeijo as a base for treks within Portugal's most isolated national park, whose edge lies just 6 miles away. Snacks can be prepared in-house for guests who request them, but more appealing are the many restaurants, reachable by car or by boat, which lie within an easy trek.

SOLAR DE CORTEGAÇA, Subportela, 4900 Viana do Castelo. Tel. 058/97-16-39. 3 rms.
$ Rates (including breakfast): 8,000$ ($48.80) single; 9,000$ ($54.90) double. No credit cards. **Parking:** Free

This 18th-century manor house stands at the center of a large tract of fertile land whose fields and barns are rented to several tenant farmers. This establishment lies about 4 miles east of Viana do Castelo, in the parish of Subportela, on the left bank of the Lima River. Recently restored, the house was built by the family of a Portuguese explorer who some sources credit with the early commercial development of Newfoundland, Canada. Today, the house is maintained by the de Abreu Coutinho family, descendants of the original builders. It has rustically comfortable guest rooms with modern comfort, but its architectural characteristics have been for the most part carefully preserved. The family welcomes visitors into their private home and do not consider it a hotel at all; rather they regard it as a private home open to temporary paying guests. To reach it, you'll have to take a private car or taxi to a point near the EN203 highway between Viana do Castelo and Ponte de Lima.

WHERE TO DINE
MODERATE

DOLCE VITA, Rua do Poço 44. Tel. 248-60.
   Cuisine: ITALIAN. **Reservations:** Not necessary.
   $ Prices: Appetizers 450$–650$ ($2.70–$4); main courses 900$–1,800$ ($5.50–$11); pizzas from 130$ (80¢). AE, DC, MC, V.
   Open: Lunch daily noon–3pm; dinner daily 7–10pm.
Dolce Vita, as its name suggests, is an Italian eatery and pizzeria. The pizzas are considered the best in town, and you might try some concoctions unfamiliar to you, including one made with *bacalhau* (codfish). You can also order some good pastas, such as lasagne Dolce Vita. Among more familiar Italian specialties are beef pizzaiola, veal cutlet bolognese, and risotto piemontese.

OS 3 POTES, Beco dos Fornos 7–9. Tel. 82-99-28.
   Cuisine: PORTUGUESE/INTERNATIONAL. **Reservations:** Recommended.
   $ Prices: Appetizers 175$–950$ ($1.10–$5.80); main courses 995$–2,500$ ($6.10–$15.30); 2,000$ ($12.20) fixed-price lunch; 2,500$ ($15.30) fixed-price dinner.
   Open: Lunch daily noon–3:30pm; dinner daily 7pm–midnight.
Like a country house in the center of town, Os 3 Potes, off Praça da República, was an old bakery before its conversion into one of the best regional restaurants in Viana do Castelo. From Praça da República, head down Rua de Sacadura Cabral (the restaurant is somewhat hard to find but worth the search). The atmosphere is rustic, and on Friday and Saturday from June to September folk dancing is offered. The food is good, too, but you should have your hotel call in advance to make a reservation. I'd suggest *caldo verde* to begin, followed by such good-tasting main dishes as codfish 3 Potes, lampreys (eels), or fondue *bourguignonne*. I always skip dessert and settle for the Irish coffee instead.

RESTAURANTE PANORAMICO, in Hotel do Parque, Praça da Galiza. Tel. 82-86-05.
   Cuisine: MINHO/INTERNATIONAL. **Reservations:** Not necessary.
   $ Prices: Appetizers 450$–850$ ($2.70–$5.20); main courses 1,500$–2,200$ ($9.20–$13.40). AE, DC, MC, V.
   Open: Lunch daily noon–3pm; dinner daily 7–10:30pm.
In addition to offering a good selection of well-prepared food, this panoramic restaurant in a previously recommended hotel offers a sweeping view of the River Lima and the famous bridge designed by Alexandre-Gustave Eiffel. The restaurant sits on the topmost floor of this hotel, reached via an elevator from the lobby. Amid a modern turquoise-and-white decor, you can enjoy a bill of fare including cream soups, pork *piri-piri*, peppersteak, and grilled turbot.

INEXPENSIVE

ALAMBIQUE, Rua Manuel Espregueira 86. Tel. 82-38-94.
   Cuisine: MINHO. **Reservations:** Not necessary.
   $ Prices: Appetizers 350$–650$ ($2.10–$4); main courses 850$–1,200$ ($5.20–$7.30); tourist menu 1,700$ ($10.40). AE, DC, MC, V.
   Open: Lunch Wed–Mon noon–3pm; dinner Wed–Mon 7–10pm.
You enter this typical Portuguese restaurant through a large wine vat. Inside you'll find many of the specialties for which the cooks of northern Portugal are known, including codfish Antiga Viana, *churrasco de porco* (pork), *cabrito* (goat), tripe Porto style, and lampreys bordelaise. One of the chef's most memorable dishes is *feijoada a transmontana,* bean-and-meat stew. For a beginning, you can order either *sopa a alentejana* or *sopa do mar.*

TÚNEL, Rua dos Manjovos 1. Tel. 82-21-88.
   Cuisine: MINHO. **Reservations:** Not necessary.
   $ Prices: Appetizers 200$–300$ ($1.20–$1.80); main courses 850$–1,500$

($5.20–$9.20); fixed-price lunch 850$ ($5.20); fixed-price dinner 950$ ($5.80). AE, DC, MC, V. **Open:** Lunch Sun–Fri 11:30am–2pm; dinner Sun–Fri 7–10pm. **Closed:** Oct 20–Nov 30.

Túnel, with an excellent regional cuisine, lies right off Avenida dos Combatantes da Grande Guerra. At certain times you can order quail or roast kid. The fish dishes are usually the best, however. You might begin with a rich-tasting vegetable soup, made with fresh vegetables from the field. The dining room is on the second floor. You pass through a simple snack bar at ground level.

MADEIRA

The island of Madeira, 530 miles southwest of Portugal, is the mountain peak of a volcanic mass. Its craggy spires and sea-coast precipices of umber-dark basalt end with a sheer drop into the blue water. The surrounding sea is so deep that large sperm whales often come near the shore.

The summit of the undersea mountain is found at Madeira's center, where Pico Ruivo, often snow-capped, rises to an altitude of 6,105 feet above sea level. From that point project the rocky ribs and ravines of the island, running to the coast. If you stand on the sea-swept balcony of Cabo Girão, one of the world's highest ocean cliffs (1,933 feet above the sea), you'll understand the Eden-like quality of Madeira. The national poet Luís Vaz de Camões called it "at the end of the world."

Madeira, now an autonomous archipelago, is only 35 miles in length and about 13 miles in breadth at its widest point. It contains nearly 100 miles of coastline but no beaches. In its volcanic soil, plants and flowers blaze like the Tahitian palette of Gauguin. From jacaranda and masses of bougain-villea to orchids and geraniums, from whortleberry to prickly pear, poinsettias, cannas, frangipani, birds of paradise, and wisteria, the land is a botanical garden. Custard apples, avocados, mangoes, and bananas grow profusely. Fragrances such as vanilla and wild fennel intermingle with sea breezes and pervade the ravines, sweeping down the rocky headlands.

Claimed by the British as a sentimental dominion, Madeira has been popular with them ever since. Post-Victorian women wore wide-brimmed hats for protection from the sun. Now that has changed: Everyone comes here specifically to enjoy the sun. Legend has it that two English lovers discovered the island about half a century before its known date of exploration. Supposedly Robert Machim and Anna d'Arfet, fleeing England, were swept off their course by a tempest and deposited on the eastern coast.

In 1419, João Gonçalves Zarco and Tristao Vaz Teixeira, captains under Henry the Navigator, discovered Madeira while exploring the African coastline, some 350 miles to the east. As it was densely covered with impenetrable virgin forests, they named it Madeira, which means "wood." Soon it was set afire to clear it for habitation. The holocaust is said to have lasted 7 years, until all but a small northern section was reduced to ashes.

The hillsides are so richly cultivated today that you would never know there had ever been a fire. Many of the groves and vineyards, protected by buffers of sugarcane, grow on stone-wall ledges, which almost spill into the sea. The farmers plant so close to the cliff's edge they must have at least a dash of goat's blood in them. The terraced mountain slopes are irrigated by a complex network of *levadas* (water channels). It is

WHAT'S SPECIAL ABOUT MADEIRA

Great Towns/Villages

☐ Funchal, the capital—founded in 1428 and opening onto a fine natural harbor on the south coast.

☐ Câmara de Lobos, west of Funchal, a fishing village of red-tile-roofed whitewashed houses—built around a cliff-protected harbor and a rock-strewn beach.

☐ Camacha, the island's highest village, northeast of Funchal—standing at an altitude of almost 2,300 feet.

☐ Machico, northeast of Funchal—where João Gonçalves Zarco and crew made their final landfall on the island in 1419.

☐ Porto Santo, "the other Madeira"—a tiny dry island a world apart but part of the same volcanic Atlantic chain.

Beaches

☐ Porto Santo's coastline, one of Europe's most unspoiled stretches of beach—4 miles of golden sand where Columbus once trod.

Ace Attractions

☐ Toboggan rides, once the major means of transportation, now used just for fun—wicker-sided sleds on wooden runners racing across cobblestone streets.

☐ Cabo Girão—considered the second-loftiest promontory of Europe.

Shopping

☐ Embroidery, wine, and wickerware—these are the products that have earned Madeira a position of honor on every shopper's world tour.

Parks/Gardens

☐ Jardim Botânico, in the hills at Caminho do Meio—almost every tree, plant, or flower on the island grows here.

---

estimated that there are some 1,330 miles of these levadas, including about 25 miles of tunnels. These levadas were originally constructed of stone by slaves and convicts. They are most often 1 to 2 feet wide and deep. Water from mountain springs is carried in them.

About 25 miles to the northeast, Porto Santo is the only other inhabited island in the Madeira archipelago. *Réalités* magazine called it "another world, arid, desolate and waterless." Unlike Madeira, Porto Santo contains beaches, but is not yet developed for mass tourism. It is previewed at the end of this chapter.

SEEING MADEIRA

Madeira is not really suited for a day trip from Lisbon, although some visitors try to achieve that frantic goal. It deserves a minimum of 3 days of your time, if you can afford that much. For more specific uses of your time, refer to "Attractions" later in this chapter for recommendations on how to occupy your time, whether sightseeing or relaxing.

Madeira is really a destination unto itself. Many British fly there directly, avoiding the mainland of Portugal altogether (see "Arriving," below). Most North Americans, however, tie in a visit to Madeira with trips to Lisbon. Madeira is an extremely popular destination in both summer and winter, and the limited number of planes flying there may not have seats at the last minute, so book well in advance.

Cruise ships sometimes anchor here, but there is no regular passenger boat service to Madeira from the mainland. That means you'll have to fly. Many charter flights link

Funchal with the capitals of Europe, although the regular route is from Lisbon to Funchal on TAP Air Portugal. See "Arriving," below, for more details.

1. ORIENTATION

ARRIVING The quickest and most convenient way to reach Madeira from Lisbon is on a **TAP** flight (the trip takes 1½ hours). The plane stops at the Madeira Airport, then goes on to Porto Santo. There are six flights daily. However, if you're booking a TAP flight from, say, New York to Lisbon, you can have the side trip to Madeira included at no extra cost, providing you have a regular—that is, not an excursion—ticket.

In addition, TAP has a weekly direct flight between Faro in the Algarve and Funchal, an extension of its Frankfurt-Faro service. TAP also flies in about four times daily from London (trip time: 4 hours).

Lately, many smaller airlines have joined in the competition. **Gibraltar Airways,** Avenida Zarco 2 (tel. 091/29-113) in Funchal, also operates a nonstop service between London and Funchal. It offers several flights a week. A local charter company, **Air Columbus,** Aeroporto Santa Catarina (tel. 091/52-30-01), at Madeira, links with an associate in Canada, **Ultra Mar Charter Corporation,** 347 College St., Suite 205, Toronto, Canada M5T 1S5 (tel. 416/921-9191), to offer flights two times monthly along a route that links Toronto with Montreal before flying on to the Azores and Funchal.

In Madeira, the planes arrive at **Aeroporto Santa Catarina** (tel. 091/52-29-41), east of Funchal at Santa Cruz. The ride into the town center takes about 35 minutes.

Since most visitors use TAP and not one of these smaller lines, you don't need to go to the airport to reconfirm your ticket but can do so right in Funchal at the TAP office on Avenida Comunidades Madeirenses 8–10 (tel. 091/301-51). Hours are daily from 9am to noon and 2 to 5:30pm.

Taxis wait to take airlines passengers anywhere they want to go on the island. However, if you're going to Funchal, you can take a bus from the airport. Buses also leave Funchal heading back to the airport. Departures are from Avenida do Mar in Funchal, and service is daily—in both directions—from 7am to 11pm.

TOURIST INFORMATION An English-speaking staff runs the desk at the **Madeira Tourist Office,** Avenida Arriaga 18 (tel. 091/22-5658) in Funchal. Hours are Monday through Friday from 9am to 8pm and Saturday and Sunday from 9am to 6pm. Here you'll be given a map of the island, and the staff will also, if asked, make suggestions about the best ways to explore their beautiful island. You can also inquire about ferry connections to the neighboring island of Porto Santo (see the last section of this chapter).

ISLAND LAYOUT The capital of Madeira, **Funchal,** is the focal point of the entire island and the gateway to outlying villages. When Zarco landed in 1419, the sweet odor of wild fennel led him to name it after the aromatic herb, called *funcho* in Portuguese. Today the southern coast city of hillside-shelved villas and narrow winding streets is the garden spot of the island. Its numerous estates, including the former residence of Zarco, the Quinta das Cruzes, are among the most exotic in Europe.

With a population of 100,000, Funchal has a long street running along the waterfront called **Avenida do Mar.** This often traffic-clogged artery runs in an east-west direction. North of this wide boulevard is **Avenida Arriaga,** considered the "main street" of Funchal. At the eastern end of this thoroughfare is the cathedral (Sé), and at the western end is a large traffic circle whose center is graced with a fountain. As the Avenida Arriaga heads west, site of most of the major hotels, it changes its name to **Avenida do Infante.** However, as it moves east it becomes known as **Rua do Aljube.** Running in a north-south direction, the other most

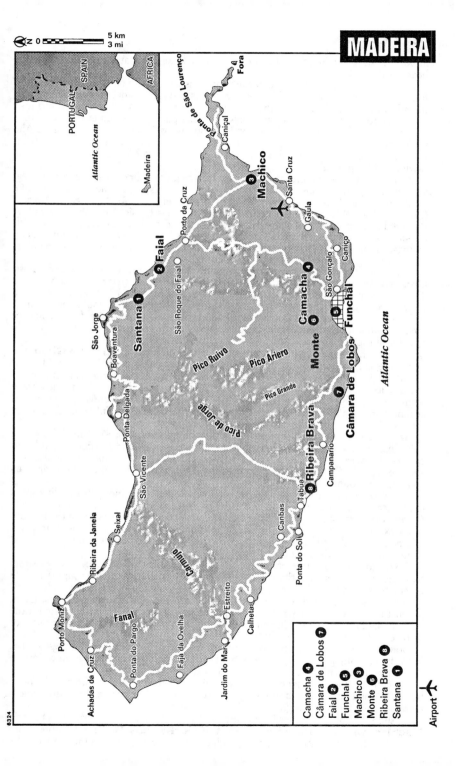

important street of Funchal, **Avenida Zarco,** links the waterfront area with the heart of the old city.

To explore and savor Madeira, the adventurous visitor with endless time will go on foot across some of the trails. Hand-hewn stones and gravel-sided embankments lead the adventurous (definitely not the queasy) along precipitous ledges, down into lush ravines, across flowering meadows. These dizzying paths are found everywhere from the hillsides of the wine-rich region of Estreito de Câmara de Lobos to the wickerwork center of Camacha. A much easier way to go, of course, is on an organized tour or via the local buses, although you may prefer to risk the hazardous driving on hairpin curves.

Heading west from Funchal, you'll pass banana groves almost spilling into the sea, women doing their laundry on rocks, and homes so tiny they're almost like dollhouses. Less than 6 miles away lies the coastal village of ✪ **Câmara de Lobos** (Room of the Wolves), the subject of several paintings by Sir Winston Churchill. A sheltered and tranquil shell-shaped cove, it is set amid rocks and towering cliffs, with hill-climbing cottages, terraces, and date palms. In the late afternoon, naked youngsters loll and play in the cove, alongside the bobbing fishing boats in such colors as sunflower gold, kelly green, and marine blue.

The road north from the village through the vineyards leads to **Estreito de Câmara de Lobos,** the heart of the wine-growing region that produces Madeira. The men who cultivate the ribbonlike terraces can be seen laboring in the fields, wearing brown stocking caps with tasseled tops. Along the way, you'll spot women sitting on mossy stone steps doing Madeira embroidery. At times, clouds move in over the mountaintops to obscure the view, but then they pass off toward the sea or tumble down a hillside.

Scaling a hill studded with pine and eucalyptus, you'll reach ✪ **Cabo Girão,** the oceanside cliff mentioned in the introduction. It is considered the second-loftiest promontory in Europe, and a belvedere overlooks the sea and the saffron-colored rocks below. Close by, you can see how the land is cultivated in Madeira, one terrace seemingly no larger than a small throw rug. (Incidentally, the blonds you see in and around here aren't peroxided; rather, the straw-colored hair was inherited from early Flemish settlers sent to the island.)

Try to return to Funchal by veering off the coastal road, past São Martinho to the belvedere at **Pico dos Parcelos.** In one of the most idyllic spots on the island, you can see the ocean, mountains, orange and banana groves, bougainvillea, poinsettias, and the capital. Whether it's roosters crowing, babies crying in faraway huts, or goats bleating, the sound carries for miles.

By heading north from Funchal, you can visit some of the most outstanding spots in the heart of the island. Going first through Santo António, you'll eventually reach **Curral das Freiras,** a petite village huddled around an old monastery at the bottom of an extinct volcanic crater. The site, whose name means Corral of the Nuns, was originally a secluded convent that protected the good sisters from sea-weary, woman-hungry mariners and pirates.

If you go north in a different direction, one of the goals is **Santana.** Many visitors have described it as something out of Disney's *Fantasia.* Picture an alpine setting complete with waterfalls, cobblestone streets, green meadows sprinkled with multi-colored blossoms, thatched cottages, swarms of roses, and plunging ravines. Of it, novelist Paul Bowles once wrote: "It is as if a 19th-century painter with a taste for the baroque had invented a countryside to suit his own personal fantasy. It is the sort of picture that used to adorn the grocer's calendar."

Southwest of the village is **Queimadas,** the site of a 3,000-foot-high rest house. From here, many people make the 3-hour trek to the apex of **Pico Ruivo** (Purple Peak), the highest point on the island, 6,105 feet above sea level.

Directly southeast of Santana leads to **Faial,** a colorful hamlet with tiny A-frame huts. The road descends in a series of sharp turns into a deep ravine. The lush terraces here are built for cows to graze.

In the east, about 18 miles from Funchal (a short drive from the airport) is historic **Machico,** with its much-visited **Church of Senhor dos Milagres,** dating from the mid-15th century. According to legend, the church was built over the tombs of the two star-crossed English lovers Robert Machim and Anna d'Arfet. Try to view the village from the belvedere of **Camoë Pequeno.** In the vicinity is a 300-foot-long grotto said to be the deepest in Madeira.

On the way back from Machico, you can detour inland to **Camacha,** perched in a setting of flowers and orchards. It's the island center of the wickerwork industry. You can buy items here (although the stores in Funchal are heavily supplied) or just watch chairs and other items being made by the local craftspeople.

2. GETTING AROUND

Remember that distances are short on Madeira, but regardless of where you're going, allow plenty of time to get there because of the winding road conditions.

BY PUBLIC TRANSPORTATION The cheapest way of getting around Madeira—providing you're not rushed—is by bus. Local buses go all over the island. A typical fare in town is 210$ ($1.30), but rides in the countryside can cost 600$ ($3.70) to 700$ ($4.30). Sometimes only one bus a day runs to the island's most distant points. A helpful reader, Herman Marcuse of Arlington, Virginia, wrote: "One of the best-kept secrets on Madeira is that you can make excursions on local buses at a fraction of the cost charged by the tour companies."

Most buses depart from the large park at the eastern part of the waterfront-bordering Avenida do Mar. If you're going to Camacha or Camico, you'll find buses leaving from a little square at the eastern sector of Rua da Alfandega, which runs parallel to Avenida do Mar near the marketplace.

BY TAXI The going taxi rate is about 12,000$ ($73.20) to 14,000$ ($85.40) per day, although this should always be negotiated and agreed on in advance. When the cost is divided among three or four passengers, it isn't so steep. Most taxis are often Peugeots or Mercedes, so you'll ride in relative safety and not have to cope with the nightmarish roads. If you're in Funchal and want a taxi to take you back to your hotel in the environs, you'll usually find a line of them waiting across from the tourist office along Avenida Arriaga. Many of the taxi drivers speak English.

BY CAR Unless you're a skilled driver used to narrow roads, reckless drivers, and hairpin turns, I don't recommend you rent a car on the island, although there are several local companies that will be only too happy to furnish you a car for a price. Most hotels can make arrangements for car rentals.

The leading car-rental companies in Madeira include **Avis** (tel. toll free 800/331-2112 in the U.S.), at the Aeroporto Santa Catarina (tel. 091/52-43-92) in Madeira. Avis also has a branch office in Funchal at Largo António Nobre 164 (tel. 091/76-34-95). **Hertz** (tel. toll free 800/654-3001 in the U.S.) also rents cars. It, too, has a branch office at the airport (tel. 091/52-43-60) in Madeira and another in Funchal at Rua Ivens 12 (tel. 091/22-60-26). Finally, **Budget Rent-a-Car** (tel. toll free 800/472-3325 in the U.S.) has a branch office at the airport in Madeira (tel. 091/96-56-19) and another in Funchal at Estrada Monumental 239 (tel. 091/76-56-19).

 MADEIRA

American Express The representative in Madeira is **Top Tours Travel Agency,** Rua Brigadero Coseiro (tel. 091/74-26-11), in Funchal. It is open Monday through Friday from 9:30am to 1pm and 2:30 to 6:30pm.

Area Code The country code for telephoning Portugal is **351,** and the area code for Madeira is **091.**

Bookstores A good English bookstore is **Livraria Inglesa,** Rua Carreira 43 (tel. 091/22-44-90), open Monday through Friday from 10am to 7pm and Saturday from 10am to 1pm.

Business Hours Most shops are open Monday through Friday from 9am to 1pm and 3 to 7pm and Saturday from 9am to 1pm; they're usually closed Sunday. **Municipal buildings** are open Monday through Friday from 9am to 12:30pm and 2 to 5:30pm.

Car Rentals See "Getting Around," earlier in this chapter.

Climate See "When to Go" in Chapter 2.

Consulates The **U.S. Consulate** is at Avenida Luís de Camões, Block D, Apt. B (tel. 091/74-38-08), off Avenida do Infante. The **British Consulate** is at Avenida de Zarco 2 (tel. 091/22-12-22).

Currency See "Information, Entry Requirements & Money" in Chapter 2.

Dentist A good English-speaking dentist is **John de Sousa, D.D.,** Marina Forum Building, Avenida Arriaga (tel. 091/23-12-77), in Funchal.

Doctor A good English-speaking doctor is **Francis Zino, M.D.,** Edifício Jasmineiro, Rua do Jasmineiro (tel. 091/74-22-27), in Funchal.

Drugstores Drugstores are open Monday through Saturday from 9am to 1pm and 3 to 7pm. There is a rotation emergency and night service schedule posted on the door of all chemists. Sunday has a special schedule, too. A centrally located and reliable local chemist is **Farmácia Honorato,** Rua da Carreira 62 (tel. 091/22-32-97). Dial 166 to locate a pharmacy that's open.

Emergencies Numbers to keep in mind include 115 for a general **emergency;** 091/22-00-64 for the **police;** 091/74-11-15 for the **Red Cross;** 091/74-21-11 for a **hospital** emergency.

Eyeglasses A well-stocked optometrist whose staff speaks English is **Oculista Synphronio,** Rua João Gaga 14 (tel. 22-29-62), in Funchal.

Hairdressers Many hotels maintain in-house beauty salons and barbershops, but a consistently reliable bet for both men and women in Funchal is **Correia,** Avenida Arriaga 30, 2nd floor D. (tel. 34-485).

Holidays See "When to Go" in Chapter 2.

Hospital The island's largest hospital is **Hospital Distrital do Funchal,** Cruz de Carvalho (tel. 74-21-11).

Information See "Tourist Information," earlier in this chapter.

Laundry/Dry Cleaning Try **Lavandaria Donini,** Rua das Pretas (tel. 091/22-44-06), in Funchal. Any clothing can be laundered or dry cleaned here within one or two days. It is open Monday through Friday from 9am to 7pm. Most hotels will also provide this service.

Libraries There is no library with a noteworthy collection of English-language books, although the **Biblioteca Municipal,** Praça de Municipio (tel. 22-00-64), in Funchal, provides a quiet place for reading and a worthy collection of Portuguese-language books and periodicals.

Lost Property If anything is found, it will likely be returned to the island's main **police station** on Rua João de Deus in Funchal (tel. 22-10-21).

Luggage There are no storage facilities other than those provided as a good-will gesture by your hotel. Ask the receptionist or concierge.

Newspapers/Magazines The island stocks a good selection of such English-language publications as *Newsweek, Time,* and *The International Herald Tribune,* as well as periodicals in French, German, and Spanish. Especially useful is a locally produced English-language publication, *Madeira Island Bulletin,* distributed free at the tourist office and within many of the island's more visible hotels.

Photographic Needs Many kiosks within large hotels will sell rolls of film and perhaps send them out for development. More specialized is **Quali Foto,** Edifício Lido Sol, Store no. 1, Estrada Monumental (tel. 76-24-00), in Funchal.

Police Dial 22-00-64.

Post Office If you've had your mail sent *poste restante* (general delivery), you can pick it up at the **Zarco Post Office,** Avenida Zarco, 9000 Funchal (tel. 091/22-90-43), near the tourist office, but you should bring your passport to identify yourself. You can also place long-distance phone calls here, which will help avoid steep hotel surcharges. It's also possible to send telegrams, faxes, and telexes. The office is open Monday through Friday from 8:30am to 8pm and Saturday from 9am to 12:30pm. Other post offices offering the same service include **Calouste Gulbenkian,** Avenida Calouste Gulbenkian (open Monday through Friday from 9am to 12:30pm and 2:30 to 6:30pm), near Monument of the Infante D. Henrîque; **Monumental,** Estrada Monumental, near the Lido swimming pool (open Monday through Friday from 9am to 7pm); and **Mercado,** Rua do Arcipreste, near the Municipal Market (open Monday through Friday from 9am to 6:30pm).

Many *correios* signs can be found in the center pointing out the way to the nearest post office.

Religious Services   Roman Catholic services are conducted all over the island, especially at St. Peter's Church, Largo São Pedro (tel. 22-25-23) in Funchal. There is no synagogue. However, services in English are conducted at the **English Church,** Rua do Quebra Costas, in Funchal, and also at the **Anglican Church,** Rua do Castanheiro, also in Funchal. Since there is no number to call for information, inquire about the times of services at the tourist office.

Restrooms   These are available at the airport, at hotels, and in some museums. There are not enough public toilets. Locals often use cafes or taverns, although in theory these facilities are reserved for customers.

Safety   In crime statistics, Madeira is safer than mainland Portugal, especially Lisbon. However, in any area that attracts thousands upon thousands of tourists, you get a criminal element who would prey on these visitors. Protect your valuables, as you would at any resort in the world. Pickpockets and purse snatchers are the major villains.

Taxes   Madeira imposes no special taxes, other than the value-added tax (VAT) imposed on all goods and services purchased in Portugal. Refer to "Fast Facts: Portugal" in Chapter 2 for more information.

Taxis   See "Getting Around," earlier in this chapter.

Weather   Call 091/331-61 24 hours a day for information.

3. ACCOMMODATIONS

In summer, when every other European resort on the seafront socks you with its highest tariffs, Madeira used to experience its "low season." And not because of bad weather, although August is still not the most desirable month to visit because of the *capacete,* a shroud of mist that often envelops the island.

Summer was traditionally considered the low season because the early British visitors, really the first tourists, set a pattern of mass descent in winter, thereby crowding the hotels and inflating its tariffs.

That long-ago pattern, however, seems to have broken, and Madeira now experiences more of a year-round popularity. In fact, it's become hard to get an airplane seat there in the peak summer months without reservations made way in advance.

Madeira's hotels, among the best in all of Portugal, range from some of the finest deluxe citadels in Europe to attractively priced and old-fashioned *quintas* for budgeteers.

Chances are you won't be staying directly in the heart of Funchal but in one of the hotels on the outskirts, where many of the best hotels are. However, for those who want to be right in the heart of the action (and not be dependent on transportation), I will have a few suggestions, all of which are reasonable in price. The most expensive hotels—that is, those with pools and resort amenities—are on the outskirts. The center of Funchal is filled with heavy traffic most of the day, which means that hotels in the center often tend to be noisy. Nevertheless, for shopping and the widest selection of restaurants, Funchal is a magnet for the visitor.

VERY EXPENSIVE

REID'S HOTEL, Estrada Monumental 139, 9000 Funchal, Madeira. Tel. 091/76-30-01, or toll free 800/223-6800 in the U.S. Fax 091/76-44-99. 167 rms, 21 suites. A/C MINIBAR TV TEL **Bus:** 5 or 6.

$ Rates (including breakfast): Winter: 32,800$ ($200.10) single; 46,800$ ($285.50) double; 67,900$ ($414.20) suite. Summer and fall: 28,200$ ($172) single; 40,500$ ($247.10) double; 58,500$ ($356.90) suite. AE, DC, MC, V. **Parking:** Free.

⭐ The legendary place to stay in Funchal is Reid's Hotel, founded in 1891 by William Reid, a young Scotsman. It's now owned by the Blandy family of wine and shipping fame. Its position is "smashing," as the British say, along the coastal road at the edge of Funchal, on 10 acres of multiterraced gardens all the way down the hillside to the rocky shores. The English who frequent the hotel in large numbers (one famous guest was Sir Winston Churchill) spend their days strolling the scented walks lined with blue and pink hydrangeas, hedges of geraniums, gardenias, banana trees, ferns, and white yuccas.

The public rooms and a wing added in 1968 are all tastefully and successfully combined. The main drawing rooms are refreshingly decorated in sea colors with country estate furnishings in either tropical prints or soft solids. All but 15 of the guest rooms face the ocean; all have radios. The spacious rooms are conservative in the finest sense, with well-chosen pieces, plenty of storage space, sitting areas, and desks. The baths have marble or tile walls and floors.

Dining/Entertainment: Afternoon tea is served on the Tea Terrace with a magnificent view of the gardens and Funchal Bay. Lunch is offered in the Garden Restaurant overlooking the pools or at the poolside buffet. The two-level main dining room is classically dignified with pink-and-white marble and Murano crystal lamps, plus the inevitable and very English silver trolley holding roast beef. Reid's gourmet restaurant, Les Faunes, on the sixth floor in the garden wing, is recommended separately under "Dining," below. Less formal is Villa Cliff, serving a typically Portuguese cuisine.

Services: Shoe shining, laundry, 24-hour room service, hairdresser.

Facilities: Three saltwater pools, a garden park, tennis courts.

HOTEL SAVOY, Avenida do Infante, 9006 Funchal, Madeira. Tel. 091/22-20-31. Fax 091/22-31-03. 350 rms, 12 suites. A/C MINIBAR TV TEL **Bus:** 2, 12, or 16.

$ Rates (including breakfast): 20,000$–36,300$ ($122–$221.40) single; 24,800$–60,500$ ($151.30–$369.10) double; 55,000$–77,000$ ($335.50–$469.70) suite. AE, DC, MC, V. **Parking:** Free.

⭐ The Savoy is one of the leading five-star hotels not only of Madeira but also of all Portugal. Long known for style and elegance, it stands at the edge of Funchal. Its origins go back to the turn of the century when it was started by a Swiss-trained hotelier, and over the years it just grew and grew. Each guest room has a balcony. The most expensive doubles are twins with sea views. Faced with escalating popularity, each generation of management has brought enlargements and improvements.

The hotel is superbly situated, opening onto the ocean and the Bay of Funchal. With its vast public facilities, it captures a peculiar kind of Madeira dolce vita.

Dining/Entertainment: For before-dinner libations, you have a choice of two bars. There are several restaurants from which to choose, or you can have lunch by the pools. Restaurants include the Bellevue, the Bakkhos Wine/Snack Bar, the Alameda coffee shop, and the Neptunus by the pool. For more deluxe dining, there is the elegantly decorated Fleur-de-Lys, a grill room with belle époque trappings. This room, closed on Sunday, has a panoramic view, as does the Galaxia nightclub on the top floor.

Services: Babysitting, room service, laundry,

Facilities: Two seawater pools (one heated), tennis courts, health center, mini-golf, shopping arcade, hairdressers for both men and women.

EXPENSIVE

CASINO PARK HOTEL, Rua Imperatriz Dahelia, 9000 Funchal, Madeira. Tel. 091/23-31-11. Fax 091/331-53. 373 rms, 30 suites. A/C MINIBAR TV TEL **Bus:** 2, 12, or 16.
$ Rates (including buffet breakfast): 25,000$ ($152.50) single; 38,000$ ($231.80) double; from 55,000$ ($335.50) suite. AE, DC, MC, V. **Parking:** Free.
The Casino Park is just a 7-minute walk from the center of town. The hotel is nestled in a subtropical garden overlooking the harbor. Designed by Oscar Niemeyer—one of the architects of Brazil's capital, Brasilia—the main building is low (only five stories) and undulating, as if poised for flight from its position on the cliff above the deep waters. The complex is made up of the hotel/conference center and a separate casino.

The guest rooms have their own balconies offering superb views of the harbor and town; there is also a radio in each room. The rooms are tastefully coordinated with bright, sunny colors that seem to bring the radiance of the island and the sea indoors. There are two comfortable lounge areas on each floor.

Dining/Entertainment: Variety in dining is thoughtfully provided—from the luxurious and spacious dining room overlooking the port and town of Funchal, to the international Grill Room with its extensive wine cellar, to the simpler coffee shop adjacent to the pool for a refreshing snack after a swim.

Services: 24-hour room service, babysitting, laundry.

Facilities: Shopping facilities, tennis courts, pools, saunas, billiards, health club; special facilities, including shallow pool, for children; arrangements for fishing, sailing, golf excursions.

MADEIRA CARLTON, Largo António Nobre, 9007 Funchal, Madeira. Tel. 091/23-10-31. Fax 091/233-77. 375 rms, 16 suites. A/C MINIBAR TV TEL **Bus:** 5 or 6.
$ Rates (including breakfast): 22,000$-26,000$ ($134.20-$158.60) single; 35,000$-43,000$ ($213.50-$262.30) double; from 55,000$ ($335.50) suite. AE, DC, MC, V. **Parking:** 200$ ($1.20).
Madeira Carlton is a luxurious 17-story structure near the casino with direct access to the sea. The hotel has some amusing eccentricities of design—two trapezium-shaped elevators that transport guests down to their rooms from the reception area. All the accommodations, many furnished in a provincial style, have private balconies and radios. The least expensive rates are for the standard mountain view, the more expensive for deluxe rooms with a sea view. The hotel lies on a promontory overlooking Funchal Bay in the fashionable Vale-Verde Garden district, next to the century-old landmark, Reid's (see above). Its oceanfront exposure to the south offers dawn-to-dusk sunlight on all pool terraces and seaside guest-room balconies and patios.

Dining/Entertainment: The hotel offers a restaurant for 500 persons, Os Arcos, plus an English pub, O Farol, and a disco.

Services: Laundry, babysitting, 24-hour room service.

Facilities: Three pools, sauna, health club, solarium.

MADEIRA PALÁCIO, Estrada Monumental 265, 9000 Funchal, Madeira. Tel. 091/76-44-76. Fax 091/76-44-77. 253 rms, 7 suites. A/C MINIBAR TV TEL **Bus:** 5 or 6.
$ Rates (including breakfast): 25,000$ ($152.50) single; 32,000$ ($195.20) double; from 40,000$ ($244) suite. AE, DC, MC, V. **Parking:** Free.
Madeira Palácio is a luxurious hotel of well-appointed rooms and suites on the seaside route to Câmara de Lobos, about 2 miles from the center of Funchal. The hotel is perched on a cliff over the sea. From here, Madeira's famous high cliff, Cabo Girão, can be seen looming in the distance. Each guest room is complete with a radio, a color TV with video systems, and a balcony. Rooms opening onto the mountains are less desirable than those facing the sea.

The star-shaped hotel is most contemporary, with three wings. The public salons and the guest rooms are colorfully coordinated, and local woods, native construction materials, and Madeiran fabrics have been used judiciously.

Dining/Entertainment: Visitors may select the hotel's main restaurant, Cristovão Colombo, with its menu of local and international dishes, or they may prefer the regional dishes of Le Terrace. International cuisine is served in the hotel's gourmet restaurant, Vicerei. Later, entertainment is provided in the nightclub; occasional folk dances are staged here as well. There's also an outdoor snack bar.

Services: Laundry, babysitting, 24-hour room service.

Facilities: Heated pool, tennis courts, shopping arcade complete with hairdresser and sauna, table tennis.

QUINTA DO BELO VISTA, Caminho do Avista Navios 4, 9000 Funchal, Madeira. Tel. 091/76-41-44. Fax 091/76-50-90. 67 rms, 5 suites. A/C TV TEL

$ Rates (including breakfast): 16,000$–21,000$ ($97.60–$128.10) single; 21,400$–26,400$ ($130.50–$161) double; 50,000$ ($305) suite. AE, DC, MC, V.

Set in the hills above Funchal, the core of this hotel was built around 1840 as a private villa. In 1991, its owner, a local surgeon, arranged for the construction of two outlying annexes in the Portuguese colonial style and added the accoutrements necessary for the establishment's later classification as a five-star hotel. Today, only four suites, a salon, a library, and the main restaurant lie within the original villa. The rest of the hotel is scattered amid a verdant garden and the comfortable guest rooms of the annexes. Furnishings include high-quality mahogany reproductions as well as a scattering of genuine English and Portuguese antiques. Since its opening, the hotel has attracted a well-heeled, well-traveled clientele—including painters from Belgium, barristers from Britain, and most of the political honchos of Madeira.

Dining/Entertainment: A well-staffed formal restaurant, Casa Mei, lies within the original villa. More relaxed is the panoramic Avistas Navios, with views sweeping out over the Port of Funchal and a cuisine that is both regional and international. There's also a very pleasant bar.

Services: Valet/laundry, babysitting, concierge, room service.

Facilities: Tennis courts, sauna, Jacuzzi, health club/gym, heated outdoor pool, garden.

MODERATE

HOTEL ALTO LIDO, Estrada Monumental 316, 9000 Funchal, Madeira. Tel. 091/76-56-23. Fax 091/76-59-50. 113 rms, 5 suites. A/C TV TEL **Bus:** 1, 2, 4, or 35.

$ Rates (including breakfast): 12,600$ ($76.90) single; 14,000$ ($85.40) double; 25,000$ ($152.50) suite. AE, DC, MC, V. **Parking:** Free.

The Alto Lido, on the road at the western end of the environs of Funchal, has staggered concrete balconies and a riot of lushly planted vines, aloe plants, and bougainvillea. Its verdant screening helps to create one of the most appealing facades in Madeira. Built in 1983, the hotel devotes about 70% of its accommodations to time-share units rented for the most part by vacationers from England, Germany, and Scandinavia. The remainder of the rooms, however, are available for daily rentals and are in high demand. Each has a balcony and comfortable summer-inspired furniture, often in wicker. The establishment maintains a marble-sheathed lobby, a pool, a restaurant where full meals cost from around 2,500$ ($15.30), a coffeeshop, two bars, a sauna, and a much-needed parking garage. Laundry and room service are available.

GIRASSOL, Estrada Monumental 256, 9000 Funchal, Madeira. Tel. 091/76-40-51. Fax 091/76-54-41. 133 rms. A/C TV TEL **Bus:** 5 or 6.

$ Rates (including breakfast): 10,000$ ($61) single; 14,000$ ($85.40) double. AE, DC, MC, V. **Parking:** Free.

The Girassol offers immaculate accommodations at reasonable tariffs. It's on the outskirts of Funchal, overlooking the Tourist Club, where guests are allowed access to the sea at a small charge. Every one of its accommodations has a sunny balcony, half overlooking the mountains, the rest viewing the sea. Each chamber also comes complete with a radio. Most double rooms are, in fact, suites, consisting of a bedroom, a bath, a small sitting room, and a veranda. The room decor is bright and cheerful.

Two pools are available, one for children. Guests can also catch the sun on the 12th-floor solarium. On the street level are a bar/social lounge and even a hairdressing salon. Ballroom dancing and floor shows are offered in the disco, and there's a tea lounge on the second floor. Two other special features are an entrance courtyard with a series of interconnected angular reflecting pools and a dining room with sea views.

HOTEL SANTA ISABEL, Avenida do Infante, 9006 Funchal, Madeira. Tel. 091/22-31-11. Fax 091/22-79-59. 69 rms. A/C MINIBAR TV TEL **Bus:** 2, 12, or 16.
$ Rates (including breakfast): 9,900$–11,400$ ($60.40–$69.50) single; 13,700$–16,500$ ($83.60–$100.70) double. AE, DC, MC, V. **Parking:** Free.
Adjacent to Hotel Savoy and under the same management, this is an excellent small hotel with a homelike feeling and a well-deserved reputation for service and comfort. In the center of the deluxe hotel belt, it has a rooftop terrace, with a small pool and solarium, a snack bar, a cocktail bar, a well-appointed lounge overlooking the gardens, and a solarium; guests can use the numerous facilities of the Savoy. The guest rooms have radios. There are two grades of accommodations: The more expensive ones face the sea, and the cheaper units open onto a garden and a mountain view. Meals are taken at the Savoy restaurants.

HOTEL SÃO JOÃO, Rua das Maravilhas 74, 9000 Funchal, Madeira. Tel. 091/74-31-11. Fax 091/74-16-25. 192 rms, 16 suites. A/C MINIBAR TV TEL **Bus:** 10, 11, or 14.
$ Rates (including breakfast): 10,500$–12,600$ ($64.10–$76.90) single; 15,000$–17,100$ ($91.50–$104.30) double; from 22,000$ ($134.20) suite. AE, DC, MC, V. **Parking:** Free.
On a hillside above the town is this modern four-star hotel with well-furnished guest rooms, each of which has a private terrace. You can quench your thirst at one of the three well-decorated bars or assuage your hunger at either the poolside self-service snack bar or the restaurant, both of which serve good Portuguese food and wine. During the day, guests have the use of two pools (one for children), and the hotel also has several planned activities, bringing in folkloric shows and bands for dancing. A courtesy bus makes frequent runs into Funchal. The hotel offers laundry, babysitting, and room service.

QUINTA DO SOL, Rua Dr. Pita 6, 9000 Funchal, Madeira. Tel. 091/76-41-51. Fax 091/76-62-87. 151 rms, 6 suites. A/C TV TEL **Bus:** 2, 12, or 16.
$ Rates (including buffet breakfast): 12,000$–15,000$ ($73.20–$91.50) single; 16,000$–22,000$ ($97.60–$134.20) double; from 38,000$ ($231.80) suite. MC, V. **Parking:** Free.
The four-star Quinta do Sol is among the best in its category in Madeira. Occupying an attractive setting, it offers well-furnished guest rooms, some have their own balconies; 30 contain minibars. The hotel has a number of public facilities that make it like a resort—including a pool; well-decorated lounges; a rooftop solarium; and a bar/restaurant, Charola, offering good food and wine, with meals costing 3,000$ ($18.30) at lunch and 3,500$ ($21.40) at dinner.

INEXPENSIVE

HOTEL DO CARMO, Travessa do Rego 10, 9000 Funchal, Madeira. Tel. 091/22-90-01. Fax 091/22-319. 80 rms. MINIBAR TV TEL **Bus:** 1, 2, 4, 5, 6, 8, 9, or 10.
$ Rates (including breakfast): 8,000$ ($48.80) single; 9,600$ ($58.60) double; 12,960$ ($79.10) triple. AE, DC, MC, V. **Parking:** Free.
Hotel do Carmo provides modern accommodations right in the center of Funchal, a

5-minute walk from the cathedral. It is erected in a cellular honeycomb fashion, each guest room opening onto its own balcony. While there is no surrounding garden, guests gather during the day for dips in the L-shaped rooftop pool, from which there is a good view of the harbor. Created by the Fernandes family, the hotel was designed for guests who have limited purses and want to be near the bazaars in the heart of the city's life. The guest rooms are simple, with contemporary furnishings. Meals, costing 2,600$ ($15.90), are served in a spacious dining room decorated with a harlequin-patterned green-tile floor. A little lounge opens onto an inner patio. Facilities include a sauna and solarium, and laundry, babysitting, and 24-hour room service are offered.

QUINTA DA PENHA DE FRANÇA, Rua da Penha de França 2, 9000 Funchal, Madeira. Tel. 091/290-87. Fax 091/292-61. 41 rms. TEL **Bus:** 2, 12, or 16.

$ Rates (including breakfast): 9,400$ ($57.30) single; 13,500$ ($82.40) double. AE, DC, MC, V. **Parking:** Free.

This gracious old manor house has been turned into a guesthouse. Like a family home, the *quinta* is chock full of antiques, paintings, and silver. Near the Savoy, it stands in a garden right on a ledge almost hanging over the harbor. It's a short walk to the center of the bazaars and is opposite an ancient chapel. The four-story *antiga casa* is bone white with dark-green shutters, plus small-panel windows overlooking the ocean. Across the front terrace is a good-sized pool with white-iron garden chairs arranged for lounging. Set on the hillside in the midst of poinsettias, bamboo, sugarcane, and coffee plants is a wine lodge and stone washhouse now converted into twin-bedded guest rooms.

HOTEL WINDSOR, Rua das Hortas 4C, 9000 Funchal, Madeira. Tel. 091/23-30-81. Fax 091/23-30-80. 67 rms. MINIBAR TV TEL **Bus:** 1, 12, or 16.

$ Rates (including breakfast): 7,800$–9,000$ ($47.60–$54.90) single; 10,400$–11,400$ ($63.40–$69.50) double. No credit cards. **Parking:** Free.

Opened with fanfare in 1987, this is one of the most stylish hotels in Funchal, rated four stars. It has a marble-sheathed lobby laden with plants, wicker chairs, and art deco accessories. The hotel was constructed in two separate buildings connected by an aerial passageway stretching above a sun-flooded enclosed courtyard. There is also a cafe/bar designed like a Jazz Age nightclub a few paces from the reception desk. The free parking garage is almost a necessity in this crowded commercial neighborhood. Also popular is a cramped but convivial rooftop pool with an outdoor bar. Because of its enclosure by the buildings in the town center, few of the guest rooms have any kind of view; but each is nicely decorated, with wall-to-wall carpeting. The Windsor Restaurant serves Madeiran cuisine, with fixed-price lunches and dinners costing 2,100$ ($12.80). Swordfish caught in local waters is a specialty.

BUDGET

ALBERGARÍA CATEDRAL, Rua do Aljube 13, 9000 Funchal, Madeira. Tel. 091/23-00-91. Fax 091/23-19-80. 25 rms. TEL **Bus:** 1, 2, 4, 5, 6, 8, 9, or 10.

$ Rates (including breakfast): 5,000$ ($30.50) single; 6,000$ ($36.60) double. AE, DC, MC, V. **Parking:** Free on street.

Albergaría Catedral, for its price bracket, is a good choice if you want to be in the center of town. Don't judge it by its narrow dark entrance, across the street from the cathedral. Climb a flight of stairs to a slickly "moderno" reception area, where you'll be assigned one of the establishment's comfortable guest rooms. They occupy five floors of a six-story building, and the quieter ones in the rear, unfortunately, don't have much of a view. In front, many of the units have balconies opening onto the street noise. The sunniest and most pleasant rooms occupy the two uppermost floors.

CASA DAS HORTAS, Rua das Hortas 55, 9000 Funchal, Madeira. Tel. 091/74-36-77. Fax 091/23-21-87. 8 rms (5 with bath or shower), 1 suite, 1 three-bedroom apt. **Bus:** 8, 9, 15, or 45.

$ Rates: 4,500$ ($27.50) single without bath or shower, 5,000$–5,500$ ($30.50–

$33.60) single with bath or shower; 5,000$ ($30.50) double without bath or shower, 5,500$–6,500$ ($33.60–$39.70) double with bath or shower; 8,000$ ($48.80) suite; 12,000$ ($73.20) apt. No credit cards. **Parking:** Free.
This is a simple but well-managed guesthouse, set near the heart of residential Funchal in a charming Madeiran house with a verdant garden. Views from many of its rooms encompass the town and its monuments. Four of the accommodations contain TVs. No meals of any kind are served, but the staff is able to direct guests to several nearby cafes. The suite is in a small house on the grounds, with a downstairs sitting room and kitchenette, plus an upstairs bedroom with private bath. The apartment contains three bedrooms, two baths, a kitchen, a large sitting room, and balconies.

HOTEL MADEIRA, Rua Ivens 21, 9009 Funchal Codex, Madeira. Tel. 091/23-00-71. Fax 091/22-90-71. 58 rms. TV TEL **Bus:** 2, 12, or 16.
$ Rates (including breakfast): 6,800$–7,500$ ($41.50–$45.80) single; 7,700$–8,500$ ($47–$51.90) double. AE, DC, MC, V. **Parking:** Free.
Hotel Madeira is in the center of Funchal behind the park and in the quietest part of the town. Its rooms are clean and comfortable. The rooftop pool has a solarium area where the bar and snack services never give you a chance to be thirsty. It has the most extraordinary panoramic view of the town, mountains, and sea. The guest rooms are arranged around a plant-filled atrium. One of the nicest aspects of this hotel, built in 1971, is the sheltered sun windows attached to each accommodation.

SANTA CLARA, Calçada do Pico 16B, 9000 Funchal, Madeira. Tel. 091/74-21-94. Fax 091/74-32-80. 20 rms. TEL **Bus:** 1, 12, or 16.
$ Rates (including breakfast): 5,500$ ($33.60) single; 6,500$ ($39.70) double. AE, DC, MC, V.
The Santa Clara, in the upper reaches of Funchal, is a breakfast-only hotel reached via the narrow winding streets of an old-fashioned residential section. Behind an iron gate, at the end of a narrow driveway bordered with fragrant vines and hibiscus, lies the kind of villa many visitors dream of owning for themselves. Prefaced with a gracefully curved double staircase, the villa was built in 1926 by a wealthy Portuguese family in an orange art nouveau style. Inside, floors crafted from Brazilian hardwoods compete for attention with trompe l'oeil ceilings and a scattering of antiques. Its only drawback is its popularity, which might make getting a room difficult without an advance reservation. Laundry and room service are provided.

NEARBY PLACE TO STAY: MACHICO

At Machico, on the east coast where the Portuguese first landed, you'll find more hotels. This part of land-scarce Madeira is being rapidly developed. Scores of tiny vacation villas climb the hillside. In the complex is a yacht club, plus an elegant bridge club. Machico is about 5 minutes from the airport but a good 30-minute run along a twisting road 18 miles west of Funchal.

Ⓕ FROMMER'S COOL FOR KIDS: HOTELS

Girassol *(see page 340)* On the outskirts of Funchal, this is a family pleaser. It not only offers reasonable rates but also has a pool set aside for children. Most doubles are, in reality, suites.

Hotel Santa Isabel *(see page 341)* This is the choice of those who'd like to enjoy the facilities of the deluxe Savoy without paying its steep tariffs. Next door, it's a satellite of the parent. Children 2 to 11 get a 50% reduction when sharing a room with their parents.

Quinta da Penha de França *(see page 342)* This family favorite is a large old manor house with charm and grace. Kids enjoy its snack bar, gardens, and pool.

MODERATE

HOTEL DOM PEDRO BAIA, Estrada de São Roque, 9200 Machico, Madeira. Tel. 091/96-57-51. Fax 091/96-68-89. 218 rms. A/C TV TEL
$ Rates (including breakfast): 12,000$ ($73.20) single; 17,500$ ($106.80) double. AE, DC, MC, V. **Parking:** Free.

The best hotel here is Dom Pedro Baia, a modern structure that boasts sea views. The comfortably furnished guest rooms are well kept and tastefully appointed. An extra meal is 2,900$ ($17.70). Good food is served in the Panoramic Restaurant. A bar, a heated saltwater pool, sun terraces, a beach, and a disco make this a nice choice.

4. DINING

Many guests eat at their hotels, but perhaps you'll be able to sneak away for a regional meal at one of the recommendations listed below. The list begins, however, with the pick of the hotel restaurants, which are all in the grill rooms, the specialty restaurants, of the three leading five-star hotels of Madeira.

EXPENSIVE

CHEZ OSCAR/RESTAURANT PANORAMICO, In Casino Park Hotel, Avenida do Infante, Funchal. Tel. 23-31-11.
   Cuisine: INTERNATIONAL. **Reservations:** Required. **Bus:** 2, 12, or 16.
$ Prices: Chez Oscar: Appetizers 1,000$–2,200$ ($6.10–$13.40); main courses 1,400$–2,600$ ($8.50–$15.90). Panoramico: Fixed-price meals 5,400$ ($32.90) without show, 7,000$ ($42.70) with show. AE, DC, MC, V.
   Open: Chez Oscar: Dinner only, Mon–Sat 7:30–11pm. Panoramico: Dinner only, nightly 7:30–9:15pm.

Both of these restaurants lie within the previously recommended confines of Casino Park Hotel. The smaller and more elegant of the two is Chez Oscar, housed within a large dark-bronze modern room that opens onto a flowering outdoor terrace. Pin lighting and candles, along with a polite and uniformed staff, add to the formal and glamorous ambience. The Panoramico is larger and somewhat less personal, but it has the added advantage of offering a cabaret performance three or four nights a week at the end of your meal. Menu specialties in Chez Oscar include an array of flambé dishes prepared beside your table. Both restaurants serve a menu based on fresh ingredients, although food at Chez Oscar's might be more exotic and experimental. Examples in either place might include piccata of pork and shellfish in saffron-flavored sauce or chateaubriand for two. Clients who want the best of both restaurants sometimes opt for a quiet and intimate dinner at Chez Oscar, then decamp to the Panoramico for after-dinner drinks in time for the cabaret, which usually begins around 9:30pm three or four nights a week. If this is your plan, be sure to phone ahead for reservations in both areas.

FLEUR-DE-LYS, in Hotel Savoy, Avenida do Infante. Tel. 22-20-31.
   Cuisine: FRENCH. **Reservations:** Required. **Bus:** 2, 12, or 16.
$ Prices: Appetizers 1,000$–6,000$ ($6.10–$36.60); main courses 2,000$–2,900$ ($12.20–$17.70). AE, DC, MC, V.
   Open: Dinner only, daily 7–11:30pm.

Its most devoted admirers claim that this restaurant serves the finest food in Madeira. It is certainly one of the most panoramic spots for dining, opening onto the twinkling lights of Funchal. Decorated in a vaguely belle époque style, it has an eclectic decor with antique reproductions and Oriental carpets. Guests can observe the activity in an open-grill kitchen covered with pewter facsimiles of the establishment's namesake. Reservations are important, and even with one you sometimes have a long wait. Meals are likely to include an array of well-prepared international dishes, such as shrimp in mustard-cream dressing, rock lobster mornay, duck *à la orange,* filet of lamb with curry sabayon, and veal medallions flavored with Calvados.

LES FAUNES, in Reid's Hotel, Estrada Monumental 139. Tel. 76-30-01.
   Cuisine: FRENCH. **Reservations:** Required. **Bus:** 5 or 6.
$ Prices: Appetizers 1,000$–3,000$ ($6.10–$18.30); main courses 2,000$–3,000$ ($12.20–$18.30). AE, DC, MC, V.
   Open: Dinner only, daily 7:30–11pm.

⭐ Try to dine at least once at Les Faunes, generally conceded to be the island's finest restaurant. It takes its name from the series of Picasso lithographs decorating the walls. On the sixth floor of the hotel's garden wing, diners have musical entertainment by a pianist. Both guests and the local gentry consider it the perfect place to celebrate a new amour or console oneself after the loss of an old love. True to English tradition, clients in winter often dress for dinner, the women perhaps in silk, the men sedate in black tie.

The chef offers a wide variety of French specialties and some typical Portuguese dishes. The menu changes daily. For your palatable preliminaries, you can try everything from Portuguese soup to the chef's own smoked fish. Particular favorites are the *caldeirada,* fish stew, and lobster (grilled or poached). To top your repast, you can select from the dessert trolley or ask for a hot soufflé, preferably made of passionfruit or strawberries.

MODERATE

BAKKHOS WINE BAR, Rua Imperatriz D. Amelia. Tel. 22-20-31.
   Cuisine: MADEIRAN. **Reservations:** Not necessary. **Bus:** 2, 12, or 16.
$ Prices: Appetizers 450$–950$ ($2.70–$5.80); main courses 1,100$–1,800$ ($6.70–$11). AE, DC, MC, V.
   Open: Daily 11am–11pm.

The popular Bakkhos Wine Bar, owned and operated by Hotel Savoy, lies at the rear entrance to that hotel. You'll dine amid Moroccan lattices at smallish tables serviced by English-speaking waiters in red coats. The menu lists "typical dishes of the islands," including tuna steaks, stewed octopus, grilled prawns, cheese fondue, and wine by the carafe. Another offering is pasta, such as lasagne, spaghetti, and macaroni, as well as salads or sandwiches, if you're dining light.

CASA DA CAROCHINHA [Lady Bird], Rua de São Francisco 2A. Tel. 23-695.
   Cuisine: MADEIRAN. **Reservations:** Not necessary. **Bus:** 2, 12, or 16.
$ Prices: Appetizers 350$–800$ ($2.10–$4.90); main courses 1,000$–1,650$ ($6.10–$10.10). AE, DC, MC, V.
   Open: Lunch Mon–Sat noon–2pm; dinner Mon–Sat 7–10pm; tea Mon–Sat 3:30–5:30pm.

Casa da Carochinha is a favorite local retreat, known especially to the British visitors and expatriates who are so fond of Madeira. The restaurant faces the Centenary Gardens, near the tourist office. The casa abounds in Edwardian English charm and serves a refined continental cuisine. This is perhaps the only place in Madeira where the chef does not use garlic. Specialties include coq au vin, beef Stroganoff, roast beef with Yorkshire pudding, and duck with orange sauce. A flag of the diner's country is also placed on the spotless white Nottingham lace tablecloth.

CASA DOS REIS, Rua Imperatriz D. Amelia 103. Tel. 22-51-81.
   Cuisine: FRENCH. **Reservations:** Required. **Bus:** 5 or 6.
$ Prices: Appetizers 800$–1,100$ ($4.90–$6.70); main courses 1,100$–2,200$ ($6.70–$13.40). AE, MC, V.
   Open: Dinner only, daily 7–10:30pm.

Casa dos Reis, in an appealing neighborhood just downhill from the Madeira Carlton, is elegant and tranquil, with polished mahogany armchairs, brass chandeliers, and the aura of an aristocratic private club. Avoid the snack bar one flight above street level and head for a table in the more formal dining room. Meals include the chef's special fish soup, grilled scabbard fish, chateaubriand, rack of lamb with *fines herbes,* fish fricassée with prawns, and nouvelle cuisine suggestions.

DOS COMBATENTES, Rua Ivens 1. Tel. 213-88.

Cuisine: MADEIRAN. **Reservations:** Not necessary. **Bus:** 2, 12, or 16.
$ Prices: Appetizers 350$–850$ ($2.10–$5.20); main courses 1,000$–2,100$ ($6.10–$12.80). AE, DC, MC, V.
Open: Lunch daily noon–3pm; dinner daily 7:30–10pm.

Dos Combatentes is a good choice for regional food, a favorite of Funchal's colony of doctors and lawyers. At the top of the Municipal Gardens, this simple restaurant serves well-prepared dishes, including rabbit stew, roast chicken, stewed squid, and codfish. The Portuguese eat a lot, so the portions are ample, and two vegetables and a green salad come with the main dish. Desserts are likely to be simple, including caramel custard and chocolate mousse or fresh fruit, and most dinners begin with a bowl of the soup of the day. The waiters are efficient.

GAVINAS, Rua do Gorgulho. Tel. 629-18.

Cuisine: PORTUGUESE. **Reservations:** Not necessary. **Bus:** 1, 2, 4, or 35.
$ Prices: Appetizers 450$–950$ ($2.70–$5.80); main courses 1,000$–2,200$ ($6.10–$13.40). AE, DC, MC, V.
Open: Daily noon–midnight.

Gavinhas is reached by heading out the Estrada Monumental to the Lido. Once this was only a little garagelike cottage, drawing the "slumming" chic of Madeira. But its popularity grew until its owners tore down the old shack and reconstructed a modern restaurant. The fish is as fresh as you can imagine. You'll find no fancy sauces, no elaborate service—just hearty sea fare that is the rule of the kitchen. Perhaps you'll be there the day when a savory *caldeirada* (fish stew) has just been prepared. Most guests, however, gravitate to one of the fresh grilled fish platters.

GOLFINHO, Largo do Corpo Santo 21. Tel. 267-74.

Cuisine: SEAFOOD. **Reservations:** Required. **Bus:** 2, 12, or 16.
$ Prices: Appetizers 450$–1,200$ ($2.70–$7.30); main courses 1,000$–2,400$ ($6.10–$14.60). AE, DC, MC, V.
Open: Lunch Mon–Sat noon–3pm; dinner daily 7–11pm.

Ⓢ Golfinho lies in the eastern section of town, near the waterfront, in the midst of the largest cluster of restaurants in Funchal. The rich and warm-textured decor cost the owners a fortune. Virtually every corner of Golfinho's compact but well-decorated interior is covered with an eye-catching array of burnished pieces that make for a visual feast. After the waiter seats you on one of the scallop-backed Portuguese chairs, you order some of the best fresh fish and shellfish served in Madeira. You might, for example, begin with smoked swordfish and then follow with either grilled steak or lobster. However, fresh lobster should be ordered in advance, as should that savory kettle of fish, *caldeirada,* since preparation takes about 3 hours. A more typical fish, and one famous in Madeira for its taste, is *espada.* The bulbous eyes and fearsome teeth of this fish belie its tasty flesh. Sometimes espada is served with a fresh banana.

KON-TIKI, Rua do Favila 9. Tel. 76-47-37.

Cuisine: MADEIRAN. **Reservations:** Required. **Bus:** 5 or 6.
$ Prices: Appetizers 1,000$–2,000$ ($6.10–$12.20); main courses 1,000$–3,000$ ($6.10–$18.30); fixed-price menu 1,750$ ($10.70). AE, DC, MC, V.
Open: Daily noon–11pm.

Kon-Tiki, near the Carlton, offers some of the best food on the island. The building is part of an old-fashioned quinta. You will be shown to a table either in the intimate restaurant or on a glassed-in terrace overlooking a well-tended garden. You can enjoy such dishes as warm home-smoked fresh mackerel, chicken with curry, and goulash soup. You can cook your own filet steak on a sizzling-hot beefstone imported from Finland or order a peppersteak or *espada* flambé with prawns. Everything seems to be good, especially the fresh fruit flambés to finish off a meal.

O ESPADARTE, Estrada da Boa Nova 5. Tel. 280-65.

Cuisine: MADEIRAN. **Reservations:** Recommended for dinner. **Bus:** 2 or 12.
$ Prices: Appetizers 350$–900$ ($2.10–$5.50); main courses 950$–1,850$ ($5.80–$11.30). No credit cards.
Open: Lunch Tues–Sun noon–3pm; dinner daily 7–11pm.

O Espadarte is an uncluttered and unpretentious restaurant in a low-slung concrete building perched between a steep road and the mountains, about a mile east of Funchal on the road to the airport. It's owned and operated by a team of Portuguese entrepreneurs who have spent time in many other parts of the world. Guests dine at long trestle tables. Portuguese specialties include grilled trout, peppersteak, beef on a skewer, grilled pork cutlets, and fresh sardines. In honor of its namesake, which means "swordfish," the restaurant does its own smoked swordfish, which is the most delectable appetizer you can order. Some nights are devoted to folklore and fado.

O PATIO JARDIM TROPICALE, Avenida Zarco 21. Tel. 22-73-76.

Cuisine: PORTUGUESE. **Reservations:** Not necessary. **Bus:** 2, 12, or 16.
$ Prices: Appetizers 450$–950$ ($2.70–$5.80); main courses 950$–1,700$ ($5.80–$10.40). AE, DC, MC, V.
Open: Lunch Mon–Sat noon–3pm; dinner Mon–Sat 7–10pm.

In the center of town, O Patio Jardim Tropicale is totally concealed within the inner courtyard of a complex of commercial buildings. Its entrance near a newspaper kiosk is easy to overlook because of its narrowness and insufficient lighting. Once inside, however, you'll enter a welcome refuge from the noise and traffic outside. You can sip coffee at one of the atrium's iron tables, but many of the local shopkeepers head every day for the pleasant restaurant. One of the best lunchtime bargains in Funchal is a heaping platter of the dish of the day, usually roast chicken or stewed codfish with onions. Meals on the well-scrubbed wooden tables might include house-style beef or squid, followed by pineapple flambé.

RESTAURANT CARAVELA, Avenida do Mar 15–17. Tel. 22-84-64.

Cuisine: PORTUGUESE/INTERNATIONAL. **Reservations:** Not necessary. **Bus:** 2, 12, or 16.
$ Prices: Appetizers 1,150$–1,500$ ($7–$9.20); main courses 1,200$–1,800$ ($7.30–$11). AE, DC, MC, V.
Open: Lunch daily noon–3pm; dinner daily 6:30–11pm.

Right on the waterfront is modern Restaurant Caravela. You can dine on a glass-enclosed terrace with an open fireplace or in the inner room where you sit in wicker chairs. Reached by elevator, the top-floor restaurant gives guests a view of the cruise ships arriving and departing. You can order both lunch and dinner, as well as afternoon tea with open-faced Danish *smorrebröd* sandwiches. Perhaps the finest regional dish is *espetada,* skewered meat flavored with garlic and bay leaves and served only on special request. Unpretentious and proud of the native Portuguese dishes, the restaurant features Caravela fish but also turns out international dishes, such as chateaubriand flambé.

RESTAURANT ROMANA, Largo do Corpo Santo 15. Tel. 289-56.

Cuisine: MADEIRAN/INTERNATIONAL. **Reservations:** Recommended for dinner. **Bus:** 5 or 6.
$ Prices: Appetizers 450$–950$ ($2.70–$5.80); main courses 1,000$–2,200$ ($6.10–$13.40). AE, DC, MC, V.
Open: Daily 11am–10:30pm.

The Romana, under French management, is one of the leading restaurants of Madeira, with excellent service. Customers have included the king and queen of Sweden, the queen mother of Denmark, the great *fadista* Amália Rodrigues, and the Prince of Monaco. Comfortable and decorated in a rustic style, the Romana is considered a top rendezvous for both residents and visitors. The owner oversees a kitchen that is based on fresh fish and top-quality meats, served in both Madeira and international style. The Romana will send a free minibus to pick you up.

INEXPENSIVE

ESCOLA DE HOTELARIA E TURISMO DA MADEIRA [Madeira Hotel

and Tourism School), Quinta Magnolia, Rua Dr. Pita 10. Tel. 76-40-13.
Cuisine: PORTUGUESE. **Reservations:** Required. **Bus:** 5 or 6.
$ Prices: Fixed-price menu 3,000$ ($18.30). AE, DC, MC, V.
Open: Lunch only, Mon–Sat 1–2:30pm.

Located in a charming old estate overlooking the bay, this is a good place to have lunch. The daily menu offers a choice of specially prepared dishes for each course. The menu changes every day. The bar opens at 12:30pm, with cocktails made by advanced students, who are attentive to the desires of the patrons. Lunch is accompanied by wine and coffee.

PENSÃO RESTAURANT UNIVERSAL, Rua de João Tavira 4. Tel. 22-06-18.
Cuisine: PORTUGUESE. **Reservations:** Not necessary. **Bus:** 2, 12, or 16.
$ Prices: Appetizers 235$–850$ ($1.40–$5.20); main courses 600$–1,200$ ($3.70–$7.30). DC, MC, V.
Open: Lunch daily noon–3pm; dinner daily 6–10pm.

The Universal stands in the center of Funchal, a minute's walk from the cathedral, amid a network of grimy commercial buildings and busy traffic. The building that contains it is said to be the oldest hotel in Madeira, probably established in the early 1800s, although no one in the neighborhood really knows for sure. Tables are maintained in three dining rooms, one of which might close when business is slow. The same menu is served throughout the establishment and features a platter of the day priced at around 600$ ($3.70); other fare includes scabbard fish prepared in several ways, roast chicken with herbs and peppers, grilled filet of swordfish, and different preparations of the ubiquitous codfish.

Upstairs, the management rents 17 basic guest rooms, none with private bath or telephone. Singles cost 3,000$ ($18.30) and doubles are 3,500$ ($21.40); no breakfast is served.

AFTERNOON TEA

INEXPENSIVE

CASA MINAS GERAIS (The Corner Shop), Avenida do Infante 2. Tel. 22-33-81.
Cuisine: INTERNATIONAL. **Reservations:** Not required. **Bus:** 2, 12, or 16.
$ Prices: Soups 260$ ($1.60); main courses 490$–1,050$ ($3–$6.40); pot of tea 150$ (90¢); pastries 200$–280$ ($1.20–$1.70). AE, DC, MC, V.
Open: Daily 9am–11pm. **Closed:** Dec 25.

An old-fashioned tea and pastry shop as well as a restaurant, Casa Minas Gerais has been around for some 50 years. At its central serving bar, waiters make pots of tea and coffee or pour Madeira wine. Before sitting at one of the little tables, clients pick out a pastry. One section of the establishment is a restaurant, serving meals with such fare as spaghetti bolognese, mixed grill, grilled chicken, and fish soup. The tall ceiling is supported by painted columns capped with vine motifs. The Corner Shop opens onto a circular fountain and the busy boulevard.

NEARBY PLACES TO DINE

While exploring Madeira, you may want to arrange a dining stopover at one of the following recommendations.

INEXPENSIVE

AQUÁRIO, Seixal São Vicente. Tel. 85-43-96.
Cuisine: MADEIRAN. **Reservations:** Not necessary.
$ Prices: Appetizers 350$–600$ ($2.10–$3.70); main courses 1,000$–1,500$ ($6.10–$9.20). AE, DC, MC, V.
Open: Lunch daily noon–3:30pm; dinner daily 7–10pm.

**FROMMER'S COOL FOR KIDS:
RESTAURANTS**

Casa da Carochinha *(see page 345)* Facing the Centenary Gardens, this has long been a family favorite of the English-speaking world, mainly because much of the fare is familiar, including roast beef with Yorkshire pudding.

O Patio Jardim Tropicale *(see page 347)* This is another family favorite in the heart of Funchal. Within an inner courtyard, it is a safe, snug haven. Meals are served on well-scrubbed tables. The menu always has something kids will go for, including juicy roast chicken.

Casa Minas Gerais *(see page 348)* This old-fashioned tea and pastry shop in Funchal is both a restaurant and a cafe. In an election, kids would vote it their number-one favorite. Not only do they get the best pastries on Madeira, but also they can order the most popular dish here: spaghetti bolognese.

Aquário is a waterfront fish restaurant too often ignored by visitors who flock to the dining spots of Porto Moniz, where they have to fight for a seat. Clients at Aquário enjoy some of the tastiest Portuguese cooking on the island. The kitchen turns out simple fare, but its cooking often outdistances the table d'hôte menus served in the deluxe hotels. Everything is prepared fresh. The proprietor oversees every serving by the waitresses. To begin, you get a heaping basket of homemade bread and a carafe of the local wine. I recommend the grilled fish of the day, served with three vegetables. Soups are hearty, the helpings generous. The decor is nautical, the walls decorated with objects rescued from the sea. On sale are handmade straw and reed baskets.

A SETA, Estrada do Livramento 80, Monte. Tel. 476-43.
    Cuisine: MADEIRAN. **Reservations:** Recommended.
$ **Prices:** Appetizers 350$–600$ ($2.10–$3.70); main courses 1,000$–1,500$ ($6.10–$9.20). AE, DC, MC, V.
    Open: Lunch Thurs–Tues noon–3pm; dinner Thurs–Tues 6–11pm.
    A Seta is for regional cuisine supreme. This mountainside restaurant, a favorite with tour groups, is a tavern where you can order inexpensive and tasty Madeiran meals. The decor is rustic, with a burnt-wood trim, walls covered with pinecones, and crude natural pine tables. An inner dining room adjoins the open kitchen, with a charcoal spit and oven, ideal for those who want to watch the action.

First, a plate of homemade coarse brown bread still warm from the oven is put at your place. Above each table is a hook to which is attached a long skewer of charcoal-broiled meat. You slip off chunks while mopping up the juices with your crusty bread. There are three specialties: beef, chicken, and grilled dry codfish. Seasoned with olive oil, herbs, garlic, and bay leaves, these concoctions are called *espetadas.* Fried potatoes are always done well here (ask for some hot sauce).

**POUSADA DOS VINHÁTICOS, Estrada de São Vicente Serra de Agua,
9350 Ribeira Brava. Tel. 95-23-44.**
    Cuisine: MADEIRAN. **Reservations:** Not necessary.
$ **Prices:** Appetizers 350$–900$ ($2.10–$5.50); main courses 950$–1,800$ ($5.80–$11). AE, DC, MC, V.
    Open: Lunch daily noon–3pm; dinner daily 7–9:30pm.
The government-owned Pousada dos Vinháticos, which opened in 1940, is near the top of a pass on the winding road to São Vicente. Guests can visit just for a meal or to spend the night. The pousada, a tavern-style building with a brick terrace, is built of solid stone. Visitors can absorb the unmarred mountain views from the terrace. The food is hearty and unpretentious, often depending on the catch of the day. Madeira specialties on the menu include *espetada* (swordfish) and local beef flavored with regional wines.

Most of the 12 guest rooms are done in Portuguese modern, although a few accommodations contain antiques. All have private baths and good views and are kept immaculate. The price of a double room is 9,900$ ($60.40) daily, and a single is 6,950$ ($42.40), including breakfast. Parking is free.

5. ATTRACTIONS

Funchal is the center of Madeira's wine industry. Grapes have grown in the region since the early 15th century, when Henry the Navigator introduced vines and sugarcane to the slopes. In Funchal, the must (fresh wine) from the black and white grapes is used to make Bual, Sercial, and Malmsey. It's cultivated for its bittersweet tang (women used to scent their handkerchiefs with it). The wine growers still transport the foot-pressed must in goatskin bottles over the rough terrain by *borracheiros*. Naturally, it undergoes extensive pasteurization in its refinement and blending.

You can visit a **lota** (fish auction) and many bazaars selling local handcrafts. At the lota, seafood is auctioned off to housewives and restaurant owners. Horse mackerel, grouper, mullet, tunny (sometimes weighing hundreds of pounds), and freshwater eels, even a slab of barracuda, will find its way to the stalls.

In the bazaars you can purchase needlepoint tapestries, Madeira wines, laces, and embroidery on Swiss organdy or Irish linen, plus all sorts of local crafts, such as goatskin boots or Camacha basketry of water willows. The **City Market,** at Praça do Comércio on Saturday, is a study in color, offering everything from yams to pawpaws.

The most exciting (and most crowded) time to visit Funchal is during the **End of the Year Festival,** December 30 to January 1. Fireworks light up the Bay of Funchal, the mountains in the background forming an amphitheater. Floodlit cruise ships anchor in the harbor to the delight of passengers who revel until dawn.

THE TOP ATTRACTIONS

MADEIRA WINE COMPANY, Avenida Arriaga 28. Tel. 22-01-21.
This richly stocked wine shop, next to the tourist office, is one of the island's most potent unofficial ambassadors of goodwill. Proud of its traditions, it offers samples from the diverse stock, which covers virtually every vintage ever produced on the island for the past 35 years. Inside this former convent, dating from 1790, are murals depicting the wine pressing (by foot) and harvesting processes, which proceed according to traditions established hundreds of years ago. You can savor the slightly burnt sweetness in a setting of old barrels, wine kegs, and time-mellowed chairs and tables made from aged wine kegs. Incidentally, Napoleon passed this way on his journey into exile on St. Helena in 1815. Bottles from a vintage year were given to him, but death came before the former emperor could sample them.
Admission: Free.
Open: Mon–Fri 9am–1pm, Sat 3–6pm.

SÉ (Cathedral), Rua Aljube. Tel. 22-81-55.
Of the churches of Funchal, the most intriguing is the rustic 15th-century Sé, with its Moorish carved cedar ceiling, stone floors, Gothic arches, stained-glass windows, and baroque altars. The cathedral lies at the junction of four busy streets in the historic heart of Funchal. The most visible of these is Rua Aljube (without number).
Admission: Free, but donation suggested.
Open: Mon–Sat 11am–6pm, Sun 8am–8:30pm. (Hours subject to change depending on church affairs.)

IGREJA DE SANTA CLARA (Church of St. Clara), Calçada de Santa Clara.
Just down the street from the Cruzes Museum (see below) is this baroque church,

with walled tiles, a painted wooden ceiling, and the tomb of João Gonçalves Zarco, the discoverer of Madeira. The church is said to have been built by the granddaughter of Zarco the year Columbus discovered America.
Admission: Free, but donation appreciated.
Open: Mon–Sat 11am–6pm, Sun 8am–8:30pm. (Hours subject to change depending on church activities.)

MUSEU DA QUINTA DAS CRUZES, Calçada do Pico 1. Tel. 223-82.

This museum is the ancient residence of Madeira's discoverer, João Gonçalves Zarco. The surrounding park is of botanical interest and contains an orchid collection of note. The museum houses many fine examples of English furniture and China trade porcelains brought to Madeira by expatriate Englishmen during the 18th century; rare Indo-Portuguese cabinets; and the unique chests, native to Madeira, fashioned from *caixas de acucar* (sugar boxes, which date from the 17th century). Also worth noting is a superb collection of antique Portuguese silver.
Admission: 100$ (60¢).
Open: Tues–Sat 10am–12:30pm and 2:30–5:30pm, Sun 10am–1pm.

MUSEU MUNICIPAL DO FUNCHAL [Municipal Museum], Rua da Mouraria 31. Tel. 22-97-61.

The land and aquatic animal life of the archipelago is represented at this Municipal Museum. Moray eels, eagle rays, scorpion fish, sea cucumbers, sea zephyrs, sharp-nosed puffers, and loggerhead turtles, as well as many of the beautifully plumed birds seen around Madeira, are represented here. Access is by either private car or taxi (no buses).
Admission: 65$ (40¢) adults; children under 12 free.
Open: Tues–Fri 10am–8pm, Sat–Sun noon–6pm.

PRAÇA DO MUNICÍPIO [Municipal Square], Funchal.

The Municipal Square is a study in light and dark, its plaza paved with hundreds of black-and-white lava half moons. The whitewashed buildings surrounding it have black-stone trim and ocher-tile roofs. On the south of the square is a former archbishopric now devoted to the museum of religious art. Rising to the east is the Câmara Municipal (City Hall), once the 18th-century palace of count Carvalhal. It is noted for its distinctive palace tower, rising over the surrounding rooftops. In all, it's an atmosphere of stately beauty.

MUSEU DE ARTE SACRA [Museum of Sacred Art], Rua do Bispo 21. Tel. 289-00.

In the center of town, in an old bishop's house, this museum is filled with "sacred art" treasures. Many of its exhibitions came from various churches on the island, some of which are no longer standing. Its most interesting collections are a series of paintings from both the Portuguese and the Flemish schools of the 15th and 16th centuries. The paintings are on wood, often oak, and an outstanding example of the collection is a 1518 painting called *Adoration of the Magi*. A rich merchant commissioned it and paid for it with sugar. A triptych depicts St. Philip and St. James, and there is an exceptional painting called *Descent from the Cross*. Ivory sculpture, gold and silver plate, and gilded wood ornamentations round out the collection.
Admission: 100$ (60¢).
Open: Tues–Sat 10am–12:30pm and 2:30–6pm, Sun 10am–1pm.

JARDIM BOTÂNICO [Botanical Garden], Caminho do Meio, about 2½ miles from Funchal. Tel. 360-37.

Located on the road to Camacha, this botanical garden is said to be one of the best in Iberia, with faraway views of the bay. Opened by the government in 1960 on the grounds of the old Quinta do Bom Sucesso plantation, the garden includes virtually every tree or plant growing on Madeira. Some of the subtropical plants were imported from around the world, including anthuriums and birds-of-paradise from such continents as Africa and South America. A heather tree, discovered near Curral das Freiras, is said to be 10 million years old. The gardens open onto beautiful views of Funchal and its port.

Admission: 300$ ($1.80).
Open: Daily 10am–6pm. **Bus:** 30.

ORGANIZED TOURS

Sun-seekers who remain either in Funchal or beside the pools of their hotels often miss most of what the island is about. If you don't care to venture out into the mountains on your own, you can take one of the many organized bus tours that cruise at regular intervals through the valleys and along the coastline of this famous and beautiful island. The most popular is a full-day island tour that incorporates virtually every accessible point in Madeira, including the island's remote northwestern tip, Porto Moniz, and the lovely shell-shaped harbor of Câmara de Lobos, a few miles to the west of Funchal. The full-day tours, which cost 6,500$ ($39.70) per person, including lunch, usually finish with a toboggan ride down steeply inclined cobble-covered slopes into Funchal. At presstime, these tours were offered on Tuesday and Saturday, although that might change by the time of your visit.

A less-strenuous half-day volcano-and-tobaggan tour costs 3,200$ ($19.50) per person; it departs twice a week, usually on Monday and Friday. An additional possibility, usually offered only on Thursday, is a visit to the wickerworks at Camacha, where thousands of pieces of locally crafted work, from small baskets to entire groupings of furniture, are offered for sale as part of the experience. Departing every Thursday, that tour costs 4,000$ ($24.40).

Clients who participate in these tours can be picked up at their hotels in Funchal or can congregate at the tourist office. Clients staying at hotels outside Funchal usually pay a small surcharge to be picked up by the bus tour. For more information, contact the tourist office or **Inter-Visa Tours,** Avenida Arriaga no. 30 (third floor) (tel. 091/22-83-44), in Funchal.

6. SPORTS & RECREATION

The pleasant climate of Madeira invites visitors to enjoy outdoor activities, even if they consist mainly of strolling through the city of Funchal and along park pathways and country lanes. There was a time when the visiting Victorians (some of the men looking like Mr. Pickwick) were carried around the islands in hammocks slung on poles and supported by two husky bearers. Nowadays this form of transport is a nostalgic memory. As one official put it: "The Communists objected to it. They consider it a form of slavery." A more popular means of transport in Funchal is to hire a bullock-pulled, wheel-less sledge on the Avenida do Mar, near the pier.

DEEP-SEA FISHING This is a popular sport in Madeira. The catch is mainly longtail tuna, blue marlin, swordfish, and several varieties of shark, along with other denizens of the deep. Boats can generally be rented for moderate costs. The tourist office will supply you with up-to-date information about boat rentals and the latest rates.

GOLF In the northeastern part of Madeira, in the hamlet of Santo da Serra, is the Campo de Golfe de Madeira (tel. 55-21-39), lying 4 miles from the airport and 15 miles from Funchal. The golf course, at more than 2,000 feet above sea level, enjoys an attractive setting in a forested area with mimosa and eucalyptus. It opened as a 6-hole course, but there was an almost immediate demand to extend it to 27 holes. There is a clubhouse room, as well as a lounge area and bar. Clubs can be rented, and local caddies are available. Greens fees cost 7,000$ ($42.70) for 18 holes.

HORSEBACK RIDING For equestrians, the Centro de Hispismo da Madeira, Caminho dos Pretos (tel. 79-25-82), arranges this increasingly popular activity. Vacationers go riding Tuesday through Sunday from 9am to 5pm. The cost is 3,000$ ($18.30) per hour.

FROMMER'S FAVORITE MADEIRA EXPERIENCES

A Toboggan Ride Madeira's most-fabled activity is to take a *carro de cesto* ride in a wicker-sided sled from the suburb of Monte to Funchal. Two drivers run alongside the sled to control its widely careening direction across slippery cobblestones for the 20-minute jaunt. It's been called Portugal's great "joyride."

The Golden Beaches of Porto Santo Since Madeira has no beaches, escape at least for the day to this relatively forgotten part of the world with its 4 miles of golden beaches, on which pirates of the Atlantic once romped.

A Morning at the Mercado dos Lavradores [Market of the Workers] Go early—at least between 7 and 8am daily, except Sunday—to see this market come alive. Flower vendors, fishermen, local terrace farmers, and frugal shoppers present an array of local colors and produce not seen anywhere else in Madeira. Check out the fish, everything from tuna to eel, that you'll be ordering later in restaurants.

Shopping for Handcrafts The prizes of Madeira—wine, wickerware, and embroidery—are but some of the merchandise lavishly displayed in the bazaars of Funchal. A whole day can be spent browsing, bargaining, and just wandering among a treasure trove with good prices on tooled leather and handmade shoes. Prices on other items can be high, so sharpen your bargaining skills.

Tasting Port Wine Go to any *taverna* (tavern) on the island and acquaint yourself with the array of local wines fortified with grape brandy. Before you leave the island, come away with having selected your particular favorite—perhaps the driest (Sercial), the olden-hued slightly sweeter Verdelho, or the definitely sweet Bual, a dessert wine good with cheese. Or perhaps your choice will be the sweetest of all Madeiras, Malmsey, rich and highly fragrant and served with dessert.

SWIMMING Since Madeira doesn't have beaches, guests use one of the pools, most often provided by a hotel. However, if your hotel doesn't have one, you can use the facilities of the Lido Swimming Pool Complex (Complexo Balnear do Lido), Rua do Gorgulho (tel. 76-22-17), which has an Olympic-size pool, plus a spacious pool for children. It is open in summer daily from 8:30am to 7pm (in the off-season from 9am to 6pm). Adults pay 200$ ($1.20) and children 100$ (60¢) to use the pool. A special ticket, which costs 50$ (30¢), is sold to visitors who want to use the upper deck only. You can rent sunbeds and umbrellas for 180$ ($1.10).

The complex is equipped with several facilities, including a cafe, a restaurant, an ice-cream parlor, bars, and a water-sports headquarters. To reach it, head out the Estrada Monumental from Funchal, turning onto the Rua do Gorgulho (the turnoff is marked). Take bus no. 6.

TENNIS Most of the first-class and deluxe establishments have their own courts. If you're in a hotel without a court, you can often obtain permission to play at a major hotel if you make a reservation (you'll be charged a small fee, of course). Naturally, guests of the hotel get priority.

TOBOGGAN RIDES By far the most famous rides are the toboggan rides. A visitor, of course, can take a taxi from anywhere to Monte, but more popular with locals is bus nos. 20 and 21, painted a *bright yellow*. They depart from Funchal every 30 minutes and sell tickets on the bus for 210$ ($1.30) each way.

Toboggans descend from Monte (the highest point) to Funchal for 2,200$ ($13.40) per passenger. Some visitors opt to get onto the toboggan midway down the slope, at *Livramento*, in which event, the price is only 1,500$ ($9.20) per passenger.

Before you begin your descent, you can visit the Church of Nossa Senhora do Monte, which contains the iron tomb of the last of the Hapsburgs, the Emperor Charles who died of pneumonia in Madeira in 1922. From a belvedere nearby, you can look down on the whole of Funchal: the narrow streets, the plazas, and especially the *cais*, that long docking pier set in deep-blue mirrorlike water.

The toboggan is a wide wicker basket with wooden runners. The baskets were the main means of transport in Monte from 1849 to 1942. The nearly 2-mile ride takes 20 minutes. As it rushes down the slippery smooth cobblestones, it is directed and sometimes propelled by two expert straw-hatted guides who yaw the ropes like nimble-footed seamen. You may need to fortify yourself with a glass or two of Madeira wine before taking the plunge. At Terreiro da Luta, at a height of 2,875 feet, you'll enjoy a splendid view of Funchal. Here also are monuments to Zarco and Our Lady of Peace.

WATER SPORTS   The activities desks of several of the major hotels, including the Savoy and Reid's, will arrange these activities for you, even if you're not a guest of the establishment. Naturally, you must pay for whatever services you book. Waterskiing can be arranged, as can windsurfing and boat rentals. Sailing dinghies can also be rented. If you want to go snorkeling or scuba diving, check with the Inter Atlas Hotel, Garajau-Caniçio (tel. 93-24-21).

7. SAVVY SHOPPING

CAMACHA WICKERWORKS, Avenida Arriaga. Tel. 34-586.
This is a showcase for the wicker work for which Madeirans have long been noted. Most of the products made here, everything from giraffes to sofas, were made in the village of Camacha, about 6 miles from Funchal. Since nearly all the items are too large to carry back home, the store will arrange shipment.

CASA DO TURISTA, Rua do Conselheiro José Silvestre Ribeiro 2. Tel. 249-07.
Located near the waterfront in Funchal, this is one of the best places on the island at which to purchase handcrafts of Madeira. Privately managed, it has a policy of clearly labeled "firm" prices, unlike many of the bazaars, which pick up added business by paying to have cruise-ship passengers directed to their establishments or having employees chase you down the street quoting lower tariffs after you've nixed their higher tabs. The setting of the Tourist House is beguiling, in an old quinta once inhabited by a distinguished local family. Its elegant rooms are a natural setting to show off the beautiful handmade items. You're treated as a guest in a private home.

In the patio, with a fountain and semitropical greenery, is a miniature village, with small-scale typical rooms furnished in the local style. Among the merchandise offered are handmade embroideries in linen or cotton (the fabric is often imported from Switzerland and Ireland), tapestries, wickerwork, Portuguese pottery and ceramics, Madeira wines, fruit, and flowers. You'll find all types of embroidery and appliqués, as well as "shadow work," the tariffs determined by the number of stitches.

Specific merchandise includes embroidered Irish linen handkerchiefs for men (some with monograms); handbags made of banana skins, in different sizes; the characteristic goatskin boots; 12-string guitars; 15-piece embroidered placemat and napkin sets; appliquéd tray cloths in shadow work; old Madeira-style tablecloths; and embroidered bridge cloths with four napkins.

In one of the rooms is a display of old wines, with ceramic jugs. Old wines (*velho*) are sold in their original bottles, some costing very little. In addition, half a pint of sugarcane brandy is for sale in souvenir packages of five miniature varieties.

CASA OLIVEIRA, Rua da Alfândega 11. Tel. 22-93-40.
There's an embroidery factory right on the premises. However, the store is primarily a retail outlet for one of the largest embroidery concerns in town. It turns out everything from a delicate negligée to an elegant "heirloom" tablecloth.

LINO AND ARAUJO LTD., Rua Dos Murcas 15. Tel. 22-07-36.
The specialty here is hand-embroideries and knitted goods. This shop is frequented by many non-Portuguese residents of Madeira.

MADEIRA SUPERBIA, Rua do Carmo 27. Tel. 22-40-23.
This shop, known for its fine embroidery (of excellent quality), is also a specialist in tapestries.

---

8. EVENING ENTERTAINMENT

THE ENTERTAINMENT COMPLEX AT CASINO PARK HOTEL, Avenida do Infante, Funchal. Tel. 23-31-11.
This glittering complex of glass, steel, roulette wheels, and gardens is the most obvious entertainment venue for first-time visitors to the island. Completely renovated in 1992 and set within its own grounds near the center of Funchal, it was designed in the late 1970s by Oscar Niemeyer, one of the main architects of Brazil's capital, Brasília. The centerpiece of the complex is a 373-room five-star hotel, which is ringed with an array of entertainment options.

Foremost among these is a casino, the only one on Madeira, which offers such "indoor sports" as roulette, French banque, craps, blackjack, and slot machines. Admission to the casino requires the presentation of a passport or some other form of identification and payment of a 350$ ($2.10) government tax.

Nearby is a dance club, Bacara, whose allure is best appreciated after 11pm; it charges a cover of 1,000$ ($6.10). If you're hungry, the hotel contains an unpretentious coffee shop and a gourmet à la carte restaurant, Chez Oscar. It charges from 4,000$ ($24.40) to 6,000$ ($36.60) for full meals, which are served Monday through Saturday from 7:30 to 9:30pm. Less expensive is the table d'hôte dining room, The Panoramic Restaurant, which charges 5,400$ ($32.90) for a fixed-price meal, served Monday through Saturday from 7:30 to 9:15pm. Three nights a week, usually on Monday, Thursday, and Friday, the Panoramic offers a Las Vegas–style cabaret show beginning at 9:30pm. Visitors who want to see just the show pay a minimum bar tab of 2,000$ ($12.20) per person; clients who want dinner, two drinks, and a view of the show pay a set price of 7,000$ ($42.70) each. In addition to these attractions, the complex contains a scattering of bars, kiosks, and boutiques.

JOE'S BAR, on the grounds of Quinta da Penha de França, Rua da Penha de França. Tel. 22-90-87.
Crowded but comfortable, Joe's Bar occupies an outbuilding on the grounds of a previously recommended hotel. Decorated in a turn-of-the-century style, with plenty of red, it presents live piano music most evenings from 7 to 11pm. Beer costs around 250$ ($1.50), mixed drinks from around 450$ ($2.70) each. Hours are daily from 11am to 2am.

O FAROL DISCO CLUB, in Madeira Carlton, Largo António Nobre. Tel. 23-10-31.
This is considered the best, most interesting, and safest disco on the island. It lies in a circular outbuilding near the lagoon-shaped pool of this already recommended five-star hotel. To reach it, most visitors pass through the hotel lobby, descending open-toed flights of stairs and passing through the hotel gardens. The disco offers current music, rows of curved windows overlooking the sea, and several tiers of curved platforms whose visual focus is the dance floor. The admission price builds up a drink credit. A scotch and soda costs 700$ ($4.30). The music lasts Monday to Saturday nights from 10pm to 3am.

Admission: 1,500$ ($9.20).

THE PRINCE ALBERT, Rua da Imperatriz D. Amelia. Tel. 35-793.

The Prince Albert is a Victorian pub in Madeira, complete with plush cut-velvet walls, tufted banquettes, and English pub memorabilia. You're greeted with a "Good evening, sir (or madam)." Next to the Savoy, the pub serves oversize mugs of beer and a cross sampling of all the accents of England. Drinks are offered at the curved bar or at one of the tables under Edwardian fringed lamps. Beer costs from 250$ ($1.50); mixed drinks cost 350$ ($2.10). The establishment is open daily from noon to 2am.

9. EASY EXCURSION TO PORTO SANTO

Another island of the little Madeira group is Porto Santo, some 24 miles northeast of the main land mass and very different from that island. It is only 9 miles long and 3 miles wide, yet it boasts a 4-mile strip of fine sandy beach along the southern shore. The island is not as hilly as Madeira: Its highest elevation is about 1,670 feet above sea level, at **Pico do Facho.**

The **Porto Santo Tourist Office** is at Avenida Vieira de Castro (tel. 98-23-62). The **telephone area code** is 091.

This island was the first on which the discoverers of Madeira, João Gonçalves Zarco and Tristao Vaz Teixiera, landed in 1418. These captains, serving Prince Henry the Navigator, took refuge here when a storm blew them off course, and they named it Porto Santo (Holy Port) to express gratitude for their survival. It was not until 1419 that they were in a condition to sail on and make the landfall at Madeira. Henry gave Teixiera and Zarco authority to run Madeira, but he placed Porto Santo in the hands of Bartolomeu Perestrello, who made his mark on the island. At least, he is reported to have brought in rabbits as a future food source, but instead, it is said, they ate everything in sight, laying waste to the vegetation already there and not helping future crops much.

Christopher Columbus slept here. He married Isobel Moniz, the daughter of Perestrello, before going on to Funchal to prepare for his planned sea exploration. The house in which he is claimed to have lived is in an alley behind the little white church in the town of **Villa Baleira,** which is also called Porto Santo.

The island gets very dry in summer, which makes it popular with beachgoers but not very good for crops. Produced in winter, the foodstuffs grown on Porto Santo include grain, tomatoes, figs, and melons, as well as grapes from which a sweet white wine is made. Islanders who don't farm go fishing. The low hills are crowned here with a few remaining unusual windmills.

The water of Porto Santo is supposed to have therapeutic values, which have made it a popular drink not only on the island but also in Madeira and Portugal. The water-bottling plants, fish canneries, and a lime kiln are industries of Porto Santo.

The little town with two names lies beneath **Pico do Castelo,** a height on which stands a ruined 16th-century castle built for defense. For a long time, Madeira let Porto Santo shift for itself in this regard, and it fell prey to pirates now and then.

Try to go to the **Fountain in the Sands (Fonte da Areia),** near cliffs above a rocky coast. Here local women wash their clothes in the water flowing out.

Good points from which to get views of the island and its surroundings are **Portela** and **Castelo Peak (Pico do Castelo). Ponta da Calheta** is another sight provided by nature, on the south of the island. This point looks to Baixo Islet across a reef-strewn channel constantly pounded by the sea. Black-basalt rocks dot the beach.

Independência, a 244-passenger catamaran, sails from Funchal to Porto Santo if the weather is good. The trip takes 1½ hours each way and costs 6,400$ ($39) round trip. Call 270-20 for reservations. Some hotels or quintas will pack a picnic lunch, which guests can enjoy on the beach. Sailings are daily from June through September and on Wednesday through Monday from October through May. They are subject to cancellation, of course. The *Independencia* leaves the port at Funchal at 8am, returning from Porto Santo at 5pm. Many visitors go over only for the day, so tickets arranged in advance are important, especially in summer. The ride is often rough, and many passengers get sick from motion sickness, so be duly warned. You can also fly over in the morning on a **TAP flight**, catching a Funchal-bound plane in Porto Santo in the early evening. In summer, at least six flights leave from Madeira. The shuttle flight on an 18-seat Dornier turboprop plane takes only 15 minutes, costing 10,800$ ($65.90) round trip; children 2 to 12 pay only half fare. In July and August, always make reservations well in advance.

WHERE TO STAY

MODERATE

HOTEL PORTO SANTO, Campo de Baixo, 9400 Porto Santo. Tel. 091/ 98-23-81. Fax 091/98-26-11. 89 rms, 1 suite. TEL
$ Rates (including half board): 11,500$–20,600$ ($70.20–$125.70) single; 18,400$ ($112.20) double; 23,700$ ($144.60) suite for two. AE, DC, MC, V. **Parking:** Free.

The four-star first-class Porto Santo has only two floors. It was constructed a little more than a mile from Vila Valeira at Suloeste, in a garden setting bordering directly on the large (4-mile-long) beach of gold-colored sand. The Porto Santo offers well-furnished guest rooms, each with a terrace overlooking the bay. A minibar is available upon request.

The hotel also has a large restaurant serving a bountiful lunch or dinner. The main lounge has been attractively furnished and, mercifully, air-conditioned. It leads to the main terrace and garden, where there is an open bar. After the hot sun retires a bit, the tennis courts are popular. A pool has been built for guests, and windsurfing is also available. Laundry, babysitting, and room service are offered.

INEXPENSIVE

HOTEL PRAIA DOURADA, Rua Dr. Pedro Lomelino, 9400 Porto Santo. Tel. 091/98-23-15. Fax 091/98-24-87. 110 rms TEL
$ Rates (including breakfast): 10,800$ ($65.90) single; 12,000$ ($73.20) double. AE, DC, MC, V. **Parking:** Free.

Built in a three-story design in the early 1980s, this is one of the most visible hotels on the island, set near the center of Vila Baleira. An unpretentious three-star hotel, it offers simply furnished, well-scrubbed guest rooms, some of which have balconies. It serves breakfast to residents but does not contain a restaurant, although it has a bar and does a thriving business with merchants and business clients visiting from th' mainland of Portugal. Laundry service is available, and there's an outdoor pool

TORRE PRAIA SUITE HOTEL, Rua Goulart Medeiros, 9400 Porto $ **Tel. 091/98-52-92.** Fax 091/98-24-87. 62 rms, 3 suites. A/C MINIBA'
$ Rates (including breakfast): 10,580$–12,000$ ($64.50–$73.20) sinc' 21,120$–24,000$ ($128.80–$146.40) suite. AE, DC, MC, V. **Pa'**

⭐ This is the best hotel on Porto Santo, set on the outskirr' adjacent to its own beach. Opened in August 1993 and ra' island's tourist authorities, it offers a three-story forma'
rooms with uncomplicated furniture in fresh colors. Despi' name (Suite Hotel), only three of its accommodations are ' are comfortably furnished individual rooms, each w' deposit box, and—in most cases—a view of the sea. ' are available. The hotel offers a health club with a' a library; a games room; and a pool with a chilu. restaurants, a bar inspired by Germany's beer garu.

BUDGET

RESIDENCIAL CENTRAL, Rua Abel Magna Vasc. **Santo. Tel. 091/98-22-26.** Fax 091/98-34-60. 37 rms,

$ Rates (including breakfast): 5,500$–6,900$ ($33.60–$42.10) single; 6,200$–7,700$ ($37.80–$47) double; 10,000$–11,000$ ($61–$67.10) suite. AE, DC, MC, V. **Parking:** Free.

⑤ Originally conceived as a simple and unpretentious pension with only 12 rooms, this establishment was radically enlarged and renovated in 1993. It's managed by several generations of an extended family from a position in the center of the island's capital, Vila Baleira. The atmosphere includes lots of children and a strong sense of family-related priorities, which may or may not suit you. The ground-floor guest rooms, because they lack a view, are slightly less expensive than rooms on the two upper floors, where in some cases vistas extend out over the village and the sea. On the premises are a sun terrace, a garden, a bar, and a restaurant.

WHERE TO DINE
MODERATE

ARSÉNIOS, Avenida Dr. Manuel Pestana Junior. Tel. 98-23-48.
  Cuisine: MADEIRAN/ITALIAN. **Reservations:** Not necessary.
$ Prices: Appetizers 450$–950$ ($2.70–$5.80); main courses 1,000$–1,500$ ($6.10–$9.20). AE, DC, MC, V.
  Open: Lunch daily 11am–3pm; dinner daily 6–11pm.

Arsénios was patterned after a restaurant owned by the same entrepreneur in Funchal, and its Madeira success formula was imported to nearby Porto Santo. It specializes in pizza, lasagne, and spaghetti. Full meals may include many fresh fish dishes (which depend on the catch of the day). The restaurant is located in town on the main road opposite the sea. It is housed in a modern building with large panoramic windows.

MARQUÉS, Rua Maximiliano de Sousa Maxç. Tel. 98-23-19.
  Cuisine: MADEIRAN. **Reservations:** Not necessary.
$ Prices: Appetizers 350$–500$ ($2.10–$3.10); main courses 950$–1,500$ ($5.80–$9.20). AE, DC, MC, V.
  Open: Daily 9:30am–midnight.

Marqués is another good choice, lying in a modern building near the center of town. It serves many varieties of grilled fish and seems to take pride in the offerings of its kitchen. Try several kinds of grilled or fried fish or *espetada* (steak on a spit).

PÔR-DO-SOL, Ponta da Calheta. Tel. 98-23-80.
  Cuisine: PORTUGUESE. **Reservations:** Not necessary.
$ Prices: Appetizers 350$–500$ ($2.10–$3.10); main courses 750$–1,500$ ($4.60–$9.20). No credit cards.
  Open: Daily noon–midnight.

Pôr-do-Sol lies on the western tip of the island near the beach. Installed in a brick-walled house, it is simply decorated. Three specialties include *espetada* (steak on a spit), *caldeirada* (fish stew made with several kinds of fish), and grilled fish (whatever the catch turned up that day). Sandwiches and burgers are among the more popular items. Wear your most casual dress here.

**A. MENU
   TRANSLATIONS**
**B. CAPSULE
   VOCABULARY**
C. METRIC MEASURES

A. MENU TRANSLATIONS

French is still traditionally spoken by guides in provincial museums, but English is increasing in popularity and is now taught in most schools. Usually in Lisbon, Estoril, Cascais, and Madeira and at the major coastal resorts of the Algarve, you'll have no problem if you speak only English. However, if you venture inland—to towns of the Alentejo, for example—you may find a few words in the following "Capsule Vocabulary" helpful. Likewise, menus tend to be bewildering, especially when a chef has named a bean-and-tripe dish after his favorite aunt. Nevertheless, a basic knowledge of the main dishes in the Portuguese cuisine is essential, especially if you're planning to stay at second-class hotels or eat at local taverns where there's nobody around to translate for you.

SOUPS *(SOPAS)*

caldo verde potato-and-cabbage soup
canja de galinha chicken soup
creme de camarao cream of shrimp soup
creme de legumes cream of vegetable soup

sopa à alentejana Alentejo soup
sopa de cebola onion soup
sopa de mariscos shellfish soup
sopa de queijo cheese soup
sopa de tomate tomato soup

EGGS *(OVOS)*

com presunto with ham
cozidos hard-boiled
escalfados poached
estrelados fried

mexicos scrambled
omeleta omelet
quentes soft-boiled
tortilha Spanish omelet

FISH *(PEIXE)*

ameijoas clams
atum tuna
bacalhau salted codfish
cherne turbot
camaraos shrimps
eiró eel
lagosta lobster
linguado sole
lulas squid

ostras oysters
peixe espada
percebes b
pescada
robalo
salm
sa

SPECIALTIES *(ES*

bife na frigideira steak with mustard sauce
caldeirada fisherman's stew

cu
st
porco
tomat

MEAT (CARNE)

bife steak
borrego lamb
cabrito kid
carneiro mutton
coelho rabbit
costeletas chops
dobrada tripe
iscas liver

lingua tongue
porco pork
presunto ham
rim kidney
salchichas sausages
vaca beef
vitela veal

POULTRY (AVES)

borracho pigeon
frango chicken
galinha fowl
ganso goose

pato duck
perdiz partridge
peru turkey

VEGETABLES (LEGUMES)

aipo celery
alcachôfra artichoke
arroz rice
azeitonas olives
batatas potatoes
berinjela eggplant
beterrabas beets
cebola onion
feijao bean
nabo turnip
cenouras carrots
cogumelo mushroom

couve-flor cauliflower
couve cabbage
ervilhas peas
espargos asparagus
espinafres spinach
favas broad beans
pepino cucumber
tomate tomato

SALAD (SALADA)

agriaos watercress
alface lettuce
salada mista mixed salad

salada verde green salad
Russa Russian salad

DESSERTS (SOBREMESA)

arroz doce rice pudding
olo cake
lados diversos mixed ice creams
ca assada baked apple
elaria pastry
ego Melba peach Melba

pudim flan egg custard
pudim de pao bread pudding
salada de frutas fruit salad
sorvetes sherbets
queijo cheese

FRUITS (FRUTAS)

avocado
apricots
um
eapple
ries

pberry

melancia watermelon
melao melon
morangos strawberries
pêras pears
pêssegos peaches
roma pomegranate
tâmara date
toronja grapefruit
uvas grapes

BEVERAGES *(BEBIDAS)*

água water
água mineral mineral water
café coffee
chá tea
cerveja beer
com gelo with ice
laranjada orangeade

leite milk
sumo de fruta fruit juice
sumo de laranja orange juice
sumo de tomate tomato juice
vinho branco white wine
vinho tinto red wine

CONDIMENTS *(CONDIMENTOS)*

açúcar sugar
alho garlic
azeite olive oil
caril curry
manteiga butter

mostarda mustard
compota jam
pimenta pepper
sal salt
vinagre vinegar

MISCELLANEOUS

chocolate chocolate
biscoito cracker
gelo ice

gelado ice cream
pao bread
pao torrado toast

COOKING TERMS

assado no forno baked
cozido boiled
estufada braised

frito fried
mal passado rare
bem passado well done

B. Capsule Vocabulary

ENGLISH	PORTUGUESE	PRONUNCIATION
Hello	**olá**	oh-*lah*
How are you?	**Como está?**	*Co*-mo esh-*tah*
Very well	**muito bem**	*muy*-toh bym
Thank you	**muito obrigado**	*muy*-toh o-bree-*gah*-do
Good-bye	**adeus**	adeush
Please	**faça favor**	*fas*-sa fah-*vohr*
Yes	**sim**	seem
No	**nao**	naion
Excuse me	**desculpe-me**	dash-*cul*-pa-meh
Give me	**dê-me**	*deh*-meh
Where is . . .	**Onde fica . . .**	*On*-jeh *fee*-cah . . .
the station?	a estaçao?	o aish-tassaion?
a hotel?	um hotel?	oom ho-*tel*?
a restaurant?	um restaurante?	om rash-taur-*an*-teh?
the toilet?	a casa de banhoah?	*cah*-zah de bahn-*hoo*?
To the right	**à direita**	aah dee-*rai*-tah
To the left	**à esquerda**	aah ash-*ker*-dah
Straight ahead	**em frente**	ym *frain*-tah
I would like . . .	**Gostaria de . . .**	Goosh-tar-*ee*-ah de . . .
to eat.	comer.	coh-*mere*.
a room.	um quarto.	oom *quarr*-toh.
How much is it?	**Quanto custa?**	Quahnto *coosh*-tah?

The check, please.	**A conta se faz, favor.**	Ah *cohn*-ta sa fahsh, fah-*vohr.*
When	**quando**	*quan*-doh
Yesterday	**ontem**	ohn-*tym*
Today	**hoje**	*hoyh*-je
Tomorrow	**amanha**	ah-*main*-hayh
Breakfast	**pequeno almoço**	pai-*kain*-oh aahl-*mohs*-soh
Lunch	**almoço**	aahl-*mohs*-soh
Dinner	**jantar**	jain-*taah*

NUMBERS

1	**um** (oom)	14	**catorze** (cah-*tohr*-zeh)	40	**quarenta** (quar-*ain*-tah)
2	**dois** (doysh)	15	**quinze** (*keen*-zeh)	50	**cinquenta** (seen-*quain*-tah)
3	**tres** (traishe)	16	**dezasseis** (dehz-ai-*saish*)	60	**sessenta** (sais-*saihn*-tah)
4	**quatro** (*quaah*-troh)	17	**dezassete** (dehz-ai-*saih*-teh)	70	**setenta** (sai-*tain*-tah)
5	**cinco** (*seen*-coh)	18	**dezoito** (dehz-*oy*-toh)	80	**oitenta** (oyh-*tain*-tah)
6	**seis** (saish)	19	**dezanove** (dehz-a-*noh*-veh)	90	**noventa** (noh-*vain*-tah)
7	**sete** (saiteh)	20	**vinte** (*veen*-teh)	100	**cem** (sym)
8	**oito** (*oy*-toh)	30	**trinta** (*treehn*-tah)		
9	**nove** (*noh*-veh)				
10	**dez** (daish)				
11	**onze** (*on*-zeh)				
12	**doze** (*do*-ze)				
13	**treze** (*traih*-zeh)				

C. METRIC MEASURES

LENGTH

1 millimeter (mm)	=	0.04 inches
1 centimeter (cm)	=	0.39 inches
1 meter (m)	=	39 inches
1 kilometer (km)	=	0.62 miles

To convert kilometers to miles, multiply the number of kilometers by 0.62. Also use to convert speeds from kilometers per hour (kmph) to miles per hour (mph).
To convert miles to kilometers, multiply the number of miles by 1.61. Also use to convert speeds from mph to kmph.

CAPACITY

1 liter	=	33.92 ounces	=	2.1 pints	=	1.06 quarts
	=	0.26 U.S. gallons				
1 Imperial gallon	=	1.2 U.S. gallons				

To convert liters to U.S. gallons, multiply the number of liters by 0.26.
To convert U.S. gallons to liters, multiply the number of gallons by 3.79.
To convert Imperial gallons to U.S. gallons, multiply Imperial gallons by 1.2.
To convert U.S. gallons to Imperial gallons, multiply U.S. gallons by 0.83.

WEIGHT

1 gram (g)	=	0.04 ounces (*or* about a paperclip's weight)
1 kilogram (kg)	=	35.2 ounces
	=	2.2 pounds
1 metric ton	=	2,205 pounds = 1.1 short ton

To convert kilograms to pounds, multiply the number of kilograms by 2.2
To convert pounds to kilograms, multiply the number of kilograms by 0.45

TEMPERATURE

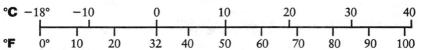

To convert degrees Celsius to degrees Fahrenheit, multiply °C by 9, divide by 5, then add 32 (example: 20°C + 9/5 = 32 × 68°F).
To convert degrees Fahrenheit to degrees Celsius, subtract 32 from °F, then multiply by 5, then divide by 9 (example: 85°F − 32 = 5/9 × 29.4°C).

Now Save Money on All Your Travels by Joining
FROMMER'S ™ TRAVEL BOOK CLUB
The World's Best Travel Guides at Membership Prices

FROMMER'S TRAVEL BOOK CLUB is your ticket to successful travel! Open up a world of travel information and simplify your travel planning when you join ranks with thousands of value-conscious travelers who are members of the FROMMER'S TRAVEL BOOK CLUB. Join today and you'll be entitled to all the privileges that come from belonging to the club that offers you travel guides for less to more than 100 destinations worldwide. Annual membership is only $25 (U.S.) or $35 (Canada and foreign).

The Advantages of Membership

1. Your choice of *three* free FROMMER'S TRAVEL GUIDES (any *two* FROM-MER'S COMPREHENSIVE GUIDES, FROMMER'S $-A-DAY GUIDES, FROMMER'S WALKING TOURS *or* FROMMER'S FAMILY GUIDES—plus *one* FROMMER'S CITY GUIDE, FROMMER'S CITY $-A-DAY GUIDE *or* FROMMER'S TOURING GUIDE).
2. Your own subscription to **TRIPS AND TRAVEL** quarterly newsletter.
3. You're entitled to a **30% discount** on your order of any additional books offered by FROMMER'S TRAVEL BOOK CLUB.
4. You're offered (at a small additional fee) our **Domestic Trip-Routing Kits.**

Our quarterly newsletter **TRIPS AND TRAVEL** offers practical information on the best buys in travel, the "hottest" vacation spots, the latest travel trends, world-class events and much, much more.

Our **Domestic Trip-Routing Kits** are available for any North American destination. We'll send you a detailed map highlighting the best route to take to your destination—you can request direct or scenic routes.

Here's all you have to do to join:

Send in your membership fee of $25 ($35 Canada and foreign) with your name and address on the form below along with your selections as part of your membership package to **FROMMER'S TRAVEL BOOK CLUB, P.O. Box 473, Mt. Morris, IL 61054-0473.** Remember to check off your *three* free books.

If you would like to order additional books, please select the books you would like and send a check for the total amount (please add sales tax in the states noted below), plus $2 per book for shipping and handling ($3 per book for foreign orders) to:

FROMMER'S TRAVEL BOOK CLUB
P.O. Box 473
Mt. Morris, IL 61054-0473
(815) 734-1104

[ ] **YES.** I want to take advantage of this opportunity to join FROMMER'S TRAVEL BOOK CLUB.
[ ] **My check is enclosed.** Dollar amount enclosed_____*
(all payments in U.S. funds only)

Name_____
Address_____
City_____ State_____ Zip_____
All orders must be prepaid.

To ensure that all orders are processed efficiently, please apply sales tax in the following areas: CA, CT, FL, IL, NJ, NY, TN, WA and CANADA.

*With membership, shipping and handling will be paid by FROMMER'S TRAVEL BOOK CLUB for the three free books you select as part of your membership. Please add $2 per book for shipping and handling for any additional books purchased ($3 per book for foreign orders).

Allow 4–6 weeks for delivery. Prices of books, membership fee, and publication dates are subject to change without notice. Prices are subject to acceptance and availability.

Please Send Me the Books Checked Below:

FROMMER'S COMPREHENSIVE GUIDES
(Guides listing facilities from budget to deluxe,
with emphasis on the medium-priced)

	Retail Price	Code		Retail Price	Code
☐ Acapulco/Ixtapa/Taxco 1993–94	$15.00	C120	☐ Japan 1994–95 (Avail. 3/94)	$19.00	C144
☐ Alaska 1994–95	$17.00	C131	☐ Morocco 1992–93	$18.00	C021
☐ Arizona 1993–94	$18.00	C101	☐ Nepal 1994–95	$18.00	C126
☐ Australia 1992–93	$18.00	C002	☐ New England 1994 (Avail. 1/94)	$16.00	C137
☐ Austria 1993–94	$19.00	C119	☐ New Mexico 1993–94	$15.00	C117
☐ Bahamas 1994–95	$17.00	C121	☐ New York State 1994–95	$19.00	C133
☐ Belgium/Holland/ Luxembourg 1993–94	$18.00	C106	☐ Northwest 1994–95 (Avail. 2/94)	$17.00	C140
☐ Bermuda 1994–95	$15.00	C122	☐ Portugal 1994–95 (Avail. 2/94)	$17.00	C141
☐ Brazil 1993–94	$20.00	C111	☐ Puerto Rico 1993–94	$15.00	C103
☐ California 1994	$15.00	C134	☐ Puerto Vallarta/Manzanillo/ Guadalajara 1994–95 (Avail. 1/94)	$14.00	C028
☐ Canada 1994–95 (Avail. 4/94)	$19.00	C145	☐ Scandinavia 1993–94	$19.00	C135
☐ Caribbean 1994	$18.00	C123	☐ Scotland 1994–95 (Avail. 4/94)	$17.00	C146
☐ Carolinas/Georgia 1994–95	$17.00	C128	☐ South Pacific 1994–95 (Avail. 1/94)	$20.00	C138
☐ Colorado 1994–95 (Avail. 3/94)	$16.00	C143	☐ Spain 1993–94	$19.00	C115
☐ Cruises 1993–94	$19.00	C107	☐ Switzerland/Liechtenstein 1994–95 (Avail. 1/94)	$19.00	C139
☐ Delaware/Maryland 1994–95 (Avail. 1/94)	$15.00	C136	☐ Thailand 1992–93	$20.00	C033
☐ England 1994	$18.00	C129	☐ U.S.A. 1993–94	$19.00	C116
☐ Florida 1994	$18.00	C124	☐ Virgin Islands 1994–95	$13.00	C127
☐ France 1994–95	$20.00	C132	☐ Virginia 1994–95 (Avail. 2/94)	$14.00	C142
☐ Germany 1994	$19.00	C125	☐ Yucatán 1993–94	$18.00	C110
☐ Italy 1994	$19.00	C130			
☐ Jamaica/Barbados 1993–94	$15.00	C105			

FROMMER'S $-A-DAY GUIDES
(Guides to low-cost tourist accommodations and facilities)

	Retail Price	Code		Retail Price	Code
☐ Australia on $45 1993–94	$18.00	D102	☐ Israel on $45 1993–94	$18.00	D101
☐ Costa Rica/Guatemala/ Belize on $35 1993–94	$17.00	D108	☐ Mexico on $45 1994	$19.00	D116
☐ Eastern Europe on $30 1993–94	$18.00	D110	☐ New York on $70 1994–95 (Avail. 4/94)	$16.00	D120
☐ England on $60 1994	$18.00	D112	☐ New Zealand on $45 1993–94	$18.00	D103
☐ Europe on $50 1994	$19.00	D115	☐ Scotland/Wales on $50 1992–93	$18.00	D019
☐ Greece on $45 1993–94	$19.00	D100	☐ South America on $40 1993–94	$19.00	D109
☐ Hawaii on $75 1994	$19.00	D113	☐ Turkey on $40 1992–93	$22.00	D023
☐ India on $40 1992–93	$20.00	D010	☐ Washington, D.C. on $40 1994–95 (Avail. 2/94)	$17.00	D119
☐ Ireland on $45 1994–95 (Avail. 1/94)	$17.00	D117			

FROMMER'S CITY $-A-DAY GUIDES
(Pocket-size guides to low-cost tourist accommodations
and facilities)

	Retail Price	Code		Retail Price	Code
☐ Berlin on $40 1994–95	$12.00	D111	☐ Madrid on $50 1994–95 (Avail. 1/94)	$13.00	D118
☐ Copenhagen on $50 1992–93	$12.00	D003	☐ Paris on $50 1994–95	$12.00	D117
☐ London on $45 1994–95	$12.00	D114	☐ Stockholm on $50 1992–93	$13.00	D022

FROMMER'S WALKING TOURS

(With routes and detailed maps, these companion guides point out
the places and pleasures that make a city unique)

	Retail Price	Code		Retail Price	Code
☐ Berlin	$12.00	W100	☐ Paris	$12.00	W103
☐ London	$12.00	W101	☐ San Francisco	$12.00	W104
☐ New York	$12.00	W102	☐ Washington, D.C.	$12.00	W105

FROMMER'S TOURING GUIDES

(Color-illustrated guides that include walking tours, cultural and historic
sights, and practical information)

	Retail Price	Code		Retail Price	Code
☐ Amsterdam	$11.00	T001	☐ New York	$11.00	T008
☐ Barcelona	$14.00	T015	☐ Rome	$11.00	T010
☐ Brazil	$11.00	T003	☐ Scotland	$10.00	T011
☐ Florence	$ 9.00	T005	☐ Sicily	$15.00	T017
☐ Hong Kong/Singapore/			☐ Tokyo	$15.00	T016
Macau	$11.00	T006	☐ Turkey	$11.00	T013
☐ Kenya	$14.00	T018	☐ Venice	$ 9.00	T014
☐ London	$13.00	T007			

FROMMER'S FAMILY GUIDES

	Retail Price	Code		Retail Price	Code
☐ California with Kids	$18.00	F100	☐ San Francisco with Kids		
☐ Los Angeles with Kids			(Avail. 4/94)	$17.00	F104
(Avail. 4/94)	$17.00	F103	☐ Washington, D.C. with Kids		
☐ New York City with Kids			(Avail. 2/94)	$17.00	F102
(Avail. 2/94)	$18.00	F101			

FROMMER'S CITY GUIDES

(Pocket-size guides to sightseeing and tourist accommodations and
facilities in all price ranges)

	Retail Price	Code		Retail Price	Code
☐ Amsterdam 1993–94	$13.00	S110	☐ Montréal/Québec		
☐ Athens 1993–94	$13.00	S114	City 1993–94	$13.00	S125
☐ Atlanta 1993–94	$13.00	S112	☐ Nashville/Memphis		
☐ Atlantic City/Cape			1994–95 (Avail. 4/94)	$13.00	S141
May 1993–94	$13.00	S130	☐ New Orleans 1993–94	$13.00	S103
☐ Bangkok 1992–93	$13.00	S005	☐ New York 1994 (Avail.		
☐ Barcelona/Majorca/Minorca/			1/94)	$13.00	S138
Ibiza 1993–94	$13.00	S115	☐ Orlando 1994	$13.00	S135
☐ Berlin 1993–94	$13.00	S116	☐ Paris 1993–94	$13.00	S109
☐ Boston 1993–94	$13.00	S117	☐ Philadelphia 1993–94	$13.00	S113
☐ Budapest 1994–95 (Avail.			☐ San Diego 1993–94	$13.00	S107
2/94)	$13.00	S139	☐ San Francisco 1994	$13.00	S133
☐ Chicago 1993–94	$13.00	S122	☐ Santa Fe/Taos/		
☐ Denver/Boulder/Colorado			Albuquerque 1993–94	$13.00	S108
Springs 1993–94	$13.00	S131	☐ Seattle/Portland 1994–95	$13.00	S137
☐ Dublin 1993–94	$13.00	S128	☐ St. Louis/Kansas		
☐ Hong Kong 1994–95			City 1993–94	$13.00	S127
(Avail. 4/94)	$13.00	S140	☐ Sydney 1993–94	$13.00	S129
☐ Honolulu/Oahu 1994	$13.00	S134	☐ Tampa/St.		
☐ Las Vegas 1993–94	$13.00	S121	Petersburg 1993–94	$13.00	S105
☐ London 1994	$13.00	S132	☐ Tokyo 1992–93	$13.00	S039
☐ Los Angeles 1993–94	$13.00	S123	☐ Toronto 1993–94	$13.00	S126
☐ Madrid/Costa del			☐ Vancouver/Victoria 1994–		
Sol 1993–94	$13.00	S124	95 (Avail. 1/94)	$13.00	S142
☐ Miami 1993–94	$13.00	S118	☐ Washington, D.C. 1994		
☐ Minneapolis/St.			(Avail. 1/94)	$13.00	S136
Paul 1993–94	$13.00	S119			

SPECIAL EDITIONS

	Retail Price	Code		Retail Price	Code
☐ Bed & Breakfast Southwest	$16.00	P100	☐ Caribbean Hideaways	$16.00	P103
☐ Bed & Breakfast Great American Cities (Avail. 1/94)	$16.00	P104	☐ National Park Guide 1994 (avail. 3/94)	$16.00	P105
			☐ Where to Stay U.S.A.	$15.00	P102

Please note: if the availability of a book is several months away, we may have back issues of guides to that particular destination. Call customer service at (815) 734-1104.